NICARAGUA

COSTA
RICA

PANAMÁ

MAR CARIBE

Barranquilla

Maracaibo

Caracas

Rio Orinoco

Medellín

VENEZUELA

Georgetown
Paramaribo

GUYANA
Cayenne

OCÉANO
ATLÁNTICO

Cali

Bogotá

COLOMBIA

GUAYANA FRANCESA

SURINAME

Quito

ECUADOR

Guayaquil

Ecuador

Manaus

Belém

CORDILLERA

OCÉANO
PACÍFICO

PERÚ

Recife

Lima

Machu Picchu
Cuzco

BRASIL

OCÉANO PACÍFICO

Isla Pinta

Isla Marchena

Isla San Salvador

Isla Santa Cruz

Isla
Isabela

Isla San
Cristóbal

LAS ISLAS
GALÁPAGOS
(ECUADOR)

Puerto
Baquerizo
Moreno

Lago Titicaca

Arequipa

BOLIVIA

La Paz

Sucre

DE

LOS

Brasília

0   100 MILLAS

0   100 KILÓMETROS

Antofagasta

PARAGUAY

São Paulo

ANDES

Asunción

Puerto Iguazú

Rio de Janeiro

Trópico de
Capricornio

0   8 MILLAS

0   8 KILÓMETROS

CHILE

Rio Paraná

Valparaíso

Cabo
Cummings

Córdoba

Hanga Roa

Santiago

Rosario

URUGUAY

Mataveri

Cabo Sur

OCÉANO
PACÍFICO

ARGENTINA

Buenos
Aires

Montevideo

OCÉANO
ATLÁNTICO

ISLA DE PASCUA
(CHILE)

Concepción

Rio de la Plata

San Carlos de
Bariloche

Bahía Blanca

OCÉANO
PACÍFICO

AMÉRICA DEL SUR

0   250   500   750 MILLAS

0   250   500   750 KILÓMETROS

Estrecho de
Magallanes

Islas
Malvinas

ELEVACIÓN

METROS   PIES

Punta Arenas

Tierra del Fuego

3050   10000

1525   5000

Cabo de Hornos

610   2000

305   1000

152.5   500

0   0

MÉXICO, AMÉRICA CENTRAL Y EL CARIBE

ESTADOS UNIDOS

Santa Fe
Albuquerque
Phoenix
Memphis
Atlanta
San Diego
Mexicali
Tijuana
Tucson
Dallas
Nogales
El Paso
Ciudad Juárez
Hermosillo
San Antonio
Austin
Houston
Mobile
Nueva Orleáns
San Agustín
Orlando
Chihuahua
Nuevo Laredo
Tampa
Monterrey
Miami
Nassau
MÉXICO
Durango
Golfo de México
BAHAMAS
Trópico de Cáncer
Cabo San Lucas
Mazatlán
La Habana
CUBA
OCÉANO ATLÁNTICO
Guadalajara
Guanajuato
México, D.F.
Mérida
Cozumel
Guantánamo
Puerto Vallarta
Cuernavaca
Puebla
Península de Yucatán
Chichén Itzá
Santiago de Cuba
HAITÍ
REPÚBLICA DOMINICANA
San Juan
Campeche
Port-au-Prince
Veracruz
JAMAICA
Kingston
Santo Domingo
PUERTO RICO
Oaxaca
Acapulco
BELICE
Belmopan
GUATEMALA
HONDURAS
MAR CARIBE
Guatemala
Tegucigalpa
San Salvador
NICARAGUA
EL SALVADOR
Managua
Barranquilla
Maracaibo
Caracas
Canal de Panamá
Cartagena
San José
COSTA RICA
Panamá
Mérida
VENEZUELA
OCÉANO PACÍFICO
PANAMÁ
Medellín
Cali
Bogotá
COLOMBIA
Ecuador

ELEVACIÓN
METROS / PIES
3050 / 10000
1525 / 5000
610 / 2000
305 / 1000
152.5 / 500
0 / 0

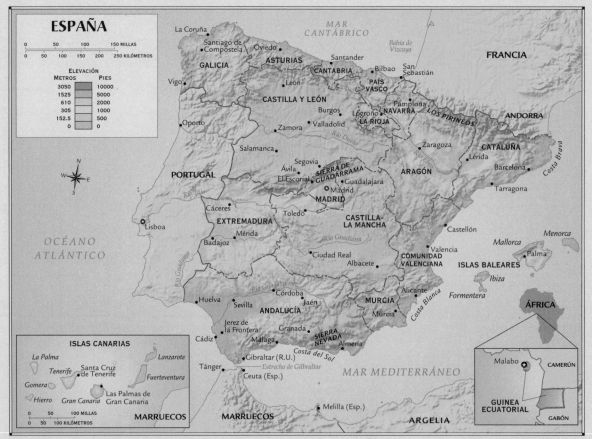

ESPAÑA

ELEVACIÓN
METROS / PIES
3050 / 10000
1525 / 5000
610 / 2000
305 / 1000
152.5 / 500
0 / 0

MAR CANTÁBRICO
La Coruña
Santiago de Compostela
Oviedo
Santander
Bahía de Vizcaya
FRANCIA
GALICIA
ASTURIAS
CANTABRIA
Bilbao
San Sebastián
Vigo
León
PAÍS VASCO
Pamplona
NAVARRA
LOS PIRINEOS
ANDORRA
CASTILLA Y LEÓN
Burgos
Logroño
LA RIOJA
Zamora
Valladolid
Río Duero
Zaragoza
CATALUÑA
Lérida
Costa Brava
PORTUGAL
Salamanca
Segovia
Ávila
SIERRA DE GUADARRAMA
El Escorial
ARAGÓN
Barcelona
Tarragona
Oporto
Guadalajara
MADRID
Madrid
Río Tajo
Cáceres
Toledo
EXTREMADURA
CASTILLA-LA MANCHA
Castellón
Menorca
Mallorca
Lisboa
Mérida
Badajoz
Río Guadiana
Valencia
ISLAS BALEARES
OCÉANO ATLÁNTICO
Ciudad Real
Albacete
COMUNIDAD VALENCIANA
Ibiza
Formentera
Río Guadalquivir
Córdoba
Jaén
MURCIA
Alicante
ÁFRICA
Huelva
Sevilla
Murcia
Costa Blanca
Jerez de la Frontera
Granada
ANDALUCÍA
SIERRA NEVADA
Almería
Málaga
Costa del Sol
Cádiz
Gibraltar (R.U.)
Malabo
Tánger
Estrecho de Gibraltar
MAR MEDITERRÁNEO
CAMERÚN
Ceuta (Esp.)
GUINEA ECUATORIAL
GABÓN
Melilla (Esp.)

ISLAS CANARIAS
La Palma
Lanzarote
Tenerife
Santa Cruz de Tenerife
Fuerteventura
Gomera
Hierro
Gran Canaria
Las Palmas de Gran Canaria
MARRUECOS
MARRUECOS
ARGELIA

Sol y viento
En breve

Bill VanPatten

Michael J. Leeser
Florida State University

Gregory D. Keating
San Diego State University

Boston   Burr Ridge, IL   Dubuque, IA   Madison, WI   New York
San Francisco   St. Louis   Bangkok   Bogotá   Caracas   Kuala Lumpur
Lisbon   London   Madrid   Mexico City   Milan   Montreal   New Delhi
Santiago   Seoul   Singapore   Sydney   Taipei   Toronto

Mc Graw Hill **Higher Education**

Published by McGraw-Hill, an imprint of The McGraw-Hill Companies, Inc., 1221 Avenue of the Americas, New York, NY 10020. Copyright © 2008 by The McGraw-Hill Companies, Inc. All rights reserved. No part of this publication may be reproduced or distributed in any form or by any means, or stored in a database or retrieval system, without the prior written consent of The McGraw-Hill Companies, Inc., including, but not limited to, in any network or other electronic storage or transmission, or broadcast for distance learning.

This book is printed on acid-free paper.

Printed in China

2 3 4 5 6 7 8 9 0 CTP CTP 0 9

Student Edition
ISBN: 978-0-07-351319-5
MHID: 0-07-351319-9

Instructor's Edition
ISBN: 978-0-07-328088-2
MHID: 0-07-328088-7

Editor-in-chief: *Emily G. Barrosse*
Publisher: *William R. Glass*
Senior sponsoring editor: *Christa Harris*
Director of development: *Scott Tinetti*
Executive marketing manager: *Nick Agnew*
Project manager: *Jackie Henry*
Production supervisor: *Richard DeVitto*
Photo research coordinator: *Alexandra Ambrose*
Freelance photo researcher: *Judy Mason*
Freelance interior designer: *Amanda Kavanaugh*
Cover designer: *Violeta Díaz*
Illustrators: *Kathryn Rathke, Diane Dempsey*
Compositor: *TechBooks*
Typeface: *10/12 Bookman*
Printer and binder: *CTPS*

Library of Congress Cataloging-in-Publication Data

VanPatten, Bill.
  Sol y viento: en breve: beginning Spanish / Bill VanPatten, Michael J. Leeser, Gregory D. Keating.
    p. cm.
  Includes index.
  ISBN-13: 978-0-07-351319-5
  ISBN-10: 0-07-351319-9
  1. Spanish language—Textbooks for foreign speakers—English. I. Leeser, Michael J. II.
Keating, Gregory D. III. Title.

PC4129.E5S64 2008
468.2′421—dc22

                                                  2006046963

www.mhhe.com

Contents

Gramática

Vistazos culturales

Gramática

Vistazos culturales

Gramática

Vistazos culturales

Preface

Sol y viento—The Film

A successful young businessman gets orders to travel abroad to secure a land deal. Occupied with other matters and unwilling to go at first, he finally accepts the assignment and soon finds himself in Chile, a country far from his native California. Here, in this Andean nation—land of fertile valleys and soaring mountains, home to the condor, a place exotic and familiar all at once—this young man regains and embraces values he had set aside years ago. He rediscovers the importance of loyalty to family and friends and learns that a person's past is part of his or her soul. He rediscovers the meaning of community and how people and their land may share a bond as strong as that between any two people. Most importantly, he comes to understand that from love, forgiveness is possible—but it is not easily dispensed. Forgiveness must be earned.

Such is the story of the exciting new movie, *Sol y viento.* Follow Jaime "James" Talavera on his unexpected journey of self-discovery. Along the way meet Mario, the talkative personal driver who becomes Jaime's first friend in a new land. Meet Carlos, the secretive administrator of the winery who is eager to sell his family's lands—and those of others. Meet doña Isabel, the matriarch of the Sol y viento winery, and don Paco, the friend of the family who travels from Mexico to aid doña Isabel as she faces a crisis that threatens to alter an entire community's way of life. Finally, meet the high-spirited María, the young woman who captures Jaime's heart and mind. However, their mutual attraction may prove to be fleeting if Jaime does not grapple with the moral issues that confront him. As events unfold and the forces of nature conspire to draw the characters together, Jaime is forced to make the most difficult decision of his life.

Dramatic and engaging, the *Sol y viento* film serves as the centerpiece for *Sol y viento: En breve.* Divided into ten episodes, consisting of a prologue and nine segments of approximately ten minutes each, the movie is easily managed for viewing in class and is fully integrated into the textbook. Students see each episode multiple times with varied accompanying activities, thus maximizing their exposure to language and greatly increasing their comprehension skills. Language is taken directly from the movie to illustrate grammar points, and the movie also provides points of departure for readings and discussions on cultural themes. In the Instructional Version of the film, approximately five hours long, on-screen activities facilitate instruction and learning.

Sol y viento: En breve—The Textbook

Equally innovative and as interesting as the movie, the *Sol y viento: En breve* textbook is firmly framed in communicative-oriented language teaching. This brief version of the highly successful *Sol y viento* textbook (2005, McGraw-Hill) presents an easily manageable text for a number of different courses, including those for high (false) beginners, intensive courses, and courses with fewer contact hours.

Completely meaning-based and drill-free, it presents the grammatical points that most instructors expect to cover in a first-year college-level Spanish course. How does it do this? *Sol y viento: En breve* borrows from the most recent innovations and research in instructed second language acquisition. Using an input-to-output approach for the presentation of vocabulary and grammar, *Sol y viento: En breve* provides instructors and students with a clear focus on the language without sacrificing meaning; or, to look at it another way, it provides a clear focus on meaning without sacrificing a focus on the language.

In short, *Sol y viento: En breve* provides the instructor with a refreshing approach to grammar instruction and practice that fits well within the tenets of communicative language teaching. The materials allow instructors to maintain a simultaneous focus on both meaning and formal properties of language as students are engaged in learning about their classmates, their instructor, and the world around them. Paired with an exciting movie, the *Sol y viento: En breve* textbook provides students with a complete and effective

beginning Spanish course that will lead them to higher levels of proficiency in comprehension and production than they might achieve with other materials. However, *Sol y viento: En breve* is not a set of learning materials focused on vocabulary and grammar alone. As a complete learning package, it presents abundant information on cultural topics relevant to the Spanish-speaking world, as well as opportunities for students to develop their reading and writing abilities.

For a more detailed description on using the film and textbook together, please refer to the *Instructor's Manual and Testing Program* or to the Instructor Edition on the Online Learning Center Website at **www.mhhe.com/syvenbreve.**

A Guided Tour of the Textbook

Episode Opener

The text is divided into eight units (**Episodios**) with two lessons each (**A** and **B**), for a total of 16 regular lessons. Thus, **Lecciones 1A** and **1B** correspond to **Episodio 1** of the film, **Lecciones 2A** and **2B** correspond to **Episodio 2,** and so forth. **Episodio 9** is covered in a three-page wrap-up of the film.

Lesson Opener

Lesson openers provide a list of goals that prepare students for what they will learn in the lesson.

Lesson Organization

Each lesson is organized into three parts (**Primera parte, Segunda parte, Tercera parte**), each of which contains a **Vocabulario** and **Gramática** presentation and accompanying activities. An audio recording of the **Vocabulario** presentations can be found on the Online Learning Center.

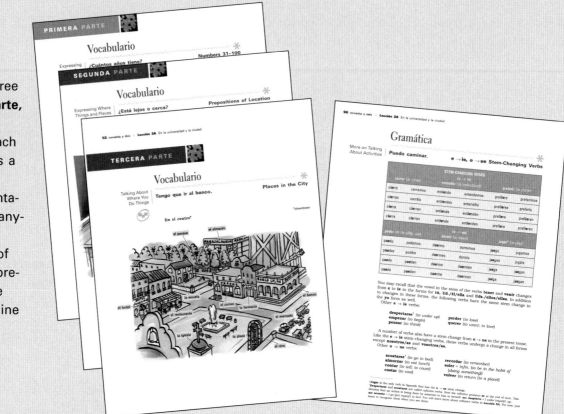

Sol y viento

Every "B" lesson concludes with a two-page **Sol y viento** section that focuses on the story line and characters of the film with pre- and post-viewing activities.

Cultural Features

- Each lesson contains three **Vistazo cultural** sections that focus on a cultural topic of interest related to the lesson theme. Topics range from "big C" culture (art, literature, and so forth) to "little c" culture (everyday life, customs, and so forth).
- *Sol y viento:* **Enfoque cultural** sections explore a cultural point illustrated in the *Sol y viento* film.

Additional Features

- **De *Sol y viento*** boxes highlight portions of dialogue from the film that illustrate grammar points presented in the text. In this way, students are able to view the grammar in context in the film. In addition, they offer "previews" of scenes that will aid student comprehension of the episode.
- **Enfoque lingüístico** features help students understand the nature of language in general. Although Spanish and English are often compared, for students to fully capture how languages work, contrasts with languages such as Chinese, Arabic, and Nahuatl also appear.
- **Más vocabulario** and **Más gramática** boxes are found in **Vocabulario** and **Gramática** sections, respectively, and present additional vocabulary and grammar that students need to know to complete the accompanying activities.
- **¡Exprésate!** boxes highlight a key element of language, whether vocabulary, useful phrases, or structures, that students will need to complete accompanying activities.
- **Comunicación útil** features present useful phrases and other tips for successfully communicating in Spanish.
- **Detrás de la cámara** boxes are found in *Sol y viento* sections and provide additional information not presented in the film, such as the characters' background, motivation, personalities, and so forth.
- **Icons** highlight partner/pair or group work, activities that require listening to the instructor for information, writing activities that require an additional sheet of paper, and content provided on the Online Learning Center.

Vistazo cultural

Diseñadores° hispanos

For decades, a number of Hispanic designers... for their elegant, high-end fashion designs... created a world-renowned fashion house in... success on both sides of the Atlantic. Venezu... can Óscar de la Renta have been at the fore... than two decades. In addition to creating ac... known for creating designs described as... Cuban-American Narciso Rodríguez gained r... for Carolyn Bessette Kennedy in 1996. His d... such as Salma Hayek and Sarah Jessica Pa...

In terms of popular fashion, perhaps the b... born entrepreneur Amancio Ortega. What st... in provincial Galicia in the early sixties has turned into an empire of more than one thousand stores worldwide and the third-largest clothing company in the world (after Gap and the Swedish HM). Ortega's flagship store is Zara, which can be found in many Spanish cities, as well as in major cities in Europe, the United States, and Asia.

°*Designers*

▲ Carolina Herre...

SOL Y VIENTO: Enfoque cultural

City parks abound in Spanish-speaking countries, as they do in this country. However, they are often used in different ways. In **Episodio 2** you will watch Jaime as he jogs through the Parque Forestal in Santiago. However, using a public park as a place to exercise is not the norm for most Spanish-speaking people. Instead, parks are often places to socialize, and on Sundays they may flourish with couples and families of all ages out for an old-fashioned Sunday afternoon stroll (**el paseo**). It is also typical to find vendors of all types in these parks selling everything from cotton candy to balloons, as well as entertainers working for donations, such as the organ-grinding fortune teller with his parrot that you will see in this episode. Some well-known parks in Spanish-speaking cities include the Retiro (Madrid), Lazema (Buenos Aires), and Chapultepec (Mexico City), among others.

▲ El parque Chapultepec (México, D.F.)

DE SOL Y VIENTO

In **Episodio 2** of *Sol y viento*, you will watch a scene in which Jaime bumps into María while he's reading a fortune. Part of their exchange appears in the dialogue.

JAIME
¡Le _____ mil disculpas!° ... distraído.

MUCHACHO
El señor estaba leyendo° el pa... la suerte.°

MARÍA
Ah. Debe ser una suerte exce...

Based on the context of the dialo... the verb that best completes Ja... ment.

1. sirvo   **2.** me visto

°*Le... I'm sorry! (lit: A thousand par...*

Enfoque lingüístico

Más sobre las inflexiones

You may recall that *inflections* are forms that are added to words that provide the listener with certain information. For example, you learned in **Lección 1A** that one way in which Spanish is an inflectionally rich language is that its verb inflections are unique for each person (e.g., *I, you, he/she, we,* and *they*). In the last few lessons, you've learned the present-tense inflections for Spanish **-ar, -er,** and **-ir** verbs. Later in *Sol y viento* you will learn other verb inflections to express various meanings and speaker perspectives. All of the Spanish verb inflections that you will learn are *suffixes;* that is, they are forms that are attached to the *end* of a word or stem. (Remember in **Lección 1A** you read that you will have to get used to listening to the ends of verbs to find out who is being talked about.)

However, not all languages use suffixes for verbal inflections. Some Native American languages like Navajo use *prefixes* (forms attached to the *beginning* of a word or ... ...ix **naal** (roughly equivalent ...o) to form **naalnish**. Instead ... inserted in the *middle* of

MÁS VOCABULARIO

comprar	to buy	Estoy buscando...	I'm looking for...
gastar	to spend	¿Puedo probarme...?	May I try on...?
regatear	to bargain	Sólo estoy mirando.	I'm just looking.
vender	to sell		
barato/a	inexpensive	¿Cuál es su talla?	What size do you wear?
caro/a	expensive		
de compras	shopping	¿Qué número calza?	What size shoe do you wear?
la marca	brand name		
el precio (fijo)	(fixed) price	¿Me queda bien?	Does it fit me?
la talla	size	Creo que le queda un poco grande.	I think it's a lit... big on you.
grande	large		
mediano/a	medium		
pequeño/a	small		

¿En q... servi...

MÁS GRAMÁTICA

Although **bien** is usually translated into English as *well* when used wit... it is usually translated as *to be OK/fine.*

Está bien. — *It's OK. / That's fine.*
Estoy bien, gracias. — *I'm fine, thanks.*

¿Necesitan algo más? — *Do you all need anything else?*
N... ...E... ...bien.

¡Exprésate!

In addition to the expression **tener que** + *infinitive,* the following expressions also take infinitives:

Hay que...	*One must...*
Es buena idea...	*It's a good idea...*
Es necesario...	*It's necessary...*

COMUNICACIÓN ÚTIL

You can use the words **aquí** (*here*) and **allí** (*there; over there*) to... tionships between people, places, and things.

—¿Te gusta esta bolsa blanca que tengo **aquí**? — *Do you like this white... have here?*

—Sí, pero prefiero esa roja en la mesa **allí**. — *Yes, but I prefer that... the table over there.*

Detrás de la cámara

Although Jaime seems happy while talking with María, have you noticed in these beginning episodes that something seems to be gnawing at him? Is it professional? Or is it something in his personal life? Jaime has had to

Supplements

As a full-service publisher of quality educational products, McGraw-Hill does much more than just sell textbooks to your students. We create and publish an extensive array of print, video, and digital supplements to support instruction on your campus. Orders of new (versus used) textbooks help us to defray the cost of developing such supplements, which is substantial. Please consult your local McGraw-Hill representative to learn about the availability of the supplements that accompany *Sol y viento: En breve*.

For Students and Instructors

- Available for purchase in VHS or DVD formats, the *Instructional Version* of the *Sol y viento* film contains on-screen pre- and post-viewing activities for each episode (written by Isabel Anievas-Gamallo and Scott Tinetti). This version also contains film clips of the **De Sol y viento** features in the text, as well as additional features such as interviews with the cast and crew, a behind-the-scenes look at the filming of *Sol y viento,* and much more.

- The *Director's Cut* is also available for those who wish to purchase it. This version of the film (in VHS or DVD formats) contains the complete, uninterrupted movie, with or without Spanish subtitles. The DVD version contains individual episodes of the film, without any on-screen activities, as well as special features.

- McGraw-Hill is proud to partner with **Quia™** in the development of the *Sol y viento: En breve, Digital Edition,* which presents all of the content from the textbook in an engaging and interactive online format. With built-in audio, video, real-time chat feature, and robust gradebook, the *Digital Edition* is ideal for distance learning or hybrid courses.

- The *Manual de actividades* offers additional practice with vocabulary, grammar, and listening comprehension. Two distinguishing features of the *Manual* are the **¡A escuchar!** section at the end of every "A" lesson and the **Para escribir** section at the end of every "B" lesson. **¡A escuchar!** provides in-depth listening comprehension practice, accompanied by listening strategies. **Para escribir** guides students through the process of writing, from jotting down ideas, to creating outlines and rough drafts, and finally to the reviewing and editing of the final written piece. Verb charts and an Answer Key provide excellent reference materials for students.

- Carefully integrated with the textbook, the *Online Manual de actividades* is a robust digital version of the printed *Manual* and is easy for students to use and great for instructors who want to manage students' course work online. Identical in practice material to the print version, the *Online Manual* contains the complete audio program and provides students with automatic feedback and scoring of their work. The Instructor Workstation contains an easy-to-use gradebook and class roster system that facilitates course management.

- The *Audio Program* to accompany the *Manual* provides additional listening comprehension practice outside of the classroom.

- The *Interactive CD-ROM to accompany Sol y viento* is available for purchase in a multiplatform format and offers students opportunities to review the vocabulary and grammar presented in the textbook, as well as the story line and characters of the *Sol y viento* film, all in an engaging multimedia environment. It also contains interactive verb charts, a glossary, and interactive maps of the Spanish-speaking world.

- The Student Edition of the Online Learning Center Website (**www.mhhe.com/syvenbreve**) provides even more practice with the vocabulary and grammar presented in the textbook. It also contains useful resources, such as interactive verb charts, grammar tutorials, and the laboratory audio program.

- The *Student Viewer's Guide* is ideal for those courses in which the *Sol y viento* film is used as a supplement to another core text. The *Student Viewer's Guide* offers a variety of pre- and post-viewing activities for use with the film, as well as cultural information and a process writing activity that accompanies each episode of the film.

For Instructors Only

- The annotated *Instructor's Edition* contains detailed suggestions for carrying out activities in class. It also offers options for expansion and follow-up.

- The combined *Instructor's Manual and Testing Program* expands on the methodology of the *Sol y viento: En breve* materials. Among other things, it offers suggestions for carrying out the activities in the textbook. It also contains the complete script of the *Sol y viento* film and information on using *Sol y viento: En breve* for distance learning courses. The *Testing Program* includes sample quizzes for each lesson as well as a comprehension quiz for each episode.

- The *Picture File* contains fifty images from the film that may be used as a springboard for student discussion about the film or related topics.

- The *instructor's section* of the Online Learning Center Website (**www.mhhe.com/syvenbreve**) contains many digital resources to assist instructors in getting the most out of the *Sol y viento: En breve* program. Such resources include the *Instructor's Manual and Testing Program*, PowerPoint® slides, Digital Transparencies, *Picture File*, and *Audioscript*.

Because the instructor's side of the Online Learning Center is password-protected, please contact your local McGraw-Hill sales representative to obtain a password.

Acknowledgments

We owe a ton of thanks to lots of people. First, to everyone at McGraw-Hill who saw this project from start to finish: Christa Harris, Thalia Dorwick, Bill Glass, Scott Tinetti, Nick Agnew, David Staloch, Violeta Díaz, and Laura Chastain. Extra thanks to Christa, who was our sponsoring editor and helped us shape this project; and other extra thanks to Scott, our development editor— always a pleasure! Thanks to Thalia for staying on after retirement as an additional pair of eyes. We would also like to thank Steve Debow, who was behind this project 100 percent and who is such an avid supporter of languages. And no less enthusiastic are our thanks to our publisher, Bill Glass. We can think of no publishing team better to work with than the people at McGraw-Hill.

We are also indebted to the members of our advisory panel who carefully read the manuscript and screened the movie during development. Their feedback along the way was invaluable. We would also like to thank all of the additional reviewers for their feedback.

A round of thanks to all the folks at Truth-Function who were involved with the filming of the movie: David Murray (our great director), Hugo Kryspin (our second unit director), Rocío Barajas (producer), Lamar Owen (director of photography), and Tom Sherer (associate producer, still photography), among others. Of course, many thanks to the local production crew in Chile, headed by Rodrigo Fernández of RF Films, as well as all of the talented actors, most notably Frank Lord (Jaime) and Javiera Contador (María). Such great professionals. Thanks also to the Gil family of the Miraflores winery in the Maipo Valley who so graciously let us film in their home and on their land. Thanks to Carlos Barón for his work on the screenplay and for being such a great source of information. Big thanks to Brendan Carollo and Mark Overstreet for their work on the CD-ROM, to María A. Pérez for her excellent work on the Testing Program (and other things, too), and finally to Enrique Álvarez for serving as a native informant and occasional reader.

Finally, thanks to all our loved ones who put up with overcommitted authors and academics. We think we can do it all, but in reality we can only do it because of your patience.

The authors and the publisher wish to express their gratitude to the following instructors across the country, whose valuable suggestions contributed to the preparation of this program. Special thanks are due to our Advisory Panel members, who provided us valuable feedback at every step of the way, from the writing of the film's script to the development of the print and media materials. The appearance of their names in this list does not necessarily constitute their endorsement of the text or its methodology.

Advisory Panel

Barbara Gatski, The Millbrook School
Kathy O'Connor, Tidewater Community College
Jeff Stevenson, University of Washington
Miguel Verano, United States Air Force Academy
Joseph Weyers, College of Charleston

Reviewers

Isabel Anievas-Gamallo, San Joaquín Delta College
Maritza Chinea-Thornberry, University of Southern Florida
Daria Cohen, Princeton University
Rosalinda Rivera Collins, Polk Community College
Georgia Decker, College of the Desert
Mary Ebuna, Colorado Mountain College
Yolanda Hernández, Community College of Southern Nevada
Jennifer Leeman, George Mason University
Gillian Lord, University of Florida, Gainesville
Gerardo Augusto Lorenzino, Temple University
Ana María Meyers, Polk Community College
Sue Pechter, Northwestern University
Stacey Powell, Auburn University
Jacobo Sefamí, University of California, Irvine
José Luis Suárez-García, Colorado State University

Survey Participants

Catalina Aguilar, Fort Lewis College
Shannon Álvarez, Monmouth College
Yuly Asención, Northern Arizona University
Larry Banducci, Cabrillo College
Kevin Beard, Richland College
Kathryn Birkhead, Pikes Peak Community
  College
Melissa S. Bronfman, Albright College
Carmela Bruni-Bossio, University of Alberta
Guada Cabedo-Timmons, Western Illinois
  University
Elizabeth Calvera, Virginia Tech
Stephen J. Clark, Northern Arizona University
José Juan Colín, University of Oklahoma
Xuchitl N. Coso, Georgia Perimeter College
Danion Doman, Truman State University
Rosalba Esparragoza-Scott, Davidson College
John L. Finan, William Rainey Harper College
Jill R. Gauthier, Miami University-Hamilton
María José Giménez, Dalhousie University
Anna Hamling, University of New Brunswick
Carmen M. Hernández, Grossmont College
Christy P. Hyland, Washington and Jefferson
  College
Shelly Jarrett-Bromberg, Miami University-
  Hamilton
Valerie Job, South Plains College
Wayne Langehennig, South Plains College

Paz Macías, Carnegie Mellon University
Ramón Magrans, Austin Peay State University
Jeanne Martínez, Arizona State University
Deanna Mihaly, Emory & Henry College
Yelgy Parada, Los Angeles City College
Inmaculada Pertusa, Western Kentucky
  University
Comfort Pratt, Texas Tech University
Rita Ricaurte, Nebraska Wesleyan University
Marcie Rinka, University of San Diego
Anthony J. Robb, Rowan University
Tara Rojas, Leeward Community College
Tracy Rutledge, Texas Tech University
Monica F. Sasscer, Northern Virginia Community
  College
José A. Sainz, University of Mary Washington
Jacquelyn Sandone, University of Missouri
Rosemary Sands, St. Norbert College
Barbara Sawhill, Oberlin College
Melissa Stewart, Western Kentucky University
Roy L. Tanner, Truman State University
Silvia N. Teodorescu, Hartnell College
Beverly Turner, Truckee Meadows Community
  College
Phyllis E. VanBuren, St. Cloud State University
Sherry Velasco, University of Kentucky
Brenda Watts, Southwest Missouri State
  University

¡Aquí estamos![a]

OBJETIVOS

IN THIS PRELIMINARY LESSON, YOU WILL:

- **learn how to greet people and make introductions in Spanish**
- **learn the verb ser and some of its basic uses**
- **talk about courses and majors**
- **learn about articles and the gender and number of nouns**
- **name common objects and people in the classroom**
- **learn the verb estar and one of its basic uses**

In addition, you will prepare for and watch the **Prólogo** of the film *Sol y viento*.

◀

This woman is a **machi,** a spiritual leader within the Mapuche tribe of Chile. What do you think she is doing? Is she telling a tale? Leading a group in song? Warning of an impending danger?

The following media resources are available for *Sol y viento: En breve*

Prólogo of
Sol y viento

Online *Manual de actividades*

Interactive CD-ROM

Online Learning Center Website

[a]¡Aquí... *Here we are!*

Vocabulario

Meeting and Greeting People | **Me llamo...**

Introductions ✳

—¡**Hola! Soy** Tomás Villa.
—¡**Hola! Me llamo** Jorge. Jorge Mateos.
—**¿Cómo se llama él?**
—**No sé.**

The most common way to greet someone in Spanish is to say **hola,** equivalent to *hello* in English. Note the following exchange in Spanish.

¡**Hola! Me llamo** Paco.	*Hi! My name is Paco.*
¡**Hola! Soy** Elena. **Mucho gusto.**	*Hi! I'm Elena. Pleased to meet you.*
Igualmente.	*Likewise.*

✳ MÁS VOCABULARIO

¿Cómo te llamas?	What's your name?
Mi nombre es Paula.*	My name is Paula.
¿Cuál es tu apellido?	What's your last name?
Mi apellido es González.	My last name is González.
¿Cómo se llama (él/ella)?	What's his/her name?
¿Cuál es su apellido?	What's his/her last name?
No sé.	I don't know.

Actividad A En orden

Put the following phrases in the order in which two speakers would most likely say them.

____ Mucho gusto.   ____ ¡Hola! Soy Pablo. ¿Cómo te llamas?

____ Mi nombre es Adriana.   ____ Igualmente.

---

*In Spanish, **mi nombre es** is a word-for-word equivalent to the English *my name is.* However, **me llamo** is literally translated as *I call myself.* When you ask **¿Cómo te llamas?** you are actually saying *How do you call yourself?* So don't make the mistake of thinking **me** means *my* and **llamo** means *name.* In Spanish *my* is **mi** and *name* is **nombre.**

Actividad B ¿Cuál es? (*Which one is it?*)

Listen as your instructor says a phrase. Then select the phrase that would most logically follow it.

1. **a.** Soy Alfredo.   **b.** Mucho gusto.   **c.** ¡Hola!
2. **a.** Me llamo Paula.   **b.** Es Rodríguez.   **c.** ¿Cómo te llamas?
3. **a.** Igualmente.   **b.** ¿Cuál es tu apellido?   **c.** ¡Hola!

Actividad C Algunas (*Some*) personas famosas

Answer the question your instructor asks about each of these photos.

▲ 1.   ▲ 2.   ▲ 3.   ▲ 4.

Actividad D ¡A conocernos! (*Let's get acquainted!*)

Move around the room, greeting and introducing yourself to at least four people. Write down their first and last names.

NOMBRE	APELLIDO
1. _____	_____
2. _____	_____
3. _____	_____
4. _____	_____

¡Exprésate!

In addition to **hola,** you might want to use the following greetings. In Hispanic cultures, these expressions are typical when meeting and greeting people. Try using them as you complete **Actividad D.**

Buenos días.
Good morning.

Buenas tardes.
Good afternoon/evening.

The expression **Buenas noches** (*Good night*) is used when saying good-bye in the evening.

≋ Vistazo cultural

Los saludos[a]

In the Spanish-speaking world, when people first meet it is customary for them to shake hands, no matter their age or sex. When friends greet each other, men generally shake hands and women kiss each other on the cheek. In Spain, a kiss on each cheek is the norm, whereas a kiss on one cheek is customary elsewhere. Kissing on the cheek between male and female friends varies from country to country but is fairly typical, especially among younger friends. As you watch the episodes of *Sol y viento,* pay attention to the ways in which people greet each other.

Un saludo entre (*between*) amigos hispanos ▶

[a]Los... *Greetings*

Gramática

Expressing Origin | **Soy de México.**   **Introduction to ser** ✳

—¿**De dónde eres,** Jorge?
—**De** Nueva York. ¿Y tú?
—**Soy de** Puerto Rico, de San Juan.

Spanish has two verbs that mean *to be.* In this section, you will focus on the verb **ser.** One very common use of **ser** is to express one's place of origin. In this case, it is used with the preposition **de,** which means *from* in this particular expression.

Jennifer López **es de** Nueva York.	*Jennifer López is from New York.*
Antonio Banderas **es de** España.	*Antonio Banderas is from Spain.*

All Spanish verbs have endings that express the English equivalents of subject pronouns (**los pronombres personales**) *I, you, he/she, we,* and so on. Spanish also uses formal and informal ways to address people. When talking to someone whom you don't know well, who is older, or who is in a position of respect, use **usted.** When talking to a friend, family member, or a person younger than you, use **tú.*** Here are the forms for **ser.**

ser (*to be*)			
(yo) **soy**	I am	(nosotros/as) **somos**	we are
(tú) **eres**	you (*informal, singular*) are	(vosotros/as) **sois**	you (*informal, plural, Spain*) are
(usted) **es**	you (*formal, singular*) are	(ustedes) **son**	you (*formal, plural*) are
(él/ella) **es**	he/she is	(ellos/ellas)† **son**	they are

✳ MÁS GRAMÁTICA

¿De dónde eres?	Where are you from?
¿Y él?	And him?
Es de Guatemala **también.**	He's from Guatemala too.

---

*You will learn more about these distinctions later. For now, you should use **tú** with your classmates; your instructor will tell you what to use with him or her.
†The issue of when to use **ellos** and when to use **ellas** is dealt with later in this book.

Actividad E   ¿De dónde eres?

Paso (*Step*) **1**   Complete each sentence with correct information for you. Your instructor will then call on some of you to present your information. How many of your classmates are from the same city or state as you? How many of you are from the same city or state as your parents? (If you opted to talk about your children, are you from the same place as they are?)

   1. Soy de _____ (*city/state/country*).

   2. Mis padres (*My parents*) son de _____.

   3. (Optativo) Mis hijos (*children*) son de _____.

Paso 2   Now ask two people next to you where they are from. Are they from the same place as you? If you want to ask about a person's parents or children you should ask **¿De dónde son tus padres (hijos)?**

Actividad F   ¿Cómo se escribe? (*How is it spelled?*)

Paso 1   You may have to spell your name or the name of the place you are from very often in Spanish. Listen as your instructor reviews the Spanish alphabet, presented on the inside front cover of the text.

Paso 2   Listen as your instructor spells the names of some countries and cities. Write down what you hear.

   1. ...   **2.** ...   **3.** ...   **4.** ...   **5.** ...   **6.** ...   **7.** ...

Paso 3   Listen as your instructor spells some names in Spanish. Write down what you hear. Do you know what their English equivalents are?

   1. ...   **2.** ...   **3.** ...   **4.** ...   **5.** ...   **6.** ...   **7.** ...

Actividad G   ¡A conocernos mejor (*better*)!

Introduce yourself to four more people in the classroom and find out the following information about each one. You may have to spell your name or place of origin (**lugar de origen**). Be prepared to present the information to the rest of the class afterward.

	NOMBRE	APELLIDO	LUGAR DE ORIGEN
1.	_____	_____	_____
2.	_____	_____	_____
3.	_____	_____	_____
4.	_____	_____	_____

Vocabulario

Talking About
Majors and Classes

Las materias

School Subjects

las humanidades y las artes*

el arte
la filosofía
los idiomas / las lenguas
  (*languages*)
    el alemán (*German*)
    el español
    el francés
    el inglés
la literatura
la música

las ciencias sociales

la antropología
las ciencias políticas
la historia
la psicología
la sociología

las ciencias naturales

la astronomía
la biología
la física
la química (*chemistry*)

el comercio (*business*)

la administración de empresas
  (*business administration*)
la contabilidad (*accounting*)
la economía (*economics*)

los estudios interdepartamentales

los estudios latinos (*Latino studies*)
los estudios sobre el género
  (*gender studies*)

otras (*other*) **materias**

las comunicaciones
la informática (*computer science*)
**la ingeniería (civil, eléctrica,
  mecánica)**
las matemáticas

✳ MÁS VOCABULARIO

¿Cuál es tu campo? **¿Qué carrera haces?**	What's your major?
¿Qué estudias?	What are you studying?
Estudio...	I'm studying . . .
Todavía no sé.	I still don't know.
¿Qué clases tienes este semestre/trimestre?	What classes do you have this semester/quarter?
Tengo una clase de...	I have a . . . class.

*When used in the singular, **el arte** takes the masculine article **el**. When pluralized, the feminine article **las** is used: **las artes.** You will learn more about gender and articles in **Segunda parte: Gramática.**

Actividad A Asociaciones

Paso 1 Indicate the item you associate with the subject matter your instructor mentions.

1. **a.** el microscopio   **b.** las guerras mundiales (*world wars*)
2. **a.** Mozart   **b.** B.F. Skinner
3. **a.** los chimpancés   **b.** las novelas
4. **a.** la Bolsa (*stock market*)   **b.** el Museo (*Museum*) del Prado
5. **a.** Friedrich Nietzsche   **b.** la calculadora
6. **a.** España   **b.** la geometría

Paso 2 Go back to the items you didn't choose. Can you give a subject matter association for each one?

Actividad B Uno estudia... (*One studies . . .*)

Using the following columns, make logical sentences according to the model.

MODELO: En economía uno estudia la Bolsa.

En...   ...uno estudia...
1. ___ historia   **a.** las reacciones nucleares.
2. ___ física   **b.** la lógica.
3. ___ arte   **c.** el comportamiento (*behavior*) de las personas.
4. ___ química   **d.** las causas y consecuencias de las guerras.
5. ___ filosofía   **e.** las propiedades de los elementos.
6. ___ psicología   **f.** el uso (*use*) del color y de la luz (*light*).

Actividad C ¿Cuál es su (*his/her*) campo?

Listen as your instructor reads statements from several people. Can you guess what that person's major is? Note: The word **sobre** means *about* (**una clase** *sobre* **Shakespeare**).

1. ...   2. ...   3. ...   4. ...

Actividad D ¿Qué clases tienes?

Following the model, interview three people to find out what classes they are taking and what they think of them. Be sure to jot down the information.

MODELO: E1*: ¿Qué clases tienes este semestre/trimestre?
E2*: Tengo una clase de biología, una de historia y una de español.
E1: ¡Gracias! (*Thanks!*)
E2: De nada. (*You're welcome.*)

---

*E1 and E2 will be used throughout *Sol y viento* to represent **Estudiante 1 (uno)** and **Estudiante 2 (dos)**, respectively.

Gramática

Naming Things │ **El cálculo y las matemáticas**

En **el escritorio** de **la profesora hay** (*there are*) **un libro, una pluma** y **una mochila.**

Unlike English, Spanish has grammatical gender. Every spanish noun (a person, a place, a thing, or an idea) is classified as being either masculine or feminine. The two categories distinguish animate beings on the basis of biological gender: **el hombre** (*the man*), **la mujer** (*the woman*). However, their application to inanimate things is arbitrary; chairs, tables, and books, for example, have no biological gender, but they have grammatical gender in Spanish.

Gender is expressed not only in the noun but in the article that accompanies it. Spanish also expresses number (singular versus plural) with its articles.

ARTICLES, GENDER, AND NUMBER		
	MASCULINO	FEMENINO
Singular	**un** libro (*a book*)	**una** pizarra (*a chalkboard*)
	el libro (*the book*)	**la** pizarra (*the chalkboard*)
	un profesor (*a male professor*)	**una** profesora (*a female professor*)
	el profesor (*the male professor*)	**la** profesora (*the female professor*)
Plural	**unos** libros (*some books*)	**unas** pizarras (*some chalkboards*)
	los libros (*the books*)	**las** pizarras (*the chalkboards*)
	unos profesores (*some professors*)	**unas** profesoras (*some professors [female only]*)
	los profesores (*the professors*)	**las** profesoras (*the professors [female only]*)

In general, any noun ending in **-o** or in most consonants is masculine. Most nouns ending in **-a** are feminine. However, biological gender takes precedence over any ending as in **una mujer** (*a woman*) versus **un señor** (*a man*), which both end in a consonant. You will continue to learn the gender of nouns throughout your study of Spanish. For now, here is a list to help you get started.

un chico	a boy	**un escritorio**	a desk
una chica	a girl	**un lápiz**	a pencil
un estudiante	a (male) student	**un libro**	a book
una estudiante	a (female) student	**una mochila**	a backpack
un hombre	a man	**una pluma**	a pen
una mujer	a woman	**una silla**	a chair

Actividad E ¿Qué es? (*What is it?*)

Listen to and answer the questions your instructor asks. Note that the verb **ser** is used to identify people, objects, and things as in *It's a pencil* = **Es un lápiz.**

MODELO: PROFESOR(A): ¿Es una pluma o (*or*) un lápiz?
TÚ: Es un lápiz.

Actividad F ¿Qué hay en una mochila típica?

Complete each statement to talk about what you might find in a typical student's backpack. Note: Your completed sentences must be both grammatical and logical, so pay attention to gender and number as well as meaning!

En una mochila hay...

1. unos...
   a. estudiantes   **b.** plumas   **c.** libros   **d.** escritorios

2. unas...
   a. plumas   **b.** sillas   **c.** lápices*   **d.** hombres

3. un...
   a. cartera (*wallet*)   **b.** cajita (*box*) de Tic-Tacs   **c.** teléfono celular   **d.** profesor

4. una...
   a. mujer   **b.** pluma   **c.** cuaderno (*notebook*)   **d.** disco compacto

¡Exprésate!

To express *there is* or *there are* and to ask *Is there . . . ?* or *Are there . . . ?* Spanish uses the verb **hay** (pronounced similar to English *eye*): **Hay unas mochilas en la clase. ¿Hay profesores excelentes en la universidad?**

Actividad G En la sala de clase (*classroom*)

With a partner, take turns pointing to two items in the room that are far away. The other should see if he or she can guess which items the first student is referring to. How many did you both guess correctly? (Note: **sí** = *yes.*)

MODELO: E1: (*points to two items*)
E2: ¿Son una mochila y una estudiante?
E1: No, son una silla y una estudiante.

---

*Nouns ending in **-z** must change this letter to a **c** when adding the plural suffix **-es.**

Vocabulario

Talking About
People and Things
in the Classroom
and on Campus

En la sala de clase

Classroom Objects

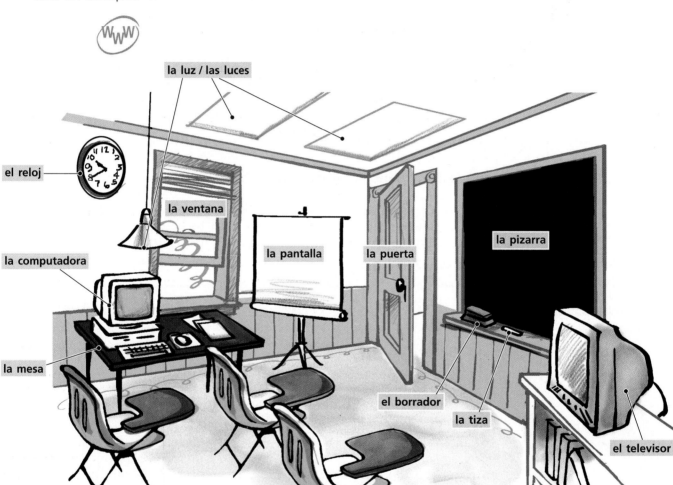

la luz / las luces

el reloj

la ventana

la computadora

la pantalla

la puerta

la pizarra

la mesa

el borrador

la tiza

el televisor

En la universidad

el auditorio	auditorium
la biblioteca	library
la cafetería	cafeteria
el edificio	building
la facultad	department
la librería	bookstore
la oficina	office
la residencia estudiantil	dormitory
el teléfono público	public phone

Actividad A ¿Sí o no?

Listen as your instructor names a classroom object. Does the object named fit the description given?

	SÍ	NO
1. Indica la hora. (*It tells the time.*)	☐	☐
2. Limpia (*It cleans*) la pizarra.	☐	☐
3. Deja entrar (*It lets in*) mucha (*lots of*) luz.	☐	☐
4. Es blanca (*white*).	☐	☐
5. Hay dos (*two*) en la sala de clase.	☐	☐

Actividad B Asociaciones

Match each item in the first column with an appropriate idea or phrase from the second.

1. ___ la librería

2. ___ la cafetería

3. ___ la residencia estudiantil

4. ___ la biblioteca

5. ___ la oficina del profesor (de la profesora)

6. ___ el teléfono público

a. comer (*to eat*)

b. vivir (*to live*)

c. hacer una cita (*to make an appointment*)

d. hacer una llamada (*to make a call*)

e. comprar (*to buy*) libros

f. sacar (*to check out*) libros

Actividad C La sala de clase y la universidad

Paso 1 Answer each question about what is in your Spanish classroom.

MODELO: ¿Hay una computadora? →
Sí, hay una computadora Macintosh. (No, no hay computadora.)

1. ¿Hay un reloj? ¿Es digital?

2. ¿Hay un televisor? ¿Con (*With*) vídeo? ¿con DVD?

3. ¿Hay una pantalla? ¿Hay un proyector (*projector*)?

4. ¿Hay una pizarra con tiza y borrador?

5. ¿Hay muchas (*many*) ventanas?

Paso 2 What do you know about your university or college? With a partner, read each question, then answer as best as you can. Prepare a brief statement to present your answers to your classmates. If you don't know the answer to a question, respond with **No sé** (*I don't know*).

MODELO: ¿Hay una Facultad de Español? →
No, no hay una Facultad de Español, pero (*but*) sí hay una Facultad de Lenguas Extranjeras.

1. ¿Cómo se llama la biblioteca?

2. ¿Cómo se llama el edificio donde tienes la clase de español?

3. ¿Hay una Facultad de Lenguas Extranjeras?

4. ¿Hay una oficina de servicios estudiantiles?

5. ¿Hay teléfonos públicos en todos (*all*) los edificios? Da (*Give*) un ejemplo.

6. ¿Hay residencias estudiantiles? ¿Cómo se llaman?

Gramática

Expressing
Location

—¿Dónde **está** la
biblioteca?
—**Está** enfrente de (*in front
of*) este edificio.

¡Están aquí!   Introduction to **estar**

You have already learned the verb **ser** and some of its uses. Here is a review of the uses you have studied so far.

1. to indicate where someone or something is from: **Soy de Chicago.
¿De dónde eres tú?**

2. to say what someone or something is: **Soy estudiante. Es una
mochila.**

Estar is another Spanish verb that is translated as *to be.* However, its uses are very different from those of **ser.** One important use of **estar** is to express location.

El libro **está** en el escritorio.	*The book is on the desk.*
Juan y Diego no **están** en clase.	*Juan and Diego are not in class.*

Here are the forms of **estar.**

estar (*to be*)			
yo	**estoy**	nosotros/as	**estamos**
tú	**estás**	vosotros/as	**estáis**
usted	**está**	ustedes	**están**
él/ella	**está**	ellos/ellas	**están**

🎞 DE SOL Y VIENTO

In the prologue of *Sol y viento* that you will soon watch, a character talks about the presence of certain beings. Here are some lines of dialogue from the prologue. Notice the use of **estar** to express location.

MACHI
¡Nuestros[a] espíritus **están** aquí! **Están**
con nosotros —¡siempre[b]!

What do you think is always with us? Do you agree with the following three statements?

1. Nuestros antepasados (*ancestors*) siempre están con nosotros.

2. El pasado (*The past*) siempre está con nosotros.

3. Nuestros hechos (*deeds*) siempre están con nosotros.

[a]*Our* [b]*always*

Actividad D   ¿Dónde está?

Listen to your instructor's questions. Answer them with one of the following phrases:

- en el escritorio / en la mesa
- en la silla
- en el suelo (*floor*)

1. ...   **2.** ...   **3.** ...   **4.** ...   **5.** ...   **6.** ...   **7.** ...   **8.** ...

Actividad E   ¿Quiénes (*Who*) están en el grupo?

Your instructor will ask several students to form a group in front of the class. Can you say who is in the group?

◉ Enfoque lingüístico

¿Dos verbos que significan lo mismo?[a]

You may wonder why Spanish needs two verbs that mean *to be* whereas English has only one. Simply put, languages vary widely. In this case, Spanish seems more complex to an English speaker. In Chinese, however, there is no verb *to be;* you would simply say something like "John here." In Arabic, the verb *to be* is used only in certain contexts and not in all tenses (e.g., present, past, future). As you continue your studies, you will see that Spanish expresses some subtle and somewhat abstract notions through the use of the two verbs that mean *to be.* Here's a sneak preview. In English, if one says "The apple is green," this could mean it isn't ripe or it could refer to its color (such as a Pippin or Granny Smith). In Spanish, the verb indicates which meaning is intended: **La manzana está verde** can only mean the apple isn't ripe, and **la manzana es verde** can only mean the apple is a green one, like a Pippin.

[a]que... *that mean the same thing*

▲ ¿Dónde está esta (*this*) persona? ¿Está en una oficina o en una sala de clase?

SOL Y VIENTO

Antes de ver[a] el episodio

[a]Antes... *Before watching*

You are about to watch the prologue of *Sol y viento*. In this brief episode, you will meet several principal characters, and a major plot line will be established. Before watching the episode, complete the activities in **Antes de ver el episodio.**

Actividad A Dos personajes (*characters*)

These are the two main characters you will meet in this episode. Try to determine which of the sentences for each character strikes you as true or likely based on a first impression from the photos.

▲ María Sánchez

1. Es profesora de economía.
2. Es española.
3. Es inteligente y dedicada.

▲ Jaime (James) Talavera

1. Es hombre de negocios (*businessman*).
2. Es español.
3. Es inteligente y sensible (*sensitive*).

Actividad B Un diálogo

In one scene, María speaks to her assistant. Read the dialogue and then select the word that you think best completes it.

MARÍA: ¿Qué quieres,[b] Diego?

DIEGO: Sólo quiero decirle[c] que _____ muy tarde.[d] Ya terminamos,[e] profesora.

[b]¿Qué... *What do you want*   [c]Sólo... *I just want to tell you*   [d]*late*   [e]Ya... *We're finished*

1. es   2. tienes   3. hay

Actividad C El episodio

Now watch the episode. Don't worry if you don't understand everything in Spanish; just try to get the gist of what is going on.

Después de ver^a el episodio

^aDespués... *After watching*

Actividad A ¿Qué recuerdas? (*What do you remember?*)

Answer each item based on what you remember from watching the **Prólogo**.

1. ¿Cómo se llama el señor que necesita viajar (*needs to travel*) a Chile?
   a. Andy   **b.** John   **c.** James

2. Él está muy contento (*He is very happy*) con la idea de viajar (*traveling*) a Chile. ¿Cierto (*True*) o falso?
   a. cierto   **b.** falso

3. ¿Cuál es la relación entre María y Diego?
   a. Ella es estudiante y él es profesor.
   b. Él es estudiante y ella es profesora.

4. Probablemente, la especialización (*specialty*) de María es...
   a. contabilidad.   **b.** ingeniería.   **c.** antropología.

Actividad B Verificación

Go back to **Actividad B** of **Antes de ver el episodio** and verify your answers. Remember: If it helps, watch the corresponding section of the episode again.

Actividad C Pistas (*Clues*) lingüísticas

One skill you will want to develop as you study Spanish is guessing the meaning of language from context. Here are the first lines of the scene between María and Diego:

> DIEGO: Es lindo, ¿no?
> MARÍA: Sí. Es muy lindo.

Go back and watch this scene again without looking up any words. What are they talking about and what do you think **lindo** means?

Actividad D Descripciones

Make statements about the following characters using the verb **ser** and the adjectives listed. For adjectives ending in **-o/a**, use **-o** with males and **-a** with females.

1. bilingüe
2. chileno/a (*Chilean*)
3. sabio/a (*wise*)
4. persistente
5. guapo/a (*good-looking*)

¡Exprésate!

You have been exposed to a number of question words. You can now understand them in context and use them in some expressions you have learned.

¿cómo?	how?
¿cuál?	which?/what?
¿dónde?	where?
¿por qué?	why?
¿qué?	what?
¿quién(es)?	who?

Notice how many of these are used in **Actividad A**.

Detrás de^b la cámara

You probably noticed that one of the main characters is addressed in the **Prólogo** as "James," but his given name (and the name with which he grew up) is "Jaime." Why do you suppose he goes by James, the English equivalent of Jaime? What might this tell you about his character?

Keep this in mind as you watch future episodes of *Sol y viento*. In what other ways may Jaime/James have left his past behind?

^bDetrás... *Behind*

▲ María

▲ Jaime (James)

▲ Andy

▲ la machi

RESUMEN DE VOCABULARIO

Las presentaciones

¿Cómo te llamas?	What's your name?
Me llamo…	My name is . . .
Mi nombre es…	
Soy…	I'm . . .
¿Cuál es tu apellido?	What's your last name?
Mi apellido es…	My last name is . . .
¿Cómo se llama (él/ella)?	What's his/her name?
¿Cuál es su apellido?	What's his/her last name?
¡Hola!	Hello! Hi!
Mucho gusto.	Pleased to meet you.
Igualmente.	Likewise.
Buenos días.	Good morning.
Buenas tardes.	Good afternoon/evening.
Buenas noches.	Good night.
¿De dónde eres?	Where are you from?
Soy de…	I'm from . . .

Las materias

la administración de empresas	business administration
la antropología	anthropology
el arte (pl. las artes)	art
la astronomía	astronomy
la biología	biology
las ciencias naturales	natural sciences
las ciencias políticas	political science
las ciencias sociales	social sciences
el comercio	business
las comunicaciones	communications
la contabilidad	accounting
la economía	economics
los estudios interdepartamentales	interdisciplinary studies
los estudios latinos	Latino studies
los estudios sobre el género	gender studies
la filosofía	philosophy
la física	physics
la historia	history
las humanidades	humanities

los idiomas / las lenguas	languages
el alemán	German
el español	Spanish
el francés	French
el inglés	English
la informática	computer science
la ingeniería (civil, eléctrica, mecánica)	(civil, electrical, mechanical) engineering
la literatura	literature
las matemáticas	mathematics
la música	music
la psicología	psychology
la química	chemistry
la sociología	sociology
¿Cuál es tu campo?	What's your major?
¿Qué carrera haces?	
¿Qué estudias?	What are you studying?
Estudio…	I'm studying . . .
Todavía no sé.	I still don't know.
¿Qué clases tienes este semestre/trimestre?	What classes do you have this semester/quarter?
Tengo una clase de…	I have a . . . class.

Verbos

estar (irreg.)	to be
hay	there is / there are
ser (irreg.)	to be

En la sala de clase

el borrador	eraser
el/la chico/a	boy/girl
la computadora	computer
el escritorio	desk
el/la estudiante	student
el hombre	man
el lápiz (pl. lápices)	pencil
el libro	book
la luz (pl. luces)	light
la mesa	table
la mochila	backpack
la mujer	woman

la pantalla	screen
la pizarra	chalkboard
la pluma	pen
el/la profesor(a)	professor
la puerta	door
el reloj	clock; watch
la silla	chair
el televisor	TV (set)
la tiza	chalk
la ventana	window

En la universidad

el auditorio	auditorium
la biblioteca	library
la cafetería	cafeteria
el edificio	building
la facultad	department
la librería	bookstore
la oficina	office
la residencia estudiantil	dormitory
el teléfono público	public telephone

Los pronombres personales

yo	I
tú	you (*inf., sing.*)
usted	you (*form., sing.*)
él	he
ella	she
nosotros/as	we
vosotros/as	you (*inf., pl., Sp.*)
ustedes	you (*form., pl.*)
ellos	they (*m. pl.*)
ellas	they (*f. pl.*)

Palabras adicionales

con	with
de	of; from
mucho/a/os/as	much, a lot; many
o	or
pero	but
sí	yes
y	and

EPISODIO 1

LECCIÓN 1A
LECCIÓN 1B

La llegada^a

Jaime has just arrived in Santiago, Chile. What do you think his mood is?

▼

▲ Who is the man talking to Jaime? Do you think Jaime is going to go see the Sánchez family at the Sol y viento winery right away?

◄

Who is the man in this office? How would you describe his expression?

^a*arrival*

Sobre los horarios^a

◄

El señor tiene una cita (*has an appointment*). ¿Llega tarde? (*Is he arriving late?*)

^aSobre... *About schedules*

Vocabulario

Talking About Your
Course Load

Llevo quince créditos.

Numbers 0–30

Los números 0–30

0 cero		
1 uno	11 once	21 veintiuno
2 dos	12 doce	22 veintidós
3 tres	13 trece	23 veintitrés
4 cuatro	14 catorce	24 veinticuatro
5 cinco	15 quince	25 veinticinco
6 seis	16 dieciséis	26 veintiséis
7 siete	17 diecisiete	27 veintisiete
8 ocho	18 dieciocho	28 veintiocho
9 nueve	19 diecinueve	29 veintinueve
10 diez	20 veinte	30 treinta

Dos y dos son cuatro
cuatro y dos son seis
seis y dos son ocho
y ocho, dieciséis

In Spanish, the numbers 16 through 19 and 21 through 29 are actually combinations of two numbers, but they are generally spelled as one. For example, **dieciséis** is actually **diez y seis, veintidós** is actually **veinte y dos,** and so forth.

✳ MÁS VOCABULARIO

¿Cuántos créditos llevas?	How many credits are you taking?
En total tengo veintiún* créditos.	I have twenty-one credits altogether.
Este semestre/trimestre llevo dieciocho créditos.	This term I'm taking eighteen credits.
Llevo doce créditos de ciencias.	I am taking twelve credits of science.
¿Tienes/Llevas muchas clases?	Do you have / Are you taking a lot of classes?
¿Tienes/Llevas muchos créditos?	Do you have / Are you taking a lot of credits?
Esteban lleva quince créditos.	Esteban is taking fifteen credits.

〰 Vistazo cultural

Los cursos y los créditos

Courses and grading in Spanish-speaking countries not only vary from systems used in this country, but they often vary from each other as well. Transcripts don't normally list credit hours, only classes. In Spain, grades are assigned using the terms **sobresaliente** (*excellent*), **notable** (*good*), **aprobado** (*passed*), and **suspendido** (*failed*). Based on this system, then, a Spanish student would never have a "G.P.A." as an American student would.

In universities throughout Latin America a numerical system is used, generally 0–10, with 10 being the highest possible grade. Unless you're in Puerto Rico, which uses a U.S.-based system, it doesn't make sense to ask someone studying in a Spanish-speaking country: **¿Cuántos créditos llevas?** Instead, you would simply ask students what year of university studies they are in and which classes they have, as in the following scene.

CLAUDIA: Manuel, ¿en qué año estás[a]?
MANUEL: Estoy en mi segundo.[b] ¿Y tú?
CLAUDIA: Igual. También estoy en mi segundo.
MANUEL: ¡Ah! Entonces tomas[c] Filosofía II, como[d] yo.
CLAUDIA: Exactamente.

[a]¿en... *what year are you in* [b]*second* [c]*you're taking* [d]*like*

***Veintiuno** shortens to **veintiún** when followed by a masculine noun, for example, **Tengo veintiún créditos.**

Actividad A ¿Qué número sigue (*follows*)?

Listen as your instructor says a number. Select the number that follows it.

1. **a.** 6 **b.** 16 **c.** 26
2. **a.** 15 **b.** 25 **c.** 5
3. **a.** 13 **b.** 3 **c.** 23
4. **a.** 7 **b.** 20 **c.** 19
5. **a.** 8 **b.** 11 **c.** 26
6. **a.** 2 **b.** 4 **c.** 14

Actividad B Números de teléfono

Paso 1 Listen as your instructor reads some telephone numbers, then write down what you hear. Can you get them all correct?

1. _____
2. _____
3. _____
4. _____

Paso 2 Look at the following ad for the Spanish magazine *Quo*. Can you say the phone number out loud? What do you think the number in parentheses is?

¡Suscríbete!

(55)9177 4342

SUSCRÍBETE y recibe 12 números de **Quo** por **$179** y te regalamos **$100** en una tarjeta electrónica para comprar lo que quieras en **Mixup**

Con tu suscripción sólo pagas **$14.90** por ejemplar y te ahorras **$121.00** sobre el precio de portada

ahorra 40%

Actividad C Una deducción

Listen as your instructor describes Marcos' schedule and total credits. Then answer these questions.

> **1.** ¿Cuántos créditos lleva Marcos en total?
>
> **2.** ¿Cuántas clases tiene (*does he have*)? ¿Y cuántas sesiones de laboratorio tiene?
>
> **3.** Sabiendo (*Knowing*) la respuesta (*answer*) al número 1, ¿cuántos créditos lleva cada (*each*) clase, probablemente? ¿y las sesiones de laboratorio?

Actividad D ¿Cuántos créditos?

Find three people to interview. Using the **Más vocabulario** from p. 21, find out what their class loads and credits are this term. Jot the information down because your instructor may call on you to present it to the rest of the class.

SOL Y VIENTO: Enfoque cultural

In **Episodio 1** of *Sol y viento*, you will see Jaime's arrival at the airport in Santiago, where he is greeted by an enthusiastic driver, Mario. Santiago, like any major city in the Spanish-speaking world, offers both private drivers like Mario as well as regular public taxis. However, taxi systems and taxi drivers vary from city to city. In Santiago, they are safe, clean, and convenient, and as in any great city there are lots of them. As in this country, in Chile the fare is calculated by meters, and there is no need to negotiate a price (unless you use a private taxi). In Mexico City, in contrast, you generally have to ask how much it will cost to get to your destination before getting in the taxi. If not, you may wind up paying much more than you should, as those taxis may not use meters. Nonetheless, in most Spanish-speaking countries outside of Spain, taxi rides tend to be less expensive than they are in this country.

▲ Hay muchos taxis en México, D.F.*

---

*D.F. = **Distrito Federal,** much like Washington, D.C. (District of Columbia)

Gramática

Talking About
Activities

Estudio y trabajo.

Regular -ar Verbs

REGULAR *-ar* VERBS llevar *(to take; to carry)*			
yo	llev**o**	nosotros/as	llev**amos**
tú	llev**as**	vosotros/as	llev**áis**
usted/Ud.*	llev**a**	ustedes/Uds.*	llev**an**
él/ella	llev**a**	ellos/ellas	llev**an**

You will remember from the **Lección preliminar** that verbs have forms for each subject pronoun in Spanish. The chart summarizes the forms that belong to what are called regular **-ar** verbs.

Present-tense verbs in Spanish can have three different meanings in English. For example, **llevo** can mean *I take* (simple present tense), *I am taking* (present progressive, indicating an action in progress), or *I will take* (near future). You will learn more about tense as you continue your studies in Spanish.

Since the verb ending expresses the subject, the subject pronoun is generally not necessary in Spanish except for emphasis or clarity. For example, it is sufficient to say **Llevo muchos créditos** without using **yo,** unless you are contrasting what you are saying with what someone else is saying, or you are emphasizing something. Note the following exchange in which Manolo contrasts what he says with what Marcos says.

> MARCOS: Llevo dieciséis créditos.
> MANOLO: Pues (*Well*), *yo* llevo veinte.
> MARCOS: ¡Uf! Es mucho.

An important thing to note is that the use of **nosotros, vosotros, ellos,** and **ellas** as pronouns depends on who is included in that particular group. **Nosotros, vosotros,** and **ellos** are used if the group is all male or of mixed sexes. **Nosotras, vosotras,** and **ellas** are used only if the group contains only females.

---

*The subject pronouns **usted** and **ustedes** are often abbreviated as **Ud.** and **Uds.,** respectively.

✳ MÁS VOCABULARIO

Here are some common regular **-ar** verbs that you will use in this lesson.

charlar	to chat
estudiar	to study
hablar	to speak; to talk
llamar (por teléfono)	to call (on the phone)
llevar	to take; to carry
navegar la red	to surf the Web
pagar (el alquiler)	to pay (the rent)
practicar (un deporte)	to practice (a sport)
preparar	to prepare
regresar (a casa)	to return (home)
tocar (la guitarra, el piano)	to play (the guitar, the piano)
tomar* (café, cerveza)	to drink (coffee, beer)
tomar* (una clase)	to take (a class)
trabajar	to work
visitar (a† la familia)	to visit (one's family)

🎞 DE SOL Y VIENTO

In **Episodio 1** of *Sol y viento* you will watch a scene in which Mario, a taxi driver eagerly waiting for a fare, rushes up to Jaime at the airport. Part of their exchange appears here.

MARIO
¡Para servirlo,ᵃ señor! ¡El mejor choferᵇ de Chile! ¿_____, señor?

JAIME
Al Hotel Bonaparte. ¿A cuánto sale?ᶜ

MARIO
Eh, um, unos diez milᵈ pesos, más o menos.ᵉ

Selecting from the list below, what do you think Mario asks in the phrase that's missing from the dialogue?

1. ¿De dónde es Ud.?

2. ¿Adónde lo llevo (*Where shall I take you*)?

3. ¿Necesita ayuda con las maletas? (*Do you need help with your luggage?*)

ᵃ¡Para... *At your service* ᵇ¡El... *The best driver* ᶜ¿A... *How much is it?* ᵈ*thousand*
ᵉmás... *more or less*

---

*You will learn that, like English, Spanish also contains words that have more than one meaning. Think of the word *run* in English. How many different meanings can you come up with? (Hint: run a mile, a run in your hose, a runny nose . . .)

†The **a** used in this phrase is called the **a personal** and has no direct equivalent in English. You will learn more about the **a personal** in subsequent lessons.

Actividad E ¿Cierto o falso? (*True or False?*)

Match each phrase in column A with one from column B to make a logical statement. Then, speculate whether each sentence is true for the *Sol y viento* character, Jaime.

	A		**B**	CIERTO	FALSO
	Jaime...				
1.	___ estudia	**a.**	la cena (*dinner*) cada noche.	☐	☐
2.	___ habla	**b.**	en un restaurante o bar.	☐	☐
3.	___ trabaja	**c.**	cuatro horas cada noche.	☐	☐
4.	___ prepara	**d.**	la guitarra en una banda.	☐	☐
5.	___ toca	**e.**	dos idiomas.	☐	☐
6.	___ toma	**f.**	café cada mañana.	☐	☐

Actividad F ¿Cuándo? (*When?*)

Paso 1 Indicate whether you do each activity daily (**cada día**), weekly (**cada semana**), monthly (**una vez al mes**), or never (**nunca**) on a normal basis.

		CADA DÍA	CADA SEMANA	UNA VEZ AL MES	NUNCA
1.	Trabajo.	☐	☐	☐	☐
2.	Regreso a la residencia / a casa.	☐	☐	☐	☐
3.	Llamo a un amigo por teléfono.	☐	☐	☐	☐
4.	Estudio español.	☐	☐	☐	☐
5.	Pago el alquiler (*rent*).	☐	☐	☐	☐
6.	Charlo con mis amigos por correo electrónico (*e-mail*).	☐	☐	☐	☐
7.	Navego la red.	☐	☐	☐	☐
8.	Visito a mi familia.	☐	☐	☐	☐

Paso 2 Now form questions using the **tú** form of the verbs, and interview someone in class to see if that person does the same thing as you. Jot down his or her responses.

MODELOS: Estudio español. → ¿Estudias español cada día?

Pago el alquiler. → ¿Pagas el alquiler una vez al mes?

Paso 3 Report to the class one thing you and your classmate do that's similar. Then indicate something the two of you do differently.

MODELOS: John y yo estudiamos español cada día.

Yo trabajo, pero John no trabaja.

Actividad G Personas célebres (*Famous people*)

For each statement, name at least two famous people who do the activity with some regularity.

MODELO: Tocan la guitarra. → Sting y Carlos Santana tocan la guitarra.

1. Tocan el piano.
2. Cantan (*They sing*) en público.
3. Bailan (*They dance*) en público.
4. Hablan español.
5. Hablan francés.
6. Practican el tenis.
7. Charlan con el presidente de los Estados Unidos.
8. Critican las películas (*movies*).

Actividad H El profesor (La profesora)

Paso 1 Using the verbs and phrases you have learned so far, create at least six questions to use in an interview with your instructor about his or her schedule.

Vocabulario útil

¿cuándo?	when?
¿cuánto/a/os/as?	how much/many?
¿dónde?	where?
enseñar	to teach
viajar	to travel

Paso 2 A volunteer will interview your instructor using his or her questions. Jot down all the information you hear. If the volunteer does not ask any of the questions you created in **Paso 1**, then ask them yourself, taking turns with the other students. Again, jot down all information.

Paso 3 Write a short paragraph in which you summarize four or five points about your instructor's schedule. At the same time, indicate what you think other instructors do.

Vocabulario útil

pero	but
solamente	only
también	also
y	and

MODELO: Mi profesor enseña tres clases. Otros (*Other*) profesores enseñan solamente una clase. Mi profesor también...

SEGUNDA PARTE

Vocabulario

More About
Schedules

Los días de la semana

Days of the Week

lunes	Monday
martes	Tuesday
miércoles	Wednesday
jueves	Thursday
viernes	Friday
sábado	Saturday
domingo	Sunday

- Note that the first day of the week is Monday (instead of Sunday) in most calendars from the Spanish-speaking world. You will read more about this in the **Vistazo cultural** in this section.

- Note too that the days of the week are not capitalized in Spanish as they are in English.

✳ MÁS VOCABULARIO

el fin de semana	weekend
el horario	schedule
el (los) lunes	on Monday(s)
por la mañana	in the morning
por la tarde	in the afternoon
por la noche	in the evening / at night
todos los días	every day
todas las noches	every night
¿Qué día es hoy?	What day is it today?

Origen de los nombres de los días

Como el español se deriva del latín, los nombres de los días son de origen latino.

lunes: día de la luna [a]

martes: día de Marte, el dios de la guerra [b]

miércoles: día de Mercurio, el dios mensajero [c]

jueves: día de Júpiter, padre y jefe [d] de los dioses

viernes: día de Venus, la diosa del amor [e]

sábado: del latín **sabbatum,** día de descanso [f]

domingo: del latín **dominicus,** día del Señor [g]

Los nombres de los días, en inglés, tienen un origen un poco diferente. Algunos[h] son de la mitología vikinga (*Thursday*, por ejemplo, se deriva del día de Thor).

▲ *Mercury,* por Simeon Solomon (inglés, 1840–1905)

[a]*moon* [b]*dios... god of war* [c]*messenger* [d]*boss* [e]*love* [f]*rest* [g]*Lord* [h]*Some*

¿Puedes nombrar (*Can you name*) las fechas (*dates*) en este calendario?

agosto	1:00	2:00	3:00	4:00
14 lunes				
15 martes				
16 miércoles				
17 jueves				
18 viernes				
19 sábado				
20 domingo				

Actividad A Las clases de Roberto

Paso 1 Listen as your instructor makes a series of statements about Roberto's class schedule. Indicate whether the statements are **cierto** or **falso** based on his schedule, provided in the following table.

1. ...   2. ...   3. ...   4. ...   5. ...   6. ...

LUNES	MARTES	MIÉRCOLES	JUEVES	VIERNES
Química II		Química II	Laboratorio de Química II	Química II
	Español III	Español III	Español III	Español III
	Historia de la Norteamérica colonial		Historia de la Norteamérica colonial	
Filosofía I		Filosofía I		Filosofía I

Paso 2 With a partner, take turns making statements about Roberto's schedule using the models below. See if each of you can make five different statements.

MODELOS: Roberto tiene una clase de química los lunes, miércoles y viernes.

Tiene dos clases los lunes.

Actividad B ¿Estás de acuerdo? (*Do you agree?*)

Indicate whether you agree or disagree with each statement.

	ESTOY DE ACUERDO.	NO ESTOY DE ACUERDO.
1. Es buena idea estudiar todas las noches.	☐	☐
2. No es buena idea estudiar los fines de semana.	☐	☐
3. Para mí (*For me*), es mejor (*better*) estudiar por la mañana.	☐	☐
4. Para mí, es mejor tomar las clases por la tarde, si (*if*) es posible.	☐	☐
5. Los mejores (*best*) programas de televisión se presentan (*are aired*) los jueves por la noche.	☐	☐
6. El peor (*worst*) día de la semana para mí es el lunes.	☐	☐

Actividad C Un horario

Using the grid that follows as a guide, interview a classmate to find out what days of the week he or she has classes and what those classes are. Also indicate whether the classes are **por la mañana, por la tarde,** or **por la noche.** Turn in the schedule to your instructor with the student's name on it.

MODELO: E1: ¿Qué clases tienes los lunes por la mañana?
E2: Dos. Una de química y una de historia.

	LUNES	MARTES	MIÉRCOLES	JUEVES	VIERNES
por la mañana					
por la tarde					
por la noche					

⧼ Vistazo cultural

Los calendarios

Although calendars in this country list Sunday as the first day of the week, in the Spanish-speaking world, Monday is traditionally shown as the first day of the week. This difference reflects the Latinate and Judeo-Christian background of the Spanish system rather than the Germanic and Scandinavian influences in English. The Romans imported the idea of a seven-day week from Jewish tradition and named the days accordingly. When the Roman empire converted to Christianity, Sunday became the last day of the week and the official "day of rest" or, as Emperor Constantine declared, "the Christian sabbath." As part of the Roman empire and as a country that emerged as strongly Catholic, Spain kept this system and took it to its empire in Africa (Equatorial Guinea), the Philippines, and the Americas.

However, due to globalization, Anglo influence has started to creep into some Hispanic cultures, and it is possible to find calendars whose first day of the week is **domingo** rather than the traditional **lunes.** But Hispanic countries still consider **domingo** the "day of rest," and many businesses (including shops and restaurants) are closed on this day. In rural areas of Mexico, Chile, and Colombia, for example, as well as in many cities, you will still find couples and families strolling through parks and plazas on Sundays.

	7:00	8:00	9:00	10:00
septiembre				
13 lunes				
14 martes				
15 miércoles				
16 jueves				
17 viernes				
18 sábado				
19 domingo				

Gramática

Necesito estudiar.

Verb + *infinitive*

EXPRESSING THE NEED OR DESIRE TO DO SOMETHING	
necesidad	deseo
necesitar + *infinitive* **Necesito estudiar** para un examen. *I need to study for a test.* **¿Necesitas comprar** un libro? *Do you need to buy a book?*	**desear** + *infinitive* **Deseo visitar** Madrid. *I want to visit Madrid.* **¿Desean** los estudiantes **hablar** bien el español? *Do the students want to speak Spanish well?*
es necesario + *infinitive* **Es necesario escuchar** bien en clase. *It's necessary to listen well in class.*	

As you saw in the previous grammar section, Spanish has verb forms that end in **-r**. These forms indicate the same thing that *to* indicates in front of an English verb (for example, *to talk* = **hablar** and *to need* = **necesitar**). These verb forms are called *infinitives.* To express the need to do something, Spanish does not require a word equivalent to the English word *to*, since it is implied in the Spanish infinitive.

Necesito viajar al Valle del Maipo.   *I need to travel to the Maipo Valley.*

In addition to using the verb **necesitar,** you can also use certain "impersonal expressions" in Spanish to convey general necessity to do something. Again, there is no equivalent word for English *to*.

Es necesario practicar mucho.   *It's necessary to practice a lot.*

The verb **desear** (*to desire, want*) can be combined with infinitive verb forms to talk about what people want to do. Again, no equivalent word for *to* is required.

Deseo visitar Buenos Aires.   *I want to visit Buenos Aires.*

¿Desean muchos estudiantes **estudiar** otro idioma?   *Do a lot of students want to study another language?*

The chart summarizes how to express necessity and desire to do something.

✳ MÁS VOCABULARIO

Here are some other regular **-ar** verbs and expressions that you will want to use in this lesson:

bailar	to dance	**mirar**	to watch
buscar	to look for	**pasar (mucho)**	to spend
cantar	to sing	**tiempo**	(a lot of) time
descansar	to rest	**repasar**	to review
escuchar	to listen (to)	**tomar apuntes**	to take notes
memorizar	to memorize		

DE SOL Y VIENTO

In **Episodio 1** of *Sol y viento,* you will watch a scene in which Jaime and his taxi driver, Mario, discuss the possibility of a trip outside the city of Santiago. Part of their exchange appears here.

JAIME
¿Ud. hace viajes fuera de Santiago?[a]

MARIO
Pero, ¡claro que sí![b]... ¿Qué se le ofrece?[c]

JAIME
Necesito _____ mañana[d]...

Selecting from the following list, what verb or activity do you think Jaime mentions in this scene?

1. viajar   **2.** visitar   **3.** charlar

[a]¿Ud.... *Do you take trips outside of Santiago?* [b]Pero... *But of course!* [c]¿Qué... *What can I do for you?* [d]*tomorrow*

Enfoque lingüístico

La importancia (o no) de las inflexiones

Some languages are "inflectionally rich." This means that they add endings (called *inflections*) to either nouns or verbs (or both) that provide the listener with information. English is inflectionally poor. For any regular verb, there are only two forms in the present tense: one with the inflection *-s* to talk about someone else (e.g., *John studies a lot*) and one "common" verb with no following *-s* to talk about everyone else (e.g., *You/We/I/They study a lot*). Some languages, such as Chinese, have no verb inflections for person, so you might consider these languages "inflectionless." Spanish, as you are beginning to learn, is inflectionally rich. Verb endings tend to be unique for each person, *person* being a term that refers to the meaning contained in the subject pronouns *I, you, he/she, they,* and *we.* A Spanish verb ending in **-o,** for example, will always refer to **yo,** a verb ending in **-mos** will always mean **nosotros/as,** and so forth.

Estudio química.	(No need to say **yo estudio** because the verb indicates who studies.)
¿**Llevas** muchos créditos?	(No need to say **llevas tú** because the verb indicates **tú**).
Trabajamos mucho en la clase de español.	(No need to say **nosotros trabajamos** because **-mos** can only refer to *we*).

For infinitives, **-r** is the inflection that means "to" (as in the English verbs *to work, to take,* and so forth). This is why Spanish does not need another word for *to* in constructions with **necesitar** and **desear:** the **-r** at the end of the second verb indicates this meaning. Learning Spanish, then, requires paying attention to the ends of verbs as you listen and read.

Actividad D ¿Qué sabes (*do you know*) de Jaime?

You already know the following about Jaime: **Mañana necesita viajar al Valle del Maipo.** What else do you know about him? Check the statements that you think apply.

Jaime...	SÍ	NO
1. necesita hablar con la familia Sánchez.	☐	☐
2. probablemente necesita descansar ahora (*now*).	☐	☐
3. desea pasar mucho tiempo en Chile.	☐	☐
4. desea regresar a California con un contrato firmado (*signed contract*).	☐	☐
5. no necesita llamar a la oficina mientras (*while*) está en Chile.	☐	☐
6. no necesita buscar un taxi mañana.	☐	☐
7. no desea probar (*to try*) los vinos chilenos.	☐	☐

Actividad E ¿Qué necesitamos hacer (*to do*)?

Paso 1 On your own, decide which of the following you think are true for studying Spanish.

	ES CIERTO.	NO ES CIERTO.
1. Uno necesita estudiar todas las noches.	☐	☐
2. Uno necesita escuchar música en español.	☐	☐
3. Uno necesita tomar apuntes en clase.	☐	☐
4. Uno necesita memorizar el vocabulario.	☐	☐
5. No es necesario pasar mucho tiempo estudiando (*studying*) la gramática.	☐	☐
6. Es necesario hablar un poco (*a little bit*) en español con otra persona todos los días.	☐	☐
7. Uno necesita mirar programas de televisión en español.	☐	☐
8. No es necesario pasar mucho tiempo en el laboratorio de lenguas.	☐	☐

Paso 2 Compare your responses to **Paso 1** with those of two other people. Together, present a final list of the statements that you all agree are true.

COMUNICACIÓN ÚTIL

Another handy expression to talk about what you like to do is **me gusta** + *infinitive.* What you are saying literally is "(*something*) is pleasing to me."

> **Me gusta estudiar** por la mañana.
> **No me gusta pagar** el alquiler.

To ask a classmate if he or she likes to do something, use **te gusta** + *infinitive.*

> **¿Te gusta navegar** la red?

Actividad F Lo que (*What*) deseamos hacer

In the previous activity, you talked about what you had to do to learn Spanish. But suppose you didn't have to do any of those things tonight. What do you *want* to do instead? Check each item that applies to you.

Esta noche...	SÍ	NO
1. deseo descansar.	☐	☐
2. deseo bailar.	☐	☐
3. deseo mirar una película.	☐	☐
4. deseo tomar cerveza con mis amigos.	☐	☐
5. deseo limpiar (*to clean*) la casa (el apartamento).	☐	☐
6. deseo quemar (*to burn*) unos discos compactos.	☐	☐
7. deseo ¿ ?	☐	☐

Actividad G Otra entrevista

Interview a classmate about what days of the week he or she needs, wants, or likes to do particular activities. Find out about at least seven activities. Then list a series of complete sentences, as in the model.

MODELO: Susie necesita trabajar en Blockbuster los fines de semana por la noche.

	LUNES	MARTES	MIÉRCOLES	JUEVES	VIERNES
por la mañana					
por la tarde					
por la noche					

▲ ¿Qué necesita hacer mañana Jaime? ¿Recuerdas? (*Do you remember?*)

TERCERA PARTE

Vocabulario

¿A qué hora?

Telling Time

Es la una de la tarde.

Son las cinco y cuarto de la mañana.

Son las siete y media de la noche.

Son las once menos veinte de la mañana.

Although you may encounter regional variation in how Spanish speakers talk about the time, you will always be understood if you use the following guidelines.

■ To tell what time it is, use forms of the verb **ser,** either **es** or **son,** depending on whether the hour is one o'clock or some other hour.

Es la una.	*It's one o'clock.*
Son las dos.	*It's two o'clock.*
Son las seis de la tarde.	*It's six o'clock in the evening.*

■ To add minutes, use **y** as in the expressions below.

Es la una **y diez.**	*It's 1:10.*
Son las tres **y veinte.**	*It's 3:20.*

■ Note that special words are used to mean quarter of the hour or half-hour.

Es la una **y cuarto.**	*It's 1:15.*
Son las ocho **y media.**	*It's 8:30.*

■ For a time that is approaching an hour, Spanish uses the expression **menos** (*less*).

Es la una **menos cuarto.**	*It's a quarter to one.*
Son las cinco **menos veinte.**	*It's twenty to five.*

EL HORARIO DE JULIA RAMÍREZ					
	LUNES	MARTES	MIÉRCOLES	JUEVES	VIERNES
9:00	Biología II		Biología II		Biología II
10:00		Inglés III	Inglés III	Inglés III	Inglés III
11:00		Historia mexicana contemporánea		Historia mexicana contemporánea	
12:00	Filosofía I		Filosofía I		Filosofía I
2:00	trabaja en la biblioteca		trabaja en la biblioteca		trabaja en la biblioteca

Julia tiene una clase **a las nueve** de la mañana.

Necesita llegar (*to arrive*) a la biblioteca **a las dos menos cinco.**

When talking about schedules and at what time you do things, use the phrases **a la** or **a las,** again depending on whether you are talking about one o'clock or some other hour.

Necesito regresar a mi casa **a la una.**	*I need to return home at one o'clock.*
Necesito llamar a mi mamá **a las tres.**	*I need to call my mom at three.*

❋ MÁS VOCABULARIO

¿A qué hora... ?	At what time . . . ? / When . . . ?
¿Qué hora es?	What time is it?
¡Uy! Es muy tarde/temprano.	Oh! It's very late/early.
llegar a tiempo	to arrive on time
ser (*irreg.*) puntual	to be on time
a la misma hora	at the same time
de la mañana	in the morning, A.M.
de la tarde/noche	in the afternoon/evening, P.M.
de las dos y cuarto hasta las tres y media	from 2:15 until 3:30
en punto	on the dot, exactly
mediodía (*m.*)	noon
medianoche (*f.*)	midnight

COMUNICACIÓN ÚTIL

One potential problem when listening to others talk about time is hearing the difference between **dos** and **doce**. For example:

Necesitamos llegar a las dos y media.

Necesitamos llegar a las doce y media.

At first, these may sound the same to you. To request clarification, you might say:

Perdón. ¿A qué hora?

Perdón. ¿A las dos o a las doce y media?

Actividad A   ¿Qué hora es?

Write down each time of day your instructor reads aloud in the spaces provided. Be sure to include A.M. or P.M. if specified.

MODELOS: *Instructor says:* Son las dos.
            You write: 2:00

            Instructor says: Es mediodía.
            You write: noon

1. _____   3. _____   5. _____   7. _____
2. _____   4. _____   6. _____

Actividad B   ¿Cierto o falso?

Your instructor will read a series of statements about what Enrique does on Mondays. Based on his schedule, which follows, indicate whether each statement is true (**cierto**) or false (**falso**).

Este lunes

8:30 clase de biología

10:00 laboratorio de biología

11:00 clase de literatura

12:30 estudiar en la biblioteca

2:30–5:30 trabajar en la librería

5:45 regresar a casa

7:15–9:45 reunión para estudiar

1. ...
2. ...
3. ...
4. ...
5. ...

Actividad C   Comparación de horarios

Paso 1   In the following schedule, write at least two things you do in the morning, in the afternoon, and at night for each day, including the time at which you do them.

MODELOS: (*under* lunes, miércoles, viernes) 10:00 clase de español
(*under* martes *and* jueves) 12:00 clase de química
(*under* sábado) trabajo de 1:00 a 9:00

	LUNES	MARTES	MIÉRCOLES	JUEVES	VIERNES	SÁBADO	DOMINGO
por la mañana yo mi compañero/a							
por la tarde yo mi compañero/a							
por la noche yo mi compañero/a							

Paso 2   Now ask a partner what he or she does at the times and days you've written down in your schedule.

MODELOS: ¿Qué haces (*do you do*) los lunes a las diez?
¿Tienes clase a las doce los martes y jueves?
¿Trabajas? ¿Cuándo?

Paso 3   With the information you have obtained in **Paso 2,** indicate which of the following is true. Be able to say at least two things that support your choice.

☐ Tenemos (*We have*) actividades y horarios parecidos (*similar*).
☐ Tenemos actividades y horarios diferentes.

〰 Vistazo cultural

De 0:00 a 24:00

Although people talk about time as you have learned in this lesson, the twenty-four hour clock is used in most Spanish-speaking countries for schedules, in the news, and in other types of official reporting. Thus, you will see train schedules with departures at 14:30 (2:30 P.M.), for example, and movie times at 22:00 (10:00 P.M.). Store hours may be given the same way: **abierto**[a] **de 10:00 a 21:00.**

In the business world, people in Spanish-speaking countries are as punctual when keeping appointments as are people in this country. On the other hand, the concept of **en punto** is relatively flexible for social occasions. For example, when two friends from Venezuela, Argentina, or Costa Rica say they'll meet **a las dos,** neither one would normally expect the other to be there right at 2:00. In fact, arriving at 2:30 would not be considered rude in some of these contexts.

[a]*open*

Gramática

Talking About Ownership | **Es mi libro.**   **Unstressed Possessive Adjectives** ✳

POSSESSIVE ADJECTIVES			
mi(s) libro(s)	my book(s)	**nuestro(s) libro(s)** **nuestra(s) vida(s)**	our book(s) our life (lives)
tu(s) libro(s)	your (*informal*) book(s)	**vuestro(s) libro(s)** **vuestra(s) vida(s)**	your (*informal, Spain*) book(s) your life (lives)
su(s) libro(s)	your (*formal*) book(s)	**su(s) libro(s)**	your (*formal*) book(s)
su(s) libro(s)	his/her book(s)	**su(s) libro(s)**	their book(s)

There are a variety of ways to talk about what is yours, someone else's, theirs, and so forth in Spanish. Unstressed possessive adjectives are the simple ones that precede nouns and are equivalent to *my, your, his, her,* and so forth in English. The chart contains the Spanish equivalents.

Note that the one word **su** can mean a variety of possessors, so context will determine who is the owner.

In the next lesson you will learn about something called *adjective agreement,* but you need to know a bit about it here for possessive adjectives. Remember that nouns have gender (e.g., **el libro, la mochila**). In Spanish, adjectives must agree in gender with the nouns they modify. Fortunately in the case of possessive adjectives, only **nuestro** and **vuestro** show this agreement. So, if a noun is feminine, you must use **nuestra** or **vuestra: nuestra/vuestra clase** (*our/your class*).

But adjectives must also agree in number (singular versus plural) with the nouns they modify. This is true for all possessive adjectives in the chart. Thus, an **-s** is added to the adjective if the noun is plural.

nuestra clase	*our class* →	nuestra**s** clase**s**	*our classes*
mi clase	*my class* →	mi**s** clase**s**	*my classes*
su estudiante	*his (her or their)* *student* →	su**s** estudiante**s**	*his (her or their)* *students*

DE SOL Y VIENTO

In an earlier **De *Sol y viento*** activity, you saw part of an exchange between Jaime and Mario regarding a trip that Jaime wants to take out of Santiago. Here is the entire exchange.

JAIME
¿Ud. hace viajes fuera de Santiago?

MARIO
Pero, ¡claro que sí! Es _____ autito, soy _____ propio jefeª...
¿Qué se le ofrece?

JAIME
Necesito viajar mañana, como a las diez de la mañana.

MARIO
¡Perfecto! ¿Adónde desea irᵇ?

JAIME
Al... al Valle del Maipo.

MARIO
¿Valle del Maipo? ¡Fantástico! Muy, muy lindo.ᶜ A propósito:ᵈ me llamo Mario
Verdejo. «Verdejín» para _____ amigos.

What forms of the possessive adjective do you think Mario is using in the blanks above?

ªpropio... *own boss* ᵇ*to go* ᶜ*pretty* ᵈA... *By the way*

Actividad D ¿Mario o Jaime?

Which of the two characters would most likely make each statement below?

	MARIO	JAIME
1. Mi compañía paga bien.	☐	☐
2. Necesito trabajar todos los días para mantener (*support*) a mi familia.	☐	☐
3. Nuestro país es lindo (*pretty*), ¿no?	☐	☐
4. Nuestros vinos son excelentes.	☐	☐
5. ¿Su señora (*wife*) también es de Santiago?	☐	☐

Actividad E   ¿Cierto o falso?

Listen to the statements your instructor makes about the people and things in your class. Then decide if each statement is true or not.

1. ...
2. ...
3. ...
4. ...
5. ...
6. ...
7. ...

Actividad F   ¿Cómo es nuestra universidad?

Paso 1   Select the response that best reflects your reaction to each statement. Note: **más o menos** = *more or less.*

	SÍ	MÁS O MENOS	NO
1. Nuestros edificios son bonitos (*pretty*).	☐	☐	☐
2. Nuestra biblioteca es grande (*big*).	☐	☐	☐
3. Nuestro equipo (*team*) de fútbol americano es excelente.	☐	☐	☐
4. Nuestras residencias son cómodas (*comfortable*).	☐	☐	☐
5. Nuestra matrícula (*tuition*) es cara (*expensive*).	☐	☐	☐
6. Nuestros profesores son buenos.	☐	☐	☐
7. Nuestro auditorio es moderno.	☐	☐	☐
8. Nuestra clase de español es interesante.	☐	☐	☐

Paso 2   Compare your responses with those of three other people. Then prepare a statement to share with the class about something you all agree upon.

MODELO: Pensamos que (*We think that*) nuestra biblioteca es grande.

Paso 3   Based on everyone's statements, what is the overall attitude (**actitud**) about the university?

☐ Nuestra actitud es buena.
☐ Nuestra actitud es más o menos buena.
☐ Nuestra actitud es bastante (*rather*) negativa.

Paso 4 (*Optativo*)   Listen as your instructor gives his or her reactions to the statements in **Paso 1**. What can you say about your instructor's attitude toward the university?

Su actitud es buena / más o menos buena / bastante negativa.

Actividad G Algunas (*Some*) de nuestras cosas (*things*) favoritas

Paso 1 First answer each of the questions in the **yo** column in the chart. Then interview a partner, asking him or her the same questions, jotting down each response under the column **mi compañero/a.**

	YO	MI COMPAÑERO/A
1. ¿Cuál es tu clase favorita?		
2. ¿Cuáles son dos de tus artistas (*performers*) favoritos?		
3. ¿Cuál es tu auto favorito?		
4. ¿Cuáles son dos de tus programas de televisión favoritos?		
5. ¿Cómo se llama tu actor favorito (actriz favorita)?		
6. ¿Cómo se llama tu profesor favorito (profesora favorita)?		
7. ¿Cuál es tu película (*movie*) favorita?		

Paso 2 Prepare three to four statements about your classmate to share with the class.

MODELO: Hablé (*I spoke*) con _____. Su auto favorito es _____. Sus programas de televisión favoritos son _____...

NAVEGANDO LA RED

Find a university's website in a Spanish-speaking country and locate *one* of the following to report on in class: (1) a schedule of classes on English literature or (2) a professor's office hours.

RESUMEN DE VOCABULARIO

Verbos

bailar	to dance
buscar	to look for
cantar	to sing
charlar	to chat
descansar	to rest
desear	to desire, want
enseñar	to teach
escuchar	to listen (to)
hablar	to speak; to talk
llamar (por teléfono)	to call (on the phone)
llegar a tiempo	to arrive on time
llevar	to take; to carry
mirar	to watch
navegar la red	to surf the Web
necesitar	to need
pagar (el alquiler)	to pay (the rent)
pasar (mucho) tiempo	to spend (a lot of) time
practicar (un deporte)	to practice (a sport)
regresar (a casa)	to return (home)
repasar	to review
ser (*irreg.*) **puntual**	to be punctual
tocar (la guitarra, el piano)	to play (the guitar, the piano)
tomar (apuntes, una clase)	to take (notes, a class)
tomar (café, cerveza)	to drink (coffee, beer)
trabajar	to work
viajar	to travel
es necesario + *infin.*	it's necessary to (*do something*)
tiene	he/she has; you (*form.*) have

Cognados: estudiar, memorizar, preparar, visitar (a la familia)

¿Qué día es hoy?

lunes, martes, miércoles, jueves, viernes, sábado, domingo

el fin de semana	weekend
el (los) lunes	on Monday(s)

Los números del 0 al 30

cero, uno, dos, tres, cuatro, cinco, seis, siete, ocho, nueve, diez, once, doce, trece, catorce, quince, dieciséis, diecisiete, dieciocho, diecinueve, veinte, treinta

¿Qué hora es?

Es la una.	It's one o'clock.
Son las dos (tres, cuatro,...)	It's two (three, four, . . .) o'clock.
¿A qué hora... ?	At what time . . . ? / When . . . ?
A la una.	At one o'clock.
A las dos (tres, cuatro,...)	At two (three, four, . . .) o'clock.
de la mañana	in the morning (A.M.)
de la tarde/noche	in the afternoon/ evening (P.M.)
y cuarto	quarter past
y media	half past
menos cuarto	quarter to
a la misma hora	at the same time
de la(s)... hasta la(s)	from (*hour*) to (*hour*)
en punto	on the dot, exactly
mañana	tomorrow
medianoche (*f.*)	midnight
mediodía (*m.*)	noon
por la mañana (tarde, noche)	in the morning (afternoon, evening / at night)
tarde	late
temprano	early
todos los días / todas las noches	every day / every night

Adjetivos posesivos

mi(s), tu(s), su(s), nuestro/a/os/as, vuestro/a/os/as

Otras palabras y expresiones

el crédito	credit (*school*)
el día	day
el horario	schedule
la película	movie
ahora	now
cada	each
mucho (*adv.*)	a lot
muy	very
solamente	only

Más sobre las actividades

OBJETIVOS

IN THIS LESSON, YOU WILL:

- review interrogative (question) words

- learn to use regular **-er** and **-ir** verbs to talk about activities

- talk about the months, seasons, and the weather

- express immediate and planned future events with **ir**

- describe people using adjectives

- learn about adjective agreement

In addition, you will watch **Episodio 1** of the film *Sol y viento.*

◄
Santiago, la capital de Chile, es una ciudad (*city*) grande y cosmopolita.

The following media resources are available for *Sol y viento: En breve*

Episodio 1 of
Sol y viento

Online *Manual de actividades*

Interactive
CD-ROM

Online Learning
Center Website

PRIMERA PARTE

Vocabulario

Asking Questions

¿Cuándo?

¿Adónde?	¿Adónde vas (*are you going*)?
¿Cómo?	¿Cómo te llamas?
¿Cuál(es)?	¿Cuál es tu apellido?
¿Cuándo?	¿Cuándo estudias?
¿Cuánto/a/os/as?	¿Cuántos estudiantes hay en la clase?
¿Dónde?	¿De dónde eres?
¿Por qué?	¿Por qué estudias español?
¿Qué?	¿Qué clase te gusta más?
¿Quién(es)?	¿Quién llama?

Summary of Interrogative Words

▲ **¿Quién** es esta (*this*) persona? **¿Cómo** se llama? **¿Dónde** vive (*does he live*)?

By now you have seen and heard many of these basic interrogative words in Spanish. Here are a few things to keep in mind when using them to ask questions.

■ Prepositions always stay with question words. They cannot be left alone as in English.

¿**De** dónde eres?	Where are you from? (the English preposition *from* can be left alone at the end of the sentence)
¿**Con** quién hablas?	Whom are you speaking with? (the English preposition *with* can be left alone at the end of the sentence)

■ You may be fooled if you rely on English translations, especially with **cómo, cuál,** and **qué.** Note the following.

¿**Cómo** te llamas?	In English we say "What's your name?" but **cómo** actually means *how.* So what you are asking literally means "How do you call yourself?" Compare with ¿**Cómo se dice... ?,** which in English *does* translate as "How do you say . . . ?"
¿**Cuál** es tu apellido?	In English we say "What's your last name?" but **cuál** literally means *which.* So you are actually asking "Which is your last name?" Contrast with the phrase ¿**Cuál de los tres desea Ud.?,** which *does* translate as "Which of the three do you want?"
¿**Qué** clases tienes por la tarde?	In English we can say either "Which classes" or "What classes do you have in the afternoon?" But in Spanish, **qué** literally means *what* as in ¿**Qué necesitas?** ("What do you need?")

- Although you will study adjective agreement later in this lesson, note that **cuánto** and **cuál** are adjectives and will agree with the noun they modify or refer to.

  ¿**Cuáles** son **los nombres** de los días de la semana?

  ¿**Cuántas clases** tienes este semestre?

- To answer a question with ¿**por qué?**, you respond with **porque** (*because*), written as a single word and no accent mark.

  —¿**Por qué** estudias español?

  —**Porque** me gusta.

COMUNICACIÓN ÚTIL

In English, when requesting repetition, we often say "What did you say?" or, depending on the context, simply "What?" In Spanish, however, a very typical way of asking for repetition or clarification is to use ¿**cómo?***

¿**Cómo?**	What? (lit: How?)
¿**Cómo dices?**	What are you saying? (lit: How are you saying it?)

With added emphasis, ¿**cómo?** can also be used to express surprise at what someone says.

¿Cómo? ¡Es imposible!

≈ Vistazo cultural

Los dialectos

Spanish, like other languages, exhibits dialectal variation. For a native speaker of Spanish, it is often easy to determine what country or region another speaker is from. Dialects are based on various features of language:

- Pronunciation: In Mexico, you would hear **estás,** but in Cuba, Puerto Rico, and other Caribbean countries you are likely to hear **ehtáh** or even **etá.**

- Vocabulary: In Spain, the word **el bebé** is used, but in Chile you would likely hear **la guagua** when the speaker refers to an infant or small child.

- Grammar: In much of Spain, **vosotros** and **ustedes** are used, whereas in Spanish-speaking America **ustedes** is used for both formal and informal situations.

As you watch *Sol y viento,* take note of differences in pronunciation and other aspects of language as you hear characters from different regions and countries interact.

---

*There are dialectical differences for expressing *what?* in the Spanish-speaking world, but you will always be understood if you use ¿**cómo?** in this way.

Actividad A Correspondencias

Choose the most logical match between the question word and a possible response.

1. ____ ¿Cuándo?   **a.** En Europa.
2. ____ ¿Dónde?   **b.** José.
3. ____ ¿Quién?   **c.** Tres.
4. ____ ¿Cuántos?   **d.** La clase de historia.
5. ____ ¿Cuál?   **e.** A las tres de la tarde.

Actividad B ¿Cuál es la diferencia entre (*between*)... ?

See if you can answer each question by selecting the appropriate answer.

1. ¿Cuál es la diferencia entre un estudiante y una estudiante?
   a. Uno es del sexo masculino y la otra es del sexo femenino.
   b. Uno es atlético y la otra no.
2. ¿Cuál es una diferencia entre el Brasil y la Argentina?
   a. El producto principal del Brasil es el chocolate. El producto principal de la Argentina es el vino.
   b. En la Argentina, hablan español. En el Brasil, hablan portugués.
3. ¿Cuál es una diferencia entre los Estados Unidos y el Canadá?
   a. En los Estados Unidos juegan al (*they play*) fútbol americano, pero en el Canadá no.
   b. El francés es una lengua oficial en el Canadá, pero en los Estados Unidos no.
4. ¿Cuál es una diferencia entre Chile y la Guinea Ecuatorial?
   a. Chile está en Sudamérica y la Guinea Ecuatorial está en África.
   b. La Guinea Ecuatorial es más grande que (*bigger than*) Chile.

▲ ¿Cuál es una diferencia entre Jaime y Mario? Jaime es estadounidense y Mario es chileno.

Actividad C Las preposiciones

Paso 1 Remembering that prepositions cannot be left alone in Spanish, insert the preposition from the list that makes the most sense for each question.

a	to	**de**	of; from
con	with	**para**	for

1. ¿_____ quién hablas si (*if*) tienes problemas?
2. ¿_____ cuál de los dos países (*countries*) deseas viajar, Chile o México?
3. ¿_____ dónde es tu mejor (*best*) amigo/a?
4. ¿_____ qué clase pasas mucho tiempo estudiando (*studying*)?
5. ¿_____ cuáles de tus amigos de la secundaria (*high school*) te mantienes (*do you maintain*) en contacto?
6. ¿_____ qué país o países hispanos importamos mucho vino?

Paso 2 With a partner, take turns asking the questions of each other. But don't ask them in the order they are listed. Make sure to pay attention to your partner!

Actividad D Otra (*Another*) entrevista

What can you find out about someone with all the question words you know now? Using the hints that follow as a guide, interview someone in the class. Jot down any information that you receive. Your instructor may call on you to make a brief presentation to the class.

- the person's favorite class
- the person's favorite professor
- where the person studies and how many hours per day/night
- how many classes the person has
- where and when the person works
- ¿ ?

▲ ¿Dónde está Mario? ¿Con quién habla?

Gramática

More on Activities
and Schedules

¿Dónde vives? **Present Tense of Regular -er and -ir Verbs**

REGULAR *-er/-ir* VERBS					
	comer *(to eat)*	vivir *(to live)*		comer	vivir
yo	com**o**	viv**o**	nosotros/as	com**emos**	viv**imos**
tú	com**es**	viv**es**	vosotros/as	com**éis**	viv**ís**
Ud.	com**e**	viv**e**	Uds.	com**en**	viv**en**
él/ella	com**e**	viv**e**	ellos/ellas	com**en**	viv**en**

In addition to regular **-ar** verbs, Spanish has two other classes of regular present-tense verbs, as the chart shows. Note the following:

■ The endings are the same except for the **nosotros/as** and **vosotros/as** forms.

■ The endings that mark person (the subject) are the same for **-ar, -er,** and **-ir** verbs in the present tense. In other words, **-o** always means **yo**, **-s** always means **tú**, **-mos** always means **nosotros/as**, some form of **-is** always means **vosotros/as, -n** always means **Uds.** or **ellos/ellas,** and a plain vowel other than **-o** with no following consonant always means **Ud.** or **él/ella.**

✳ **MÁS VOCABULARIO**

Here are some common verbs ending in **-er** and **-ir** that you will use in this lesson:

abrir	to open
aprender	to learn
asistir (a)	to attend (*a class*)
beber	to drink
comer	to eat
comprender	to understand
correr	to run
creer (que)	to think, believe (that)
escribir	to write
leer	to read
recibir	to receive
ver (*irreg.*)*	to see; to watch
vivir	to live

*Note that regular verbs drop the **-er** and add **-o: bebo, corro. Ver,** however, keeps an **e** as part of the stem of the verb in the **yo** form. Thus, the **yo** form of **ver** is **veo** and not **vo. Ver** has irregularities in other tenses as well, which is why it's often classified as an irregular verb.

DE SOL Y VIENTO

By now you are somewhat familiar with the scene between Jaime and Mario in the hotel lobby. Examine the exchange that follows and see if you can select the correct verb to fit in the blank.

MARIO
A propósito,ª me llamo Mario Verdejo. «Verdejín» para mis amigos.

JAIME
Yo soy Jaime. Jaime Talavera. Bueno, Mario. Lo* _____ mañana. Hasta luego.

MARIO
Hasta mañana.

Is the missing verb **creo, veo,** or **leo?**

ªA... *By the way*

◯ Enfoque lingüístico

El tiempo verbal

What does the term *tense* mean? *Tense* refers to the general time frame in which something happens, such as the present, the past, or the future. English distinguishes all three (*I eat / I am eating, I ate / I was eating, I will eat / I will be eating*) as does Spanish, but differently, as you will learn later. Some languages do not mark tense at all; they let other words such as *right now, later today,* and *last week* carry the full responsibility of indicating tense.

Languages also vary as to the functions assigned to verb inflections that indicate tense. For example, in Spanish, **¿Qué lees?** can mean any one of the following English equivalents: *What are you reading* (*at this moment*)?, *What are you reading* (*these days*)?, and *What do you read* (as in "What do you like to read?")? Another way to think of this is that Spanish is less restrictive than English in the possible interpretations of a present-tense verb form. For example, to which of the following English statements could you add the phrase *this week?:* a. *John is running a lot.* b. *John runs a lot.* The answer, of course, is that only sentence **a** lets you add *this week.* In Spanish, however, you could add **esta semana** to the sentence **Juan corre mucho** to mean the same as *Juan is running a lot this week.* Context, then, is important to determine the function of a present-tense verb form. If someone interviews you and asks **¿Qué estudias?,** you will know that the meaning is something like "What's your major?" If someone walks in on you while you have a book open and asks the very same question, you will understand that the person means "What are you studying (at this moment)?" What is more, Spanish present-tense verb forms can also take on a future meaning, as in the following: **Mañana escribo la carta** (*Tomorrow I'll write the letter*).

---

*Lo is what is called an *object pronoun,* something you will study in a later lesson. Here it means formal *you* as in "I'll _____ you tomorrow."

Actividad E ¿Cómo es Jaime Talavera?

Indicate whether you agree with each statement about Jaime Talavera or not. Then share your answers with the class. How many people agree with you?

Probablemente, Jaime...	ESTOY DE ACUERDO.	NO ESTOY DE ACUERDO.
1. escribe muchos informes (*reports*).	☐	☐
2. lee el *Wall Street Journal* todos los días.	☐	☐
3. ve *The Real World* en la televisión cada semana.	☐	☐
4. vive en un apartamento modesto.	☐	☐
5. cree que su trabajo (*job*) con Bartel Aquapower es muy importante.	☐	☐
6. recibe muchos mensajes (*messages*) por correo electrónico (*e-mail*).	☐	☐
7. come en un restaurante elegante todos los días.	☐	☐

▲ Jaime corre para hacer ejercicio (*to exercise*).

Actividad F ¿Cuándo?

Paso 1 Indicate the frequency with which you do each activity listed. Note: **una vez al mes** = *once a month.*

	CADA DÍA	CADA SEMANA	UNA VEZ AL MES	NUNCA
1. Escribo una carta (*letter*).	☐	☐	☐	☐
2. Como en un restaurante.	☐	☐	☐	☐
3. Bebo cerveza en un bar.	☐	☐	☐	☐
4. Aprendo algo nuevo (*something new*).	☐	☐	☐	☐
5. Abro el libro de español.	☐	☐	☐	☐
6. Asisto a clase por la tarde.	☐	☐	☐	☐
7. Corro para no llegar tarde a clase.	☐	☐	☐	☐
8. Leo el periódico (*newspaper*).	☐	☐	☐	☐

Paso 2   Now, form questions using the **tú** form and interview someone in class to see the frequency with which that person completes these activities. Jot down his or her responses.

MODELO: Bebo cerveza en un bar. → ¿Con qué frecuencia bebes cerveza en un bar?

Paso 3   Report to the class one thing you and your classmate do the same. Then report something you two do differently.

MODELOS: Jeff y yo leemos el periódico cada día.

Yo como en un restaurante cada semana, pero John no.

Actividad G   Los animales

For each statement, indicate whether it applies to dogs (**los perros**), cats (**los gatos**), or both (**los perros y los gatos**). If you disagree with what someone says, speak up!

MODELO: Aprenden fácilmente (*easily*) →

TÚ: Los perros aprenden fácilmente, pero los gatos no.
OTRO/A ESTUDIANTE: No, no. Los gatos también aprenden fácilmente.

1. Aprenden fácilmente.
2. Viven dentro de (*inside*) la casa.
3. Comen de todo (*everything*).
4. Beben agua del inodoro (*toilet*).
5. Asisten a clases de obediencia.
6. Creen que son humanos.
7. Comprenden todo lo que decimos (*everything we say*).

Actividad H   El profesor (La profesora)

Paso 1   Using the verbs and phrases you have learned so far, create at least six questions to use in an interview with your instructor about his or her activities.

Paso 2   A volunteer will interview your instructor using his or her questions. Jot down all information obtained. If the volunteer does not ask any of the questions you created in **Paso 1,** then ask them yourself, taking turns with other students. Again, jot down all information.

Paso 3   Write a short paragraph in which you summarize four to five points about your instructor's activities. At the same time, indicate what you think other instructors do. The model shows some useful words.

MODELO: La profesora lee mucho. Lee revistas (*magazines*), novelas (*novels*) y otras cosas. Otros profesores también leen mucho, pero creo que no leen novelas.

SEGUNDA PARTE

Vocabulario

| **¡Hace calor en junio!** | **Months, Weather, and Seasons**

Hace mucho calor.

Hace calor.

Hace buen tiempo.

Hace fresco.

Hace frío.

Hace mucho frío.

Hace sol. Hace muy buen tiempo. **Está despejado** (*clear*), no **nublado** (*cloudy*). Es un día perfecto para **tomar el sol** (*sunbathe*).

Llueve. (Está lloviendo.) Hace mal tiempo. Es un día perfecto para leer una novela o ver una película en casa.

Hace mucho viento. No es buen tiempo para los peinados (*hairdos*).

Nieva. (Está nevando.) No es un buen día para muchas actividades afuera (*outdoors*).

Los meses y las estaciones del año

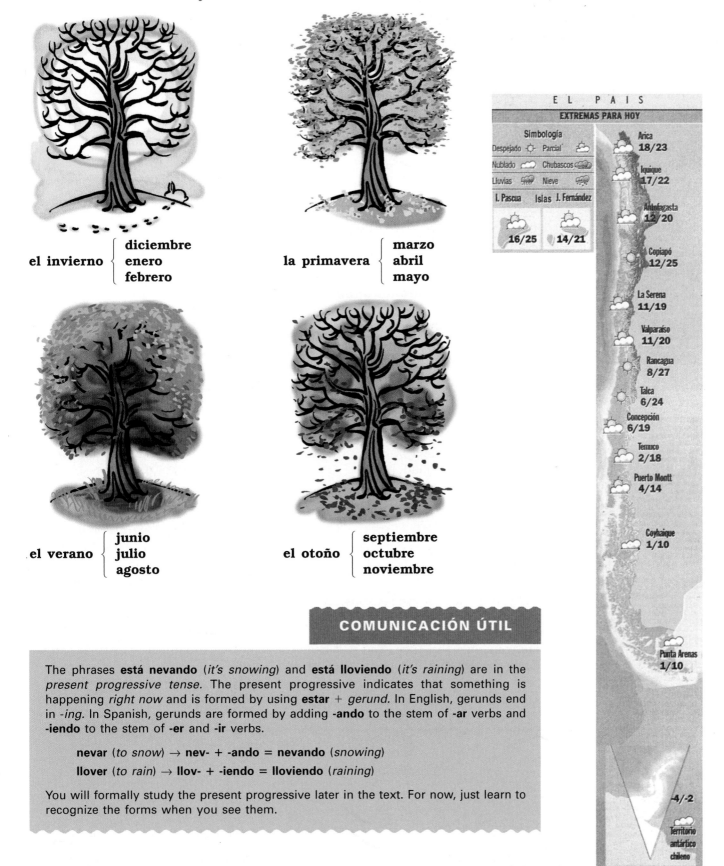

el invierno { diciembre, enero, febrero }

la primavera { marzo, abril, mayo }

el verano { junio, julio, agosto }

el otoño { septiembre, octubre, noviembre }

EL PAIS

EXTREMAS PARA HOY

Simbología

Despejado ☼ Parcial ⛅
Nublado ☁ Chubascos 🌦
Lluvias 🌧 Nieve 🌨

| I. Pascua | Islas J. Fernández |
| 16/25 | 14/21 |

Arica 18/23
Iquique 17/22
Antofagasta 12/20
Copiapó 12/25
La Serena 11/19
Valparaíso 11/20
Rancagua 8/27
Talca 6/24
Concepción 6/19
Temuco 2/18
Puerto Montt 4/14
Coyhaique 1/10
Punta Arenas 1/10
-4/-2
Territorio antártico chileno

COMUNICACIÓN ÚTIL

The phrases **está nevando** (*it's snowing*) and **está lloviendo** (*it's raining*) are in the *present progressive tense*. The present progressive indicates that something is happening *right now* and is formed by using **estar** + *gerund*. In English, gerunds end in *-ing*. In Spanish, gerunds are formed by adding **-ando** to the stem of **-ar** verbs and **-iendo** to the stem of **-er** and **-ir** verbs.

nevar (*to snow*) → **nev-** + **-ando** = **nevando** (*snowing*)

llover (*to rain*) → **llov-** + **-iendo** = **lloviendo** (*raining*)

You will formally study the present progressive later in the text. For now, just learn to recognize the forms when you see them.

El pronóstico (*forecast*) del tiempo en Chile se da (*is given*) en grados centígrados (*Celsius*). ▶

Actividad A ¿Qué actividad?

Listen as your instructor makes a statement about the weather. Select from the activities that follow to describe what the day is good for and what it is not good for. More than one response may be possible.

Es / No es un buen día para...

1. ...   **2.** ...   **3.** ...   **4.** ...

    a. abrir las ventanas de la casa.

    b. beber algo (*something*) muy frío.

    c. comer en el patio.

    d. correr.

    e. lavar (*wash*) el auto.

    f. manejar (*drive*) un auto descapotable (*convertible*).

    g. asistir a clase.

Actividad B Asociaciones

Listen as your instructor names a month, then select from the following items to indicate what you associate with that month.

1. **a.** el Día de San Valentín   **b.** el Día de la Independencia   **c.** el Día de Acción de Gracias (*Thanksgiving*)

2. **a.** las vacaciones de invierno   **b.** un nuevo año académico   **c.** las ceremonias de graduación

3. **a.** regresar a la universidad   **b.** tomar el sol   **c.** beber limonada

4. **a.** descansar entre semestres/ trimestres   **b.** tomar chocolate caliente (*hot*)   **c.** tomar exámenes finales

Actividad C Los hemisferios

Did you know that the seasons are reversed in the northern and southern hemispheres? Listen to each statement your instructor makes about the weather. Then respond by selecting elements from each of the following columns to create your own sentence. You will hear the following unfamiliar words: **las hojas** (*leaves*), **cambian** ([*they*] *change*), **el sur** (*south*).

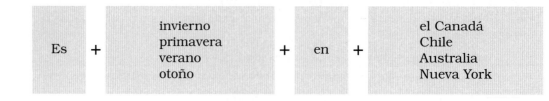

Es	+	invierno primavera verano otoño	+	en	+	el Canadá Chile Australia Nueva York

Actividad D ¿Cuál es tu estación favorita?

Paso 1 Think about your favorite season and months. Write a short description of them, according to the model.

MODELO: Me gusta (*I like*) el invierno. Hace frío, pero me gusta el frío. También me gusta el mes de diciembre porque hay vacaciones.

Paso 2 Interview a classmate, using the following questions as a guide. Then determine if you have the same ideas in common. Your instructor may call on you to present what you've found out.

- ¿Cuál es tu estación favorita? ¿y tu mes favorito?
- ¿Te gusta (*Do you like*) el calor? ¿Te gusta el frío? ¿Qué tiempo te gusta?

 Vistazo cultural

Los días festivos[a]

I n the United States there are few official holidays, such as New Year's Day, Presidents' Day, Easter, Memorial Day, the Fourth of July, Labor Day, Thanksgiving, and Christmas. In contrast, in many Spanish-speaking countries, many more days are celebrated— although with increasing globalization there is change and variety among Hispanic countries. In addition to national holidays (such as independence day in countries other than Spain), many local holidays are also celebrated. In Spain, for example, it is typical to find towns closed on patron saint days. For example, almost everyone has heard of the running of the bulls in Pamplona, officially known as **la fiesta de San Fermín,** or **los sanfermines,** which takes place the second week of July. In Valencia, for the day of **San José,** the locals celebrate **las fallas,** which consist of huge *papier-mâché* caricatures that are then set ablaze on the last evening of the festival. Also, August is a popular vacation month for Spaniards, as many head out for vacation homes at the coasts and close their local businesses. In Mexico and other parts of Spanish-speaking America, similar local holidays are observed in addition to national holidays. Before you travel to a Spanish-speaking country, be sure to find out if any holidays occur during your stay and plan accordingly!

[a]Los... *Holidays*

▲ La celebración de las fallas en Valencia, España

---

*Note that the preposition **a** contracts with **el** to make the word **al.** De and **el** also contract to form **del.** You may have noticed this elsewhere in the film and in the text.

Gramática

| **¿Vas a estudiar esta noche?** **Ir** + **a** + *infinitive*

ir (*to go*)			
yo	**voy**	nosotros/as	**vamos**
tú	**vas**	vosotros/as	**vais**
Ud.	**va**	Uds.	**van**
él/ella	**va**	ellos/ellas	**van**

One way to express future intent is by using the verb **ir** (*to go*), plus the preposition **a**, plus an infinitive, as in **Voy a ver una película esta noche** (*tonight*). The verb **ir**, however, is rather irregular. The **yo** form ends in **-oy** instead of **-o**, and all the other forms use the **-ar** endings!

Unlike **necesitar** and **desear**, **ir** requires **a** when followed by an infinitive.

Vamos a viajar a México en el verano.	*We're going to travel to Mexico in the summer.*
¿Deseas visitar un país de habla española?	*Do you want to visit a Spanish-speaking country?*
Necesito estudiar esta noche.	*I need to study tonight.*

Another way to express future intent, as you may recall from the previous **Enfoque lingüístico,** is with the present tense. This use is less frequent, often used with verbs that express movement or going from one place to another, and it is generally used when the event is to happen very soon.

Mañana voy a España.	*Tomorrow I'm going to Spain.*
Esta noche vamos todos a una fiesta. ¿Deseas ir?	*Tonight we're all going to party. Do you want to go?*
Pasado mañana llegan mis padres.	*My parents arrive the day after tomorrow.*

✳ **MÁS VOCABULARIO**

esta noche	tonight
pasado mañana	the day after tomorrow
la semana entrante	next week
el próximo verano (invierno, mes,...)	next summer (winter, month, . . .)
en unos (cuantos) días	in a few days
dentro de poco	soon
en un (dos, tres) año(s)	in one (two, three) year(s)

DE SOL Y VIENTO

When Jaime finally gets to his hotel room, he needs to make a phone call to the winery that is the object of his company's acquisition bid. Read what he says here. What verb is missing?

JAIME

¿Aló, la viña «Sol y viento»?... Don* Carlos Sánchez... Ah, con él. Bien. Soy Jaime Talavera, de los Estados Unidos. Compañía Bartel Aquapower... Sí, claro que[a] hablo español. Ya estoy aquí... No, en Santiago. Mañana _____ a verlo, como a mediodía.

CARLOS

Muy bien, señor Talavera. Lo espero[b] mañana. Hasta entonces. Chau.

[a]claro... *of course*   [b]Lo... *I'll be expecting you*

Enfoque lingüístico

Las frases verbales

As you have probably guessed, there are basically four ways in which a speaker may indicate that an event will take place in the future. The first is with words that signal a future event, such as *tomorrow* and *next week,* with no verb inflection. The second is with verb inflection, as you will see later in your studies. The third is with what are called *modals,* small words that accompany verbs such as English *will,* as in *I will arrive tomorrow at 8:00.* The fourth is with what are called *paraphrastic phrases,* such as *going to.* These phrases combine verbs in particular ways to express a meaning that is normally not part of the verb's function. For example, *go* normally means "to get from place X to place Y," but when combined with verbs it expresses some kind of future event. So, technically what you are learning in this lesson is called the "Paraphrastic Future with **ir** + **a** + infinitive"—quite a mouthful for something so simple as saying *going to,* right? Spanish has a variety of paraphrastic phrases that express different meanings and grammatical concepts. See if you can spot them as you continue your studies.

---

*In Spanish, the words **don** and **doña** are terms of respect used in front of a man's and a woman's name, respectively. There is no direct equivalent in English.

Actividad E Va a...

Do you think Jaime is going to be successful in his venture? Do you think some interesting things are going to happen to him? Decide which of the following best represents what you think.

1. Va a tener éxito (*be successful*). Va a conseguir (*get*) un contrato firmado y va a regresar a San Francisco en unos días.

2. Va a tener dificultades. Al final, va a conseguir lo que (*what*) desea, pero no va a ser fácil (*easy*).

3. Va a fracasar (*fail*) y la compañía va a despedirlo (*fire him*).

Actividad F Lo que voy a hacer esta noche

Think about the things you are going to do tonight. Check off any on the list that apply.

1. ☐ Voy a estudiar con un amigo (una amiga).
2. ☐ Voy a estudiar a solas (*alone*).
3. ☐ Voy a llamar a mi familia por teléfono.
4. ☐ Voy a escribir algo.
5. ☐ Voy a leer algo.
6. ☐ Voy a ver la televisión.
7. ☐ Voy a asistir a una reunión (*meeting*).
8. ☐ Voy a salir (*go out*) con mis amigos / mi familia.

Actividad G ¿Qué vamos a hacer?

Paso 1 Do you know what you and your Spanish classmates are going to do during the next class session? Select a possibility for each item below.

1. Vamos a...
   a. aprender algo nuevo.
   b. ver un episodio de *Sol y viento.*
2. Vamos a...
   a. tomar un examen.
   b. trabajar en grupos.
3. Vamos a...
   a. hablar y escuchar mucho.
   b. leer un **Vistazo cultural.**

Paso 2 Now answer the following questions about your class, depending on what you know. Report your answers to the class. Does everyone agree?

1. ¿Van (Uds.) a tomar un examen final? ¿Cuándo?
2. ¿Van a escribir una composición? ¿Cuándo?
3. ¿Van a necesitar más/otros libros para la clase de español el próximo semestre/trimestre?
4. ¿Cuántos episodios de *Sol y viento* van a ver este semestre/trimestre?

Actividad H En el futuro

Paso 1 Review the expressions in the **Más vocabulario** section on p. 58. Then interview someone about his or her future plans. Jot down what he or she says. Here are some questions to ask.

1. ¿Cuándo vas a terminar (*finish*) los estudios en la universidad?
2. ¿Cuándo vas a hacer tu próximo viaje (*take your next trip*)? ¿Adónde vas?
3. ¿Cuándo vas a comprar (*buy*) un auto nuevo?
4. ¿Cuándo vas a ver una película en el cine (*movie theater*)?

Paso 2 Based on what the person responded, which of the following seems true for that person? Be prepared to present your findings to the class.

☐ Tiene muchos planes fijos (*fixed plans*).

☐ Tiene unos planes fijos.

☐ No tiene planes fijos.

▲ ¿Cuándo van a ir a la viña «Sol y viento» Jaime y Mario? ¿Qué van a hacer allí (*do there*)?

NAVEGANDO LA RED

Find a Spanish-speaking country's tourism website and report on the average weather conditions for each of the four seasons. Report on whether it mentions a rainy season or not. (Remember that the seasons in the northern hemisphere are reversed from those in the southern hemisphere.)

TERCERA PARTE

Vocabulario

Describing Personalities

Es un hombre serio.

Adjectives*

La personalidad

◀ Abraham Lincoln

honesto
serio
trabajador (*hardworking*)

◀ Robin Williams

cómico
enérgico
caótico

◀ Salvador Dalí

excéntrico
extrovertido
egoísta

◀ Bill Gates

ambicioso
astuto
cerebral

◀ Thomas Edison

inteligente
creador (*creative*)
imaginativo

◀ Don Quijote

soñador (*dreamer*)
sencillo (*simple*)
confiado (*confident*)

---

*In this section, you will just describe males for now. In the next **Gramática** section, you will learn about adjective placement and agreement and about describing females.

✳ MÁS VOCABULARIO

aburrido (*boring*)	frente a (*versus*)	**interesante, estimulante** o **divertido** (*fun*)
alegre (*happy*)	frente a	**triste** (*sad*)
apasionado (*passionate*)	frente a	**indiferente**
arrogante	frente a	**humilde** (*humble*)
calmado	frente a	**explosivo**
conservador	frente a	**liberal**
caótico	frente a	**metódico, organizado, preciso**
discreto	frente a	**indiscreto** o **chismoso** (*gossipy*)
gregario	frente a	**introvertido, tímido, reservado**
leal (*loyal*)	frente a	**desleal**
malicioso	frente a	**simpático** (*nice*), **agradable** (*pleasant*)
pesimista	frente a	**optimista**
sabio (*wise*)	frente a	**ingenuo** (*naive*)
sospechoso, desconfiado (*untrusting*)	frente a	**confiado**
tonto (*dumb, foolish*)	frente a	**listo** (*clever*)
era	*he/she was*	
parece ser	*he/she seems to be*	

COMUNICACIÓN ÚTIL

You can use adjectives with **qué** to express either surprise or a reaction to how extreme something or someone is.

¡Qué interesante!	How interesting!
¡Qué desconfiado!	How untrusting!

¿Qué adjetivos describen a estos personajes (*these characters*) de *Sol y viento*? ¿Cómo es Jaime? ¿y Mario? ¿y Carlos?

Actividad A ¿De quién hablamos?

Listen as your instructor describes some well-known men. Select the person you think is being described. Note: You may hear some new adjectives, but they are cognates, and you should be able to deduce their meanings.

1. a. Harrison Ford	**b.** Woody Allen	**c.** Mark Wahlberg
2. a. Harry Potter	**b.** Elmer Fudd	**c.** Darth Vader
3. a. Ralph Nader	**b.** Bill Clinton	**c.** Pat Robertson
4. a. David Letterman	**b.** Prince	**c.** Tom Hanks
5. a. Franklin D. Roosevelt	**b.** Adolph Hitler	**c.** Winston Churchill

Actividad B ¿Qué adjetivo?

Select the adjectives you think matches the personality of each film character.

1. Darth Vader: ¿agradable o malicioso? ¿astuto o tonto?
2. Terminator: ¿calmado o explosivo? ¿apasionado o indiferente?
3. Forrest Gump: ¿sabio o tonto? ¿discreto o indiscreto?
4. Frodo Baggins: ¿arrogante o humilde? ¿pesimista u* optimista?
5. Shrek: ¿listo o ingenuo? ¿organizado o caótico?

Actividad C La personalidad y las actividades

Which activities best match the personality trait listed?

1. cerebral:
   a. leer mucho
   b. comprender poco
2. metódico:
   a. tener el impulso de organizar
   b. tocar el piano
3. enérgico:
   a. correr
   b. ver la televisión
4. gregario:
   a. estudiar a solas
   b. necesitar estar con otras personas
5. ambicioso:
   a. beber cerveza
   b. trabajar
6. imaginativo:
   a. tomar apuntes
   b. escribir novelas

---

*The word **u** (*or*) is substituted for **o** when the word immediately following it begins with an **o** or **ho.**

To talk about what sign of the zodiac you are, you use the verb **ser.**

—¿Qué signo **eres?**

—¿Yo? **Soy** Acuario. Somos muy cerebrales.

Here are the names of the signs of the zodiac in Spanish:

Capricornio	Tauro	Virgo
Acuario	Géminis	Libra
Piscis	Cáncer	Escorpio
Aries	Leo	Sagitario

Actividad D   Personas famosas

Paso 1 In groups of three, select a famous male celebrity, politician, or character from a movie or book. Using the adjectives you have learned so far, describe him in three to four sentences, without mentioning who it is.

MODELO: Este (*This*) hombre es... y... También...

Paso 2 Present your description to the class. Can everyone guess who it is? If not, provide three possibilities for them to choose from.

 Vistazo cultural

La personalidad y la cultura

It is often said that people from various regions display certain characteristics. These trait descriptions may not necessarily be true. However, sometimes stereotypes are a matter of degree: We may all be hardworking people, but perhaps one group is even more so. For example, the stereotype of people from Great Britain is that they are reserved, whereas the typical American is considered to be much more outgoing or simply less reserved. In the Spanish-speaking world, various regions also carry stereotypes. People from Spain are often said to be more outspoken and less guarded in what they say compared to those from Latin America, the U.S., and other places where Spanish is spoken. In fact, there is an expression used to describe this: **no tener pelos en la lengua** (lit: *to not have hairs on your tongue*). What this expression means is that people will say what they are thinking or feeling. As one example, although we might not want to comment on someone's recent weight gain or appearance, it would not be unusual for someone in Spain to do exactly that. A relative or friend might say right to your face, **¡Hombre! ¡Qué gordo estás! ¿Qué te pasa?** (*Man! You're fat! What's going on?*). Again, this does not mean that every Spaniard would be so frank with others, nor does it mean that there aren't people in other parts of the Spanish-speaking world who are equally frank. But perhaps there is a grain of truth in the statement that the typical Spaniard **no tiene pelos en la lengua.**

Gramática

Es una mujer seria.   Adjective Placement and Agreement

As you know, adjectives are words used to describe people, places, things, and ideas: *intelligent woman, wise old man.* Spanish is a language in which verbs must not only agree with subjects, but adjectives must also agree with the noun or pronoun they modify. This means that they must agree in gender and number, just as articles (**el, la, los, las**) do. Also note the following.

- Agreement is relatively straightforward with adjectives that end in **-o.** Change the **-o** to **-a** for agreement with a feminine noun and add **-s** if the noun is plural. However, not all adjectives end in **-o.** For example, adjectives that end in **-e** do not change the vowel to **-a.** And most that end in **-l** do not add an **-a,** but do add **-es** if the noun is plural.

- However, adjectives that end in **-r** (and other consonants) do add an **-a** for agreement with feminine nouns. Adjectives ending in **-ista** do not mark gender, just number.

The preceding explanation is summarized in the chart. Here are some additional points regarding adjective use.

- Adjectives normally follow the noun they modify.

   un **libro cómico**   una **mujer trabajadora**

- The adjectives **bueno** and **malo** can appear before nouns, but they are shortened in the masculine form.

Es un **chico** muy **bueno.**	Es muy **buen chico.**
Es una **chica** muy **buena.**	Es muy **buena chica.**
Es un **administrador malo.**	Es **mal administrador.**
Es una **administradora mala.**	Es **mala administradora.**

- The adjectives **grande** and **pobre** (*poor*) can be placed in front of nouns, but the meaning for each changes. Note that **grande** shortens to **gran** when placed in front of a noun, whether masculine or feminine.

   un **señor grande** (**grande** = physical stature)

   un **gran señor,** una **gran mujer** (**gran** = great)

   un **chico pobre** (**pobre** = broke, without money)

   un **pobre chico** (**pobre** = unfortunate)

- The words **alguien** (*someone*) and **persona** are masculine and feminine, respectively. When using adjectives with these nouns, remember that the adjective modifies these words and not a particular person you have in mind.

   alguien simpátic**o**

   una **persona** simpátic**a**

   Juan es una **persona** gregari**a,** pero no muy trabajador**a.**

- When gender is mixed (that is, men and women), use masculine agreement.

   Héctor y Mariela son muy **serios,** pero también son **simpáticos.**

NOUN AND ADJECTIVE AGREEMENT		
	MASCULINO	FEMENINO
para los adjetivos que terminan en -o		
singular	un señor ambicios**o**	una mujer ambicios**a**
plural	unos señores ambicios**os**	unas mujeres ambicios**as**
para los adjetivos que terminan en -e		
singular	un señor inteligent**e**	una mujer inteligent**e**
plural.	unos señores inteligent**es**	unas mujeres inteligent**es**
para los adjetivos que terminan en -l		
singular	un señor libera**l**	una mujer libera**l**
plural	unos señores libera**les**	unas mujeres libera**les**
para los adjetivos que terminan en -r		
singular	un señor conservado**r**	una mujer conservado**ra**
plural	unos señores conservado**res**	unas mujeres conservado**ras**
para los adjetivos que terminan en -ista		
singular	un señor pesim**ista**	una mujer pesim**ista**
plural	unos señores pesim**istas**	unas mujeres pesim**istas**

DE SOL Y VIENTO

At one point in **Episodio 1,** Mario implies that he knows Jaime's desired destination well:

MARIO
¿Valle del Maipo? ¡Fantástico! Muy, muy
_____. A propósito: me llamo Mario
Verdejo. «Verdejín» para mis amigos.

Do you remember the word that Mario used to describe the valley?

1. lindo
2. grande
3. turístico

Actividad E ¿Qué tipo de mujer necesita Jaime?

By now you may have a general impression of Jaime, but did you know he's single? What kind of person would be a good match for him? Number the descriptive adjectives in the order of importance you think they would be for him (**1** = most important, **5** = least important). Then share with the class.

Jaime necesita una mujer...

a. ___ activa y enérgica

b. ___ inteligente y ambiciosa

c. ___ seria y trabajadora

d. ___ apasionada y confiada

e. ___ honesta y discreta

Actividad F Mujeres famosas

For each person or persons listed, select the description you think fits. More than one may be possible. In some cases, none may fit!

1. Hillary Clinton

  a. Es ambiciosa.

  b. Es conservadora.

  c. Es honesta.

2. Madonna

  a. Es extrovertida.

  b. Es creadora.

  c. Es humilde.

3. Oprah Winfrey

  a. Es cerebral.

  b. Es trabajadora.

  c. Es organizada.

4. Madame Curie

  a. Era inteligente.

  b. Era imaginativa.

  c. Era caótica.

5. Serena y Venus Williams

  a. Son ambiciosas.

  b. Son tímidas.

  c. Son apasionadas.

6. Drew Barrymore, Lucy Liu y Cameron Díaz

  a. Son gregarias.

  b. Son enérgicas.

  c. Son cerebrales.

7. Salma Hayek y Jennifer López

  a. Son inteligentes y listas.

  b. Son confiadas.

  c. Son cómicas.

8. Joan y Melissa Rivers

  a. Son cómicas.

  b. Son chismosas.

  c. Son discretas.

Actividad G Parejas (*Couples*) famosas

Paso 1 How would you describe some famous couples? Complete each sentence by selecting an adjective that you think describes the couple. If more than one adjective is possible, use **y** or **pero** to connect them. You can also add **muy, bastante,** or **poco** if you'd like.

1. Brad Pitt y Angelina Jolie son...

   a. trabajadores.   **b.** simpáticos.   **c.** egoístas.

2. Barbra Streisand y James Brolin son...

   a. reservados.   **b.** desconfiados.   **c.** extrovertidos.

3. Bill y Melinda Gates son...

   a. crueles.   **b.** generosos.   **c.** indiferentes.

Paso 2 For each statement that follows, can you think of a famous couple that fits the description? If not a couple, can you list famous friends or family members that fit the description? Note that some adjectives will require that at least one of the people in the pair or group must be a male!

1. Son bastante gregarios.
2. Son muy conservadores.
3. Son muy liberales.
4. Son arrogantes.
5. Son bastante humildes.

Actividad H ¿Cómo somos?

Paso 1 From the adjectives you've learned so far, select five that you think describe you (or don't!) and write out five sentences.

MODELOS: Soy bastante organizado.

Soy poco optimista.

Paso 2 Get together with another classmate and read him or her each adjective without revealing the sentences that you wrote. Can the other person deduce what you have said about yourself? Afterward, rate the person on the following scale (remembering that you have been in class together for only several weeks).

MODELO: E1: organizado, optimista.

E2: Eres organizado y optimista.

E1: Sí, soy organizado, pero no soy muy optimista.

Mi compañero/a es...

☐ muy observador(a).

☐ bastante observador(a).

☐ observador(a).

☐ poco observador(a).

Antes de ver el episodio

Actividad A ¿Qué recuerdas? (*What do you remember?*)

Think briefly about what you know regarding the movie *Sol y viento* thus far. Which of the following are true?

1. ☐ Jaime desea ir a Chile.
2. ☐ Jaime habla inglés y español.
3. ☐ Jaime trabaja para una compañía norteamericana.
4. ☐ María es antropóloga y profesora.
5. ☐ La machi habla de un conflicto.

Actividad B ¿Qué falta? (*What's missing?*)

Paso 1 Here is part of the exchange between Mario and Jaime in the hotel lobby that you haven't yet seen or read. Select from the choices below to fill in each blank.

MARIO: _____¹ diez mil pesos, señor.

JAIME: Aquí tiene. _____² (*Mario turns and walks away. Jaime calls to him.*) ¡Oiga! ¡Espere!

MARIO: ¿Sí, señor? Diga, nomás.ᵃ

JAIME: ¿Ud. hace viajes fuera de Santiago?

ᵃDiga... *Just say the word.*

1.	**a.** Es	**2.**	**a.** Por favor (*Please*)
	b. Hay		**b.** Gracias (*Thank you*)
	c. Son		**c.** De nada (*You're welcome*)
	d. Están		

Paso 2 Look at the exchange one more time. What do you think Jaime is saying when Mario turns and walks away?

Actividad C El episodio

Now watch the episode. Remember that it's OK to let some words and expressions slip by you, especially since this is the first time you are watching the episode. You should be able to follow along without understanding every single word.

Después de ver el episodio

Actividad A ¿Qué recuerdas?

Answer each item according to what you remember from the episode.

1. Cuando Jaime llega a su habitación (*room*), está cansado (*tired*). ¿Sí o no?
2. ¿Cómo se llama el hotel donde se queda (*is staying*) Jaime?
3. Mañana Jaime necesita ir al Valle del _____.
4. ¿Cuál es el apellido de Jaime? ¿Y el de Mario?
5. En su habitación, Jaime habla por teléfono con...
   a. Andy, de Bartel Aquapower **b.** Carlos Sánchez, de «Sol y viento»
6. ¿Qué palabra describe mejor (*best*) la expresión de Carlos al final?
   a. preocupación (*worry*) **b.** alegría (*happiness*) **c.** indiferencia

Actividad B ¿Lo captaste? (*Did you get it?*)

Go back to **Actividad B** of **Antes de ver el episodio** to verify your answers. If you need to, watch that particular section of the episode again.

Actividad C Utilizando (*Using*) el contexto

Paso 1 You have already begun to learn the skill of guessing the meaning of language in context. Did you deduce the meanings of the following phrases in italics? Watch this scene in the episode again if it helps.

> JAIME: Al Hotel Bonaparte. *¿A cuánto sale?*
> MARIO: Eh, um, unos 10.000 (diez mil) pesos, más o menos. *¿Le parece bien?*
> JAIME: Sí. Vamos.

Paso 2 Another skill you have begun to work on is noting that a word or phrase can have multiple meanings. For example, Jaime says **Sí. Vamos.** in response to Mario. You know that **vamos** means *we go* or *we are going*, but does that make sense in this context? What do you think is the equivalent of **vamos** in this context?

Actividad D Primeras (*First*) impresiones

Paso 1 You have now been introduced to Jaime and Mario. How would you describe their personalities, based on your initial impressions? Using what you have learned in this lesson, describe each in several sentences.

Paso 2 Share your descriptions with two other people. Decide what you all agree on and present your descriptions to the class. Does everyone else agree?

RESUMEN DE VOCABULARIO

Verbos

abrir	to open
aprender	to learn
asistir (a)	to attend (*a class*)
beber	to drink
comer	to eat
comprender	to understand
correr	to run
creer (que)	to think, believe (that)
escribir	to write
ir (*irreg.*)	to go
ir a + *infin.*	to be going to (*do something*)
leer	to read
recibir	to receive
tomar el sol	to sunbathe
ver (*irreg.*)	to see; to watch
vivir	to live

Los meses y las estaciones del año

enero, febrero, marzo, abril, mayo, junio, julio, agosto, septiembre, octubre, noviembre, diciembre

el invierno	winter
el otoño	autumn
la primavera	spring
el verano	summer

Para hablar del tiempo

Está despejado.	It's clear.
Está nublado.	It's cloudy.
Hace buen/mal tiempo.	It's good/bad weather.
Hace (mucho) calor.	It's (very) hot.
Hace fresco.	It's cool.
Hace (mucho) frío.	It's (very) cold.
Hace sol.	It's sunny.
Hace (mucho) viento.	It's (very) windy.
Llueve. / Está lloviendo.	It's raining.
Nieva. / Está nevando.	It's snowing.

Para describir la personalidad

aburrido/a	boring
agradable	pleasant
alegre	happy
apasionado/a	passionate
chismoso/a	gossipy
confiado/a	confident
creador(a)	creative
desconfiado/a	untrusting
desleal	disloyal
divertido/a	fun
enérgico/a	energetic
gregario/a	gregarious
humilde	humble
ingenuo/a	naive
leal	loyal
listo/a	clever
sabio/a	wise
sencillo/a	simple
simpático/a	nice
soñador(a)	dreamer
sospechoso/a	untrusting
tonto/a	dumb, foolish
trabajador(a)	hardworking
triste	sad

era	he/she was
parece ser	he/she seems

Cognados: ambicioso/a, arrogante, astuto/a, calmado/a, caótico/a, cerebral, cómico/a, conservador(a), discreto/a, egoísta, estimulante, excéntrico/a, explosivo/a, extrovertido/a, honesto/a, imaginativo/a, indiferente, indiscreto/a, inteligente, interesante, introvertido/a, liberal, malicioso/a, metódico/a, optimista, organizado/a, pesimista, preciso/a, reservado/a, serio/a, tímido/a

Las palabras interrogativas

¿Adónde?	Where (*to*)?
¿Cómo?	How? What?
¿Cuál(es)?	Which?
¿Cuándo?	When?
¿Cuánto/a/os/as?	How much? How many?
¿Dónde?	Where?
¿Por qué?	Why?
¿Qué?	What?
¿Quién(es)?	Who? Whom?

Otras palabras y expresiones

alguien	someone, anyone	**dentro de poco**	soon
el año	year	**en unos (cuantos) días**	in a few days
la novela	novel	**esta noche**	tonight
el periódico	newspaper	**pasado mañana**	the day after tomorrow
la persona	person	**poco** (*adv.*)	not very
la revista	magazine	**un poco**	a little
		la semana entrante	next week
bueno/a (buen)	good	**una vez al mes**	once a month
grande (gran)	large, big; great		
malo/a (mal)	bad	**a**	to
otro/a	other, another	**entre**	between
pobre	poor; unfortunate	**para**	for
próximo/a	next	**porque**	because
a solas	alone	**Repaso** (*Review*): **con, de, muy, pero**	
bastante	rather		
		lo que	what, that which
		si	if

El encuentro[a]

Jaime and María meet in the park. What do you think brought them together? How did they meet?

▲ What is Jaime doing in this photo? Where do you think he is?

◄

Jaime is reading something on a small piece of paper. What does this look like? Is it a note? Something else?

[a]El... *The encounter*

En la universidad y la ciudad

OBJETIVOS

IN THIS LESSON, YOU WILL LEARN:

- the numbers 31–100 and how to express age
- more on talking about activities using verbs that end in **-go** (**yo** forms, present tense)
- prepositions of location to express where things and places are
- more on expressing location using the verbs **estar** and **quedar**
- names of places in a university and city
- more on talking about activities using stem-changing verbs

In addition, you will prepare for **Episodio 2** of the film *Sol y viento.*

◀

La Universidad de Salamanca (España) es una de las más antiguas (*oldest*) y más importantes de Europa.

The following media resources are available for *Sol y viento: En breve*

Episodio 2 of *Sol y viento*

Online *Manual de actividades*

Interactive CD-ROM

Online Learning Center Website

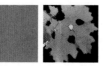

PRIMERA PARTE

Vocabulario

Expressing Age | **¿Cuántos años tiene?** | **Numbers 31–100**

In **Lección 1A** you learned that most numbers between 16 and 29 are combinations of two numbers but are generally spelled as one. For example, you learned that **veintiséis** is actually **veinte y seis.** For numbers 31–99, the numbers are written separately: **cuarenta y dos, cincuenta y tres,** and so forth.

Los números 31–100

31 treinta y uno	37 treinta y siete	70 setenta
32 treinta y dos	38 treinta y ocho	80 ochenta
33 treinta y tres	39 treinta y nueve	90 noventa
34 treinta y cuatro	40 cuarenta	100 cien
35 treinta y cinco	50 cincuenta	
36 treinta y seis	60 sesenta	

✳ MÁS VOCABULARIO

la edad	age
¿Cuántos años tienes?	How old are you?
Tengo... años.	I am . . . years old.
¿Cuántos años tiene... ?	How old is . . . ?

ANTONIO: ¡Feliz cumpleaños (*Happy birthday*), papá! **¿Cuántos años tienes?**

JOSÉ LUIS: **Cincuenta y dos.**

ANTONIO: ¡Uy! ¡Qué viejo (*old*) eres!

JOSÉ LUIS: Pero, recuerda (*remember*): ¡todavía soy más fuerte (*stronger*) y más guapo (*more handsome*) que tú!

Vistazo cultural

La esperanza de vida[a] en los países[b] hispanohablantes

How long can people from different countries expect to live? The following table shows the life expectancies for women and men in Spanish-speaking countries. What trends do you notice?

PAÍS	ESPERANZA DE VIDA		PAÍS	ESPERANZA DE VIDA	
	MUJERES	HOMBRES		MUJERES	HOMBRES
la Argentina	78	71	la Guinea Ecuatorial	54	50
Bolivia	65	62	Honduras	69	63
Chile	79	73	México	76	70
Colombia	75	69	Nicaragua	72	67
Costa Rica	80	75	Panamá	77	73
Cuba	79	75	el Paraguay	73	69
el Ecuador	74	68	el Perú	72	67
El Salvador	74	68	Puerto Rico	80	71
España	82	75	la República Dominicana	70	64
los Estados Unidos	80	75	el Uruguay	79	72
Guatemala	69	63	Venezuela	77	71

Source: United Nations Statistics, 2003.

[a]La... *Life expectancy*   [b]*countries*

Actividad A ¿Qué número es?

Listen as your instructor says some numbers. Write down what you hear.

1. ...   **2.** ...   **3.** ...   **4.** ...   **5.** ...   **6.** ...   **7.** ...

Actividad B ¿Edades típicas?

Paso 1 Decide whether you think the ages shown are typical or not for the following events.

En tu opinión, ¿es típico en este país...

		SÍ	NO
1.	casarse (*to get married*) a los treinta años?	☐	☐
2.	graduarse (*to graduate*) de la universidad a los veintitrés años?	☐	☐
3.	vivir hasta los noventa y cinco años?	☐	☐
4.	tener el primer hijo (*child*) a los veintiún años?	☐	☐
5.	tener nietos (*grandchildren*) a los cuarenta y seis años?	☐	☐
6.	jubilarse (*to retire*) a los cincuenta y cinco años?	☐	☐

Paso 2 If you checked "no" for any of the above items, write out in Spanish the age that you think is typical for that event.

Paso 3 Compare your answers with those of three other classmates. Do you all agree about what are typical ages for those events? Be prepared to share your answers with the class.

MODELO: Creemos que es típico casarse a los treinta años.

Actividad C ¿Tantos (*So many*) años?

Paso 1 Listen as your instructor tells you the approximate ages of some famous people, then jot down the names and the ages that you hear.

		CREO QUE SÍ.	NO, TIENE MÁS AÑOS.	NO, NO TIENE TANTOS AÑOS.
1.	_____ tiene entre ____ años.	☐	☐	☐
2.	_____ tiene ____ años.	☐	☐	☐
3.	_____ tiene ____ años.	☐	☐	☐
4.	_____ tiene ____ años.	☐	☐	☐
5.	_____ tiene ____ años.	☐	☐	☐
6.	_____ tiene entre ____ años.	☐	☐	☐
7.	_____ tiene entre ____ años.	☐	☐	☐

¡Exprésate!

To say that someone is between certain ages, is approximately a certain age, or is older or younger than a certain age, Spanish uses the following expressions:

tiene entre veinte y treinta años (*between 20 and 30*)

tiene aproximadamente cincuenta años (*approximately 50*)

tiene más/menos de cuarenta años (*older/younger than 40*)

Paso 2 Now decide whether you think the age of each person is correct or not by selecting the appropriate column for each, listed in **Paso 1.** If you disagreed with your instructor, how old do you think the person is?

Actividad D ¿Cuántos años tienen?

Paso 1 Fill out the **yo** line of the chart below for yourself, then indicate the ages of your parents and grandparents. If someone has died, you may either write the age that person would be today or write **ya murió** (*he/she already died*).

NOMBRE	EDAD DE LA MADRE (*mother*)	EDAD DEL PADRE (*father*)	EDAD DE LA(S) ABUELA(S) (*grandmother[s]*)	EDAD DEL ABUELO / DE LOS ABUELOS (*grandfather[s]*)
yo				
(compañero/a 1)				
(compañero/a 2)				
(compañero/a 3)				

Paso 2 Now complete the chart by talking with three other classmates.

MODELO: E1: ¿Cuántos años tiene tu _____?
E2: Tiene _____ años.

Paso 3 Based on the information you gathered, calculate the following average ages. Be prepared to share your answer with the class.

la edad media (*average age*)   _____
de las madres

la edad media de los padres   _____

la edad media de las abuelas   _____

la edad media de los abuelos   _____

En general, ¿son mayores (*older*) las mujeres (las madres y las abuelas) o los hombres (los padres y los abuelos)?

Paso 4 Compare the average age of your parents and grandparents with those of your classmates. Then prepare one statement based on the clues below that describes the age of either your parents or your grandparents.

Mi _____ tiene una edad típica.

Mi _____ es joven (*young*) en comparación con
(los/las _____) de mis compañeros.

Mi _____ es viejo/a (*old*) en comparación con
(los/las _____) de mis compañeros.

Gramática

Vengo de los Estados Unidos.   **Verbs that End in -go**

A number of common verbs in Spanish end in **-go** in the first-person singular (**yo**). Among these are **hacer** (*to do; to make*), **poner** (*to put, place*), **salir** (*to leave; to go out*), **traer** (*to bring*). The rest of the verb forms follow the normal pattern of using the stem of the infinitive. Other verbs also end in **-go** in the **yo** form, but they have changes in the stem of some forms. Pay careful attention to the pattern of these *stem-changing verbs*.

VERBS THAT END IN *-go*			
hacer (*to do; to make*): ha**go**, haces, hace, hace, hacemos, hacéis, hacen, hacen			
poner (*to put, place*): pon**go**, pones, pone, pone, ponemos, ponéis, ponen, ponen			
salir (*to leave; to go out*): sal**go**, sales, sale, sale, salimos, salís, salen, salen			
traer (*to bring*): tra**igo**,* traes, trae, trae, traemos, traéis, traen, traen			
venir (*to come*) e → ie		**tener** (*to have*) e → ie	
ven**go**	venimos	ten**go**	tenemos
vi**e**nes	venís	ti**e**nes	tenéis
vi**e**ne	vi**e**nen	ti**e**ne	ti**e**nen
vi**e**ne	vi**e**nen	ti**e**ne	ti**e**nen
oír (*to hear*) i → y		**decir** (*to say; to tell*) e → i	
oi**go**	oímos	di**go**	decimos
o**y**es	oís	d**i**ces	decís
o**y**e	o**y**en	d**i**ce	d**i**cen
o**y**e	o**y**en	d**i**ce	d**i**cen

*Note that the **yo** form of **traer** contains another irregularity: An **i** is added as part of the stem: **traigo.**

DE SOL Y VIENTO

In **Episodio 2** of *Sol y viento,* you will watch a scene in which Jaime meets María, an anthropologist at a local university. Part of their exchange appears in the dialogue.

JAIME
¡Perdón! Soy Jaime Talavera. **Vengo** de los Estados Unidos.

MARÍA
Encantada. ____... señor Talavera. ¿O prefiere «Míster Talavera»?

JAIME
Prefiero «Jaime». Y ojalá que nos veamos de nuevo.[a]

Selecting from the following list, what do you think María says in the missing phrase?

1. Yo vengo del Perú.

2. Tengo que irme (*I have to leave*).

3. Tengo ganas de (*I feel like*) visitar los Estados Unidos.

[a]ojalá... *I hope that we see each other again*

◉ Enfoque lingüístico

¿*Tener* años?

You may wonder why Spanish uses the verb **tener** (*to have*) to express age (*Tengo dieciocho años*), whereas English uses *to be* (*I am* eighteen years old). The literal translation is, of course, *I have eighteen years.* Spanish is not the only language that does this. Other Romance languages (languages that have evolved from Latin) also use the verb *to have* to express age, including Catalan, Italian, French, and Portuguese. Although English has some Latin influences, English belongs to a family of Germanic languages. Modern German also comes from this same language family, and both English and German use the verb *to be* to express age. Look at the translations of *I am eighteen years old* in these languages, and see if you can notice other similarities among languages in the same family in addition to the use of *to have* or *to be.*

Spanish	**Tengo dieciocho años.**	Portuguese	**Tenho dezoito anos.**
Catalan	**Tinc divuit anys.**	English	**I am eighteen years old.**
French	**J'ai dix-huit ans.**	German	**Ich bin achtzehn Jahre alt.**
Italian	**Ho diciotto anni.**		

Actividad E ¿Quién es?

Match the statements with the appropriate character from *Sol y viento*.

▲ **a.** Jaime

▲ **b.** María

▲ **c.** Mario

1. ___ Sale con Mario para el Valle del Maipo.
2. ___ Tiene un auto.
3. ___ Dice que es su propio (*own*) jefe.
4. ___ Viene de los Estados Unidos.
5. ___ Tiene muchos estudiantes.

Actividad F ¿Con qué frecuencia?

Paso 1 Indicate the frequency with which you do the following activities related to your Spanish class.

	SIEMPRE (*always*)	MUCHAS VECES	A VECES	NUNCA (*never*)
1. Vengo a la clase de español preparado/a.	☐	☐	☐	☐
2. Salgo de la clase de español confundido/a (*confused*).	☐	☐	☐	☐
3. Hago la tarea (*homework*) para la clase de español.	☐	☐	☐	☐
4. Oigo a mi profesor(a) y comprendo bien lo que dice.	☐	☐	☐	☐
5. Traigo comida (*food*) a la clase.	☐	☐	☐	☐
6. Pongo mucho esfuerzo (*effort*) en aprender español.	☐	☐	☐	☐
7. Tengo que estudiar mucho.	☐	☐	☐	☐
8. Tengo ganas de asistir a clase.	☐	☐	☐	☐
9. Le digo a mi profesor(a): «No comprendo» o «Repita, por favor».	☐	☐	☐	☐

¡Exprésate!

Note the following common expressions with the verb **tener.**

tener que + *infin.* = to have to (*do something*)
Tengo que hacer más ejercicio.

tener ganas de + *infin.* = to feel like (*doing something*)
No tengo ganas de estudiar más.

Paso 2 In groups of three or four, compare your answers. Do you all agree? Find at least two statements that you agree on and present them to the class. **¡OJO!** (*Watch out! Be careful!*) Be sure to use the **nosotros** form of the verb.

MODELO: Ponemos mucho esfuerzo en aprender español.

Actividad G ¿De dónde vengo?

Listen as your instructor reads statements made by students from various Spanish-speaking countries. Then decide where you think each one comes from.

1. **a.** la Guinea Ecuatorial   **b.** Bolivia   **c.** España
2. **a.** El Salvador   **b.** México   **c.** Bolivia
3. **a.** el Perú   **b.** Cuba   **c.** el Ecuador
4. **a.** el Uruguay   **b.** Nicaragua   **c.** el Brasil
5. **a.** México   **b.** Venezuela   **c.** la Argentina

Actividad H ¿Qué haces?

Paso 1 Here is a list of activities. Use it to prepare at least five questions for another student to answer. Come up with at least one question about an activity that is not listed.

- hacer ejercicio (*to exercise*) en el gimnasio
- hacer la tarea en la biblioteca
- salir a los bares los fines de semana
- salir a las discotecas los fines de semana
- oír música mientras (*while*) estudias
- traer amigos a la habitación (*room*) (a casa, al apartamento)
- poner muy alto el volumen (*to turn up the volume a lot*) de la música
- tener fiestas en la habitación (la casa, el apartamento)
- decir secretos de otros amigos
- ¿ ?

Paso 2 Interview two different classmates using the questions you prepared. Be sure to note their answers.

Paso 3 How would you answer the questions you posed to your classmates, and how similar are you to the two classmates you interviewed? Write a short paragraph comparing the three of you. Here are some statements to help you.

MODELOS: (Nombre 1) y (Nombre 2) son muy parecidos/as (*similar*) en cuanto a (*regarding*) salir a los bares los fines de semana. Los/Las dos salen…

(Nombre 1), (Nombre 2) y yo somos muy parecidos/as en cuanto a… Los/Las tres (*The three of us*)…

Mis compañeros y yo somos (muy) diferentes en cuanto a…

Vocabulario

Expressing Where
Things and Places
Are Located

¿Está lejos o cerca?

Prepositions of Location

1. El reloj está **en la pared** (*wall*).
2. Los estudiantes están **alrededor de** la profesora.
3. Los libros de la profesora están **encima del** escritorio.
4. Los libros del estudiante están **debajo de** la silla.
5. El escritorio está **entre** la profesora y la pizarra.
6. El lápiz está **al lado de** la pluma.
7. La profesora está **delante del** escritorio.

✳ MÁS VOCABULARIO

a la izquierda de	to the left of
a la derecha de	to the right of
cerca de	close to
detrás de	behind
enfrente de	across from; in front of
lejos de	far from
al norte de	to the north of
al sur de	to the south of
al este de	to the east of
al oeste de	to the west of

Here is a list of common places in a university, including ones that you have already seen in the **Lección preliminar**:

el bar	bar
la biblioteca	library
la cafetería	cafeteria; dining hall
la capilla	chapel
el centro estudiantil	student center/union
el edificio de (ciencias, lenguas extranjeras)	(science, foreign languages) building
el estadio	stadium
el gimnasio	gym
la habitación	(dorm) room
la librería	bookstore
la residencia estudiantil	residence hall, dormitory
la torre	tower

≋ Vistazo cultural

Las universidades en el mundo hispano

If you spend any time at a university in a Spanish-speaking country, you will notice a number of differences from universities in this country. First, many public universities in Spanish-speaking countries are not residential. In other words, the students do not live in university dormitories or housing, and there are no fraternities or sororities. If students attend universities close to home (usually less than an hour away), it is not uncommon for them to live at home and commute using public transportation. If the university is far from home, many students have to find housing on their own. Some may rent a room from a family; others may look for an apartment with other students. Because university students live "off campus," it is rare to have meal plans or to find a dining hall, as in many schools in North America.

Another difference is that students in most universities in Spanish-speaking countries take classes in their specialty only. Students apply to a particular **facultad** or *school* such as **derecho** (*law*), **bellas artes** (*fine arts*), **medicina, filosofía y letras** (*humanities*), or **ciencias naturales** or **sociales,** and take classes within that **facultad** only. There are usually no general education requirements, given that most students have already taken these in their final years of high school.

An additional difference is that there are no university-sponsored athletic teams on campus. Although sports are extremely popular (especially soccer), athletes belong to local club teams instead. If your college or university has study abroad programs with universities in Spanish-speaking countries, consider spending a summer, semester, or year abroad!

Actividad A ¿Cierto o falso?

Listen as your instructor describes where places are on the following campus map. Indicate whether the description is true or not.

1. ...
2. ...
3. ...
4. ...
5. ...
6. ...
7. ...

LA UNIVERSIDAD DE LAS AMÉRICAS

Facultad de medicina

Capilla

Facultad de ciencias naturales

Avenida Colón

Oficinas de Administración

Librería

Facultad de ciencias sociales

Calle San José

Centro estudiantil

Torre

Facultad de filosofía y letras

Biblioteca

Calle Bolívar

Avenida de los Reyes

✗ Ud. está aquí

Actividad B ¿Dónde estás?

Your instructor will describe a location on your campus or in your town/city using prepositions of place but will not tell you what that place is. Based on your instructor's description, write down the name of the location.

1. ...
2. ...
3. ...
4. ...
5. ...
6. ...
7. ...

Actividad C ¡Te toca a ti!

Paso 1 Now it's your turn to describe the location of places in and around your campus. Write five questions that ask about a particular location, including the point of reference.

MODELO: Estás enfrente del gimnaso. ¿Qué edificio está a la derecha del gimnasio?

Paso 2 In groups of three, take turns reading your questions to each other. Each of you should write down the building that each question describes.

Paso 3 Now each group should read the statements again to check to see if everyone wrote down correct answers.

◀ La biblioteca de la Universidad Nacional Autónoma de México (UNAM) en México, D.F.

SOL Y VIENTO: Enfoque cultural

City parks abound in Spanish-speaking countries, as they do in this country. However, they are often used in different ways. In **Episodio 2** you will watch Jaime as he jogs through the Parque Forestal in Santiago. However, using a public park as a place to exercise is not the norm for most Spanish-speaking people. Instead, parks are often places to socialize, and on Sundays they may flourish with couples and families of all ages out for an old-fashioned Sunday afternoon stroll (**el paseo**). It is also typical to find vendors of all types in these parks selling everything from cotton candy to balloons, as well as entertainers working for donations, such as the organ-grinding fortune teller with his parrot that you will see in this episode. Some well-known parks in Spanish-speaking cities include the Retiro (Madrid), Lazema (Buenos Aires), and Chapultepec (Mexico City), among others.

▲ El parque Chapultepec (México, D.F.)

Gramática

Mi trabajo está cerca.

✳ More on **estar** + *location;* **quedar** + *location*

USES OF *estar* AND *quedar* TO EXPRESS LOCATION	
Estar se usa para objetos animados...	**Quedar** se usa...
Juan está aquí. **El perro** (*dog*) **está** en la habitación.	
y para lugares y objetos no animados.	sólo para lugares y objetos no animados inmóviles.
Bogotá está muy lejos. **El banco está** en la calle Verde.	**Bogotá queda** muy lejos. **El banco queda** en la calle Verde.

You have already used the verb **estar** to talk about where people, places, and objects are located. Another verb that can also express location is **quedar** (lit: *to stay, remain*). **Quedar** can only be used to express the location of immovable places and objects like buildings, cities, and so forth.

La universidad **está** muy cerca.
 La universidad **queda** muy cerca. } *The university is very close by.*

Although **estar** can be used in the same contexts as **quedar,** when expressing the location of movable objects, especially people or animals, only **estar** can be used.

Mi padre está en el hospital.

Jaime está en Chile.

✳ **MÁS GRAMÁTICA**

Although the verbs **estar** and **quedar** are used in Spanish to talk about the location of buildings, people, and objects, the verb **ser** is used to talk about the location of events. In other words, to say where an event *takes place,* **ser** must be used, as in the following examples.

El partido de fútbol **es** en el estadio.	*The soccer game is (takes place) in the stadium.*
¿Dónde **es** el concierto?	*Where is the concert? (Where does the concert take place?)*
La fiesta **es** en casa de Ramón.	*The party is (takes place) at Ramón's house.*

If you want to express where the stadium or someone's house is *located,* then use **estar** or **quedar.**

El estadio **está** cerca del gimnasio.	*The stadium is (located) near the gym.*
La casa de Ramón **queda** en la calle Verdugo.	*Ramón's house is on Verdugo Street.*

 DE SOL Y VIENTO

In **Episodio 2** of *Sol y viento,* you will watch a scene in which María asks Jaime about what he's doing in Santiago. Part of their exchange appears in the following dialogue.

JAIME

¡Qué coincidencia! Para allá voy… al Valle del Maipo, como turista, con mi conductor.ᵃ

MARÍA

¿Su conductor? ¿Está de vacaciones o tiene negociosᵇ en Maipo?

JAIME

Bueno, la verdad es que _____ aquí por placerᶜ… y un poco de negocio.

Keeping in mind what you just learned about expressing location, what verb do you think is missing from the dialogue?

1. estoy

2. soy

3. quedo

ᵃ*driver* ᵇ*business* ᶜ*por… for pleasure*

COMUNICACIÓN ÚTIL

You will find that the verb **quedar** has many different meanings and uses. In this lesson, you will be using it to talk about the location of places and objects, but here are some other common uses:

quedar con
  Elisa **queda con** Juan a las ocho.
  ¿A qué hora quedamos?

to arrange to meet
  Elisa arranges to meet Juan at eight o'clock.
  What time are we planning to meet?

quedar en + *infin.*
  ¿Quedamos en salir a las ocho?

to agree to (*do something*)
  Shall we agree to leave at eight o'clock?

Actividad D ¿Dónde están?

Answer these questions with the names of one or more of the following characters.

Carlos   Diego   Jaime   Mario

1. En el **Prólogo,** ¿quiénes están en el sitio de excavación?
2. En el **Episodio 1,** ¿quién está en su oficina en la viña?
3. ¿Quién está siempre cerca de su auto?
4. En el **Episodio 1,** ¿quiénes están en la recepción del Hotel Bonaparte?

Actividad E Un poco de geografía

Paso 1 How well do you know where Latin American countries are located? Read each of the descriptions below and decide whether the statement is true or not.

	SÍ	NO
1. Los Estados Unidos quedan al norte de México.	☐	☐
2. Cuba queda en el mar Caribe, al sur de la Florida.	☐	☐
3. Chile queda al oeste de la Argentina.	☐	☐
4. Venezuela está al oeste de Colombia.	☐	☐
5. Costa Rica queda al sur de Panamá.	☐	☐
6. Colombia está al norte de Chile.	☐	☐

Paso 2 If you checked "no" for any of the statements in **Paso 1,** change the statements to make them true.

Actividad F ¿Cierto o falso?

Paso 1 Listen as your instructor describes where some places on your campus are located. Indicate whether each description is true or not.

   1. ...   **2.** ...   **3.** ...   **4.** ...   **5.** ...   **6.** ...   **7.** ...

Paso 2 If any of the descriptions were false, can you provide your instructor with the correct description? If you don't remember the original statement, ask **¿Puede(s) repetir el número... , por favor?**

Actividad G ¡Adivina qué es! (*Guess what it is!*)

Working in groups of four, each student will think of one classroom object but will not tell the others what it is. The other members of the group have to think of yes or no questions using as many different prepositions of location as possible to figure out where the object is. The questions must contain either **estar** or **quedar** and a preposition of location. When the exact location of the object is determined, only then may someone say what the object is. Use the following rules as you work through this activity:

- If a student gets an answer of **sí** to his or her question, that student may ask another question.
- If a student repeats a question that another student has already asked, that student is disqualified from that round.
- If a student guesses the object incorrectly, that student is disqualified from that round.
- The student who guesses the object correctly wins.

MODELO: E1: ¿Está encima del escritorio?
         E2: Sí.
         E1: ¿Está al lado de los libros de la profesora?
         E2: Sí.
         E1: ¿Es la pluma?
         E2: ¡Sí!

▲ ¿Dónde está el maletín (*briefcase*) de Jaime? Está encima del mostrador (*counter*).

Vocabulario

Talking About
Where You
Do Things

Tengo que ir al banco.

Places in the City ✳

En el centro[a]

[a]*downtown*

el parque

el almacén

REBAJALANDIA   REBAJA

el hotel

Hotel Josefina

la Bodega

la escuela

CORREOS

FARMACIA GÓMEZ

BANCO COLÓN   BANCO COLÓN

el banco

el restaurante

el correo

la farmacia

el mercado

la iglesia

la plaza

CINE

el cine

✳ MÁS VOCABULARIO

las afueras	outskirts, suburbs
el barrio	neighborhood
el cajero automático	ATM machine
la catedral	cathedral
el centro comercial	shopping center, mall
la discoteca	dance club
la estación del tren	train station
el estanco	tobacco stand
el hospital	hospital
el lugar	place
la parada de autobuses	bus stop
el rascacielos	skyscraper
el supermercado	supermarket
la tienda	store, shop

〰 Vistazo cultural

Los mercados y supermercados

In this country, it's common to go to a large supermarket even if one only needs a loaf of bread or some milk. In many Spanish-speaking countries, large indoor **supermercados** have become popular only in the last twenty years or so, and they are normally found on the outskirts of cities and towns. In smaller towns and in the center of cities, shoppers usually go to smaller stores or shops (**tiendas**). For example, many people will buy their meat at a local **carnicería** (*butcher shop*), their bread at a **panadería** (*bakery*), and their fruit and vegetables at a **frutería**. In many cities, each neighborhood has a number of each of these smaller stores. This provides a community atmosphere within larger cities. In smaller towns, it's common to see an open-air market (**mercado**). Farmers, bakers, butchers, and artisans travel to different towns within a region and set up a stand (**puesto**) to sell their products one or two days a week. Similarly to what has happened in this country, large supermarkets often offer a larger selection of items in one store. Consequently, many smaller, family-owned **tiendas** suffer financially, and some have had to close.

▲ Un mercado típico de Bolivia

Actividad A Lugares en la ciudad

Match each city building or location with a name that represents it.

1. ___ el hotel
2. ___ el supermercado
3. ___ el restaurante
4. ___ la catedral
5. ___ el almacén
6. ___ la farmacia
7. ___ el rascacielos
8. ___ la tienda

a. St. Patrick's, Notre Dame
b. Walgreens, CVS
c. Holiday Inn, Hilton
d. Abercrombie & Fitch, Gap
e. Winn Dixie, IGA, Safeway
f. Empire State, la Torre de Sears
g. Olive Garden, Pizza Hut
h. Bloomingdale's, Macy's

Actividad B ¿Dónde?

Listen as your instructor describes the activities of different people. Then choose where the activity takes place or where the person needs to go.

1. **a.** al supermercado   **b.** al almacén   **c.** al centro comercial
2. **a.** en un hotel   **b.** en un restaurante   **c.** en una tienda
3. **a.** en el centro   **b.** en un barrio   **c.** en las afueras
4. **a.** a la escuela   **b.** a la iglesia   **c.** al cine
5. **a.** a un bar   **b.** a un estanco   **c.** a una farmacia
6. **a.** al teatro   **b.** al cine   **c.** al almacén
7. **a.** a la farmacia   **b.** a la tienda   **c.** al hospital
8. **a.** a un cajero   **b.** a un bar   **c.** a una tienda
   automático

Actividad C Alrededor de tu universidad

Paso 1 What do you know about the town or city in which your university is located? With a partner, review each question and then answer as best you can.

1. ¿Hay un supermercado cerca del campus? ¿Cómo se llama?
2. ¿Cuántos bares hay en el campus o alrededor del campus?
3. ¿Cuántas escuelas secundarias (*high schools*) hay en la ciudad? ¿Cómo se llaman?
4. ¿Dónde queda tu universidad? ¿En una ciudad? ¿en las afueras de una ciudad? ¿en un pueblo?
5. ¿Hay hoteles de lujo (*luxury*) cerca de la universidad? ¿Cómo se llaman?
6. ¿Cuántos cines hay?
7. ¿Cuántos centros comerciales importantes hay en tu ciudad o pueblo?

¡Exprésate!

To say that your town or city does not have something, you can say the following:

No hay ningún (cine, centro comercial, hotel, etcétera).

There's not a single… (*masc. noun*).

No hay ninguna (tienda, escuela, etcétera).

There's not a single… (*fem. noun*).

Paso 2 Prepare a brief statement to share with the class about the city or town where your university is located.

MODELO: (Nombre de la ciudad o pueblo) es (muy) interesante porque hay...
(Nombre de la ciudad o pueblo) es (un poco) aburrido/a porque no hay...

Actividad D Nuestros lugares preferidos

Paso 1 Complete the following survey by writing down the names of the places that you go to for different things in the city or town where your university is located.

1. Cuando necesito una farmacia, voy a _____.
2. Si tengo que comprar ropa nueva (*buy new clothes*), voy a la tienda de _____.
3. Si deseo tomar unas cervezas, voy al bar de _____.
4. Si voy a la iglesia, voy a _____.
5. Si necesito comprar comida, voy al mercado/supermercado de _____.
6. Cuando deseo comer en un restaurante con mis amigos, normalmente vamos a _____.
7. Si deseo descansar o jugar (*to play*) en un parque voy a _____.
8. Si voy al cine, voy a _____.

Paso 2 With three or four classmates, compare your answers for **Paso 1** and take note of your classmates' answers. Be prepared to share with your instructor the most popular places in your town or city for each of the items in **Paso 1.**

▲ Santiago de Chile es una ciudad con edificios modernos y antiguos (*old*).

NAVEGANDO LA RED 〜〜〜〜〜〜〜〜〜〜〜〜〜〜

Look for information about a Hispanic university and print out a map of its campus. Briefly describe where the buildings are in relation to others at the university. Is the layout of that campus similar to the layout of your campus?

Gramática

More on Talking
About Activities

Puedo caminar.   **e →ie, o →ue Stem-Changing Verbs**

STEM-CHANGING VERBS (e → ie)					
cerrar (*to close*)		**entender** (*to understand*)		**preferir** (*to prefer*)	
cierro	cerramos	entiendo	entendemos	prefiero	preferimos
cierras	cerráis	entiendes	entendéis	prefieres	preferís
cierra	cierran	entiende	entienden	prefiere	prefieren
cierra	cierran	entiende	entienden	prefiere	prefieren
(o → ue)					
poder (*to be able, can*)		**dormir** (*to sleep*)		**jugar*** (*to play*)	
puedo	podemos	duermo	dormimos	juego	jugamos
puedes	podéis	duermes	dormís	juegas	jugáis
puede	pueden	duerme	duermen	juega	juegan
puede	pueden	duerme	duermen	juega	juegan

You may recall that the vowel in the stem of the verbs **tener** and **venir** changes from **e** to **ie** in the forms for **tú, Ud./él/ella** and **Uds./ellos/ellas.** In addition to changes in these forms, the following verbs have the same stem change in the **yo** form as well.

Other **e → ie** verbs:

despertarse† (*to wake up*)	**perder** (*to lose*)
empezar (*to begin*)	**querer** (*to want; to love*)
pensar (*to think*)	

A number of verbs also have a stem change from **o → ue** in the present tense. Like the **e → ie** stem-changing verbs, these verbs undergo a change in all forms except **nosotros/as** and **vosotros/as.**

Other **o → ue** verbs:

acostarse† (*to go to bed*)	**recordar** (*to remember*)
almorzar (*to eat lunch*)	**soler** + *infin.* (*to be in the habit of*
contar (*to tell; to count*)	[*doing something*])
costar (*to cost*)	**volver** (*to return* [*to a place*])

*****Jugar** is the only verb in Spanish that has the **u → ue** stem change.
†**Despertarse** and **acostarse** are called *reflexive* verbs. Note the reflexive pronoun **se** at the end of each. This denotes that an action is being done by someone to him or herself: **me despierto** = *I wake* (*myself*) *up,* **me acuesto** = *I go* (*put myself*) *to bed.* You will learn more about reflexive verbs in **Lección 5A.** For now, just learn to recognize them when you see them.

✳ MÁS GRAMÁTICA

A number of stem-changing verbs take prepositions and/or infinitives to form a variety of useful expressions.

empezar a + *infin.*	to begin to (*do something*)	Manuel **empieza a trabajar** a las nueve.
pensar en	to think about	**Pienso** mucho **en** mi familia.
pensar de	to think of/about	¿Qué **piensas de** la película?
pensar que	to think (that)	**Pienso que** es una buena película.
pensar + *infin.*	to plan, intend to (*do something*)	Alicia **piensa trabajar** en el hospital.
querer + *infin.*	to want to (*do something*)	¿Dónde **quieres comer**?

DE SOL Y VIENTO

In **Episodio 2** of *Sol y viento,* you will watch a scene in which Jaime and Mario talk about Jaime's encounter with María. Part of their exchange appears here in the dialogue.

MARIO
¡Bonita la muchacha, don Jaime!

JAIME
Sí, bonita e inteligente... Vayamos a lo nuestro.ª _____ en dos minutos.

Selecting from the list below, what do you think is the verb that's missing from the dialogue?

1. Duermo

2. Pierdo

3. Vuelvo

ªVayamos... *Let's get back to business.*

Actividad E En orden

Put Jaime's activities in order according to what you've seen so far and also what makes sense.

____ Se despierta al día siguiente (*the next day*).

____ Prefiere tomar el primer vuelo (*flight*) a Santiago.

____ Quiere ir a correr un poco por el parque.

____ No entiende por qué tiene que viajar a Chile.

____ Vuelve al hotel después de correr.

____ Duerme en el Hotel Bonaparte.

Actividad F ¿Con qué frecuencia?

Paso 1 When do you do the following activities? (Note: **durante** = *during*, [**casi**] **nunca** = [*almost*] *never*)

	DURANTE LA SEMANA	DURANTE EL FIN DE SEMANA	TODOS LOS DÍAS	(CASI) NUNCA
1. Vuelvo muy tarde a casa.	☐	☐	☐	☐
2. Duermo hasta mediodía.	☐	☐	☐	☐
3. Me despierto a las siete de la mañana o antes.	☐	☐	☐	☐
4. Empiezo las clases a las nueve.	☐	☐	☐	☐
5. Juego al* tenis por la mañana.	☐	☐	☐	☐
6. Me acuesto antes de (*before*) medianoche.	☐	☐	☐	☐
7. Suelo estudiar por la noche.	☐	☐	☐	☐
8. Pienso en mis notas (*grades*).	☐	☐	☐	☐

Paso 2 Compare your answers with those of a classmate. Based on your answers, decide when you are both most active. Use the following clues to help you, and share your answers with the class.

Nosotros/as preferimos... Por ejemplo,...

(Nombre) prefiere... , pero yo no. Por ejemplo,...

Prefiero... , pero (nombre) no. Por ejemplo,...

---

*Note that **a** + *definite article* is used with **jugar** when talking about games and sports.

Actividad G ¿A quién describe?

Read the following descriptions and decide what kind of person best fits each description.

1. _____ pierde las cosas con mucha frecuencia y no recuerda dónde están.

   a. Una persona irresponsable **b.** Una persona responsable **c.** Una persona organizada

2. _____ quiere ser muy puntual y hacer buen trabajo.

   a. Una persona sociable **b.** Una persona introvertida **c.** Una persona dedicada

3. _____ prefiere estar a solas todo el tiempo.

   a. Una persona responsable **b.** Una persona introvertida **c.** Una persona extrovertida

4. _____ no piensa nunca (*never*) en las necesidades de otras personas.

   a. Una persona egoísta **b.** Una persona generosa **c.** Una persona sociable

5. _____ juega al basquetbol y al tenis.

   a. Una persona atlética **b.** Una persona artística **c.** Una persona sedentaria

6. _____ suele tener muchos amigos y prefiere pasar mucho tiempo con ellos.

   a. Una persona introvertida **b.** Una persona egoísta **c.** Una persona extrovertida

Actividad H Entrevista

¡Exprésate!

To ask a friend a question using a verb that ends in **-se**, place **te** directly before the conjugated verb.

¿A qué hora **te despiertas**?

¿A qué hora **te acuestas**?

To answer the question, place **me** directly before the conjugated verb.

Me despierto a las ocho.

Me acuesto a las doce.

To report the information about your partner, place **se** in front of the conjugated verb.

Ángela **se despierta** a las seis.

No **se acuesta** hasta medianoche.

Paso 1 You will be interviewing another classmate about his or her activities. First you need to come up with questions to ask. Use the list of question words and the list of activities to help you write ten questions. Create questions about at least four activities that are not in the list.

MODELO: ¿Dónde prefieres estudiar?

PALABRAS INTERROGATIVAS

¿adónde?
¿a qué hora?
¿con qué frecuencia?
¿cuándo?
¿dónde?

ACTIVIDADES

acostarse
despertarse
empezar las clases
preferir estudiar
soler...
volver a casa (al apartamento, a la residencia)

Paso 2 Using the questions you have prepared, interview someone in the class with whom you have not worked before. Be sure to note his or her answers.

Paso 3 Write a paragraph describing your partner's activities. Include information about yourself as well so that you can decide how much you have in common.

RESUMEN DE VOCABULARIO

Verbos

acostarse (ue)	to go to bed
almorzar (ue)	to eat lunch
cerrar (ie)	to close
contar (ue)	to tell; to count
costar (ue)	to cost
decir (*irreg.*)	to say; to tell
despertarse (ie)	to wake up
dormir (ue)	to sleep
empezar (ie)	to begin
entender (ie)	to understand
hacer (hago)	to do; to make
jugar (ue)	to play (*a sport*)
oír (*irreg.*)	to hear
pensar (ie)	to think
perder (ie)	to lose
poder (ue)	to be able, can
poner (pongo)	to put, place
preferir (ie)	to prefer
quedar	to be (*location*)
querer (ie)	to want; to love
recordar (ue)	to remember
salir (salgo)	to leave; to go out
soler (ue) + *infin.*	to be in the habit of (*doing something*)
tener (*irreg.*)	to have
traer (traigo)	to bring
venir (*irreg.*)	to come
volver (ue)	to return (*to a place*)

Los números del 31 al 100

treinta y uno, treinta y dos... , cuarenta, cincuenta, sesenta, setenta, ochenta, noventa, cien

Lugares en la universidad

la capilla	chapel
el centro estudiantil	student center/union
el estadio	stadium
la habitación	(dorm) room
la torre	tower

Cognados: el bar, el gimnasio
Repaso: la biblioteca, la cafetería, el edificio, la facultad, la librería, la residencia estudiantil

Lugares en la ciudad

las afueras	outskirts, suburbs
el almacén	department store
el barrio	neighborhood
el cajero automático	ATM machine
el centro	downtown
el centro comercial	shopping center, mall
el cine	movie theater
el correo	post office
la escuela	school
el estanco	tobacco stand
la iglesia	church
el mercado	market
la parada de autobuses	bus stop
el rascacielos	skyscraper
la tienda	store, shop

Cognados: el banco, la catedral, la discoteca, la estación del tren, la farmacia, el hospital, el hotel, el parque, la plaza, el restaurante, el supermercado

Preposiciones de lugar

a la derecha de	to the right of
a la izquierda de	to the left of
al lado de	next to
alrededor de	around
cerca de	close to
debajo de	under
delante de	in front of
detrás de	behind
en	on; in
encima de	on top of
enfrente de	across from; in front of
lejos de	far from
al este de	to the east of
al norte de	to the north of
al oeste de	to the west of
al sur de	to the south of

Otras palabras y expresiones

la edad	age
el país	country
la tarea	homework
tener (*irreg.*)... **años**	to be . . . years old

¡Vamos de compras!ᵃ

ᵃ¡Vamos... *Let's go shopping!*

Vocabulario

Talking About What People Wear | **La ropa**

Clothing ✳

los pantalones

la gorra
el cinturón
el impermeable
la chaqueta
la corbata
los calcetines
el traje
la camisa
la camiseta
los vaqueros
las sandalias
los zapatos de tenis

✳ MÁS VOCABULARIO

llevar	to wear
la bufanda	scarf
la cartera	wallet
las medias	stockings; pantyhose
la prenda de ropa	article of clothing
los zapatos de tacón alto	high-heeled shoes
Es/Son de...	It's/They're made of . . .
algodón (*m.*)	cotton
cuero	leather
lana	wool
poliéster (*m.*)	polyester
seda	silk

la bata

el pijama

las zapatillas

la blusa

el vestido

el abrigo

la bolsa

el suéter

la sudadera

los zapatos

las botas

la falda

el traje de baño

los pantalones cortos

〰 Vistazo cultural

Diseñadores[a] hispanos

For decades, a number of Hispanic designers have enjoyed international recognition for their elegant, high-end fashion designs. Cristóbal Balenciaga (Spain, 1895–1972) created a world-renowned fashion house in Paris, and his designs continue to enjoy success on both sides of the Atlantic. Venezuelan-born Carolina Herrera and the Dominican Óscar de la Renta have been at the forefront of the U.S. fashion industry for more than two decades. In addition to creating accessory and fragrance lines, both are well-known for creating designs described as both wearable and stylish. More recently, Cuban-American Narciso Rodríguez gained notoriety after designing the wedding gown for Carolyn Bessette Kennedy in 1996. His designs are often worn by famous actresses such as Salma Hayek and Sarah Jessica Parker.

In terms of popular fashion, perhaps the biggest success story is that of the Spanish-born entrepreneur Amancio Ortega. What started out as a small dress-making business in provincial Galicia in the early sixties has turned into an empire of more than one thousand stores worldwide and the third-largest clothing company in the world (after Gap and the Swedish HM). Ortega's flagship store is Zara, which can be found in many Spanish cities, as well as in major cities in Europe, the United States, and Asia.

[a]*Designers*

▲ Carolina Herrera

Actividad A ¿De qué es/son?

Listen as your instructor names an item of clothing. Then write the number of the item mentioned next to what it's normally made of. **¡OJO!** You may put more than one item in the blank.

_____ Es/Son de lana.

_____ Es/Son de cuero.

_____ Es/Son de seda.

_____ Es/Son de algodón.

_____ Es/Son de una mezcla (*mix*) de algodón y poliéster.

¡Exprésate!

You can use the preposition **para** plus an infinitive to express "in order to (*do something*)."

Para comprar ropa de última moda, necesitas mucho dinero.

In order to buy the latest fashions, you need lots of money.

Actividad B ¡No lleves eso! (*Don't wear that!*)

Choose the article of clothing that you would *not* wear for each situation or condition below.

1. para ir a la playa (*beach*)
   a. un traje de baño
   b. un sombrero
   c. unas botas

2. para acostarse
   a. un traje
   b. el pijama
   c. una camiseta

3. para ir a clase
   a. una sudadera
   b. unos vaqueros
   c. una bata

4. cuando hace mucho frío
   a. una gorra
   b. pantalones cortos
   c. un abrigo

5. cuando llueve
   a. unas zapatillas
   b. un impermeable
   c. unas botas

6. cuando hace mucho calor
   a. unas sandalias
   b. una camiseta
   c. un suéter

7. para ir al gimnasio
   a. unos zapatos de tenis
   b. una falda
   c. unos calcetines

Actividad C ¿Qué llevan los compañeros?

Paso 1 Count the number of men and women in the class that are wearing each of the clothing items listed in the chart.

PRENDA DE ROPA	NÚMERO DE HOMBRES	NÚMERO DE MUJERES	TOTAL
vaqueros			
camisetas			
camisas			
zapatos de tenis			
zapatos			
sandalias			
sudaderas			
suéteres			
gorras			
calcetines			
chaquetas			
pantalones			
botas			
¿ ?			
Total			

Paso 2 With a partner, compare your numbers and answer the following questions.

1. ¿Hay un conjunto (*outfit*) típico de los estudiantes? ¿Cuál es?
2. ¿Hay diferencia entre lo que llevan las mujeres y lo que llevan los hombres en la clase? ¿Cuál es la diferencia?
   - ☐ Los hombres llevan más (*more*)/menos (*less*) _____.
   - ☐ Las mujeres llevan más/menos _____.
   - ☐ Los hombres y las mujeres se visten (*dress*) más o menos (*more or less*) igual. Llevan...

NAVEGANDO LA RED

Search for a clothing store in a Spanish-speaking country, and decide what clothes you would buy for yourself with $200. Make sure you know what the exchange rate is between the dollar and the currency of the country in which the store is located.

Gramática

More on Talking About People's Activities

¿Qué dices?   e → i Stem-Changing Verbs

In **Lección 2A,** you learned about a number of verbs that undergo a stem change (**e → ie, o → ue**) in all forms except for **nosotros/as** and **vosotros/as.** Instead of changing from **e → ie,** some **-ir** verbs change from **e → i.** You may recall from **Lección 2A** that **decir** is one of these verbs.

PRESENT TENSE OF *e → i* STEM-CHANGING VERBS					
decir (*to say; to tell*)		**repetir** (*to repeat*)		**servir** (*to serve*)	
digo	decimos	repito	repetimos	sirvo	servimos
dices	decís	repites	repetís	sirves	servís
dice	dicen	repite	repiten	sirve	sirven
dice	dicen	repite	repiten	sirve	sirven
pedir (*to ask for; to order*)		**seguir*** (*to follow; to continue*)		**vestir** (*to dress*)	
pido	pedimos	sigo	seguimos	visto	vestimos
pides	pedís	sigues	seguís	vistes	vestís
pide	piden	sigue	siguen	viste	visten
pide	piden	sigue	siguen	viste	visten

COMUNICACIÓN ÚTIL

To say *to get dressed* or *to dress oneself,* use the verb **vestir** with reflexive pronouns, just like the verbs **despertarse** and **acostarse** that you learned in **Lección 2A.** You will learn more about reflexive pronouns and verbs in **Lección 5A.** For now, just learn these common expressions with **vestirse.**

Me visto rápidamente.	*I get dressed quickly.*
¡Vístete!	*Get dressed!*
¿Cómo **nos vestimos**?	*How do/should we dress?*

---

*The **u** in **seguir** is found in all forms except the **yo** form in order to maintain a hard **g** sound.

 DE SOL Y VIENTO

In **Episodio 2** of *Sol y viento,* you will watch a scene in which Jaime bumps into María while he's reading a fortune. Part of their exchange appears in the dialogue.

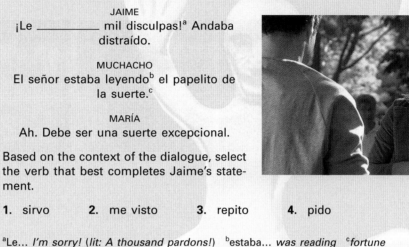

JAIME
¡Le _____ mil disculpas!ᵃ Andaba distraído.

MUCHACHO
El señor estaba leyendoᵇ el papelito de la suerte.ᶜ

MARÍA
Ah. Debe ser una suerte excepcional.

Based on the context of the dialogue, select the verb that best completes Jaime's statement.

1. sirvo　　**2.** me visto　　**3.** repito　　**4.** pido

ᵃLe... *I'm sorry!* (*lit: A thousand pardons!*)　ᵇestaba... *was reading*　ᶜ*fortune*

⦿ Enfoque lingüístico

Más sobre las inflexiones

You may recall that *inflections* are forms that are added to words that provide the listener with certain information. For example, you learned in **Lección 1A** that one way in which Spanish is an inflectionally rich language is that its verb inflections are unique for each person (e.g., *I, you, he/she, we,* and *they*). In the last few lessons, you've learned the present-tense inflections for Spanish **-ar, -er,** and **-ir** verbs. Later in *Sol y viento* you will learn other verb inflections to express various meanings and speaker perspectives. All of the Spanish verb inflections that you will learn are *suffixes;* that is, they are forms that are attached to the *end* of a word or stem. (Remember in **Lección 1A** you read that you will have to get used to listening to the ends of verbs to find out who is being talked about.)

However, not all languages use suffixes for verbal inflections. Some Native American languages like Navajo use *prefixes* (forms attached to the *beginning* of a word or stem). For example, to say *he is going* in Navajo, the prefix **naal** (roughly equivalent to *-ing* used with *is* in English) is added to the stem **nish** (*go*) to form **naalnish.** Instead of prefixes or suffixes, some languages use *infixes,* a form inserted in the *middle* of a word or stem. Tagalog, a language spoken in the Philippines, uses infixes to form commands (i.e., telling someone to do something). For example, to say to someone *Read!,* Tagalog inserts **-um-** after the first consonant of the verb *read,* **basa,** to form **Bumasa!** If you were learning a language like Tagalog, you would have to get used to listening to the middle of verbs to understand different meanings!

Actividad D ¿Quién es?

You have already been introduced to a number of characters from *Sol y viento*. Can you identify them, based on the descriptions below? Pay close attention to the stem-changing verbs.

▲ Jaime   ▲ María   ▲ Mario   ▲ Carlos   ▲ la machi

1. _____ pide disculpas.

2. _____ repite una historia (*tale, story*).

3. _____ se viste con pantalones cortos en el parque.

4. _____ dice que es «el mejor (*best*) chofer de Chile».

5. _____ pide una reunion (*meeting*) con Carlos.

6. _____ se viste con una blusa y una chaqueta.

Actividad E Acciones típicas

Choose whether the actions listed are typical for students, professors, or both.

	LOS ESTUDIANTES	LOS PROFESORES	LOS DOS
1. Se visten de manera informal (*informally*).	☐	☐	☐
2. Siguen instrucciones.	☐	☐	☐
3. Piden ayuda (*help*) a los compañeros.	☐	☐	☐
4. Dicen que les gustan unas clases más que otras.	☐	☐	☐
5. Se visten de manera formal.	☐	☐	☐
6. Repiten instrucciones.	☐	☐	☐
7. Piden respuestas (*answers*).	☐	☐	☐
8. Dicen que van a tomar una clase.	☐	☐	☐

Actividad F ¿Sigues la moda (*fashion*)?

Paso 1 Indicate whether the following statements are true for you (**Sí**), are sometimes true (**A veces**), or not true at all (**No**).

	SÍ	A VECES	NO
1. Leo revistas de moda.	☐	☐	☐
2. Sigo las modas de los diseñadores famosos.	☐	☐	☐
3. Me visto con ropa de marcas (*brand names*) famosas.	☐	☐	☐
4. Pido ropa de ciertas marcas para mi cumpleaños (*birthday*) y otros días festivos (*holidays*).	☐	☐	☐
5. Llevo zapatos de muy buena calidad (*quality*).	☐	☐	☐
6. Compro ropa sólo en ciertas tiendas.	☐	☐	☐
7. Tardo mucho en (*I take a long time to*) vestirme.	☐	☐	☐

Paso 2 Give yourself two points each time you answered **Sí,** one point for **A veces,** and zero for **No,** then add up your total number of points. Based on your total (between 0 and 14), check one of the following statements:

☐ (11–14 puntos) Sigo mucho la moda. No siempre puedo (*I can't always*) comprar ropa de moda, pero me gusta mucho.

☐ (5–10 puntos) A veces sigo la moda.

☐ (0–4 puntos) Casi nunca (*Almost never*) sigo la moda. No me importa para nada. (*It doesn't matter to me at all.*)

Actividad G ¿Cómo nos vestimos?

Paso 1 For each of the following situations, state how one should dress. Then, write what you think would be both appropriate and inappropriate for men and women to wear.

MODELO: (*you see*) la clase de español
(*you write*) Uno se viste con ropa informal.
Los hombres pueden llevar... No deben (*They shouldn't*) llevar...
Las mujeres pueden llevar... No deben llevar...

1. una fiesta universitaria
2. una entrevista (*interview*) de trabajo
3. la boda (*wedding*) de un miembro de la familia
4. una primera cita (*date*) en ____
5. para ir de compras

Paso 2 Compare your list with three other classmates of the same sex. Do you agree with what they listed? Do you wish to modify or change your list?

Paso 3 Your instructor will ask a member from two men's groups and two women's groups to write their lists on the board. Does one sex dress more formally or informally than the other? Are there different expectations about what men and women expect each other to wear in certain circumstances?

¡Exprésate!

With reflexive verbs, use **uno** to mean *one* as in *one dresses,* as in the following expressions:

Uno se viste...

con ropa (in)formal	(in)formal(ly)
con ropa elegante	elegant(ly)
con ropa cómoda	in comfortable clothing
de forma atrevida	daringly

SEGUNDA PARTE

Vocabulario

More on Describing | **Hay doscientas blusas rojas.** **Colors; Numbers 100–1,000**

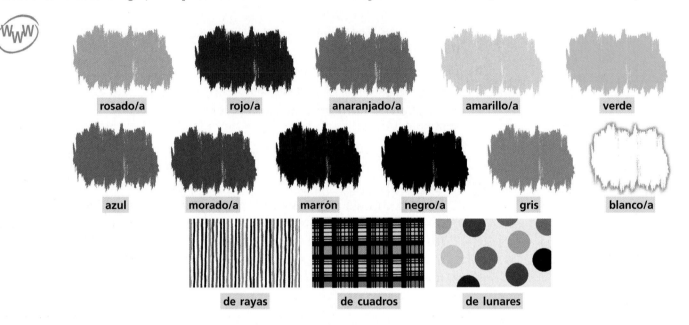

rosado/a rojo/a anaranjado/a amarillo/a verde

azul morado/a marrón negro/a gris blanco/a

de rayas de cuadros de lunares

Like all adjectives, colors need to agree in gender and number with the noun they modify.

> los vaqueros azul**es**
> las zapatillas negr**as**
> la blusa roj**a**

Los números del 100 al 1.000

100	cien	600	seiscientos/as
101	ciento uno/a	700	setecientos/as
200	doscientos/as	800	ochocientos/as
300	trescientos/as	900	novecientos/as
400	cuatrocientos/as	1.000*	mil
500	quinientos/as		

When the numbers 200 through 900 modify a noun, they must agree in gender.

> doscient**as** personas
> quinient**os** hombres

---

*In Spanish, a decimal point (**punto**) is often used where you would use a comma (**coma**) in English, and vice-versa: **$1.000; 64,9%.**

≋ Vistazo cultural

La moneda[a] de los países hispanos

Below is a list of the different currencies of Spanish-speaking countries. You may notice that the currency names of some countries are linked to important historical and/or cultural references. Do you know what they are?

COUNTRY	CURRENCY	COUNTRY	CURRENCY
la Argentina	el peso	Honduras	el lempira
Bolivia	el peso boliviano	México	el nuevo peso
Chile	el peso	Nicaragua	el córdoba
Colombia	el peso	Panamá	el dólar estadounidense
Costa Rica	el colón	el Paraguay	el guaraní
Cuba	el peso	el Perú	el nuevo sol
el Ecuador	el dólar estadounidense	Puerto Rico	el dólar estadounidense
El Salvador	el dólar estadounidense	la República Dominicana	el peso
la Guinea Ecuatorial	el franco	el Uruguay	el peso
España	el euro	Venezuela	el bolívar
Guatemala	el quetzal		

You may have also noticed that a number of countries use the **peso**; however, the value of each country's **peso** is not the same. You may wish to do an Internet search to find out how much your country's unit of currency is worth in some of these countries.

[a]La... *Currency*

Actividad A ¿Combinan bien?

Paso 1 Read the following clothing and color combinations. Then decide whether the combination is appropriate or if it depends on the situation.

		SÍ	NO	DEPENDE
1.	una camiseta blanca con vaqueros azules	☐	☐	☐
2.	un traje verde con una corbata morada	☐	☐	☐
3.	unos pantalones negros con calcetines blancos	☐	☐	☐
4.	una falda anaranjada sobre (*over*) unos vaqueros azules	☐	☐	☐
5.	unas medias rosadas con una falda negra de cuero	☐	☐	☐
6.	unos zapatos negros con un traje negro	☐	☐	☐
7.	una camisa de cuadros con vaqueros azules	☐	☐	☐
8.	unos pantalones de rayas con una blusa de lunares	☐	☐	☐
9.	un vestido rojo con zapatos negros de tacón alto	☐	☐	☐

Paso 2 In groups of four, compare your answers. If you all said certain combinations are not acceptable, indicate why. Also, if some of the outfits depend on the situation, for which situations are they acceptable? Use the following cues to help you.

¡El _____ (*color*) y el _____ (*color*) nunca combinan bien!

Es una combinación horrible.

Depende de la situación. En _____, está bien.

Paso 3 Report your discussion to the class.

Creemos que _____ siempre combinan bien, pero _____ no.

Actividad B ¿Quiénes lo llevan (*wear it*)?

Listen as your instructor names an article of clothing. Then choose who is more likely to wear or have it.

	LAS MUJERES	LOS HOMBRES	LOS DOS
1.	☐	☐	☐
2.	☐	☐	☐
3.	☐	☐	☐
4.	☐	☐	☐
5.	☐	☐	☐
6.	☐	☐	☐
7.	☐	☐	☐
8.	☐	☐	☐

Actividad C   ¿Cuánto cuesta?

Paso 1   First, listen as your instructor tells you the prices of certain items in **nuevos** (*new*) **pesos,** then write down the prices that you hear. After you have written down the prices, go back and decide if the price is too high (**demasiado caro**), about right (**buen precio**), or a real bargain (**una ganga**). ¡OJO! Ten Mexican **nuevos pesos** equal about one U.S. dollar.

PRECIO	DEMASIADO CARO	BUEN PRECIO	UNA GANGA
1. La mochila cuesta _____ nuevos pesos.	☐	☐	☐
2. El diccionario cuesta _____ nuevos pesos.	☐	☐	☐
3. El reloj cuesta _____ nuevos pesos.	☐	☐	☐
4. El teléfono celular cuesta _____ nuevos pesos.	☐	☐	☐
5. El televisor cuesta _____ nuevos pesos.	☐	☐	☐
6. La pluma cuesta _____ nuevos pesos.	☐	☐	☐
7. El disco compacto cuesta _____ nuevos pesos.	☐	☐	☐

Paso 2   Compare your selections with those of three other people. Do you agree on what is a good price for these items? If you think something is too expensive, what would be a reasonable price?

Actividad D   Una prueba (*quiz*) para tu compañero/a

Paso 1   Prepare a quiz consisting of at least five questions about what people are wearing in your class. Use the following model to help you.

MODELO: ¿Quién lleva sandalias marrones, pantalones cortos verdes y camiseta blanca?

Paso 2   With a partner, ask and answer the questions you prepared. A question should only be given once. If one of you needs to hear the question again, you must say **Repite, por favor.**

◀ ¿Qué llevan Mario, María y Jaime en esta (*this*) foto?

Gramática

¿Qué es esto?   **Demonstrative Adjectives and Pronouns**

DEMONSTRATIVE ADJECTIVES					
SINGULAR			PLURAL		
this	**este** suéter	**esta** camiseta	these	**estos** pantalones	**estas** blusas
that	**ese** suéter	**esa** camiseta	those	**esos** pantalones	**esas** blusas
that (over there)	**aquel** suéter	**aquella** camiseta	those (over there)	**aquellos** pantalones	**aquellas** blusas

DEMONSTRATIVE PRONOUNS			
SINGULAR		PLURAL	
este suéter → **este** esta camiseta → **esta**	*this one*	estos pantalones → **estos** estas blusas → **estas**	*these ones*
ese suéter → **ese** esa camiseta → **esa**	*that one*	esos pantalones → **esos** esas blusas → **esas**	*those ones*
aquel suéter → **aquel** aquella camiseta → **aquella**	*that one*	aquellos pantalones → **aquellos** aquellas blusas → **aquellas**	*those ones*

Demonstrative adjectives are used to point out people and things. As you can see from the chart, they always precede the noun they modify and they agree in gender and number. Forms of **este** (*this/these*) are used to indicate that an object or person is close to the speaker. Unlike English, Spanish has two ways to indicate that something is not close to the speaker. Forms of **ese** (*that/those*) are used to indicate something that is not near the speaker but may be close to the listener. Forms of **aquel** (*that/those* [*over there*]) are used to communicate that something is far away from both the speaker and the listener.

All of the demonstrative adjectives can stand alone as pronouns, but as the chart shows, they must still agree in gender and number with the noun they are replacing. *Demonstrative pronouns* take the place of the person or thing being mentioned in order to avoid repetition.

¿Cuál de los dos abrigos   *Which of the two coats do you want,*
   quieres, **este** o **ese***?   *this one or that one?*

The neuter demonstrative pronouns (**esto, eso, aquello**) are used to refer to an unspecified object, an idea, or an entire situation:

¿Qué es **esto**?   *What is this (thing/situation)?*
Eso es increíble.   *That (situation) is unbelievable.*
Aquello fue horrible.   *That (situation) was awful.*

---

*Until 1994, demonstrative pronouns were usually written with accents (**éste, ése**) in order to distinguish them from demonstrative adjectives. However, context will generally determine meaning. You may still see accents on these pronouns from time to time, but the nonaccented pronouns will be used in *Sol y viento*.

DE SOL Y VIENTO

In **Episodio 2** of *Sol y viento,* Jaime returns a business card that María has dropped. Part of their exchange appears in the dialogue.

JAIME
¡Señorita Sánchez!

MARÍA
¿Viene a chocarse conmigo^a otra vez?

JAIME
Eh, no. Creo que _____ es suyo.^b

MARÍA
¡Ah! Por eso sabe^c mi nombre. Si quiere, la guarda.^d

Selecting from the following list, which demonstrative pronoun belongs in the space above?

1. esto   **2.** eso   **3.** aquello

^achocarse... *bump into me* ^b*yours* ^c*Por... That's how you know* ^dla... *you can keep it*

In the exchange between Jaime and María, Jaime used the possessive **suyo.** In **Lección 1A** you learned the possessive adjectives **mi, tu, su,** and so forth. Just like demonstrative pronouns, *stressed possessives* (**los posesivos tónicos**) can also take the place of the noun, indicating to whom something belongs.

mío/a/os/as	*mine*	**nuestro/a/os/as**	*ours*
tuyo/a/os/as	*yours*	**vuestro/a/os/as**	*yours*
suyo/a/os/as	*yours (formal); his, hers*	**suyo/a/os/as**	*yours; theirs*
Son mis libros.	Son **míos.**	*They're mine.*	
¿Es tu cartera?	¿Es **tuya**?	*Is it yours?*	
Es nuestro auto.	Es **nuestro.**	*It's ours.*	
Es su casa.	Es **suya.**	*It's yours/his/hers/theirs.*	

Actividad E ¿Cerca o lejos?

Decide whether Mario, Jaime, or María would say the following statements. Then indicate whether the speaker is talking about something close (**cerca**), far (**lejos**), or even farther away (**muy lejos**).

		SPEAKER	CERCA	LEJOS	MUY LEJOS
1.	Este auto es mío.	_____	☐	☐	☐
2.	Creo que esta tarjeta es suya.	_____	☐	☐	☐
3.	Sí, esa tarjeta es mía.	_____	☐	☐	☐
4.	Me quedo (*I'm staying*) en aquel hotel.	_____	☐	☐	☐
5.	Claro que conozco (*Of course I know*) ese hotel. Está cerca de mi trabajo.	_____	☐	☐	☐

Actividad F ¿Quién lo dice? (*Who says it?*)

Look at the following drawing and indicate who says what.

1. Me gustan mucho esas camisetas blancas.

2. Son bonitas, pero me gustan más esas negras.

3. Estas camisetas blancas están en rebaja (*on sale*), pero esas negras no.

4. Aquellas camisetas rojas también están en rebaja.

Actividad G ¿Cierto o falso?

Listen as your instructor points out and describes the clothing your classmates are wearing. Then decide whether the description is correct (**es correcto**) or not (**no es correcto**).

1. ...   **2.** ...   **3.** ...   **4.** ...   **5.** ...   **6.** ...   **7.** ...

Actividad H ¿Es suyo?

Listen as your instructor points out various items and indicates to whom they belong. Then indicate if the statement is true or not by responding **sí** o **no.**

1. ...   **2.** ...   **3.** ...   **4.** ...   **5.** ...   **6.** ...   **7.** ...

COMUNICACIÓN ÚTIL

You can use the words **aquí** (*here*) and **allí** (*there; over there*) to talk about spatial relationships between people, places, and things.

—¿Te gusta esta bolsa blanca que tengo **aquí**?

Do you like this white purse I have here?

—Sí, pero prefiero esa roja en la mesa **allí**.

Yes, but I prefer that red one on the table over there.

Actividad I Otra prueba para tu compañero/a

Paso 1 You are going to prepare a true/false quiz for a classmate. First, choose seven different clothing items from the following people: you, someone near you, and someone far from you. Then come up with a true or false statement about each item indicating what it is made of, the brand name, or to whom it belongs. Your partner has to respond with **cierto** or **falso.**

MODELOS: (*for an item you're wearing*) Estos vaqueros son de algodón.
(*for an item away from you*) Esos vaqueros son Levis.
(*for an item far away from you*) Aquellos vaqueros son del profesor.

Paso 2 Take turns reading your items to a classmate. When indicating an item, be sure to point to it so that the other person knows exactly what and where it is. Are you able to stump your classmate on any item?

◄

¿Sabes (*Do you know*) de qué material es esta chaqueta que lleva María? Es de pana (*corduroy*).

Vocabulario

Talking About
Buying Things

De compras

Shopping

la cliente · probarse (ue) · el probador · el dinero

la tarjeta de crédito

el dependiente

la caja

las rebajas

20% de descuento

100 pesos

la ganga

el cliente · pagar en efectivo · la dependienta

✳ MÁS VOCABULARIO

comprar	to buy	Estoy buscando…	I'm looking for . . .
gastar	to spend	¿Puedo probarme…?	May I try on . . . ?
regatear	to bargain	Sólo estoy mirando.	I'm just looking.
vender	to sell		
barato/a	inexpensive		
caro/a	expensive	¿Cuál es su talla?	What size do you wear?
de compras	shopping	¿Qué número calza?	What size shoe do you wear?
la marca	brand name		
el precio (fijo)	(fixed) price		
la talla	size	¿Me queda bien?	Does it fit me?
grande	large	Creo que le queda un poco grande.	I think it's a little big on you.
mediano/a	medium		
pequeño/a	small		
¿En qué puedo servirle?	How may I help you?		

≋ Vistazo cultural

Los precios y el regateo[a]

Prices in department stores (**almacenes**) and most other shops (**tiendas**) in Spanish-speaking countries are **precios fijos**. However, you will also find **mercados** in Latin America or **rastros** in Spain where you can buy flowers, clothing, furniture, music, souvenirs (**recuerdos**), and even animals. In many of these markets, the prices are not fixed; rather, it is necessary and even expected to bargain (**regatear**) with the salesperson or vendor in

▲ ¿Crees que se puede regatear en este mercado en Guatemala?

order to get a good price. If you are unsure whether or not the prices are fixed, you can always ask **¿Son fijos los precios?** If they are not, be prepared to bargain! If you do bargain, a good strategy is to offer a price considerably lower than what you are willing to pay. The vendor will then offer a higher price, and you and the vendor can work out a compromise—you raise your original price a bit and the vendor lowers his or hers. Below is a sample exchange that might be heard in a typical Hispanic market:

CLIENTE
¿Cuánto cuesta esta bolsa?

VENDEDOR
Trescientos pesos.

CLIENTE
¡Ay, no! Es muy cara. Le doy[b] doscientos.

VENDEDOR
¿Cómo? Es muy poco; está hecha a mano.[c] Doscientos setenta y cinco, y es suya.

CLIENTE
Doscientos veinticinco y ya.[d]

VENDEDOR
Déme[e] doscientos cincuenta.

CLIENTE
Bueno. Aquí tiene.[f] Gracias.

Although some tourists find bargaining tiresome, most think it's fun and an excellent way to put their Spanish to use!

[a]el... *bargaining* [b]Le... *I'll give you* [c]está... *it's handmade* [d]*that's it* [e]*Give me* [f]Aquí... *Here you are.*

Actividad A Descripciones

Listen as your instructor says the name of a person or thing related to shopping. Then write the number of the item mentioned next to the appropriate description.

a. ___ en vez de (*instead of*) pagar en efectivo uno puede usar esto

b. ___ donde uno puede probarse la ropa

c. ___ donde uno paga las compras

d. ___ la persona que compra algo (*something*)

e. ___ la persona que trabaja en una tienda

f. ___ un precio muy barato

g. ___ muchas veces indica la calidad (¡o el precio!) de algo

Actividad B ¿Quién lo dice?

Listen as your instructor reads some common expressions you might hear while shopping. Then decide who would most likely say them.

	UN(A) DEPENDIENTE/A	UN(A) CLIENTE	LOS DOS
1.	☐	☐	☐
2.	☐	☐	☐
3.	☐	☐	☐
4.	☐	☐	☐
5.	☐	☐	☐
6.	☐	☐	☐
7.	☐	☐	☐
8.	☐	☐	☐

¡Exprésate!

In addition to the expression **tener que** + *infinitive,* the following expressions also take infinitives:

Hay que...	*One must...*
Es buena idea...	*It's a good idea...*
Es necesario...	*It's necessary...*

Actividad C ¿Qué hay que hacer? (*What must one do?*)

Match each verb with an appropriate situation.

1. ___ Si uno quiere un precio más barato, hay que...

2. ___ Antes de salir de la tienda con algo, es necesario...

3. ___ Si uno compra algo pero luego le encuentra un defecto (*finds a defect in it*), hay que...

4. ___ Si uno quiere ver si algo le queda bien o no, es buena idea...

5. ___ Si una tienda quiere ganar (*earn*) dinero, tiene que... mucho.

a. probárselo*
b. regatear
c. vender
d. pagarlo
e. devolverlo (*return it*)

---

*The **lo** that you see attached to **probarse, pagar,** and **devolver** is a direct object pronoun, meaning *it* in this context. You will learn more about the uses of **lo** and other direct object pronouns in **Lección 3A.**

Actividad D En orden

Imagine that a friend is narrating her account of a trip to a store to buy a pair of jeans. Put her statements in order so that her story makes sense.

___ El dependiente tiene que buscar si hay más.

___ Me quedan muy bien.

___ Me pruebo los vaqueros en el probador.

___ Busco la talla que necesito.

___ Pago los vaqueros con tarjeta de crédito y me voy a casa.

___ Entonces le pregunto (*I ask*) al dependiente si tienen mi talla.

___ Tengo que regresar a la tienda para devolver los vaqueros.

___ Después de (*After*) unos minutos vuelve con unos vaqueros de mi talla.

___ Pero no encuentro (*I can't find*) mi talla.

___ En casa veo que están rotos (*torn*) los vaqueros.

Actividad E Entrevista

Paso 1 Using the cues in columns A and B, write down five questions (in addition to the model) to use in an interview with a classmate to find out what kind of shopper he or she is. **¡OJO!** Many of the items in column A go with more than one expression in column B. Also, some questions can be formed without using an item from column A.

MODELO: ¿Cuáles son tus marcas preferidas de ropa?

A	B
¿Adónde... ?	ir de compras
¿Qué... ?	comprar
¿Te gusta... ?	pasar mucho tiempo de compras
¿Cuáles son... ?	gastar mucho dinero
¿Con qué frecuencia... ?	tus marcas preferidas de ropa
¿Dónde... ?	te gusta comprar

Paso 2 Take turns asking and answering the questions that you and a classmate have prepared. Be sure to jot down your classmate's responses.

Paso 3 Based on your classmate's answers, what adjectives from the following list would you choose to describe him or her as a shopper? Be prepared to provide information that would support your conclusions. Would he or she agree?

☐ pragmático/a   ☐ materialista   ☐ compulsivo/a

☐ decidido/a (*decisive*)   ☐ típico/a   ☐ fanático/a

☐ indeciso/a (*indecisive*)   ☐ extraño/a (*strange*)   ☐ obsesionado/a

Gramática

Está bien.   **More on ser and estar**

Up to this point you have been using the verb **ser** with adjectives to describe someone's physical characteristics or his or her personality.

Elena **es** elegante.	*Elena is elegant (by nature).*
Marcos **es** inteligente.	*Marcos is (has always been) intelligent.*

These examples communicate inherent or fundamental qualities of someone or something. To put it another way, they answer the question *What is he/she/it like?* (**¿Cómo es?**)

The verb **estar** can also be used with many adjectives to describe an unexpected change in someone's personality or physical appearance at a given point in time. Note that English often uses verbs other than *to be* to describe these changes.

Elena **está** muy elegante.	*Elena looks very elegant.*
Marcos **está** más delgado.	*Marcos looks (seems) thinner.*

When someone uses **estar** with **delgado/a** or **guapo/a,** the message normally conveyed is that a person looks particularly thin or good-looking at a particular time, not that the person is normally overweight or unattractive. In other words, these statements answer the question *How does she/he look or seem?* (**¿Cómo está?**)

Some adjectives that can be expressed with either **ser** or **estar** have different equivalents in English, depending on which verb is used. When used with **estar,** the meaning of **verde** is *green* as in *unripe.* The chart summarizes some of these common adjectives for you.

✳ **MÁS GRAMÁTICA**

Although **bien** is usually translated into English as *well* when used with the verb **estar,** it is usually translated as *to be OK/fine.*

Está bien.	*It's OK. / That's fine.*
Estoy bien, gracias.	*I'm fine, thanks.*
¿Necesitan algo más?	*Do you all need anything else?*
No, gracias. **Estamos bien.**	*No, thank you. We're fine.*

ser AND estar WITH ADJECTIVES	
¿Cómo es? (*What's he/she like?*)	**¿Cómo está?** (*How's he/she doing? / How does he/she look?*)
Es muy guapo. (*He's very good-looking.*)	**Está** muy guapo con ese traje. (*He looks very handsome in that suit.*)
Es seria. (*She's serious / a serious person.*)	**Está** seria hoy. (*She looks/seems serious today.*)
Es delgado. (*He's thin.*)	**Está** más delgado. (*He looks thinner.*)

DIFFERENCES IN MEANING WITH ser AND estar		
ADJECTIVE	WITH **ser**	WITH **estar**
aburrido/a	María **es** aburrida. (*María's boring. [She's a boring person.]*)	María **está** aburrida. (*María's bored.*)
listo/a	**Somos** listos. (*We're smart/clever.*)	**Estamos** listos. (*We're ready.*)
malo/a	**Son** muy malos. (*They're very bad/malicious.*)	**Están** malos. (*They're in bad shape, sick.*)
rico/a	La familia Ruiz **es** muy rica. (*The Ruiz family is very wealthy.*)	La comida **está** rica. (*The food tastes delicious.*)
verde	El suéter **es** verde. (*The sweater is green.*)	El plátano **está** verde. (*The banana is unripe, green.*)

DE SOL Y VIENTO

In **Episodio 3** of *Sol y viento,* you will watch a scene in which Jaime and Mario arrive in the Valle del Maipo. Part of their exchange appears here.

MARIO
¿Se siente bien,[a] don Jaime? ¿Eh?

JAIME
Sí, Mario. Un recuerdo lejano.[b]

MARIO
Tan[c] serio que _____ ...

JAIME
Nah, no es nada. Vamos.

Selecting from the following list, which verb belongs in the space above?

1. eres   **2.** es   **3.** estás   **4.** está

[a]¿Se... *Do you feel OK*   [b]recuerdo... *distant memory*   [c]*So*

Actividad F ¿*Ser* o *estar*?

Complete Jaime's statements with the correct form of **ser** or **estar.**

1. Creo que Santiago (es / está) muy interesante. Me gustaría (*I would like*) pasar más tiempo aquí.

2. Conocí a (*I met*) una mujer que (es / está) bonita e inteligente.

3. (Es / Está) bien, Carlos. Nos vemos (*We'll see each other*) mañana.

4. Mario, ya (soy / estoy) listo. Podemos salir ahora.

Actividad G ¿Esperado o inesperado?

Listen as your instructor describes different people and things. Decide whether the description represents something *expected* (**esperado**) or *unexpected* (**inesperado**).

1. ...   2. ...   3. ...   4. ...   5. ...   6. ...

Actividad H ¿Cómo está?

Choose the appropriate response to each description.

1. ____ Esta mañana el profesor lleva un traje muy elegante.

2. ____ Para Juan, hoy todo es malo.

3. ____ Mi padre es una persona muy alegre, pero esta mañana no sonríe (*he isn't smiling*).

4. ____ Marta piensa que va a tener una buena nota (*grade*) en el examen.

5. ____ Hoy Elena no tiene interés en nada (*anything*).

6. ____ A Marcos no le gusta estudiar, pero mañana tiene un examen y hoy pasa todo el día en la biblioteca.

a. Está serio.
b. Está indiferente.
c. Está pesimista.
d. Está muy estudioso.
e. Está optimista.
f. Está guapo.

Actividad I ¿*Es* o *está*?

Listen as your instructor reads each of the following statements and then poses a question. Select the best option from his or her question.

1. Marta estudia mucho y siempre saca (*she always gets*) buenas notas en sus clases.

2. José no tiene interés en la clase hoy y no puede prestar atención (*pay attention*).

3. Las chicas quieren salir ahora.

4. Verónica tiene mucho dinero y cada año compra un coche nuevo.

5. Miguel tiene fiebre (*fever*).

6. Me gusta mucho el color de esa chaqueta.

¡Exprésate!

The verb **ser** is often used with the adjectives **barato/a** and **caro/a**; however, to say that something is a good price, **está a buen precio** is used.

Es barato/a.	*It's cheap.*
Es caro/a.	*It's expensive.*
Está a buen precio.	*It's a good price.*

Actividad J ¿Es caro o está a buen precio?

Imagine that you are in a department store in Spain and encounter the following prices. For this activity, consider that one euro equals approximately $1.10. How would you respond to these prices?

1. Unos zapatos de cuero elegantes cuestan doscientos euros.
   - ☐ Son baratos.   ☐ Están a buen precio.   ☐ Son caros.

2. Un disco compacto cuesta veinte euros.
   - ☐ Es barato.   ☐ Está a buen precio.   ☐ Es caro.

3. Un televisor grande cuesta cien euros.
   - ☐ Es barato.   ☐ Está a buen precio.   ☐ Es caro.

4. Un ordenador portátil (*laptop*) cuesta dos mil (2.000) euros.
   - ☐ Es barato.   ☐ Está a buen precio.   ☐ Es caro.

5. Un traje de Armani cuesta mil euros.
   - ☐ Es barato.   ☐ Está a buen precio.   ☐ Es caro.

6. Unos vaqueros Levis cuestan setenta euros.
   - ☐ Son baratos.   ☐ Están a buen precio.   ☐ Son caros.

7. Un cinturón de cuero cuesta diez euros.
   - ☐ Es barato.   ☐ Está a buen precio.   ☐ Es caro.

8. Un traje de baño cuesta cinco euros.
   - ☐ Es barato.   ☐ Está a buen precio.   ☐ Es caro.

Actividad K La ropa y la personalidad

Paso 1 How does what someone wears express his or her personality or mood? For each description of outfits listed, write a sentence that could describe that person's personality or mood today. You may use the following adjectives or others you have learned.

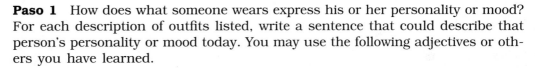

alegre	excéntrico/a	perezoso/a	soñador(a)
elegante	listo/a	perfeccionista	tonto/a
enérgico/a	optimista	profesional	

MODELO: Felipe siempre se viste de negro. → Es pesimista.

1. Para ir a clase hoy, Federico lleva sudadera, vaqueros, gorra y zapatos de tenis.
2. Para ir al trabajo, mi madre (*mother*) siempre lleva blusa, falda y chaqueta.
3. Para salir a la calle (*street*), un hombre de cincuenta años generalmente lleva un abrigo anaranjado y un gorra verde.
4. Para ir a un restaurante con su novio (*boyfriend*) esta noche, Ángela lleva un vestido negro y zapatos de tacón alto.
5. Para ir a correr esta tarde, Juan lleva una camisa de flores (*floral*) y unos pantalones cortos de cuadros.
6. Mi hermano (*brother*) siempre combina bien los colores de su ropa cuando se viste.

Paso 2 Compare your answers with a classmate's. Are there certain colors or clothes that project a particular personality or mood?

MODELO: El rojo da (*gives*) una imagen (*image*) enérgica.

SOL Y VIENTO

Antes de ver el episodio

Actividad A   ¿Qué recuerdas?

Indicate whether the following statements are **cierto** or **falso,** based on what you've seen so far in *Sol y viento*.

	CIERTO	FALSO
1. Jaime tiene ganas de ir a Santiago.	☐	☐
2. Jaime ya sabe (*already knows*) mucho de vinos.	☐	☐
3. Mario no puede llevar a Jaime al Valle del Maipo.	☐	☐
4. El hotel donde Jaime se aloja (*is staying*) se llama el Hotel Bonaparte.	☐	☐
5. Jaime necesita hablar con Andrés Sánchez de la viña «Sol y viento».	☐	☐

Actividad B   ¿Qué falta?

Here is part of the exchange that you have not yet seen between Jaime, María, and Mario in front of the hotel. Select from the choices to fill in each blank.

> MARIO: Buenos días, don Jaime... ¡Lo esperaba!ª
> JAIME: Fuiᵇ a _____¹ un poco. Bueno, hasta aquí llego yo. ¿_____² que la llevemosᶜ a algún sitio?
> MARÍA: No, gracias. Mi trabajo _____³ cerca de aquí. Puedo _____.⁴

ªLo... *I was waiting for you!* ᵇ*I went* ᶜque... *us to take you*

1. a. charlar	**b.** correr	**c.** levantar pesas (*lift weights*)
2. a. Quiere	**b.** Tiene	**c.** Puede
3. a. es	**b.** no es	**c.** está
4. a. caminar (*walk*)	**b.** regresar	**c.** descansar

Actividad C   El episodio

Now watch the episode. Don't worry if there are things you don't understand. You should be able to follow most of what happens without understanding every single word.

Después de ver el episodio

Actividad A ¿Qué recuerdas?

Answer each question according to what you remember from the episode.

1. ¿Qué ejercicio hace Jaime en el parque?
   - **a.** Juega al fútbol (*soccer*).
   - **b.** Corre.
   - **c.** Hace ejercicios aeróbicos.

2. ¿Cuánto cuesta el papelito de la suerte (*little fortune*)?
   - **a.** tres pesos
   - **b.** trece pesos
   - **c.** trescientos (300) pesos

3. ¿Cómo sabe (*knows*) Jaime el nombre de María? Lo sabe por (*because of*)...
   - **a.** el papelito de la suerte.
   - **b.** los libros de ella.
   - **c.** su tarjeta.

4. María trabaja en dos lugares: en la universidad y en...
   - **a.** el Hotel Bonaparte.
   - **b.** un sitio de excavación.
   - **c.** el Parque Forestal.

5. El papelito dice que _____ es un torbellino (*whirlwind*).
   - **a.** el amor
   - **b.** la antropóloga
   - **c.** el tiempo

6. Al final del episodio, ¿quién parece tener más interés en el papelito de la suerte?
   - **a.** Jaime
   - **b.** Mario

Actividad B ¿Lo captaste?

Go back to **Actividad B** of **Antes de ver el episodio** to verify your answers. If you need to, watch that particular section of the episode again.

Actividad C Utilizando el contexto

You have already begun to learn the skill of guessing the meaning of language in context. Did you deduce the meanings of the following phrases in italics? Watch this scene between Jaime, the boy (**el muchacho**), and María again if you think it will help.

> JAIME: ¡Le pido mil disculpas! *Andaba distraído.*
> MUCHACHO: El señor *estaba leyendo* el papelito de la suerte.
> MARÍA: Ah. Debe ser una suerte excepcional.

Detrás de la cámara

Although Jaime seems happy while talking with María, have you noticed in these beginning episodes that something seems to be gnawing at him? Is it professional? Or is it something in his personal life? Jaime has had to work hard to arrive where he is professionally, and his work has kept him from having much of a social life. Although he's had a few girlfriends in the past, Jaime has never had a serious relationship. When his friends bug him about settling down, his response is always "When I find someone, I'll know it."

RESUMEN DE VOCABULARIO

Verbos

combinar bien/mal	to go well/poorly with (*clothing*)
comprar	to buy
encontrar (ue)	to find
gastar	to spend
llevar	to wear
pedir (i)	to ask for; to order
probarse (ue)	to try on
regatear	to bargain
repetir (i)	to repeat
seguir (i)	to follow; to continue
servir (i)	to serve
vender	to sell
vestir(se)	to dress (get dressed)

Repaso: costar (ue), decir (*irreg.*)**, pagar**

Las prendas de ropa

el abrigo	coat
la bata	robe
la blusa	blouse
la bolsa	purse
las botas	boots
la bufanda	scarf
los calcetines	socks
la camisa	shirt
la camiseta	T-shirt
la cartera	wallet
el cinturón	belt
la corbata	tie
la falda	skirt
la gorra	baseball cap
el impermeable	raincoat
las medias	stockings; pantyhose
los pantalones	pants
los pantalones cortos	shorts
la sudadera	sweatshirt
el traje	suit
el traje de baño	bathing suit
los vaqueros	jeans
el vestido	dress
las zapatillas	slippers
los zapatos	shoes
de tacón alto	high-heeled shoes
de tenis	tennis shoes, sneakers

es/son de...	it's/they're made of . . .
algodón (*m.*)	cotton
cuero	leather
lana	wool
poliéster (*m.*)	polyester
seda	silk

Cognados: la chaqueta, el pijama, las sandalias, el suéter

De compras

la caja	cashier's station, checkout counter
el/la cliente	customer
el/la dependiente/a	clerk
de compras	shopping
el dinero	money
el efectivo	cash
la ganga	bargain
la marca	brand name
el precio (fijo)	(fixed) price
el probador	fitting room
las rebajas	sale(s)
la talla	size
mediano/a	medium
pequeño/a	small
la tarjeta de crédito	credit card

barato/a	inexpensive
caro/a	expensive

¿Cuál es su talla?	What size do you wear?
¿En qué puedo servirle?	How may I help you?
¿Puedo probarme... ?	May I try on . . . ?
¿Qué número calza?	What size shoe do you wear?

Estoy buscando...	I'm looking for . . .
Sólo estoy mirando.	I'm just looking.

¿Me queda bien?	Does it fit me?
Creo que le queda un poco grande.	I think it's a bit big on you.

Repaso: grande

Los colores

amarillo/a	yellow
anaranjado/a	orange
azul	blue
blanco/a	white
gris	gray
marrón	brown
morado/a	purple
negro/a	black
rojo/a	red
rosado/a	pink
verde	green

de cuadros	plaid
de lunares	polka-dotted
de rayas	striped

Los números del 100 al 1.000

ciento uno/a, doscientos/as, trescientos/as, cuatrocientos/as, quinientos/as, seiscientos/as, setecientos/as, ochocientos/as, novecientos/as, mil

Repaso: cien

Los adjetivos y pronombres demostrativos

aquel, aquella	that; that one (over there)
aquellos/as	those; those ones (over there)
ese/a	that; that one
esos/as	those; those ones
este/a	this; this one
estos/as	these; these ones
eso	that (*neuter*)
esto	this (*neuter*)
aquello	that (over there) (*neuter*)

Los posesivos tónicos

mío/a/os/as	mine, of mine
tuyo/a/os/as	yours, of yours (*informal*)
suyo/a/os/as	yours, of yours (*formal*); his, hers, their

Repaso: nuestro/a, vuestro/a

Otras palabras y expresiones

la moda	fashion

aburrido/a	boring
listo/a	clever, smart
malo/a	bad; sick
rico/a	rich, wealthy; delicious

allí	there; over there
aquí	here

es buena idea + *infin.*	it's a good idea (*to do something*)
es necesario + *infin.*	it's necessary (*to do something*)
hay que + *infin.*	one must (*do something*)
para + *infin.*	in order to (*do something*)

A la viña[a]

MARIO: ¿Se siente[b] bien, don Jaime?
JAIME: Sí, Mario. Un recuerdo lejano...[c]

▲ Jaime y Mario llegan a la viña «Sol y viento». ¿Con quién van a hablar? ¿Cómo va a ser la reunión[d]?

◄

CARLOS: ¿Quisiera hacer un breve recorrido?[e] ¿Le gusta el vino chileno?
JAIME: Sí, me gusta mucho, pero prefiero esperar. Tenemos negocios[f] importantes. ¿No es cierto?
CARLOS: Bueno, sí. Es cierto. ¿Por qué no vamos a mi oficina para tener así más privacidad?

[a]A... *To the winery* [b]*Se... Do you feel*
[c]*recuerdo... distant memory* [d]*meeting*
[e]*¿Quisiera... Would you like to take a quick tour?* [f]*business*

La familia

OBJETIVOS

IN THIS LESSON, YOU WILL LEARN:

- vocabulary to talk about members of your immediate and extended family

- how to talk about knowing people, places, and factual information using the verbs **saber** and **conocer**

- how to use direct object pronouns to eliminate redundancy

- vocabulary to describe how people look

- to make comparisons to describe people and things

In addition, you will prepare for **Episodio 3** of the film *Sol y viento*.

◄

La mujer a la izquierda, ¿es la madre o la abuela (*grandmother*) de esta familia?
(*Waiting for the Virgin*, por Nancie King-Mertz [estadounidense])

The following media resources are available for *Sol y viento: En breve*

Episodio 3 of
Sol y viento

Online *Manual de actividades*

Interactive CD-ROM

Online Learning Center Website

Vocabulario

Describing Families | **Mi familia**   **Members of the Immediate Family; Pets** ✳

La familia de Antonio Trujillo

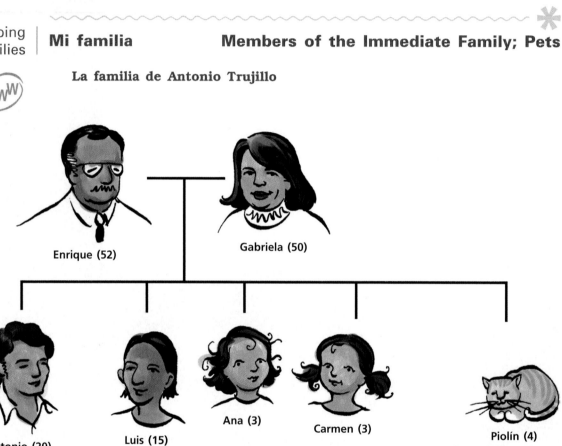

Enrique (52)   Gabriela (50)

Antonio (20)   Luis (15)   Ana (3)   Carmen (3)   Piolín (4)

COMUNICACIÓN ÚTIL

To talk about all the members of a family, English uses the plural form of the last name, as in *The Simpsons* or *The Osbournes*. Spanish uses the definite article **los** followed by the singular form of the last name, as in **los Trujillo** and **los Alexander.**

- Enrique es **el padre** de Antonio.
- Gabriela es **la madre** de Antonio.
- Enrique y Gabriela son **los padres.**
- Luis es **hermano** de Antonio.
- Ana es **una hermana** de Antonio.
- Carmen es otra **hermana** de Antonio.
- Piolín es **el gato** de la familia.
- Antonio tiene tres **hermanos** en total: un hermano (Luis) y dos hermanas (Ana y Carmen). Ana y Carmen son **gemelas.**
- Antonio, Luis, Ana y Carmen son **los hijos** de Enrique y Gabriela. Luis es **un hijo** y Carmen es **una hija.**

La familia de Patricia Alexander

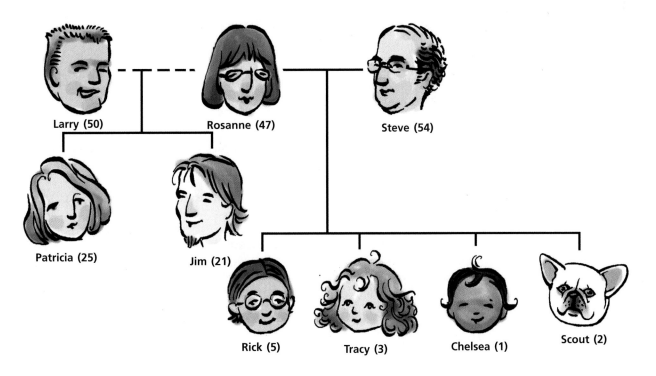

- Larry es **el padre** de Patricia. Es un **padre soltero.**
- Rosanne es **la madre** de Patricia.
- Larry y Rosanne son **los padres** de Patricia.
- Jim es el **hermano** de Patricia.
- Patricia no tiene **hermanas.**
- Patricia tiene **un hermano** y tres **medio hermanos:** Rick, Tracy y Chelsea. Chelsea es **la hija adoptiva** de Rosanne y Steve.
- Scout es **el perro** de la familia.
- Patricia tiene **un padrastro,** Steve.
- Patricia y Jim son **los hijos** de Larry y Rosanne.
- Rick, Tracy y Chelsea son **los hijos** de Rosanne y Steve.

✳ MÁS VOCABULARIO

el esposo / el marido	husband
la esposa / la mujer	wife
el hermanastro / la hermanastra	stepbrother, stepsister
el hijastro / la hijastra	stepson, stepdaughter
el hijo único / la hija única	only child
la madrastra	stepmother
la madre soltera	single mother
la mascota	pet
mayor	older
menor	younger

Actividad A ¿Cierto o falso?

Lee cada descripción sobre los Trujillo e indica si es cierta o falsa.

		CIERTO	FALSO
1.	Luis es el hermano mayor de Antonio.	☐	☐
2.	Los padres se llaman Enrique y Gabriela.	☐	☐
3.	Piolín es el perro de Antonio.	☐	☐
4.	En la familia Trujillo hay dos hijos gemelos y dos hijas, cuatro hijos en total.	☐	☐
5.	Antonio no tiene hermanastros.	☐	☐
6.	Ana y Carmen son las menores de la familia.	☐	☐

Actividad B ¿A quién se describe?

Paso 1 Escucha las descripciones que lee el profesor (la profesora) sobre la familia de Patricia Alexander y escribe el nombre de la persona que corresponde a cada descripción.

1. _____   5. _____
2. _____   6. _____
3. _____   7. _____
4. _____

Paso 2 Ahora compara tus respuestas (*answers*) con las de un compañero (una compañera) de clase.

Actividad C ¿Conoces (*Do you know*) bien a los famosos?

Indica a quién(es) se refiere cada oración (*sentence*) a continuación (*following*).

1. Son gemelas.
   a. Venus y Serena Williams
   b. Paris y Nicky Hilton
   c. Barbara y Jenna Bush

2. Es el ex marido de Demi Moore.
   a. Tom Cruise
   b. Bruce Willis
   c. Brad Pitt

3. Es madre soltera.
   a. Jodie Foster
   b. Winona Ryder
   c. Oprah Winfrey

4. Es hijo único.
   a. Michael Jackson
   b. Alec Baldwin
   c. Tiger Woods

5. No tiene ni hijos ni hijastros.
   a. Jay Leno
   b. Mel Gibson
   c. Madonna

6. Su hermano es cantante (*singer*).
   a. Rob Lowe
   b. Janet Jackson
   c. Ben Affleck

Actividad D Un árbol genealógico (*family tree*)

Paso 1 Entrevista (*Interview*) a un compañero (una compañera) de clase sobre su familia. Apunta (*Jot down*) los nombres y edades en los espacios en blanco, según (*according to*) el modelo.

	PADRES/PADRASTROS	HERMANOS/HERMANASTROS	MASCOTAS
MODELO:	Joseph (49)	Carolyn (17)	Wolfgang (3)
Nombre y edad	_____	_____	_____
	_____	_____	_____
	_____	_____	_____
	_____	_____	_____

Paso 2 Con la información que tienes, dibuja (*draw*) el árbol genealógico de la familia de tu compañero/a de clase.

La familia de _____

Paso 3 Entrégale (*Hand over*) a tu compañero/a el árbol genealógico. ¿Están correctas todas las relaciones?

≈ Vistazo cultural

Dos apellidos

En los países de habla inglesa los hijos suelen usar solamente el apellido de su padre, por ejemplo, Andrew *Knight* o Kelly *Croft*. En el mundo hispano los hijos toman el apellido del padre seguido por[a] el apellido de la madre, por ejemplo, Gabriel *García Márquez* o Ramón *del Valle Inclán*. En el primer ejemplo, el apellido paterno es García y el materno es Márquez. En el segundo ejemplo, del Valle es el apellido paterno e* Inclán es el apellido materno. En algunos países y en los Estados Unidos los hispanos tienden a[b] eliminar el apellido materno (por ejemplo: Evita Perón, Sammy Sosa, Salma Hayek), excepto en ocasiones oficiales o formales.

En los Estados Unidos es común ver nombres compuestos[c] como Cynthia Sánchez-Jones o Mary Higgins-Taylor. Los apellidos separados por guión[d] por lo general indican un matrimonio.[e] En el primer ejemplo, Sánchez es el nombre de soltera[f] y Jones es el nombre de casada.[g] En el otro ejemplo, el nombre de soltera es Higgins y el nombre de casada es Taylor.

María Teresa Sánchez Prieto

Cátedra de Antropología
Universidad del Sur

Teléfono: 555 39 63
Cel: 651 25 65

[a]seguido... *followed by* [b]tienden... *tend to* [c]compound [d]por... *by a hyphen* [e]*marriage*
[f]nombre... *maiden name* [g]nombre... *married name*

---

*The word **e** is used instead of **y** when the word immediately following it begins with **i** or **hi**.

Gramática

**Sí, conozco a la familia.
¿Sabes dónde están?**

**Saber and conocer;
Verbs That End in -zco**

USES OF *saber* AND *conocer*	
Saber expresses knowledge of facts or pieces of information.	**Conocer** expresses familiarity with a person, place, or thing; note the possible English equivalents.
¿Sabes la hora? *Do you know what time it is?*	No **conocemos** a la nueva profesora. *We don't know the new professor.*
No **sabemos** el número de teléfono del profesor. *We don't know the professor's phone number.*	**¿Conoces** el restaurante «Salpicón»? *Are you familiar with (Have you been to) the restaurant Salpicón?*
¿Sabes el origen de la palabra *chocolate* en español? *Do you know the origin of the word chocolate in Spanish?*	Juan **conoce** las obras de Shakespeare. *Juan knows (is familiar with, has read) the works of Shakespeare.*
saber + *infin.* = to know how to (*do something*) **Sé tocar** la guitarra. *I know how to play the guitar.*	**Conozco** bien la Ciudad de México. *I know Mexico City well.*

Unlike English, Spanish has two verbs that mean *to know:* **saber** and **conocer.** Their uses are summarized in the chart. Both **saber** and **conocer** are irregular in the **yo** form: **sé** and **conozco,** respectively.

✳ MÁS GRAMÁTICA

When **conocer** is used to talk about knowing a person, groups of people, or pets, it may be difficult to distinguish who knows whom because objects can come before verbs in Spanish. Compare the following sentences, both of which mean *Consuela knows your best friend.*

Consuela conoce a tu mejor amigo.
A tu mejor amigo lo conoce Consuela.

Consuela is the subject of both sentences (she does the knowing) and **mejor amigo** is the object (the one who is known), but in the second sentence the object precedes the verb. Spanish uses **a** to mark the object in both sentences so that there is no confusion as to who knows whom. This is called the **a personal,** and it has no English equivalent. You will learn more about objects and the **a personal** in the **Segunda parte** of this lesson.

Other Spanish verbs ending in **-cer** also show the same **-zco** irregularity in their first-person forms.

VERBS THAT END IN *-zco*		
VERB	MEANING	FIRST-PERSON SINGULAR (**yo**) FORM
agradecer	*to thank*	agrade**zco**
(des)obedecer	*to (dis)obey*	(des)obede**zco**
merecer	*to deserve*	mere**zco**
ofrecer	*to offer*	ofre**zco**
parecerse* (a)	*to resemble*	me pare**zco** (a)
reconocer	*to recognize*	recono**zco**

DE SOL Y VIENTO

In **Episodio 3** of *Sol y viento,* you will watch a scene in which Jaime and Mario are talking about the Sol y viento winery. Part of their exchange appears in the following dialogue.

MARIO
Bueno, don Jaime. Ya estamos en el Valle del Maipo. ¿Quiere visitar algún lugar en particular?

JAIME
Sí. Vamos a la viña «Sol y viento». ¿La **conoce**?

MARIO
¡Por supuesto! La «Sol y viento» es chiquita,ª pero produce buen vino. Y créameᵇ don Jaime: ¡_____ los vinos!

Selecting from the following options, what verb do you think Mario says in the sentence above?

1. conozco
2. sé

ªpequeña ᵇ*believe me*

---

*This is another example of a reflexive verb. You will learn more about these types of verbs in **Lección 5A.** For now, just learn to recognize their forms.

Actividad E ¿Qué sabe María? ¿A quién conoce?

Paso 1 Basándote en (*Based on*) tus primeras impresiones, indica si las siguientes (*following*) oraciones sobre María (personaje de *Sol y viento*) son probables o no.

	SÍ, ES PROBABLE.	NO, NO ES PROBABLE.
1. Sabe cocinar (*to cook*) muy bien.	☐	☐
2. Sabe hablar la lengua mapuche.	☐	☐
3. Sabe mucho de la política (*politics*).	☐	☐
4. Sabe practicar un deporte.	☐	☐
5. Conoce los Estados Unidos.	☐	☐
6. Conoce los mejores vinos de Chile.	☐	☐
7. Conoce a muchos hombres guapos (*handsome*).	☐	☐
8. Conoce las películas de Hollywood.	☐	☐

Paso 2 Comparte (*Share*) tus respuestas con un compañero (una compañera) de clase. ¿Tienen Uds. las mismas (*same*) impresiones de María?

Actividad F ¿Qué saben hacer los famosos?

Tu profesor(a) va a leer una serie de oraciones. Indica a quién se refiere (*refers*) cada una.

1.	**a.** Derek Jeter	**b.** Shaquille O'Neal	**c.** Tiger Woods
2.	**a.** Danielle Steele	**b.** John Grisham	**c.** Stephen King
3.	**a.** Adam Sandler	**b.** Howard Stern	**c.** Katie Couric
4.	**a.** Annika Sorenstam	**b.** Sasha Cohen	**c.** Anna Kournikova
5.	**a.** Bette Midler	**b.** Jennifer López	**c.** Cher
6.	**a.** Bill Gates	**b.** Donald Trump	**c.** Jimmy Carter

Actividad G Asociaciones

Empareja (*Match*) una frase de la columna A con una frase de la columna B para formar oraciones lógicas.

A	**B**
1. ___ Merezco una «A» en mis clases porque...	**a.** me dan (*they give me*) dinero.
2. ___ Me parezco...	**b.** invito a un amigo a tomar un café.
3. ___ Ofrezco pagar la cuenta (*bill*) cuando...	**c.** no llevo los lentes (*glasses*).
4. ___ Les agradezco a mis padres cuando...	**d.** estudio mucho.
5. ___ No reconozco bien a las personas cuando...	**e.** para evitar (*avoid*) un accidente.
6. ___ Obedezco las leyes de tráfico (*traffic laws*)...	**f.** a mi madre, pero no a mi padre.

Actividad H La clase de español

Paso 1 Indica si cada oración es cierta o falsa para ti.

		CIERTO	FALSO
1.	Conozco a todas las personas de mi clase de español.	☐	☐
2.	Sé el número de ausencias (*absences*) que tengo en esta clase.	☐	☐
3.	Conozco un país del mundo hispano.	☐	☐
4.	Conozco bien al profesor (a la profesora).	☐	☐
5.	Sé cuántos exámenes y composiciones tenemos que hacer.	☐	☐
6.	Sé cuántas mujeres hay en mi clase.	☐	☐
7.	Conozco bien a los personajes de *Sol y viento*.	☐	☐
8.	Conozco la geografía de Chile.	☐	☐

Paso 2 Entrevista a dos compañeros/as de clase sobre las oraciones del **Paso 1**. Anota sus respuestas.

MODELO: E1: ¿Conoces un país del mundo hispano?
E2: Sí. Conozco Costa Rica.

Paso 3 Prepara un breve resumen para presentárselo a la clase.

MODELO: Hablé (*I spoke*) con Ana y Miguel. Nosotros sabemos cuántas ausencias tenemos. Ana y Miguel conocen un país hispano, pero yo no...

⦿ Enfoque lingüístico

¿Dos verbos que significan lo mismo?

In the **Lección preliminar** you learned that Spanish has two verbs meaning *to be.* You now know that Spanish also uses **saber** and **conocer** to convey all of the meanings encompassed by the one English verb *to know.* This is not unique to Spanish. In fact, all Romance languages (French, Italian, Portuguese, and Romanian, among others) make this distinction, as do German and Russian. **Saber** and **conocer** also differ as to the types of direct objects they can take. **Saber** can take a clause (a phrase that contains a subject and a verb) as a direct object, as in **Sé que Juan es inteligente,** but **conocer** cannot. It would be incorrect to use a clause like **que Juan es inteligente** after **conocer.**

There are also cases in which English uses two verbs to express meanings conveyed by a single verb in other languages. For example, English distinguishes between doing something (*to do*) and making something (*to make*). We *do homework* but *make a bed.* In the Romance languages, Russian, and Hebrew, the same verb communicates the idea of making and doing. Spanish speakers say **hacer la tarea** and **hacer la cama.** Distinguishing between *doing* and *making* is very difficult for second-language learners of English whose first language uses just one verb for both meanings.

Vocabulario

More on Describing Families | **Los otros parientes**　　　　**Extended Family Members**

La familia extendida de Antonio Trujillo

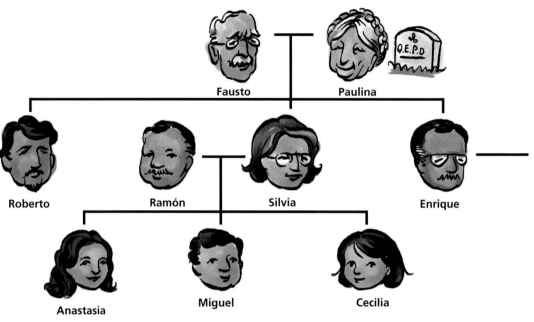

- Fausto, Paulina, Ignacio y Esperanza son **los abuelos** de Antonio.
- Fausto y Paulina son sus **abuelos paternos.**
- Ignacio y Esperanza son sus **abuelos maternos.**
- Paulina es su **abuela paterna** y Esperanza es su **abuela materna.**
- Paulina, su **abuela paterna, ya murió.**
- Ignacio, su **abuelo materno,** ya murió también.
- Antonio tiene seis **tíos** en total, cuatro **tíos** y dos **tías.**
- **Los tíos** de Antonio son: Roberto, Ramón, Freddie y Samuel. Silvia y Mónica son sus **tías.**
- Su tía Silvia y su tío Ramón tienen tres hijos: Anastasia, Miguel y Cecilia. Ellos son **los primos** de Antonio.

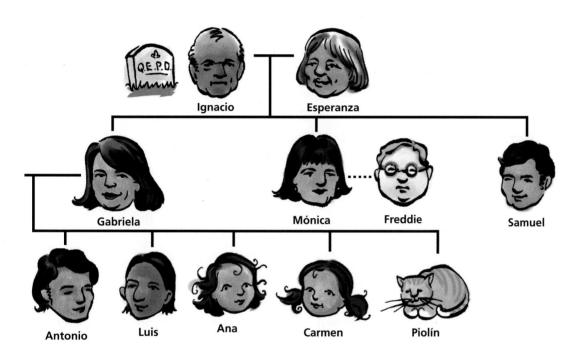

Ignacio · Esperanza · Gabriela · Mónica · Freddie · Samuel · Antonio · Luis · Ana · Carmen · Piolín

✳ MÁS VOCABULARIO

el cuñado / la cuñada	brother-in-law, sister-in-law
el nieto / la nieta	grandson, granddaughter
los parientes	relatives
el sobrino / la sobrina	nephew, niece
el suegro / la suegra	father-in-law, mother-in-law
casado/a	married
divorciado/a	divorced
separado/a	separated
soltero/a	single
viudo/a	widowed
vivo/a	alive
ya murió	he/she already died

Actividad A La familia extendida

Estudia el dibujo (*drawing*) de la familia extendida de Antonio Trujillo. El profesor (La profesora) va a leer unas descripciones. Indica si son ciertas o falsas.

1. ... **2.** ... **3.** ... **4.** ... **5.** ... **6.** ...

Actividad B Relaciones familiares

Tu profesor(a) va a leer una definición. Selecciona la palabra que se define.

1. **a.** soltera   **b.** casada
2. **a.** suegro/a   **b.** abuelo/a
3. **a.** divorciado/a   **b.** viudo/a
4. **a.** cuñado   **b.** sobrino
5. **a.** divorciados   **b.** solteros
6. **a.** tía   **b.** cuñada
7. **a.** prima   **b.** hijastra

Actividad C Más sobre los Trujillo

Empareja una frase de la columna A con otra de la columna B para formar oraciones ciertas sobre la familia Trujillo.

A	**B**
1. ___ Silvia es	**a.** la suegra de Enrique.
2. ___ Mónica es	**b.** la cuñada de Gabriela.
3. ___ Fausto y Paulina son	**c.** sobrinas de Mónica.
4. ___ Esperanza es	**d.** viudos.
5. ___ Enrique y Samuel son	**e.** una tía divorciada de Antonio.
6. ___ Roberto es	**f.** un tío soltero de Antonio.
7. ___ Ana y Carmen son	**g.** nietos de Ignacio y Esperanza.
8. ___ Antonio y Luis son	**h.** cuñados.
9. ___ Fausto y Esperanza son	**i.** los suegros de Gabriela.

▲ ¿Qué sabes de Jaime? ¿Tiene familia? ¿Es numerosa?
¿Dónde están sus padres? ¿Están vivos sus abuelos?

Actividad D Mi familia

Paso 1 En una hoja de papel (*sheet of paper*) dibuja el árbol genealógico de tu familia extendida. Incluye a tus tíos, primos y abuelos. Si quieres, ¡puedes inventar una familia!

Paso 2 En otra hoja aparte, escribe una lista de seis a ocho oraciones del tipo cierto/falso sobre tu familia. Sigue los ejemplos a continuación.

MODELOS: Mi abuela materna se llama Marisa.

Tengo una tía soltera.

Hay ocho nietos en mi familia.

Paso 3 Intercambia (*Exchange*) el dibujo de tu familia extendida con el dibujo de la familia de un compañero (una compañera) de clase. Luego (*Then*), léele a tu compañero/a las oraciones que escribiste (*you wrote*) sobre tu familia. Él/Ella va a indicar si las oraciones son ciertas o falsas. Cuando termines, cámbiense los papeles. (*When finished, switch roles.*)

MODELO: E1: Tengo una tía soltera.
E2: Es cierto.
E1: ¡Correcto!

≋ Vistazo cultural

El habla[a] popular

Las palabras que suelen usarse para denotar relaciones familiares (**padre, madre, tío**) también tienen otros significados en el habla popular de varios países. En la Argentina y España, por ejemplo, las palabras **tío** y **tía**, además de[b] sus significados estrictos, se utilizan también como equivalentes de **hombre** y **mujer**, como se ve en los ejemplos a continuación.

Mariela es una **tía** bien simpática.	*Mariela is a really nice girl.*
No conozco a ese **tío**.	*I don't know that guy.*

En el español coloquial de México, la palabra **padre** se usa como adjetivo para expresar que algo parece muy bueno.

¡Qué **padre** coche!	*What a cool/awesome car!*

La palabra **madre** en el español coloquial mexicano se usa con el verbo **estar** para expresar algo parecido.

¡Está a toda **madre**!	*That's so cool/awesome!*

Estas expresiones son muy informales y sólo se usan entre personas que se tratan de[c] **tú**. Además, estas expresiones son particulares de su país de origen; es decir, no se usan en todos los países del mundo hispano.

[a]*speech* [b]*además... besides* [c]*se... address each other as*

Gramática

Eliminating Redundancy

¿La conoce?

Direct Object Pronouns

English avoids redundancy of nouns by using pronouns. For example, in the statements: *Where's John? Oh, he called. He's running late,* the answers to the question avoid the repetition of *John* by using the pronoun *he*. English also avoids redundancy with objects of verbs, as in *When did you see John? I saw him last night.* Here, John is the object of the verb *see* (object meaning that he is the person or thing seen), and English avoids redundancy in the answer by using the object pronoun *him.*

Spanish also uses object pronouns to avoid redundancy.

> ANA: ¿Llamas a tus padres con frecuencia?
> CECILIA: Pues, sí. **Los** llamo (*I call them*) todos los sábados.

Object pronouns in Spanish precede conjugated verbs but may be attached to infinitives.

¿Mi sobrina? **La** respeto mucho.	*My niece? I respect her a lot.*
¿Mi perro? **Lo** abrazo todos los días.	*My dog? I hug him every day.*
Mi tío quiere invitar**nos** a una fiesta.	*My uncle wants to invite us to a party.*

SUBJECT VERSUS OBJECT PRONOUNS	
yo: Conozco bien a mis padres.	**me**: Mis padres **me** conocen bien.
tú: ¿Conoces bien a tus padres?	**te**: ¿Tus padres **te** conocen bien?
Ud.: ¿Conoce Ud. bien a sus padres?	**lo/la**: ¿Sus padres **lo/la** conocen bien?
él/ella: Conoce bien a sus padres.	**lo/la**: Sus padres **lo/la** conocen bien.
nosotros/as: No conocemos a los abuelos.	**nos**: Nuestros abuelos no **nos** conocen.
vosotros/as: ¿Conocéis a los abuelos?	**os**: ¿Vuestros abuelos **os** conocen?
Uds.: ¿Conocen Uds. a sus abuelos?	**los/las**: ¿Sus abuelos **los/las** conocen?
ellos/ellas: No conocen a sus abuelos.	**los/las**: Sus abuelos no **los/las** conocen.

OBJECT AND SUBJECT CAN PERFORM THE ACTION; *a personal* IS REQUIRED	OBJECT CANNOT PERFORM THE ACTION; *a personal* IS NOT REQUIRED
Juana conoce **a** mis primos. *Juana knows my cousins.*	Juana conoce las obras de Cervantes. *Juana knows Cervantes' works.*
El perro caza **al** gato. *The dog chases the cat.*	El perro caza su cola. *The dog chases his tail.*
Julia besa **al** perro. *Julia kisses the dog.*	Julia besa la foto. *Julia kisses the photo.*

Remember that Spanish uses the **a personal** to mark full direct object nouns (but not pronouns). This is done to distinguish an object from a subject when both are capable of performing the action. This comes in handy when word order in Spanish is different from that in English. See the chart for examples.

DE SOL Y VIENTO

In **Episodio 3** of *Sol y viento,* you will watch a scene in which Traimaqueo, the foreman of the winery, informs Carlos of Jaime's arrival. Part of their exchange appears in the dialogue.

CARLOS
¡Traimaqueo! Ve qué quiere ese tipo.[a]

TRAIMAQUEO
El caballero[b] viene de los Estados Unidos, Carlos. Y dice que tú ____ esperas.

Selecting from the following options, what pronoun do you think Traimaqueo says in the sentence above? Whom does this pronoun refer to?

1. lo

2. la

3. me

4. nos

[a]*guy* [b]*gentleman*

Actividad E ¿Qué hace?

Contesta las preguntas a continuación sobre los personajes de *Sol y viento*. Marca todas las respuestas posibles.

1. ¿Cómo se siente (*feels*) Jaime con respecto a María?

    a. La respeta.   **b.** La quiere   **c.** La detesta.
                          (*he's fond of*).

2. ¿Qué crees que hace María cuando ve a sus amigas?

    a. Las critica.   **b.** Las besa   **c.** Las abraza (*she*
                       (*she kisses*).   hugs).

3. ¿Qué hace Andy cuando llama por teléfono a Jaime?

    a. Lo escucha bien.   **b.** Lo obedece.   **c.** Lo critica.

4. ¿Qué hace Mario cuando recoge (*he picks up*) a los clientes?

    a. Los trata (*he*   **b.** Los saluda   **c.** Los molesta (*he*
        treats) mal.   (*he greets*).   bothers).

Actividad F Mi familia

Paso 1 Llena los espacios en blanco con información verdadera (*true*) sobre tu familia, según el modelo.

MODELO: Mi prima Ángela me llama frecuentemente.

    1. Mi(s) _____ me abraza(n) cuando me ve(n).
    2. Mi(s) _____ me molesta(n) (*annoy*).
    3. Mi(s) _____ me visita(n) frecuentemente.
    4. Mi(s) _____ me critica(n).
    5. Mi(s) _____ me comprende(n) bien.
    6. Mi(s) _____ me escucha(n).

Paso 2 Entrevista a un compañero (una compañera) de clase con las frases del **Paso 1.**

MODELO: ¿Te critican tus tías?

Actividad G Mi profesor(a)

Indica la respuesta adecuada para cada situación a continuación.

    1. Cuando tu profesor(a) llega a clase, ¿qué hace con sus cosas?
        Las pone _____.
    2. ¿Con qué frecuencia da (*gives*) exámenes tu profesor(a)?
        Los da _____.
    3. Cuando llega a clase, ¿qué hace tu profesor(a) con el libro de texto?
        Lo pone _____.
    4. ¿Con qué frecuencia asigna las tareas tu profesor(a)?
        Las asigna _____.

Actividad H ¿Nos comprenden las mascotas?

Paso 1 Indica si los gatos nos hacen las siguientes cosas.

	SÍ, LO HACEN.	NO, NO LO HACEN.
1. Nos reciben con saltos (*jumping*).	☐	☐
2. Nos besan (*they kiss*).	☐	☐
3. Nos lamen (*they lick*).	☐	☐
4. Nos comprenden.	☐	☐
5. Nos obedecen.	☐	☐
6. Nos quieren.	☐	☐
7. Nos molestan.	☐	☐
8. Nos escuchan.	☐	☐

Paso 2 Ahora indica si los perros nos hacen las cosas del **Paso 1.** ¿Son diferentes las respuestas?

Actividad I Personas famosas

Paso 1 Piensa en una mujer famosa (una actriz, mujer política, cantante [*singer*], etcétera) y escribe tres oraciones que indican tu opinión sobre ella. Los siguientes verbos pueden ser útiles.

> admirar
> adorar
> apreciar (*to appreciate*)
> detestar
> estimar (*to think highly of*)
> odiar (*to hate*)
> querer (*to be fond of*)
> respetar

Nombre: _____

1. _____
2. _____
3. _____

Ahora piensa en un hombre famoso y haz lo mismo (*do the same*).

Nombre: _____

1. _____
2. _____
3. _____

Paso 2 Léele a una persona de la clase el nombre de las personas y tus oraciones. ¿Está de acuerdo contigo?

TERCERA PARTE

Vocabulario

Describing How
People Look | **No es muy alto.**

✳ **Physical Traits**

los ojos castaños

las orejas pequeñas

el pelo castaño

Es moreno.

Es de estatura mediana.

Miguel

el pelo canoso

la nariz larga

Es alto.

Thomas

el pelo rubio

el pelo lacio

los ojos verdes

la nariz pequeña

Es baja.

Abigail

Es pelirroja.

el pelo rizado

los ojos azules

las pecas

Kaitlin

✳ **MÁS VOCABULARIO**

las mejillas	cheeks
el mentón	chin
la piel	skin
los rasgos	traits
calvo/a	bald
corto/a	short (*except for height*)
delgado/a	thin
feo/a	ugly
gordito/a	chubby
guapo/a	handsome; good-looking
largo/a	long
¿Cómo es?	What does he/she look like? / What's it like? (e.g., hair, nose)

To describe physical characteristics related to parts of the body, Spanish uses the definite article (**el, la, los, las**), not a possessive, before a body part that is followed by an adjective. When an adjective is not used, the definite article is omitted.

Ricardo tiene pelo.

Ricardo tiene **el** pelo castaño.

Vistazo cultural

El mestizaje[a]

Entre las personas del mundo hispano hay mucha variedad de rasgos físicos. Esta variedad se debe[b] en parte a un fenómeno llamado **el mestizaje,** que se refiere a la mezcla[c] de razas[d] diferentes. En México, Centroamérica y Sudamérica el mestizaje se basa en la mezcla de la herencia[e] española con la indígena. Estas personas se llaman **mestizos.** Es cierto que muchos mestizos tienen la piel morena y los ojos oscuros,[f] pero no todos los hispanos son así. Por ejemplo, hay muchos mexicanos, peruanos y centroamericanos que tienen los ojos azules y el pelo rubio.

▲ Un mestizo peruano

En los países caribeños como Puerto Rico, Cuba y la República Dominicana, el mestizaje se refiere a la mezcla de la herencia española con la africana. Durante el período colonial, los españoles importaron[g] a muchos esclavos de África para trabajar en las minas y en los cañaverales de azúcar.[h] Por eso, muchas personas del Caribe, Venezuela, Colombia y Panamá tienen rasgos físicos que reflejan el mestizaje de estas dos culturas.

▲ Una mexicana de Guadalajara

Los uruguayos y paraguayos tienen características físicas europeas debido al[i] gran número de inmigrantes que llegaron[j] a sus países durante los siglos XIX y XX. Entre ellos había[k] muchos españoles, italianos y portugueses, así como japoneses y canadienses. En el Uruguay y el Paraguay hay pocos mestizos de herencia indígena o africana.

[a]El... *Mixing of races* [b]se... *is due* [c]*mixture* [d]*races* [e]*heritage* [f]*dark* [g]*imported* [h]cañaverales... *sugar cane fields* [i]debido... *due to the* [j]*arrived* [k]*there were*

▲ Un hispano del Caribe

▲ Un chico uruguayo

Actividad A ¿A quién describe?

Paso 1 Estudia los dibujos en la página 148. En los espacios a continuación escribe el nombre de la persona que se describe.

1. _____ tiene las orejas pequeñas.
2. _____ tiene el pelo lacio.
3. _____ es alto.
4. _____ tiene los ojos castaños.
5. _____ es pelirroja.
6. _____ es baja.
7. _____ tiene pecas.
8. _____ tiene el pelo canoso.

Paso 2 Tu profesor(a) va a hacer una serie de preguntas. Contesta cada una con el nombre de la persona apropiada.

1. ...   **2.** ...   **3.** ...   **4.** ...   **5.** ...   **6.** ...

Actividad B Las estrellas de Hollywood

Tu profesor(a) va a leer una serie de descripciones. Selecciona la foto que corresponde a cada descripción y escribe el número de la descripción debajo de cada foto.

▲ Susan Sarandon _____   ▲ Danny DeVito _____   ▲ Cameron Díaz _____   ▲ Salma Hayek _____

▲ Will Smith _____   ▲ Jay Leno _____

Actividad C   Veinte preguntas

Piensa en una persona de la clase sin mencionar su nombre. Un compañero (Una compañera) de clase va a hacerte preguntas del tipo sí/no para adivinar (*guess*) quién es esa persona. Luego, cambien de papeles.

MODELO: E1: ¿Tiene el pelo lacio?
          E2: Sí.
          E1: ¿Es alto?
          E2: No.
          E1: ¿Es mujer?
          E2: Sí.
          E1: Es baja... Es mujer... ¿Es Carolina?
          E2: ¡Sí!

Actividad D   ¿A quién se parece más?

Paso 1   Haz una lista de las características físicas de un compañero (una compañera) de la clase de español. Escribe sus características (los ojos azules, es alto, etcétera) en los espacios en blanco a continuación.

LOS RASGOS DE MI COMPAÑERO/A	PADRE	MADRE	LOS DOS	OTRO PARIENTE
1. _____	☐	☐	☐	☐
2. _____	☐	☐	☐	☐
3. _____	☐	☐	☐	☐
4. _____	☐	☐	☐	☐
5. _____	☐	☐	☐	☐
6. _____	☐	☐	☐	☐
7. _____	☐	☐	☐	☐
8. _____	☐	☐	☐	☐

Paso 2   Entrevista a esa persona para determinar si cada característica es heredada (*inherited*) de su padre, de su madre, de los dos o de otro pariente. Marca la caja (*box*) apropiada para cada característica física.

MODELO: E1: ¿Quién tiene los ojos azules?
          E2: Mi madre.
          E1: ¿Quién tiene pecas?
          E2: Mi padre.

Paso 3   Con la información que tienes de los **Pasos 1** y **2,** indica cuál de las siguientes oraciones describe mejor a tu compañero/a de clase.

Mi compañero/a de clase se parece...

☐ más a su padre que a su madre.

☐ más a su madre que a su padre.

☐ tanto (*equally*) a su padre como a su madre.

☐ más a otro pariente.

NAVEGANDO LA RED

Busca información en la red sobre la composición racial de cinco países latinoamericanos. Incluye dos países centroamericanos, dos sudamericanos y uno del Caribe. Indica el porcentaje (%) de la población que es mestizo, indígena y africano para cada país.

Gramática

| **Es más alto que yo.**

✳ **Comparisons of Equality and Inequality**

COMPARISONS OF INEQUALITY		COMPARISONS OF EQUALITY	
Adjectives	Juanita es **más baja que** su madre. *Juanita is shorter than her mother.*	**Adjectives**	Claudia es **tan delgada como** María. *Claudia is as thin as María.*
	Marcos es **menos atlético que** su hermano. *Marcos is less athletic than his brother.*		Mis tíos son **tan cómicos como** mis padres. *My uncles are as funny as my parents.*
Adverbs	¿Hablas **más rápido que** el profesor? *Do you speak faster than the professor?*	**Adverbs**	Escriben **tan claramente como** nosotros. *They write as clearly as we do.*
	Salgo **con menos frecuencia que** ellos. *I go out less frequently than they do.*		No manejo **tan lento como** mis padres. *I don't drive as slowly as my parents do.*
Nouns	Tengo **más hermanos que** tú. *I have more siblings than you.*	**Nouns**	María tiene **tanto* trabajo como** Miguel. *María has as much work as Miguel.*
	Tengo **menos dinero que** otros estudiantes. *I have less money than other students.*		Pati compra **tanta ropa como** su hermana. *Pati buys as much clothing as her sister.*
			Tienes **tantos amigos como** yo. *You have as many friends as I do.*
			Tengo **tantas clases como** tú. *I have as many classes as you do.*

Comparisons of inequality compare differences involving adjectives, adverbs, and nouns using the expressions **más... que** and **menos... que.**

Comparisons of equality express similarities between things. Spanish uses **tan... como** with adjectives and adverbs and **tanto... como** with nouns, as indicated in the chart.

---

*Note that **tanto** must agree in gender and number with the noun that is being discussed.

When comparing similarities that do not involve an adjective, an adverb, or a noun, use **tanto como** (*as much as*).

Mis abuelos no trabajan **tanto como** mis padres.

My grandparents don't work as much as my parents.

DE SOL Y VIENTO

In **Episodio 5** of *Sol y viento,* you will watch a scene in which Jaime tells María more about himself. Part of their exchange appears here.

JAIME

Oh, mi vida no es **tan fascinante como** la suya. Trabajo con una compañía de exportaciones, sigo la Bolsa[a] y corro para hacer un poco de ejercicio.

MARÍA

Tiene razón.[b] ¡Su vida no es **tan fascinante como** la mía!

Using **más... que** or **menos... que,** write one sentence in which you compare Jaime with María based on what you know about both of them.

[a]*stock market* [b]*Tiene... You're right.*

COMUNICACIÓN ÚTIL

To say that someone is *extremely* tall, happy, tired, and so forth, Spanish adds **-ísimo/a/os/as** to the end of adjectives. If the adjective ends in a consonant, simply add a form of **-ísimo** to the end of it.

La clase de literatura es **facilísima.**   *The literature class is extremely easy.*

If the adjective ends in a vowel, drop the final vowel, then add the correct form of **-ísimo.**

Roberto es **altísimo.**   *Roberto is extremely tall.*

If an adjective ends in **-c, -g,** or **-z,** a spelling change is necessary to maintain the original pronunciation of the adjective.

rico → ri**qu**ísimo

largo → lar**gu**ísimo

feliz (*happy*) → feli**c**ísimo

Actividad E Más sobre Mario

Lee las siguientes oraciones sobre Mario de *Sol y viento* y llena cada espacio en blanco con **tan** o una forma apropiada de **tanto.** Luego indica si cada oración es cierta o falsa, en tu opinión.

Mario...	CIERTO	FALSO
1. es _____ trabajador en su profesión como lo es María en la suya.	☐	☐
2. no cena en restaurantes _____ frecuentemente como Jaime.	☐	☐
3. tiene _____ oportunidades para ganar dinero como Jaime.	☐	☐
4. es _____ respetuoso como los taxistas de mi ciudad.	☐	☐
5. no consume _____ vino como María.	☐	☐
6. sufre (*suffers*) _____ presión en su trabajo como la sufre Andy en el suyo.	☐	☐

Actividad F Mi universidad

Paso 1 Indica si las siguientes oraciones son ciertas o falsas para ti.

En mi universidad...	CIERTO	FALSO
1. el equipo (*team*) de fútbol americano es mejor que el equipo de basquetbol.	☐	☐
2. las residencias estudiantiles son tan feas como los apartamentos fuera del (*off*) campus.	☐	☐
3. el rector (la rectora) (*president of the university*) es menor que mis padres.	☐	☐
4. las humanidades son tan importantes como las ciencias naturales.	☐	☐
5. el gimnasio es peor que un gimnasio privado.	☐	☐
6. la vida social es tan importante como los estudios.	☐	☐
7. las clases de español son tan grandes como las clases de psicología o sociología.	☐	☐
8. la comida de la cafetería es mejor que comida rápida (*fast food*).	☐	☐

Paso 2 Escribe de nuevo (*Rewrite*) cada oración falsa para que sea verdadera (*so that it's true*) para ti.

MODELO: El equipo de fútbol es peor que el equipo de basquetbol.

Actividad G   Los hermanos Alexander

Tu profesor(a) va a leer una serie de oraciones basadas en los dibujos de Patricia y Jim Alexander a continuación. Indica si cada oración es cierta o falsa.

1. ...   **2.** ...   **3.** ...   **4.** ...   **5.** ...   **6.** ...

Actividad H   Comparaciones

Paso 1   Entrevista a dos compañeros/as de clase para averiguar (*find out*) el tamaño (*size*) de su familia. Apunta el número de parientes de cada categoría a continuación.

MODELO: E1: ¿Cuántos hermanastros tienes?
          E2: Dos. Un hermanastro y una hermanastra.

	E1	E2
hermanos	_____	_____
hermanastros	_____	_____
tíos solteros	_____	_____
primos	_____	_____
abuelos vivos	_____	_____
hijos	_____	_____
mascotas	_____	_____

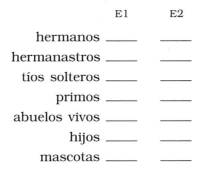

Paso 2   Con la información del **Paso 1,** escribe tres afirmaciones con **tan/tanto... como** para hacer comparaciones sobre la familia de cada compañero/a de clase.

MODELO: Joe (no) tiene tantas hermanastras como hermanas.
          La familia de Jen (no) es tan grande como la familia de Rob.

RESUMEN DE VOCABULARIO

Verbos

agradecer (zc)	to thank
conocer (zc)	to know, be familiar with
(des)obedecer (zc)	to (dis)obey
merecer (zc)	to deserve
ofrecer (zc)	to offer
parecerse (zc) (a)	to resemble
reconocer (zc)	to recognize
saber (*irreg.*)	to know (*facts, information*)
saber (*irreg.*) + *infin.*	to know how (*to do something*)

La familia

el/la abuelo/a	grandfather, grandmother
el/la cuñado/a	brother-in-law, sister-in-law
la esposa / la mujer	wife
el esposo / el marido	husband
el/la gemelo/a	twin
el/la hermanastro/a	stepbrother, stepsister
el/la hermano/a	brother, sister
el/la hijastro/a	stepson, stepdaughter
el/la hijo/a (único/a)	son, daughter; only child
la madrastra	stepmother
la madre (soltera)	(single) mother
el/la medio/a hermano/a	half brother, half sister
el/la nieto/a	grandson, granddaughter
el padrastro	stepfather
el padre (soltero)	(single) father
el/la primo/a	cousin
el/la sobrino/a	nephew, niece
el/la suegro/a	father-in-law, mother-in-law
el/la tío/a	uncle, aunt

el gato	cat
la mascota	pet
los parientes	relatives
el perro	dog

casado/a	married
soltero/a	single
viudo/a	widowed
vivo/a	alive

ya murió	he/she already died

Cognados: adoptivo/a, divorciado/a, extendido/a, materno/a, paterno/a, separado/a

¿Cómo es?

alto/a	tall
bajo/a	short
calvo/a	bald
castaño/a	brown (*hair, eyes*)
de estatura mediana	of medium height
delgado/a	thin
feo/a	ugly
gordito/a	chubby
guapo/a	handsome; good-looking
largo/a	long
moreno/a	dark-skinned
pelirrojo/a	redheaded

las pecas	freckles
los rasgos	traits

Algunas partes del cuerpo

las mejillas	cheeks
el mentón	chin
la nariz	nose
los ojos	eyes
las orejas	ears
el pelo	hair
canoso	gray
lacio	straight
rizado	curly
rubio	blond
la piel	skin

corto/a	short (*except for height*)

Las comparaciones

más... que	more . . . than
menos... que	less . . . than
tan... como	as . . . as
tanto/a/os/as... como	as much/many . . . as

mayor	older
mejor	better
menor	younger
peor	worse

3B

¡A comer!

OBJETIVOS

IN THIS LESSON, YOU WILL LEARN:

- vocabulary to talk about what you eat for breakfast

- how to express negation

- vocabulary to talk about what you eat for lunch and for snacking

- more about the uses of ser and **estar**

- vocabulary to talk about what you eat for dinner

- to use indirect object pronouns

In addition, you will watch **Episodio 3** of the film *Sol y viento*.

◄

Las empanadas son una comida típica chilena.

The following media resources are available for *Sol y viento: En breve*

Episodio 3 of
Sol y viento

Online *Manual
de actividades*

Interactive
CD-ROM

Online Learning
Center Website

PRIMERA PARTE

Vocabulario

Talking About What You Eat in the Morning

El desayuno

Breakfast

Lo que **desayuna** Elsa Moreno, una estudiante de cine y televisión en la Universidad del Sur de California.

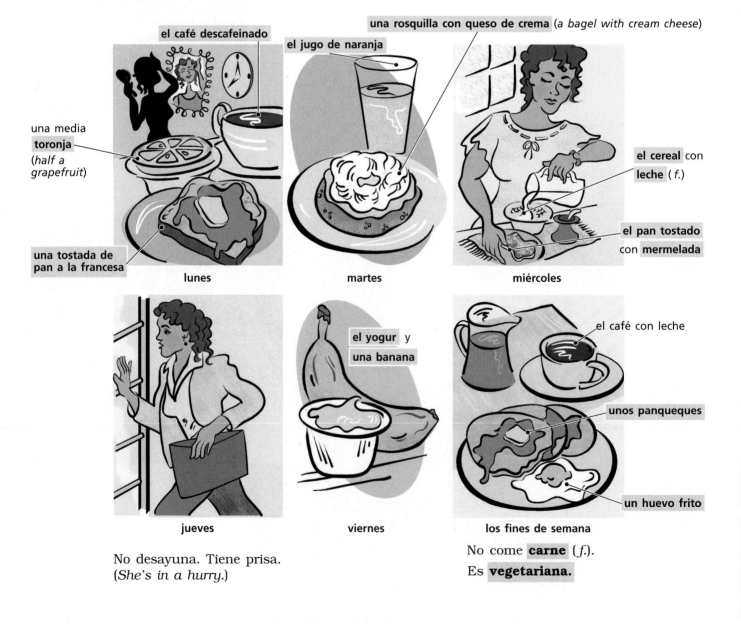

el café descafeinado

el jugo de naranja

una rosquilla con queso de crema (*a bagel with cream cheese*)

una media **toronja** (*half a grapefruit*)

el cereal con **leche** (*f.*)

el pan tostado con **mermelada**

una tostada de pan a la francesa

lunes

martes

miércoles

el yogur y **una banana**

el café con leche

unos panqueques

un huevo frito

jueves

viernes

los fines de semana

No desayuna. Tiene prisa. (*She's in a hurry.*)

No come **carne** (*f.*). Es **vegetariana.**

Lo que desayuna Franco Obregón, un estudiante de antropología en la Universidad Nacional Autónoma de México.

el jugo de naranja

el café con leche

los chilaquiles*

el jugo de toronja

el tocino

unos huevos revueltos

con **cebolla** (*onion*) y **tomate** (*m.*)

una tortilla española (*an omelette*)

el pan con **mantequilla** (*butter*)

lunes

martes

miércoles

unos huevos revueltos con **salchichas**

el café

el jugo de **manzana** (*apple*)

el pan dulce (*sweet bread*)

jueves

unas tortillas de **maíz** (*m.*) (*corn*)

viernes

los frijoles

los fines de semana

No desayuna. Duerme hasta muy tarde.

✳ | **MÁS VOCABULARIO**

desayunar	to eat/have (for) breakfast
la barra de frutas/granola	fruit/granola bar
el cereal cocido	hot cereal
el té (caliente)	(hot) tea

---

*These are a Mexican specialty of strips of fried corn tortillas mixed with red or green salsa, onions, oregano, and crumbled cheese. They are sometimes mixed with scrambled eggs or shredded chicken.

Actividad A   ¿Qué día es?

Tu profesor(a) va a mencionar unos alimentos (*food items*) que desayuna Elsa Moreno. Indica qué día de la semana corresponde a cada desayuno.

MODELO: PROFESOR(A): el jugo de naranja
ESTUDIANTE: Es martes.

1. ...   **2.** ...   **3.** ...   **4.** ...   **5.** ...   **6.** ...   **7.** ...   **8.** ...

Actividad B   ¿Cierto o falso?

Tu profesor(a) va a leer unas descripciones sobre los desayunos de Franco Obregón. Indica si cada oración es cierta o falsa.

1. ...   **2.** ...   **3.** ...   **4.** ...   **5.** ...   **6.** ...   **7.** ...

Actividad C   ¿Elsa o Franco?

Escucha las descripciones que lee el profesor (la profesora) e indica si la descripción se refiere a Elsa o a Franco.

1. ...   **2.** ...   **3.** ...   **4.** ...   **5.** ...   **6.** ...   **7.** ...   **8.** ...

Actividad D   ¿Qué desayunas tú?

Paso 1 Indica con qué frecuencia desayunas los siguientes alimentos.

	CON FRECUENCIA	DE VEZ EN CUANDO (*once in a while*)	RARAS VECES	NUNCA (*never*)
1. rosquillas	☐	☐	☐	☐
2. pan tostado	☐	☐	☐	☐
3. salchichas	☐	☐	☐	☐
4. jugo de naranja	☐	☐	☐	☐
5. yogur	☐	☐	☐	☐
6. huevos	☐	☐	☐	☐
7. cereal con leche	☐	☐	☐	☐
8. café	☐	☐	☐	☐
9. tocino	☐	☐	☐	☐
10. barra de frutas	☐	☐	☐	☐
11. No desayuno.	☐	☐	☐	☐
12. ¿ ?	☐	☐	☐	☐

Paso 2 Entrevista a un compañero (una compañera) de clase para ver con qué frecuencia desayuna los alimentos del **Paso 1.**

MODELO: E1: ¿Con qué frecuencia desayunas pan tostado?
E2: De vez en cuando.

Paso 3 Escribe un breve resumen en el cual (*in which*) comparas tus preferencias con las de tu compañero/a de clase.

MODELO: Desayuno huevos y salchichas de vez en cuando, pero Miguel desayuna huevos y tocino con frecuencia. Nunca desayuno rosquillas, pero Miguel...

〜 Vistazo cultural

El horario de las comidas

El horario de las comidas varía de país a país. En los EE.UU.[a] y México, por ejemplo, la gente suele desayunar entre las 7:00 y las 9:00 de la mañana, pero en España desayunan a las 7:00. En los EE.UU., la gente almuerza a eso del[b] mediodía, pero en el mundo hispano suelen almorzar entre las 2:00 y las 4:00. La cena[c] típica norteamericana se come entre las 5:00 y las 7:00 de la tarde, pero en el mundo hispano tienden a cenar entre las 8:00 y las 11:00 de la noche, dependiendo del país y de otros factores.

Para los hispanos, el almuerzo tiende a ser la comida más fuerte[d] del día. Para el norteamericano, la cena es la comida más fuerte. Presta atención a[e] estas diferencias mientras estudias lo que comen Elsa y Franco en esta lección.

[a]Estados Unidos [b]a... *around* [c]*dinner*
[d]más... *heaviest* [e]Presta... *Pay attention to*

▲ Los churros (*fried dough with sugar*) con chocolate son un desayuno típico español.

	DESAYUNO	ALMUERZO	CENA
EE.UU.	7:00–9:00	11:00–1:00	5:00–7:00
España	7:00–8:00	2:00–4:00	10:00–11:00
México	7:00–9:00	2:00–4:00	8:00–10:00

Gramática

| **No lo sé tampoco.**   **Indefinite and Negative Words** ✳

In prior lessons of *Sol y viento* you have used indefinite words like **algo** and **alguien** and negative words like **nada** and **nunca.** The chart on the next page lists the indefinite and negative words commonly used in Spanish.

The simplest way to express negation in Spanish or English is to use the word **no.** Although English typically does not use double negation, Spanish must if **no** is used.

—¿Quieres desayunar **algo**?   *Do you want something for breakfast?*

—**No, no** quiero desayunar **nada.**   *No, I don't want anything for breakfast.*

—¿Tiene **algún** mensaje para la profesora?   *Do you have a message for the professor?*

—**No, no** tengo **ninguno.**   *No, I don't have any.*

Similar to subjects, negative words in Spanish can come before or after a verb. When a negative word comes after a verb, a **no** must precede the verb.

Nunca desayuno salchichas.   ⎫
No desayuno salchichas **nunca.**   ⎬   *I never have sausage for breakfast.*
  ⎭

Tampoco voy a comer en ese restaurante.   ⎫
     ⎬   *I'm not going to eat in that restaurant either.*
No voy a comer en ese restaurante **tampoco.**   ⎭

▲ **¿Siempre** comes una ensalada con tu comida?
¿O **no** la comes **nunca**?

INDEFINITE AND NEGATIVE WORDS	
LAS PALABRAS INDEFINIDAS	LAS PALABRAS NEGATIVAS
algo (*something*) ¿Deseas **algo**?	**nada** (*nothing*) **No, no** quiero **nada**.
alguien (*someone, anyone*) **Alguien** viene.	**nadie** (*no one, not anyone*) **No** viene **nadie**. **Nadie** viene.
algún* (**alguno/a/os/as**) (*some, any*) Tengo **algunos** libros rusos.	**ningún*** (**ninguno/a**) (*none, not any*) **No** tengo **ningún** libro ruso.
siempre (*always*) **Siempre** veo a Juan en su oficina.	**nunca, jamás** (*never*) **Nunca** veo a Juan en su oficina. **No** veo a Juan **nunca** en su oficina. Juan **jamás** está en su oficina. Juan **no** está **jamás** en su oficina.
también (*also, too*) **También** conozco a Rudolfo.	**tampoco** (*neither, not either*) **Tampoco** conozco al chico nuevo. **No** conozco al chico nuevo **tampoco**.

DE SOL Y VIENTO

In **Episodio 3** of *Sol y viento,* Mario asks Jaime why he looks so reflective. Part of their exchange appears in the dialogue.

MARIO
¿Se siente bien,[a] don Jaime? ¿Eh?

JAIME
Sí, Mario. Un recuerdo lejano[b]...

MARIO
Tan serio que está.

JAIME
No es _____. Vamos.

Selecting from the following list, what word do you think Jaime says in this scene?

1. nadie
2. ninguno
3. nada

[a]¿Se... *Do you feel OK* [b]recuerdo... *distant memory*

*The adjectives **alguno** and **ninguno** shorten to **algún** and **ningún** before masculine singular nouns. The plural forms **ningunos** and **ningunas** are not used.

Actividad E Los desayunos de Jaime Talavera

Basándote en (*Based on*) lo que sabes de Jaime Talavera de *Sol y viento*, indica si las siguientes oraciones son ciertas o falsas.

		CIERTO	FALSO
1.	Nunca desayuna en restaurantes de comida rápida.	☐	☐
2.	Siempre toma un jugo de naranja por la mañana.	☐	☐
3.	Desayuna un vaso (*glass*) de leche también.	☐	☐
4.	No desayuna pizza o sobras (*leftovers*) de pollo frito (*fried chicken*).	☐	☐
5.	Tampoco come mucha carne por la mañana.	☐	☐
6.	No sale de casa sin (*without*) desayunar algo.	☐	☐
7.	Jamás desayuna cereales para niños (*children*), como Trix o Lucky Charms.	☐	☐
8.	Tampoco desayuna leche con chocolate.	☐	☐
9.	En su refrigerador no hay ningún desayuno congelado (*frozen*).	☐	☐
10.	Nadie le hace (*makes him*) el desayuno. Él mismo lo prepara.	☐	☐

▲ ¿Crees que Jaime siempre toma café con azúcar (*sugar*) o nunca toma café con azúcar?

Actividad F ¿Dedicado o no?

Tu profesor(a) va a leer unas oraciones. Indica si cada una se refiere a **un estudiante dedicado** o a **un estudiante perezoso** (*lazy*).

	UN ESTUDIANTE DEDICADO	UN ESTUDIANTE PEREZOSO
1.	☐	☐
2.	☐	☐
3.	☐	☐
4.	☐	☐
5.	☐	☐
6.	☐	☐

Actividad G El profesor (La profesora) ideal

Paso 1 Usa expresiones indefinidas (**algo, siempre,** etcétera) y palabras negativas (**nada, nunca,** etcétera) para escribir cuatro oraciones sobre lo que el profesor (la profesora) ideal hace o no hace.

MODELO: El profesor (La profesora) ideal siempre llega a clase a tiempo.

Paso 2 En grupos de tres personas comparen sus oraciones. ¿Están de acuerdo con lo que dicen todos? Hagan una lista de las oraciones con las que todos están de acuerdo para presentársela a la clase.

▲ ¿Siempre escucha a sus estudiantes María? ¿Crees tú que ella es una profesora ideal?

⦿ Enfoque lingüístico

Más sobre la negación

Although negation may seem like a simple concept, different languages make negative statements in different ways. English uses a form of the auxiliary verb *do* and the adverb *not* before the verb, as in the following sentences: *I don't know you, James does not speak Japanese,* and *Don't we need to go now?* French is somewhat different than English in that it uses a two-part adverb that surrounds the verb. To make a sentence negative in French, you place *ne* in front of a conjugated verb and the adverb *pas* after it. The French equivalent of *James does not speak Japanese* is *James **ne** parle **pas** japonais.*

Negation in Spanish is interesting because it allows (and in some cases requires) what English forbids: double negation. Whenever a negative word is used after a verb in Spanish, another negative word must precede the verb, as in **Juan no sabe nada.** An English speaker can say *Juan doesn't know anything* or *Juan knows nothing* but cannot combine both *doesn't* and *nothing.* This is not to say that double negatives never happen in English. Few would fault the Rolling Stones for saying they "can't get no satisfaction," nor would we be surprised to hear someone say "You ain't seen nothing yet." On the whole, however, most double negatives are seen as bad use of language by English speakers.

SEGUNDA PARTE

Vocabulario

El almuerzo y la merienda

Lunch and Snacking

Lo que come Elsa durante el día

A las 10:00 A.M. Elsa **merienda...**

pasas (*raisins*)

o **nueces** (*f.*) (*nuts*)

o **una fruta.**

A las 12:00 P.M. almuerza...

un sándwich de atún (*tuna*), una manzana y **té** (*m.*) **helado**

o **una porción** de **pizza** vegetariana con **champiñones** (*m.*) (*mushrooms*), cebollas, tomates y **espinacas** (*spinach*) y **un refresco dietético**

o **una hamburguesa** vegetariana con queso, **papas fritas** y **agua** (*f.*).*

A las 2:00 P.M. merienda...

palomitas de maíz

o **galletas**

o algunos **dulces** (*m.*) (*candy*).

*The word **agua** is feminine, but the article **el** is used with it in its singular form: **el agua fría** but **las aguas frías.**

Lo que come Franco durante el día

A las 12:00 P.M. Franco merienda...

papitas (*potato chips*)

o unos dulces

o una manzana.

A las 2:00 P.M. almuerza...

sopa de espinacas, **bistec** (*m.*) con frijoles, **ensalada mixta,** tortillas de maíz, **helado** (*ice cream*) de frutas, **una cerveza** o **vino tinto** (*red wine*)

o **arroz** (*m.*) con **zanahorias** (*carrots*) y **chícharos** (*peas*), **chuleta de cerdo** (*pork chop*) con **puré** (*m.*) **de papas** (*mashed potatoes*), **verduras** mixtas, **flan** (*m.*) (*baked custard*) y agua

o sopa de **camarones** (*m.*) (*shrimp*), **pescado frito** (*fried fish*) con **limón** (*m.*) y **salsa,** ensalada de **aguacate** (*m.*) (*avocado*) y tomate y **vino blanco.**

A las 5:00 P.M. merienda...

pan dulce con café

o una fruta

o **galletas saladas** (*crackers*).

✱ MÁS VOCABULARIO

almorzar (ue)	to eat/have (for) lunch
merendar (ie)	to snack / have (for) a snack
la mantequilla de cacahuete	peanut butter
el sándwich de	
jamón (*m.*)	ham sandwich
pavo	turkey sandwich
pollo	chicken sandwich
rosbif (*m.*)	roast beef sandwich

Actividad A   ¿Almuerzo o merienda?

Tu profesor(a) va a mencionar unos alimentos. Indica si cada alimento se come para el almuerzo, para la merienda o para los dos, según los dibujos anteriores.

1. **a.** almuerzo   **b.** merienda   **c.** los dos
2. **a.** almuerzo   **b.** merienda   **c.** los dos
3. **a.** almuerzo   **b.** merienda   **c.** los dos
4. **a.** almuerzo   **b.** merienda   **c.** los dos
5. **a.** almuerzo   **b.** merienda   **c.** los dos
6. **a.** almuerzo   **b.** merienda   **c.** los dos
7. **a.** almuerzo   **b.** merienda   **c.** los dos
8. **a.** almuerzo   **b.** merienda   **c.** los dos
9. **a.** almuerzo   **b.** merienda   **c.** los dos
10. **a.** almuerzo   **b.** merienda   **c.** los dos

Actividad B   ¿Almuerzo norteamericano o almuerzo mexicano?

Escucha las comidas que menciona tu profesor(a) e indica si cada una se refiere al almuerzo norteamericano (lo que comería [*would eat*] Elsa) o al almuerzo mexicano (lo que comería Franco).

   1. …   **2.** …   **3.** …   **4.** …   **5.** …   **6.** …   **7.** …

Actividad C   ¿Qué almuerza mi profesor(a)?

Paso 1   Repasa la información en la pirámide de las comidas en la siguiente página.

Paso 2   La clase va a hacerle preguntas al profesor (a la profesora) para saber si come para el almuerzo y la merienda alimentos de todos los grupos básicos. ¿Cuánta información pueden Uds. obtener en sólo cinco minutos? Usen **tú** o **Ud.**, según la preferencia de tu profesor(a).

MODELO: ¿Almuerza Ud. manzanas? / ¿Almuerzas manzanas?

Paso 3   En grupos de dos personas, indiquen la cantidad de alimentos de cada categoría de la pirámide de las comidas que consume su profesor(a).

El grupo de...	MUCHOS ALIMENTOS	POCOS ALIMENTOS
1. grasas, aceites y dulces	☐	☐
2. leche, yogur y queso	☐	☐
3. carne, aves, pescado, frijoles, huevos y nueces	☐	☐
4. verduras	☐	☐
5. frutas	☐	☐
6. pan, cereales, tortillas, arroz y pasta	☐	☐

Paso 4   Usando las frases **más/menos... que** y **tanto... como**, escribe dos oraciones en las cuales comparas tu dieta con la de tu profesor(a).

MODELO: Yo como menos frutas que mi profesor(a).

Grasas,[a] aceite[b] y dulces

El grupo de la leche, el yogur y el queso

El grupo de la carne, las aves,[c] el pescado, los frijoles, los huevos y las nueces

El grupo de las verduras

El grupo de las frutas

El grupo del pan, los cereales, las tortillas, el arroz y la pasta

[a]*Fats* [b]*oil*
[c]*poultry*

 ## Vistazo cultural

Las palabras préstamo[a]

Muchas palabras que se usan en español para nombrar las comidas tienen su origen en otros idiomas como el náhuatl y el árabe. El náhuatl es el idioma hablado por los aztecas de México. Muchas palabras del náhuatl se incorporaron[b] al español durante la conquista de México en el siglo XVI. ¿Puedes adivinar[c] el significado en español de estas palabras?

- ahuakatl
- chokolatl
- tomatl

▲ Un mercado mexicano típico

Estás en lo correcto si dices que estas palabras quieren decir **aguacate, chocolate** y **tomate,** respectivamente. Hay también muchas palabras de origen árabe en el español moderno. Estas palabras se incorporaron a la lengua española entre 711 y 1492 (mil cuatrocientos noventa y dos), cuando los moros[d] dominaban[e] el territorio que hoy día es España y Portugal. Del árabe tenemos las siguientes palabras relacionadas con las comidas y bebidas.

| aceite | alcohol | arroz | azúcar[g] | café | naranja |
| alcachofa[f] | alfalfa | atún | berenjena[h] | espinacas | zanahoria |

[a]*Las... Loan words* [b]*se... were incorporated* [c]*guess* [d]*Arabs* [e]*were in control of*
[f]*artichoke* [g]*sugar* [h]*eggplant*

Gramática

Talking About
Conditions and
Traits

Está muy serio.　　　　Ser Versus estar with Adjectives

You learned in the **Lección preliminar** and in **Lección 2B** that Spanish has two verbs for English *to be*—**ser** and **estar**—and you have been using these verbs in different contexts throughout *Sol y viento*. The chart on the next page shows a summary of how you have seen or used each verb so far.

Although the chart summarizes most of the uses of **ser** and **estar,** in this lesson you will use **ser** and **estar** with adjectives to talk primarily about food. Remember that **ser** is used to talk about inherent qualities and **estar** is used to talk about qualities that are not inherent in nature.

Los limones **son** agrios.	*Lemons are sour.*
Estas nueces **están** saladas.	*These nuts are salty.*

Here are some common adjectives you will use to describe food.

agrio/a	sour
amargo/a	bitter
cocido/a	cooked
crudo/a	raw
dulce	sweet
pasado/a	spoiled
picante / picoso/a	hot, spicy
salado/a	salty

Note that very often we use the verbs *taste, seem, look* where Spanish uses **estar.**

No **está** cocido.	*It doesn't seem cooked.*
Está bastante dulce.	*It tastes rather sweet.*

✳ MÁS GRAMÁTICA

In addition to being used with adjectives like **cansado, contento,** and **sucio, estar** is also used with past participles to describe people and things. Past participles are words derived from verbs. Most English past participles end in *-ed* or *-en* (*cooked, served, ordered, frozen, written, broken*). Spanish past participles are formed by adding **-ado** to the stem of **-ar** verbs and by adding **-ido** to the stem of **-er** and **-ir** verbs. When used with **estar,** past participles function as adjectives and must agree in gender and number with the nouns they modify.

lavar (*to wash*) → lav**ado**	Las papas **están lavadas.**
vender → vend**ido**	No **está vendido** el restaurante.
servir → serv**ido**	La sopa ya (*already*) **está servida.**

SUMMARY OF THE USES OF *ser* AND *estar*		
ser		
to express origin (with **de**)	**Soy de** Cuba. ¿**De** dónde **eres**?	*I'm from Cuba.* *Where are you from?*
to express time	¿Qué hora **es**? **Son** las dos y quince. Hoy **es** lunes.	*What time is it?* *It's 2:15.* *Today is Monday.*
to express possession (with possessive adjectives or with **de**)	**Es** mi libro. ¿**De** quién **es**? La mochila **es de** Juan.	*It's my book.* *Whose is this?* *The backpack is Juan's.*
to describe people and things	**Somos** inteligentes. **Es** una mujer seria. La clase **es** interesante.	*We're intelligent.* *She's a serious woman.* *The class is interesting.*
to identify people and things	¿**Sois** estudiantes? ¿Qué **es** esto? Tú y yo **somos** amigos.	*Are you students?* *What is this?* *You and I are friends.*
to talk about inherent qualities with adjectives	El suéter **es** verde. **Son** muy malos.	*The sweater is green.* *They're very bad (malicious)* *people.*
estar		
to express the location of objects and people	Mi tío **está** en México. ¿Dónde **están**?	*My uncle is in Mexico.* *Where are they?*
to express a condition or quality that is subject to change or that is not characteristic	La banana **está** verde. **Están** malos.	*The banana is green (unripe).* *They're in bad shape (sick).*

DE SOL Y VIENTO

In **Episodio 3** of *Sol y viento,* Carlos explains to Jaime why he wants to sell the winery. Part of their exchange appears in the dialogue.

CARLOS
Una viña siempre **es** mucho trabajo. Llevo muchos años entre toneles[a] y botellas.[b] Mi madre ya _____ muy vieja, y mi hermana no tiene ningún interés en estos asuntos. Prefiero hacer el negocio con Uds. y salirme de esto.[c]

JAIME
Por eso vine,[d] para finalizar el negocio.

What verb do you think Carlos uses in the preceding blank, **es** or **está?**

[a]*barrels* [b]*bottles* [c]*salirme... get out of all of this* [d]*Por... That's why I came*

Actividad D ¿Cómo reacciona Jaime?

Empareja una frase de la primera columna con una de la segunda columna para formar oraciones lógicas sobre lo que probablemente hace Jaime Talavera en las siguientes situaciones.

Cuando...

1. ____ está pasada la leche en el refrigerador
2. ____ está malo el servicio en un restaurante
3. ____ está bien vestida María
4. ____ está muy ocupado (*busy*) con su trabajo
5. ____ está fresco el aire

Jaime probablemente...

a. corre en el parque.
b. la tira en la basura (*he throws it in the garbage*).
c. no vuelve a almorzar allí.
d. trabaja toda la noche sin dormir.
e. le da un cumplido (*he gives her a compliment*).

Actividad E Correspondencias

Tu profesor(a) va a mencionar un alimento o una bebida. Indica la oración que mejor describe ese alimento o bebida.

1. **a.** Es agria. **b.** Es dulce.
2. **a.** Son picosos. **b.** Son salados.
3. **a.** Es cara. **b.** Es barata.
4. **a.** Es amargo. **b.** Es agrio.
5. **a.** Son duras (*hard*). **b.** Son blandas (*tender*).
6. **a.** Es picante. **b.** Es dulce.
7. **a.** Son saladas. **b.** Son crudas.

Actividad F En un restaurante elegante

Paso 1 Indica si las siguientes oraciones se dirían (*would be said*), en general, en un restaurante de cinco estrellas (*stars*) o en un restaurante de dos estrellas.

	CINCO ESTRELLAS	DOS ESTRELLAS
1. La leche para el café está pasada.	☐	☐
2. Las bebidas alcohólicas están aguadas (*watered down*).	☐	☐
3. La ensalada está fresca.	☐	☐
4. El servicio está muy malo.	☐	☐
5. Los baños (*bathrooms*) están limpios (*clean*).	☐	☐
6. El bistec está blando.	☐	☐
7. El pan está seco (*dry*) y duro.	☐	☐
8. El pollo está crudo.	☐	☐
9. La sopa está fría.	☐	☐

Paso 2 Con otra persona de la clase, escriban dos oraciones más para agregarlas a la lista del **Paso 1.** Una oración debe referirse a un restaurante de cinco estrellas y la otra debe referirse a un restaurante de dos estrellas.

Actividad G ¿Te molesta? (*Does it bother you?*)

Paso 1 Indica si las siguientes cosas te molestan en un restaurante.

> 5 = Me molesta mucho.
>
> 3 = Me molesta un poco.
>
> 0 = No me molesta para nada.

1. ___ Los refrescos están aguados.
2. ___ Las papas fritas están muy saladas.
3. ___ Los cubiertos (*silverware*) no están bien lavados.
4. ___ La mantequilla no está fría.
5. ___ El jugo de naranja está agrio.
6. ___ La salsa está muy picosa.
7. ___ El bistec está quemado (*burned*).
8. ___ La ensalada está servida en un tazón (*bowl*) y no en un plato (*plate*).

Paso 2 Ahora entrevista a un compañero (una compañera) de clase, según el modelo.

MODELO: E1: ¿Te molesta si los refrescos están aguados?
          E2: Sí, me molesta mucho.

Paso 3 Ahora compara tus respuestas con las de tu compañero/a. ¿Quién se molesta más en cuanto al (*with regard to the*) servicio en los restaurantes?

▲ ¿Crees que el restaurante en este hotel es de dos o cinco estrellas? (Santillana, España)

NAVEGANDO LA RED

Busca un menú en español de un restaurante en *una* de las siguientes regiones: 1) la costa mediterránea de España; 2) el Caribe; 3) La Pampa (la Argentina). Menciona algunas comidas y bebidas interesantes del menú y sus ingredientes principales.

TERCERA PARTE

Vocabulario

Talking About What
You Eat at Night | **La cena**

✳ **Dinner**

Unas cenas típicas de Elsa

A las 6:00 P.M. Elsa **cena**...

(1)

una hamburguesa de **soja** (*soy*), una papa **al horno** (*baked*), maíz (1), una cerveza y un helado (2)

(2)

(3)

o **mariscos** (*seafood*) como **la langosta** (3), los camarones y el pescado, **brócoli** (*m.*) y **coliflor** (*f.*) **al vapor** (*steamed*), arroz, una porción de **pastel** (*m.*) (4) y vino blanco

(4)

(5)

o **los espaguetis** con salsa roja, **judías verdes** (5) y una ensalada mixta.

Como es vegetariana, Elsa no come ni bistec ni pollo para la cena.

Unas cenas típicas de Franco

A las 9.00 P.M. Franco cena...

(6)

un sándwich de carne (pavo, jamón o rosbif) y un refresco o unos tamales* con **chocolate** (*m.*) **caliente** (6)

o **las sobras** (*leftovers*) del almuerzo y una cerveza

o pan dulce o **pasteles** (7) con café.

(7)

* MÁS VOCABULARIO

cenar	to eat/have (for) dinner
la carne de res	beef
los espárragos	asparagus
la lechuga	lettuce
los postres	desserts

◀ ¿Es esta una cena norteamericana o mexicana? ¿Cómo lo sabes?

---

*Tamales are cornmeal dough filled with seasoned meat or other ingredients that are then wrapped in corn husks and steamed.

Actividad A Asociaciones

Empareja un alimento de la primera columna con el estado de los Estados Unidos con que se asocia en la segunda columna.

1. ___ Las naranjas		**a.** California
2. ___ Las papas		**b.** Maine
3. ___ El maíz		**c.** Wisconsin
4. ___ Las manzanas		**d.** Florida
5. ___ El bistec	se asocia(n) con el estado de	**e.** Colorado
6. ___ La langosta		**f.** Washington
7. ___ Los vinos		**g.** Idaho
8. ___ La cerveza Coors		**h.** Texas
9. ___ El queso		**i.** Iowa

Actividad B ¿Quién habla?

Escucha lo que dicen las siguientes personas sobre lo que van a cenar esta noche. Luego, indica si lo dice un norteamericano o un mexicano.

1. ...

2. ...

3. ...

4. ...

Actividad C Categorías

Tu profesor(a) va a leer una lista de comidas. Escribe cada comida en la categoría apropiada. Es posible que algunas comidas pertenezcan a (*belong to*) más de una categoría.

LOS CARBOHIDRATOS	LAS PROTEÍNAS	LOS PRODUCTOS LÁCTEOS (*dairy products*)	LAS GRASAS	LOS DULCES

Actividad D Un menú

Paso 1 Repasa brevemente lo que cenan Elsa, la estudiante de California, y Franco, el estudiante de México. ¿Crees que estas cenas son típicas de los estudiantes de tu universidad? En grupos de dos, hagan los cambios necesarios para crear un menú que refleje lo que los estudiantes de su universidad cenan.

Paso 2 Presenten su menú a la clase. ¿Están de acuerdo sus compañeros de clase con respecto a lo que cenan los estudiantes de esta universidad?

⬚ Vistazo cultural

Las comidas regionales

En varias partes del mundo hispano se comen alimentos que para los norteamericanos son exóticos. En Santander, Colombia, por ejemplo, las hormigas[a] fritas son una de las meriendas populares. Según los residentes de esa región, saben a[b] palomitas o nueces.

Una especialidad del estado de Oaxaca, México, son los chapulines[c] fritos. Se comen como merienda (**botana** en México) o como aperitivo.[d] La ciudad de Dolores Hidalgo en el estado de Guanajuato, México, es conocida por sus helados de sabores[e] raros. Además de chocolate, vainilla, fresa[f] y otros sabores conocidos, también son populares los helados de aguacate, tequila, camarón, maíz, queso, chicharrón[g] y cerveza.

En el Perú y otros países andinos, la carne del cuy[h] es un alimento de los nativos desde la época precolonial. El cuy es alto en proteínas y muy bajo en grasas, y por eso es una carne ideal para muchos andinos. ¿A qué crees que sabe el cuy?

▲ Los chapulines fritos son una merienda típica en México.

[a]*ants* [b]*saben... they taste like* [c]*grasshoppers* [d]*appetizer* [e]*flavors* [f]*strawberry*
[g]*fried pork skin* [h]*guinea pig*

Gramática

¿Le gusta el vino?   Indirect Object Pronouns and **gustar**

In addition to subject and direct object pronouns, Spanish also has a system of *indirect* object pronouns. Indirect objects usually indicate *to whom* or *for whom* as in *Alberto writes letters to me.* In this example, *me* is the indirect object pronoun. The Spanish equivalent of this sentence is **Alberto me escribe cartas.** Alberto is the subject (the one writing), **cartas** are the direct object (the things being written), and **me** is the indirect object (to whom the letters are written). The chart contains the list of Spanish indirect object pronouns.

Like direct objects, indirect objects precede conjugated verbs or can be attached to infinitives.

> Juan **me** quiere hablar.
>
> Juan quiere hablar**me.**

You will note in Spanish that with the verbs **dar** (*to give*) and **decir,** indirect object pronouns are often redundant. That is, they are used at the same time as the indirect object noun is used.

> **Les** doy* consejos (*advice*) **a mis amigos.**
>
> **Le** voy a decir la verdad **a Jorge.**

Indirect object pronouns are required with **gustar** to express likes and dislikes. Although it is often translated into English as *to like*, **gustar** really means *to be pleasing to.*

> A mis tíos **les gusta** la música rock.   *Rock music is pleasing to my uncles.* (*My uncles like rock music.*)
>
> **Nos gustan** las películas de horror.   *Horror movies are pleasing to us.* (*We like horror movies.*)

Note that **gusta** is used in the first sentence because **la música rock** is the subject and is singular. In the second example, **gustan** is used because the subject is **las películas de horror** and is plural.

COMUNICACIÓN ÚTIL

Le and **les** can also refer to things other than people. When used with the verbs **poner** (*to put*) and **quitar** (*to remove, take away*), they acquire the meaning of *to put in* or *on* and *to take off*, respectively.

> —¿**Le** pones azúcar al café?   *Do you put sugar in your coffee?*
>
> —No, no **le** pongo nada.   *No, I don't put anything in it.*
>
> —¿**Les** quitas las cebollas a las hamburguesas?   *Do you take onions off your burgers?*
>
> —Sí, y **les** pongo tomates extras.   *Yes, and I add extra tomatoes.*

---

*Note the irregular **yo** form of **dar: doy.** All other forms of the verb are regular in the present tense.

INDIRECT OBJECT PRONOUNS	
me	**nos**
María **me** dice la verdad. *María tells me the truth.*	Los padres **nos** compran ropa y comida. *Parents buy us clothing and food.*
te	**os**
El profesor **te** da una «A». *The professor gives you an A.*	Los amigos **os** ofrecen consejos. *Friends offer you advice.*
le	**les**
¿Ud.? **Le** tengo mucho respecto. *You? I have a lot of respect for you.*	¿Uds.? No **les** digo mentiras. *You all? I don't tell you lies.*
¿Mi tío? No **le** cuento mis problemas. *My uncle? I don't tell him my problems.*	¿Mis abuelos? **Les** mando tarjetas. *My grandparents? I send them cards.*
¿Mi mejor amiga? **Le** cuento muchas cosas. *My best friend? I tell her lots of things.*	¿Mis hermanas? **Les** presto dinero. *My sisters? I lend them money.*

DE SOL Y VIENTO

You are about to watch **Episodio 3** of *Sol y viento*, in which Jaime emphasizes how important it is for the Sánchez family to close the deal soon. Part of their exchange appears below.

JAIME
La venta tiene que suceder[a] en los próximos días. ¿Y su familia? ¿Aceptan la venta?

CARLOS
Bueno, a mi madre ya casi la tengo convencida.

JAIME
¿Y su hermana?

CARLOS
Con ella no hay problema. Si firma[b] mi madre, firma mi hermana. Como ya ____1 dije,[c] a mi hermana no ____2 interesan los asuntos de la viña.

What indirect object pronouns do you think Carlos uses in the blanks above? Whom do these pronouns refer to?

[a]*take place* [b]*signs* [c]*I told*

Actividad E ¿A quién se refiere?

Imagina que Jaime Talavera menciona las siguientes cosas sobre su viaje a Chile. Indica el personaje de *Sol y viento* que es el sujeto de cada oración.

MODELO: Me da mucho trabajo. (Rassner)

▲ Rassner   ▲ Carlos   ▲ María   ▲ Mario   ▲ el adivino (*fortune-teller*)

1. Me da su tarjeta. _____
2. Me hace un brindis (*makes a toast*). _____
3. Me cobra (*charges*) precios justos (*fair*). _____
4. Me da un papelito que dice «El amor es un torbellino». _____
5. No me ofrece la opción de no ir a Chile. _____

Actividad F El/La dentista

A continuación hay una lista de las cosas que nos hace el/la dentista cuando vamos a su consultorio (*office*). Pon (*Put*) las actividades en orden cronológico, del 1 al 6.

El/La dentista...

____ nos limpia (*cleans*) los dientes (*teeth*).

____ nos toma rayos X para mejor examinar los dientes.

____ nos dice «Buenos días. ¿Cómo estás?»

____ nos regala (*gives as a gift*) un cepillo (*brush*) nuevo al salir del consultorio.

____ nos examina los dientes.

____ nos pide información sobre el seguro (*insurance*) antes de examinarnos.

Actividad G Asociaciones

Empareja una oración de la primera columna con una de la segunda columna para formar oraciones lógicas.

Si a una persona...

1. ____ le gustan los mariscos,
2. ____ no le gusta la carne,
3. ____ no le gustan los huevos,
4. ____ le gusta la comida rápida,   probablemente...
5. ____ le gustan las bebidas alcohólicas,
6. ____ le gustan los postres,

a. no le gusta la tortilla española.
b. le gusta la langosta.
c. le gusta el helado.
d. le gustan las cervezas importadas.
e. le gustan las comidas grasosas.
f. no le gusta el bistec.

Actividad H ¿Qué te gusta merendar?

Paso 1 Escribe en los espacios en blanco a continuación seis comidas y/o bebidas que te gusta merendar.

	E1		E2	
De merienda me gusta(n)...	SÍ	NO	SÍ	NO
1. _____.	☐	☐	☐	☐
2. _____.	☐	☐	☐	☐
3. _____.	☐	☐	☐	☐
4. _____.	☐	☐	☐	☐
5. _____.	☐	☐	☐	☐
6. _____.	☐	☐	☐	☐

Paso 2 Entrevista a dos compañeros de clase para averiguar si les gustan las mismas comidas como merienda que a ti. Anota sus respuestas en las columnas apropiadas.

MODELO: ¿Te gustan las galletas saladas con queso como merienda?

Paso 3 Con la información de los **Pasos 1** y **2**, escribe dos oraciones con **nos** y dos con **les** para presentárselas a la clase.

MODELO: A Juan y a Ana les gusta la leche como merienda. A nosotros tres nos gustan las frutas frescas como merienda.

SOL Y VIENTO: Enfoque cultural

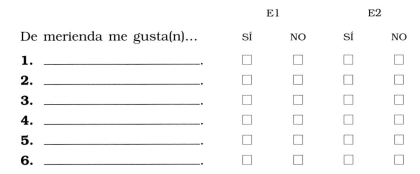

En el **Episodio 3,** Jaime y Mario llegan al Valle del Maipo, y Mario compra unas empanadas para Jaime y para él. En muchos países hispanos, sobre todo en Latinoamérica, son típicos estos puestos[a] pequeños donde se vende comida. En Puerto Rico, al lado de algunas carreteras[b] hay puestos con letreros hechos a mano[c] que anuncian «pollo asado y frutas». En México, es típico ver en la ciudad puestos pequeños en forma de «carritos»[d] donde se venden tacos y tortas (sándwiches). En las zonas rurales, son más comunes los lugares pequeños como el puesto en donde Mario compró[e] las empanadas. Este tipo de comida tiene mucha demanda: es barata y se encuentra por todas partes en los países latinos. Pero, lo principal[f] es que les ofrece a personas de pocos recursos[g] la oportunidad de ganar algún dinero.

▲ Unos puestos de comida en México

[a]*stands* [b]*highways* [c]*letreros... hand-made signs* [d]*carts* [e]*bought* [f]*lo... the main thing*
[g]*financial resources*

SOL Y VIENTO

Antes de ver el episodio

Actividad A ¿Qué recuerdas?

Indica si las siguientes oraciones son ciertas o falsas según lo que recuerdas del **Episodio 2** de *Sol y viento.*

	CIERTO	FALSO
1. Jaime juega al frisbee en un parque de Santiago.	☐	☐
2. Jaime se choca con (*bumps into*) María mientras lee un papelito de la suerte.	☐	☐
3. María trabaja en una excavación en el Valle del Maipo.	☐	☐
4. María permite que Jaime se quede con (*keep*) su tarjeta.	☐	☐
5. A Jaime no le importa (*Jaime doesn't care about*) la inteligencia de María.	☐	☐

Actividad B ¿Qué falta?

En el **Episodio 3** de *Sol y viento* vas a ver una escena en que Carlos y Jaime toman una copa de vino mientras hablan. A continuación hay unos fragmentos de su diálogo.

CARLOS: ¡Salud![a]

JAIME: Hmmm... Delicioso... y un _____[1] color. Un merlot, si no me equivoco.[b]

CARLOS: Correcto. Una cosecha[c] muy especial, del 88. ¿Ud. _____[2] algo de vinos?

JAIME: Sí, algo. _____[3] pronto se dejará de producir.[d]

[a]*Cheers!* [b]*si... if I'm not mistaken* [c]*harvest* [d]*se... it won't be produced anymore*

Indica la respuesta más adecuada para cada espacio en blanco.

1. **a.** tan claro **b.** excelente **c.** monótono (*drab*)
2. **a.** dice **b.** lee **c.** sabe
3. **a.** Qué bueno que (*Good thing that*) **c.** Es cierto que (*It's certain that*)
   b. Lástima que (*Too bad that*)

Actividad C El episodio

Ahora mira el episodio. Si hay algo que no entiendes bien, puedes volver a ver la escena en cuestión.

Después de ver el episodio

Actividad A ¿Qué recuerdas?

Contesta cada pregunta basándote en lo que recuerdas del **Episodio 3.**

1. ¿Quién es Traimaqueo?
   - **a.** un miembro de la familia Sánchez
   - **b.** un trabajador de la viña
2. Don Carlos está nervioso al reunirse con (*on meeting*) Jaime. ¿Cierto o falso?
   - **a.** cierto
   - **b.** falso
3. Carlos le dice a Jaime que su madre y su hermana están...
   - **a.** en Santiago.
   - **b.** en casa.
4. Según Carlos, su hermana no tiene interés en los asuntos (*matters*) de la viña. ¿Cierto o falso?
   - **a.** cierto
   - **b.** falso
5. Don Carlos y sus trabajadores están planeando...
   - **a.** una recepción para celebrar un vino nuevo.
   - **b.** una fiesta de cumpleaños (*birthday party*).
6. Jaime le dice a don Carlos que la venta (*sale*) tiene que suceder (*happen*) en los próximos días. ¿Cierto o falso?
   - **a.** cierto
   - **b.** falso

Actividad B ¿Lo captaste?

Vuelve a la **Actividad B** en **Antes de ver el episodio** para verificar tus respuestas. Si es necesario, vuelve a ver el episodio.

Actividad C Utilizando el contexto

Ya sabes que es difícil interpretar pronombres directos sin contexto. Al ver (*Upon watching*) más episodios de *Sol y viento*, trata de usar tus conocimientos (*knowledge*) del trama (*plot*) para ayudarte a identificar los pronombres. Considera el diálogo a continuación.

JAIME: ¿Le molesta si primero doy[a] un tour por la viña?
CARLOS: No, para nada. Pero yo necesito quedarme aquí en la oficina. Traimaqueo lo puede guiar. Yo lo voy a llamar a su celular. ¿Sabe llegar?

[a]*I take*

Basándote en el contexto, ¿a quién se refiere **lo** en **Traimaqueo lo puede guiar**? ¿Y en **Yo lo voy a llamar a su celular**?

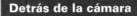

RESUMEN DE VOCABULARIO

Verbos

cenar	to eat/have (for) dinner
dar (*irreg.*)	to give
desayunar	to eat/have (for) breakfast
gustar	to be pleasing to
merendar (ie)	to snack / have for a snack
regalar	to give (*as a gift*)

Repaso: almorzar (ue)

Las carnes y las aves

el bistec	steak
la carne de res	beef
la chuleta de cerdo	pork chop
los huevos (fritos, revueltos)	(fried, scrambled) eggs
el jamón	ham
el pavo	turkey
el pollo	chicken
la salchicha	sausage
el tocino	bacon
la tortilla española	omelette

Cognados: la hamburguesa, el rosbif

El pescado y los mariscos

el atún	tuna
los camarones	shrimp
la langosta	lobster

Las verduras

el aguacate	avocado
la cebolla	onion
los champiñones	mushrooms
los chícharos	peas
la ensalada mixta	tossed salad
las espinacas	spinach
los frijoles	beans
las judías verdes	green beans
la lechuga	lettuce
el maíz	corn

la papa	potato
las papas fritas	French fries
el puré de papas	mashed potatoes
la soja	soy(bean)
las zanahorias	carrots

Cognados: el bróculi, la coliflor, los espárragos, el tomate

Las frutas

la manzana	apple
la naranja	orange
las pasas	raisins
la toronja	grapefruit

Cognados: la banana, el limón

Los productos lácteos

la leche	milk
la mantequilla	butter
el queso (de crema)	(cream) cheese
el yogur	yogurt

Los carbohidratos

el arroz	rice
el cereal (cocido)	(hot) cereal
el pan	bread
el pan dulce	sweet bread (*Mex.*)
el pan tostado	toast
la rosquilla	bagel
la tortilla (de maíz)	(corn) tortilla
la tostada de pan a la francesa	French toast

Cognados: los espaguetis, los panqueques

Los postres

el flan	flan (*baked custard*)
el helado	ice cream
el pastel	cake
los pasteles	pastries

Las meriendas

los dulces	candy
la galleta	cookie
la galleta salada	cracker
la nuez (*pl.* **las nueces**)	nut
las palomitas de maíz	popcorn
las papitas	potato chips

Las bebidas

el agua (*f.*)	water
el café (descafeinado)	(decaffeinated) coffee
el chocolate caliente	hot chocolate
el jugo	juice
el refresco (dietético)	(diet) soft drink
el té (caliente, helado)	(hot, iced) tea
el vino (blanco, tinto)	(white, red) wine

Repaso: la cerveza

Otros alimentos

la barra de frutas / granola	fruit / granola bar
la mantequilla de cacahuete	peanut butter
la mermelada	jam
la sopa	soup

Cognados: la pizza, la salsa, el sándwich

Adjetivos

agrio/a	sour
amargo/a	bitter
blando/a	soft, tender
cocido/a	cooked
crudo/a	raw
dulce	sweet
duro/a	hard
pasado/a	spoiled
picante	hot, spicy
picoso/a	hot, spicy
salado/a	salty

Palabras indefinidas y negativas

algo	something
algún (alguno/a/os/as)	some, any
siempre	always
jamás	never
nada	nothing
nadie	no one, not anyone
ningún (ninguno/a)	none, not any
nunca	never
tampoco	neither, not either

Repaso: alguien, también

Otras palabras y expresiones

el almuerzo	lunch
la cena	dinner
el desayuno	breakfast
la comida rápida	fast food
la porción (de pastel, pizza)	slice (of cake, pizza)
las sobras	leftovers
el/la vegetariano/a	vegetarian
al horno	baked
al vapor	steamed
de vez en cuando	once in a while

Otro encuentro

TRAIMAQUEO: Así es la tierra: el sol, la lluvia, las cepas[a]... Todo en armonía, todo trabajando junto[b]...

JAIME: ¿Tiene algún significado esta figura?

TENDERA:[c] Sí, esta figura simboliza un espíritu protector de los mapuches.

JAIME: ¿Los mapuches? Son una cultura indígena, ¿no?

¿Qué pasa en esta foto? ¿Lo pasan bien Jaime y María?[d] ¿Crees que a Jaime le gusta mucho María? ¿Y qué piensa ella de él?

[a]*vine stocks* [b]*together* [c]*Shopkeeper*
[d]*¿Lo... Are Jaime and María having a good time?*

Cuando no trabajo...

IN THIS LESSON, YOU WILL LEARN:

- how to talk about pastimes and leisure activities

- vocabulary related to sports and fitness activities

- how to talk about special occasions and holidays

- how to talk about activities in the past using the preterite tense

In addition, you will prepare for **Episodio 4** of the film *Sol y viento.*

◀

Esta es una celebración de la Noche Vieja (*New Year's Eve*) en la Puerta del Sol (Madrid, España).

The following media resources are available for *Sol y viento: En breve*

Episodio 4 of *Sol y viento*

Online *Manual de actividades*

Interactive CD-ROM

Online Learning Center Website

Vocabulario

Talking About What
You Do When You
Don't Study or Work

El tiempo libre

Leisure Activities ✳

En las fiestas

Roberto

A Roberto no le gustan **las fiestas.** Es un poco tímido y no le gusta **rozarse con la gente.** No hace más que **tomar** y **picar.** ¿Eres tú como él?

bailar	to dance
dar (*irreg.*) **una fiesta**	to throw a party
picar	to nibble
rozarse con la gente	to mingle with people
tocar (el piano, la guitarra)	to play (the piano, the guitar)
tomar	to drink

✳ MÁS VOCABULARIO

divertir (ie)	to entertain	**el juego**	game (*as in chess*)
pasarlo bien/mal	to have a good/bad time	**los ratos libres**	free (spare) time
		divertido/a	fun
el aguafiestas	party pooper		
el equipo	equipment		

En casa

En sus ratos libres, Roberto y sus compañeros de casa hacen diferentes actividades. Roberto ve películas. A Tomás le gusta **pintar** (tiene aspiraciones artís-
ticas). A Jaime le gusta **limpiar la casa** (dice que es relajante). Alicia **practica
el yoga** y **medita.** ¿Cuál de los cuatro es más como tú?

cocinar	to cook
coleccionar (estampillas, monedas)	to collect (stamps, coins)
dibujar	to draw
jugar (ue) al* ajedrez	to play chess
limpiar la casa	to clean the house
pintar	to paint
sacar un vídeo/DVD	to rent a video/DVD

Fuera de casaª

ªFuera... *Outside*

En el parque, la gente hace varias actividades. Unos **patinan en línea.** Otros
dan un paseo. A unos les gusta **andar en bicicleta.** En el lago, otros prefieren
navegar en barco. ¿Dónde está Roberto? Ah, ¡claro! Probablemente está en casa.

andar en bicicleta	to ride a bicycle
dar (*irreg.*) **un paseo**	to take a walk; to stroll
navegar en barco	to sail
patinar (en línea)	to (inline) skate
visitar un museo	to visit a museum

*Remember that **a** + *definite article* is used with **jugar** when talking about games and sports.

Actividad A ¿Cómo lo ves?

Paso 1 Escucha mientras tu profesor(a) menciona una actividad. ¿En qué categoría la pondrías (*would you put*)?

Se necesita equipo especial	Se puede hacer a solas
Se necesita cierto talento	Se requiere mucho esfuerzo (*effort*) físico

Paso 2 Mirando (*Looking at*) las actividades que has escrito (*you have written*), indica para cuáles, en tu opinión, se necesitan (*are needed*) dos personas y para cuáles se necesita un grupo de personas.

MODELO: Para jugar al ajedrez se necesitan dos personas.

Actividad B Las personas célebres

¿Qué personas célebres o personajes conocidos asocias con cada actividad?

1. cocinar
2. pintar
3. tocar el piano
4. ir a una discoteca
5. bailar
6. andar en bicicleta
7. dar fiestas
8. dibujar

Actividad C En una fiesta

Paso 1 Indica cuáles de las siguientes oraciones se te aplican a ti (*apply to you*) en una fiesta.

	SE ME APLICA.	NO SE ME APLICA.
1. Me gusta mucho rozarme con la gente.	☐	☐
2. No me gusta bailar.	☐	☐
3. Me gusta picar la comida.	☐	☐
4. Me gusta divertir a los demás (*others*) (y ser el centro de la atención de todos).	☐	☐
5. Me gusta escuchar a otra persona tocar el piano o la guitarra. Y siempre canto con esa persona.	☐	☐
6. Me gusta dar fiestas tanto como ser invitado/a a una.	☐	☐
7. No me gustan las fiestas. Soy un aguafiestas.	☐	☐

¡Exprésate!

To make impersonal statements, ones in which the verb is singular and the subject is not specified, use the reflexive pronoun **se.** The rough equivalent in English is *one, you,* or *they.*

Se puede llamar a la profesora si hay preguntas.

One (You, They) can call the professor if there are questions.

Se necesita practicar el español todos los días.

One (You, They) need to practice Spanish every day.

Paso 2 Escoge las cuatro oraciones del **Paso 1** que mejor te caracterizan y conviértelas en preguntas para otra persona. ¿Son sus respuestas iguales a las tuyas?

MODELO: ¿Te gusta dar fiestas tanto como ser invitada a una?

Actividad D En busca de amigos

Imagina que se podría (*one could*) entrevistar a las personas al conocerlas para ver si son compatibles como amigos. Utilizando el nuevo vocabulario, escribe diez preguntas para entrevistar a dos personas. Luego, indica quién de las dos personas (o ninguna) podría ser buena compañía para ti.

Vistazo cultural

Las fiestas

Cuando un hispano viene a los Estados Unidos por primera vez y es invitado[a] a una fiesta, una de las cosas que suele notar es que para él las fiestas parecen un poco aburridas. Algunos hispanos han comentado[b] que a los estudiantes norteamericanos, sólo les interesa beber y emborracharse.[c] En el mundo hispano, la idea de «beber para emborracharse» no es parte de la mentalidad estudiantil. Claro, los estudiantes toman cerveza o vino, pero el concepto de un *keg party,* por ejemplo, es algo ajeno[d] a su experiencia. En contraste, salen a «tomar copas», lo cual quiere decir que unos amigos salen en la noche y disfrutan de[e] una o dos copas de vino (o cerveza) mientras charlan y pican comidas ligeras.[f]

En las fiestas, tanto de los jóvenes[g] como de los mayores, es muy común poner música y bailar o tocar la guitarra y cantar. Así que si vas a una fiesta hispana, no te sorprendas[h] si alguien te dice «Vamos a bailar» o si te llama «aguafiestas» si dices que no quieres bailar.

▲ En las fiestas hispanas, bailar es casi una obligación.

[a]es... *is invited* [b]han... *have mentioned* [c]*getting drunk* [d]*foreign* [e]disfrutan... *enjoy* [f]*light*
[g]*young people* [h]no... *don't be surprised*

Gramática

Lo pasé muy bien.   **Preterite Tense of Regular -ar Verbs**

REGULAR -ar VERBS IN THE PRETERITE bailar			
yo	bail**é**	nosotros/as	bail**amos**
tú	bail**aste**	vosotros/as	bail**asteis**
Ud.	bail**ó**	Uds.	bail**aron**
él/ella	bail**ó**	ellos/ellas	bail**aron**

To talk about past events in Spanish, at a minimum you will need to know how to use two sets of verb forms: the *preterite* and the *imperfect*. This lesson will focus solely on the preterite. In this section of the lesson, you will learn the forms of the preterite for regular **-ar** verbs.

The preterite (**el pretérito**) has several equivalents in English to express a single event in the past. Look at the examples that follow.

Lo **pasé** muy bien.	*I had a good time.*
De veras, lo **pasé** muy bien.	*Honestly, I did have a good time.*

What you see is that the preterite is used to talk about finished or completed events in the past. If the action or event is viewed by the speaker as completed by a certain time point—no matter how long the action or event lasted—it will be expressed in the preterite.

Sólo **canté** una canción.	*I sang only one song.*
Los dinosaurios **reinaron** por millones de años.	*Dinosaurs reigned for millions of years.*

Note the following about **-ar** verb forms of the preterite.

1. The **nosotros** form is the same as that used in the present tense. Context usually lets you know whether past or present is intended.

Ayer **visitamos** el Museo del Prado.	*Yesterday we visited the Prado Museum.*

2. Verbs that end in **-car, -gar,** and **-zar** have spelling changes in the **yo** form to keep the *k*, hard *g*, and soft *c* sounds, respectively.

tocar: -car → qu	to**qu**é, tocaste,...
pagar: -gar → gu	pa**gu**é, pagaste,...
empezar: -zar → c	empe**c**é, empezaste,...

3. Verbs with present-tense stem changes show no stem changes in the preterite.

    com**ie**nza *but* comenzó

    alm**ue**rza *but* almorzó

4. Note the accent marks on the **yo, Ud.,** and **él/ella** forms. These are important to demonstrate the shift of stress from the stem of the verb to the verb ending.

DE SOL Y VIENTO

In **Episodio 4,** Jaime runs into María again by chance. She asks him about his trip to the Maipo Valley, and he responds. Read part of their exchange below.

MARÍA

Ya volvió[a] de su viaje. ¿Cómo le fue?[b]

JAIME

_____.

Which response do you think Jaime gave María?

1. Lo pasé muy bien, gracias. **2.** Lo paso muy bien, gracias.

[a]*you returned* [b]¿Cómo... *How was it?*

Enfoque lingüístico

Más sobre los tiempos verbales

Remember that *tense* (**el tiempo**) refers to the relative time frame in which an event or action occurs: past, present, and future. The word *tense* can be confusing because actions or states that are all part of the same time frame (past, present, future) are often called tenses as well. For example, in this lesson you are learning how to use the preterite tense. Why not just say "past tense"? This is because, as you will learn later, there is another very important verb form used to talk about the past, the *imperfect,* which you may hear referred to as the *imperfect tense.* These really aren't tenses but sets of forms that refer to past tense events.

What's the difference between the preterite and the imperfect? As a preview, look at the following English sentence: *The phone rang just as I was walking out the door.* Here you have two events that relate to each other in a past time frame. But note that the speaker uses *was walking* rather than *walked.* This is because the speaker is conveying the fact that the action of walking out the door was in progress when the phone rang. The imperfect is used to express this concept, among others. The preterite is used only for events that are reported as completed. Note that in this example you can easily answer the question "Did the phone ring?" with yes, because the speaker reports the action as completed: the phone *rang.* This is the preterite. With the imperfect, you cannot so easily answer "Did the speaker walk out?" because the verb form does not indicate that the action has ended. The speaker may have stayed to answer the phone, or he may have decided to ignore the call and continue walking out the door. For now, you will focus on the idea of events viewed as completed.

Actividad E   ¿Quién lo diría (*would say*)?

Basándote en episodios previos de *Sol y viento*, ¿quién podría (*could*) decir las siguientes oraciones?

1. Trabajé con mis estudiantes.
2. Llegué a Santiago el lunes.
3. Lo llevé al Hotel Bonaparte.
4. Compré un papelito de la suerte.
5. Caminé y hablé con un hombre simpático.
6. Grité (*I yelled*) a un empleado.
7. Busqué a la señorita para darle su tarjeta.
8. Después de llevar al señor a la viña, almorcé con algunos amigos en nuestro bar favorito.

¡Exprésate!

To express the concept of *ago*, Spanish uses **hace** plus the amount of time elapsed. For example, **hace unos días** means *a few days ago,* and **hace unas semanas** means *a few weeks ago.* How would you say *a month ago? several years ago?*

Actividad F   ¿Cuándo?

Paso 1   Indica cuándo fue (*was*) la última vez que hiciste (*you did*) cada actividad.

	ANOCHE O AYER (*last night or yesterday*)	HACE UNOS DÍAS	HACE _____
1. Bailé en una fiesta.	☐	☐	☐
2. Bailé en una discoteca.	☐	☐	☐
3. Cociné.	☐	☐	☐
4. Limpié la casa.	☐	☐	☐
5. Saqué un DVD.	☐	☐	☐
6. Visité un museo.	☐	☐	☐
7. Estudié toda la noche para un examen.	☐	☐	☐
8. Lo pasé súperbien con mis amigos.	☐	☐	☐

Paso 2   Convierte las oraciones del **Paso 1** en preguntas para hacérselas a tus compañeros. Luego, busca a personas que dieron (*gave*) respuestas iguales a las tuyas en por lo menos cinco de las actividades.

MODELO: ¿Cuándo fue la última vez que estudiaste toda la noche?

Actividad G El estudiante y el profesor

Paso 1 Agrupa las siguientes actividades según lo que crees que hizo (*did*) anoche un estudiante o un profesor o los dos. Todas las oraciones se refieren a posibles actividades de anoche. Compara tus respuestas con las de un compañero (una compañera) para ver si son iguales.

1. Tomó una cerveza.
2. Habló con un amigo por teléfono.
3. Navegó la red para buscar información.
4. Charló con alguien por correo electrónico.
5. Regresó a casa después de las 5:00 de la tarde.
6. Preparó la cena.
7. Bailó en una fiesta.

Paso 2 Entrevisten al profesor (a la profesora) entre todos para ver si hizo las actividades anteriores anoche. Usen **tú** o **Ud.,** según la costumbre (*custom*) de la clase. ¿Creen Uds. que su profesor(a) es típico/a?

Actividad H En el pasado

Da el nombre de dos o más personas que hicieron (*did*) cada actividad a continuación.

MODELO: Actuaron en muchas películas de horror. → Boris Karloff y Bela Lugosi actuaron en muchas películas de horror.

1. Inventaron aparatos o máquinas importantes.
2. Pintaron cuadros (*paintings*) famosos durante el Renacimiento (*Renaissance*).
3. Viajaron grandes distancias en un avión (*airplane*).
4. Actuaron en las películas de James Bond.
5. Buscaron su fortuna en el Nuevo Mundo (*New World*).
6. Tocaron la guitarra en bandas de música rock en los años 60 (*the sixties*).

Actividad I Las personas famosas

Paso 1 ¿Qué sabes de los «célebres»? Escribe dos o tres preguntas sobre una persona famosa. **¡OJO!** Debes usar el pretérito en tus preguntas.

MODELO: ¿En qué película cantó John Travolta *Greased Lightning*?

Paso 2 Cada persona va a presentar sus preguntas a la clase. ¿Cuáles son las preguntas más difíciles?

SEGUNDA PARTE

Vocabulario

| **El ejercicio y el gimnasio**

Sports and Fitness

Raúl y Elena

Juan Ignacio

Antonia

Marisela

José

Susanita, Carol, Juan Pablo, Billy

Algunas actividades

caminar	to walk
competir (i)	to compete
correr	to run
esquiar (esquío)	to ski
ganar	to win
hacer (*irreg.*) **ciclismo estacionario**	to ride a stationary bike
hacer (*irreg.*) **ejercicio (aeróbico)**	to exercise (do aerobics)
hacer (*irreg.*) **gimnasia**	to work out
jugar (ue) (gu) al golf	to play golf
levantar pesas	to lift weights
nadar	to swim
perder (ie)	to lose
sudar	to sweat
trotar	to jog

Lugares y objetos

el campeonato	championship
la cancha (de tenis)	(tennis) court
el equipo	team
el estadio	stadium
el gimnasio	gymnasium
la natación	swimming
el partido	game, match
la piscina	swimming pool
la pista	track
la rueda de andar	treadmill

✳ MÁS VOCABULARIO

estar (*irreg.*) **en (buena) forma**	to be in (good) shape
fortalecer (zc)	to strengthen
quemar calorías	to burn calories
ser (*irreg.*) **aficionado/a (a)**	to be a fan (of)
el/la atleta	athlete
el kilómetro	kilometer
el metro	meter
la milla	mile
fuerte	strong

Cognados: el basquetbol, el béisbol, el fútbol,* el fútbol americano, el tenis, el vólibol

---

***El fútbol** is the term for *soccer*, whereas **el fútbol americano** is used for *football*.

Actividad A ¿Quién es?

Escucha las descripciones que da tu profesor(a). Todas tienen que ver (*have to do*) con las actividades en la página 196. ¿Puedes indicar a quién se refiere cada descripción?

1. ...   **2.** ...   **3.** ...   **4.** ...   **5.** ...   **6.** ...

Actividad B ¿Qué es?

Escucha lo que dice el profesor (la profesora). Luego indica lo que se describe.

1. a. el verano
   b. el Super Bowl
   c. la piscina
2. a. la cancha
   b. el partido
   c. la pista
3. a. trotar
   b. sudar
   c. esquiar
4. a. pierde
   b. juega
   c. es aficionado
5. a. levantar pesas
   b. correr
   c. el ciclismo
6. a. la piscina
   b. la rueda de andar
   c. el invierno

Actividad C ¿Para qué sirve?

Indica a qué tipo de ejercicio corresponde cada descripción. En algunos casos, hay más de una respuesta posible.

1. Este ejercicio fortalece el corazón y quema calorías.
2. Este ejercicio fortalece los músculos (*muscles*).
3. Este deporte requiere mucha concentración. Como normalmente compiten dos personas, los jugadores tienen que anticipar lo que va a hacer su contrario (*opponent*). Entonces, desarrolla (*it develops*) la planificación y la observación.
4. Este deporte no sirve para quemar muchas calorías. De hecho (*In fact*), hay personas de 60 y 70 años de edad que lo practican.
5. Este deporte requiere bastante esfuerzo y coordinación entre los miembros del equipo. Como los jugadores corren mucho, también es bueno para quemar calorías.

Actividad D ¿Son importantes los deportes?

Paso 1 Utilizando las preguntas a continuación como guía, entrevista a dos personas de la clase sobre la importancia del ejercicio y los deportes en su vida.

1. ¿Haces ejercicio regularmente? ¿Cuántas veces a la semana? ¿Qué haces?

2. ¿Practicas algún deporte? ¿Cuándo lo practicas?

3. ¿Cuál es tu deporte favorito? ¿Ves muchos partidos en la televisión? ¿Cuáles?

4. ¿Vas a muchos partidos?

5. ¿Eres aficionado/a a algún equipo o a algún (alguna) atleta en particular? ¿Cuál es el equipo o quién es el/la atleta? ¿Por qué te gusta?

6. ¿ ?

Paso 2 Basándote en la información que obtuviste (*you obtained*) en el **Paso 1**, contesta la siguiente pregunta en un párrafo de entre 25 y 50 palabras.

¿Son el ejercicio y los deportes importantes para las dos personas?

〰 Vistazo cultural

El fútbol y otros deportes

Ya sabes que en los Estados Unidos los deportes más populares son el fútbol americano, el basquetbol y el béisbol. Las universidades grandes y también muchas ciudades tienen equipos que compiten para ganar un campeonato al final de la temporada.[a] Pero en los países hispanos, el fútbol es el rey[b] de los deportes y la Copa Mundial[c] es tan importante como el Super Bowl lo es en los Estados Unidos. Los niños juegan al fútbol en la calle, en los parques y, claro, en las escuelas.

También uno puede ver que el tenis gana más importancia cada día, sobre todo en España, Chile y la Argentina. En los campeonatos del Grand Slam, es frecuente ver a un jugador de origen hispano. Y el béisbol todavía es importante en el Caribe, sobre todo en la República Dominicana. El gran beisbolista Sammy Sosa es dominicano.

[a](*sport*) *season* [b]*king*
[c]*Copa... World Cup*

▲ La selección (*national team*) argentina juega en la Copa Mundial.

Gramática

More on Talking
About the Past

Volví tarde.

Preterite of Regular -er and -ir Verbs

REGULAR -er AND -ir VERBS IN THE PRETERITE volver, escribir			
yo	volví escribí	**nosotros/as**	volvimos escribimos
tú	volviste escribiste	**vosotros/as**	volvisteis escribisteis
Ud.	volvió escribió	**Uds.**	volvieron escribieron
él/ella	volvió escribió	**ellos/ellas**	volvieron escribieron

As in the preterite forms of **-ar** verbs, the stress shifts from the stem of the verb to the vowel in the ending of **-er/-ir** verbs.

Note the following.

1. Unlike those for the present tense, the preterite endings for **-er** and **-ir** verbs are exactly the same, including the **nosotros** and **vosotros** forms.

2. As with stem-changing **-ar** verbs, **-er** verbs do not change in the preterite. However, some **-ir** verbs do show a stem change in the preterite, but only in the **Ud., él/ella, Uds.,** and **ellos/ellas** forms. This is true of two verbs you have learned in this lesson.

   competir (i, i):* yo competí, ella compitió, Uds. compitieron

   divertir (ie, i):* tú divertiste, Ud. divirtió, ellas divirtieron

   You will learn more about stem-changing **-ir** verbs in the preterite in **Lección 4B.** For now, just keep in mind the changes for these two verbs as you work through this lesson.

3. An unstressed **i** between vowels becomes **y** for spelling and pronunciation purposes.

   leí, leíste, le**y**ó, leímos, leísteis, le**y**eron

4. Note that the verb **conocer** in the preterite translates as *met.*

   Conocí al nuevo estudiante.   *I met the new student.*

---

*The first vowel in parentheses is the stem change for the present tense. The second vowel shows the stem change in the preterite.

DE SOL Y VIENTO

At the beginning of **Episodio 4,** Traimaqueo concludes a tour of the winery with Jaime. Read the following exchange. Use the following verbs to aid your comprehension of the exchange and to complete the activity.

Vocabulario útil

nacer	to be born
enterrar*	to bury

JAIME
Muy interesante, señor. Es evidente su pasión por la viña.

TRAIMAQUEO
¿Pasión? No sé. Pero nací en estos terrenos^a y me enterrarán en estos terrenos, señor. ¿No es así como debe ser?

Examine Traimaqueo's statement beginning with **Pero nací... .** Knowing that the verb **enterrar** is in the future tense, what is the English equivalent of this sentence?

^a*lands*

✳ MÁS GRAMÁTICA

Although you will learn irregular past tense forms later, here are two irregular verbs in the preterite that are useful at this point.

hacer: hice, hiciste, hizo,[†] hicimos, hicisteis, hicieron

ir/ser: fui, fuiste, fue, fuimos, fuisteis, fueron

Note that **ir** and **ser** share the same forms in the preterite. Context will determine meaning.

¿**Fue** Roberto al cine?	*Did Roberto go to the movies?*
Bill Clinton **fue** presidente de 1993 a 2001.	*Bill Clinton was president from 1993–2001.*

---

*This is an example of a cognate that you may not immediately recognize. Do you know another term for *to bury*? How about *to inter*, as in *She was interred at Hill Crest Cemetery in 1906*? Be on the lookout for such cognates of less frequent English words.
[†]Note that for **Ud., él,** and **ella, hizo** is spelled with a **z** to maintain the soft **c** sound of the other forms.

Actividad E   Jaime

Paso 1   ¿Cuáles de las siguientes oraciones sobre las actividades de Jaime en los **Episodios 2** y **3** son ciertas?

		C	F
a. ____ Bebió vino en la viña.		☐	☐
b. ____ Comió un sándwich.		☐	☐
c. ____ Conoció a Carlos.		☐	☐
d. ____ Conoció a María.		☐	☐
e. ____ Corrió en el parque.		☐	☐
f. ____ Leyó su correo electrónico.		☐	☐
g. ____ Recibió un mensaje de los Estados Unidos.		☐	☐
h. ____ Salió para el Valle del Maipo.		☐	☐

Paso 2   De las que son ciertas, ¿puedes ponerlas en el orden en que ocurrieron?

▲ ¿Cuándo salió Jaime para la viña «Sol y viento», en el **Episodio 2** o en el **Episodio 3**?

Actividad F   Lo que hice en el pasado

Paso 1   Completa las oraciones a continuación con información verdadera (*true*) para ti. No le reveles tus respuestas a nadie.

Una vez en el pasado, yo...

1. comí _____.

2. perdí _____.

3. conocí a _____.

4. leí _____.

5. salí con mis amigos y no volví a casa hasta _____.

Paso 2   Una persona servirá de (*will serve as a*) voluntaria. Los demás (*The rest*), utilizando lo que ya saben de esa persona, más sus impresiones de él/ella, tratarán de (*will try*) adivinar lo que hizo haciéndole preguntas del tipo **sí/no**. El profesor (La profesora) puede ayudar con el vocabulario.

MODELOS: ¿Comiste algo malo?

¿Comiste algo vivo?

¿Comiste algo y luego te llevaron al hospital?

Actividad G En la escuela secundaria (*high school*)

Contesta las siguientes preguntas con información verdadera sobre lo que tú y tus compañeros hicieron en la escuela secundaria.

1. ¿Qué novela o novelas leyeron en sus clases de inglés?
2. ¿Escribieron alguna composición de más de diez páginas? ¿de más de veinte páginas?
3. ¿Resistieron la tentación de tomar las drogas? ¿de tomar el alcohol? ¿de usar el tabaco?
4. ¿Asistieron al baile de promoción (*prom*) el último año?
5. ¿Salieron todos contentos con la educación que recibieron?

Actividad H La semana pasada

Paso 1 Contesta las siguientes preguntas sobre la semana pasada con información verdadera.

1. ¿Hiciste ejercicio? ¿Qué ejercicio hiciste?
2. ¿Cuántas veces saliste con los amigos?

Paso 2 Utilizando las preguntas del **Paso 1**, entrevista a dos personas en la clase y apunta sus respuestas.

Paso 3 Haz una comparación de lo que hiciste tú la semana pasada con lo que hicieron las personas que entrevistaste, a base de la información que tienes de los **Pasos 1** y **2**. Usa las frases **fue activa** ([*it*] *was active*) y **fue solitaria** ([*it*] *was solitary, quiet*).

MODELO: Para mí, la semana pasada fue bastante activa. Hice mucho ejercicio cada día. También salí cuatro veces con mis amigos. Para Anne, la semana fue menos activa y más solitaria...

NAVEGANDO LA RED

Busca información en la red sobre algún equipo de fútbol en un país hispano. En clase, indica cuántos partidos ganó el equipo la última temporada y un dato (*fact*) interesante más sobre el equipo. Aquí hay algunas sugerencias:

- Real Madrid (España)
- Cobreloa (Chile)
- Boca Juniors (la Argentina)
- Peñarol (el Uruguay)
- Guadalajara (México)

TERCERA PARTE

Vocabulario

Talking About
Special Events
¿Cuándo celebras tu cumpleaños?
❋ **Special Occasions
and Holidays**

Los días festivos

el Día de San Valentín	St. Valentine's Day
(de los Enamorados)	
el Martes de Carnaval	Mardi Gras
el Día de San Patricio	St. Patrick's Day
la Pascua (de los judíos)	Passover
la Pascua (Florida)	Easter
el Día de Acción de Gracias	Thanksgiving
la Fiesta de las Luces	Hanukkah
la Nochebuena	Christmas Eve
la Navidad	Christmas
la Noche Vieja	New Year's Eve

▲ Los brindis (*toasts*) son comunes en las fiestas
hispanas, como esta en Chile.

Algunos brindis populares

«¡Salud,ᵃ amor y dinero, y tiempo
para disfrutarlosᵇ!»

«Por don Pablo:
¡Que cumpla muchos más!»

«Para arriba, para abajo,
para el centro, ¡para adentro!»ᶜ

ᵃ*Health* ᵇ*enjoy
them* ᶜ*Para... Up,
down, to the center,
inside!*

✱ MÁS VOCABULARIO

celebrar	to celebrate
cumplir... años	to be . . . old (*on a birthday*)
regalar	to give (*a gift*)
el brindis	toast
el cumpleaños	birthday
la fiesta (de sorpresa)	(surprise) party
el regalo	gift
la tarjeta	card
¿Cuándo es... ?	When is . . . ?
¿Cuántos (años) cumples?	How old are you (turning)?

≈ Vistazo cultural

Los días festivos en el mundo hispano

Es verdad que todos tenemos un día especial: el cumpleaños. Pero en el mundo hispano también existe el día del santo. En el calendario católico, cada día corresponde a un santo y si tú llevas un nombre igual al del[a] santo, ese día es el día de tu santo. Por ejemplo, una persona llamada Juan o Juanita tiene el mismo nombre que San Juan el Bautista. El día de San Juan es el 24 de junio. Entonces, el día del santo para los Juanes y las Juanitas es el 24 de junio. Así que en el mundo hispano se celebran tu cumpleaños y el día de tu santo.

Muchos creen que el Cinco de

▲ En San Francisco, como en otras partes de los Estados Unidos y el Canadá, el Cinco de Mayo es un día festivo importante para la comunidad mexicoamericana.

Mayo es el día de la independencia de México. La verdad es que el día de la independencia de México es el 16 de septiembre, el día en que los mexicanos se declararon independientes del Imperio Español en 1810 (mil ochocientos diez). El Cinco de Mayo corresponde a otra fecha[b] importante. En 1862 (mil ochocientos sesenta y dos) los franceses invadieron México. El cinco de mayo de ese año, los mexicanos derrotaron[c] a las tropas francesas en la ciudad de Puebla, y todo el país celebró la victoria.

Aunque en el mundo hispano se celebra la Navidad tanto como en los Estados Unidos y el Canadá, en muchos países de habla española el día para intercambiar[d] regalos no es el 25 de diciembre. El día en que las personas se hacen regalos es el 6 de enero, el Día de los Reyes Magos.[e] ¿Por qué? Porque este día marca la llegada de los Reyes Magos con sus regalos para el Niño Jesús.

[a]al... *to that of the* [b]*date* [c]*defeated* [d]*exchanging* [e]Reyes... *Three Wise Men*

¡Exprésate!

Some holidays don't fall on a specific date but rather on the first, second, third, or fourth Monday, Tuesday, and so forth, of a particular month. To express this concept use **el primer, el segundo, el tercer, el cuarto,** or **el último.** For example, **el tercer lunes de febrero es el Día de los Presidentes.**

Actividad A ¿En qué día cae... ?

Indica en qué día cae (*what day is*) cada día festivo.

1. el Día de San Valentín
2. la Navidad
3. la Noche Vieja
4. el Día de San Patricio
5. el Día del Padre
6. el cumpleaños del Dr. Martin Luther King, Jr.
7. el Día de los Veteranos
8. el Día del Trabajo (*Labor*)
9. el Día de la Madre
10. el Día de Acción de Gracias

¡Exprésate!

As you find out about people's birthdays in **Actividad B**, see if you can tell what zodiac sign that person is. Once again, here are the names in Spanish (in alphabetical, not chronological, order).

Acuario	Leo
Aries	Libra
Cáncer	Piscis
Capricornio	Sagitario
Escorpio	Tauro
Géminis	Virgo

Actividad B Mi cumpleaños

Paso 1 Indica lo que pasa regularmente el día de tu cumpleaños.

1. ☐ Recibo muchos/algunos regalos.
2. ☐ Recibo muchas/algunas tarjetas.
3. ☐ Lo anuncio de antemano (*ahead of time*). Así las personas no se olvidan (*don't forget*).
4. ☐ Doy una fiesta.
5. ☐ Salgo con mis amigos.
6. ☐ Los miembros de mi familia me llaman para felicitarme (*congratulate me*).
7. ☐ Mis amigos me llaman para felicitarme.
8. ☐ Lo considero como un día festivo. No voy a clases y no trabajo.
9. ☐ ¿ ?

Paso 2 Presenta a la clase las oraciones apropiadas del **Paso 1.** ¿Pasan todos el cumpleaños más o menos de igual forma?

Paso 3 Utilizando las expresiones apropiadas de **Más vocabulario** en la página 205, trata de encontrar a dos personas en la clase cuyo (*whose*) cumpleaños cae en el mismo mes que el tuyo.

MODELO: E1: ¿Cuándo es tu cumpleaños?
E2: Es el 22 de octubre.
E1: ¡Ah! Entonces, eres Libra, como yo.

Actividad C ¿Es importante?

Paso 1 Por orden de importancia (del 1 al 6), indica si cada día o evento es muy importante (1–2), algo importante (3–4) o poco importante (5–6) para ti.

_____ una ceremonia de graduación

_____ el nacimiento (*birth*) del hijo de un amigo / de un pariente

_____ la muerte (*death*) de una persona célebre

_____ el Día de San Valentín

_____ el Día de San Patricio

_____ el Martes de Carnaval

Paso 2 ¿Qué indican las respuestas sobre la personalidad de una persona?

☐ La persona piensa más en sí misma (*him/herself*) que en los otros.

☐ La persona piensa más en los otros que en sí misma.

Actividad D Un perfil (*profile*) personal

Entrevista a un compañero (una compañera) de clase para hacer un breve perfil de él/ella. Utiliza el siguiente cuadro como guía. Luego, entrégale el perfil a tu profesor(a).

Nombre de la persona: _____

Día de su cumpleaños: _____

　Cómo le gusta celebrarlo: _____

　_____

　_____

Día festivo favorito: _____

　Cómo le gusta celebrarlo: _____

　_____

　_____

Gramática

| ¿Qué hiciste? **Irregular Preterite Forms**

IRREGULAR VERB FORMS IN THE PRETERITE		
VERB	STEM	FORMS (yo, tú, Ud./él/ella, nosotros/as, vosotros/as, Uds./ellos/ellas)
andar	**anduv-**	anduve, anduviste, anduvo, anduvimos, anduvisteis, anduvieron
decir	**dij-**	dije, dijiste, dijo, dijimos, dijisteis, dijeron
estar	**estuv-**	estuve, estuviste, estuvo, estuvimos, estuvisteis, estuvieron
poder	**pud-**	pude, pudiste, pudo, pudimos, pudisteis, pudieron
poner	**pus-**	puse, pusiste, puso, pusimos, pusisteis, pusieron
querer	**quis-**	quise, quisiste, quiso, quisimos, quisisteis, quisieron
saber	**sup-**	supe, supiste, supo, supimos, supisteis, supieron
tener	**tuv-**	tuve, tuviste, tuvo, tuvimos, tuvisteis, tuvieron
traer	**traj-**	traje, trajiste, trajo, trajimos, trajisteis, trajeron
venir	**vin-**	vine, viniste, vino, vinimos, vinisteis, vinieron

Many common verbs have irregular preterite forms. You will notice that the forms in the chart are irregular in that (1) the stem is different from that of the present tense; (2) that there is no stress shift in the **yo, Ud.,** and **él/ella** forms; and (3) that all endings are the same regardless of whether the verb is **-ar, -er,** or **-ir.**

Note the following about some irregular preterites.

1. The verb **saber** in the preterite translates as *to find out* or *to come to know* in English.

   ¿Y cuándo **supiste** eso?   *And when did you find that out?*

2. Verbs whose irregular preterite stems end in **j** or a vowel drop the **i** in the **Uds./ellos/ellas** form: **dijeron, trajeron.**

Another irregular verb is the verb **dar.** It takes regular **-er/-ir** endings in the preterite. There are no accent marks on the **yo** and **Ud./él/ella** forms because they consist of one syllable.

dar: di, diste, dio, dimos, disteis, dieron

✳ MÁS GRAMÁTICA

You learned earlier that **conocer** and **saber** in the preterite are translated as *to meet* and *to find out,* respectively. Here are some other verbs whose meanings change in the preterite.

querer: normally translates as *to want*, but in the preterite it means *to try*

> **Quise** hacerlo.   *I tried to do it.*

no querer: normally translates as *not to want*, but in the preterite it means *to refuse*

> **No quise** hacerlo.   *I refused to do it.*

poder: normally translates as *to be able, can*, but in the preterite it means *to succeed* or *to manage to* (*do something*)

> Por fin **pude** hacerlo.   *Finally I managed to do it.*

no poder: normally translates as *not to be able, can't*, but in the preterite means *to fail* (*in doing something*)

> **No pude** hacerlo.   *I failed to do it.*

DE SOL Y VIENTO

You know that Jaime runs into María again in **Episodio 4**. Look over the exchange here, then select the verbs that you think fit best in each blank.

MARÍA
¡Don Jaime Talavera! ¿Qué hace aquí?
¿Me anda siguiendo?[a]

JAIME
¿Yo? No, es una feliz casualidad.[b] Bueno,
feliz para mí, por lo menos...
No sé si lo es para Ud....

MARÍA
A mí también me hace muy feliz verlo
de nuevo.

JAIME
¡Whoo! Me alegra[c] oír eso...

MARÍA
Ya _____[1] de su viaje. ¿Cómo
le _____[2]?

JAIME
Lo pasé muy bien, gracias.

1. a. volvió   **b.** volviste

2. a. estuvo   **b.** fue

[a]¿Me... *Are you following me?* [b]feliz... *happy coincidence* [c]Me... *I'm glad*

Actividad E ¿A quién se refiere?

Basándote en los episodios anteriores de *Sol y viento,* ¿a qué personaje se refiere cada oración a continuación?

1. Hizo ejercicio.

2. Dijo: «Bonita la muchacha... »

3. Le trajo a Jaime algo de comer.

4. Fue a la universidad a pie (*on foot*).

5. No tuvo éxito (*success*) con su primera visita con Carlos.

6. No vino a la conversación con el contrato firmado.

Actividad F ¿Qué sabes?

Haz las correspondencias correctas para formar oraciones verdaderas.

1. ____ Muchos inmigrantes mexicanos...

2. ____ Los españoles...

3. ____ Washington y Adams...

4. ____ Los mexicanos del siglo XIX...

5. ____ Adán y Eva...

6. ____ Neil Armstrong y Buzz Aldrin...

a. trajeron el caballo (*horse*) al Nuevo Mundo.

b. tuvieron dos hijos.

c. hicieron el primer viaje a la luna.

d. fueron los dos primeros presidentes de los Estados Unidos.

e. no pudieron impedir (*stop*) la ocupación francesa.

f. vinieron a los Estados Unidos durante la Revolución de 1910.

Actividad G Historietas incompletas

Completa las siguientes «historietas» de manera lógica. Luego compáralas con las de otras dos personas. ¿Quién tiene la historieta más imaginativa?

Marta quiso _____,[1] pero no pudo. De repente[a] vino su mamá y _____,[2] arruinando sus planes.

Anoche Juan supo que _____.[3] Pues, claro, en seguida[b] fue a ver a _____[4] para contárselo.[c] ¡Ese Juan es un metiche[d]!

Para mi cumpleaños, Elisa me trajo _____.[5] Cuando la miré perplejo,[e] ella me dijo «_____».[6] En fin, no creí su excusa.

[a]De... *Suddenly* [b]en... *right away* [c]*tell him/her/them about it* [d]*gossip* [e]*perplexed*

Actividad H La Noche Vieja pasada

Paso 1 ¿Qué hicieron tú y tu familia o tú y tus amigos la Noche Vieja pasada? Indica las oraciones que se te aplican.

1. ☐ Dimos una fiesta en casa.
2. ☐ Fuimos a una fiesta.
3. ☐ Fuimos a un bar.
4. ☐ Tuvimos que cancelar nuestros planes.
5. ☐ No hicimos nada en especial.

Paso 2 Comparte tus respuestas con la clase. ¿Cúantos dieron una fiesta? ¿Cuántos no hicieron nada en especial? ¿Qué indican las respuestas en cuanto a la actitud de la clase hacia este día festivo?

Actividad I Entrevista

Paso 1 Utilizando las siguientes preguntas como guía, entrevista a otra persona y apunta sus respuestas.

1. ¿Cuándo es tu cumpleaños?
2. ¿Hiciste algo especial para tu último cumpleaños?
3. ¿Cuánto tiempo estuvieron Uds. allí?
4. ¿A qué hora terminó la fiesta / volviste a casa?

Paso 2 Ahora contesta la siguiente pregunta: «¿Quién lo pasó mejor en su cumpleaños, mi compañero/a de clase o yo?» ¿Por qué? Da algunos ejemplos.

SOL Y VIENTO: Enfoque cultural

En el **Episodio 4,** vas a ver a María colocar carteles[a] para una reunión a favor de los mapuches. Como muchas personas en Latinoamérica, María lucha[b] por los derechos[c] de los grupos indígenas que no tienen voz[d] ni mucha influencia en la política de su país. El activismo por los indígenas no se limita a Chile sino también se observa en México, el Paraguay, Guatemala, el Perú y otros países. Muchas veces estos indígenas no tienen suficiente conocimiento del idioma español, lo cual impide su participación activa en la sociedad. En tales[e] casos necesitan de personas como María que los ayudan a obtener los beneficios que les corresponden según las leyes[f] del país.

▲ Un indígena ecuatoriano

Además, luchan por un sistema de educación bilingüe o, por lo menos, cursos de español como segunda lengua.

[a]colocar... *hanging up posters* [b]*fights* [c]*rights* [d]*voice* [e]*such* [f]*laws*

RESUMEN DE VOCABULARIO

Verbos

andar (*irreg.*) en bicicleta	to ride a bicycle
caminar	to walk
cocinar	to cook
coleccionar (estampillas, monedas)	to collect (stamps, coins)
cumplir... años	to be . . . old (*on a birthday*)
dar (*irreg.*) una fiesta	to throw a party
dar (*irreg.*) un paseo	to take a walk; to stroll
dibujar	to draw
divertir (ie, i)	to entertain
esquiar (esquío)	to ski
estar (*irreg.*) en (buena) forma	to be in (good) shape
fortalecer (zc)	to strengthen
ganar	to win
hacer (*irreg.*) ciclismo estacionario	to ride a stationary bike
hacer (*irreg.*) ejercicio (aeróbico)	to exercise (do aerobics)
hacer (*irreg.*) gimnasia	to work out
levantar pesas	to lift weights
limpiar la casa	to clean the house
nadar	to swim
navegar (gu) en barco	to sail
pasarlo bien/mal	to have a good/bad time
patinar (en línea)	to (inline) skate
picar (qu)	to nibble
pintar	to paint
quemar calorías	to burn calories
rozarse (c) con la gente	to mingle with people
sacar (qu) un vídeo/DVD	to rent a video/DVD
ser (*irreg.*) aficionado/a (a)	to be a fan (of)
sudar	to sweat
trotar	to jog

Cognados: celebrar, competir (i, i), meditar; el golf, el museo, el yoga
Repaso: bailar, correr, leer, perder (ie), regalar, tocar (qu) (el piano, la guitarra), tomar

Sobre los deportes

el campeonato	championship
la cancha (de tenis)	(tennis) court
el equipo	equipment; team
la milla	mile
la natación	swimming
el partido	game, match
la piscina	swimming pool
la pista	track
la rueda de andar	treadmill

Cognados: el/la atleta, el basquetbol, el béisbol, el fútbol, el fútbol americano, el kilómetro, el metro, el tenis, el vólibol
Repaso: el estadio, el gimnasio

Los días festivos

el Día de Acción de Gracias	Thanksgiving
el Día de San Patricio	St. Patrick's Day
el Día de San Valentín (de los Enamorados)	St. Valentine's Day
la Fiesta de las Luces	Hanukkah
el Martes de Carnaval	Mardi Gras
la Navidad	Christmas
la Noche Vieja	New Year's Eve
la Nochebuena	Christmas Eve
la Pascua (de los judíos)	Passover
la Pascua (Florida)	Easter
¿Cuántos (años) cumples?	How old are you (turning)?

Otras palabras y expresiones

el aguafiestas	party pooper
el ajedrez	chess
el brindis	toast
el cumpleaños	birthday
los/las demás	others
la fiesta (de sorpresa)	(surprise) party
el juego	game (*as in chess*)
los ratos libres	free (spare) time
el regalo	gift
la tarjeta	card
anoche	last night
ayer	yesterday
fuerte	strong

Repaso: divertido/a

En casa

OBJETIVOS

IN THIS LESSON, YOU WILL:

- learn how to talk about dwellings and buildings
- continue talking about activities in the past with stem-changing **-ir** verbs in the preterite
- learn how to talk about rooms, furniture, and other items found in a house
- learn how to avoid redundancy by using direct and indirect object pronouns together
- describe typical household chores
- learn some preliminary distinctions between **por** and **para**

In addition, you will watch **Episodio 4** of the film *Sol y viento.*

◄

Los pisos (*apartments*) y casas del Barrio de Santa Cruz en Sevilla, España, son muy impresionantes (*impressive*).

The following media resources are available for *Sol y viento: En breve*

Episodio 4 of *Sol y viento*

Online *Manual de actividades*

Interactive CD-ROM

Online Learning Center Website

PRIMERA PARTE

Vocabulario

Talking About
Buildings and
Where People Live

¿Dónde vives?

Dwellings and Buildings

Lugares

el apartamento	apartment
el barrio / la vecindad	neighborhood
la casa	house; home
la casa particular/privada	private residence
el condominio	condo(minium)
el cuarto	room (*general*)
el edificio	building
el hogar	home (*as in home, sweet home*)
la oficina	office
la residencia	residence
la residencia estudiantil	dormitory
la torre	tower
la vivienda	housing

Las personas

el/la compañero/a de cuarto (casa)	roommate (housemate)
el/la dueño/a	owner; landlord, landlady
el/la inquilino/a	tenant
el/la portero/a	doorperson; building manager
el/la vecino/a	neighbor

▲ El centro de Bogotá, Colombia, tiene edificios altos y modernos.

▲ El centro de Guanajuato, México, está rodeado de (*surrounded by*) barrios pequeños y casas particulares.

✳ MÁS VOCABULARIO

el alquiler	rent
el balcón	balcony
la dirección	address
el piso (*Sp.*)	flat, apartment
el piso, la planta (*Sp.*)	floor (*of a building*)
la vista	view
alquilar	to rent
firmar (un contrato)	to sign (a lease)

≋ Vistazo cultural

¿Primer piso?

En los Estados Unidos, *ground floor* y *first floor* tienden a ser lo mismo. Y en algunos edificios, entre el *ground floor* y el segundo piso, tienen el *mezzanine*. El sistema de nombrar los pisos es diferente en el mundo hispano. Examina los equivalentes a continuación.

En un país hispano	En edificios norteamericanos	En ciertos edificios norteamericanos
la planta baja	first floor, ground floor	first floor, ground floor
el primer piso	second floor	mezzanine
el segundo piso	third floor	second floor
el tercer piso	fourth floor	third floor
el cuarto piso	fifth floor	fourth floor

Así que cuando entras en un ascensor[a] en el mundo hispano, el botón marcado **B** o **PB** no quiere decir *basement* sino[b] **baja (planta baja)** y el botón marcado **1** no se refiere a *ground floor* sino al primer piso (*second floor*).

▲ ¿En qué piso está la recepción del Hotel Bonaparte? ¿Está en la planta baja o en el primer piso?

[a]*elevator* [b]*but rather*

Actividad A ¿A qué se refiere?

El profesor (La profesora) va a leer algunas descripciones. ¿A cuál de las opciones se refiere cada descripción?

1. **a.** el barrio   **b.** el hogar
2. **a.** la dueña   **b.** la inquilina
3. **a.** el edificio   **b.** la residencia estudiantil
4. **a.** la vecina   **b.** la portera
5. **a.** el piso   **b.** la vista
6. **a.** la dirección   **b.** la torre
7. **a.** la casa particular   **b.** el condominio
8. **a.** la vivienda   **b.** el alquiler

Actividad B ¿Cierto o falso?

Indica si cada oración es cierta o falsa para los edificios y viviendas en tu universidad y ciudad.

		CIERTO	FALSO
1.	Si no pagas el alquiler a tiempo, te pueden poner una multa (*fee*).	☐	☐
2.	Para alquilar un apartamento o una casa en esta ciudad, es necesario firmar un contrato de un año.	☐	☐
3.	La residencia estudiantil más alta de la universidad tiene sólo cuatro pisos.	☐	☐
4.	La universidad tiene una torre. Es un campanario (*bell tower*).	☐	☐
5.	Si vives en un apartamento, eres dueño y no inquilino.	☐	☐
6.	No hay barrios peligrosos (*dangerous*) en esta ciudad.	☐	☐
7.	En esta universidad, la Facultad de Psicología tiene su propio (*own*) edificio. No lo comparte (*share*) con otras facultades.	☐	☐
8.	En esta ciudad, $500 por el alquiler de un apartamento de un cuarto es mucho.	☐	☐

NAVEGANDO LA RED

Busca información en la red sobre algún pueblo o ciudad en España que data de (*dates back to*) la Edad Media (*Middle Ages*) o algún pueblo o ciudad colonial en Latinoamérica. Describe la parte central del pueblo o de la ciudad.

Actividad C Un anuncio (*advertisement*)

Paso 1 Con un compañero (una compañera), inventen un anuncio para un apartamento disponible (*available*). Incluyan toda la información necesaria: el número de cuartos, el aquiler, el piso en que está, el tipo de barrio, etcétera.

Paso 2 Los anuncios deben circular en la clase. ¿Ves uno interesante? ¿Qué tiene que te gusta?

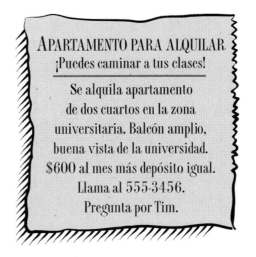

APARTAMENTO PARA ALQUILAR
¡Puedes caminar a tus clases!

Se alquila apartamento
de dos cuartos en la zona
universitaria. Balcón amplio,
buena vista de la universidad.
$600 al mes más depósito igual.
Llama al 555-3456.
Pregunta por Tim.

Actividad D Comparaciones

Paso 1 Mira las fotos en la página 214. ¿Puedes describir las dos ciudades utilizando el vocabulario nuevo? Escribe dos o tres oraciones que describan lo que ves en las fotos.

Paso 2 Algunos estudiantes van a leer sus descripciones. ¿Hay otras oraciones que la clase pueda añadir (*could add*) a las descripciones de estos lugares? ¿Cómo se comparan los dos lugares?

Paso 3 Ahora imagina que una estudiante viene a los Estados Unidos a estudiar por un año. Ha sido aceptada (*She's been accepted*) en dos universidades. Una está en la Ciudad de Nueva York y la otra en Iowa. Entre todos, ¿qué le podrían decir (*could you tell her*) sobre la vivienda, el costo, etcétera, de los dos lugares?

Actividad E Entrevista

Paso 1 Entrevista a otra persona utilizando las siguientes preguntas como guía. Puedes añadir otras preguntas si quieres.

1. Para ti, ¿es necesario vivir cerca de la universidad?
2. ¿Qué prefieres, un apartamento, una residencia estudiantil o una casa?
3. Para ti, ¿es importante el barrio donde vives? ¿Qué barrio o zona de esta ciudad prefieres?
4. ¿Te molestan las alturas (*heights*)? ¿Puedes vivir en un piso alto?
5. ¿Cuánto puedes pagar de alquiler?

Paso 2 Utilizando la información que obtuviste en el **Paso 1,** escribe un breve párrafo sobre las preferencias y necesidades de la persona a quien entrevistaste.

Gramática

No durmió bien.   e → i, o → u Preterite Stem Changes

-ir STEM CHANGES IN THE PRETERITE e → i, o → u			
yo	pedí repetí seguí	**nosotros/as**	pedimos repetimos seguimos
	dormí morí		dormimos morimos
tú	pediste repetiste seguiste	**vosotros/as**	pedisteis repetisteis seguisteis
	dormiste moriste		dormisteis moristeis
Ud.	pidió repitió siguió	**Uds.**	pidieron repitieron siguieron
	durmió murió		durmieron murieron
él/ella	pidió repitió siguió	**ellos/ellas**	pidieron repitieron siguieron
	durmió murió		durmieron murieron

As you have learned, **-ar** and **-er** verbs with stem changes in the present do not have stem changes in the preterite.

¿**P**erdiste algo?	*Did you lose something?*
Ya emp**e**zó la clase.	*Class already started.*

As you saw briefly in the previous lesson, the **-ir** stem-changing verbs do have a stem change in the preterite but only in the **Ud., él/ella,** and the **Uds., ellos/ellas** forms. Verbs whose stem changes from **e → ie** in the present change from **e → i** in the preterite in the forms just mentioned. Similarly, **-ir** verbs that in the present tense have **o → ue** stem changes have the following stem change in the **Ud., él/ella,** and **Uds., ellos/ellas** forms: **o → u.**

MÁS GRAMÁTICA

Here are some other verbs that undergo **e → i** stem changes. You will encounter others throughout *Sol y viento.*

conseguir (*to get, obtain*)*: consiguió, consiguieron
divertir: divirtió, divirtieron
mentir (*to lie, tell a lie*): mintió, mintieron
preferir: prefirió, prefirieron
sentir (*to feel*): sintió, sintieron
servir: sirvió, sirvieron
sugerir (*to suggest*): sugirió, sugirieron
vestirse: se vistió, se vistieron

DE SOL Y VIENTO

In a future episode of *Sol y viento,* you will meet doña Isabel, Carlos' mother. As Carlos talks about running the winery, she reminds him of why he took on the duties he has. Read their exchange and then answer the questions that follow.

ISABEL
Cuando **murió** tu papá, te encargaste de los negocios.[a] Yo ya estaba[b] vieja y tu hermana tenía[c] otros intereses.

CARLOS
Sí. Ella siempre ha tenido[d] otros intereses.

ISABEL
¡Carlos! ¡Estás grande para estar resentido!

1. ¿Se sabe cuándo murió el padre de Carlos?
2. ¿Crees que murió joven o que murió viejo?

[a]te... *you took over the business* [b]*was* [c]*had* [d]ha... *has had*

***Conseguir** + *infinitive* means *to succeed in* (*doing something*).

Actividad F ¿Qué crees tú?

Para cada oración a continuación, indica si es **probable, improbable, posible** o **imposible** según lo que recuerdas de los personajes y la historia de *Sol y viento.*

1. Durante el viaje a Chile, Jaime no durmió. Leyó y trabajó un poco.
2. Cuando conoció a María, Jaime sintió una gran atracción por ella.
3. Carlos sirvió unas copas de vino antes de hablar con Jaime de los negocios porque quería distraerlo (*he wanted to distract him*).
4. Jaime no le pidió un contrato firmado a Carlos porque entendía (*he understood*) que Carlos no lo tenía (*didn't have it*).
5. Los padres de Jaime murieron hace unos años.

Actividad G ¿A quién(es) se refiere?

Paso 1 ¿Puedes identificar a quién(es) se refiere cada oración? Escoge entre las siguientes personas o personajes.

- María Antonieta y Luis XVI
- el Mad Hatter
- Rip Van Winkle
- Butch Cassidy y el Sundance Kid
- Marilyn Monroe
- los Ángeles de Carlitos
- Robin Hood
- Elvis Presley

1. Murió joven, a los 36 años, de un aparente suicidio.
2. Murieron en la guillotina.
3. Murió de un infarto cardíaco (*heart attack*).
4. Consiguió robarles dinero a los ricos para luego dárselo a los pobres.
5. Murieron en la última escena de la película.
6. Durmió 20 años.
7. Sirvió té en una fiesta muy conocida.
8. Divirtieron a muchos televidentes (*TV viewers*) de los años 70.

Paso 2 Inventa una o dos oraciones como las del **Paso 1** y léelas en voz alta. ¿Pueden adivinar los demás a quién(es) se refiere(n)?

Actividad H ¿Cuánto sabes?

¿Crees que sabes mucho de historia? ¿de eventos importantes en los deportes? ¿de hechos (*facts*) triviales relacionados con las películas y las novelas? Contesta cada pregunta a continuación para ver cuánto sabes sobre estos temas.

1. ¿Qué sirvieron los peregrinos (*pilgrims*) el primer Día de Acción de Gracias? ¿Pavo o pato (*duck*)?

2. ¿Qué estrella (*star*) siguieron los Reyes Magos para llegar a Belén (*Bethlehem*)? La del oeste, del norte, del sur o del este?

3. ¿Qué le pidió el Mago de Oz a Dorotea como prueba de la muerte de la bruja (*witch*)? ¿Sus zapatos, su escoba (*broom*) o su sombrero?

4. ¿Qué presidente mintió cuando anunció que no sabía (*he didn't know*) nada del robo (*break-in*) en el Hotel Watergate?

5. ¿Qué consiguió hacer Andre Agassi que no consiguió Pete Sampras? ¿Ganar el trofeo en cada uno de los campeonatos del Grand Slam? ¿O ser la primera persona en ganar dos trofeos seguidos (*back to back*) del Australian Open?

¡Exprésate!

In case you aren't sure about something, you can say

Creo que... or

No estoy seguro/a, pero creo que...

If you are sure, you can say

Eso lo sé muy bien.

and then give your answer.

Actividad I ¿Mienten los políticos (*politicians*)?

Paso 1 Muchas personas dicen que los políticos mienten. Con un compañero (una compañera) de clase, indiquen si las siguientes personas mintieron o no, sobre qué mintieron y si su mentira (*lie*) fue grande o no. Si quieren, pueden hablar de otro político también. El profesor (La profesora) les puede ayudar (*help*) con el vocabulario necesario.

1. Richard Nixon
2. Ronald Reagan
3. Bill Clinton
4. George W. Bush
5. ¿ ?

Paso 2 Cada grupo debe presentar sus ideas a la clase. ¿Están todos de acuerdo?

SEGUNDA PARTE

Vocabulario

Talking About
Things in the House

Es mi sillón favorito.

Furniture and Rooms

Los cuartos y los mueblesᵃ

ᵃ*furniture*

el cartel

la habitación*

el armario

el baño

la cómoda

el estante

el espejo

la lámpara

la ducha

el lavabo

la bañera

el inodoro

la mesita

el escritorio

la cama

la silla

la alfombra

el cuadro

el sillón

la mesa

el sofá

la sala

---

*Other terms for *bedroom* used in various parts of the Spanish-speaking world are **la alcoba**, **el dormitorio**, and **la recámara**.

✳ MÁS VOCABULARIO

la cama matrimonial*	queen bed
la cama sencilla	twin bed
la cocina	kitchen
el comedor	dining room
los pies (metros) cuadrados	square feet (meters)
el tamaño	size
Cognados: el garaje, el jardín, el patio	
amueblado/a	furnished
¿De qué tamaño es... ?	What size is . . . ?
de venta	for sale
se alquila	for rent

▲ 1.

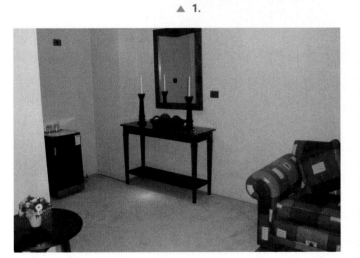

▲ 2.

▲ 3.

Aquí están tres fotos de la *suite* de Jaime en el Hotel Bonaparte en Santiago.
¿Cuántos muebles y objetos del vocabulario nuevo puedes identificar?

---

*In some parts of the Spanish-speaking world, the English words *queen* and *king* have been adopted as bed sizes: **una cama queen, una cama king**.

Actividad A ¿Te importa?

Paso 1 Indica si te importa o no que una casa tenga (*has*) cada una de estas cosas. Añade algo más en los números 9 y 10.

	ME IMPORTA.	NO ME IMPORTA.
1. un armario amplio (de tipo *walk-in*)	☐	☐
2. una cocina grande	☐	☐
3. una bañera sin ducha	☐	☐
4. un espejo largo	☐	☐
5. una habitación privada	☐	☐
6. alfombra de pared a pared (*wall to wall*)	☐	☐
7. una sala aparte (*separate*) del comedor	☐	☐
8. inodoro aparte del resto del baño	☐	☐
9. ¿ ?	☐	☐
10. ¿ ?	☐	☐

Paso 2 Convierte las oraciones en preguntas y busca personas que tengan las mismas respuestas que tú.

MODELO: ¿Te importa tener un inodoro aparte del resto del baño?

Actividad B Busco piso amueblado

Paso 1 Mira el siguiente anuncio. Utiliza el vocabulario nuevo para llenar los espacios en blanco con palabras apropiadas.

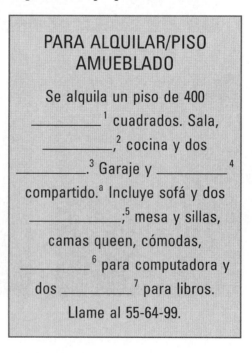

PARA ALQUILAR/PISO
AMUEBLADO

Se alquila un piso de 400
_____ [1] cuadrados. Sala,
_____, [2] cocina y dos
_____. [3] Garaje y _____ [4]
compartido.[a] Incluye sofá y dos
_____; [5] mesa y sillas,
camas queen, cómodas,
_____ [6] para computadora y
dos _____ [7] para libros.
Llame al 55-64-99.

[a]*shared*

Paso 2 Di a la clase si este apartamento parece ser más grande, más pequeño o casi igual de tamaño comparado con tu propia vivienda. Describe las diferencias.

Actividad C ¿Qué tienes?

Paso 1 Combina las frases de las dos columnas para formar oraciones lógicas.

En...   hay...

1. ____ mi mesita   **a.** una mesa con cuatro sillas.
2. ____ mi habitación   **b.** fotos, una lámpara y un reloj despertador.
3. ____ el comedor   **c.** sólo dos sillones. No tengo sofá.
4. ____ la sala   **d.** una cama matrimonial y una cómoda.
5. ____ mi armario   **e.** ropa, cajas (*boxes*) y zapatos.

Paso 2 Indica si las oraciones que formaste en el **Paso 1** son verdaderas para ti o no.

Actividad D Busco compañero/a de casa

Paso 1 Imagina que necesitas mudarte (*to move*) de casa y vas a hablarle a un compañero (una compañera) para ver si Uds. son compatibles o no. Tu decisión no depende de la personalidad de la persona sino de la casa y lo que incluye el precio. Por ejemplo, ¿te importa tener tu propio baño? ¿Necesitas un cuarto amueblado? ¿Qué tienes que necesitas llevar a la nueva casa? ¿Qué tamaño de cuarto esperas tener? ¿Necesitas un armario amplio? Escribe por lo menos cinco preguntas pensando en estas ideas.

Paso 2 Entrevista a varias personas en la clase. ¿Encuentras a la persona y el lugar apropiados? Presenta la información a la clase.

≋ Vistazo cultural

Hogar, dulce hogar

No hay casas o apartamentos «típicos» del mundo hispano. Como en muchos otros países, el tipo de vivienda depende principalmente del lugar geográfico. En las ciudades grandes, predominan los apartamentos y edificios altos. En las zonas rurales y los suburbios, las casas particulares son más prevalentes. Algo que sí es común en el mundo hispano es el concepto del jardín, balcón o terraza. A los hispanos, en general, les gusta tener un lugar fuera de la casa para sentarse[a] y gozar del[b] tiempo. Es frecuente ver casas con patios interiores y balcones llenos[c] de plantas y flores, con sillas cómodas[d] donde la gente puede pasar una tarde con amigos o familiares tomando una bebida y charlando.

[a]*sit down* [b]*gozar... enjoy the* [c]*full*
[d]*comfortable*

▲ ¿Te gustaría (*Would you like*) tener una casa con patio y fuente (*fountain*), como esta en Ponce, Puerto Rico?

Gramática

Ya te lo dije.

Double-Object Pronouns

DOUBLE-OBJECT PRONOUNS
The Indirect Object Precedes the Direct Object

me lo (la, los, las)	nos lo (la, los, las)
te lo (la, los, las)	os lo (la, los, las)
se lo (la, los, las)	se lo (la, los, las)

¿Los libros? **Te los** doy más tarde.	Sí, la lámpara. **¿Nos la** vendes?

le/les → se

¿Le diste el sofá a tu mamá?

Sí. Se lo di la semana pasada.

Mis hermanos quieren los dos sillones que tenemos.

¿Por qué no se los regalamos de sorpresa?

It is typical to use two object pronouns together to avoid redundancy.

> Do you have my book?
>
> Yes. I'll give it to you right now.

In the preceding exchange, the response includes a direct object pronoun, *it,* and an indirect object pronoun, *you.* In Spanish, when both direct and indirect object pronouns appear together, the indirect object pronoun always precedes the direct object pronoun.

> ¿Tienes mi libro?
>
> Sí. Ahora mismo **te lo** doy.

The order is always indirect object followed by direct object no matter whether the pronouns appear before the verb, as in the above example, or are attached to the end of an infinitive.

> ¿Tienes mi libro?
>
> Sí, pero no quiero dár**telo** ahora.

When both indirect and direct object pronouns begin with the letter **l** (i.e., **le/les** and **lo, la, los, las**), the indirect object changes to **se**. This is not a reflexive construction. Look at the chart to see how this works.

There are several other points to keep in mind about double-object pronouns.

- Given that **se** can refer to both singular and plural indirect objects, it is often accompanied by a phrase with **a** that explains who the indirect object is if context does not make the meaning clear.

  Ya **se** lo di **a mi hermano.**

  Se la escribimos **a mis padres.**

- With the verb **decir,** it is typical to use **lo** when a direct object is implied, that is, that something was said.

  ¿No te **lo dije**?   *Didn't I tell you?* (lit: *Didn't I tell it to you?*)

- Remember that these pronouns are not subjects of the verb, so **se** does not translate as *you/he/she/them* but rather as *to* or *for you/him/her/them.*

COMUNICACIÓN ÚTIL

The use of two pronouns with **decir** is common in Spanish. Examine the following sentences.

Ya te lo dije.   *I already told (it to) you.*

¿Me lo vas a decir?   *Are you going to tell me (it)?*

The **lo** represents the "thing" that was said or is to be said. Note that the pronoun is always masculine singular.

DE SOL Y VIENTO

At the end of his tour of the winery, Jaime notes the deep feelings Traimaqueo has about wine, wine making, and the Sol y viento vineyard. Read the following exchange and then answer the questions.

TRAIMAQUEO
¡El vino es un regalo de los dioses,[a] don Jaime! ¡Algo maravilloso! Como decía[b] el poeta, don Pablo Neruda:
«Vino color de día,
vino color de noche,
vino con pies de púrpura
o sangre de topacio,[c]
vino... »

JAIME
Ya _____ lo dije, señor. Su pasión es evidente.

Which indirect object pronoun do you think Jaime uses here, **te** or **se**? What does this sentence mean literally?

[a]*gods* [b]*said* [c]*sangre... topaz blood*

Actividad E ¿Qué pasó?

Escoge la respuesta correcta según lo que recuerdas de *Sol y viento*.

1. ¿Qué hizo María con la tarjeta que encontró Jaime en el parque?
   a. Se la dio.
   b. Se la quitó (*She took it away*).
2. Cuando Jaime habló con Carlos por teléfono, ¿le dio su número en el hotel?
   a. Sí, se lo dio.
   b. No, no se lo dio.
3. Al final del **Episodio 2,** ¿qué hizo Jaime con el papelito de la suerte que decía «El amor es un torbellino»?
   a. Se lo dio a María.
   b. Se lo dio a Mario.
4. ¿A quién le dijo Jaime «Lo veo mañana, como a las diez»?
   a. Se lo dijo a María.
   b. Se lo dijo a Mario.

Actividad F Preguntas

Paso 1 Escoge las respuestas que se te aplican a ti.

1. ¿Te dan dinero tus padres o amigos cuando lo necesitas?
   a. Sí. Me lo dan sin problema.
   b. Depende. Me lo dan sólo cuando es algo urgente.
   c. No. Nunca me lo dan.
2. ¿Te piden dinero tus hijos o amigos cuando lo necesitan?
   a. Sí. Me lo piden porque tenemos relaciones muy estrechas (*we're very close*).
   b. Depende. Me lo piden, pero les da vergüenza (*shame*).
   c. No. Nunca me lo piden.

Paso 2 Ahora escoge las respuestas para continuar las ideas del **Paso 1.**

1. ¿Se lo pides frecuentemente? (el dinero a tus padres o amigos)
   a. Sí. Se lo pido con frecuencia.
   b. Sólo se lo pido de vez en cuando.
   c. Nunca se lo pido.
2. ¿Se lo das? (el dinero a tus hijos o amigos)?
   a. Sí. Se lo doy sin problema.
   b. Sólo se lo doy si puedo.
   c. No. No se lo doy. Creo que causa problems.

Paso 3 Comparte tus respuestas con otras personas. ¿Hay algunas tendencias comunes entre los miembros del grupo?

Actividad G ¿Se lo/la pasas?

Imagina que es hora de hacer las cosas a continuación. ¿Las haces tú o se las pasas a tu compañero/a de cuarto (o a otra persona que vive contigo)?

1. limpiar el garaje

    a. Lo limpio yo.

    b. Se lo paso a _____.

2. limpiar la cocina

    a. La limpio yo.

    b. Se la paso a _____.

3. lavar los platos (*to wash the dishes*)

    a. Los lavo yo.

    b. Se los paso a _____.

4. mover el sofá

    a. Lo muevo yo.

    b. Se lo paso a _____.

5. pagar las cuentas

    a. Las pago yo.

    b. Se las paso a _____.

Actividad H ¿Dónde está?

Esta actividad consiste de un juego.

1. La clase va a dividirse en dos grupos, A y B. Una persona del grupo A y otra del grupo B deben ir al frente de la clase. Estas personas serán (*will be*) «los capitanes» de sus respectivos grupos.

2. A cada persona, menos a los capitanes, se le va a dar un papel con el nombre de algún objeto de casa (por ejemplo, la alfombra, el espejo, la lámpara, etcétera). Esta información (nombre de la persona y el objeto) se verá (*will be displayed*) en la pizarra también.

3. Los capitanes deben cerrar los ojos o no mirar a los demás.

4. Mientras los capitanes no miran, los demás deben hablar con otras personas (o hacer algún tipo de ruido) y, si quieren, pueden intercambiar sus «objetos».

5. Luego los capitanes abrirán (*will open*) los ojos y por turnos van a escoger a personas de su grupo diciendo: «Barbara, el profesor (la profesora) te dio el cartel. Lo tienes todavía / Se lo diste a otra persona», dependiendo de lo que el capitán crea (*believes*).

6. El objetivo: el grupo del capitán que primero se equivoque (*is wrong*) tres veces, pierde.

¡BONO! Si el capitán adivina (*guesses*) que una persona le pasó el objeto a otra persona y también *adivina a quién*, a su grupo se le va a asignar un bono. Entonces, si hace un error después, el bono cancela ese error. No se toma como error si el capitán no adivina el nombre de la persona que recibió el objeto.

TERCERA PARTE

Vocabulario

Talking About
Domestic Tasks

¿Te gusta lavar la ropa?

Los quehaceres domésticos[a]

Domestic Chores and Routines

[a]Los… *Household chores*

la cafetera   lavar los platos   el microondas   la estufa

la nevera

el refrigerador

el horno

el lavaplatos

sacar (qu) la basura

✳ **MÁS VOCABULARIO**

los aparatos domésticos	household appliances
los productos de limpieza	cleaning products
el detergente	detergent
el jabón	soap
la lejía	bleach
las toallas de papel	paper towels

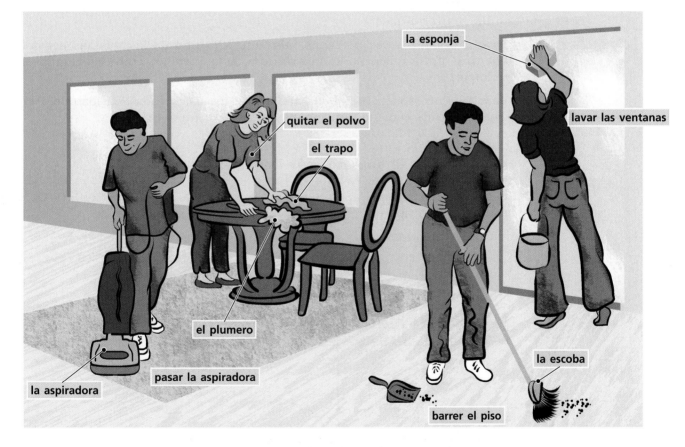

fregar (ie) (gu)	to scrub
hacer (*irreg.*) **la cama**	to make the bed
limpiar la casa (entera)	to clean the (whole) house
pintar las paredes	to paint the walls
poner (*irreg.*) **las cosas en orden**	to put things in order
pulir	to polish

Actividad A   ¿Lo quieres hacer?

Paso 1   Indica lo que piensas de cada actividad, poniendo un círculo alrededor del número apropiado de la escala a continuación. Nota: **odiar** = *to hate.*

	ODIO HACERLO.	NO ME IMPORTA HACERLO.	ME GUSTA HACERLO.
1. pasar la aspiradora	1	2	3
2. lavar los platos	1	2	3
3. lavar las ventanas	1	2	3
4. planchar la ropa	1	2	3
5. quitar el polvo	1	2	3
6. limpiar el inodoro	1	2	3
7. lavar la ropa	1	2	3
8. limpiar el horno	1	2	3
9. sacar la basura	1	2	3
10. barrer el piso	1	2	3

Paso 2   Busca a dos personas, una que odia una de las mismas actividades que tú y otra a quien no le importa una de las mismas actividades que a ti no te importa.

Paso 3   Entre todos, indiquen cuándo se debe hacer cada actividad del **Paso 1:** cada día, cada semana, en semanas alternas o una vez al mes.

Actividad B   El aparato más importante

Paso 1   Clasifica cada aparato según las categorías a continuación. **¡OJO!** Solamente pueden aparecer en la misma categoría tres aparatos.

la aspiradora	la nevera	la secadora
la cafetera	el refrigerador	la plancha eléctrica
el microondas	la lavadora	el lavaplatos

INDISPENSABLES (*essential*)	IMPORTANTES	NO SON NECESARIOS

Paso 2   Todos deben compartir sus ideas. ¿Hay consenso entre todos? ¿Qué indican sus selecciones?

Actividad C Los productos de limpieza

Indica para qué sirve cada producto y luego di si lo utilizas o no.

MODELOS: Eso sirve para limpiar el baño. (No) Lo utilizo porque...
Ese es un tipo de _____. (No) Lo utilizo porque...

1. Windex
2. Soft Scrub
3. Dawn
4. Lemon Pledge
5. Clorox
6. Bounty
7. Tide

Actividad D ¿Quién hace qué?

Paso 1 Imagina que compartes un cuarto o una casa con una persona de la clase. ¿Quién hace qué en la casa? Vuelvan a la lista de quehaceres domésticos en las páginas 230–231 y hagan un plan indicando quién hace qué y cuándo.

MODELO: E1: ¿No te importa limpiar el baño? Porque a mí no me gusta.
E2: No. No me importa. ¿Lo hago una vez a la semana?

Paso 2 Una de las parejas (*pairs*) debe presentar su plan a la clase. ¿Les parece razonable a los demás? ¿Es justa la distribución del trabajo? ¿Es suficiente la frecuencia con que se hace cada actividad?

Vistazo cultural

Ayudar a mamá

En muchos lugares del mundo hispano es típico que las niñas ayuden a su mamá con los quehaceres domésticos, mientras que los hombres y los niños se ocupan de otras cosas. Es poco frecuente, por ejemplo, ver a un niño lavar platos o limpiar el polvo. En fin, «cuidar la casa» es trabajo de la mujer mucho más que del hombre. Y en los hoteles, igual que en este y en otros países, los quehaceres domésticos son reservados casi exclusivamente para las mujeres.

Claro, con el tiempo y la modernización, las cosas cambian. Las jóvenes parejas[a] en las ciudades grandes hoy tienden a compartir[b] los quehaceres, sobre todo si la mujer tiene una ocupación profesional fuera de la casa. Y cada vez más,[c] los niños tanto como las niñas aprenden a utilizar muchos aparatos domésticos y, en algunos casos, hasta a cocinar.

▲ En México, los quehaceres domésticos suelen ser dominio de la mujer.

[a]*couples* [b]*share* [c]*cada... more and more*

Gramática

Talking About What
Something Is For

¿Para mí? Introduction to **por** Versus **para**

The prepositions **por** and **para** can be confusing, especially given that both can be translated into English as *for.*

Lo hice **por** mi familia. ⎫
Lo hice **para** mi familia. ⎭   *I did it for my family.*

What's the difference? In such cases, the general distinction is one of motivation versus outcome. The use of **por** in the first example implies that the speaker was motivated by his family. In this case, the sentence could also be translated as *I did it on behalf of my family* or *I did it because (on account) of my family.* The use of **para** in the second example suggests the speaker did something for which his family would receive some benefit. In this case, there is no other translation in English except *for.* So, the rule of thumb is that if you can substitute *because of, on account of,* and *on behalf of* for the word *for* and your meaning is retained, then the equivalent in Spanish is **por.**

The distinction becomes clear when one compares the compounding of the two prepositions with **que.** Note the English equivalents.

Lo hago **porque** eres mi amigo.   *I do it because you are my friend.* (The friendship is motivating my behavior.)

Lo hago **para que** seas* mi amigo.   *I do it so that you'll be my friend.* (There is a desired outcome.)

When the meaning of *for* is similar to *in lieu of, instead of, in place of,* or something similar, as in trading one thing for another, **por** is used.

Te cambio la cafetera **por** el microondas.

I'll trade you my coffeemaker for your microwave.

In terms of physical or metaphorical space, as well as time, **por** is used to indicate passage *through* or *by way of* something. **Para** functions much like the preposition **a** and implies a destination (again, an outcome) or goal.

Pasé **por** Chicago **para** llegar a Nueva York.

I went to New York by way of Chicago.

Voy **para** Guanajuato.

I'm going to Guanajuato.

Estudié **por** la noche.

I studied during the night.

Tengo que entregar esto **para** mañana.

I have to turn this in by tomorrow.

---

*The use of **para que** requires a verb form called the subjunctive that you will study later.

SOME CONTRASTS BETWEEN *por* AND *para*

With People

por = motivo (*on behalf of, on account of*)
Lo hago **por** mi hermano.

para = destino
Este regalo es **para** mi hermano.

With Things

por = cambio (*in lieu of, instead of*)
Sustituimos *Nutrasweet* **por** el azúcar.

para = destino
Esta taza (*cup*) es **para** café.

In Space and Time

por = transición (*through, by way of, during*)
Pasamos **por** Chicago.
Lo puedes hacer **por** la tarde.

para = destino (*to, by a determined time*)
Vamos **para** Chicago.
Lo voy a hacer **para** las 2:00.

✳ MÁS GRAMÁTICA

Subject pronouns can be used with most prepositions, as in **para él, para Ud., por ellos, por vosotros,** and so forth. The exceptions are **yo** and **tú.** After prepositions, the special pronouns **mí** and **ti** are required. With the preposition **con,** the endings **-migo** and **-tigo** are added.

—Esto es **para ti.**   —¿Quieres ir **conmigo?**
—¿**Para mí?** ¡Gracias!   —No, no puedo ir **contigo.**

Here is a summary of common prepositions. You already know most of them.

a	to; at	**para**	for; to
con	with	**por**	for; because of
de	of; from	**sin**	without
en	in; at; on	**sobre**	about; over

🎞 DE SOL Y VIENTO

Just before Jaime leaves the winery, Traimaqueo presents him and Mario with bottles of wine on behalf of Carlos. Read what Traimaqueo says and select whether **Ud.** or **ti** should be placed in the blanks.

TRAIMAQUEO
Don Carlos quiere hacerles un regalito. Sí.
(*a Jaime*) Un merlot **para** _____... (*a Mario*) Y
un cabernet sauvignon **para** _____.

In **Episodio 4** there is also an exchange in which Jaime asks María about a poster she is hanging. How would you translate **por** in María's response?

MARÍA
Bueno, además de ser[a] profesora, trabajo **por** los derechos del pueblo mapuche.

[a]además... *besides being a*

Actividad E Por...

Escoge la respuesta que complete mejor cada oración. Después, explica el uso de **por.**

   1. Carlos quiere vender la viña por...
       a. su propios intereses.
       b. el bien de la familia.

   2. Jaime hace su visita a la viña por...
       a. la mañana.
       b. la tarde.

   3. Para ir al Valle del Maipo, Jamie y Mario tuvieron que pasar por...
       a. unas colinas (*hills*).
       b. un desierto.

   4. Traimaqueo le da a Jaime un tour por...
       a. la bodega (*wine cellar*) y las viñas.
       b. las viñas solamente.

Actividad F ¿Por o para?

Escoge la mejor opción en cada situación.

   1. Un soldado (*soldier*) levanta la bandera (*flag*) de su país. ¿Qué dice el soldado?
       a. ¡Por mi patria!   **b.** ¡Para mi patria!

   2. Una persona acaba de comprar algo que su amigo admira. La persona le dice entonces:
       a. Toma (*Here*). Es por ti.   **b.** Toma. Es para ti.

   3. Llegas a casa con un detergente. Luego recuerdas que ese detergente es malo para el medio ambiente (*environment*). Vuelves a la tienda y le dices al empleado:
       a. Debo cambiar (*exchange*) este detergente por otro.
       b. Debo cambiar este detergente para otro.

   4. Alguien llega a tu casa con una gran cantidad de ajos (*garlic*). Le preguntas para qué y te contesta:
       a. Es bueno por la salud (*health*).   **b.** Es bueno para la salud.

   5. Hay una reunión importante de estudiantes. Una persona bastante egoísta y desagradable está presente, pero no contribuye nada a la discusión. Entonces, tú le preguntas algo, y él te responde:
       a. Déjame en paz. (*Leave me alone.*) No estoy aquí por ti.
       b. Déjame en paz. No estoy aquí para ti.

Actividad G Rutas y destinos

Paso 1 Completa cada oración con información verdadera o falsa.

   1. Para llegar a la biblioteca desde (*from*) aquí, es necesario pasar por _____.

   2. Para llegar a la librería desde aquí, es necesario pasar por _____.

   3. Yo vivo en _____. Para llegar a mi casa desde aquí es más fácil pasar por _____.

Paso 2 Presenta tus oraciones a la clase. ¿Pueden decir los demás si cada oración es cierta o falsa?

Paso 3 Completa otra vez cada oración con información real o imaginaria.

1. Mañana salgo para _____. Necesito _____. Quiero _____.

2. La próxima semana salgo para _____. Tengo boletos para ver _____.

Paso 4 Presenta tus oraciones a la clase. ¿Pueden decir los demás si lo que dice cada oración es real o imaginario?

Actividad H Cambios

Paso 1 Imagina que estás en varias situaciones en que puedes cambiar una cosa por otra. Indica si lo haces o no.

1. Mañana hay que entregar una composición importante. Un amigo necesita tu ayuda, pero tú sabes que ese tipo de ayuda no es permitido. Tu amigo te dice «Te cambio un DVD por tu ayuda.» ¿Lo aceptas?

2. Te gusta mucho una camisa que tiene un amigo. ¿Qué ofreces cambiar por esa camisa?

3. Necesitas pintar las paredes de tu casa. ¿Qué cambias con tu amigo por su ayuda? ¿Una cena? ¿Otra cosa?

Paso 2 Compara tus ideas con las de otra persona. ¿En qué coinciden?

⬤ Enfoque lingüístico

Las preposiciones

Prepositions are called that because they are "preposed" (i.e, placed in front of something). Prepositions are generally followed by nouns (think of nouns as representatives of some entity or thing in the real world) because prepositions show the relationship of a noun to verbs and other nouns. In Spanish, for example, the preposition **de** signals, among other things, ownership between one entity and something else (**el sillón favorito *de* mi papá**) or direction away from an entity (**salió *del* apartamento**).

Some languages don't have prepositions—or at least have fewer than languages like Spanish and English—and signal such relationships through inflections on nouns or what are called *postpositions.* Nahuatl, the language of the Aztecs and one that is still spoken in certain areas of Mexico, is a language of this type. Note the differences with Spanish.

Spanish	Nahuatl
la casa	cal-li
de la casa	cal-pa
en la casa	cal-co
sobre la casa	cal-pan
con la casa	cal-tica

Whereas in Spanish you are learning to pay attention to the ends of verbs for lots of information, in Nahuatl you would also have to pay attention to the ends of nouns.

SOL Y VIENTO

Antes de ver el episodio

Actividad A ¿Qué recuerdas?

¿Qué recuerdas hasta el momento? Escribe el nombre de los personajes apropiados en los espacios.

1. Después de correr, _____ compró una fortuna.
2. Al leer (*Upon reading*) su fortuna, se chocó con (*he bumped into*) _____, una profesora de antropología.
3. _____ lo llevó a la viña «Sol y viento». Allí habló con _____ sobre la venta de la viña.
4. No pudo ver a _____. _____ le dijo a Jaime que ella se fue a Santiago.

Activdad B Repaso

Revisa las escenas en las varias secciones **De *Sol y viento*** en esta lección para comprender mejor lo que vas a ver en el episodio.

Actividad C ¿Qué falta?

En este episodio, Jaime oye a Traimaqueo decir que doña Isabel lo espera en la casa. Lee el diálogo entre Jaime y Traimaqueo.

YOLANDA: Oye, viejo.* ¿Vas a llegar muy tarde?
TRAIMAQUEO: Un poquito. La señora Isabel me espera en la casa.
JAIME: Creía que la señora Isabel estaba[†] en Santiago.
TRAIMAQUEO: No, no, no. La señora Isabel no hace muchos viajes en estos días. _____.

¿Qué razón crees que va a ofrecer Traimaqueo para explicar por qué doña Isabel no hace muchos viajes?

a. La señora está muy ocupada (*busy*) con la viña.
b. La señora no está de muy buena salud (*health*).

Actividad D El episodio

Ahora mira el episodio. Si hay algo que no entiendes bien, puedes volver a ver la escena en cuestión.

---

*Viejo/a is a term of endearment often used among people who have known each other for a long time. It is used more typically among married people.
[†]Estaba is a past-tense verb form you will learn in the next lesson. In this context, it means (*she*) *was*.

Después de ver el episodio

Actividad A   ¿Qué recuerdas?

Contesta cada pregunta sobre el **Episodio 4.**

1. ¿Quién le dio un tour de la viña a Jaime? ¿Los acompañó Mario?
2. Cuando Jaime oyó que la señora Isabela estaba en casa, decidió ir a verla en seguida. ¿Sí o no?
3. ¿Le dijo Carlos la verdad a Jaime? ¿Sí o no?
4. ¿Para quién compró Jaime la figurita del espíritu mapuche?

Actividad B   ¿Lo captaste?

Ahora verifica tu respuesta a la **Actividad C** de **Antes de ver el episodio.** Puedes ver esa escena de nuevo si quieres.

Actividad C   Usando el contexto

¿Pudiste deducir el significado de las palabras y expresiones que aparecen *en letra cursiva,* según el contexto en que aparecen?

1.   TRAIMAQUEO: Pasemos a la viña, *¿le parece?*
2.   JAIME: ¿Tiene algún significado esta figurita? ... *¿A cuánto me sale?*
   TENDERA (*Shopkeeper*): Diecinueve mil quinientos pesos.
           JAIME: Perfecto. *Me la llevo.*

Actividad D   En resumen

Completa la siguiente narración con las palabras y expresiones apropiadas de la lista a la derecha.

En este episodio, Jaime _____[1] la viña «Sol y viento» gracias a un tour que le da Traimaqueo. Al final del tour, Traimaqueo recita parte de un _____[2] sobre el vino, demostrando[a] su _____[3] por el vino. Jaime llega a saber que Carlos no es una persona honesta, pues le mintió sobre su _____.[4] Más tarde, Jaime tiene un encuentro _____[5] con María. Ella está en el mercado colocando[b] anuncios en apoyo[c] del _____.[6] Jaime le da una sorpresa: una figurita del _____[7] protector de los mapuches. ¿Cómo crees que van las relaciones entre Jaime y María?

agradable
conoce
espíritu (*m.*)
madre
pasión (*f.*)
poema (*m.*)
pueblo mapuche

[a]*showing* [b]*hanging* [c]*support*

Detrás de la cámara

Who is Traimaqueo? Having worked for the winery ever since he was young (as did his father), Traimaqueo is close to doña Isabel, but he is not considered a "member" of the family. He has little respect for Carlos but says nothing. Part Mapuche, he has learned to have patience and also that bad situations work themselves out. He is a simple man, but not stupid and certainly not ignorant of what goes on around him. In fact, he most likely has an idea about why Jaime is visiting.

RESUMEN DE VOCABULARIO

Verbos

alquilar	to rent
conseguir (i, i) (g)	to get, obtain
conseguir + *infin.*	to succeed in (*doing something*)
firmar	to sign
mentir (ie, i)	to lie, tell a lie
morir (u, ue)	to die
odiar	to hate
sentir (ie, i)	to feel
sugerir (ie, i)	to suggest

Repaso: repetir (i, i), vestirse (i, i)

Los cuartos, muebles y aparatos domésticos

el balcón	balcony
el baño	bathroom
la alfombra	rug; carpet
la bañera	bathtub
la ducha	shower
el espejo	mirror
el inodoro	toilet
el lavabo	(bathroom) sink
la cocina	kitchen
la cafetera	coffeemaker
la estufa	stove
el horno	oven
el lavaplatos	dishwasher
el microondas	microwave
la nevera	freezer
el refrigerador	refrigerator
el comedor	dining room
la habitación	bedroom
el armario	closet
la cama (matrimonial, sencilla)	(queen, twin) bed
el cartel	poster
la cómoda	dresser
el estante	bookshelf
la lámpara	lamp
la mesita	end table
la sala	living room
el cuadro	painting
el sillón	armchair
el sofá	sofa

Cognados: el garaje, el jardín, el patio
Repaso: el escritorio, la mesa, la silla

Los quehaceres domésticos

barrer el piso	to sweep the floor
fregar (ie) (gu)	to scrub
hacer (*irreg.*) **la cama**	to make the bed
lavar (los platos)	to wash (the dishes)
limpiar la casa (entera)	to clean the (whole) house
pasar la aspiradora	to vacuum
pintar las paredes	to paint the walls
planchar la ropa	to iron the clothing
poner (*irreg.*) **las cosas en orden**	to put things in order
pulir	to polish
quitar el polvo	to dust
sacar (qu) la basura	to take out the garbage
la aspiradora	vacuum cleaner
la escoba	broom
la esponja	sponge
el jabón	soap
la lavadora	washing machine
la lejía	bleach
la plancha	iron
el plumero	feather duster
los productos de limpieza	cleaning products
la secadora	dryer
las toallas de papel	paper towels
el trapo	rag

Cognado: el detergente
Repaso: la ropa, la ventana

La vivienda

la casa	house; home
la casa particular/privada	private residence
el compañero/a de cuarto (casa)	roommate (housemate)
el contrato	lease
la dirección	address
el/la dueño/a	owner; landlord, landlady
el hogar	home (*as in home, sweet home*)
el/la inquilino/a	tenant
los pies (metros) cuadrados	square feet (meters)
el piso	flat, apartment (*Sp.*)

el piso / la planta (*Sp.*)	floor (*of a building*)
el/la portero/a	doorperson; building manager
el tamaño	size
la vecindad	neighborhood
el/la vecino/a	neighbor
la vista	view

Cognados: el apartamento, el condominio, la residencia
Repaso: el alquiler, el barrio, el edificio, la oficina, la residencia estudiantil, la torre

Otras palabras y expresiones

amueblado/a	furnished
mí	me (*obj. of prep.*)
por	for; because of
sin	without
sobre	about; over
ti	you (*obj. of prep.*)
¿De qué tamaño es... ?	What size is . . . ?
de venta	for sale
se alquila	for rent

EPISODIO 5

LECCIÓN 5A

LECCIÓN 5B

Un día perfecto

Jaime y María suben[a] al Cerro[b] San Cristóbal en el funicular. ¿Crees que lo pasan bien? ¿De qué están hablando? ¿Qué van a hacer cuando llegan a la cima[c]?

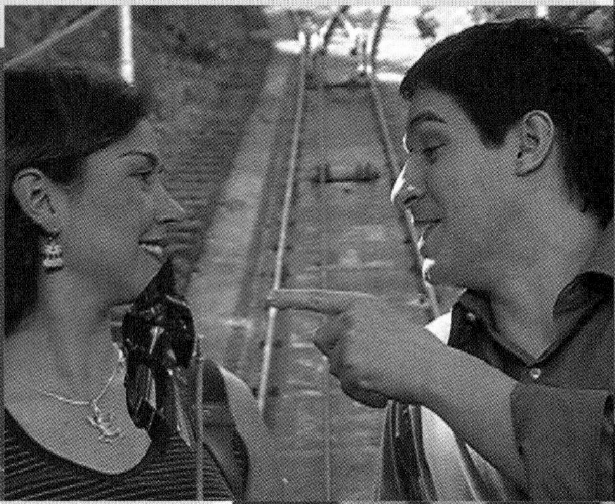

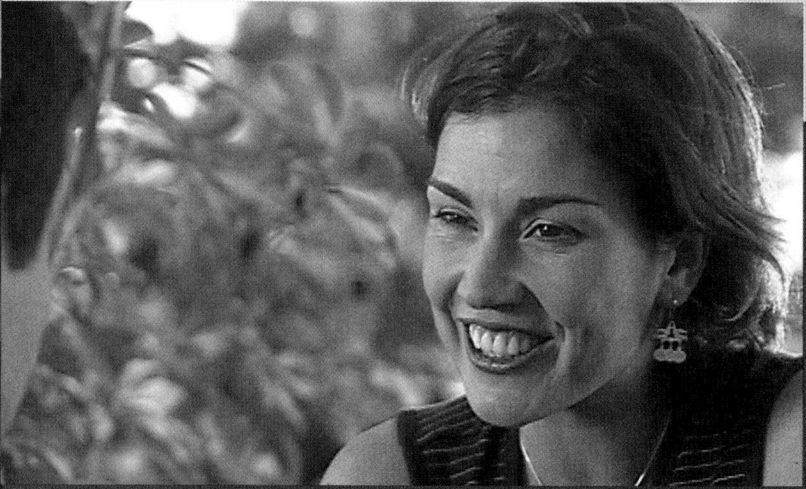

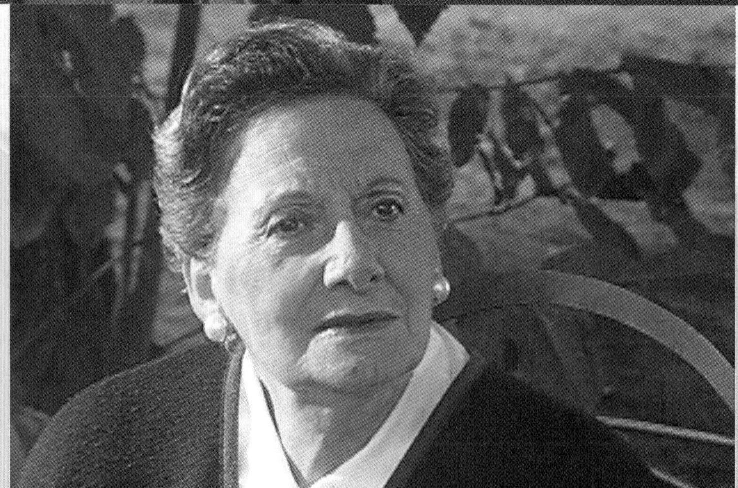

MARÍA: Tú eres gente de la tierra, como los mapuches.

JAIME: ¿Por qué como los mapuches?

MARÍA: *Mapu* significa «tierra». *Che* significa «gente». «Gente de la tierra», como tu familia.

En este episodio vas a conocer a doña Isabel, la madre de Carlos. ¿De qué crees que están hablando ella y su hijo? ¿Crees que ella sabe algo de la venta de «Sol y viento»? ¿Está ella de buen o mal humor[d]?

[a]*go up* [b]*Hill* [c]*top* [d]de... *in a good or bad mood*

La tecnología y yo

OBJETIVOS

IN THIS LESSON, YOU WILL LEARN:

- words and expressions associated with computers and the Internet
- more verbs like **gustar** to talk about what interests you, bothers you, and so forth
- to talk about useful electronic devices
- about reflexive pronouns and their uses
- to talk about your pastimes and activities now and when you were younger
- about imperfect verb forms and how to use them to talk about what you used to do

In addition, you will prepare for **Episodio 5** of the film *Sol y viento.*

◄

¿Usas una agenda electrónica? ¿Cuáles son otros aparatos electrónicos que sueles usar?

The following media resources are available for *Sol y viento: En breve*

Episodio 5 of *Sol y viento*

Online *Manual de actividades*

Interactive CD-ROM

Online Learning Center Website

Vocabulario

Mi computadora	**Computers and Computer Use** ✳

La computadora*

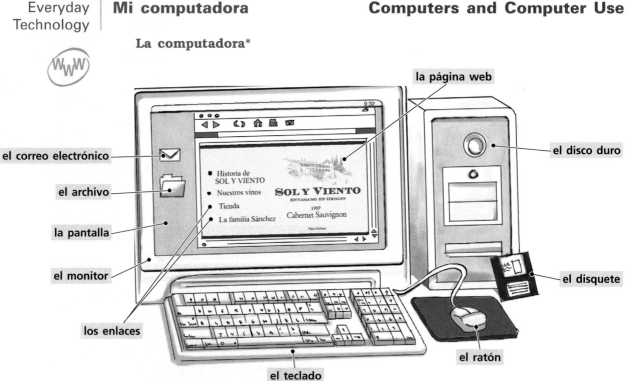

- la página web
- el correo electrónico
- el archivo
- la pantalla
- el monitor
- los enlaces
- el teclado
- el disco duro
- el disquete
- el ratón

Historia de
SOL Y VIENTO
- Nuestros vinos
- Tienda
- La familia Sánchez

SOL Y VIENTO
ENVASADO EN ORIGEN
1997
Cabernet Sauvignon

✳ MÁS VOCABULARIO

la contraseña	password
el Internet / la red	Internet
el mensaje	message
el módem	modem
apagar (gu)	to turn off
conectar	to connect
congelarse	to freeze up (*screen*)
copiar	to copy
descargar (gu)	to download
encender (ie)	to turn on (*machines*)
enviar (envío) / mandar	to send
guardar (documentos)	to save (documents)
hacer (*irreg.*) clic	to click
hacer (*irreg.*) una búsqueda	to do a search
navegar (gu) la red	to surf the Web

*In Spain, **el ordenador** is used for *computer*.

≋ Vistazo cultural

Periódicos hispanos en el Internet

Una de las muchas ventajas[a] del Internet es que uno puede informarse de lo que está pasando en otros países del mundo. Además, es posible informarse de noticias[b] en los Estados Unidos, pero desde otra perspectiva. Muchos periódicos de los países hispanos tienen versiones electrónicas de sus publicaciones. En algunos casos es necesario pagar una tarifa[c] para poder leer los artículos de ciertos periódicos, pero el acceso para la mayoría es gratis.[d] A continuación hay una lista de periódicos en español.

PAÍS	PERIÓDICO	PAÍS	PERIÓDICO
la Argentina	*Clarín*	Honduras	*La Tribuna*
Bolivia	*La Razón*	México	*Reforma*
Chile	*El Mercurio*	Nicaragua	*El Nuevo Diario*
Colombia	*El Tiempo*	Panamá	*El Siglo*
Costa Rica	*La Nación*	el Paraguay	*La Nación*
Cuba	*La Nueva Cuba*	el Perú	*Diario La Razón*
el Ecuador	*Hoy*	Puerto Rico	*El Nuevo Día*
El Salvador	*El Mundo*	la República Dominicana	*Diario Libre*
España	*El País*	el Uruguay	*El País*
Guatemala	*Prensa Libre*	Venezuela	*El Nacional*
la Guinea Ecuatorial	*La Gaceta*		

Además de noticias nacionales e internacionales, estos periódicos presentan el tiempo regional, información cultural y otra información de interés. ¡Entérate de[e] lo que pasa en el mundo hispano!

[a]*advantages* [b]*news* [c]*fee* [d]*free* [e]¡Entérate... *Find out about*

Actividad A Asociaciones

Empareja cada sustantivo con el verbo apropiado. **¡OJO!** Algunos verbos van con más de un sustantivo.

1. _____ el teclado		**a.** navegar
2. _____ un mensaje		**b.** hacer clic
3. _____ la red		**c.** congelarse
4. _____ un programa		**d.** escribir
5. _____ el ratón		**e.** descargar
6. _____ el documento		**f.** enviar
7. _____ la pantalla		**g.** conectar
8. _____ la computadora		**h.** guardar
9. _____ el módem		**i.** apagar

Actividad B Descripciones

Tu profesor(a) va a mencionar un objeto relacionado con la computadora. Pon (*Place*) el número del objeto mencionado al lado de su descripción.

a. _____ Se hace clic aquí para ir de una página web a otra página interesante.

b. _____ Se usa para guardar documentos relacionados.

c. _____ Se usa para mover el cursor en la pantalla.

d. _____ Se usa para escribir en la computadora.

e. _____ Contiene todos los programas y documentos guardados en la computadora.

f. _____ Se usa para conectar la computadora con el Internet.

g. _____ Se ven todos los documentos y páginas web aquí.

h. _____ Se usa para proteger (*protect*) el correo electrónico.

Actividad C ¿Qué debes hacer (*should you do*)?

Las situaciones a continuación ocurren cuando usamos la computadora. Algunas son muy frecuentes y otras menos frecuentes. Primero, lee las situaciones. Luego, escucha las soluciones que lee tu profesor(a) y elige (*select*) la mejor solución para cada situación.

¿Qué pasa cuando...

a. _____ ...la computadora se congela?

b. _____ ...la conexión va muy lenta (*slow*)?

c. _____ ...tienes un virus en un documento?

d. _____ ...quieres mandarle a otra persona un mensaje que recibiste?

e. _____ ...quieres buscar información sobre alguien?

f. _____ ...quieres escuchar tu música favorita?

g. _____ ...necesitas guardar un documento en un disquete?

¡Exprésate!

To say *to spend time doing something,* Spanish uses **pasar tiempo** + *participle.* As you saw earlier, the participle (or *gerund*) is formed by adding **-ando** to the stem of **-ar** verbs and **-iendo** to **-er** and **-ir** verbs and is translated as the *-ing* form of the verb in English. The verb **leer,** however, adds **-yendo** instead of **-iendo.** The examples below will help you with **Actividad D.**

¿Cuánto tiempo **pasas leyendo** y **contestando** el correo electrónico?
How much time do you spend reading and answering e-mail?

Paso mucho tiempo haciendo investigaciones por el Internet.
I spend a lot of time doing research on the Internet.

You will learn more about the present participle in **Lección 8A.**

Actividad D ¿Cuánto tiempo pasamos en la computadora?

Paso 1 A continuación hay una tabla con varias actividades relacionadas con la computadora. Llena la primera columna (**yo**) con las horas que tú pasaste haciendo cada actividad la semana pasada.

	YO	(NOMBRE)	(NOMBRE)	(NOMBRE)	PROMEDIO DE HORAS
1. leyendo y contestando el correo electrónico					
2. escribiendo tareas/trabajos					
3. haciendo investigaciones para las clases					
4. charlando en las salas de chat o con mensajero instantáneo					
5. descargando música o imágenes					
6. jugando (juegos / por dinero)					
7. haciendo compras					
8. leyendo las noticias					
Número de horas en total					

Paso 2 En un grupo, comparte tus respuestas con otras tres personas. Apunta las respuestas de tus compañeros en las tres columnas correspondientes.

Paso 3 Ahora calcula el promedio (*average*) de las horas de cada actividad de tu grupo. Tu grupo va a compartir esta información con toda la clase. Además de presentar el promedio de las actividades, contesta las siguientes preguntas:

1. ¿En qué actividad pasan Uds. más tiempo?
2. ¿Hay diferencias entre las mujeres y los hombres? ¿Cuáles son?

Paso 4 (Optativo) Escribe un párrafo en que compares el uso que tú haces de la computadora con el de tus compañeros.

Gramática

¡Me fascina!

Verbs Like gustar

OTHER VERBS LIKE *gustar*		
agradar	*to please*	**Me agrada** mucho. *It pleases me a lot.*
apetecer (zc)	*to appeal, be pleasing*	**¿Os apetece?** *Does it appeal to you (all)?*
caerle (*irreg.*) **bien/mal a alguien**	*to (dis)like someone* (lit: *to strike someone well or poorly*)	Julio **me cae bien.** *I like Julio.* (lit: *Julio strikes me well.*)
encantar	*to love* (lit: *to enchant*)	**Nos encanta** la música. *We love music.* (lit: *Music enchants us.*)
fascinar	*to love, be fascinated by* (lit: *to fascinate*)	A Jorge **le fascinan** las computadoras. *Jorge loves (is fascinated by) computers.* (lit: *Computers fascinate Jorge.*)
importar	*to be important; to matter*	**¿Les importa?** *Does it matter to you (all) / them?*
interesar	*to interest, be interesting*	**¿Te interesan** las lenguas? *Do languages interest you? / Are languages interesting to you?*
molestar	*to annoy, bother*	A nosotros **nos molestan** las conexiones lentas. *Slow connections annoy us.*
parecer (zc)	*to seem (like)*	**¿Te parece** buena idea? *Does it seem like a good idea to you?*

You have already been talking about your likes and dislikes using the verb **gustar.** As you may remember, **gustar** literally means *to be pleasing.* In order to say *I like to surf the Internet,* you say **Me gusta navegar el Internet** (literally: *Surfing the Internet pleases me.*) You may also remember that **gustar** always takes an indirect object pronoun in order to indicate *to whom* something is pleasing. The new verbs in this section, many of which you've already seen, function the same way. And as with **gustar,** the preposition **a** must be used if the indirect object noun is mentioned.

A Juan le importa mucho su familia.   *Juan's family really matters to him.*

A mis amigos les encantó la fiesta.   *My friends loved the party.*

COMUNICACIÓN ÚTIL

To respond in agreement or disagreement when someone uses a verb like **gustar,** the following expressions are used. Note the use of the preposition **a.**

—Me encantó la película.	*I loved the movie.*
—**A mí también.**	*Me too.*
—No me apetece ir.	*I don't feel like going.*
—**A mí tampoco.**	*Me neither. / Neither do I.*
—No me interesa nada.	*It doesn't interest me at all.*
—**A mí sí.**	*It does (interest) me.*
—Me fascina navegar la red.	*I love surfing the Web.*
—**A mí no.**	*Not me. / I don't.*

DE SOL Y VIENTO

In **Episodio 5** of *Sol y viento,* you will see a segment in which Jaime gives something to María. Part of their conversation appears here. Before watching the segment, decide which verbs like **gustar** could be placed in the blanks.

MARÍA
¡Un remolino! ¡Me _____[1] los remolinos!

JAIME
Lo compré allí. Me _____[2] bonito.

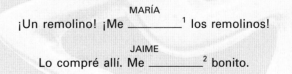

Actividad E ¿Estás de acuerdo?

Indica si estás de acuerdo o no con las oraciones a continuación.

	ESTOY DE ACUERDO.	NO ESTOY DE ACUERDO.
1. A Jaime le encanta Santiago.	☐	☐
2. A María no le agrada mucho su trabajo en la universidad.	☐	☐
3. A Mario le cae bien Jaime.	☐	☐
4. A María le interesa conocer mejor a Jaime.	☐	☐
5. A Jaime le importa más el aspecto físico de las mujeres que la inteligencia.	☐	☐
6. A Mario le molesta ser conductor de Jaime.	☐	☐
7. A Carlos le apetece vender «Sol y viento».	☐	☐

Actividad F Reacciones

Paso 1 Elige la oración que expresa tu reacción a cada situación.

1. comprar una computadora nueva
   ☐ Me apetece mucho.   ☐ Me apetece un poco.
   ☐ No me apetece para nada.

2. navegar el Internet por muchas horas
   ☐ Me fascina.   ☐ Me gusta de vez en cuando.
   ☐ No me gusta para nada.

3. descargar música del Internet
   ☐ Me encanta.   ☐ Me gusta un poco.
   ☐ No me interesa para nada.

4. recibir *spam*
   ☐ Me molesta mucho.   ☐ Me molesta un poco.
   ☐ No me molesta en absoluto (*at all*).

5. conocer a alguien en una sala de chat
   ☐ Me interesa mucho.   ☐ Me interesa un poco.
   ☐ No me interesa nada.

6. las computadoras Dell
   ☐ Me parecen buenas.   ☐ Me parecen malas.
   ☐ No tengo opinión.

Paso 2 Compara tus respuestas con las de un compañero (una compañera) de clase, según los modelos.

MODELOS: E1: Me molestan mucho las computadoras.
          E2: A mí también. / ¿De veras? (*Really?*) A mí no. No me molestan nada.

o

          E1: No me molestan nada las computadoras.
          E2: A mí tampoco. / ¿De veras? A mí sí. Me molestan mucho.

Actividad G ¿Qué le molesta al profesor (a la profesora)?

Paso 1 A continuación hay una lista de los posibles gustos de tu profesor(a). En grupos de tres, elijan la oración que (en su opinión) describa mejor los sentimientos (*feelings*) de él o ella.

	SÍ	A VECES	NO
1. A mi profesor(a) le caen bien todos sus estudiantes.	☐	☐	☐
2. A mi profesor(a) le caen mal algunos colegas.	☐	☐	☐
3. A mi profesor(a) le encanta enseñar español.	☐	☐	☐
4. A mi profesor(a) le fascinan otras culturas.	☐	☐	☐
5. A mi profesor(a) le molestan las llamadas por teléfono de los vendedores (*telemarketing calls*).	☐	☐	☐
6. A mi profesor(a) le importa mucho la puntualidad (*punctuality*).	☐	☐	☐
7. A mi profesor(a) le fascina la película *Sol y viento.*	☐	☐	☐
8. A mi profesor(a) le apetece viajar a África.	☐	☐	☐
9. A mi profesor(a) le gustan las películas de ciencia ficción.	☐	☐	☐

Paso 2 Trabajando en los mismos grupos, piensen en por lo menos tres oraciones más sobre los gustos de su profesor(a). Usen las oraciones del **Paso 1** como modelo.

Paso 3 Compartan sus oraciones de los **Pasos 1** y **2** con su profesor(a). ¿Acertaron Uds. (*Were you right*) en sus opiniones?

MODELO: Creemos que a (nombre del profesor [de la profesora]) le...

Actividad H Entrevista

Paso 1 Piensa en cuatro o cinco preguntas para hacerle a un compañero (una compañera) sobre sus gustos y sobre el uso de la computadora y/o el Internet. Usa verbos de cada columna.

MODELO: ¿Te gusta navegar la red?

caer bien	caer mal
encantar	molestar
fascinar	
gustar	
importar	
interesar	

Paso 2 Hazle a tu compañero/a las preguntas que preparaste y anota sus respuestas. Contesta también las preguntas que te hace tu compañero/a.

Paso 3 Escribe un párrafo con la información de tu compañero/a. Di (*Say*) también si estás de acuerdo o no con él/ella. En general, ¿tienen los/las dos una actitud positiva o negativa hacia las computadoras y el Internet?

Vocabulario

Talking About
Reliance on
Technology

Mi celular

Electronic Devices

el estéreo

el (teléfono) celular

el reproductor de CD

el mando a distancia

el televisor

el reproductor de DVD

hacer (*irreg.*) *zapping*

el vídeo

la computadora portátil

el reproductor de vídeo

el contestador automático

la videocámara

la cámara digital

✳ **MÁS VOCABULARIO**

la agenda electrónica	electronic organizer (*PDA: personal digital assistant*)
la calculadora	calculator
el estéreo portátil	portable stereo
la máquina fax	fax machine
cambiar de canal	to change channels
funcionar	to work, function (*machines*)
grabar	to record

≋ Vistazo cultural

El uso de los teléfonos celulares en Latinoamérica

Aunque el uso de los teléfonos celulares en este país ha aumentado[a] en los últimos años, en Latinoamérica ha aumentado aún[b] más. Son muchas las razones de este fenómeno. Primero, a diferencia de los teléfonos tradicionales, los celulares no requieren una infraestructura de cables, la cual[c] no existe en muchas zonas rurales. Por eso, es más fácil y menos caro instalar sistemas celulares que instalar cables en cada casa. Además, en las zonas rurales más aisladas,[d] es común tener que esperar meses hasta poder usar un teléfono de casa a causa de los gastos y el tiempo que se requieren para instalar los cables. Lo que más ha impactado[e] el uso de los celulares es el cambio en cuanto a[f] quién paga. Como sucede[g] en este país (y antes en Latinoamérica), tanto la persona que llama como la persona que recibe la llamada tienen que pagar por los minutos de uso. Ahora, en muchos países latinoamericanos, sólo la persona que llama paga la llamada.

Renueva
tu móvil
por uno
con cámara

Infórmate en el
4636

Telefónica
MoviStar

[a]ha... *has increased* [b]*even* [c]la... *which* [d]*isolated* [e]ha... *has impacted*
[f]en... *regarding* [g]*happens*

¡Exprésate!

Actividad A ¿Para qué se usa?

Empareja las descripciones con los aparatos correspondientes.

1. ___ el celular
2. ___ la máquina fax
3. ___ la calculadora
4. ___ la videocámara
5. ___ el contestador automático
6. ___ el reproductor de DVD
7. ___ el mando a distancia
8. ___ la cámara digital

a. Se usa para cambiar de canal en el televisor.

b. Se usa para dejar un mensaje cuando nadie contesta una llamada.

c. Se usa para grabar eventos personales y luego verlos en el televisor.

d. Se usa para recibir y mandar documentos.

e. Se usa para llamar a otras personas, especialmente cuando uno está fuera de la casa.

f. Se usa para sacar fotos y verlas en la computadora.

g. Se usa para ver películas.

h. Se usa para hacer cálculos.

Actividad B Asociaciones

Escucha las actividades que menciona tu profesor(a) y pon el número de la actividad al lado del aparato correspondiente.

a. ___ el reproductor de vídeo

b. ___ el mando a distancia

c. ___ la agenda electrónica

d. ___ el televisor

e. ___ el estéreo portátil

NAVEGANDO LA RED

Busca información sobre los precios de las computadoras y otros aparatos electrónicos en algún país hispanohablante. Teniendo en cuenta (*Keeping in mind*) el cambio de moneda, ¿qué te parecen los precios? ¿Son más caros o más baratos que en este país? Menciona los nombres de tres aparatos que no conocieras (*you didn't know*) antes.

¡Exprésate!

To say that one *needs* or *misses* something, Spanish uses the expression **hacerle falta (a alguien).**

Me hace falta.	*I miss/need it.*
No me hace falta.	*I don't miss/need it.*

Actividad C ¿De qué dependes más?

Paso 1 Elige la oración que mejor representa tu opinión sobre cada aparato electrónico.

	NO PUEDO VIVIR SIN ESTO.	PUEDO VIVIR SIN ESTO; NO ME SERÍA (*it wouldn't be*) DIFÍCIL.	NO LO/LA USO Y NO ME HACE FALTA.
1. el celular	☐	☐	☐
2. la computadora	☐	☐	☐
3. la agenda electrónica	☐	☐	☐
4. el televisor	☐	☐	☐
5. la calculadora	☐	☐	☐
6. la cámara digital	☐	☐	☐
7. el mando a distancia	☐	☐	☐
8. el contestador automático	☐	☐	☐
9. el reproductor de DVD	☐	☐	☐
10. el estéreo	☐	☐	☐

Paso 2 Compara tus respuestas con las de tres compañeros/as y prepara unas oraciones para compartir con la clase.

MODELOS: No podemos vivir sin _____.

Para nosotros no sería difícil vivir sin _____.

No usamos y tampoco necesitamos _____.

Actividad D ¿Qué necesita un estudiante nuevo?

Paso 1 En grupos de tres o cuatro personas, hagan una lista de los aparatos electrónicos que va a necesitar un estudiante de primer año en la universidad.

Paso 2 Ahora indiquen si cada aparato mencionado en el **Paso 1** es **absolutamente necesario** o **no es necesario pero sería** (*it would be*) **bueno tenerlo.** Justifiquen el uso de cada aparato.

MODELO: Un estéreo portátil es absolutamente necesario. Hay mucho trabajo y estrés con las clases y un nuevo estudiante necesita relajarse (*to relax*).

Gramática

Me conozco bien.   **True Reflexive Constructions** ✳

In **Lecciones 3A** and **3B,** you learned about objects and object pronouns. Can you identify the subjects and objects in each sentence below?

RAMÓN: No sé si Elena conoce bien a Juan.
SILVIA: Pues sí. Elena lo conoce bien porque son vecinos.

Cuando el gato está ausente, los ratones **se divierten.**

In the preceding example, the subjects and objects are different people. **Elena** is the subject of **conoce** and **Juan/lo** are the objects. But what if the subject and object are the same? What happens when María is talking about knowing herself? What if you are looking at yourself? When the subject and object are the same, the sentence is called a *reflexive* sentence. In Spanish, you can use regular object pronouns for reflexive sentences except for **Ud./Uds.** and **él/ella/ellos/ellas,** all of which require **se.** That is, the reflexive pronouns are **me, te, se, nos,** and **os.** Look at the chart to see how this works.

REFLEXIVE AND NONREFLEXIVE SENTENCES	
SUBJECT AND OBJECT ARE DIFFERENT	SUBJECT AND OBJECT ARE THE SAME
Juan **me conoce** bien. *Juan knows me well.*	**Me conozco** bien. Sé mis puntos fuertes y débiles. *I know myself well. I know my strong and weak points.*
¿**Te pone** restricciones tu trabajo? *Does your job put restrictions on you?*	¿**Te pones** restricciones? *Do you put restrictions on yourself?*
No **le hablo** a Roberto. *I don't speak to Roberto.*	Roberto **se habla** constantemente. *Robert speaks to himself constantly.*
No **sabemos** cómo expresar **eso.** *We don't know how to express that.*	**Nos expresamos** muy bien. *We express ourselves very well.*
Ramona no **os ve** mucho, ¿verdad? *Ramona doesn't see you (all) much, right?*	¿Cómo **os veis** en tres años? *How do you (all) see yourselves in three years?*
Elena **les prepara** el desayuno a los hijos. *Elena prepares breakfast for her kids.*	Los hijos **se preparan** el desayuno. *The kids prepare breakfast for themselves.*

Just as with direct and indirect object pronouns, reflexive pronouns precede the conjugated verb, but they may also be attached to the end of an infinitive.

Miguel no **se quiere mirar** en el espejo.

Miguel no **quiere mirarse** en el espejo.

✳ MÁS VOCABULARIO

Here are some useful reflexive verbs that you may use to talk about things that people do to or for themselves. Note that many of them have to do with daily routines.

acostarse (ue)	to go to bed
afeitarse	to shave
bañarse	to take a bath
despertarse (ie)	to wake up
dormirse (ue, u)	to fall asleep
ducharse	to take a shower
lavarse los dientes	to brush one's teeth
levantarse	to get up
sentirse (ie, i)	to feel
vestirse (i, i)	to get dressed

DE SOL Y VIENTO

In **Episodio 5** of *Sol y viento,* you will watch a scene in which Jaime tells María that she's not a typical professor. Part of their conversation appears in the dialogue.

JAIME
De verdad me parece muy interesante lo que hace Ud. No es una profesora... típica.

MARÍA
¿«Típica» cómo? ¿Porque no uso anteojos gruesosª y vestidos formales?

JAIME
¡Exactamente! ¡Nah! No, no es eso, precisamente. Es que Ud. no **se limita** a _____.

¿A qué no se limita María?

1. a su especialización

2. a su trabajo con la comunidad indígena

3. a la sala de clase y a sus libros

¿Estás de acuerdo con Jaime en que María no es una profesora típica? ¿Conoces a profesores como María? ¿Cómo son?

ªanteojos... *thick glasses*

Actividad E   Descripciones

Empareja los nombres con las oraciones para describir a algunos personajes de *Sol y viento.* **¡OJO!** Algunas oraciones son apropiadas para más de una persona.

1. _____ Jaime
2. _____ María
3. _____ Mario

a. Se siente cómodo/a con Jaime.
b. No se limita a su trabajo en la universidad.
c. Se apoda (*He/She is nicknamed*) «Verdejín».
d. Se viste de manera cómoda (*comfortable*).
e. Se levanta temprano para hacer ejercicio.

Actividad F   ¿Una mañana típica?

Paso 1   Mira los dibujos y pon en orden lo que dice Ángela, una mujer profesional, de una mañana típica.

____ Me visto para ir al trabajo.

____ Me conecto con el Internet para leer las noticias y mi correo electrónico.

____ Me levanto temprano, como a las cinco y media.

____ Salgo para el trabajo.

____ Me preparo un café para despertarme porque siempre estoy muy cansada por la mañana.

____ Me lavo los dientes.

____ Me ducho rápidamente.

____ Desayuno algo ligero (*light*), normalmente sólo pan tostado.

Paso 2   Mira otra vez lo que dice Ángela y prepara tres oraciones comparando su mañana con una mañana típica tuya.

MODELOS: Como Ángela, me preparo un café para despertarme.

Ángela se despierta a las seis y media, pero yo no. Me despierto a las nueve.

Actividad G Más descripciones

Elige la frase más lógica para completar cada descripción.

1. Roberto pasa mucho tiempo solo, pero habla mucho. Entonces Roberto...
   ☐ habla con otra persona.
   ☐ se habla.

2. El cumpleaños de la madre de Sara es el próximo sábado. Entonces Sara...
   ☐ le compra un regalo.
   ☐ se compra un regalo.

3. El compañero de casa de Marcos nunca oye su despertador (*alarm clock*) y tiene una clase a las ocho. Entonces Marcos...
   ☐ tiene que despertarlo.
   ☐ tiene que despertarse.

4. Elisa sabe muy bien cuáles son sus virtudes y cuáles son sus defectos. Entonces Elisa...
   ☐ la conoce bien.
   ☐ se conoce bien.

5. El hijo de Ramón sólo tiene un año. Entonces, obviamente, este niño...
   ☐ no puede vestirlo.
   ☐ no puede vestirse.

6. A Juan le cae muy bien su profesor de filosofía. No sólo es famoso e inteligente, sino también (*but also*) es muy bueno. Entonces Juan...
   ☐ lo respeta mucho.
   ☐ se respeta mucho.

7. Diana rompió con (*broke up with*) su novio porque lo vio con otra mujer. Diana está furiosa con él y en este momento ella...
   ☐ lo detesta.
   ☐ se detesta.

Actividad H Ayer...

Paso 1 Hazle las siguientes preguntas a un compañero (una compañera) de clase y apunta sus respuestas. Todas las preguntas tienen que ver con lo que hizo ayer.

1. ¿A qué hora te levantaste?
2. ¿Te duchaste o te bañaste por la mañana?
3. ¿Te afeitaste?
4. ¿Te compraste algo? ¿Qué te compraste?
5. ¿Cuántas veces te conectaste con el Internet? ¿Qué hiciste?
6. ¿Te acostaste muy tarde? ¿A qué hora? ¿Te dormiste en seguida (*right away*)?
7. ¿Cuántas veces te lavaste los dientes?

Paso 2 Usando la información del **Paso 1,** escribe tres oraciones comparando lo que hiciste tú y lo que hizo tu compañero/a.

MODELOS: (Nombre) y yo nos acostamos tarde.

(Nombre) se compró un libro, pero yo no me compré nada.

Vocabulario

Talking About When
You Were Younger | **Mi niñez y juventud**

**Typical Childhood and
Adolescent Activities**

Algunas actividades típicas de los niños y los jóvenes

dibujar y colorear

jugar (ue) (gu) a los videojuegos

meterse en líos

sacar (qu) la licencia de conducir

subirse a los árboles

enamorarse (de)

❋ MÁS VOCABULARIO

hacer (*irreg.*) **novillos**	to skip/cut school
jugar (ue) (gu) al escondite	to play hide and seek
llevarse bien/mal con	to get along well/poorly with
pelearse	to fight
portarse bien/mal	to behave well/poorly
soñar (ue) con	to dream about
la cita	date (*social*)
la juventud	youth; adolescence
el/la mentiroso/a	liar
las muñecas	dolls
el/la niñero/a	baby-sitter
la niñez	childhood
el recreo	recess
las tiras cómicas	comics

Características de los niños y los adolescentes

adaptable	adaptable
cabezón (cabezona)	stubborn
(im)paciente	(im)patient
obediente	obedient
precavido/a	cautious
torpe	clumsy
travieso/a	mischievous

〰 Vistazo cultural

Las muñecas Barbie: populares y problemáticas en toda América

La muñeca Barbie siempre ha sido[a] una de las muñecas favoritas entre las niñas norteamericanas desde que apareció por primera vez en 1959 (mil novecientos cincuenta y nueve). La muñeca Barbie no sólo es un fenómeno norteamericano sino que es exportada a todo el mundo. Las características de la Barbie norteamericana (rubia, ojos azules, etcétera) no reflejan la realidad de las mujeres latinoamericanas ni tampoco la de la mayor parte de las mujeres norteamericanas. Por esa razón en 1980 (mil novecientos ochenta) la compañía que fabrica las muñecas Barbie introdujo versiones de la muñeca que sí parecen más «latinas», y ahora hay Barbies brasileñas, chilenas, quechuas (un grupo indígena en el Perú y Bolivia), mexicanas, peruanas y puertorriqueñas. La Barbie puertorriqueña, por ejemplo, es mulata, tiene ojos almendrados,[b] una nariz gruesa, labios[c] más grandes y pelo moreno y rizado. A pesar de[d] estos cambios, la muñeca todavía ha sido criticada por varios grupos y organizaciones por tener ideales norteamericanos como una cintura[e] muy delgada y senos[f] grandes. Estas críticas se hacen no sólo en Latinoamérica sino también en este país.

[a]ha... *has been* [b]*almond-shaped* [c]*lips* [d]A... *In spite of* [e]*waist* [f]*breasts*

Actividad A Definiciones

Pon el número de cada descripción que lee tu profesor(a) al lado de la palabra
o expresión correspondiente.

a. ___ la cita

b. ___ el escondite

c. ___ el/la niñero/a

d. ___ el recreo

e. ___ hacer novillos

f. ___ las muñecas

g. ___ las tareas domésticas

Actividad B ¿En qué etapa (*stage*) de la vida?

Indica la etapa de la vida en que generalmente ocurre o se hace lo siguiente.

	LA NIÑEZ	LA JUVENTUD	LAS DOS
1. jugar con las muñecas	☐	☐	☐
2. leer tiras cómicas	☐	☐	☐
3. llevarse mal con los padres	☐	☐	☐
4. colorear	☐	☐	☐
5. sacar la licencia de conducir	☐	☐	☐
6. tener amigos imaginarios	☐	☐	☐
7. hacer novillos	☐	☐	☐
8. jugar al escondite	☐	☐	☐
9. pelearse con los hermanos	☐	☐	☐
10. enamorarse por primera vez	☐	☐	☐

¿Cómo afecta la tecnología las actividades de los niños? ¿Son menos activos ahora que antes?

Actividad C Asociaciones

Un niño que...

1. no dice la verdad es ____.
2. tiene muchos accidentes es ____.
3. se mete en muchos líos es ____.
4. hace lo que le dicen los padres es ____.
5. se acostumbra fácilmente es ____.
6. es muy creativo es ____.
7. no quiere obedecer a nadie es ____.
8. no sabe esperar es ____.
9. no es impulsivo es ____.

a. precavido
b. travieso
c. impaciente
d. mentiroso
e. cabezón
f. torpe
g. adaptable
h. imaginativo
i. obediente

Actividad D Los pasatiempos favoritos

Paso 1 Completa la tabla con una lista de las actividades o pasatiempos favoritos de tu niñez y de ahora.

LAS ACTIVIDADES FAVORITAS DE MI NIÑEZ	MIS PASATIEMPOS FAVORITOS AHORA

Paso 2 Compara tus actividades con las de tres compañeros/as. ¿Qué actividades tienen en común para la niñez y para ahora?

Paso 3 ¿En cuál de las dos etapas son más comunes actividades o pasatiempos que tienen que ver con la tecnología? ¿Por qué?

Gramática

Talking About What You Used to Do

¿En qué trabajabas?   Introduction to the Imperfect Tense

Thus far you have been using the preterite to talk about what you did yesterday, last weekend, and so forth. But to talk about repeated, habitual, ongoing events and activities in the past (i.e., what you *used to do*), Spanish uses a different verb form: the *imperfect.** As the chart indicates, the imperfect is formed by adding **-aba** to the stem of **-ar** verbs and **-ía** to the stem of **-er** and **-ir** verbs. Verbs that have a stem change in the present tense do not change in the imperfect. Furthermore, the imperfect has only three irregular verbs: **ir, ser,** and **ver.**

Cuando **era** niño, **jugaba** mucho al escondite.	*When I was a child, I used to play hide and seek a lot.*
¿**Te metías** en muchos líos?	*Did you used to / Would you get in a lot of trouble?*
Me **gustaba** mucho leer las tiras cómicas.	*I used to like to read comics.*

Notice that this use of the imperfect is normally translated as *would . . .* or *used to . . .* and is used to communicate actions that used to be normal or habitual occurrences in the past.

The imperfect of **hay** is **había** (*there was / there were*).

THE IMPERFECT OF REGULAR VERBS					
jugar		comer		vivir	
jugaba	jugábamos	comía	comíamos	vivía	vivíamos
jugabas	jugabais	comías	comíais	vivías	vivíais
jugaba	jugaban	comía	comían	vivía	vivían
jugaba	jugaban	comía	comían	vivía	vivían
IRREGULAR VERBS IN THE IMPERFECT					
ir		ser		ver	
iba	íbamos	era	éramos	veía	veíamos
ibas	ibais	eras	erais	veías	veíais
iba	iban	era	eran	veía	veían
iba	iban	era	eran	veía	veían

---

*Although there are a number of uses of the imperfect, in this section you will be using the imperfect to talk about activities that you *used to do.* You will learn more uses of the imperfect in **Lección 5B.**

✱ MÁS GRAMÁTICA

There are two uses of the verb *would* in English: to express habitual actions in the past such as *When I was younger, I would always get into trouble,* and unreal conditions such as *I would go if I could.* For the first kind of *would,* Spanish uses the imperfect **(Cuando era más joven, siempre me metía en líos.)** For the second kind, Spanish uses a different verb form called the conditional **(Yo iría...).** You will learn more about this second kind of *would* and conditional forms in **Lección 8A.**

DE SOL Y VIENTO

In **Episodio 5** of *Sol y viento,* you will watch a scene in which Jaime explains to María why he knows so much about wine. Part of their conversation appears here.

MARÍA
Parece que sabes mucho de vino.

JAIME
Algo. He estado rodeado[a] de uvas,[b] o jugo de uvas, toda mi vida.

MARÍA
¿Cómo?

JAIME
Mis padres _____ ... campesinos.[c] En el Valle Central de California.

Which verb in the imperfect would you put in the blank above?

[a]He... *I've been surrounded*   [b]*grapes*   [c]*farm workers*

Actividad E   ¿Cómo eran?

¿Cómo eran las vidas de Jaime y María hace quince o veinte años? Completa las oraciones sobre lo que piensas de las juventudes de Jaime y María.

   1. Jaime vivía en _____ y era muy _____.
      Le gustaba _____.
   2. María vivía en _____ y era muy _____.
      Le gustaba _____.

Actividad F   Generaciones diferentes

Paso 1   A continuación hay una lista de oraciones que describen lo que dos estudiantes hacían con sus amigos durante sus años en la universidad. Con otra persona, indiquen si cada descripción se refiere a estudiantes que se graduaron en el año 1980 (mil novecientos ochenta) o veinticinco años más tarde, en 2005 (dos mil cinco) o en los dos.

	1980	2005	LOS DOS
1. «Leíamos el correo electrónico tres veces al día.»	☐	☐	☐
2. «Usábamos un catálogo para buscar libros en la biblioteca.»	☐	☐	☐
3. «Escribíamos los trabajos a mano (*by hand*) o a máquina (*typewriter*).»	☐	☐	☐
4. «Descargábamos mucha música, vídeos y juegos.»	☐	☐	☐
5. «Escuchábamos música en cintas (*tapes*).»	☐	☐	☐
6. «Salíamos a tomar cerveza.»	☐	☐	☐
7. «Llamábamos a los amigos por teléfono celular.»	☐	☐	☐
8. «Les escribíamos cartas (*letters*) a amigos de otras universidades.»	☐	☐	☐
9. «Dejábamos (*We would leave*) las tareas hasta el último momento.»	☐	☐	☐
10. «Teníamos acceso al Internet en la residencia estudiantil.»	☐	☐	☐

Paso 2 ¿A qué conclusiones puedes llegar sobre los estudiantes que se graduaron en 1980 y los que se graduaron en 2005? Elige una de las opciones a continuación y completa las oraciones.

☐ No había muchas diferencias entre los estudiantes de las dos épocas. Los estudiantes de las dos épocas...

☐ Había muchas diferencias entre los estudiantes de las dos épocas. Por ejemplo, en los años ochenta los estudiantes... , pero a principios del siglo XXI los estudiantes...

☐ Había algunas diferencias entre los estudiantes de las dos épocas, pero no muchas. En los años ochenta... , pero a principios del siglo XXI los estudiantes...

Actividad G ¿Cómo eras tú?

Paso 1 Hazle a un compañero (una compañera) de clase las preguntas a continuación y apunta sus respuestas.

Cuando tenías catorce años...	SÍ, SIEMPRE/ MUCHO	A VECES	NO
1. ¿obedecías a tus padres?	☐	☐	☐
2. ¿jugabas a los videojuegos?	☐	☐	☐
3. ¿estudiabas mucho?	☐	☐	☐
4. ¿te metías en líos?	☐	☐	☐
5. ¿les decías mentiras a tus padres?	☐	☐	☐
6. ¿te portabas bien en la escuela?	☐	☐	☐
7. ¿te llevabas bien con tus hermanos/amigos?	☐	☐	☐
8. ¿te subías a los árboles?	☐	☐	☐
9. ¿hacías novillos?	☐	☐	☐
10. ¿practicabas algún deporte?	☐	☐	☐

Paso 2 Tomando en cuenta (*Keeping in mind*) las respuestas de tu compañero/a en el **Paso 1,** ¿cómo crees que era tu compañero/a a los catorce años? Elige uno o dos de los siguientes adjetivos, pero no lo(s) compartas (*share*) con tu compañero/a.

☐ obediente

☐ tranquilo/a (*calm*)

☐ rebelde (*rebellious*)

☐ trabajador(a)

☐ travieso/a

Paso 3 Prepara una o dos oraciones que justifiquen tu selección de esos adjetivos. Luego vas a leer las oraciones a la clase.

MODELO: <u>(Nombre)</u> era muy travieso/a porque hacía novillos y les decía mentiras a sus padres.

RESUMEN DE VOCABULARIO

Verbos

afeitarse	to shave
agradar	to please
apetecer (zc)	to appeal, be pleasing
bañarse	to take a bath
caerle (*irreg.*) **bien/mal a alguien**	to (dis)like someone
dormirse (ue, u)	to fall asleep
ducharse	to take a shower
encantar	to love
lavarse los dientes	to brush one's teeth
levantarse	to get up
parecer (zc)	to seem (like)
sentirse (ie, i)	to feel

Cognados: fascinar, importar, interesar
Repaso: acostarse (ue), despertarse (ie), gustar, molestar, vestirse (i, i)

Las computadoras y el Internet

apagar (gu)	to turn off
congelarse	to freeze up (*screen*)
descargar (gu)	to download
encender (ie)	to turn on (*machines*)
enviar (envío)	to send
guardar (documentos)	to save (documents)
hacer (*irreg.*) **clic**	to click
hacer (*irreg.*) **una búsqueda**	to do a search
mandar	to send

el archivo	file
la contraseña	password
el correo electrónico	e-mail
el disco duro	hard drive
el enlace	link
el mensaje	message
la página web	Web page
el ratón	mouse
el teclado	keyboard

Cognados: conectar, copiar; la computadora portátil, el disquete, el módem, el monitor
Repaso: navegar (gu) la red; la computadora, la pantalla

Otros aparatos electrónicos

cambiar de canal	to change channels
funcionar	to work, function (*machines*)
grabar	to record
hacer (*irreg.*) ***zapping***	to channel surf
la agenda electrónica	electronic organizer (*PDA: personal digital assistant*)
el contestador automático	answering machine
el mando a distancia	remote control
el reproductor de CD (DVD, vídeo)	CD (DVD, video) player

Cognados: la calculadora, la cámara digital, el estéreo (portátil), la máquina fax, el (teléfono) celular, la videocámara
Repaso: el televisor, el vídeo

Los niños y jóvenes

dibujar	to draw
enamorarse (de)	to fall in love (with)
hacer (*irreg.*) **novillos**	to skip/cut school
jugar (gu) al escondite	to play hide and seek
jugar (gu) a los videojuegos	to play video games
llevarse bien/mal con	to get along well/poorly with
meterse en líos	to get into trouble
pelearse	to fight
portarse bien/mal	to behave well/poorly
sacar (qu) la licencia de conducir	to get a driver's license
soñar (ue) con	to dream about
subirse a los árboles	to climb trees

la cita	date (*social*)
la juventud	youth; adolescence
el/la mentiroso/a	liar
las muñecas	dolls
el/la niñero/a	baby-sitter
la niñez	childhood
el recreo	recess
las tiras cómicas	comics

cabezón (cabezona)	stubborn
precavido/a	cautious
torpe	clumsy
travieso/a	mischievous

Cognados: colorear; el/la adolescente; adaptable, impaciente, obediente, paciente

Érase una vez...[a]

OBJETIVOS

IN THIS LESSON, YOU WILL LEARN:

- to express years, decades, and centuries
- to use the preterite and the imperfect together to narrate events
- to talk about important historical events
- to talk about important personal events

In addition, you will watch **Episodio 5** of the film *Sol y viento*.

◀ La llegada de Cristóbal Colón a América fue un evento histórico importante y controvertido (*controversial*).

The following media resources are available for *Sol y viento: En breve*

Episodio 5 of *Sol y viento*

Online *Manual de actividades*

Interactive CD-ROM

Online Learning Center Website

[a]Érase... *Once upon a time . . .*

PRIMERA PARTE

Vocabulario

Expressing
Years

En 1972...   Numbers 1,000 and Higher

1.000	mil	102.000	ciento dos mil
1.001	mil uno	200.000	doscientos mil
1.002	mil dos	300.000	trescientos mil
1.998	mil novecientos	400.000	cuatrocientos mil
	noventa y ocho	500.000	quinientos mil
2.000	dos mil	600.000	seiscientos mil
2.005	dos mil cinco	700.000	setecientos mil
3.000	tres mil	800.000	ochocientos mil
10.000	diez mil	900.000	novecientos mil
100.000	cien mil	1.000.000	un millón
101.000	ciento un mil	2.000.000	dos millones

Years are expressed in Spanish by saying the whole number.

1898	mil ochocientos noventa y ocho
1985	mil novecientos ochenta y cinco
2008	dos mil ocho

Remember that when numbers 200 through 900 modify a noun, they must agree in gender:

30.200 personas   treinta mil doscient**as** person**as**

Mil does not have a plural form when used in front of a noun, but **millón** does. Also, when used with a noun, **millón** must be followed by **de.**

5.000	cinco **mil** habitantes
5.000.000	cinco **millones de** habitantes

✳ MÁS VOCABULARIO

los años veinte (treinta)	the 20s, 30s (*decades*)
la década	decade
la fecha	date (*calendar*)
el siglo	century
el siglo XXI	the 21st century

≋ Vistazo cultural

Fechas importantes en el mundo hispano

¿Cuánto sabes de la historia de los países hispanohablantes? A continuación hay una lista de algunas fechas históricas importantes de España y de Latinoamérica.

1492	Cristóbal Colón llegó a América
1519–1521	La conquista del Imperio azteca por Hernán Cortés
1531–1533	La conquista del Imperio inca por Francisco Pizarro
1808–1826	Guerras[a] de independencia; los países hispanoamericanos se independizaron de España
1898	Guerra Hispano-Americana; Puerto Rico se convirtió en territorio de los Estados Unidos
1910–1917	La Revolución mexicana
1914	Fin de la construcción del Canal de Panamá
1936–1939	Guerra Civil española; comienzo de 36 años de dictadura[b] bajo el General Francisco Franco
1952	Puerto Rico se hizo[c] Estado Libre Asociado de los Estados Unidos
1959	Fidel Castro subió al poder[d] en Cuba
1973	El presidente de Chile, Salvador Allende, fue asesinado; empezó la dictadura de Augusto Pinochet
1979–1988	Revolución sandinista en Nicaragua
1979–1991	Guerra civil en El Salvador
1985	Terremoto[e] en México; murieron más de ocho mil personas
1992	Rigoberta Menchú, activista indígena guatemalteca, ganó el Premio Nóbel de la Paz[f]
1994	Se firmó el Tratado de Libre Comercio de América del Norte (TLCAN)[g] entre México, los Estados Unidos y el Canadá
1999	El huracán[h] Mitch causó destrucción y muerte en Honduras, Nicaragua y Guatemala
2002	La Argentina pasó por una seria crisis económica con graves consecuencias en todos los sectores del país
2004	Ataques terroristas en los trenes de Madrid, España

[a]*Wars* [b]*dictatorship* [c]*se... became* [d]*subió... rose to power* [e]*Earthquake* [f]*Peace*
[g]Tratado... *North American Free Trade Agreement (NAFTA)* [h]*hurricane*

¿Quiénes son estas famosas personas históricas? ¿Con qué evento histórico se asocia cada una?

Actividad A   ¿Qué año?

Paso 1   Escribe los años que lee tu profesor(a).

1. _____   3. _____   5. _____   7. _____

2. _____   4. _____   6. _____

Paso 2   ¿Sabes la importancia en el mundo hispano de los años del **Paso 1**? Empareja cada evento a continuación con el año correspondiente del **Paso 1**.

a. el comienzo de la Guerra Civil española

b. la Revolución mexicana

c. la llegada de Colón a América

d. la llegada de Hernán Cortés a México

e. el Tratado de Libre Comercio de América del Norte

f. la Revolución cubana

g. la Guerra Hispano-Americana

Actividad B   ¿Cuántos habitantes?

Paso 1   Pensando en la geografía del mundo hispano, ¿sabes cuál de los siguientes países tiene más habitantes? ¿menos habitantes? Pon en orden los países según el número de habitantes que crees que es correcto (1 = más habitantes, 7 = menos habitantes).

a. ___ Colombia

_____

b. ___ Cuba

_____

c. ___ la Guinea Ecuatorial

_____

d. ___ México

_____

e. ___ Panamá

_____

f. ___ España

_____

g. ___ el Uruguay

_____

Paso 2   Tu profesor(a) va a leer el número de habitantes de los países del **Paso 1**. Escribe ese número debajo del nombre de cada país.

Paso 3   Compara el número que escribiste en el **Paso 1** con las poblaciones que leyó tu profesor(a). ¿Adivinaste (*Did you guess*) bien cuáles son los países con más y menos habitantes?

Actividad C   Los precios

Paso 1   Con un compañero (una compañera) de clase, indiquen un precio razonable para las siguientes cosas.

MODELO: un libro de texto → cincuenta dólares

1. un auto nuevo   _____
2. un auto usado   _____
3. una nueva computadora portátil   _____
4. una casa de tres habitaciones   _____
5. el alquiler de un apartamento de dos habitaciones   _____
6. un televisor con pantalla amplia (*wide*)   _____
7. un reproductor de DVD   _____

Paso 2   Ahora conviertan esos precios en dólares a la moneda que les dé su profesor(a).

Paso 3   Cada grupo va a compartir cuánto costarían (*would cost*) algunas de las cosas del **Paso 1** en la moneda de un país hispano. ¿En qué país les sería (*would it be*) más difícil manejar la tasa de cambio (*to manage the exchange rate*)?

Actividad D   ¿En qué año fue?

Paso 1   Elige algún año histórico. Luego, prepara una lista de tres eventos importantes que ocurrieron en ese año.

MODELO: mil novecientos ochenta y nueve →
Cayó (*Fell*) el muro (*wall*) de Berlín.
Hubo una invasión en Panamá.
Inició su presidencia George Bush (padre).

Paso 2   Lee tu lista de eventos a cinco compañeros. ¿Pueden adivinar (*guess*) el año que describes?

Paso 3   Ahora tu profesor(a) va a describir la época en que él/ella nació. ¿Puedes adivinar *el año* en que nació?

NAVEGANDO LA RED

Busca información sobre uno de los siguientes personajes importantes en la historia: José Martí (Cuba), Violeta Chamorro (Nicaragua), Pancho Villa (México), Ernesto «Che» Guevara (la Argentina) o Felipe II (España). ¿En qué año nació (*was he/she born*) y/o murió? ¿Con qué evento(s) histórico(s) se asocia este personaje? ¿Qué hizo para ganar tanta fama?

Gramática

¿Qué hacías cuando te llamé?　　　**Contrasting the Preterite and Imperfect**

THE IMPERFECT: ONGOING ACTIONS	
Anoche a las diez yo **estudiaba** en la biblioteca.	Last night at 10:00 I was studying in the library.
Mientras María **trabajaba** en la excavación, Jaime **visitaba** la ciudad de Santiago.	While María was working at the excavation site, Jaime was visiting Santiago.

THE PRETERITE: COMPLETED ACTIONS	
La Guerra Civil española **duró** tres años.	The Spanish Civil War lasted three years.
«**Vine, vi, vencí.**» (Julio César)	"I came, I saw, I conquered."
Anoche **trabajé** hasta las nueve y luego **salí** con unos amigos.	Last night I worked until nine, and then I went out with some friends.

THE PRETERITE AND IMPERFECT TOGETHER: NARRATING A STORY OR DESCRIBING A SITUATION	
IMPERFECT (actions in progress, gives background information)	PRETERITE (specific events in the past, advances the story)
Mis amigos y yo **jugábamos** afuera... _My friends and I were playing outside . . ._	cuando **empezó** a llover. _when it began to rain._
Lo **pasábamos** muy bien... _We were having a very good time . . ._	hasta que los vecinos **se quejaron**. _until the neighbors complained._
Ya **existían** grandes civilizaciones en América... _Great civilizations already existed in America . . ._	cuando **llegaron** los españoles. _when the Spaniards arrived._

You have already learned the two main Spanish verb forms used to talk about the past: the preterite and the imperfect. So far, you have used each tense separately, as in the following examples.

Preterite

El sábado **fui** al cine.　　　_On Saturday I went to the movies._

Vimos una película muy buena.　　　_We saw a very good movie._

Imperfect

Mi hermana y yo **jugábamos** al escondite.	*My sister and I used to play hide and seek.*
Mi familia **iba** a la playa todos los veranos.	*My family used to (would) go to the beach every summer.*

Besides expressing repeated and habitual actions in the past, the imperfect is also used to signal that an event or condition was in progress at a specific point in time or that two events were simultaneously in progress in the past. The words **mientras** (*while*) and **cuando** are often used with the imperfect. The English equivalent of this use of the imperfect is usually *was/were -ing* (e.g., *was studying, were playing, were living,* and so forth).

The preterite and imperfect may be used together in the same sentence. In fact, it is often difficult to tell a story in the past without using both. The imperfect describes an activity or condition in progress (i.e., provides background information), whereas the preterite communicates an interruption of that activity or condition. As such, it is the verb form that moves the narrative along in time. Note that the preterite is almost always used when a specific time frame or other information limits the event, as in *it rained **for three days**, I ran **six miles**, he lived **his whole life** in Mexico City.*

DE SOL Y VIENTO

In **Episodio 5** of *Sol y viento,* Carlos complains to his mother about the work that he has at the vineyard. Part of their conversation appears in the dialogue. Before watching the segment, think about which verb forms you think the characters will use.

CARLOS
Entonces sabrás[a] que tengo mucho
trabajo con la viña, mamá.

ISABEL
Cuando _____[1] tu papá, _____[2] de
los negocios. Yo ya _____[3] vieja y tu
hermana _____[4] otros intereses.

1. a. murió **b.** moría

2. a. te encargaste[b] **b.** te encargabas

3. a. estuve **b.** estaba

4. a. tuvo **b.** tenía

[a]*you must know* [b]*encargarse = to take over*

Actividad E Mientras...

Mientras unos personajes de *Sol y viento* hacían ciertas actividades, otros personajes hacían otras cosas. Empareja las frases de la columna A con las de la columna B para formar oraciones completas y lógicas.

<table>
<tr><td align="center">**A**</td><td align="center">**B**</td></tr>
</table>

Mientras...

1. ...Mario esperaba a Jaime, ____
2. ...Jaime y María subían en el funicular, ____
3. ...Traimaqueo le enseñaba (*showed*) la viña a Jaime, ____
4. ...Jaime corría por el parque, ____
5. ...Jaime hacía unas compras, ____

a. hablaban del trabajo de María.
b. María caminaba hacia la universidad.
c. María colgaba (*was hanging*) unos carteles.
d. María y Jaime caminaban hacia el hotel.
e. doña Isabel descansaba en casa.

Actividad F ¿Qué hacías?

Paso 1 Indica las actividades que hacías anoche a las diez.

Anoche a las diez yo...

☐ dormía.
☐ estudiaba.
☐ leía.
☐ estaba en un bar.
☐ veía una película.
☐ regresaba a mi casa.

☐ escuchaba música.
☐ practicaba un deporte.
☐ hablaba por teléfono con _____.
☐ navegaba la red.
☐ leía mi correo electrónico y lo contestaba.
☐ ¿ ?

Paso 2 Pregúntales a algunos de tus compañeros qué hacían anoche a las diez y apunta sus respuestas.

MODELO: E1: ¿Qué hacías anoche a las diez?
E2: Yo dormía. ¿Y tú?
E1: Escuchaba música y estudiaba para un examen.

Paso 3 ¿Qué hacía la mayoría de tus compañeros según tus apuntes? ¡Ahora adivina lo que hacía tu profesor(a)!

Actividad G Un poco de historia

Paso 1 Empareja las condiciones en proceso de la columna A con los eventos de la columna B.

A	B
1. ___ Ya existía una civilización muy avanzada en México cuando...	**a.** los conquistó Francisco Pizarro.
2. ___ George W. Bush era presidente de los Estados Unidos cuando...	**b.** los Estados Unidos ganaron una guerra contra México.
3. ___ Los incas vivían en la región andina cuando...	**c.** un grupo terrorista atacó las torres gemelas en Nueva York.
4. ___ La Argentina era un país muy próspero hasta que...	**d.** murió el General Franco.
5. ___ Texas era territorio mexicano hasta que...	**e.** entró en la Segunda Guerra Mundial
6. ___ España vivía bajo una dictadura militar hasta que...	**f.** llegó Hernán Cortés.
7. ___ Los Estados Unidos sufría una depresión económica cuando...	**g.** sufrió una gran crisis económica.

Paso 2 ¿Hay algunos eventos del **Paso 1** que no sabías antes? ¿Cuáles son?

MODELO: No sabía que...

Actividad H Un evento inolvidable (*unforgettable*)

Paso 1 Toda la clase va a identificar algún evento que todos recuerdan muy bien. Puede ser algo que tuvo impacto en la universidad, en la ciudad donde viven, en el país y/o el mundo.

Paso 2 Contesta las preguntas a continuación acerca del (*about the*) evento.

1. Cuando ocurrió, ¿dónde estabas?
2. ¿Qué hora era cuando te enteraste (*you found out*) del evento?
3. ¿Con quién(es) estabas?
4. ¿Cómo te sentías? (feliz, triste, enojado/a, confundido/a [*confused*], emocionado/a, asustado/a [*frightened*])
5. ¿Qué hiciste después de enterarte de lo que pasó?

Paso 3 Comparte tus respuestas con un compañero (una compañera) de clase y apunta lo que él/ella te dice. Luego, escribe un párrafo sobre el evento incluyendo la información que diste en el **Paso 2** y la de tu compañero/a.

SEGUNDA PARTE

Vocabulario

Talking About
Historical Events

Durante la guerra... **Important Events and Occurrences** ✳

Algunos eventos históricos importantes

▲ **El encuentro** de dos culturas:
Hernán Cortés con el emperador
azteca Moctezuma

▲ **La guerra** (*Los fusilamientos* [shootings]
del 3 de mayo por Francisco de Goya
[español, 1746–1828])

✳ MÁS VOCABULARIO

celebrar	to celebrate	**la invasión**	invasion
colonizar (c)	to colonize	**la llegada**	arrival
conquistar	to conquer	**la migración**	migration
descubrir	to discover	**la revolución**	revolution
establecer (zc)	to establish		
explorar	to explore	**difícil**	difficult
invadir	to invade	**emocionante**	exciting
		estable	stable
la conquista	conquest	**feliz**	happy
la depresión (económica)	(economic) depression	**oscuro/a**	dark; scary
		pacífico/a	peaceful
el descubrimiento	discovery	**tumultuoso/a**	tumultuous; unstable
el encuentro	encounter; meeting		
la exploración	exploration		
la fundación	founding		
la guerra	war		
la independencia	independence		
el/la inmigrante	immigrant		

Los desastres naturales

▲ Los efectos del **huracán** Mitch (Honduras)

▲ Los efectos de un **terremoto** en México

▲ Las **inundaciones,** el resultado de lluvias excesivas (Puerto Rico)

〜 Vistazo cultural

¿Un descubrimiento?

Muchos aprenden desde una edad temprana que el año 1492 es la fecha del «descubrimiento de América», o que Cristóbal Cólon «descubrió» América en ese año. Pero hay que tener en cuenta[a] que este acontecimiento[b] es un descubrimiento sólo desde el punto de vista[c] europeo. A muchos indígenas y latinoamericanos no les agrada el término **descubrimiento.** Para ellos, la llegada de los europeos no representa ningún descubrimiento del continente americano, ya que[d] los indígenas vivían allí durante muchos siglos. Según la perspectiva de una persona americana, los europeos que vinieron *invadieron* y *conquistaron* los terrenos[e] nativos de los indígenas. Por eso, en vez de hablar del «descubrimiento de América en 1492», se habla del «encuentro» de los dos mundos: el mundo europeo y el indígena americano.

▲ ¿Descubrimento o encuentro?

[a]tener... *keep in mind*   [b]*event*   [c]punto... *point of view*   [d]ya... *since*   [e]*lands*

Actividad A Definiciones

Empareja cada palabra con la definición apropiada.

1. ___ el terremoto
2. ___ la fundación
3. ___ la independencia
4. ___ la exploración
5. ___ la migración
6. ___ el descubrimiento
7. ___ la guerra

a. el movimiento (*movement*) de personas de un lugar a otro
b. un conflicto violento entre dos países
c. un movimiento de la tierra
d. el encuentro de algo nuevo
e. cuando un país ya no está bajo el control de otro
f. el proceso de aventurarse en un territorio nuevo
g. el establecimiento de una ciudad o una organización

Actividad B Algunos ejemplos

Paso 1 Escribe el primer ejemplo que te venga a la mente (*comes to mind*) de cada evento a continuación. Incluye la fecha si la sabes.

MODELO: un encuentro → 1492, Cristóbal Colón en América

1. una lucha (*struggle*) por la independencia
2. una migración
3. una guerra
4. un terremoto
5. una invasión
6. un descubrimiento
7. una exploración

Paso 2 Compara los ejemplos que escribiste en el **Paso 1** con los de tres compañeros/as. ¿Tienen los mismos ejemplos? Si todos tienen los mismos ejemplos para algunos eventos, ¿cuál puede ser la razón?

Paso 3 Comparte los ejemplos de tu grupo con la clase. Da una posible explicación en caso de que haya (*there are*) ejemplos comunes.

Actividad C ¿Cómo era durante esa época?

Paso 1 Con un compañero (una compañera) de clase, indiquen los adjetivos de la siguiente lista que describan mejor las siguientes épocas de la historia norteamericana.

MODELO: los años treinta del siglo XX → difíciles, oscuros, espantosos

difícil	espantoso/a (*scary*)	feliz	pacífico/a
emocionante	estable	oscuro/a	tumultuoso/a

1. la Revolución norteamericana
2. la Guerra Civil
3. los años veinte
4. la Guerra Fría

5. los años sesenta
6. los años noventa
7. los meses después del 11 de septiembre de 2001

Paso 2 Piensa en los adjetivos que escribiste en el **Paso 1.** ¿Cuáles son los eventos que influyeron en tu selección de adjetivos?

MODELO: los años treinta del siglo XX → la depresión económica, conflictos en Europa

Actividad D Esperanzas y preocupaciones (*Hopes and worries*)

Paso 1 ¿Cuáles son las esperanzas y preocupaciones que tienes acerca del mundo de hoy? En grupos de tres o cuatro personas, llenen la tabla a continuación.

TENEMOS LA ESPERANZA DE...	NOS PREOCUPA(N)...
MODELO: encontrar vida en otros planetas.	MODELO: la posibilidad de un terremoto en California.

Paso 2 ¿Cómo ven Uds. el mundo de hoy? ¿Son Uds. optimistas o pesimistas?

SOL Y VIENTO: Enfoque cultural

En el **Episodio 5** vas a ver un parque con una estatua enorme de la Virgen María. Los habitantes de Chile son, en su mayoría, católicos, como en la mayoría de los demás países hispanos. Por ejemplo, en España el 94% de la población es católica; en Chile, el 89%; en Venezuela, el 96%; y en Puerto Rico, el 85%.* Hasta en la Guinea Ecuatorial, donde hay una fuerte influencia de las culturas africanas, la mayoría de las personas se identifica con la Iglesia católica. Compara esas cifras[a] con el número de personas estadounidenses que se identifican como católicos: sólo llega al 28%. Claro, la manera en que se practica el catolicismo varía de país a país. Por ejemplo, en México la devoción a la Virgen de Guadalupe es casi más fuerte que la devoción a Jesucristo. Y en la zona andina (el Perú, Bolivia, el Ecuador) los indígenas han forjado[b] un catolicismo con restos[c] de la mitología y creencias de sus antepasados,[d] los incas.

[a]*figures* [b]*han... have created* [c]*remnants*
[d]*ancestors*

▲ La estatua de la Virgen María en el Cerro San Cristóbal en Santiago

*C.I.A. World Fact Book, 2003.

Gramática

¡No lo sabía!

More on Using the Preterite and Imperfect Together

When using verbs that express states or conditions in the past, Spanish often uses the imperfect. This is because states and conditions are usually ongoing, and they provide background information in relation to a specific event or action in the past.

Tenía dieciséis años cuando...	**aprendí** a conducir.
I was sixteen years old when . . .	*I learned to drive.*
Eran las ocho cuando...	me **llamaron.**
It was eight o'clock when . . .	*they called me.*

You have already learned that when some verbs that express states or conditions are used in the preterite, the English equivalent may be different.

—¿**Sabías** que Julio y María eran novios?	*Did you know that Julio and María were boyfriend and girlfriend?*
—Lo **supe** ayer.	*I found out about it yesterday.*
Quería ir al concierto, pero no **pude.**	*I wanted to go to the concert, but I couldn't.*
No **quiso** oírme.	*He refused to hear me.*

You will learn more about the uses of verbs that describe states and conditions in **Lección 7A.**

VERBS WITH MEANING CHANGES IN THE IMPERFECT AND PRETERITE			
IMPERFECT		PRETERITE	
conocía	I knew (*a person*)	**conocí**	I met (*a person*)
podía	I was able, could	**pude**	I could (and did)
no podía	I wasn't able, couldn't	**no pude**	I couldn't (and didn't)
quería	I wanted	**quise**	I tried
no quería	I didn't want	**no quise**	I refused
sabía	I knew (*something*)	**supe**	I found out
no sabía	I didn't know	**no supe**	I never knew / found out

DE SOL Y VIENTO

In **Episodio 4** of *Sol y viento,* you watched a scene in which Jaime talked with Traimaqueo at the vineyard. Part of their conversation appears in the dialogue. Which form of the verb would you put in the blank?

TRAIMAQUEO
La señora Isabel me espera en
la casa.

JAIME
Creía que la señora
Isabel _____ en Santiago.

TRAIMAQUEO
No, no, no. La señora Isabel no hace muchos viajes en estos días. No está de muy buena salud.

1. estuvo
2. estaba

⊙ Enfoque lingüístico

El tiempo y el aspecto

Thus far in *Sol y viento* you have seen two different verb forms that communicate that something occurred in the past: the preterite and the imperfect. The difference between the two is not one of *tense* but rather of *aspect*. Tense is a grammatical expression of time (usually verb endings in Romance languages and in English). You will recall from **Lección 4A** that tense locates an event or situation in the present, past, or future. Aspect, on the other hand, is a grammatical expression that communicates a speaker's perspective of a situation or event. For example, consider the difference in perspective of these sentences:

John sang.   John was singing.   John used to sing.

All of these sentences are in the past tense (as opposed to the present or future) but represent different perspectives. In *John sang*, the perspective communicated is of completion. The event is viewed from the "outside." The singing is over. The speaker communicates that it ended in some moment in the past. But in *John was singing*, the perspective is different. The event is viewed from the "inside" as an event in progress and may leave us expecting more information about what happened while he was singing. In *John used to sing*, the event is viewed as habitual or recurring. Unlike *John sang*, this last sentence communicates that the singing occurred more than one time in the past. Languages vary as to whether they express aspectual distinctions or not and in what way. Keep in mind that in Spanish you need to distinguish between an event being "in progress" or "recurring" in the past and the event being completed.

Actividad E ¿Quién lo diría (*would say it*)?

Indica cuál de los personajes de *Sol y viento* diría cada oración a continuación. Presta atención al uso del pretérito y del imperfecto.

> **a.** Jaime   **b.** María   **c.** Carlos

1. ___ Leía un papelito de la suerte cuando me choqué con (*I bumped into*) alguien en el parque.
2. ___ Colgaba (*I was hanging*) unos carteles cuando vi al norteamericano otra vez.
3. ___ Estaba en la oficina cuando me llamó el norteamericano.
4. ___ Estaba enfrente de la bodega cuando llegó el Sr. Talavera.
5. ___ Hablaba con Traimaqueo cuando supe que doña Isabel estaba en casa.
6. ___ Me dijo que trabajaba por los derechos de los mapuches.

Actividad F ¿Cuántos años tenías?

Paso 1 Llena los espacios en blanco con la edad que tenías cuando cada evento ocurrió.

1. Tenía _____ años cuando supe que Papá Noel (*Santa Claus*) no existía.
2. Tenía _____ años cuando aprendí a conducir un auto.
3. Tenía _____ años cuando tuve mi primera cita romántica.
4. Tenía _____ años cuando hice mi primer viaje en avión.
5. Tenía _____ años cuando empecé a asistir a la universidad.
6. Tenía _____ años cuando empecé a afeitarme la cara / las piernas (*my face / my legs*).
7. Tenía _____ años cuando mis padres me permitieron usar el auto a solas.
8. Tenía _____ años cuando mis padres me dejaron solo/a (*alone*) en casa sin niñero/a.
9. Tenía _____ años cuando mis padres me permitieron salir con mis amigos hasta medianoche.

Paso 2 Compara tus respuestas con las de tres compañeros. ¿Tienen las mismas respuestas? ¿Hay una edad típica en que ocurren ciertos eventos?

MODELO: Nosotros teníamos dieciocho años cuando empezamos a asistir a la universidad. Nos parece una edad típica.

Actividad G ¿A quién conociste?

Paso 1 Piensa en el momento en que conociste a alguien que ha tenido (*has had*) gran influencia en tu vida. Puede ser una persona famosa, un novio (una novia), tu mejor amigo/a o cualquier persona importante en tu vida.

Nombre de la persona _____

Paso 2 Escribe cuatro o cinco oraciones que describen el momento en que lo/la conociste. Usa las preguntas a continuación para organizar lo que vas a decir.

1. ¿En qué año lo/la conociste?
2. ¿Dónde estabas cuando lo/la conociste?
3. ¿Con quién estabas?
4. ¿Cómo era esa persona? (simpático/a, guapo/a, bonito/a, etcétera)
5. ¿Quién habló primero, tú o la otra persona?
6. ¿Cómo te sentías? (nervioso/a, emocionado/a, contento/a, etcétera)

Paso 3 Cuéntales tu historia a tres compañeros/as.

MODELO: Conocí a _(nombre)_ en el año... Estaba en...

Paso 4 ¿De quiénes hablaron tus compañeros? ¿Hablaron de personas famosas? ¿de profesores? ¿de novios/as?

Actividad H ¿Qué querías hacer?

Paso 1 Cuando estabas en el último año de la escuela secundaria, ¿qué planes tenías para ese año o para después de graduarte? ¿Qué querías hacer? Escribe cinco oraciones que describan tus planes.

MODELO: En el año 2003 quería asistir a la universidad de...

Paso 2 ¿Pudiste realizar (*achieve*) lo que querías hacer? Ahora añade más información a las oraciones del **Paso 1** para indicar lo que pasó.

MODELOS: En el año 2003 quería asistir a la universidad de _____ y lo hice. ¡Aquí estoy!

En el año 2003 quería asistir a la universidad de _____, pero no pude. No pude pagar la matrícula (*tuition*).

Paso 3 Compara la información que tienes en los **Pasos 1** y **2** con la de un compañero (una compañera). Luego prepara dos oraciones para compartir con la clase.

MODELOS: (Nombre) y yo queríamos asistir a la universidad de _____, y lo hicimos.

(Nombre) quería asistir a la universidad de _____ y yo quería asistir a la universidad de _____, pero no pudimos. A (nombre) no lo/la aceptaron y yo no pude pagar la matrícula.

TERCERA PARTE

Vocabulario

| **Me gradué en 2000.**

Personal Events, Triumphs, and Failures

  Algunos eventos importantes de la vida

la graduación

graduarse (me gradúo)

la boda

la novia

el novio   casarse (con)

el nacimiento

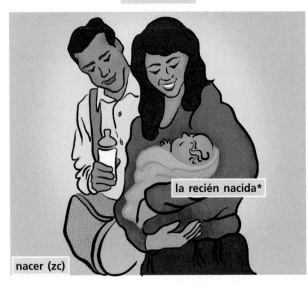

la recién nacida*

nacer (zc)

la mudanza

mudarse

---

*A newborn boy would be referred to as **el recién nacido.**

✳ MÁS VOCABULARIO

divertirse (ie, i)	to have fun
divorciarse (de)	to get divorced (from)
fracasar	to fail
morir (ue, u)	to die
tener (*irreg.*) **éxito**	to succeed, be successful
el divorcio	divorce
el éxito	success
el fracaso	failure
el matrimonio	marriage
la muerte	death

〰 Vistazo cultural

Las bodas en los países hispanos

Como en muchos países del mundo, las bodas en los países hispanos son grandes celebraciones y es común invitar a más de doscientas personas para celebrarlas. Si tienes la oportunidad de asistir a una boda en un país hispano, puedes notar algunas diferencias con las bodas norteamericanas. Por ejemplo, muchas bodas hispanas empiezan a eso de las siete de la tarde, y el novio va al altar acompañado de su madre o madrina.[a] Muchas veces no hay ni padrinos de boda[b] ni damas de honor.[c] Durante la ceremonia, el sacerdote[d] pone un rosario largo alrededor de los hombros[e] y las manos[f] de la pareja para simbolizar la unión y la protección del matrimonio. En algunos países el novio le da a la novia trece monedas o **arras** para simbolizar la habilidad del novio de sostener[g] y cuidar a[h] su esposa. La ceremonia no suele durar más de una hora, pero la fiesta después de la boda puede durar hasta la madrugada[i] del día siguiente.

▲ Una boda española

[a]*godmother* [b]padrinos... *groomsmen* [c]damas... *bridesmaids* [d]*priest* [e]*shoulders* [f]*hands*
[g]*support* [h]cuidar... *care for* [i]*dawn*

Actividad A ¿Qué evento se describe?

Tu profesor(a) va a leer descripciones de algunos eventos importantes. Escribe el número de la descripción al lado del evento correspondiente.

a. ___ la mudanza

b. ___ la muerte

c. ___ la boda

d. ___ el fracaso

e. ___ la graduación

f. ___ el nacimiento

g. ___ el divorcio

Actividad B ¿Cómo te sentías?

Paso 1 Empareja las emociones de la columna B con cada evento de la columna A. Hay más de una respuesta posible en muchos casos.

A	B
Uno se siente...	
1. ___ después de un divorcio.	**a.** feliz
2. ___ antes de casarse.	**b.** deprimido/a
3. ___ al conseguir un trabajo.	**c.** nervioso/a
4. ___ al graduarse.	**d.** enojado/a
5. ___ después de un nacimiento.	**e.** triste
6. ___ al cumplir veintiún años.	**f.** orgulloso/a
7. ___ al cumplir cuarenta años.	
8. ___ antes de mudarse a otra ciudad.	
9. ___ en la boda de unos amigos.	

Paso 2 Con un compañero (una compañera), comenten las respuestas posibles para los eventos del **Paso 1**. ¿Es posible sentir emociones opuestas (*opposite*) en algunas circunstancias? ¿Por qué?

Paso 3 Elige tres de los eventos del **Paso 1** que te han pasado (*that have happened to you*) y describe cómo te sentías. Comparte tus descripciones con tres compañeros.

MODELO: E1: Al cumplir veintiún años me sentía muy feliz.
E2: Yo también me sentía muy feliz

o

¿Ah, sí? Yo no. Me sentía muy deprimida.

¡Exprésate!

Important events often provoke certain emotions, which can be described using the verb **sentirse**.

Me siento...

ansioso/a	*anxious*
deprimido/a	*depressed*
enojado/a	*angry*
feliz, contento/a	*happy*
nervioso/a	*nervous*
orgulloso/a (de)	*proud (of)*
triste	*sad*

Also, **al** + *infinitive* in Spanish means *upon/while/when* (*doing something*). For example, **al cumplir veintiún años** means *upon turning* (*when turning*) *twenty-one*.

Actividad C   Un éxito memorable

Paso 1   Piensa en algún éxito personal que has experimentado (*you've experienced*). Puede ser la graduación de la escuela secundaria, ganar una competición, conseguir un trabajo, una carta de aceptación para ir a la universidad, salir con el hombre / la mujer de tus sueños (*dreams*), etcétera. Escribe el evento en el siguiente espacio en blanco.

_____

Paso 2   Escribe cuatro oraciones que describan el evento. Puedes usar las preguntas a continuación para organizar tus ideas.

> ¿En qué año ocurrió?
>
> ¿Cuántos años tenías?
>
> ¿Cómo te sentías?
>
> ¿Qué hiciste para celebrar el éxito?

Paso 3   Comparte tu experiencia con otras tres personas. Luego, escucha bien las experiencias de tus compañeros/as y apunta algunos momentos importantes.

Paso 4   ¿Cómo clasificas los éxitos de tus compañeros?

☐ éxito(s) académico(s)   ☐ éxito(s) en la vida personal
☐ éxito(s) deportivo(s)   ☐ ¿otro(s)?
☐ éxito(s) profesional(es)

▲ El equipo Real Madrid (España) celebra uno de sus muchos éxitos en el fútbol. El equipo tiene algunos de los mejores jugadores del mundo, como David Beckham.

Gramática

Tenía 30 años cuando nació mi primer hijo.

Summary of the Preterite and Imperfect

The chart in this section summarizes the basic uses of the preterite and imperfect that you have learned.

USES OF THE PRETERITE
• to communicate that an event happened at a particular point in time
Ramón **llegó** temprano. *Ramón arrived early.*
La fiesta no **terminó** hasta las 2:00 de la mañana. *The party didn't end until 2:00 in the morning.*
• to communicate an event that was confined by time limits
El partido **duró** tres horas. *The game lasted three hours.*
Viví allí desde 1995 hasta 2003. *I lived there from 1995 to 2003.*
• to communicate a series of completed or consecutive events
Preparé un café y **leí** el periódico. *I made coffee and read the newspaper.*
• to express that one event occurred while another was in progress
Mi madre **llamó** mientras comíamos. *My mom called while we were eating.*
USES OF THE IMPERFECT
• to communicate that an event was in progress at a certain time
A las 8:00 todavía **estudiaba.** *I was still studying at 8:00.*
• to communicate that two events were taking place at the same time
Mientras **comía, veía** la tele. *While I ate (was eating), I watched (was watching) TV.*
• to communicate that an event occurred repeatedly in the past
Mis amigos y yo **nos metíamos** en muchos líos. *My friends and I used to get into a lot of trouble.*
• to provide background information (time, weather, age, physical/mental characteristics, states) while narrating an event
Hacía muy buen tiempo el día de la fiesta. **Había** mucha gente allí que **tenía** entre 25 y 40 años. *The weather was very good on the day of the party. There were lots of people there who were between 25 and 40 years old.*

COMUNICACIÓN ÚTIL

To ask about an event ("How was . . . ?"), Spanish uses the expression **qué tal** with the preterite of the verb **estar.**

¿Qué tal estuvo el partido (la película, la boda, la clase...)?

How was the game (the movie, the wedding, the class . . .)?

Estuvo bien (mal, interesante, aburrido/a, divertido/a...).

It was good (bad, interesting, boring, fun . . .).

Spanish can also use **fue,** but only with indirect objects.

¿Cómo te fue en la entrevista?

How did it go for you in the interview? / How was the interview?

Me fue muy bien, gracias.

It went really well for me, thanks. / It was great, thanks.

DE SOL Y VIENTO

In **Episodio 5** of *Sol y viento,* María remembers that she had previously made plans with Diego and has to leave suddenly. Part of their conversation appears here. Before watching the segment, indicate which verb forms you think belong in the blanks.

MARÍA

Diego es un estudiante, es mi ayudante en la excavación. Lo _____¹ pasando tan bien contigo que no _____² en la hora.

JAIME

_____³ que... pues, que...

MARÍA

¿Que... que Diego _____⁴ mi novioª? ¿Que _____⁵ contigo sólo para investigar quién _____⁶ este especimen norteamericano?

1. **a.** estaba **b.** estuve
2. **a.** me fijabaᵇ **b.** me fijé
3. **a.** Pensaba **b.** Pensé
4. **a.** era **b.** fue
5. **a.** venía **b.** vine
6. **a.** era **b.** fue

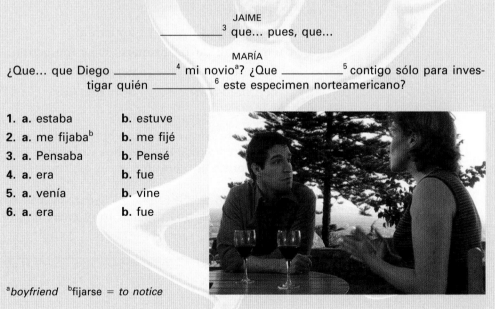

ª*boyfriend* ᵇfijarse = *to notice*

Actividad D Lo que piensa Jaime

Completa los pensamientos (*thoughts*) de Jaime con la forma correcta de cada verbo entre paréntesis.

> Antes de llegar a Chile, mi trabajo (fue / era)¹ mi vida. No (tuve / tenía)² mucha vida social y (salí / salía)³ muy poco. Pero desde queª (conocí / conocía)⁴ a María, lo veo todo diferente. Lo (pasé / pasaba)⁵ muy bien hoy con ella en el parque, ¡y espero verla otra vez!

ªdesde... *since*

Actividad E Mis primeras impresiones

Paso 1 Completa las oraciones a continuación sobre tus primeros días en la universidad.

1. Cuando llegué a la universidad por primera vez, el campus me parecía...

    ☐ grande.   ☐ pequeño.   ☐ confuso (*confusing*).
    ☐ emocionante.   ☐ _____

2. Cuando conocí a mi compañero/a de cuarto (una persona en una de mis clases) él/ella me parecía...

    ☐ simpático/a.   ☐ tímido/a.   ☐ distante.
    ☐ extrovertido/a. ☐ _____

3. Mi primera clase en la universidad fue (nombre) y era a la(s) _____

    ☐ de la mañana.   ☐ de la tarde.

4. La clase era...

    ☐ interesante.   ☐ aburrida.   ☐ _____

5. Cuando salí de mi primera clase me sentía...

    ☐ ansioso/a.   ☐ contento/a.   ☐ preocupado/a (*worried*).
    ☐ deprimido/a.   ☐ aburrido/a.   ☐ entusiasmado/a.
    ☐ _____

Paso 2 Comparte tus respuestas con las de tres compañeros. ¿Tuvieron Uds. las mismas impresiones? Escribe dos oraciones sobre una experiencia que tú y otra persona tienen en común.

MODELO: Cuando (nombre) y yo llegamos a la universidad por primera vez, el campus nos parecía muy emocionante.

Actividad F   La primera cita

Paso 1   Pon en orden lógico las siguientes oraciones, que narran la primera cita entre dos personas. Presta atención a los verbos en el pretérito y en el imperfecto.

_____ Entonces, el sábado, Arturo llegó a la casa de Raquel y salieron para el restaurante.

_____ Mientras caminaban por el parque hablaban de sus gustos personales.

_____ Un día Raquel trabajaba en casa cuando Arturo la llamó.

_____ Todo iba muy bien hasta que...

_____ Arturo le preguntó a Raquel si quería salir a cenar con él el sábado por la noche.

_____ Después de cenar, Arturo la invitó a dar un paseo por el parque.

_____ Como Raquel estaba nerviosa, no tenía mucha hambre y sólo pidió una ensalada.

_____ Raquel le dijo que sí y que estaba muy contenta.

Paso 2   Compara el orden de las oraciones con el de un compañero (una compañera). Luego escribe tres oraciones para terminar la historia.

Paso 3   Tu profesor(a) va a pedir que varios grupos lean sus historias a la clase. ¿Qué grupo tiene el final de la historia más creativo?

Actividad G   Eventos importantes en mi vida

Paso 1   Elige cinco eventos importantes en tu vida. Pueden ser éxitos, una tragedia, un nacimiento, una boda, etcétera. Indica el año de cada evento en una línea como la de abajo, pero no escribas el evento.

MODELO:

1981   1999   Hoy

Paso 2   Prepara de tres a cinco oraciones para cada evento. Puedes usar las preguntas a continuación para organizar tus ideas.

¿Qué ocurrió?

¿Cuántos años tenías?

¿Cómo te sentías?

¿Dónde / Con quién estabas?

¿Qué pasó después?

Paso 3   Con un compañero (una compañera) compartan los eventos que describieron. Sigan el modelo a continuación para empezar su conversación. Además de la pregunta inicial, tienen que pensar en por lo menos una pregunta para hacerle a su compañero/a sobre cada evento.

MODELO: E1: ¿Qué ocurrió en mil novecientos noventa y nueve?
          E2: Me gradué de la escuela secundaria. Tenía dieciocho años y estaba muy contento. Estaba con toda mi familia y mis amigos. Después de la ceremonia tuvimos una fiesta en mi casa.
          E1: ¿De qué escuela te graduaste?

SOL Y VIENTO

Antes de ver el episodio

Actividad A ¿Qué recuerdas?

¿Recuerdas lo que viste en el **Episodio 4**? Indica si las oraciones a continuación son ciertas o falsas. Si la oración es falsa, cámbiala.

	CIERTO	FALSO
1. Jaime pudo conocer a doña Isabel.	☐	☐
2. Carlos le regaló a Jaime una botella de vino.	☐	☐
3. Diego no sabe si va a continuar con sus estudios por presiones familiares.	☐	☐
4. La figura que compró Jaime simboliza un espíritu azteca.	☐	☐
5. Jaime y María quedaron en reunirse en el bar del hotel de Jaime.	☐	☐

Actividad B ¿Qué falta?

A continuación hay parte de una conversación entre doña Isabel y Carlos que no has visto (*that you haven't seen*). Antes de ver el episodio, escoge la opción apropiada para llenar cada espacio en blanco.

> CARLOS: Mamá, ¿qué te parecería
> si vendiéramos[a] la viña?
> ISABEL: ¿Vender «Sol y viento»?
> ¿Tú sabes cuánto _____[1]
> tu papá, cuánto _____[2] yo, para tener esta viña? ¡_____[3]
> este país sin nada!

[a]¿qué... *how would you feel if we sold*

    1. a. trabajaba   **b.** trabajó   **c.** trabaja

    2. a. trabajaba   **b.** trabajé   **c.** trabajo

    3. a. Vinimos a   **b.** Vivimos en   **c.** Salimos de

Actividad C El episodio

Ahora mira el episodio. Si hay algo que no entiendes bien, puedes volver a ver la escena en cuestión.

Después de ver el episodio

Actividad A ¿Qué recuerdas?

Contesta cada pregunta según lo que recuerdas del episodio.

1. ¿Qué hacía Jaime mientras esperaba a María?

  a. Hablaba por teléfono con Andy.

  b. Leía un artículo en el periódico.

2. Jaime piensa que María tiene una vida más interesante que la suya.

  a. cierto   **b.** falso

3. ¿Con quién habló doña Isabel después de la salida (*exit*) de Carlos?

4. ¿Qué significa la palabra «mapuche»?

5. ¿En qué trabajaba Jaime en su juventud?

  a. Trabajaba en la exportación de los vinos.

  b. Trabajaba en la fermentación de los vinos.

6. María tiene muchos amigos norteamericanos.

  a. cierto   **b.** falso

7. ¿Por qué colgó (*hung up*) el teléfono Jaime mientras hablaba con Andy?

  a. Porque había una mala conexión.

  b. Porque no quería seguir hablando con Andy.

Detrás de la cámara

You will notice that Jaime is extremely cautious when giving information about himself, both about his work and his personal life. In the past, Jaime's caution and discretion have served him well in his business practices and in keeping boundaries between his personal and professional lives. But how might his guardedness affect his personal relationships? Will María find it intriguing and attractive or will she think that Jaime has something to hide?

Actividad B ¿Lo captaste?

Ahora verifica tus respuestas a la **Actividad B** en **Antes de ver el episodio.** Puedes ver esa escena de nuevo si quieres.

Actividad C En resumen

Completa la siguiente narración con las palabras y expresiones apropiadas de la lista a la derecha.

En este episodio, las cosas _____[1] con la viña. Carlos le dice a su madre que _____[2] «Sol y viento», pero a doña Isabel _____[3] la idea.

Mientras tanto,[a] Jaime y María _____[4] la tarde juntos. Hablan de sus profesiones y a Jaime _____[5] el trabajo de María es más interesante que el suyo. Mientras toman una copa de vino, Jaime _____[6] a María por qué sabe tanto de los vinos. Las cosas _____[7] entre ellos hasta que María recibe una llamada de Diego y tiene que salir. Pero antes de despedirse[b] _____[8] un beso[c] a Jaime.

le cuenta
le da
le parece que
no le gusta nada
no van bien
pasan
quiere vender
van bien

[a]Mientras... *In the meantime* [b]*saying good-bye* [c]*kiss*

RESUMEN DE VOCABULARIO

Eventos históricos e importantes

colonizar (c)	to colonize
conquistar	to conquer
descubrir	to discover
establecer (zc)	to establish
explorar	to explore
invadir	to invade

los años veinte (treinta)	the 20s (30s) (*decades*)
la conquista	conquest
la década	decade
el desastre natural	natural disaster
el descubrimiento	discovery
el encuentro	encounter; meeting
la fecha	date (*calendar*)
la fundación	founding
la guerra	war
el huracán	hurricane
la inundación	flood
la llegada	arrival
el siglo (XXI)	(the 21st) century
el terremoto	earthquake

Cognados: la depresión (económica), la exploración, la independencia, el/la inmigrante, la invasión, la migración, la revolución

Eventos personales

casarse (con)	to get married (to)
divertirse (ie, i)	to have fun
divorciarse (de)	to get divorced (from)
fracasar	to fail
graduarse (me gradúo)	to graduate
mudarse	to move (*to a new house*)
nacer (zc)	to be born
tener (*irreg.*) éxito	to succeed, be successful

la boda	wedding
el divorcio	divorce
el éxito	success
el fracaso	failure
la graduación	graduation
el matrimonio	marriage
la mudanza	move (*to a new house*)
la muerte	death
el nacimiento	birth
el/la novio/a	groom, bride
el/la recién nacido/a	newborn baby

Repaso: celebrar, morir (ue, u), pasarlo bien/mal, sentirse (ie, i)

Adjetivos

ansioso/a	anxious
contento/a	happy
deprimido/a	depressed
difícil	difficult
emocionante	exciting
enojado/a	angry
estable	stable
feliz (*pl.* **felices**)	happy
nervioso/a	nervous
orgulloso/a (de)	proud (of)
oscuro/a	dark; scary
pacífico/a	peaceful
tumultuoso/a	tumultuous; unstable

Repaso: triste

Los números del 1.000 al 2.000.000

dos (tres,...) mil, diez mil, cien mil, doscientos mil, trescientos mil, cuatrocientos mil, quinientos mil, seiscientos mil, setecientos mil, ochocientos mil, novecientos mil, un millón (de), dos millones (de)
Repaso: mil

Otras palabras y expresiones

al + *infin.*	upon/while/when (*doing something*)
mientras	while

EPISODIO 6

Confrontación

¿Quién es el hombre con María? ¿Es un colega de la universidad? ¿un viejo amigo? ¿Qué papel[a] crees que va a desempeñar[b] en la historia?

▲ JAIME: Nuestra oferta es muy buena, señora. Su hijo quiere vender, y me ha indicado[c] que Ud. tal vez estaría de acuerdo.[d] Piénselo bien, por favor.

◄ ¿Por qué crees que Jaime está tan enojado? ¿Ha descubierto[e] que Carlos le mintió sobre la venta de «Sol y viento»?

[a]role [b]play [c]ha... he has indicated [d]tal... perhaps you would agree [e]¿Ha... Has he discovered

Vamos al extranjero[a]

IN THIS LESSON, YOU WILL LEARN:

- vocabulary related to taking trips and traveling
- how to give someone instructions using formal commands
- vocabulary related to giving and receiving directions
- vocabulary related to restaurants and ordering food
- to talk about what has happened using the present perfect

You will also prepare for **Episodio 6** of the film *Sol y viento*.

◄

El Aeropuerto Internacional de Maiquetía «Simón Bolívar» en Caracas, Venezuela

The following media resources are available for *Sol y viento: En breve*

Episodio 6 of *Sol y viento*

Online *Manual de actividades*

Interactive CD-ROM

Online Learning Center Website

[a]al... *abroad*

Vocabulario

Talking About
Taking Trips and
Traveling

Para hacer viajes

Travel Vocabulary

PERÚ

DESPIERTA · TVS · SEIS · SENTIDOS

El transporte

el autobús	bus
el avión	airplane
el barco	boat

En la agencia de viajes

el/la agente de viajes	travel agent
el boleto*	ticket
de ida	one-way
de ida y vuelta	round-trip
la clase turística	coach
el pasaporte	passport
la primera clase	first class
la reservación	reservation

En el aeropuerto

el asiento	seat
el/la asistente de vuelo	flight attendant
el equipaje	luggage
el maletero	skycap, porter
el/la pasajero/a	passenger
la sala de espera	waiting area
el/la viajero/a	traveler
el vuelo (directo)	(direct) flight

***El boleto** is used throughout Latin America, whereas **el billete** is used in Spain.

✳ MÁS VOCABULARIO

bajar (de)	to get off (of)
facturar el equipaje	to check luggage
hacer (*irreg.*) **cola**	to wait in line
hacer (*irreg.*) **escala**	to make a stopover
hacer (*irreg.*) **la maleta**	to pack a suitcase
hacer (*irreg.*) **un viaje**	to take a trip
ir (*irreg.*) **al extranjero**	to go abroad
marearse	to get nauseated, sick (*in a boat, car, plane*)
pasar por la aduana	to go through customs
pasar por seguridad	to go through security
subir (a)	to board, get on

◀

En el sur de España se nota la influencia árabe en la arquitectura, como en este hotel en Marbella.

El alojamiento[a]

[a]El... *Lodging*

alojarse / quedarse	to stay (*in a place*)
el botones*	bellhop
la cama matrimonial	double bed
la cama sencilla	single bed
la habitación	room
con baño (privado)	with (private) bathroom
el hotel (de lujo)	(luxury) hotel
la pensión	boardinghouse
completa	room and all meals
la media pensión	room and one other meal (usually breakfast)
la propina	tip
el servicio de cuarto	room service

***El mozo** is also commonly used to mean *bellhop*.

Actividad A   El transporte

Empareja las descripciones de la primera columna con la palabra o frase apropiada en la segunda columna.

1. ____ la persona que sirve las bebidas en el avión
2. ____ cuando un vuelo no es directo
3. ____ ponerse enfermo/a en un auto o avión
4. ____ el documento que se presenta al pasar por la aduana de otro país
5. ____ el lugar donde uno se queda antes de subir al avión
6. ____ viajar a otro país
7. ____ la persona que te ayuda con el equipaje

a. ir al extranjero
b. el pasaporte
c. marearse
d. el maletero
e. el/la asistente de vuelo
f. la sala de espera
g. hacer escala

Actividad B   ¿En qué orden?

Indica en qué orden (del 1 al 12) sueles hacer los siguientes preparativos para un viaje en avión.

____ Hago cola para pasar por seguridad.

____ Le pido una almohada (*pillow*) al asistente de vuelo.

____ Hago la reservación.

____ Hago la maleta.

____ Me duermo durante el vuelo.

____ Llego al aeropuerto.

____ Busco mi asiento en el avión.

____ Facturo el equipaje con el maletero.

____ Llego a mi destino (*destination*).

____ Tomo asiento en la sala de espera.

____ Hago cola antes de subir al avión.

____ Bajo del avión.

Actividad C   ¿A quién se refiere?

Tu profesor(a) va a leer una serie de oraciones sobre el transporte y el alojamiento. Indica si cada una se refiere lógicamente a un estudiante o a un hombre de negocios (*businessman*).

1. ...   2. ...   3. ...   4. ...   5. ...   6. ...   7. ...

Actividad D ¿Conoces bien al profesor (a la profesora)?

Paso 1 Indica si las siguientes oraciones sobre tu profesor(a) son ciertas (C) or falsas (F), según tu opinión.

Mi profesor(a) de español...	CIERTO	FALSO
1. viaja en primera clase con frecuencia.	☐	☐
2. se aloja en hoteles de lujo cuando viaja.	☐	☐
3. se marea cuando viaja en avión o auto.	☐	☐
4. pide servicio de cuarto en los hoteles.	☐	☐
5. ha hecho autostop (*has hitchhiked*).	☐	☐
6. ha perdido (*has lost*) un boleto del avión.	☐	☐
7. le pide una bebida alcohólica al asistente de vuelo.	☐	☐
8. se lleva las toallas (*towels*), el jabón o el champú de los hoteles.	☐	☐
9. ha hecho (*has taken*) un viaje en barco.	☐	☐
10. no viaja nunca en autobús.	☐	☐

Paso 2 La clase va a entrevistar al profesor (a la profesora) para saber si hace las actividades del **Paso 1.** Usen tú o Ud. según la preferencia de su profesor(a). Anoten sus respuestas.

MODELO: ¿Viaja Ud. / Viajas en primera clase con frecuencia?

≋ Vistazo cultural

Las propinas

La costumbre[a] de dar propinas varía mucho de país a país. En los hoteles de este país se les dan propinas a los botones cuando ayudan al cliente con el equipaje o cuando le consiguen un taxi. Sin embargo, no es tan común dejarle propina al personal de limpieza.[b] En México, al contrario, es muy buena costumbre darle propina al personal de limpieza, sea[c] en un hotel barato o en un hotel de lujo. Esta costumbre también se practica en los países asiáticos como el Japón y la China, pero de manera muy discreta: el cliente pone la propina en un sobre[d] y lo deja en la habitación.

En cuanto al transporte, los taxistas hispanos por lo general no esperan[e] propina a menos que ayuden al[f] cliente con las maletas. Los taxistas norteamericanos suelen recibir propinas del 10 ó 15 por ciento. En el aeropuerto Changi de Singapur, sin embargo, es ilegal darles propinas a los maleteros, y en las islas Fiji y Salomón, darle una propina a alguien quiere decir que esa persona te debe[g] algo.

Como se puede ver, cuando se trata de propinas, tanto el dar como el no dar puede ser causa de gran ofensa. Si estás en un país hispano y tienes dudas[h] en cuanto a la manera apropiada de dar propinas, pregúntale a un nativo del país.

[a]*custom* [b]*personal... cleaning staff* [c]*whether it be* [d]*envelope* [e]*expect* [f]*a... unless they help the* [g]*owes* [h]*doubts*

Gramática

| **Vuelva Ud. mañana.** **Affirmative Formal Commands**

—**Recuerde** Ud.: Como va al extranjero, **llegue** al aeropuerto con dos horas de anticipación (*two hours in advance*) antes de la salida de su vuelo.

Affirmative formal commands (**los mandatos formales**) directed at one person (**Ud.**) are formed by taking the **yo** form of the present-tense indicative, dropping the **-o** or **-oy** ending, and adding the "opposite" vowel. If the verb is an **-ar** verb, the opposite vowel is **-e.** If the verb is an **-er** or **-ir** verb, the opposite vowel is **-a,** as indicated in the chart. Commands directed at more than one person (**Uds.**) add **-en** to **-ar** verbs and **-an** to **-er** and **-ir** verbs.

Hable más despacio, por favor.	*Speak more slowly, please.*
Abra la puerta.	*Open the door.*
Vengan (Uds.) para las 2:00.	*Come at around 2:00.*

Verbs ending in **-car, -gar,** and **-zar** have a spelling change in order to maintain the original pronunciation of the **-c, -g,** and **-z** sounds.

Busque en el cajón.	*Look in the drawer.*
Paguen en la caja.	*Pay at the cashier.*
Empiecen ahora.	*Begin now.*

Ir and **ser** have irregular command forms.

Vaya para allá.	*Go over there.*
Sean pacientes.	*Be patient.*

The formal **Ud.** command for **dar** requires a written accent to distinguish it from the preposition **de.**

Dé un paseo por el parque.	*Take a walk through the park.*

Estar requires an accent on both **Ud.** and **Uds.** forms.

Esté aquí a mediodía.	*Be here at noon.*
Estén tranquilos.	*Be calm.*

Direct and indirect object pronouns, as well as reflexive pronouns, are attached to the end of affirmative formal commands. Remember that when both a direct and an indirect object pronoun are used, indirect objects come before direct objects. Note the written accents, which indicate where the stress would normally fall on the verb if there were no pronouns included.

¿La tarea? **Háganla.**	*The homework? Do it.*
Despiértense.	*Wake up.*
¿El libro? **Démelo.**	*The book? Give it to me.*

FORMAL COMMANDS				
INFINITIVE	**yo** FORM	STEM	ADD THE "OPPOSITE" VOWEL FOR **Ud.**	ADD THE "OPPOSITE" VOWEL AND **-n** FOR **Uds.**
hablar	hablo	habl-	+ e = **hable**	**hablen**
beber	bebo	beb-	+ a = **beba**	**beban**
abrir	abro	abr-	+ a = **abra**	**abran**
decir	digo	dig-	+ a = **diga**	**digan**
conducir	conduzco	conduzc-	+ a = **conduzca**	**conduzcan**
VERBS ENDING IN *-car*, *-gar*, AND *-zar*				
INFINITIVE	**yo** FORM	STEM	SPELLING CHANGES BEFORE ADDING THE "OPPOSITE" VOWEL FOR **Ud.**	ADD THE "OPPOSITE" VOWEL AND **-n** FOR **Uds.**
sacar	saco	sac-	c → qu + e = **saque**	**saquen**
pagar	pago	pag-	g → gu + e = **pague**	**paguen**
comenzar	comienzo	comienz-	z → c + e = **comience**	**comiencen**

DE SOL Y VIENTO

In **Episodio 6** of *Sol y viento,* you will watch a scene in which a new character, don Francisco (Paco) Aguilar, buys vegetables in a Mexico City street market. Part of his conversation with Lourdes, a vendor, is repeated in the dialogue.

PACO
¡Estos sí que son jitomates[a]! ¡Firmes y de buen color! Así me gustan.

LOURDES
Como le dije: los mejores del mercado.

PACO
_____ dos kilos, por favor.

Selecting from the following list, what command do you think don Paco says in this scene?

1. Págueme
2. Cómpreme
3. Déme

[a]*red tomatoes* (*Mex.*)

Actividad E ¿A quién se lo diría Jaime (*would Jaime say it to*)?

Desde el principio (*beginning*) de la película hasta finales del **Episodio 5,** Jaime les habla de Ud. a los otros personajes. Basándote en lo que sabes de Jaime hasta ahora, indica a quién le diría cada mandato a continuación.

1. Tenga este regalo. Es para Ud.   Se lo diría a _____.
2. Lléveme al Valle del Maipo, por favor.   Se lo diría a _____.
3. Déme el contrato firmado.   Se lo diría a _____.
4. Hábleme de su trabajo aquí en la viña.   Se lo diría a _____.

Actividad F Una receta (*recipe*)

A continuación hay una receta para preparar una ensalada de frutas. Ordena las instrucciones lógicamente, del 1 al 7.

Vocabulario útil

cortar	to cut
pelar	to peel
los pedacitos	small pieces
el tasón	large bowl

____ Ponga el tasón en el refrigerador por dos horas.
____ Pele las bananas y naranjas antes de cortarlas.
____ Lave las frutas con agua fría.
____ Sirva la ensalada bien fría.
____ Corte las manzanas, naranjas y bananas en pedacitos.
____ Compre manzanas, naranjas, bananas y uvas en el supermercado.
____ Ponga las frutas cortadas y las uvas en un tasón.

Actividad G En mi ciudad

Paso 1 Lee la lista de instrucciones e indica si cada una se dirige a (*is directed at*) un turista que visita Los Ángeles o a un turista que visita Nueva York.

	LOS ÁNGELES	NUEVA YORK
1. Visite la Estatua de la Libertad.	☐	☐
2. Dé un paseo por el Camino de la Fama en Hollywood.	☐	☐
3. Pase por las mansiones de Beverly Hills.	☐	☐
4. Vea un espectáculo (*show*) en Broadway.	☐	☐
5. Corra en el Parque Central.	☐	☐
6. Asista a un partido de los Lakers.	☐	☐

Paso 2 Usa mandatos afirmativos para hacer una lista de las seis cosas que un turista debe hacer si hace un viaje a tu ciudad u otra ciudad que conoces bien. Presenta tus resultados a la clase.

Nombre de la ciudad: _____

Actividad H   Situaciones y recomendaciones

A continuación hay una lista de situaciones en que se encuentran muchos viajeros en el aeropuerto. Empareja cada situación con la recomendación apropiada.

Situación

1. ____ Cuando hacemos reservaciones en la agencia de viajes, siempre nos salen muy caras.
2. ____ Cuando pasamos por seguridad siempre suena (*sounds*) la alarma.
3. ____ No podemos dormir bien durante los vuelos porque tenemos miedo de volar (*we're afraid of flying*).
4. ____ Siempre nos lleva mucho tiempo facturar el equipaje.
5. ____ Los maleteros son groseros (*rude*) y tiran (*they throw*) nuestras maletas.
6. ____ Tenemos que viajar a una ciudad grande y no queremos llevar mucho dinero en efectivo.

Recomendación

a. Lleven cheques de viajero.
b. Tomen un calmante (*tranquilizer*) antes de subir al avión.
c. Hablen con el gerente (*manager*) de la línea aérea.
d. Hagan una sola maleta.
e. Busquen boletos más baratos en el Internet.
f. Pongan las llaves (*keys*) y la joyería (*jewelry*) en la maleta.

Actividad I   Consejos para los profesores

Paso 1 En grupos de tres, escriban cuatro consejos afirmativos sobre lo que los profesores deben hacer para llevarse bien (*get along well*) con los estudiantes.

MODELO: Lleguen a clase a tiempo.

Paso 2 Presenten su lista a la clase. La clase va a decidir cuáles son las instrucciones más importantes.

Vocabulario

Getting Around Town | **¿Cómo llego?** **Giving and Receiving Directions**

Cruce la calle.	Cross the street.
Doble a la derecha.	Turn right.
Doble a la izquierda.	Turn left.
Siga derecho.	Go straight.
¿Cómo se llega a... ?	How do you get to . . . ?
¿Cuánto hay de aquí a... ?	How far is it to . . . ?

✳ MÁS VOCABULARIO

cruzar (c)	to cross
doblar	to turn
seguir (i, i) (g) derecho	to continue, go straight
la cuadra / la manzana	block
el mapa	map (*in general*)
el plano	city map

Repaso: el norte, el sur, el este, el oeste

〰 Vistazo cultural

¿A cuántas curvas está?

Como en los países hispanos se usa el sistema métrico, las distancias se dan en kilómetros, no en millas. En las áreas montañosas de Chile, el Perú y otros países andinos, las carreteras[a] son muy sinuosas.[b] En estas regiones las distancias se dan en **curvas** y no en kilómetros. Si le preguntas a un andino: «Cuánto hay de aquí al pico[c] de la montaña?», es probable que te diga[d] algo como: «Está a 22 curvas.» Es decir, hay que dar la vuelta a 22 curvas para llegar al destino final.

Debido a[e] las carreteras sinuosas, es muy peligroso[f] conducir en los Andes y son frecuentes los accidentes. El Perú emplea un sistema de señales preventivas[g] para advertirles[h] de curvas peligrosas a los conductores.

Estas son sólo unas de las muchas señales que uno debe conocer para conducir con cautela[i] en las montañas de Sudamérica. ¿Crees que eres lo suficientemente aventurero/a para conducir en los Andes?

[a]*highways* [b]*winding* [c]*top* [d]*es... he will probably tell you* [e]*Debido... Due to* [f]*dangerous* [g]*señales... warning signs* [h]*warn (them)* [i]*caution*

Actividad A ¿Adónde vamos?

Mira el plano de México, D.F., a continuación. Tu profesor(a) va a leer una serie de direcciones. Sigue sus direcciones e indica cuál es el punto de llegada.

MODELO: PROFESOR(A): ¿Adónde vamos? Comiencen en la Iglesia de San Lorenzo. Sigan derecho en la calle Belisario Domínguez. Doblen a la derecha en la calle República de Chile. Doblen a la izquierda en González Obregón. Sigan derecho una cuadra y doblen a la izquierda. ¿Dónde estamos?

ESTUDIANTES: Estamos en la plaza Santo Domingo.

MODELO:

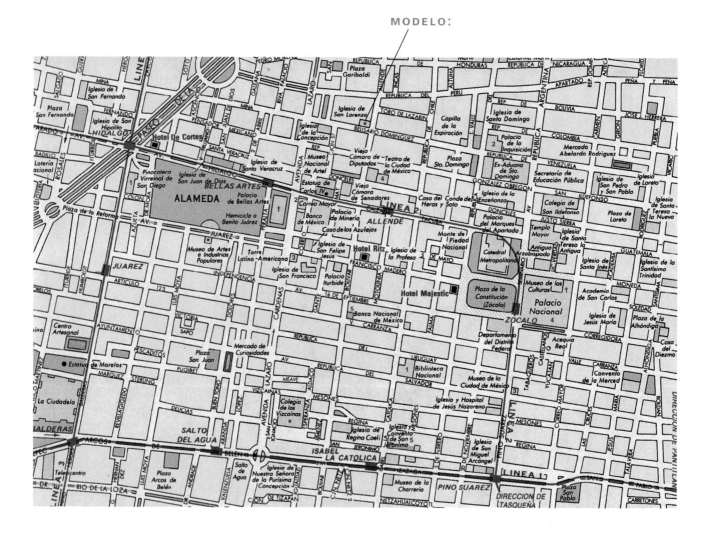

Actividad B ¿En qué sentido (*direction*)?

Escucha las descripciones que da tu profesor(a) e indica si son ciertas o falsas.

1. ...   **2.** ...   **3.** ...   **4.** ...   **5.** ...   **6.** ...   **7.** ...   **8.** ...

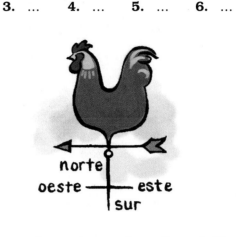

Actividad C ¿Conoce el campus mi profesor(a)?

Paso 1 En grupos de tres, piensen en un edificio o sitio muy conocido de su campus, pero no lo mencionen. Luego, escriban instrucciones sobre cómo llegar a ese edificio o sitio. Las instrucciones deben ser apropiadas para dárselas a una persona que visita el campus.

MODELO: Ud. está enfrente de la biblioteca. Siga derecho en la calle Speedway. Doble a la derecha en la calle Randolf. Doble a la izquierda en Riverside y cruce la calle.

Paso 2 Los grupos van a leerle las instrucciones al profesor (a la profesora) a ver si él/ella puede adivinar el punto de llegada. ¿Conoce muy bien el campus su profesor(a)?

▲ La Universidad de Cartagena (Cartagena, Colombia).

NAVEGANDO LA RED ～～～～～～～

Busca un mapa del viaje (de los viajes) que hizo un explorador español al Nuevo Mundo (por ejemplo: Álvar Núñez Cabeza de Vaca, Hernán Cortés, Francisco Pizarro, Ponce de León, Hernando de Soto) y describe una de las rutas de su expedición.

Gramática

More on Giving Instructions

¡No vuelvan tarde!

Negative Formal Commands

FORMAL COMMANDS USED WITH OBJECT AND REFLEXIVE PRONOUNS			
PRONOUNS ARE ATTACHED TO THE END OF FORMAL COMMANDS		PRONOUNS COME BEFORE NEGATIVE FORMAL COMMAND FORMS	
Háble**le**.	*Talk to him (her).*	No **le** hable.	*Don't talk to him (her).*
Cómpren**la**.	*Buy it. (it = la comida)*	No **la** compren.	*Don't buy it.*
Dé**melo**.	*Give me it. (it = el libro)*	No **me lo** dé.	*Don't give it to me.*
Siénten**se**.	*Sit down.*	No **se** sienten.	*Don't sit down.*

Negative formal commands are formed in the same way as affirmative commands. Drop the **-o** or **-oy** from the first-person form (**yo**) of the present-tense indicative and add the "opposite" vowel, plus an additional **-n** for plural (**Uds.**) forms.

No lleguen tarde.	*Don't arrive late.*
No vaya sin mí.	*Don't go without me.*
No sean ridículos.	*Don't be ridiculous.*

The principal difference between affirmative and negative formal commands is the placement of object and reflexive pronouns. These pronouns come *before* negative command forms, not after them. When both a direct and an indirect object are used, the indirect object pronoun precedes the direct object pronoun, as indicated in the chart.

No me mire así.	*Don't look at me that way.*
No me lo dé ahora, por favor.	*Don't give it to me now, please.*
No se despierten tarde.	*Don't wake up late.*

COMUNICACIÓN ÚTIL

Formal commands can also be used to express what you want yourself and others to do (or not to do) together, as in *Let's make a toast* or *Let's not go out tonight*. These types of commands (often called **nosotros** commands) are formed by dropping the **-o** or **-oy** from the first-person form of the present-tense indicative and adding the "opposite" vowel plus **-mos**. The irregular forms for **ir** and **ser** can be used in this way too.

¡Comamos!	*Let's eat!*
Hablemos en serio.	*Let's talk seriously.*
No lo **molestemos**.	*Let's not bother him.*
No **seamos** pesimistas.	*Let's not be pessimistic.*
Vayamos a lo nuestro.	*Let's get back to our business.*

Cómo viajar en avión sin problemas

- Verifique el estatus de su vuelo antes de ir al aeropuerto.

- Llegue al aeropuerto con dos horas de anticipación.[a]

- Escriba su nombre y dirección en todas las maletas.

- Quítese las joyas[b] antes de pasar por seguridad.

- No ponga cosas frágiles en la maleta.

- No haga más maletas de las que pueda llevar.

- No se olvide de llevar su teléfono celular para emergencias.

- No descuide[c] su equipaje.

[a]con... *two hours in advance* [b]*jewelry* [c]*leave unattended*

DE SOL Y VIENTO

In **Episodio 3** of *Sol y viento,* you viewed a scene in which Carlos barks out some orders to his workers after inviting Jaime to his office to talk. Part of his dialogue appears here.

CARLOS
¿Por qué no vamos a mi oficina para tener así más privacidad? ¡Traimaqueo! _____ y sigan trabajando ¡Ya vuelvo!

Do you remember what Carlos says to his workers?

1. No presten atención (*Don't pay attention*)
2. No se distraigan (*Don't get distracted*)
3. No me molesten (*Don't bother me*)

Actividad D ¿A quién se lo diría?

Basándote en lo que sabes de los personajes de *Sol y viento*, indica a quién Jaime le diría cada mandato a continuación.

1. No me dé más pretextos (*excuses*). Necesito las firmas.

Se lo diría a _____.

2. No se limite solamente a carteles. Haga una campaña (*campaign*) efectiva para ayudar a los mapuches.

Se lo diría a _____.

3. No me deje (*drop me off*) en el hotel. Déjeme en el parque.

Se lo diría a _____.

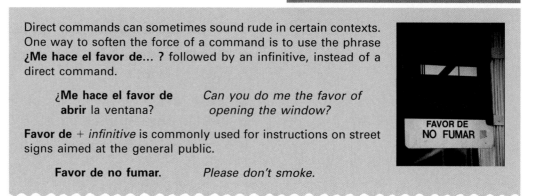

COMUNICACIÓN ÚTIL

Direct commands can sometimes sound rude in certain contexts. One way to soften the force of a command is to use the phrase **¿Me hace el favor de... ?** followed by an infinitive, instead of a direct command.

¿Me hace el favor de abrir la ventana? *Can you do me the favor of opening the window?*

Favor de + *infinitive* is commonly used for instructions on street signs aimed at the general public.

Favor de no fumar. *Please don't smoke.*

Actividad E La etiqueta del uso de los teléfonos celulares

Paso 1 A continuación hay una lista de consejos dirigidos (*directed*) a un consumidor sobre la etiqueta apropiada en cuanto al uso de los teléfonos celulares. Indica si estás de acuerdo o no con cada consejo.

	ESTOY DE ACUERDO.	NO ESTOY DE ACUERDO.
1. No hable de cosas privadas en público.	☐	☐
2. No conteste el celular en el cine o en un restaurante.	☐	☐
3. No haga llamadas telefónicas en el auto.	☐	☐
4. No hable en voz muy alta (*loudly*) en el transporte público.	☐	☐
5. No seleccione un tono de timbre (*ring tone*) irritante (*annoying*).	☐	☐
6. No invada (*invade*) el espacio personal de alguien.	☐	☐

Paso 2 Usa la frase **favor de** + infinitivo para crear un aviso (*sign*) sobre el uso de teléfonos celulares en lugares públicos. La siguiente palabra puede ser útil: **prender** = *to turn on*.

MODELOS: Favor de no prender el teléfono celular en el cine.

Favor de apagar el teléfono celular en el restaurante.

Actividad F ¿Niños o adolescentes?

Lee la siguiente lista de algunos consejos que los padres suelen darles a sus hijos. Luego, indica si cada consejo es para los niños, para los adolescentes o para los dos.

	NIÑOS	ADOLESCENTES	LOS DOS
1. No coman comida chatarra (*junk food*).	☐	☐	☐
2. No corran con tijeras (*scissors*) en la mano.	☐	☐	☐
3. No se sienten cerca del televisor.	☐	☐	☐
4. No conduzcan bajo la influencia del alcohol.	☐	☐	☐
5. No hablen con desconocidos (*strangers*).	☐	☐	☐
6. No salten (*jump*) en la cama.	☐	☐	☐
7. No crucen la calle sin mirar primero en ambos sentidos (*both directions*).	☐	☐	☐
8. No salgan de la casa con el pelo mojado (*wet*) o se van a enfermar.	☐	☐	☐

▲ ¡No salten en la cama!

Actividad G En el extranjero

Paso 1 Con un compañero (una compañera), diseñen (*design*) un folleto (*brochure*) en el cual indican lo que un turista norteamericano debe o no debe hacer cuando viaja al extranjero. Mencionen cinco cosas que debe hacer (con mandatos afirmativos) y cinco cosas que no debe hacer (con mandatos negativos).

Paso 2 Entreguen su folleto al profesor (a la profesora). Su profesor(a) va a leer algunos mandatos a la clase. Entre todos, indiquen si cada consejo es válido para **todos los países** que visita o sólo para **algunos países.**

MODELO: PROFESOR(A): Pídales direcciones a los nativos.
TODOS: Para todos los países.
PROFESOR(A): No beba agua del grifo (*tap water*).
TODOS: Para algunos países.

Vocabulario

Los vinos y licores se sirven en **copas,** pero el agua, los refrescos, la leche y otras bebidas frías se sirven en **vasos.** Las bebidas calientes se sirven en **tazas.** Por eso, cuando se habla de las bebidas, se dice **una copa** de vino, **un vaso** de agua y **una taza** de café.

---

*__La carta__ is also used for *menu.*

✳ MÁS VOCABULARIO

los cubiertos	silverware
la cuenta	bill, check (*in a restaurant*)
el primer (segundo, tercer) plato	first (second, third) course
atender (ie)	to wait on
dejar (una) propina	to leave a tip
ordenar / pedir (i, i)	to order
traer (*irreg.*)	to bring
¿Me podría traer... ?	Could you bring me . . . ?
¿Qué trae... ?	What does . . . come with?

≋ Vistazo cultural

En los restaurantes hispanos

Comer en un restaurante en el mundo hispano es una experiencia muy diferente de lo que es en este país. Una costumbre norteamericana que no es común en los países hispanos es la de servir la comida al estilo bufé, donde el cliente paga un solo precio por comer todo lo que quiera.[a]

En cuanto a las bebidas, en el mundo hispano no existe el concepto del relleno gratis.[b] En muchos restaurantes de este país el cliente puede consumir cuatro refrescos, pero sólo paga uno. En los restaurantes hispanos, si uno toma cuatro refrescos tiene que pagarlos todos. La costumbre del relleno gratis también influye en[c] la manera en que los meseros atienden a los clientes. En muchos restaurantes norteamericanos, los meseros se afanan[d] por rellenar[e] las bebidas (¡aun cuando no están vacías[f]!) con la intención de recibir una buena propina. En los restaurantes hispanos, los meseros no rellenan las bebidas; no le traen al cliente una bebida nueva hasta que termina la primera, y aun así es frecuente tener que pedirla. En general, los meseros hispanos no apresuran[g] a los clientes. Y a diferencia de los restaurantes norteamericanos, los meseros hispanos no traen la cuenta a la mesa hasta que el cliente diga:[h] «La cuenta, por favor.»

[a]todo... *whatever he wants*   [b]relleno... *free refill*   [c]influye... *influences*   [d]se... *hurry*   [e]*refill*
[f]*empty*   [g]no... *don't rush*   [h]*says*

Actividad A ¿Alta cocina (*Gourmet cooking*) o comida rápida?

Lee las oraciones a continuación e indica si se refieren a un restaurante de alta cocina o a un restaurante de comida rápida.

	RESTAURANTE DE ALTA COCINA	RESTAURANTE DE COMIDA RÁPIDA
1. La cuenta incluye la propina si hay más de ocho personas en la mesa.	☐	☐
2. Los cubiertos son de plástico.	☐	☐
3. Es común pagar la comida al momento de pedirla.	☐	☐
4. Los meseros visten trajes elegantes.	☐	☐
5. La comida se sirve en bandeja (*tray*) de plástico.	☐	☐
6. El/La cliente puede leer el menú y pedir la comida desde el auto.	☐	☐
7. El menú incluye una lista de bebidas alcohólicas.	☐	☐
8. Ofrece servicio de valet para estacionar (*valet parking*).	☐	☐

mis antojitos

Cameron Díaz

La rubia peligrosa de los *Ángeles de Charlie 2* es una chica de sorpresas. Adora el caviar y el champán, pero también las papas fritas y la cerveza. Cobra 20 millones por película, pero prefiere estar con su gato...

▲ Según este recorte (*clipping*) de una revista, ¿qué tipo de restaurante prefiere Cameron Díaz, uno de alta cocina, uno de comida rápida o los dos?

Actividad B ¿En qué orden?

A continuación hay una lista de frases que los meseros les dicen a los clientes. Pon las frases en el orden en que ocurren, del 1 al 7.

____ ¿Les retiro (*May I take away*) los platos?

____ ¿Están listos para pedir?

____ Les dejo la cuenta. Fue un placer (*pleasure*) servirles.

____ ¿Desean algo de tomar mientras leen el menú?

____ ¿Desean algún postre o una taza de café?

____ El bistec para el señor y el pescado para la señora. Buen provecho. (*Enjoy your meal.*)

____ ¿Está bien la comida?

Actividad C Cuando el servicio es malo

Paso 1 Lee cada situación a continuación e indica cómo reaccionarías (*you would react*).

1. El mesero te trae la comida y al probarla (*tasting it*), te das cuenta de (*you realize*) que tiene un pelo encima.
   a. Lo saco (*I remove it*) y sigo comiendo.
   b. Le pido otro plato de comida al mesero.
   c. Me quejo (*I complain*) con el gerente (*manager*).
   d. ¿ ?

2. Al rellenarte (*refilling*) la taza, el mesero derrama (*spills*) el café sobre tu camisa.
   a. Lo perdono.
   b. Le doy menos propina.
   c. No le doy ninguna propina.
   d. ¿ ?

3. Recibes la cuenta de otra mesa y es mucho más pequeña que la tuya.
   a. Le digo al mesero que se equivocó (*he made a mistake*).
   b. Pago la cuenta como si fuera (*as if it were*) mía.
   c. Pago la cuenta como si fuera mía, pero le doy al mesero una buena propina.
   d. ¿ ?

4. El mesero te trae un plato de comida, y al probarla te das cuenta de que está bien fría.
   a. La como sin decirle nada al mesero.
   b. Pido otro plato de comida.
   c. Me quejo con el gerente.
   d. ¿ ?

5. Tienes más de 40 minutos de esperar y la comida no ha llegado (*has not arrived*) todavía. El mesero llega, te pide perdón (*he apologizes*) y te explica que sólo hay un cocinero y que las órdenes se han atrasado (*have backed up*).
   a. Lo perdono y espero un rato más.
   b. Le pido al mesero que me dé (*gives me*) la comida para llevar (*to go*).
   c. Me desahogo con (*I take it out on*) el mesero y no le doy propina.
   d. ¿ ?

 Paso 2 Con un compañero (una compañera) de clase, compartan (*share*) sus reacciones ante (*when faced with*) estas situaciones.

MODELO: ¿Cómo reaccionas si el mesero te trae un plato de comida que tiene un pelo encima?

Paso 3 Escoge una situación del **Paso 1** y describe brevemente cómo tú y tu compañero/a de clase reaccionan ante esa situación.

Gramática

Talking About What Has Happened

¡Lo he pasado muy bien!

Introduction to the Present Perfect

«He cometido el peor pecado que uno puede cometer: no he sido feliz.»*
—Jorge Luis Borges (1899–1986), escritor argentino

To talk about what has happened, Spanish uses a form of the verb **haber** (*to have*)[†] plus a past participle. Past participles are formed by removing the **-ar**, **-er**, and **-ir** verb endings and adding **-ado, -ido,** and **-ido,** respectively.

He tomado dos aspirinas hoy.	*I have taken two aspirins today.*
¿Has conocido a una persona famosa?	*Have you met a famous person?*
Hemos salido tres veces esta semana.	*We have gone out three times this week.*

Verbs whose stems end in a vowel require a written accent in the past participle.

leer → **leído**

oír → **oído**

traer → **traído**

Some common verbs have irregular past participles, as indicated in the chart.

PRESENT PERFECT OF REGULAR VERBS				
haber		+	PAST PARTICIPLE	
(yo)	he	(nosotros/as)	hemos	viajado
(tú)	has	(vosotros/as)	habéis	conocido
(Ud.)	ha	(Uds.)	han	vivido
(él/ella)	ha	(ellos/ellas)	han	

IRREGULAR PAST PARTICIPLES		
VERB	PAST PARTICIPLE	EXAMPLES
decir	**dicho**	Mi novio no me **ha dicho** la verdad.
escribir	**escrito**	**¿Has escrito** la carta?
hacer	**hecho**	**Hemos hecho** un viaje a Nueva York.
morir	**muerto**	Mis abuelos ya **han muerto.**
poner	**puesto**	**He puesto** dinero en el banco.
ver	**visto**	No **he visto** la nueva película de Brad Pitt.
volver	**vuelto**	Los niños no **han vuelto** del parque.

---

*"I have committed the worst sin there is: I have not been happy."

[†]**Haber** is an auxiliary verb that is *not* interchangeable with **tener.** It is also an irregular verb. You already know several of its forms: **hay** (*there is / there are*), **hubo** (*there was*), **había** (*there was / there were*).

DE SOL Y VIENTO

In **Episodio 6** of *Sol y viento,* you will watch a scene in which Jaime and doña Isabel talk about the sale of the winery. Part of their exchange appears here.

JAIME
Nuestra oferta es muy buena, señora. Su hijo quiere vender, y me **ha indicado** que Ud. tal vez estaría de acuerdo.[a] Piénselo bien, por favor.

ISABEL
Ya se lo ____. «Sol y viento» no está a la venta. Hasta luego, señor Talavera.

What do you think doña Isabel says in the space above?

1. he dicho
2. he vendido
3. he pagado

[a]tal... *perhaps you would agree*

⊙ Enfoque lingüístico

Los verbos perfectos

Contrary to its meaning in everyday use, the word *perfect* does not mean *without flaw* when applied to languages. The term *perfect* connotes the meaning *completed*. When used in relationship to the present time, it is used to express that an event began sometime in the past but is either still ongoing in the present or is somehow closely related to the present time. Note, for example, the difference between *I once ran a marathon* and *I have recently run a marathon.* The former clearly situates a completed event sometime in the remote past; the latter situates the event closer to the present time. Note how certain adverbs of time cannot be used with the present perfect in English: *I once have run a marathon, A long time ago I have lived in Arizona, Three weeks ago I have run a marathon.*

Spanish and English are similar in their use of the present perfect, although not completely identical. For example, in Spain, the present perfect is often used as a substitute for the preterite. This reflects a tendency common to Latinate languages. For example, both French and Italian no longer have active simple past-tense forms in spoken language; instead, the present-perfect forms function both as preterites and present perfects. Thus, *j'ai fini* in French can mean either *I have finished* or *I finished.*

One of the things you will notice about Spanish, French, and Italian on the one hand and English on the other is that English can drop the past participle in structures with *and* or *but;* the other languages cannot. Thus, *I have eaten, but John hasn't* is a grammatically correct sentence in English. To drop **comido** in Spanish would render the sentence ungrammatical.

Actividad D ¿Quiénes lo podrían (*could*) decir?

Basándote en los episodios de *Sol y viento* que has visto hasta ahora, indica los personajes que podrían decir las siguientes oraciones.

1. Hemos subido el funicular juntos (*together*).

☐ Jaime y María ☐ Jaime y Mario

2. Hemos hablado de contratos y negocios.

☐ Jaime y Carlos ☐ María y Jaime

3. Hemos hecho varios viajes en auto.

☐ Carlos y María ☐ Jaime y Mario

4. No hemos conocido a doña Isabel.

☐ Traimaqueo y Carlos ☐ Jaime y Mario

Actividad E Hispanas famosas

Empareja las oraciones y los nombres de las dos columnas para formar oraciones con información verdadera.

1. __c__ Ha escrito varias novelas, siendo la más popular *La casa de los espíritus*.

2. ____ Ha ganado varios campeonatos del *Grand Slam* de tenis.

3. __a__ Ha grabado música en español e inglés.

4. __e__ Ha hecho el papel (*She has played the role*) de Frida Kahlo.

5. __b__ Ha diseñado (*designed*) una colección muy exitosa de ropa y complementos para mujeres.

6. __d__ Ha trabajado por los derechos de los indígenas de Guatemala.

a. Shakira
b. Carolina Herrera
c. Isabel Allende
d. Rigoberta Menchú
e. Salma Hayek
f. Arantxa Sánchez-Vicario

Actividad F ¿Quiénes son?

Usando cada una de las expresiones a continuación, escribe oraciones con información verdadera.

MODELO: Han escrito una autobiografía. →
Hillary Clinton y Nelson Mandela han escrito una autobiografía.

1. Han grabado una canción (*song*) juntos.
2. Han hecho el papel de James Bond en las películas Agente Secreto 007.
3. Han dicho estupideces (*stupid things*) en público.
4. Han sido anfitriones (*hosts*) de un programa de entrevistas (*talk show*).
5. Han recibido un premio Emmy.
6. Han hecho una película de tema deportivo (*sport*).

Actividad G La clase de español

Paso 1 Indica si las siguientes oraciones sobre la clase de español se te aplican o no.

	SÍ, SE ME APLICA.	NO, NO SE ME APLICA.
1. No he llegado tarde a clase más de tres veces.	☐	☐
2. He entregado (*turned in*) todas mis tareas.	☐	☐
3. He hecho los ejercicios del Manual.	☐	☐
4. No he hablado mucho en inglés con mis compañeros de clase.	☐	☐
5. He visto todos los episodios de *Sol y viento*.	☐	☐
6. No he faltado a (*missed*) clase más de tres veces.	☐	☐
7. He saludado (*greeted*) a mi profesor(a) en español todos los días.	☐	☐
8. He leído la lección antes de venir a clase.	☐	☐

Paso 2 Entrevista a un compañero (una compañera) de clase para averiguar si se le aplican las oraciones del **Paso 1** o no. Escribe sus respuestas en una hoja de papel aparte (*another sheet of paper*).

MODELO: E1: ¿Has visto todos los episodios de *Sol y viento*?
E2: Sí, los he visto.

Paso 3 Suma (*Add up*) el número de tus respuestas afirmativas en el **Paso 1**. Suma también el número de respuestas afirmativas que te dio tu compañero/a de clase. Luego, indica dónde quedan Uds. en la siguiente escala.

Muy dedicado/a   Dedicado/a   No muy dedicado/a
5————————————————3————————————————1

Paso 4 Escribe un breve párrafo en el cual resumes los datos de tu entrevista.

MODELO: Miguel y yo somos estudiantes dedicados. Miguel ha... yo también he...

COMUNICACIÓN ÚTIL

To express what *had* happened or what you *had* done at a particular point in time in the past, use the imperfect of **haber** plus a past participle. The imperfect forms of **haber** are **había, habías, había, habíamos, habíais, habían.**

Yo **había esperado** dos semestres antes de tomar una clase de español.	*I had waited for two semesters before taking a Spanish class.*
Clinton y Bush (hijo) **habían sido** gobernadores antes de ser presidentes.	*Clinton and Bush (son) had been governors before becoming presidents.*

RESUMEN DE VOCABULARIO

El transporte y los viajes

bajar (de)	to get off (of)
facturar el equipaje	to check luggage
hacer (*irreg.*) **cola**	to wait in line
hacer (*irreg.*) **escala**	to make a stopover
hacer (*irreg.*) **la maleta**	to pack a suitcase
hacer (*irreg.*) **un viaje**	to take a trip
ir (*irreg.*) **al extranjero**	to go abroad
marearse	to get nauseated, sick (*in a boat, car, plane*)
pasar por la aduana	to go through customs
pasar por seguridad	to go through security
subir (a)	to board, get on

el aeropuerto	airport
la agencia de viajes	travel agency
el/la agente de viajes	travel agent
el asiento	seat
el/la asistente de vuelo	flight attendant
el avión	airplane
el boleto	ticket
de ida	one-way
de ida y vuelta	round-trip
la clase turística	coach
el equipaje	luggage
el maletero	skycap, porter
el/la pasajero/a	passenger
la primera clase	first class
la sala de espera	waiting area
el/la viajero/a	traveler
el vuelo (directo)	(direct) flight

Cognados: el autobús, el pasaporte, la reservación
Repaso: el barco

El alojamiento

alojarse	to stay (*in a place*)
quedarse	to stay (*in a place*)

el botones	bellhop
la pensión	boardinghouse
completa	room and all meals
la media pensión	room and one other meal (usually breakfast)
la propina	tip
el servicio de cuarto	room service

con baño (privado)	with a (private) bathroom
de lujo	luxury

Repaso: la cama (sencilla, matrimonial), la habitación, el hotel

¿Cómo se llega a... ?

cruzar (c)	to cross
doblar	to turn
seguir (i, i) (g) derecho	to continue, go straight

¿Cuánto hay de aquí a... ?	How far is it to . . . ?

la calle	street
la cuadra / la manzana	block
el plano	city map

Cognado: el mapa
Repaso: a la derecha/izquierda, el este, el norte, el oeste, el sur

En el restaurante

atender (ie)	to wait on
dejar (una) propina	to leave a tip

¿Me podría traer... ?	Could you bring me . . . ?
¿Qué trae... ?	What does . . . come with?

el/la cocinero/a	cook
la copa	glass (*wine, liquor*)
los cubiertos	silverware
la cuchara	spoon
el cuchillo	knife
la cuenta	bill, check (*in a restaurant*)
el/la mesero/a	waiter, waitress
el primer (segundo, tercer) plato	first (second, third) course
la servilleta	napkin
la taza	coffee cup
el tenedor	fork
el vaso	glass (*water*)

Cognados: ordenar; el menú, el plato
Repaso: pedir (i, i), traer (*irreg.*)

La naturaleza y el medio ambiente [a]

OBJETIVOS

IN THIS LESSON, YOU WILL LEARN:

- vocabulary to talk about geography and geographical features

- to give instructions to someone you address as **tú,** using informal commands

- vocabulary related to ecology and the environment

- vocabulary for things to do on vacation

- to talk about extremes using superlative expressions

In addition, you will watch **Episodio 6** of the film *Sol y viento.*

◄

La Pampa es una provincia argentina con grandes llanuras (*plains*).

The following media resources are available for *Sol y viento: En breve*

Episodio 6 of
Sol y viento

Online *Manual
de actividades*

**Interactive
CD-ROM**

**Online Learning
Center Website**

[a]La... *Nature and the Environment*

PRIMERA PARTE

Vocabulario

Talking About the
Natural World | **¿Cómo es el paisaje?**

**Geography and
Geographical Features**

Algunas características de la geografía de Sudamérica

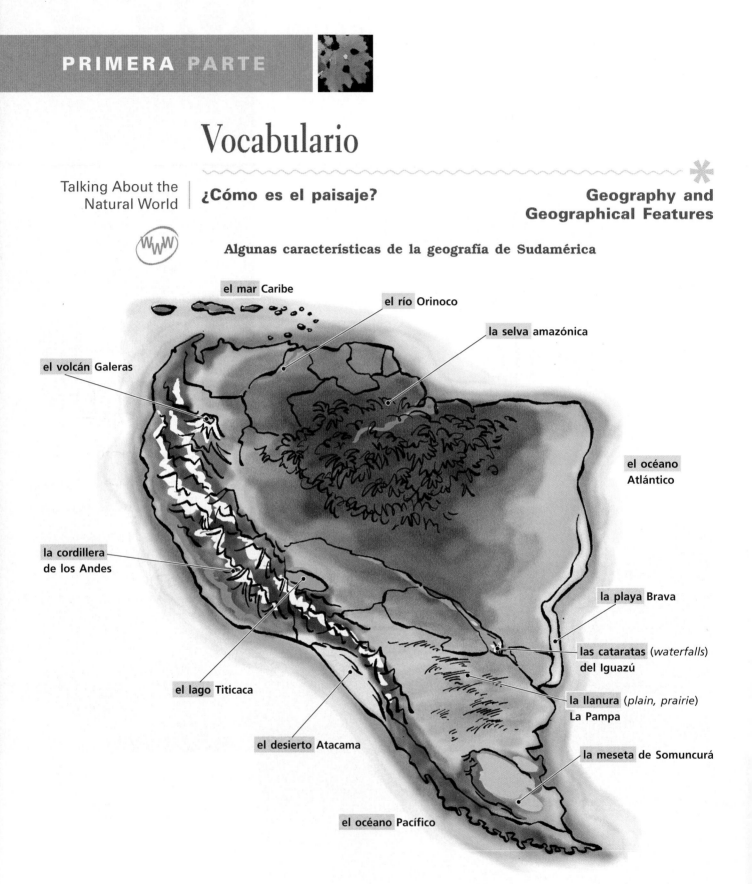

el mar Caribe

el río Orinoco

la selva amazónica

el volcán Galeras

el océano
Atlántico

la cordillera
de los Andes

la playa Brava

las cataratas (*waterfalls*)
del Iguazú

el lago Titicaca

la llanura (*plain, prairie*)
La Pampa

el desierto Atacama

la meseta de Somuncurá

el océano Pacífico

✳ MÁS VOCABULARIO

el bosque (lluvioso)	(rain)forest
la colina	hill
la costa	coast
el golfo	gulf
la isla	island
la montaña	mountain
el paisaje	landscape
el valle	valley

los continentes: África, Antártida, Asia, Australia, Europa, Norteamérica, Sudamérica

〰 Vistazo cultural

Los volcanes

Cuando se habla de volcanes, muchas personas piensan en las islas del Pacífico como Hawai, Japón, Indonesia y Nueva Zelandia. Sin embargo, en México, Centroamérica y Sudamérica también hay numerosos volcanes, muchos de ellos activos. En el norte de Chile, por ejemplo, está Ojos del Salado, el volcán activo más alto del mundo. Otro de los volcanes de la misma región, el Llullaillaco, también es uno de los volcanes activos más altos del mundo.

Otros países hispanos donde hay muchos volcanes son México, Guatemala, Costa Rica, El Salvador, Nicaragua y el Ecuador. El Popocatépetl, uno de los volcanes activos de México, se encuentra entre la Ciudad de México y Puebla. El Popo, como le dicen los mexicanos, ha estado activo desde la época de los aztecas, quienes le pusieron el nombre de[a] Popocatépetl, que significa «montaña humeante[b]» en náhuatl. Desde la llegada de los españoles en 1519, el Popo ha hecho erupción quince veces. Su actividad más reciente incluye una serie de frecuentes erupciones de gases y cenizas[c] volcánicos que comenzaron en 1994 y siguen hasta hoy día. Actualmente[d] hay un equipo de científicos que vigila[e] la actividad del Popocatépetl. Debido a su ubicación,[f] una erupción grande afectaría[g] a más de 20 millones de habitantes.

▲ El volcán Ojos del Salado, en la Puna* de Atacama, Chile

[a]*le... named it*   [b]*smoking*   [c]*ash*   [d]*Currently*   [e]*is monitoring*   [f]*location*   [g]*would affect*

****Puna** is a word used in certain regions of South America to describe high, desolate regions. Due to the bleak cold of these regions, they're often not suitable for human populations.

Actividad A   Asociaciones

Repasa el mapa y las expresiones en la lista de vocabulario en las páginas 326–327. Luego, empareja los nombres de la columna A con su definición en la columna B.

	A		**B**
1.	___ Titicaca	**a.**	un volcán muy activo de Colombia
2.	___ Atacama	**b.**	unas cataratas enormes entre la Argentina y el Brasil
3.	___ Galeras	**c.**	una meseta de la Patagonia, en el sur de la Argentina
4.	___ la Pampa	**d.**	un lago en la frontera (*border*) entre el Perú y Bolivia
5.	___ Iguazú	**e.**	el nombre de un río y también de una selva
6.	___ Somuncurá	**f.**	una llanura grande en la Argentina
7.	___ los Andes	**g.**	una cordillera que extiende por muchos países sudamericanos
8.	___ el Amazonas	**h.**	un desierto de Chile
9.	___ el Pacífico y el Atlántico	**i.**	océanos grandes que rodean (*surround*) Sudamérica

Actividad B   Los paisajes

Tu profesor(a) va a mencionar el nombre de algunos lugares conocidos. Indica la palabra que se asocia con cada lugar.

1. **a.** lago   **b.** mar   **c.** río
2. **a.** bosque   **b.** desierto   **c.** volcán
3. **a.** playa   **b.** meseta   **c.** montaña
4. **a.** mar   **b.** océano   **c.** río
5. **a.** colina   **b.** selva   **c.** llanura
6. **a.** valle   **b.** volcán   **c.** océano
7. **a.** lago   **b.** playa   **c.** isla
8. **a.** valle   **b.** isla   **c.** meseta

Actividad C   Más geografía

Tu profesor(a) va a mencionar un lugar pintoresco (*picturesque*) de la naturaleza. Indica el nombre que corresponde a cada lugar.

1. **a.** Nile   **b.** Tahoe   **c.** Pacific
2. **a.** Fuji   **b.** Euphrates   **c.** Caspian
3. **a.** Kilimanjaro   **b.** Mojave   **c.** Daytona
4. **a.** Amazon   **b.** Rhine   **c.** Gobi
5. **a.** Death Valley **b.** Niagara   **c.** Sierra Madre
6. **a.** Yangtze   **b.** Pompeii   **c.** Baltic
7. **a.** Napa   **b.** Asia   **c.** Rockies
8. **a.** Colorado   **b.** Bermuda   **c.** Persian

Actividad D ¿Cuánto sabes de geografía?

Paso 1 En una hoja de papel aparte, escribe una pregunta de geografía. Escribe la respuesta entre paréntesis.

MODELOS: ¿Cómo se llama el río que separa los estados de Texas y Oklahoma? (Red River)

¿Qué estado de los EE.UU. tiene fama de tener 10.000 lagos? (Minnesota)

¿En qué continente está el río Nilo (*Nile*)? (África)

Paso 2 Entrégale tu hoja al profesor (a la profesora) y saca otra hoja de papel. Tu profesor(a) va a leer todas las preguntas a la clase. Escribe la respuesta de cada pregunta en tu propia hoja. Al final, tu profesor(a) va a leer las respuestas de todas las preguntas de la clase. El estudiante que tiene más respuestas correctas les gana a sus compañeros de clase.

SOL Y VIENTO: Enfoque cultural

En el **Episodio 6,** Jaime le dice a Carlos: «¡A que tampoco ha hecho nada con la comunidad mapuche!» Evidentemente, Carlos había prometido[a] conseguir las tierras de los mapuches que vivían en la zona. En cambio,[b] su hermana María lucha[c] por esa comunidad indígena para preservar su cultura.

El indigenismo y los derechos de los indígenas en Latinoamérica son temas muy importantes en muchos países como el Perú, Chile, México y otros. Por seis siglos los indígenas han sufrido discriminación que los ha mantenido en las capas[d] más bajas de la sociedad. Afortunadamente, en el siglo XX empezó a demostrarse interés[e] en el indigenismo a través del arte del mexicano Diego Rivera y el novelista ecuatoriano Jorge Icaza, entre otros. En el Perú empezaron a reconocer la importancia de ofrecer a los indígenas educación en su lengua nativa, el quechua, y establecieron programas de educación bilingüe en el año 1972. Es más,[f] en 1979 la constitución peruana reconoció el español como lengua oficial del país, pero a la vez que el quechua forma parte integral de la cultura del país, y los dos idiomas quedaron como lenguas oficiales, con restricciones. Aun con estos avances, la situación no está completamente resuelta.[g] Por ejemplo, en 1994 los indígenas del estado mexicano de Chiapas se sublevaron[h] contra el gobierno, reclamando más tierra y más inclusión en el sistema político. Seguramente, la situación de los grupos minoritarios indígenas seguirá siendo[i] un tema central en varios países hispanos por muchos años.

▲ El indigenismo sigue siendo un tema central en la vida de los indígenas, como estas en el Ecuador.

[a]*promised* [b]*En... On the other hand* [c]*fights* [d]*layers* [e]*empezó... interest began to appear* [f]*Es... What's more* [g]*resolved* [h]*se... rose up* [i]*seguirá... will continue to be*

Gramática

More on Giving
Instructions

¡Ten paciencia!   **Affirmative Informal Commands**

AFFIRMATIVE INFORMAL COMMANDS

- use the third-person present-tense form as the command

  tomar → toma →
  Toma café si estás cansado.   *Drink some coffee if you're tired.*
  escribir → escribe →
  Escribe un párrafo de 50 palabras.   *Write a 50-word paragraph.*

- attach object and reflexive pronouns to the end of the command

  Dámelo, por favor.   *Give it to me, please.*
  Levántate ya. Es tarde.   *Get up already. It's late.*

IRREGULAR INFORMAL COMMAND FORMS		

VERB	COMMAND FORM	EXAMPLE	
decir	di	**Di** mi nombre.	*Say my name.*
hacer	haz	**Haz** la cama.	*Make the bed.*
ir	ve*	**Ve** al supermercado.	*Go to the supermarket.*
poner	pon	**Pon** las flores allí.	*Put the flowers there.*
salir	sal	**¡Sal** de mi casa!	*Get out of my house!*
ser	sé	**Sé** bueno.	*Be good.*
tener	ten	**Ten** paciencia.	*Have patience. (Be patient.)*
venir	ven	**Ven** aquí.	*Come here.*

COMUNICACIÓN ÚTIL

In addition to using third-person singular verbs to make informal commands, it is also common for Spanish speakers to give instructions in the form of a question using second-person singular verb forms. Instead of saying **Pásame la sal, por favor,** a Spanish speaker might say **¿Me pasas la sal, por favor?** This less direct way of giving instructions is commonly used to soften a request.

---

*The affirmative **tú** command form of the verb **ir** is identical to the regular **tú** command form for the verb **ver.** Context will determine meaning.

Ve a la biblioteca para estudiar.   *Go to the library to study.*
Ve las estrellas.   *Look at the stars.*

To give instructions to someone whom you address as **tú** (such as a friend, family member, or pet), Spanish uses third-person singular verb forms in the present tense. When used in this way, these forms are called affirmative **tú** commands or simply informal commands (**los mandatos informales**). You have already noticed the use of affirmative **tú** commands in the directions to many activities in this text.

Habla con un compañero de clase.	*Speak with a classmate.*
Escribe dos o tres oraciones.	*Write two or three sentences.*

All object and reflexive pronouns are attached to the end of affirmative **tú** commands, as they are to formal commands. Note the written accents to maintain the original stress.

Bébela.	*Drink it. (it = **la leche**)*
Háblale.	*Talk to him.*
¡Despiértate!	*Wake up!*

As with formal commands, when both a direct and an indirect object pronoun are used, the indirect object comes before the direct object.

Dímela ahora mismo.	*Tell it to me right now.*
	*(it = **la verdad**)*

Many commonly used affirmative **tú** commands have irregular forms, as indicated in the chart.

DE SOL Y VIENTO

At the end of **Episodio 5,** you saw a scene in which María has to leave her date with Jaime to meet up with her student, Diego. Jaime gets up to follow María, but she stops him. Part of their conversation appears below.

MARÍA
No, no, no, _____.
Aprovecha la puesta del sol.ᵃ

JAIME
¿Solo?

MARÍA
¡Llámame!

Do you remember what María says to Jaime in the space above? Select the most logical response from the following choices, then check your answer by watching the scene again.

1. levántate

2. quédate

3. duérmete

ᵃAprovecha... *Enjoy the sunset.*

Actividad E ¿María o doña Isabel?

A finales del **Episodio 5,** Jaime tutea (*addresses as* **tú**) a María pero trata de Ud. a doña Isabel. Tu profesor(a) va a mencionar una serie de instrucciones que Jaime podría (*could*) dar. Indica si cada una se dirige a (*is directed to*) María (informal) o a doña Isabel (formal).

1. ... **2.** ... **3.** ... **4.** ... **5.** ... **6.** ... **7.** ... **8.** ...

Actividad F Consejos

Paso 1 Lee rápidamente la primera sección (**Habla con tus hijos...**) del anuncio a continuación y contesta las preguntas.

Vocabulario útil

fumar   to smoke
dañar   to harm
la salud   health

1. El tema de este anuncio es/son _____ .

   a. el alcohol   **b.** las drogas   **c.** los cigarrillos

2. El anuncio se dirige a _____ .

   a. un niño   **b.** un padre o una madre   **c.** un amigo

Paso 2 Lee el anuncio entero y subraya (*underline*) todos los mandatos que encuentres.

Vocabulario útil

arriesgar   to risk
sano/a   healthy

Paso 3 Con un compañero (una compañera), inventen dos mandatos más para dárselos a un padre o a una madre que quiere hablar con sus hijos sobre el fumar.

Habla con tus hijos...

● para abrir un diálogo sobre el tabaco

● para explicarles cómo fumar daña la salud

Hazles saber...

● que no deben arriesgar la vida así

● que tú puedes escucharlos si te necesitan

Dales la confianza...

● que necesitan para decir «no» a los cigarrillos

● que necesitan para tomar decisiones fuertes y sanas

**Comunícate con ellos.
Te van a escuchar.**

Actividad G En este país

Paso 1 Con un compañero (una compañera), hagan una lista de seis de las cosas que debe hacer un estudiante de intercambio (*exchange*) de tu universidad para disfrutar (*enjoy*) de los paisajes de este país. Usen verbos diferentes.

MODELO: Maneja por el desierto de Arizona.

Paso 2 Intercambien su lista con la de otro grupo. Lean la lista de recomendaciones de sus compañeros y ordénenlas por su proximidad geográfica. La primera actividad deber ser la que está más cerca de su campus.

Enfoque lingüístico

La sociolingüística

Sociolinguistic competence refers to one's ability to use socially accepted forms of language in proper contexts. Many languages use different pronouns and verb forms to address people in different social contexts. Spanish, for example, distinguishes between **tú** and **Ud.** in all verb forms, including command forms. This distinction is also tied to notions of politeness. Simply put, it would not be polite to use informal commands to give instructions to someone you should address as **Ud.** If you think learning this distinction is difficult, try learning Japanese, which has four affirmative command forms that vary in degree of politeness!

Language that is socially appropriate in one region or country may not necessarily be so in another. Spaniards, for example, are often direct when making requests. A client in a restaurant might tell a waiter **Dame un tenedor** or may just catch the waiter's attention and say **¡Un tenedor!** This client would likely come across as brusque or rude in Latin America. In a similar circumstance a Mexican would likely say **¿Me podría traer un tenedor?** or even **¿Sería tan amable de traerme un tenedor?** (*Would you be so kind as to bring me a fork?*).

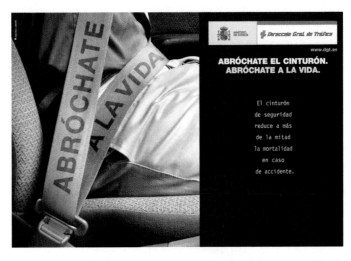

▲ ¿Qué significa «Abróchate el cinturón. Abróchate a la vida.»?

SEGUNDA PARTE

Vocabulario

Talking About the Environment | **El medio ambiente**

*
Environmental and Ecological Matters

los combustibles fósiles

la deforestación

la contaminación del aire

los pesticidas

la fábrica

la basura

el basurero

las cajas de cartón

la botella de vidrio

la botella de plástico

la contaminación del agua

el periódico

las latas de aluminio

* MÁS VOCABULARIO

conservar	to conserve
construir (y)	to build
contaminar	to pollute
descomponer (*like* **poner**)	to decompose
desperdiciar	to waste
echar / tirar	to throw out
proteger (j)*	to protect
reciclar	to recycle
salvar	to save (*from danger*)
la capa de ozono	ozone layer
los desperdicios	wastes

***Proteger** uses a **j** in the **yo** form to maintain the [h] sound: **protejo.**

≋ Vistazo cultural

Las islas Galápagos

El archipiélago Galápagos es una serie de islas de origen volcánico ubicadas[a] al oeste de la costa ecuatoriana en el océano Pacífico. La región consiste en un parque terrestre[b] y una reserva marina. Desde la época de los estudios de Darwin,* los cuales resaltaron[c] la flora y la fauna de la región, el factor humano ha llegado a ser una gran amenaza[d] a las islas. Por ejemplo, la intensa industria pesquera[e] (a veces ilegal) en la región ha reducido el número de muchas especies, entre ellas el pepino de mar[f] y la langosta. Además, la población de las islas ha aumentado mucho por la llegada de inmigrantes. Debido a una planificación inadecuada para acomodar a los habitantes nuevos, las comunidades han generado grandes cantidades de desechos[g] sólidos y líquidos que se echan al mar sin ser tratados[h] adecuadamente.

Debido a la situación peligrosa[i] de las islas, en 1998 el Ecuador aprobó[j] la Ley de Régimen Especial para la Conservación de las Islas Galápagos. La ley fomenta[k] tanto la conservación del medio ambiente como el desarrollo sustentable[l] de las Galápagos. Hoy día el Instituto Nacional Galápagos (INGALA) regula la inmigración a las islas y las actividades humanas dentro del archipiélago. Está también la Autoridad Interinstitucional (AI) que regula las actividades de la reserva marina. Como se puede ver, conservar el medio ambiente requiere un delicado balance entre los intereses humanos y los de la naturaleza.

▲ Una iguana en las islas Galápagos

[a]*located* [b]*terrestrial* [c]*highlighted* [d]*threat* [e]*fishing* [f]*pepino... sea cucumber* [g]*wastes* [h]*treated* [i]*dangerous* [j]*passed* [k]*encourages* [l]*desarrollo... sustainable development*

el efecto invernadero	greenhouse effect
la escasez (*pl.* **las escaseces**)	shortage
las especies en peligro de extinción	endangered species
la falta	lack
el medio ambiente	environment
la naturaleza	nature
el petróleo	petroleum
el producto biodegradable (desechable)	biodegradable (disposable) product
el reciclaje	recycling
los recursos naturales	natural resources

*Charles Darwin (1809–1882) fue un naturalista británico que escribió *El origen de las especies*, un estudio sobre sus investigaciones en las islas Galápagos.

Actividad A Definiciones

Empareja una definición de la primera columna con la palabra apropiada de la segunda columna.

1. _____ describe un producto que descompone rápida y naturalmente
2. _____ químicas que se usan para eliminar insectos
3. _____ la falta de una cosa
4. _____ describe algo que se usa una o dos veces y luego se tira
5. _____ el agua, el aire, los árboles, los combustibles fósiles
6. _____ se necesita hacer esto a favor de las especies en peligro de extinción
7. _____ lo que tiramos porque ya no sirve
8. _____ lugar donde se hacen productos como autos o televisores
9. _____ la temperatura global aumenta (*is increasing*) a causa de esto
10. _____ lo opuesto de conservar

a. la escasez
b. desperdiciar
c. el efecto invernadero
d. la fábrica
e. biodegradable
f. la basura
g. los recursos naturales
h. proteger
i. desechable
j. los pesticidas

Actividad B ¿Qué importancia tienen para ti?

A continuación hay una lista de problemas medioambientales que afectan a todo el planeta. Pon los problemas en orden de importancia para ti, del 1 al 10.

_____ la falta de basureros

_____ la escasez de combustibles fósiles

_____ la deforestación

_____ las especies en peligro de extinción

_____ el uso de pesticidas en los productos alimenticios

_____ la contaminación del aire

_____ la contaminación del agua

_____ la destrucción de la capa de ozono

_____ el efecto invernadero

_____ la escasez de los recursos naturales

Actividad C ¿Qué hacemos con la basura?

Paso 1 A continuación hay una lista de soluciones posibles para resolver el problema de los basureros repletos (*overflowing*) de basura. Indica si cada solución te parece buena idea o mala idea.

Para resolver el problema de los basureros repletos de basura debemos...	BUENA IDEA	MALA IDEA
1. enterrar (*bury*) la basura en el desierto.	☐	☐
2. contratar (*hire*) compañías para reciclar la basura.	☐	☐

	BUENA IDEA	MALA IDEA
3. quemar la basura, como lo hacen en otros países.	☐	☐
4. enviar la basura a otro planeta.	☐	☐
5. echar la basura al océano.	☐	☐
6. comprar más basureros en otros países.	☐	☐

Paso 2 En grupos de tres personas, expliquen sus opiniones acerca de las soluciones del **Paso 1.** Cada grupo debe decidir cuál es la mejor solución para resolver el problema de los basureros repletos de basura.

Actividad D ¿Conservas o desperdicias?

Paso 1 Indica si las siguientes afirmaciones son ciertas o falsas para ti.

	CIERTO	FALSO
1. Voy en auto a lugares que están a una milla más o menos de mi casa.	☐	☐
2. Dejo que corra el agua (*I leave the water running*) mientras me lavo los dientes.	☐	☐
3. No uso los dos lados de una hoja de papel antes de tirarla.	☐	☐
4. Echo latas de aluminio y botellas de plástico y vidrio.	☐	☐
5. Subo el regulador del termostato en el invierno y lo bajo en el verano.	☐	☐
6. No apago el monitor de mi computadora.	☐	☐
7. Uso muchos productos desechables.	☐	☐
8. Dejo prendidas (*turned on*) las luces al salir de casa.	☐	☐

Paso 2 Entrevista a un compañero (una compañera) de clase para averiguar si las oraciones del **Paso 1** son ciertas o falsas para él/ella.

Paso 3 Date un punto para cada respuesta que marcaste «cierto». Suma el número de puntos que tú y tu compañero/a de clase sacaron e indica dónde quedan en la siguiente escala.

> 0–2 = EXCELENTE: Conservas muchos recursos naturales.
>
> 3–5 = BIEN: Conservas algunos recursos, pero desperdicias otros.
>
> 6–8 = MAL: Desperdicias muchos recursos naturales.

MODELO: Yo saqué tres puntos y Joe sacó cinco. Los dos conservamos algunos recursos, pero desperdiciamos otros.

NAVEGANDO LA RED 〰〰〰〰〰〰〰〰〰〰〰〰〰

Busca un sitio hispano en la red de una organización dedicada a proteger el medio ambiente. Describe las regiones donde está trabajando y cuáles son las actividades que hace en protección del medio ambiente.

Gramática

¡No me hables!   **Negative Informal Commands**

Si pierdes el cabello, no pierdas el tiempo

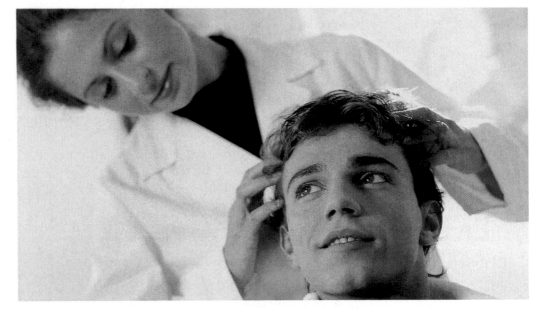

To tell someone whom you address as **tú** *not* to do something, Spanish uses negative informal commands. These are formed in the same way that formal negative commands are: by taking the present-tense **yo** form, dropping the **-o** or **-oy** ending, and adding the "opposite" vowel plus **-s.**

No me **vengas** con tus quejas.	*Don't come to me with your complaints.*
No hables de esas cosas.	*Don't talk about such things.*

Ir and **ser** have irregular forms.

No vayas a casa sin mí.	*Don't go home without me.*
No seas tan perezoso.	*Don't be so lazy.*

As with negative formal commands, all object and reflexive pronouns precede negative commands. Remember that when both a direct and an indirect object are present, the indirect object precedes the direct object. Examples are in the following chart.

NEGATIVE INFORMAL COMMANDS			
INFINITIVE	**yo** FORM	STEM	ADD THE "OPPOSITE" VOWEL AND -s
hablar	hablo	habl-	+ **es** = **hables**
beber	bebo	beb-	+ **as** = **bebas**
abrir	abro	abr-	+ **as** = **abras**
decir	digo	dig-	+ **as** = **digas**
estar	estoy	est-	+ **es** = **estés***
conducir	conduzco	conduzc-	+ **as** = **conduzcas**

USING PRONOUNS WITH INFORMAL COMMANDS			
PRONOUNS ARE PLACED AFTER AFFIRMATIVE COMMANDS		PRONOUNS ARE PLACED BEFORE NEGATIVE COMMANDS	
Dile la verdad.	*Tell him the truth.*	**No le digas** la verdad.	*Don't tell him the truth.*
Cómprala.	*Buy it. (it =* **la comida***)*	**No la compres.**	*Don't buy it.*
Dámelo.	*Give me it. (it =* **el libro***)*	**No me lo des.**	*Don't give it to me.*
Acuéstate.	*Go to bed.*	**No te acuestes.**	*Don't go to bed.*

DE SOL Y VIENTO

In **Episodio 6** of *Sol y viento,* María talks with don Paco at the airport. Part of their exchange appears here.

MARÍA
Mamá me dijo que venías e insistí en venir a buscarte.

PACO
A ver.[a] Mis ojos no lo creen. Tan bella[b] como siempre.

MARÍA
Ay, tío. No _____.

From the following options, choose the one that best fits the blank in the conversation.

1. exageres
2. seas cruel
3. me ofendas

[a]*A... Let me see.* [b]*beautiful*

---

*Note that the command form **estés** carries a written accent.

Actividad E Consejos

Considerando las frustraciones de varios personajes de *Sol y viento*, indica si los siguientes consejos son buenos o malos para cada uno de ellos.

	BUEN CONSEJO	MAL CONSEJO
1. Jaime, no llegues a conclusiones falsas; María no tiene novio.	☐	☐
2. María, no confíes en (*don't trust*) Jaime; tiene malas intenciones.	☐	☐
3. Diego, no seas cabezón; tu familia te necesita.	☐	☐
4. Carlos, no escuches a tu mamá; ella no sabe las frustraciones de manejar la viña hoy en día.	☐	☐
5. Carlos, no le digas nada más a tu madre; no debe preocuparse (*worry*) tanto.	☐	☐
6. Jaime, no tengas confianza en lo que dice Andy; lo más importante para él es el trabajo.	☐	☐

Actividad F Mi mejor amigo/a

Empareja una situación de la primera columna con un mandato apropiado de la segunda columna.

Si mi mejor amigo/a...

1. ___ quiere ponerse un suéter cuando hace calor afuera

2. ___ no ha dormido bien y tiene un examen mañana

3. ___ se pelea con su novio/a todos los días

4. ___ me cuenta algo que no puedo creer

5. ___ está deprimido/a y quiere llorar (*to cry*)

6. ___ quiere darme un regalo que no quiero aceptar

yo le digo...

a. ¡no me digas!*

b. no me lo des, por favor.

c. no te lo pongas.

d. no le hables más.

e. no te acuestes tarde.

f. no estés tan triste.

Actividad G   ¿Qué desperdicia o contamina?

Paso 1 Lee los mandatos a continuación e indica cuál es el recurso natural que el oyente (*listener*) desperdicia o contamina.

---

*In addition to its literal meaning of *Don't tell me*, **¡No me digas!** also has the colloquial meaning *You're kidding!* or *You don't say!* It is often said in response to something surprising or unexpected.

MODELOS: «No laves el auto en la calle.» → Esta persona desperdicia el agua.

«No compres otro auto diesel.» → Esta persona contamina el aire.

1. «No compres servilletas de papel para usar en la mesa.»
2. «No le pongas muchos fertilizantes (*fertilizers*) al jardín.»
3. «No uses productos en forma de aerosol.»
4. «No conduzcas un vehículo SUV.»
5. «No te duches por más de diez minutos.»
6. «No tires los periódicos a la basura.»

Paso 2 Con un compañero (una compañera) de clase, escriban un mandato informal negativo para cada problema medioambiental a continuación.

MODELO: la contaminación del aire →
No uses tanto el auto cuando puedes caminar.

1. la contaminación del aire
2. la contaminación del agua
3. la destrucción de la capa de ozono
4. el efecto invernadero

Actividad H   Un cartel

Paso 1 Con un compañero (una compañera), hagan una lista de diez consejos que le sirvan a un estudiante de tu universidad para conservar energía. Usen mandatos afirmativos en cinco de los consejos, y usen mandatos negativos en los otros cinco.

MODELOS: Dúchate rápidamente.

No dejes las luces prendidas cuando sales de casa.

Paso 2 En otra hoja de papel, diseñen (*design*) un cartel titulado «Cómo conservar energía». Incluyan los diez consejos que escribieron y unos dibujos creativos.

TERCERA PARTE

Vocabulario

More on Talking About Trips | **De vacaciones**

Activities to Do While on Vacation

Actividades al aire libre^a

^aal... *outdoors*

escalar montañas

montar a caballo

pescar (qu)

practicar (qu) el alpinismo de rocas

acampar / hacer (*irreg.*) camping

ir (*irreg.*) de excursión

bucear

ir (*irreg.*) a un parque de diversiones

remar en canoa

Actividades interiores

ver (*irreg.*) un espectáculo

charlar en un café

comprar recuerdos

ir (*irreg.*) a un concierto

cenar en un restaurante elegante

degustar vinos

✳ MÁS VOCABULARIO

hacer (*irreg.*) **kayak**	to go kayaking
hacer (*irreg.*) **el salto bungee**	to bungee jump
hacer (*irreg.*) **rafting**	to go rafting
practicar (qu) el paracaidismo	to sky dive
surfear	to surf

Actividad A   Clasificaciones

Paso 1   Tu profesor(a) va a leer una lista de actividades. Escribe cada actividad en la caja apropiada.

ACTIVIDADES ACUÁTICAS	ACTIVIDADES TERRESTRES (*land*)

Paso 2   Tu profesor(a) va a leer otra lista de actividades. Escribe cada actividad en la caja apropiada.

REQUIERE MUCHA ENERGÍA	NO REQUIERE MUCHA ENERGÍA

Actividad B   ¿Dónde se hace?

Indica dónde se hace cada una de las actividades que menciona tu profesor(a).

1. **a.** en la selva   **b.** en el océano
2. **a.** en el museo   **b.** en el teatro
3. **a.** en un lago   **b.** en un bosque
4. **a.** en las montañas   **b.** en la playa
5. **a.** en un río   **b.** en el desierto
6. **a.** en la llanura   **b.** en un volcán
7. **a.** en un café   **b.** en una tienda
8. **a.** en un auditorio   **b.** en un restaurante

Actividad C ¿Eres arriesgado/a (*daring*)?

Paso 1 Indica si has hecho las siguientes actividades o no.

	SÍ	NO
1. He practicado el paracaidismo.	☐	☐
2. He practicado el alpinismo de rocas.	☐	☐
3. He buceado con tiburones (*sharks*).	☐	☐
4. He acampado donde había osos (*bears*) o coyotes.	☐	☐
5. He hecho el salto bungee.	☐	☐
6. He practicado el parapente (*hang gliding*).	☐	☐
7. He practicado la escalada (*rappeling*).	☐	☐
8. He montado un caballo indómito (*untamed*).	☐	☐

Paso 2 Entrevista a un compañero (una compañera) de clase para averiguar si ha hecho las actividades del **Paso 1.**

MODELO: ¿Has practicado el paracaidismo alguna vez?

Paso 3 Ahora, indica si las siguientes oraciones son ciertas o falsas.

1. Soy una persona arriesgada.

2. Mi compañero/a de clase es una persona arriesgada.

Vistazo cultural

El ecoturismo

En muchos países del mundo hispano, el ecoturismo se ha hecho[a] un gran negocio en los últimos años. El ecoturismo se refiere al desarrollo[b] de una industria turística con fines de lucro[c] que pone a los turistas en contacto con la naturaleza. La mayoría de los ecoturistas son personas urbanas que viajan con el deseo de ver paisajes, animales y flores que no pueden ver en su propio país. Algunas de las actividades ecoturísticas comunes son: bucear con peces tropicales, remar en canoa en un río que va por un bosque tropical, ir de excursión a una selva, montar a caballo e ir en un safari fotográfico.

El ecoturismo tiene dos metas:[d] una es estimular la economía de países que tienen muchas riquezas biológicas, y la otra es proteger esas riquezas, incluyendo especies que ahora están en peligro de extinción. La idea es que el ecoturismo crea trabajos nuevos y genera fondos[e] para crear programas cuyo[f] fin es proteger el medio ambiente. Los países que tienen programas establecidos de ecoturismo son México, Costa Rica, Panamá, Venezuela, Bolivia y el Ecuador, entre otros. El ecoturismo como se conoce en el mundo hispano no existe en los Estados Unidos, con excepción de Alaska, que ofrece muchos viajes para gozar de[g] la flora y la fauna y de sus paisajes. La próxima vez que te dé la gana[h] hacer un viaje, ¡piensa en un viaje ecológico en el mundo hispano!

[a]se... *has become*   [b]*development*   [c]con... *for profit*   [d]*goals*   [e]*funds*   [f]*whose*
[g]gozar... *enjoying*   [h]te... *you feel like*

Gramática

Es el más guapo de todos.

Superlatives

Superlative expressions are those used to denote the extreme state expressed by a particular adjective. Take the adjective *smart,* for example. You may think your brother is smart and you are smarter, but that your uncle Bob is the smartest person in the family. *The smartest* is called a superlative expression. English forms most superlatives by adding *-est* to the ends of adjectives and using the definite article *the* before the adjective. Some adjectives take a different form using *most*—for example, *popular, more popular, the most popular.*

Superlatives can also be used to talk about negative qualities. For example, maybe you think you are smart, that your cousin is less smart than you, and that of the three your brother is the *least smart.* In English, adjectives like *funny* and *popular* don't have a direct opposite adjective to which one could add *-est.* Adjectives like these use the word *least* before them: *John is the least funny person I know,* or *Mary is the least popular girl in school.*

Spanish forms superlatives by joining the following words: *definite article* + *noun* + **más/menos** + *adjective* + **de,** as indicated in the chart on the next page. The noun may be left out if the person or thing being talked about has already been established.

—¿Quién es **la persona más alta de** tu familia?	*Who is the tallest person in your family?*
—Sin duda mi hermana es **la más alta.**	*Without a doubt, my sister is the tallest (person).*

Mejor (*Best*) and **peor** (*worst*) can be used in superlative constructions, but without an adjective.

La mejor clase de mi horario es la geografía.	*The best class in my schedule is geography.*
La peor actriz del año fue Madonna.	*The worst actress of the year was Madonna.*
Sí, fue **la peor.**	*Yes, she was the worst.*

In a previous lesson you learned another form of the superlative, one that consists of adding **-ísimo/a/os/as** to the end of an adjective, as in **La montaña es altísima.** Note that adjectives ending in **-ísimo/a/os/as** are already in a superlative form and therefore cannot be used with the structure you just learned.

◄ La escasez de agua potable[a] es uno de los problemas **más graves** que debe resolver la humanidad, pues su consumo crece[b] y los recursos hídricos[c] están altamente contaminados.

[a]*drinkable* [b]*is growing* [c]*water*

SUPERLATIVES					
ARTICLE +	NOUN +	**más/menos** +	ADJECTIVE +	**de**	
el	volcán	**más**	alto	de	México
los	ríos	**más**	grandes	de	Sudamérica
la	persona	**menos**	apreciada	de	mi familia
las	canciones	**menos**	populares	del	año
SUPERLATIVES WITH *mejor* AND *peor*					
el **mejor** amigo			del hombre		
la **peor** idea			de la reunión		

DE SOL Y VIENTO

In **Episodio 6** of *Sol y viento,* you saw a conversation between a waiter and some patrons in don Paco's restaurant in Mexico City. Their exchange appears here.

MESERO
El vino de la casa: «Sol y viento».

CLIENTE 1
Hmmm… ¿De dónde es?

MESERO
De Chile. Es _____ de todos los
vinos importados.

CLIENTE 2
Un vino chileno. ¡Qué interesante!

Which of the following expressions does the waiter use in the preceding blank?

1. el mejor
2. el peor

Actividad D Opiniones

Indica lo que opinas de las siguientes oraciones sobre los personajes de *Sol y viento*.

1. La característica más fascinante de María es su _____.

   a. belleza (*beauty*)   **b.** dedicación   **c.** inteligencia   **d.** ¿ ?
                     al trabajo

2. El momento más difícil (*awkward*) entre Jaime y María fue cuando _____.

   a. se chocaron   **b.** Diego llamó   **c.** Jaime le regaló   **d.** ¿ ?
       (*they bumped*   durante su   el remolino en
       into each other)   cita   el parque
       en el parque

3. El personaje menos respetado de *Sol y viento* es _____.

   a. Mario   **b.** Traimaqueo   **c.** Carlos   **d.** ¿ ?

4. El problema más serio que enfrenta (*faces*) Jaime es/son _____.

   a. su relación con   **b.** las mentiras   **c.** las demandas   **d.** ¿ ?
       María   de Carlos   de sus jefes

5. La mejor característica de Mario es _____.

   a. su sentido   **b.** su lealtad   **c.** su compasión   **d.** ¿ ?
       (*sense*) del   (*loyalty*)
       humor

Actividad E Los famosos

Indica si estás de acuerdo o no con las afirmaciones sobre los siguientes personajes famosos.

	ESTOY DE ACUERDO.	NO ESTOY DE ACUERDO.
1. La mujer más dinámica de los Estados Unidos es Hillary Clinton.	☐	☐
2. Halle Berry es la mujer más guapa del mundo.	☐	☐
3. Steven Spielberg es el director más creativo de Hollywood.	☐	☐
4. El hombre más influyente de nuestro país es Bill Gates.	☐	☐
5. El atleta más conocido del mundo es Tiger Woods.	☐	☐
6. La mujer más cómica del mundo es Reese Witherspoon.	☐	☐
7. Eminem es el músico más controvertido de todos.	☐	☐
8. La persona famosa más fotografiada es Jennifer López.	☐	☐

Actividad F Más sobre el medio ambiente

Indica la respuesta adecuada a cada declaración a continuación.

1. El problema más serio para el medio ambiente es _____.
   - **a.** la deforestación
   - **b.** el uso de pesticidas
   - **c.** ¿ ?

2. La mejor manera de protegernos contra los pesticidas es _____.
   - **a.** lavar bien la comida
   - **b.** comprar alimentos orgánicos
   - **c.** ¿ ?

3. La actividad más dañina (*harmful*) para la capa de ozono es _____.
   - **a.** manejar un SUV
   - **b.** usar productos en forma de aerosol
   - **c.** ¿ ?

4. La peor manera de desperdiciar el papel es _____.
   - **a.** usar servilletas de papel
   - **b.** echar los periódicos a la basura
   - **c.** ¿ ?

5. La solución menos eficaz (*effective*) para conservar energía es _____.
   - **a.** no usar el aire acondicionado
   - **b.** desconectar los aparatos domésticos
   - **c.** ¿ ?

Actividad G Una entrevista

Paso 1 Lee las preguntas a continuación y escribe tus respuestas en la primera columna.

En tu opinión,...	YO	E1	E2
1. ¿cuál es la mejor película del año? ¿y la peor?	____	____	____
2. ¿quién es el actor más guapo? ¿y la actriz más guapa?	____	____	____
3. ¿quién es la cantante más talentosa? ¿y el cantante más talentoso?	____	____	____
4. ¿cuál es el programa de televisión más cómico? ¿y el más serio?	____	____	____
5. ¿cuál es la canción más irritante (*annoying*) en la radio en estos momentos? ¿y la más popular?	____	____	____
6. ¿cuál es el videojuego más interesante en estos momentos? ¿y el más difícil de ganar?	____	____	____

Paso 2 Luego, hazles las mismas preguntas a dos de tus compañeros/as de clase. Indica sus respuestas en las columnas dos y tres.

Paso 3 Escribe un breve resumen comparando tus opiniones con las de tus compañeros de clase.

MODELO: Mis compañeros de clase creen que los actores más guapos son Tom Cruise y Colin Farrell. En mi opinión, el más guapo es Matt Damon.

SOL Y VIENTO

Antes de ver el episodio

Actividad A ¿Qué recuerdas?

Indica si las siguientes oraciones sobre la trama (*plot*) de *Sol y viento* son ciertas o falsas.

	C	F
1. María trabaja por los derechos de la comunidad mapuche.	☐	☐
2. Los padres de Jaime también eran personas de negocios.	☐	☐
3. Doña Isabel está de acuerdo con Carlos en vender la viña porque es demasiado (*too much*) trabajo mantenerla (*to maintain it*).	☐	☐
4. Carlos cree que la familia lo obligó a encargarse de (*take over*) la viña.	☐	☐
5. María y Jaime lo pasaron muy bien en la cita.	☐	☐

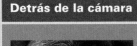

Detrás de la cámara

In **Episodio 6** of *Sol y viento* you will meet don Francisco (Paco) Aguilar, an old friend of the Sánchez family and owner of a fine restaurant in Mexico City. In addition to being a restaurateur, don Paco is also a distributor of fine wines. His job is to make contacts with wineries throughout the world and import their products into Mexico. He established a relationship with the Sánchez family many years ago on a trip through the Maipo Valley. He was so impressed with the wine produced at Sol y viento that he made it the house wine at his establishment.

Actividad B ¿Qué falta?

A continuación hay un fragmento de una conversación telefónica que tiene don Paco.

> PACO: ¿Bueno?[a]... ¿Bueno?... ¡Si no lo oigo bien! ¡_____[1] más fuerte!... ¿Bueno?... ¿Bueno?... Sí, _____[2] tantito[b]... ¿Bueno?... ¿Con quién?... ¡Ah, Isabel! ¡Qué sorpresa!

[a]*Hello? (Mex.)* [b]*a second (coll.)*

Escoge entre las palabras que siguen la más apropiada para cada espacio en blanco.

1. **a.** Hable
   b. Habla
2. **a.** espérame
   b. espéreme

Actividad C El episodio

Ahora mira el episodio. Si hay algo que no entiendes bien, puedes volver a ver la escena en cuestión.

Después de ver el episodio

Actividad A ¿Qué recuerdas?

Contesta cada pregunta a continuación según lo que recuerdas del episodio.

1. ¿A quién llama por teléfono doña Isabel?
   a. a Jaime, en su hotel **b.** a don Paco, en México
2. ¿Cuál es la relación entre don Paco y María?
   a. Son amigos. **b.** Son parientes.
3. Jaime se da cuenta de que María y Carlos son _____.
   a. primos **b.** hermanos **c.** cuñados
4. Jaime está harto de (*fed up with*) los pretextos (*excuses*) de Carlos y demanda _____ de la familia.
   a. las bodegas **b.** las firmas **c.** las cosechas (*harvests*)
5. María comprende que Jaime no sabía quién era Carlos y lo perdona.
   a. cierto **b.** falso

Actividad B El episodio

Vuelve a la **Actividad B** de **Antes de ver el episodio** para verificar tus respuestas. Si es necesario, vuelve a ver la escena en cuestión.

Actividad C Utilizando el contexto

Paso 1 Ya sabes que la frase **¿Qué tal?** es un saludo que quiere decir algo como *How's it going?* Repasa lo que dice don Paco en el mercado a continuación. ¿Qué crees que significa **¿Qué tal... ?** en este contexto?

PACO: ¡Buenas, doña Lourdes! *¿Qué tal* están sus jitomates hoy?

Paso 2 A diferencia de otros hispanos, los mexicanos dicen **¿Bueno?** al contestar el teléfono. ¿Qué dice Jaime cuando contesta su teléfono celular? ¿Sabes lo que dicen los españoles? Si no, pregúntaselo a tu profesor(a).

Actividad D En resumen

Completa la siguiente narración con las palabras y expresiones apropiadas de la lista a la derecha.

En este episodio, doña Isabel _____[1] por lo que pasa en la viña. Por eso le pide ayuda a don Francisco (Paco) Aguilar, un amigo de la familia que vive en México. Se nota que a María _____[2] su «tío» Paco y que _____[3] mucho. Entretanto,[a] Jaime va a la viña donde _____[4] doña Isabel, la madre de Carlos. Doña Isabel afirma que «Sol y viento» no _____[5] y Jaime y Carlos entran en una conversación agitada. Luego, María llega del _____[6] con don Paco y presencia[b] la confrontación. Pensando que Jaime la está engañando,[c] María se enoja[d] y deja caer[e] _____[7] que Jaime le regaló.

aeropuerto
el amuleto
conoce a
está a la venta
está preocupada
(*worried*)
le cae bien
lo respeta

[a]*Meanwhile* [b]*(she) witnesses* [c]*deceiving* [d]*se... gets angry* [e]*deja... drops*

RESUMEN DE VOCABULARIO

La geografía

el bosque (lluvioso)	(rain)forest
las cataratas	waterfalls
la colina	hill
la cordillera	mountain range
el lago	lake
la llanura	plain, prairie
el mar	sea
el paisaje	landscape
la playa	beach
el río	river
la selva (tropical)	(tropical) jungle
el valle	valley

los continentes: África, Antártida, Asia, Australia, Europa, Norteamérica, Sudamérica
Cognados: la costa, el desierto, el golfo, la isla, la meseta, la montaña, el océano, el volcán

El medio ambiente

construir (y)	to build
contaminar	to pollute
descomponer (*like* **poner**)	to decompose
desperdiciar	to waste
echar	to throw out
proteger (j)	to protect

salvar	to save (*from danger*)
tirar	to throw out

el basurero	landfill
la botella (de plástico/ vidrio)	(plastic/glass) bottle
la caja de cartón	cardboard box
la capa de ozono	ozone layer
los combustibles fósiles	fossil fuels
la contaminación (del agua/aire)	(water/air) pollution
los desperdicios	wastes
el efecto invernadero	greenhouse effect
la escasez (*pl.* **las escaseces**)	shortage
las especies en peligro de extinción	endangered species
la fábrica	factory
la falta	lack
la lata de aluminio	aluminum can
la naturaleza	nature
el producto desechable	disposable product
el reciclaje	recycling
los recursos naturales	natural resources

Cognados: conservar, reciclar; la deforestación, los pesticidas, el petróleo, el producto biodegradable
Repaso: la basura, el periódico

Actividades turísticas

acampar	to camp, go camping
bucear	to snorkel
cenar en un restaurante elegante	to eat in a fancy restaurant
charlar en un café	to chat in a café
comprar recuerdos	to buy souvenirs
degustar vinos	to go wine tasting
escalar montañas	to mountain climb
hacer (*irreg.*) **el salto bungee**	to bungee jump
ir (*irreg.*) **a un concierto**	to go to a concert
ir (*irreg.*) **a un parque de diversiones**	to go to an amusement park
ir (*irreg.*) **de excursión**	to go on a hike, go hiking
montar a caballo	to ride a horse, go horseback riding
pescar (qu)	to fish
practicar (qu) el alpinismo de rocas	to rock climb
practicar (qu) el paracaidismo	to sky dive
remar en canoa	to go canoeing
ver (*irreg.*) **un espectáculo**	to see a show

Cognados: hacer (*irreg.*) **camping, hacer** (*irreg.*) **kayak, hacer** (*irreg.*) **rafting, surfear**

Otras palabras y expresiones

al aire libre	outdoor
interior (*adj.*)	indoor

Repaso: mejor, peor

EPISODIO 7

Bajo el sol

Camino a[a] «Sol y viento», Mario y Jaime sufren un pinchazo.[b] Como Jaime se apresura por[c] llegar a la viña, decide ir caminando. ¿Crees que es buena idea o debe esperar hasta que arreglen[d] el auto?

▼

JAIME: Ud. me recuerda a[e] mi mamá. Ella siempre me hablaba de la tierra. Era campesina.

ISABEL: ¿Entonces no aprendió nada de su mamá? ¿Por qué está trabajando con esa gente que quiere cambiar nuestras vidas?

PACO: He averiguado que su compañía quiere construir una represa[f] en esta zona. ¿Comprende Ud. el daño[g] que eso causaría[h] por estas tierras?

◄

Jaime habla por teléfono con Andy, quien está en San Francisco. ¿Qué crees que le está diciendo? ¿Ha convencido a la familia Sánchez a que vendan[i] la viña?

[a]Camino... *On the way to* [b]*flat tire* [c]*se... is in a hurry* [d]*they fix* [e]*me... remind me of* [f]*dam* [g]*harm* [h]*would cause* [i]*a... to sell*

¿Cómo te sientes?

The following media resources are available for *Sol y viento: En breve*

Episodio 7 of *Sol y viento*

Online *Manual de actividades*

Interactive CD-ROM

Online Learning Center Website

Vocabulario

Talking About Feelings and Mental Conditions

Estoy tenso.

Emociones y condiciones

Describing Emotions

alegre, contento/a

avergonzado/a

cansado/a

confundido/a

enamorado/a (de)

enojado/a

frustrado/a

furioso/a

irritado/a

nervioso/a

perplejo/a

preocupado/a

relajado/a

triste

afectar	to affect
alegrar	to make happy
cansar	to tire
confundir	to confuse
enojar	to anger
frustrar	to frustrate
irritar	to irritate
molestar	to bother
ofender	to offend
preocupar	to worry
reaccionar	to react

✱ MÁS VOCABULARIO

estar (*irreg.*) **celoso/a**	to be jealous
llorar	to cry
reírse (i, i) (me río)	to laugh
tener(le) (*irreg.*) **envidia* (a alguien)**	to be envious (of someone)
tener(le) (*irreg.*) **miedo* (a alguien)**	to be afraid (of someone)
tener (*irreg.*) **sueño***	to be sleepy
tomarse algo muy a pecho	to take something to heart; to feel something intensely

〰 Vistazo cultural

Las telenovelas

Las telenovelas son programas televisivos muy populares en Latinoamérica. Son melodramas parecidos a las *soap operas* de este país. Ambos tipos de programas presentan los mismos conflictos sentimentales: emociones exageradas, pasiones tormentosas,[a] amores celosos, envidia, homicidios...

Una de las diferencias entre las novelas (como suelen llamarse) y las *soap operas* es que las novelas tienen mucha más aceptación entre el público. De hecho,[b] estos programas se transmiten en la tarde y en la noche, horas que en este país equivalen a la hora estelar.[c] Las estrellas de las novelas son muy populares en el mundo hispano. Muchos de estos actores aceptan papeles en novelas y películas alternativamente, mientras que en este país, el ideal de muchos actores es salir de la pantalla pequeña para lanzarse a[d] la pantalla grande.

Otra diferencia importante es que las novelas corren por un tiempo limitado. La idea de una telenovela de la misma longitud[e] de, por ejemplo, *All My Children,* es ajena[f] en el mundo hispano. La telenovela es una historia que tiene un principio,[g] un medio y un fin.

▲ La cadena (*network*) hispana Univisión tiene varias páginas en la red dedicadas a las telenovelas.

[a]*stormy* [b]*De... In fact* [c]*hora... prime time* [d]*lanzarse... break into* [e]*length* [f]*foreign* [g]*beginning*

---

*The words used in these **tener** expressions are not adjectives but nouns. Their literal meaning is *to have envy, to have fear,* and *to have sleepiness,* respectively. To qualify these expressions, use **mucho/a/os/as** or **un poco de** and not **muy** or **poco: Tengo mucho sueño.**

Actividad A　Oraciones lógicas

Paso 1　Escucha lo que dice el profesor (la profesora). Luego indica la frase que completa cada oración lógicamente.

1. **a.** ...tiene un auto nuevo.
   b. ...estudia mucho, pero no entiende la lección.

2. **a.** ...no durmió bien anoche.
   b. ...sacó una A en su examen.

3. **a.** ...necesitan pagar el alquiler y no tienen suficiente dinero.
   b. ...mañana van a comenzar las vacaciones de verano.

4. **a.** ...lo que le dijo el profesor es diferente de lo que dice el libro.
   b. ...necesita planear una fiesta de sorpresa y tiene mucho que hacer.

5. **a.** ...trabaja demasiado y no tiene suficiente tiempo libre.
   b. ...lo van a expulsar de la universidad.

Paso 2　Ahora indica si cada oración es lógica o no.

	SÍ	NO
1. Si uno está enojado, normalmente se ríe de la situación.	☐	☐
2. Si uno está muy triste, típicamente llora.	☐	☐
3. Si uno está enamorado de alguien, piensa mucho en esa persona.	☐	☐
4. Si uno está perplejo, está seguro de sus acciones.	☐	☐
5. Si uno está relajado, se come las uñas (*fingernails*).	☐	☐

Actividad B　¿Se te aplica o no?

Paso 1　Indica si se te aplica cada oración o no.

> ## ¡Exprésate!
>
> Verbs such as **preocupar** and **molestar,** among others in this section's vocabulary list, require an indirect object pronoun.
>
> Eso **me preocupa.**
>
> **¿Te molestan** las personas tensas?

	SE ME APLICA.	NO SE ME APLICA.
1. Me enoja cuando otras personas hablan durante una película.	☐	☐
2. Me preocupa la economía del país.	☐	☐
3. Me confunden los planos.	☐	☐
4. Me frustran las matemáticas.	☐	☐
5. Me molesta cuando otros me piden ayuda con su tarea académica.	☐	☐
6. Me irrita el humo (*smoke*) de los cigarrillos en los lugares públicos.	☐	☐
7. Me enoja el uso flagrante de teléfonos celulares en lugares públicos.	☐	☐
8. Me ofenden las palabras verdes (*swearwords*) y temas sexuales que se presentan en muchos programas televisivos.	☐	☐

Paso 2　Ahora entrevista a un compañero (una compañera) de clase para saber si se le aplican las oraciones del **Paso 1** o no. ¿Coinciden sus respuestas con las tuyas?

¡Exprésate!

To say that someone is *too frustrated, sad, angry,* and so forth, use the adverb **demasiado.**

Elena está **demasiado tensa** estos días.	*Elena is too tense these days.*

Actividad C Situaciones y consejos

Paso 1 Empareja el consejo más apropiado para responder a cada problema o situación a continuación.

PROBLEMA/SITUACIÓN

1. ___ Siempre tengo sueño en clase.
2. ___ Estoy celoso/a de los amigos de mi pareja (*partner*).
3. ___ Me tomo todo a pecho.
4. ___ Le tengo envidia a mi compañero de cuarto. Es muy inteligente y para él todo es fácil.
5. ___ No le tengo miedo a nada.

CONSEJO

a. Eso está mal. Habla con él o ella sobre tus sentimientos de inseguridad. Si la situación no mejora (*improves*), busca ayuda profesional.

b. Puede ser bueno, pero puede ser problemático si crees que eres invincible y que nada te puede pasar.

c. Eso es natural. Pero no debe llegar a tal punto que sientes un odio porque él tiene más éxito que tú.

d. Debes consultar con un médico (*doctor*) para ver qué lo está causando. Si no tienes ninguna enfermedad (*disease*), quizás (*perhaps*) no duermes lo suficiente.

e. Eres demasiado sensible (*sensitive*). Necesitas distinguir entre lo que es importante y lo que no es importante.

Paso 2 Con un compañero (una compañera) de clase, indiquen cuál es el problema o la situación más grave (*serious*) y cuál es el/la menos grave. Luego determinen si los consejos son buenos o no. Compartan lo que piensan con los demás miembros de la clase.

Actividad D ¿Cómo te sientes?

Paso 1 Completa cada oración con algo verdadero para ti.

1. Una de las cosas que más me molesta o me irrita es cuando...
2. Me frustra(n)...
3. Me ofende cuando alguien...
4. A veces estoy nervioso/a cuando...
5. Me preocupa(n)...

Paso 2 Basándote en las oraciones del **Paso 1,** entrevista a otra persona.

MODELO: ¿Cuál es una de las cosas que más te molesta o irrita?

Paso 3 Escribe un párrafo de unas 100 palabras en el que comparas tus respuestas con las de la persona que entrevistaste.

MODELO: Una de las cosas que más me irrita es cuando las personas no llegan a tiempo a una cita. En cambio (*On the other hand*), a Robert le molesta más cuando su compañero de cuarto le cambia el canal cuando está viendo la televisión...

Gramática

¿Cómo se siente?

Pseudo-Reflexive Verbs

There is a class of verbs in Spanish called pseudo-reflexives that are used to express a change in emotion. The equivalent in English is *to get* or *to become* + a state or condition. The English equivalent does not normally contain *-self/ -selves*, which would be a true reflexive. Compare the following.

Juan **se vio**.	*John saw himself.* (true reflexive)
Juan **se enojó**.	*John got angry.* (pseudo-reflexive)
Me hablo constantemente.	*I talk to myself constantly.* (true reflexive)
Me ofendo fácilmente.	*I get offended easily.* (pseudo-reflexive)

Regular reflexive pronouns (**me, te, se, nos,** and **os**) are still required. Many of the verbs you learned earlier in this lesson, as well as others, can be used in pseudo-reflexive constructions.

aburrirse	to get bored
alegrarse	to become happy
cansarse	to get tired
confundirse	to become confused
deprimirse	to get depressed
frustrarse	to get frustrated
irritarse	to get irritated
ofenderse	to get offended
preocuparse	to become worried
sentirse (ie, i)	to feel

FORMS OF PSEUDO-REFLEXIVE VERBS	
enojarse (*to get angry*) **sentirse (ie, i)** (*to feel*)	
me enojo **me** siento	**nos** enojamos **nos** sentimos
te enojas **te** sientes	**os** enojáis **os** sentís
se enoja **se** siente	**se** enojan **se** sienten
se enoja **se** siente	**se** enojan **se** sienten

In Spanish, several verbal phrases also express the equivalent of *to get* or *to become* + a state or condition. One of these is **ponerse,** which can be used with a number of adjectives to express the same meanings as certain pseudo-reflexive verbs.

Me puse muy enojado.	*I got (became) very angry.*
Marta **se puso** bien frustrada.	*Marta got (became) really frustrated.*

In addition, **volverse** can be used with adjectives like **loco/a** (*crazy*) to express a more permanent type of change, one that is often but not always sudden. Such expressions don't usually mean *crazy* in the temporary sense of *he went nuts.* This would be rendered by **ponerse** or **actuar,** often with another adjective.

El señor **se volvió loco.**	*The man went crazy (insane).*
Se puso furioso.	*He went nuts.*
Actuó de una manera loca.	*He was (acting) crazy.*

Finally, **hacerse** is used to express changes such as *getting rich, becoming famous,* and so forth. In such cases, the subject tends to directly cause the action, which is why **hacer** is used.

Se hizo millonario.	*He became a millionaire.*

DE SOL Y VIENTO

In **Episodio 7,** you will see a scene in which Mario asks an upset Jaime about María. Part of their exchange is presented here.

MARIO
Don Jaime, no entiendo. Esa señorita que _____ con Ud., María, es la misma que yo vi con Ud. el otro día, ¿no es cierto?

JAIME
Sí, es cierto...

MARIO
¿Y? ¿Por qué _____ con Ud.? ¿Lo vio con otra mujer?

JAIME
Mario, calla y maneja.[a]

Based on what you remember from the previous episode, which of the following makes the most sense to fill in both blanks?

a. se enojó   **b.** se volvió   **c.** se ofendió

[a]calla... *shut up and drive*

Actividad E   ¿Quién es?

Indica el nombre del personaje de *Sol y viento* que contesta cada pregunta a continuación. **¡OJO!** Hay más de una respuesta posible en algunos casos.

¿Qué personaje...

1. se enojó con Jaime?
2. se siente mal por lo que piensa María?
3. se cansa de las excusas de Carlos?
4. se confunde por la discusión (*argument*) entre María y Jaime?
5. se preocupa por Carlos?

Actividad F   ¿Eres equilibrado/a (*well-balanced*) o no?

Paso 1 Indica si las siguientes afirmaciones se te aplican o no.

	SÍ	NO
1. Cuando me enojo, suelo explotar (*explode*).	☐	☐
2. Cuando me ofendo, siempre se lo digo a la persona ofensiva.	☐	☐
3. Cuando me aburro, veo la televisión.	☐	☐
4. Cuando me frustro, suelo dejar (*stop*) lo que hago para concentrarme en otra cosa.	☐	☐
5. Si me confundo, siempre pido aclaración (*clarification*), especialmente en clase.	☐	☐
6. Si me irrito, busco algo para cambiar de humor (*mood*).	☐	☐

Paso 2 Ahora escucha las instrucciones y comentarios del profesor (de la profesora).

Actividad G   ¿Cómo te sientes? ¿Cómo te pones?

Paso 1 Utilizando adjetivos como **aburrido/a, nervioso/a,** etcétera, o las palabras **bien** o **mal,** indica cómo te sientes o cómo te pones en cada circunstancia.

MODELO: cuando sales bien en un examen →
Me siento bien. / Me pongo alegre.

1. antes de la primera cita con alguien que te gusta mucho
2. cuando tienes que hablar en público o enfrente de la clase
3. después de hacer ejercicio
4. cuando un profesor (una profesora) no contesta bien tu pregunta
5. cuando caminas a solas por la noche en tu barrio
6. cuando caminas a solas por la universidad por la noche

Paso 2 Ahora entrevista a un compañero (una compañera) de clase para ver cómo reacciona ante las situaciones del **Paso 1,** según el modelo. ¿Se sienten Uds. iguales o hay mucha diferencia entre sus reacciones a las situaciones?

MODELO: ¿Cómo te sientes cuando sales bien en un examen?

Actividad H ¿Reacciones apropiadas?

Paso 1 En grupos de tres, contesten cada pregunta a continuación.

¿Cuándo es apropiado...

1. ofenderse y confrontar a la persona ofensiva?

2. ofenderse y no decirle nada a la persona ofensiva?

3. preocuparse por el comportamiento (*behavior*) de un amigo (una amiga)?

4. no preocuparse por el comportamiento de un amigo (una amiga)?

5. sentirse mal por algo que uno dice?

6. no sentirse mal por algo que uno dice?

Paso 2 Los grupos deben reportar sus ideas a la clase. Luego voten para determinar cuáles de las ideas representan reacciones más apropiadas y cuáles no, según el caso.

SOL Y VIENTO: Enfoque cultural

En el **Episodio 7** don Paco va a mencionar el Internet. La imagen que muchas personas tienen de los países hispanos es una de países pobres, del «tercer mundo» y con poca modernización. En general, los países hispanos no gozan de[a] los excesos tecnológicos de una cultura como la de este país, pero no son tan atrasados[b] como algunos creen. España es tan moderna como cualquier otro país de Europa y las ciudades de Santiago, Buenos Aires, Caracas, México, D.F. y San Juan, entre otras, ofrecen casi todo lo que se podría[c] encontrar en las grandes ciudades norteamericanas. Por ejemplo, hay «cibercafés» donde la gente va para tomar un café y leer su correo electrónico. También, los negocios y bancos están tan bien equipados de tecnología como cualquier negocio en este país. Además, la viña donde se filmó *Sol y viento* poseía de[d] todo lo moderno como cualquier viña en Napa o Sonoma, California, por ejemplo. Finalmente, varios Premios Nóbel de Ciencia se han otorgado[e] a científicos de países hispanos. Claro, en las zonas rurales es un poco diferente, pero ¿no es así en casi cualquier país del mundo?

▲ Los cibercafés, como este en México, D.F., son muy populares en todas partes del mundo.

[a]no... *don't enjoy* [b]*backward* [c]*se... one could* [d]poseía... *possessed* [e]*awarded*

Vocabulario

Talking About
Health

Estoy un poco enfermo.

**Parts of the Body and
Physical Health**

Las partes del cuerpo^a

La cabeza y la cara^{b†}

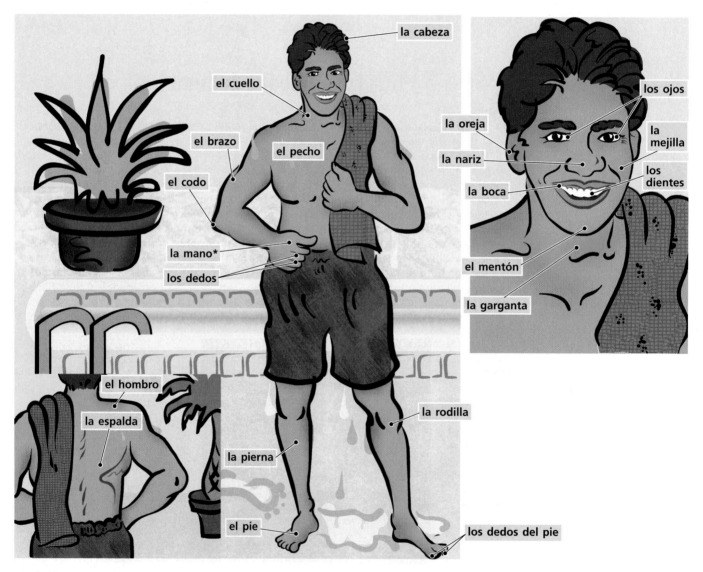

la cabeza

el cuello

el brazo

el pecho

el codo

la mano*

los dedos

el hombro

la espalda

la mano*

la pierna

la rodilla

el pie

los dedos del pie

los ojos

la oreja

la mejilla

la nariz

la boca

los dientes

el mentón

la garganta

^a*body* ^b*face*

*Note that **mano** is actually a feminine noun, despite the fact that it ends in **-o: la mano derecha.**
†Many of the vocabulary items presented here are review, but they will be useful to talk about physical health.

La salud[a] y el estado físico

[a]*health*

cortar(se)	to cut (oneself)
enfermarse	to get sick
estar (*irreg.*) **enfermo/a**	to be sick
hacer (*irreg.*) **gárgaras**	to gargle
lastimar(se)	to hurt (oneself)
romper(se)	to break
tener (*irreg.*) **fiebre** (*f.*)	to have a fever
tener (*irreg.*) **la nariz tapada**	to have a stuffed-up nose
tener (*irreg.*) **un resfriado**	to have a cold
la aspirina	aspirin
el hueso	bone
la medicina	medicine

COMUNICACIÓN ÚTIL

When talking about parts of the body, native speakers of Spanish typically use the definite article where an English speaker would use a possessive adjective. Compare the following examples.

Tengo **la** nariz tapada.	*My nose is stuffed up.*
Rebeca se lastimó **la** pierna.	*Rebeca hurt her leg.*
¿Cuándo te rompiste **el** brazo?	*When did you break your arm?*

≋ Vistazo cultural

Los hospitales y las clínicas

La imagen que muchas personas tienen de Latinoamérica es de países en vías de desarrollo[a] con problemas de salud, agua no potable[b] y limitados recursos médicos. En realidad, esto se puede decir de casi cualquier zona rural del mundo, pero no es apropiada en cuanto a[c] los centros urbanos de Latinoamérica. En las grandes ciudades como Santiago de Chile, Buenos Aires y México, D.F., hay hospitales y clínicas modernos, bien equipados, adonde uno puede recurrir[d] si sufre de algo que requiere atención médica. En Costa Rica y México, entre otros países, hay escuelas de medicina que preparan a médicos excelentes. Costa Rica, en particular, es un lugar conocido para la cirugía cosmética.

[a]en... *developing* [b]*drinkable* [c]en... *in regard to* [d]*go*

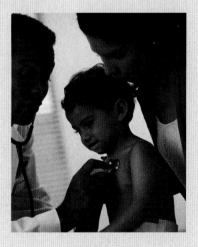

▲ San José, Costa Rica

Actividad A Asociaciones

Paso 1 ¿Qué parte del cuerpo asocias con cada enfermedad o condición?

1. la poliomielitis (*polio*)	**a.** la cabeza	**b.** las piernas
2. el resfriado	**a.** el pecho y la nariz	**b.** los brazos y las manos
3. el mal aliento (*breath*)	**a.** los ojos	**b.** la boca
4. la escoliosis	**a.** las orejas	**b.** la espalda
5. las caries (*cavities*)	**a.** los dientes	**b.** la garganta
6. necesitar muletas (*crutches*)	**a.** las piernas	**b.** el codo
7. llevar yeso (*a cast*)	**a.** la cara	**b.** el brazo
8. cortarse	**a.** los dedos	**b.** los dientes

Paso 2 ¿Qué prenda(s) de ropa o complemento(s) (*accessory*[*ies*]) asocias con cada parte del cuerpo a continuación?

1. Con la cabeza asocio...

2. Con los pies asocio...

3. Con el cuello asocio...

4. Con las piernas asocio...

5. Con los hombros, la espalda y el pecho asocio...

¡Exprésate!

The verb **romper** can be used in two ways when talking about the breaking of a bone. It can be used reflexively to imply that someone caused or was involved in the breaking of his or her own bone.

Roberto **se rompió** una pierna.   *Roberto broke his leg.*

You can also use a construction with **se** and an indirect object to imply that the break happened to Roberto without any cause or involvement (that is, that it was completely accidental and he can't be blamed for it).

A Roberto **se le rompió** una pierna.   *Roberto broke his leg. (lit: Roberto's leg was broken to him.)*

The same is also true for the verb **cortar**, among others.

Me corté un dedo. }
Se me cortó un dedo. }   *I cut my finger.*

Actividad B ¿Es inconveniente o no?

Con un compañero (una compañera) de clase, indiquen en qué categoría pondrían (*you would place*) cada una de las siguientes situaciones: **muy inconveniente, inconveniente** o **un poco inconveniente.** Luego, presenten sus ideas a la clase. ¿Están todos de acuerdo? ¿Pueden explicar sus razones?

MODELO: Si a uno se le rompe el dedo pequeño del pie, es un poco inconveniente. Uno puede caminar todavía y no necesita equipo especial.

Vocabulario útil

la muleta	crutch
la vendaje	bandage
el yeso	cast

1. si a uno se le rompe la nariz
2. si a uno se le rompe un brazo
3. si a uno se le rompe una mano
4. si a uno se le rompe una pierna
5. si a uno se le rompe un pie
6. si a uno se le rompe un diente
7. si a uno se le corta un dedo
8. si a uno se le corta la mejilla / la pierna (mientras se afeita)

Actividad C ¿Qué producto o medicina?

Paso 1 Indica qué producto usas o qué medicina tomas en cada situación.

1. Tienes resfriado. También tienes la nariz tapada.
2. Tienes dolor de cabeza (*headache*).
3. Tienes dolor de garganta.
4. Estás mareado/a (*nauseated*). No te sientes bien del estómago (*stomach*).
5. Tienes fiebre.
6. Te cortas un dedo.
7. Se te lastima la espalda.

Paso 2 Vuelve a las situaciones del **Paso 1.** ¿Hay remedios caseros (*home reme-dies*) o naturales que conoces para cada una? ¿Cuáles son? También indica si haces algo más para aliviar la situación y sentirte mejor.

MODELO: Dicen que si tienes dolor de garganta, debes hacer gárgaras de (*gargle with*) agua tibia (*warm*) con un poco de sal.

Actividad D ¡Firma aquí, por favor!

Paso 1 Busca personas que contesten **sí** a las siguientes preguntas. Pide sus firmas (**¡Firma aquí, por favor!**). No puedes hacerle dos preguntas seguidas (*in a row*) a la misma persona.

1. ¿Se te rompió un brazo alguna vez? _____
2. ¿Se te rompió una pierna alguna vez? _____
3. ¿Has estado enfermo/a por más de dos semanas alguna vez? _____
4. ¿Te cortaste un dedo alguna vez? _____
5. ¿Te lastimaste la espalda alguna vez? _____

Paso 2 Reporta a la clase lo que aprendiste en el **Paso 1.**

MODELO: A Juan se le rompió una pierna una vez.

Gramática

Estaban contentos, ¿no?   **Review of the Imperfect**

As you know, the imperfect is used to talk about repeated actions in the past. It is also used to express any action, state of being, or condition that was in progress at a particular point in the past. Examine the following.

> No me presenté al examen porque **estaba** enferma. **Tenía** un poco de fiebre y **tenía** la nariz tapada.
> *I didn't show up for the test because I was sick. I had a bit of a fever and my nose was stuffed up.*

In the previous example, the reference point is the test—or rather the time that the person should have shown up for the test. At that point in time, there were three existent states described: being sick, having a fever, and having nasal congestion.

States and conditions in Spanish are typically described with **ser** and **estar.** However, many other verbs that you already know also represent states of being, such as those in the following list.

conocer	to know, be familiar with (*someone or something*)
hacer buen/mal tiempo	to be good/bad weather
parecer	to seem, resemble
poder	to be able to, can
quedar	to stay, remain
saber	to know (*facts, information*)
tener	to have
verse	to appear to be, look

> Al llegar al consultorio, me **parecía** que los síntomas disminuían.
> *When I arrived at the doctor's office, it seemed like the symptoms were going away.*

> Vi a Miguel ayer. No **se veía** muy bien.
> *I saw Miguel yesterday. He didn't look very well.*

> No hablé con el médico porque no lo **conocía.**
> *I didn't speak with the doctor because I didn't know him.*

As is the case with many other verbs, the use of the preterite with states of being implies one of two things: (1) the state is viewed as completed at a particular point in time; or (2) the state is viewed as just beginning at that point in time.

> No me **pareció** tan grave.
> *It didn't seem that serious to me.*
> (At that particular moment, it didn't seem that serious.)

> **Estuve** enferma por una semana entera.
> *I was sick for a whole week.*
> (The preterite is used because the state is confined to a particular time frame, for two weeks.)

> Por fin **conocí** al médico.
> *I finally met the doctor.*
> (The state of knowing the doctor began at a particular moment.)

George Washington **fue** el primer presidente de los Estados Unidos.
George Washington was the first president of the United States.
(He was president for a specific period of time, then it ended.)

Tuvo un hijo.
She had a boy.
(The use of the preterite indicates that she gave birth to the boy.)

For the most part, you will continue to use the imperfect to describe states of being and conditions in the past. Used in this way, the imperfect describes background information, not the events that cause a narrative to move forward (which are described by the preterite). In the following chart, you can see how time almost stands still as the imperfect is used to describe a number of states and conditions that were all happening at the same time.

USING THE IMPERFECT TO DESCRIBE STATES AND CONDITIONS

Eran las dos de la tarde y no **me sentía** muy bien. **Tenía** un poco de fiebre y **tenía** la garganta seca.[a] Tampoco **podía** ver muy bien. **Me parecía** que todo el mundo **se oscurecía**.[b] **Necesitaba** tomar medicina rápidamente antes de que me pusiera peor aún.[c]

[a]*dry* [b]se... *was getting dark* [c]antes... *before I got any worse*

DE SOL Y VIENTO

Here is the complete exchange between Mario and Jaime as Mario inquires about María's being upset. Note the use of the imperfect in their dialogue.

MARIO
Don Jaime, no entiendo. Esa señorita que se enojó con Ud., María, es la misma que yo vi con Ud. el otro día, ¿no es cierto?

JAIME
Sí, es cierto.

MARIO
Y Uds. **se veían** muy contentos.

JAIME
Así **creía** yo.

MARIO
¿Y? ¿Por qué se enojó con Ud.?
¿Lo vio con otra mujer?

JAIME
Mario, calla y maneja.

In the dialogue, Mario remarks that **"Y Uds. se veían muy contentos."** What must he have noticed beforehand to make this comment? Complete the following sentence with forms of **sonreír** (*to smile*) and **llevarse**.

Antes, Mario notó que María y Jaime _____¹ y _____² muy bien.

Actividad E ¿Qué pasaba?

Completa cada oración para describir la escena enfrente de la casa al final del **Episodio 6** de *Sol y viento.*

1. Cuando María se enojó con Jaime y le devolvió (*returned*) la figurita, estaban presentes _____.
2. Al recoger la figurita, seguramente Jaime se sentía _____.
3. Don Paco y Carlos estaban perplejos porque no sabían nada de _____.

Actividad F El primer día de la clase de español

¿Eran verdaderos para ti los siguientes estados y condiciones cuando llegaste a la clase de español por primera vez?

	SÍ	NO
1. Yo estaba un poco nervioso/a. No quería estudiar español.	☐	☐
2. Ya tenía los libros y cuadernos.	☐	☐
3. No sabía ni una palabra de español.	☐	☐
4. Ya conocía a algunas personas en la clase.	☐	☐
5. Sabía algo del profesor (de la profesora).	☐	☐
6. Me parecía que el español era difícil porque no podía entender mucho.	☐	☐

Actividad G ¡Sean creativos!

Escoge una de las siguientes historias breves y escribe una forma correcta de los verbos alistados en los espacios en blanco. Luego, agrega una oración más para continuar la historia y pásasela a otra persona. Esa persona debe agregar una oración más y pasársela a otra persona. Esto se debe repetir con dos personas más. La última persona debe devolverte la historia. ¿Cómo es la historia? ¿Es tal como la imaginabas? Por último, lee la versión final a la clase.

Vocabulario útil

creer, estar, hacer, sentir

Versión A

Para Manuel, el día era perfecto. _____[1] buen tiempo. Brillaba[a] el sol de manera que la Madre Naturaleza parecía estar contenta con todo. Manuel se _____[2] bien. Ya no _____[3] nervioso ante la situación que le esperaba.[b] De hecho, _____[4] que estaba listo para enfrentar[c] cualquier problema. Entonces sonó[d] el teléfono. Era Miguel —y quería darle una noticia.[e]

[a]*Was shining* [b]*le... awaited him* [c]*face* [d]*rang* [e]*piece of news*

Versión B

Para Susana, el día era un catástrofe desde el comienzo. _____[1] mal tiempo. Llovía sin parar[a] y el cielo[b] estaba poblado de nubes[c] oscuras, dando la sensación de que la Madre Naturaleza estaba irritada. Susana no se _____[2] bien. _____[3] nerviosa ante la situación que le esperaba.[d] _____[4] que su futuro estaba en manos de otras personas, lo cual no le gustaba para nada. Pero su suerte estaba por cambiar.[e] Sonó[f] el teléfono. Era Miguel —y quería darle una noticia.[g]

[a]sin... *without stopping*   [b]*sky*   [c]*clouds*   [d]le... *awaited her*   [e]su... *her luck was about to change*
[f]*Rang*   [g]*piece of news*

Actividad H   La última vez

Paso 1   Describe la última vez que no fuiste a clases o al trabajo porque estabas enfermo/a o porque te lastimaste en alguna parte del cuerpo. Usa las siguientes preguntas como guía.

1. ¿Cuántos años tenías? ¿Estudiabas en la escuela secundaria o en la universidad?
2. ¿Qué síntomas tenías o qué te pasó? ¿Cómo te sentías?
3. ¿Cuánto tiempo duró la enfermedad (*sickness*) o la herida (*injury*)? ¿Cuándo pudiste regresar a las clases o al trabajo?

Paso 2   Algunos voluntarios deben leer sus descripciones en voz alta (*aloud*). ¿Quién estaba más enfermo o tenía la herida más grave?

◉ Enfoque lingüístico

La adquisición del aspecto

In **Lección 5B** you learned that the difference between the preterite and the imperfect is not one of *tense,* but rather one of *aspect.* Investigations in second-language acquisition have shown that it takes learners a long time to control aspectual distinctions in Romance languages, and it has been hypothesized that learners tend to go through particular stages in acquiring these distinctions, regardless of whether they learn a second language in a structured environment (such as a classroom) or naturalistically (i.e., living and working in a different language community).

One hypothesis claims that preterite endings emerge in learners' speech first, but not with all types of verbs. Learners are more likely to start using preterite endings with certain "punctual" events such as *break, arrive, begin, end,* then gradually use these endings with verbs expressing activities (*run, play, work*), and then finally with states or conditions (*be, have, know, want*). This hypothesis also claims that imperfect endings appear later and, like the preterite, they tend to appear on certain types of verbs before others.

The imperfect tends to emerge first on verbs representing states or conditions, then on verbs expressing activities, and finally to "punctual" verbs—the opposite order of how preterite endings emerge.

If you encounter problems knowing when to use the preterite and the imperfect in spontaneous speech in Spanish, be patient! By working carefully through the activities in these sections and by paying attention to how the forms are used in *Sol y viento* and in other communicative contexts, you will be well on your way to a better (and faster!) understanding of aspectual distinctions in Spanish.

TERCERA PARTE

Vocabulario

Telling the Doctor
How You Feel

Me duele la garganta.

In the Doctor's Office

Algunos órganos internos importantes

el cerebro	brain
el corazón	heart
el estómago	stomach
el hígado	liver
el pulmón	lung

En el consultorio del médico

examinar	to examine; to test
poner(le) (*irreg.*) **una inyección (a alguien)**	to give (someone) a shot
respirar	to breathe
sacar (qu) la lengua	to stick out one's tongue
sacar(le) (qu) sangre (a alguien)	to draw (someone's) blood
tomar(le) la temperatura (a alguien)	to take a (someone's) temperature
la alergia	allergy
el/la enfermero/a	nurse
el examen médico	checkup; medical examination
el/la médico/a	doctor
el/la paciente	patient
la pastilla	pill
la presión arterial	blood pressure
los rayos X	X-rays
la receta	prescription

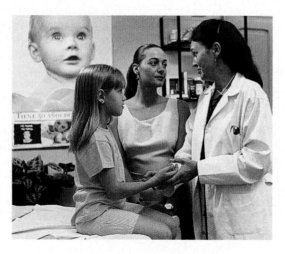

◀

A muchos niños no les gustan **los exámenes médicos.** ¡Tienen miedo de **las inyecciones**!

✱ MÁS VOCABULARIO

doler (ue)	to hurt, ache
Me duele la cabeza.	*My head hurts.*
padecer (zc) de	to suffer from
el/la farmacéutico/a	pharmacist
la farmacia	pharmacy

COMUNICACIÓN ÚTIL

When using verbs such as **examinar, poner,** and so forth to talk about medical examinations, an indirect object pronoun is often used. Note that the definite article is also used instead of a possessive adjective. Compare the following.

Me examinaron los ojos.	*They examined my eyes.*
¿Te pusieron una inyección?	*Did they give you an injection?*
Le sacaron sangre.	*They drew blood from him.*

 Vistazo cultural

Las recetas

Algo que les sorprende[a] a muchos norteamericanos cuando viajan por o viven en un país extranjero es la facilidad con que se puede obtener medicinas en algunos lugares. En los Estados Unidos las medicinas y drogas son reguladas por la Administración Federal de Drogas y es necesario tener una receta firmada por un médico para obtener muchas de ellas. En cambio, en varios países hispanos no es necesario tener la receta de un médico para comprar muchas de las medicinas. Uno puede entrar a la farmacia y decirle a un farmacéutico lo que necesita (o los síntomas que tiene). El farmacéutico, que tiene entrenamiento especial, le recomienda una medicina a la persona. De hecho, a veces ni siquiera[b] es necesario consultar con un médico de antemano[c] —la farmacia puede servir tanto de consultorio como de distribuidor de medicinas.

▲ El farmacéutico le recomienda a este estudiante una medicación. (Lima, el Perú)

[a]*surprises* [b]ni... *neither* [c]de... *beforehand*

Actividad A Definiciones

Escucha las definiciones que da tu profesor(a) y escribe su número al lado de la palabra o frase que describe.

a. ___ los rayos X

b. ___ el corazón

c. ___ el cerebro

d. ___ los pulmones

e. ___ el estómago

f. ___ la pastilla

g. ___ la receta

h. ___ la enfermera

Actividad B En el consultorio del médico

Indica si cada oración se refiere a algo que dice un paciente o un médico en el consultorio.

		PACIENTE	MÉDICO
1.	Vamos a sacarle sangre para chequear el nivel (*level*) del colesterol.	☐	☐
2.	No, no tengo alergias a ninguna medicina.	☐	☐
3.	¿Me van a poner una inyección?	☐	☐
4.	Veo que su presión arterial está bien.	☐	☐
5.	Me duele el estómago.	☐	☐
6.	Le doy una receta.	☐	☐
7.	¿Le duele aquí?	☐	☐
8.	¿Padece su familia de la diabetes?	☐	☐

▲ ¿Cuáles son las preguntas que te hace el médico (la médica) en su consultorio?

Actividad C ¿Cierto o falso?

Indica si cada oración es cierta o falsa.

	CIERTO	FALSO
1. Si uno padece de alta presión arterial, debe tomar medicina y hacer ejercicio.	☐	☐
2. La hepatitis es una enfermedad que afecta el hígado.	☐	☐
3. Durante un examen médico típico, no es necesario sacar la lengua.	☐	☐
4. En varios países hispanos una farmacéutica te puede dar medicinas sin receta.	☐	☐
5. Si padeces de alergias, es importante decírselo al médico.	☐	☐
6. Se puede comprar algunos jarabes para la tos (*cough syrups*) sin receta.	☐	☐
7. Si el médico te toca (*touches*) el área de los riñones (*kidneys*) y te duele, puede haber un problema grave.	☐	☐
8. Por lo general, en un examen médico te ponen una inyección.	☐	☐

Actividad D Un juego de charadas (*charades*)

Paso 1 La clase debe dividirse en dos grupos, el grupo A y el grupo B. El profesor (La profesora) repartirá (*will hand out*) palabras o expresiones de la lista de vocabulario de las páginas 372–373. Cada persona tiene que describir su palabra o expresión (¡sin hablar!) con gestos (*gestures*) para que los demás de su grupo puedan (*can*) adivinar esa palabra o expresión. ¿Quiénes son los mejores actores de la clase?

Paso 2 En grupos de dos, indiquen si una visita del perro al veterinario es diferente de o similar a una visita de su dueño/a al consultorio del médico. Luego, presenten sus ideas a la clase.

MODELOS: Una manera en que las dos visitas son similares es que...

Una manera en que las dos visitas son diferentes es que...

NAVEGANDO LA RED 〜〜〜〜〜〜〜〜〜〜〜〜〜〜〜

Busca un sitio de una compañía de seguros (*insurance*) médicos. Imprime (*Print out*) una lista de servicios médicos que cubre (*covers*) la compañía y comparte la información con tus compañeros de clase.

Gramática

Talking About When
Something
Happened

Hace dos años que se me rompió el brazo.

Hacer in Expressions of Time

hacer IN EXPRESSIONS OF TIME		
PRESENT	PRETERITE	IMPERFECT
Hace mucho tiempo **que vivo** en Chicago. *I've lived in Chicago for a long time.*	**Me enfermé hace** unos días. / **Hace** unos días **que me enfermé.** *I got sick a few days ago.*	**Hacía** varios meses **que trabajaba** en la novela. *I'd been working on the novel for several months.*
Hace más de un año **que no veo** al médico. *It's been over a year since I've seen the doctor.*		**Hacía** unos meses **que no veía** a Ramón. *It had been several months since I saw Ramón.*

You may recall from **Lección 4A** that **hacer** can be used with the preterite to express the concept of *ago.* However, **hacer** can also be used with other tenses and verb forms to express various temporal relationships. Examine the chart.

Note the following based on the examples in the chart.

1. With the present and the imperfect, **hace** and **hacía** are used to express *for* if the sentence is affirmative and *since* if the sentence is negative. When used with the preterite, only **hace** is used, and the meaning expressed is *ago.*

2. When used with the present and the imperfect, **que** is typically used. **Que** can be optional with the preterite. If it is used, the **hace** phrase appears before the verb. If it is omitted, the **hace** phrase comes after the verb.*

3. When used with the present and the imperfect, both verbs are in the same tense. That is, **hace** is used with the present tense to express *since* in a present time context, and **hacía** is used with the imperfect to express *since* in a past time context.

4. With the present and imperfect constructions, the English equivalent requires a helping verb (e.g., *have, has, had*). No helping verb is needed in Spanish in these constructions.

*****Que** is also sometimes omitted in the present and imperfect, but more rarely than with the preterite. Rules of placement of **hacer** apply as with the preterite.

To ask *for how long* or *since when*, use a version of **¿Cuánto tiempo hace/hacía que... ?**

> ¿Cuánto tiempo hace que estudias español?
>
> ¿Cuánto tiempo hace que no hablas con Julio?
>
> ¿Cuánto tiempo hacía que tenían problemas cuando se divorciaron?

DE SOL Y VIENTO

In **Episodio 7,** you will see don Paco and doña Isabel confront Jaime about his company's plans to build a dam. Read the following exchange and insert either **hace** or **hacía** in the blank. Do you understand what don Paco is saying?

PACO
He averiguado que su compañía quiere construir una represa en esta zona.
¿Comprende Ud. el daño que eso causaría por estas tierras?

ISABEL
Mi amigo Paco ha estado haciendo averiguaciones.[a] Hemos sabido muchas cosas
interesantes con respecto a su compañía.

PACO
La magia del Internet y unas llamadas por teléfono. Pero obviamente a su compañía
no le importa mucho el daño a la ecología... ni a la comunidad humana que habita
estas tierras. ¡Lo que hicieron en Bolivia _____ dos años no tiene perdón!

[a]*investigations*

Actividad E ¿Qué sabes? ¿Qué crees?

Completa las siguientes oraciones según lo que sabes o crees sobre *Sol y viento* hasta el momento.

1. Hace _____ que Jaime llegó a Chile.

    a. unos días   **b.** unas semanas   **c.** un mes

2. Hace _____ que doña Isabel y su esposo se establecieron en Chile.

    a. diez años   **b.** veinte años   **c.** más de treinta años

3. Hace _____ que Carlos intenta (*has been trying*) vender la viña.

    a. unas horas   **b.** varios meses   **c.** varios días

4. Hacía _____ que la familia Sánchez planeaba la recepción para la nueva cosecha.

    a. unos meses   **b.** unos años   **c.** unos días

▲ ¿Cuánto tiempo hace que Jaime llegó a Chile? ¿Unos días? ¿una semana? ¿más?

Actividad F ¿Cuánto tiempo hace que... ?

Paso 1 Completa cada oración con información verdadera para ti.

1. Hace _____ que vivo en _____.

2. Hace _____ que estoy interesado/a en _____.

3. Hace _____ que visité al dentista.

4. Hace _____ que no _____.

Paso 2 Convierte las oraciones del **Paso 1** en preguntas y busca personas que contesten igual que tú. Luego presenta la información a la clase.

MODELO: E1: ¿Cuánto tiempo hace que vives en Ann Arbor?
          E2: Hace dos años.
          E1: (más tarde) Hace sólo un año que vivo en Ann Arbor, pero hace dos años que Tracy vive aquí.

Actividad G   ¿Cuánto tiempo hacía que... ?

¿Cuánto sabes de eventos históricos? Contesta cada pregunta con información verdadera.

1. ¿Cuánto tiempo hacía que George W. Bush era presidente cuando ocurrieron los atentados terroristas del 11 de septiembre?

2. ¿Cuánto tiempo hacía que Abraham Lincoln era presidente cuando lo asesinaron?

3. ¿Cuánto tiempo hacía que los Estados Unidos no participaban en una guerra cuando entraron en la Primera Guerra Mundial en 1917?

4. ¿Cuánto tiempo hacía que la Primera Guerra Mundial consumía al continente europeo cuando por fin entraron los Estados Unidos en el conflicto?

5. ¿Cuánto tiempo hacía que Julio César era «dictador vitalicio (*for life*)» cuando lo asesinaron?

Actividad H   Los exámenes médicos

Paso 1   Contesta las siguientes preguntas.

1. ¿Cuánto tiempo hace que tuviste un examen médico?

2. Cuando fuiste, ¿cuánto tiempo hacía que no tenías un examen médico?

3. ¿Te tomaron la presión arterial? Si no, ¿cuánto tiempo hace que no te examinan la presión?

4. ¿Te hicieron un examen completo? Si no, ¿cuánto tiempo hace que tuviste un examen completo?

5. ¿Te examinaron el nivel de colesterol en la sangre? Si no, ¿cuánto tiempo hace que te examinaron el colesterol?

Paso 2   Algunos voluntarios deben leer sus respuestas a la clase. ¿Son las respuestas de otras personas más o menos iguales? Como clase, determinen a qué edad es importante tener un examen médico completo regular (por ejemplo, cada año).

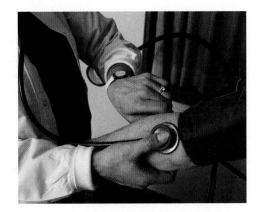

▲ ¿Cuánto tiempo hace que te tomaron la presión arterial?

RESUMEN DE VOCABULARIO

Las emociones y condiciones

aburrir(se)	to bore (get bored)
alegrar(se)	to make happy (become happy)
cansar(se)	to tire (get tired)
confundir(se)	to confuse (become confused)
deprimirse	to get depressed
enojar(se)	to anger (get angry)
estar (*irreg.*) **celoso/a**	to be jealous
llorar	to cry
preocupar(se)	to worry (become worried)
reírse (i, i) (me río)	to laugh
tener(le) (*irreg.*) **envidia (a alguien)**	to be envious (of someone)
tener(le) (*irreg.*) **miedo (a alguien)**	to be afraid (of someone)
tener (*irreg.*) **sueño**	to be sleepy
tomarse algo muy a pecho	to take something to heart; to feel something intensely
avergonzado/a	embarrassed
cansado/a	tired
confundido/a	confused
enamorado/a (de)	in love (with)
perplejo/a	perplexed
preocupado/a	worried

Cognados: afectar, frustrar(se), irritar(se), ofender(se), reaccionar; frustrado/a, furioso/a, irritado/a, relajado/a, tenso/a
Repaso: molestar, sentirse (ie, i); alegre, contento/a, enojado/a, nervioso/a, triste

Las partes del cuerpo

la boca	mouth
el brazo	arm
la cabeza	head
la cara	face
el cerebro	brain
el codo	elbow
el corazón	heart
el cuello	neck
los dedos (del pie)	fingers (toes)
la espalda	back
el estómago	stomach
la garganta	throat
el hígado	liver
el hombro	shoulder

el hueso	bone
la mano	hand
el órgano interno	internal organ
el pecho	chest
el pie	foot
la pierna	leg
el pulmón	lung
la rodilla	knee

Repaso: los dientes, la mejilla, el mentón, la nariz, los ojos, las orejas

La salud y el estado físico

cortar(se)	to cut (oneself)
doler (ue)	to hurt, ache
enfermarse	to get sick
estar (*irreg.*) **enfermo/a**	to be sick
lastimar(se)	to hurt (oneself)
padecer (zc) de	to suffer from
poner(le) (*irreg.*) **una inyección (a alguien)**	to give (someone) a shot
respirar	to breathe
romper(se)	to break
sacar (qu) la lengua	to stick out one's tongue
sacar(le) (qu) sangre (a alguien)	to draw (someone's) blood
tener (*irreg.*) **fiebre**	to have a fever
tener (*irreg.*) **la nariz tapada**	to have a stuffed-up nose
tener (*irreg.*) **un resfriado**	to have a cold
tomar(le) la temperatura (a alguien)	to take a (someone's) temperature
el consultorio (del médico)	doctor's office
el/la enfermero/a	nurse
el/la médico/a	doctor
la pastilla	pill
la presión arterial	blood pressure
la receta	prescription

Cognados: examinar; la alergia, la aspirina, el examen médico, el/la farmacéutico/a, la medicina, el/la paciente, los rayos X
Repaso: la farmacia

Otras palabras y expresiones

hace + *time*	*time* ago

Los demás y yo

OBJETIVOS

IN THIS LESSON, YOU WILL LEARN:

- vocabulary to express your feelings toward others
- to talk about what people do to and for each other using **nos** and **se**
- vocabulary to talk about how people act in relationships
- to talk about your wishes and desires using the subjunctive mood
- vocabulary related to positive and negative aspects of relationships
- to talk about contingencies and conditions using the subjunctive with conjunctions

In addition, you will watch **Episodio 7** of the film *Sol y viento*.

◀

Dos personas se besan (*are kissing each other*). ¿Crees que este beso es romántico o es solamente la manera en que se saludan (*greet each other*) estas personas?

PRIMERA PARTE

Vocabulario

Talking About How
You Feel About
Someone

Te tengo mucho cariño.

Feelings

▲ Esta mujer **le tiene mucho cariño** a su novio. Y él la **adora**.

Los sentimientos^a positivos

^aLos... *Feelings*

adorar	to adore
amar	to love
caerle (*irreg.*) **bien a alguien**	to make a good impression on someone
estimar	to think highly of
extrañar	to miss (*someone*)
gustar	to be pleasing to
querer (*irreg.*)	to love
respetar	to respect
tenerle (*irreg.*) **cariño a alguien**	to be fond of someone

Los sentimientos negativos

caerle (*irreg.*) **mal a alguien**	to make a bad impression on someone
despreciar	to despise
detestar	to detest
no aguantar	not to be able to stand, put up with
odiar	to hate
tenerle (*irreg.*) **envidia a alguien**	to be envious of someone

As you know, the verb **gustar** and the phrase **caerle bien** can be used in Spanish to talk about liking someone. However, these expressions do not mean the same thing. **Gustar** means *to like* in the general sense that someone is agreeable to you, but it can also express romantic or physical attraction. Spanish speakers will often use their tone of voice for emphasis when saying **gustar** with the meaning of physical attraction.

Miguel, ¿**te gusta** Cecilia o **te gusta** Cecilia?	*Miguel, do you like Cecilia or do you <u>like</u> Cecilia?*

Caerle bien means *to like* in the sense of making a good impression on. Its opposite, **caerle mal,** means *to make a bad impression on.*

Nos caen bien los padres de Eduardo.	*We like Eduardo's parents. (They make a good impression on us.)*
Me cae mal Jorge.	*I don't like Jorge. (I have a bad impression of him.)*

Spanish also uses two verbs to talk about loving someone: **querer** and **amar.** Use **querer** to express love for anyone you care a lot about, including friends, pets, family members, boyfriends, and so forth. **Amar** is much stronger and is used to express a deep, intense love between people in a romantic relationship.

Quieren mucho a sus abuelos.	*They love their grandparents a lot.*
Amas mucho a Ricardo, ¿no?	*You love Ricardo a lot, don't you?*

✳ MÁS VOCABULARIO

abrazar (c)	to hug
acariciar	to caress
besar	to kiss
darle (*irreg.*) **escalofríos a alguien**	to give someone chills
ponérsele (*irreg.*) **la piel de gallina a alguien**	to get goosebumps*
sonrojarse	to blush
trabársele la lengua a alguien	to get tongue-tied

COMUNICACIÓN ÚTIL

As you know, **tener** is used with **cariño,** a noun meaning *affection*. **Tener** can also be used with other nouns like **respeto** (*respect*), **envidia** (*envy*), and **celos** (*jealousy*). Some of these expressions are used with indirect object pronouns.

Le tengo respeto a Paul.	*I respect Paul.*
Les tiene envidia a sus primos.	*She envies her cousins.*
Los Trujillo **tienen celos** de nosotros.	*The Trujillos are jealous of us.*

---

*This Spanish phrase can be translated literally as *to get chicken skin.*

Actividad A   ¿Cómo reaccionabas?

Paso 1 Indica cómo reaccionabas de (*as an*) adolescente cuando veías a una persona que te gustaba mucho.

Cuando veía a alguien que me gustaba mucho,...	SIEMPRE	A VECES	NUNCA
1. me sonrojaba.	☐	☐	☐
2. se me trababa la lengua cuando le hablaba.	☐	☐	☐
3. me sudaban (*sweat*) las manos.	☐	☐	☐
4. me sentía muy inseguro/a (*insecure*).	☐	☐	☐
5. se me ponía la piel de gallina.	☐	☐	☐

Paso 2 Explica con dos o tres oraciones cómo reaccionas ahora cuando ves a una persona que te gusta mucho.

MODELO: Cuando veo a alguien que me gusta mucho, todavía estoy nerviosa, pero no me pongo insegura como antes...

Actividad B   ¿Te gusta o te cae bien?

Paso 1 Forma cinco oraciones verdaderas sobre algunas personas famosas usando las frases **(no) me gusta(n)** y **me cae(n) bien/mal.**

MODELO: No me gusta Matthew McConaughey, pero me cae bien Edward Norton.

Paso 2 Comparte tus oraciones con un compañero (una compañera) de clase. ¿Tienen Uds. algo en común?

Actividad C   Mi familia

Paso 1 Llena los espacios en blanco a continuación con información verdadera sobre los miembros de tu familia (o de la familia de un amigo).

1. Le tengo mucho cariño a _____.

2. Quiero mucho a _____.

3. Le tengo mucho respeto a _____.

4. Le tengo envidia a _____.

5. No me cae bien _____.

6. Estimo a _____.

7. Adoro a _____.

8. No aguanto a _____.

Paso 2 Entrevista a un compañero (una compañera) de clase, usando las frases del **Paso 1.**

MODELO: ¿A quién de tu familia le tienes mucho cariño?

Paso 3 Presenta a la clase uno o dos datos (*pieces of information*) interesantes de tu entrevista.

MODELO: Jennifer le tiene mucho cariño a su abuelo Stephenson.

〰 Vistazo cultural

Pablo Neruda y los sonetos de amor

El poeta chileno Pablo Neruda (1904–1973), ganador del Premio Nóbel de Literatura, es uno de los poetas más reconocidos[a] de la literatura hispanoamericana moderna. Como la película *Sol y viento,* la poesía[b] de Neruda entrelaza[c] el tema del amor con elementos de la naturaleza. Uno de sus poemarios[d] más románticos es *Cien sonetos de amor* (1960), una colección de sonetos dedicados a su tercera esposa, Matilde Urrutia. En esta obra Neruda hace referencias a la naturaleza para expresar su profundo[e] amor por Matilde. En sus versos figuran[f] las hierbas,[g] las semillas,[h] la espuma[i] y las flores, para mencionar algunas. A continuación está el primer verso del soneto XXXIV, en el que Neruda compara a Matilde con unos elementos básicos de la naturaleza.

▲ Pablo Neruda

> Eres hija del mar y prima del orégano,
> nadadora,[j] tu cuerpo es de agua pura,
> cocinera, tu sangre es tierra viva
> y tus costumbres son floridas[k] y terrestres.[l]

¿Qué opinas de la poesía de Neruda? ¿Crees que es profunda o superficial? ¿apasionada o indiferente?

[a]*renowned* [b]*poetry* [c]*intertwines* [d]*collections of poetry* [e]*profound, deep* [f]*appear* [g]*herbs* [h]*seeds* [i]*sea foam* [j]*swimmer* [k]*flowery, ornate* [l]*earthly*

NAVEGANDO LA RED 〰〰〰

Busca información en español sobre los boleros, que tradicionalmente tratan (*deal with*) temas del amor. Describe el origen de este género (*genre*) musical y los temas específicos que tratan en su letra (*lyrics*). Menciona también algunos cantantes importantes y sus países de origen.

Gramática

Talking About What
People Do to and for
Each Other

Se conocen bien.

Reciprocal Reflexives

▲ Estos novios **se miran** cariñosamente (*lovingly*).

In **Lección 5A** you learned that the pronouns **nos** and **se** are used with reflexive verbs to express *ourselves* and *themselves*, respectively. **Nos** and **se** are also used to describe what people do or have done to or for each other, actions known as *reciprocal reflexives* (**los reflexivos recíprocos**).

You will notice that a sentence like **Ed y yo nos cantamos mientras trabajamos** can also be interpreted as *Ed and I sing to each other while we work*. Context will usually determine if the **se** means *themselves* or *each other* or if **nos** means *ourselves* or *each other*.

To emphasize a reciprocal action, Spanish can add the phrase **el uno al otro / los unos a los otros** (or **la una a la otra / las unas a las otras** if all of the people are female), phrases that literally mean *the one to the other*.

Nos saludamos **el uno al otro.***

We greet each other (*the one to the other*).

Se admiran **la una a la otra.**

They admire each other (*the one to the other*).

---

*This construction is used for a group of males or a mixed group of males and females.

REFLEXIVE AND RECIPROCAL EXPRESSIONS	
REFLEXIVE **se** = *THEMSELVES*	RECIPROCAL **se** = *EACH OTHER*
Mis amigos **se miran** mucho en el espejo. *My friends look at themselves a lot in the mirror.*	Mis amigos **se hablan** mucho por teléfono. *My friends talk to each other a lot on the phone.*
Los profesores **se escriben** notas. *The professors write notes to themselves.*	Juan y Laura **se escriben** cada semana. *Juan and Laura write each other every week.*
REFLEXIVE **nos** = *OURSELVES*	RECIPROCAL **nos** = *EACH OTHER*
Ed y yo **nos cantamos** mientras trabajamos. *Ed and I sing to ourselves while we work.*	Mis hermanos y yo **nos abrazamos.** *My siblings and I hug each other.*
No **nos tomamos** demasiado en serio. *We don't take ourselves too seriously.*	**Nos vemos** todos los días. *We see each other every day.*

DE SOL Y VIENTO

In **Episodio 7** of *Sol y viento,* Jaime asks Mario how far it is to the winery. Part of their conversation appears here.

JAIME
¿Estamos lejos?

MARIO
En automóvil, a siete minutos. A pie, cuarenta y cinco minutos, más o menos. Menos si se toma un atajo[a] por ahí.

JAIME
¿Un atajo, eh?

MARIO
Si uno atraviesa[b] el campo,[c] se llega en media hora.

JAIME
Me voy a pie. _____ en la viña.

What do you think best fits in the preceding blank?

1. Nos extrañamos
2. Nos ayudamos
3. Nos vemos

[a]*shortcut* [b]*goes through* [c]*countryside*

Actividad D ¿Qué se hacen?

Indica si cada una de las siguientes oraciones describe o no la relación entre Jaime y María, según lo que crees.

Jaime y María...   SÍ   NO

1. se hablan por teléfono. ☐ ☐
2. se saludan con un beso. ☐ ☐
3. se gritan (*shout at each other*). ☐ ☐
4. se quieren. ☐ ☐
5. se guardan (*keep*) secretos. ☐ ☐
6. se mienten. ☐ ☐
7. se respetan. ☐ ☐
8. se estiman. ☐ ☐
9. se abrazan. ☐ ☐
10. se detestan. ☐ ☐

Actividad E ¿Se respetan?

Escribe, con cada una de las expresiones a continuación, oraciones con información verdadera, según lo que crees de algunas personas famosas.

MODELO: Se estiman. → Peter Jennings y Dan Rather se estiman.

1. Se detestan.
2. Se besan en público.
3. Se respetan.
4. Se tienen envidia.
5. Se adoran.
6. No se aguantan.
7. Se desprecian.
8. Se odian.
9. Se tienen envidia.
10. Se quieren.

Actividad F En un bar

A continuación hay una lista de las cosas que una persona y sus amigos hacen cuando se reúnen (*they get together*) en un bar. Pon las actividades en un orden lógico, del 1 al 6.

Mis amigos y yo...

____ nos hablamos mientras tomamos algo.

____ nos saludamos.

____ nos vemos.

____ nos despedimos (*say good-bye*) el uno del otro.

____ nos damos la mano (*shake hands*) o nos abrazamos.

____ nos compramos unas cervezas.

Actividad G Una entrevista

Paso 1 Llena los espacios en blanco con el nombre de una persona (o una mascota), según el caso. Usa información verdadera para ti.

MODELO: Mi jefe (*boss*) Roberto y yo nos hablamos todos los días.

1. _____ y yo nos vemos todos los días.
2. _____ y yo nos damos la mano cuando nos saludamos.
3. _____ y yo nos enojamos mucho.
4. _____ y yo nos odiamos.
5. _____ y yo nos queremos mucho.
6. _____ y yo nos extrañamos cuando no estamos juntos.

Paso 2 Usa las oraciones del **Paso 1** para entrevistar a un compañero (una compañera) de clase y averiguar si sus experiencias son como las tuyas.

MODELO: E1: ¿Se ven todos los días tú y tu jefe?
          E2: No. Mi jefe y yo no nos vemos los fines de semana.

Paso 3 Escribe un breve párrafo en el cual mencionas uno o dos datos interesantes de tu entrevista.

◉ Enfoque lingüístico

Las acciones recíprocas

Have you noticed that ambiguity seems to be inherent in languages and that the interpretation of meaning may often rely on context? For example, the sentence **Se respetan** can mean either *they respect themselves* or *they respect each other*. English doesn't have this ambiguity in this case because it relies on distinct pronouns or phrases: *themselves* versus *each other*. Of course, the reverse is also true: There are ambiguous structures in English that are rendered in Spanish in different ways. And there are equivalent structures in both languages that are ambiguous in meaning.

   Why do languages allow such ambiguity? Wouldn't it be easier if languages obeyed the simple rule "one structure = one meaning/interpretation"? Of course this would be easier. But languages are evolving entities. They change over time in bits and pieces. As long as communication is a fluid and contextually based enterprise among two or more people, language is likely to contain structures that result in ambiguity. What is more, the human mind also computes frequencies of structures, or what is more "typical." Thus, in addition to knowing that **Se respetan** means two things, the Spanish speaker's mind identifies *They respect each other* as the more frequent interpretation and thus it is the first one to come to mind.

   Here's an example in English to try on your friends. Ask them to complete the following sentence: *The lawyer examined . . .* What do your friends say? The typical way to complete the sentence is with an object such as *the witness* or *the evidence: The lawyer examined the witness.* But note that the incomplete phrase is structurally ambiguous without an object. It can just as easily be completed in the following way: *The lawyer examined by the Bar Association was found to be innocent of fraud.* As you can deduce, this last structure is less frequent and less typical than the other sentences. In short, your friends' minds are "predisposed" to one structure as opposed to the other.

SEGUNDA PARTE

Vocabulario

More on Describing People's Traits | **Eres muy romántico.**

Describing People

celosa
seductora (*seductive*)
vengativa (*vengeful*)

▲ Afrodita

coqueto (*flirtatious*)
cruel
engañador (*deceitful*)

▲ Don Juan Tenorio

cariñosa (*affectionate*)
nostálgica
sentimental

▲ Julieta

fiel (*faithful*)
porfiado (*persistent*)
romántico

▲ Romeo

cabezona
emocional
resuelta (*determined*)

▲ Scarlett O'Hara

apasionado
divertido
encantador (*charming*)

▲ Casanova

✳ MÁS VOCABULARIO

atento/a	considerate
comprensivo/a	understanding
detallista	detail-oriented
entrometido/a	nosy; meddlesome
mandón (mandona)	bossy
orgulloso/a	proud
sensible	sensitive
tacaño/a	stingy

Cognados: espontáneo/a, generoso/a, íntimo/a, posesivo/a

Vistazo cultural

Don Juan

El mito de Don Juan tiene su origen en España a principios del siglo XVII. Aunque existen muchas versiones de esta leyenda,[a] todas relatan la historia de un hombre mujeriego,[b] seductor, engañador y libertino[c] llamado Don Juan, quien seduce a las mujeres. En una ocasión Don Juan seduce a la hija de un comandante militar. En un acto mórbido, Don Juan mata[d] al comandante y luego invita a la estatua del comandante muerto a cenar con él. Durante la cena, la estatua se anima[e] y se lleva a Don Juan al infierno[f] en donde paga por sus pecados.[g]

Don Juan es uno de los mitos de la literatura que de España se difundió[h] a otras partes del mundo. Don Juan apareció en la literatura española por primera vez en el drama *El Burlador de Sevilla* (1630) por Tirso de Molina, y más tarde en el drama *Don Juan Tenorio* (1844) de José Zorrilla. El francés Molière escribió *Dom Juan, ou le Festin de Pierre*[i] (1665) y el italiano Lorenzo da Ponte escribió el libreto[j] para una ópera de Mozart, *Don Giovanni* (1787). Lord Byron y George Bernard Shaw escribieron sus versiones de Don Juan en lengua inglesa. Una de las interpretaciones más recientes es la del actor Johnny Depp en la película *Don Juan De Marco* (1995). Como puedes ver, el mito de Don Juan es una parte importante de la literatura universal que sigue evolucionando hasta hoy en día.

▲ Una presentación de *Don Giovanni*, ópera de Mozart

[a]*legend* [b]*womanizer* [c]*libertine (morally or sexually unstrained)* [d]*kills* [e]*se... comes to life* [f]*hell* [g]*sins* [h]*se... spread* [i]*ou... or the Stone Guest* [j]*libretto, text of an opera*

Actividad A   Acciones

Tu profesor(a) va a mencionar algunas acciones. Indica el adjetivo que se asocia con cada acción.

1. **a.** engañador **b.** fiel
2. **a.** posesivo **b.** nostálgico
3. **a.** atento **b.** cariñoso
4. **a.** resuelto **b.** cabezón
5. **a.** detallista **b.** entrometido
6. **a.** espontáneo **b.** mandón
7. **a.** tacaño **b.** porfiado
8. **a.** coqueto **b.** vengativo

Actividad B   ¿Cómo es?

Paso 1 Indica qué adjetivo o adjetivos se le aplican a cada personaje a continuación. A veces hay más de una respuesta posible.

1. James Bond
   a. seductor
   b. atento
   c. posesivo
2. Elizabeth Taylor
   a. apasionada
   b. celosa
   c. cabezona
3. Austin Powers
   a. vengativo
   b. divertido
   c. coqueto
4. Prince William
   a. generoso
   b. íntimo
   c. resuelto
5. Sarah Jessica Parker
   a. encantadora
   b. romántica
   c. fiel
6. Halle Berry
   a. sensible
   b. espontánea
   c. porfiada

Paso 2 Ahora indica dos adjetivos más para describir a los personajes del **Paso 1.**

MODELO: Austin Powers también es _____ y _____.

Actividad C ¿Eres casamentero/a (*matchmaker*)?

Paso 1 A continuación hay una lista de parejas (*couples*) famosas de la televisión. Escribe una oración describiendo cómo (no) es cada una de estas parejas.

MODELO: Cliff y Clair Huxtable → Cliff y Clair Huxtable son comprensivos.

1. Ozzy y Sharon Osbourne
2. Ricky y Lucy Ricardo
3. Fox Mulder y Dana Scully (de los *X Files*)
4. Ross Geller y Rachel Green (de *Friends*)
5. Clark Kent y Lois Lane
6. Will Truman y Grace Adler (de *Will and Grace*)

Paso 2 Con un compañero (una compañera), piensen en dos personas famosas que hacen una buena pareja aunque ya estén (*even though they are*) casadas con otras personas o no se conozcan. Mencionen por qué hacen una buena pareja.

MODELO: Cameron Díaz y Conan O'Brien hacen una buena pareja porque los dos son divertidos.

Actividad D ¿Con quién haces una buena pareja?

Paso 1 Piensa en una persona famosa con la cual haces una buena pareja. Describe en un párrafo de cinco o seis oraciones por qué crees que eres el novio (la novia) ideal para esa persona y viceversa. (O si quieres, menciona a una persona famosa con la cual *no* haces una buena pareja y explica por qué.) Puedes comenzar tu párrafo de la siguiente manera:

_____ y yo (no) hacemos una buena pareja por varias razones.

Puedes usar las siguientes palabras para pasar de una idea a otra.

primero **luego** (*next*) **por último / por fin** (*finally*)

Paso 2 Presenta tu párrafo a la clase. Tus compañeros van a indicar si están de acuerdo o no con tu análisis.

▲ ¿Crees que Jaime y María hacían una buena pareja? ¿Quieres que Jaime haga las paces con (*to make up with*) María?

Gramática

Espero que sea divertido.

✳

Introduction to the Subjunctive

So far you have been working with verb forms that are part of what is called the *indicative mood,* whose function is to report events, ask questions, and so forth. The present, preterite, and imperfect that you've already learned are all part of the indicative. Spanish also uses the *subjunctive mood,* which expresses things such as wants, desires, doubt, uncertainty, and other events that cannot be confirmed or verified. The subjunctive almost always appears in what is called a *dependent clause.* In the sentence *I hope that Mark can come, I hope* is the main or independent clause (because it can stand alone as a complete thought) and *that Mark can come* is the dependent clause (because it cannot stand alone as a complete thought).

In this lesson, you will learn to use the subjunctive mood in the present tense to talk about hopes and desires. The "trigger" for the subjunctive will be expressed in the main clause. The dependent clause in Spanish will begin with the Spanish conjunction **que** (*that*) and employ a subjunctive verb form. Note that the Spanish word **ojalá** is an invariable verb form meaning *I hope, wish.**

Espero que **vengas** a la fiesta.	*I hope (that) you come to the party.*
Ojalá que **saque** una A en el examen.	*I hope (that) I get an A on the test.*
Ojalá que **podamos** ir a Las Vegas.	*I hope (that) we can go to Las Vegas.*

The forms of the subjunctive are derived in the same manner as those used for formal commands, which you already know.

- Some irregular verbs in the subjunctive include the following.

  haber: haya, hayas, haya, hayamos, hayáis, hayan

  ir: vaya, vayas, vaya, vayamos, vayáis, vayan

  saber: sepa, sepas, sepa, sepamos, sepáis, sepan

  ser: sea, seas, sea, seamos, seáis, sean

- Some forms of the verbs **dar** and **estar** have accent marks.

  dar: dé, des, **dé,** demos, deis, den

  estar: esté, estés, esté, estemos, **estéis, estén**

- Stem-changing **-ir** verbs like **dormir, servir,** and **preferir** have an altered stem in the **nosotros** and **vosotros** forms.

  dormir: duerma, duermas, duerma, durmamos, durmáis, duerman

  servir: sirva, sirvas, sirva, sirvamos, sirváis, sirvan

  preferir: prefiera, prefieras, prefiera, prefiramos, prefiráis, prefieran

---

*Spanish also allows **ojalá** without **que,** but **que** will be used with **ojalá** throughout this textbook, except in some cases when characters in the film don't use it.

FORMATION OF THE PRESENT SUBJUNCTIVE				
INFINITIVE	**yo** FORM	STEM	ADD THE "OPPOSITE" VOWEL	ADD THE APPROPRIATE ENDINGS
hablar	hablo	habl-	+ e = **hable**	hable* hablemos hables habléis hable* hablen hable* hablen
beber	bebo	beb-	+ a = **beba**	beba bebamos bebas bebáis beba beban beba beban
abrir	abro	abr-	+ a = **abra**	abra abramos abras abráis abra abran abra abran
decir	digo	dig-	+ a = **diga**	diga digamos digas digáis diga digan diga digan
conducir	conduzco	conduzc-	+ a = **conduzca**	conduzca conduzcamos conduzcas conduzcáis conduzca conduzcan conduzca conduzcan

DE SOL Y VIENTO

In **Episodio 7** of *Sol y viento,* doña Isabel and don Paco inform Jaime about the harm his company could do to the Maipo Valley. Part of their exchange appears in the dialogue.

PACO
Pero obviamente a su compañía no le importa mucho el daño a la ecología... ni a la comunidad humana que habita estas tierras...

JAIME
He cometido un grave error. Ojalá no _____ tarde para ayudarles a Uds....

What verb best fits in the preceding space?

1. haya   **2.** esté   **3.** sea

*Note that the **yo** and **Ud., él/ella** forms are the same in the subjunctive.

Actividad E   Ojalá que...

Indica el nombre del personaje de *Sol y viento* de la lista que probablemente piensa lo siguiente. En algunos casos, es posible indicar más de un nombre.

Andy   Carlos   doña Isabel   Jaime   María   don Paco   Rassner

1. Ojalá que María me perdone pronto.
2. Espero que Carlos no haya hecho nada grave (*serious*).
3. Espero que María no sepa nada del contrato con Bartel Aquapower.
4. Ojalá que Jaime no me vuelva a hablar (*doesn't speak to me again*).
5. Ojalá que salga bien la recepción para degustar el vino nuevo.
6. Espero que Jaime finalice el negocio pronto.

Actividad F   ¿Dónde se dice?

Indica dónde se dice lo siguiente.

1. Ojalá que no llueva.
   a. en una reunión (*meeting*)   **b.** en un picnic
2. Esperamos que haya suficiente comida para todos.
   a. en una recepción   **b.** en una oficina
3. Espero que ganemos el partido.
   a. en el estadio   **b.** en el cine
4. Ojalá que los invitados (*guests*) lleguen a tiempo.
   a. en un concierto   **b.** en una fiesta
5. Espero que Ud. me pueda dar un reembolso (*refund*).
   a. en una biblioteca   **b.** en una tienda

Actividad G   La política (*Politics*)

Indica si estás de acuerdo o no con las siguientes afirmaciones.

Espero que los políticos (*politicians*)...	ESTOY DE ACUERDO.	NO ESTOY DE ACUERDO.
1. nombren a una mujer como candidata para la presidencia.	☐	☐
2. prohíban fumar en los lugares públicos.	☐	☐
3. tomen más medidas (*measures*) para combatir el terrorismo.	☐	☐
4. aprueben leyes (*pass laws*) que limiten el uso de teléfonos celulares en autos y ciertos lugares públicos.	☐	☐
5. suban a 80 millas por hora el límite de la velocidad (*speed*) máxima en las carreteras (*highways*).	☐	☐
6. permitan el consumo legal de bebidas alcohólicas al llegar a los 18 años de edad.	☐	☐

Actividad H Mi trabajo

Paso 1 Indica si las siguientes oraciones son ciertas o falsas para ti.

Espero que mi trabajo futuro...	CIERTO	FALSO
1. requiera el uso del español.	☐	☐
2. esté cerca de mi familia.	☐	☐
3. me permita viajar por todo el mundo.	☐	☐
4. me dé muchas oportunidades para avanzar (*move up*).	☐	☐
5. esté relacionado con la carrera que hago en la universidad.	☐	☐
6. contribuya de alguna manera a la sociedad.	☐	☐

Paso 2 Entrevista a un compañero (una compañera) de clase para averiguar si las oraciones del **Paso 1** son ciertas o falsas para él/ella.

Paso 3 Escribe dos datos interesantes de la entrevista para presentárselos a la clase.

MODELO: Miguel espera que su trabajo esté cerca de su familia, pero yo no.

Actividad I Las personas famosas

Paso 1 Piensa en alguna persona famosa sin mencionar su nombre. Escribe cinco oraciones sobre esa persona usando **ojalá que** y **espero que.**

MODELOS: Espero que no haga otra película como *Gigli.*

Ojalá que venda muchos discos compactos.

Paso 2 Ahora léele tus oraciones a un compañero (una compañera). ¿Puede adivinar a quién describes? Si tu compañero/a no sabe, dale unas opciones: ¿Es Jennifer López o Jennifer Aniston?

COMUNICACIÓN ÚTIL

With **esperar** (and other verbs), if there is no change of subject between the main and dependent clauses, the subjunctive is not used. Instead, **esperar** is followed by an infinitive.

Espero ver a Claudia mañana.   *I hope to see Claudia tomorrow.*

TERCERA PARTE

Vocabulario

Talking About Good and Bad Relationships

¡Me engañó!

More on Relationships

Cuando las relaciones van bien

comprometerse (con)	to get engaged (to)
confiar (confío) (en)	to trust (in)
hacer (*irreg.*) **las paces con**	to make up with
perdonar	to forgive
salir (*irreg.*) **con**	to go out with

Cuando las relaciones van mal

discutir	to argue
engañar	to deceive; to cheat on
guardar(le) rencor (a alguien)	to hold a grudge (against someone)
ocultar(le) secretos (a alguien)	to hide secrets (from someone)
romper con	to break up with
terminar	to end (*a relationship*)
traicionar	to betray

✳ MÁS VOCABULARIO

arrepentirse (ie, i) (de)	to be sorry (about); to regret
castigar (gu)	to punish
conquistar	to succeed in seducing someone
seducir (zc)	to seduce
la amistad	friendship
el noviazgo	engagement

Repaso: casarse (con), divorciarse de, enamorarse de, estar enamorado/a de, lastimar, llevarse bien/mal con, mentir (ie, i), merecer (zc), pelearse; la boda, el divorcio

▲ Cuando las relaciones entre dos personas van bien, confían la una en la otra.

≋ Vistazo cultural

Más sobre el engaño

Además de las palabras **engañar** y **traicionar,** el español tiene varias expresiones para expresar el verbo inglés *to cuckold.* Esta expresión se refiere al hecho de que una esposa le es infiel a su marido.

Una de las expresiones en español es **poner los cuernos,**[a] lo cual se aplica al hombre traicionado. Por alguna razón u otra, durante siglos la imagen del *cuckold* se ha asociado con los cuernos. Según se cuenta, cuando una mujer le es infiel a su esposo, a él le salen[b] cuernos en la cabeza. Así que los cuernos son un símbolo de la humillación. Hoy en día muchos usan la expresión **poner los cuernos** como sinónimo de **engañar** y se dice de las relaciones tanto entre esposos como entre novios.

[a]*horns (of an animal)*   [b]*a… he sprouts*

Actividad A Descripciones

Indica el adjetivo más apropiado para cada descripción a continuación.

Una persona que...

1. se deja seducir fácilmente es ___.
   a. porfiada   **b.** entrometida   **c.** ingenua
2. miente a sus amigos no es ___.
   a. honesta   **b.** desconfiada   **c.** indiferente
3. castiga a otros sin motivo es ___.
   a. cruel   **b.** humilde   **c.** gregaria
4. le pone los cuernos a otra es ___.
   a. fiel   **b.** conservadora   **c.** engañadora
5. no guarda un secreto es ___.
   a. introvertida   **b.** reservada   **c.** chismosa
6. se lleva bien con todos es ___.
   a. detallista   **b.** encantadora   **c.** celosa
7. guarda rencor por algo trivial es ___.
   a. generosa   **b.** cabezona   **c.** atenta
8. hace las paces con otra es ___.
   a. comprensiva   **b.** vengativa   **c.** divertida

Actividad B ¿Perdonas o guardas rencor?

Paso 1 ¿Cuánto tiempo tardas en (*do you take*) perdonar a alguien que...

	UN DÍA	2–3 DÍAS	UNA SEMANA	NUNCA LO PERDONO.
1. se pelea contigo cuando está estresado (*stressed out*)?	☐	☐	☐	☐
2. te oculta un secreto importante?	☐	☐	☐	☐
3. discute contigo en un lugar público?	☐	☐	☐	☐
4. se olvida de (*forgets*) darte un mensaje importante?	☐	☐	☐	☐
5. te miente sobre tu novio/a o tu familia?	☐	☐	☐	☐
6. te pone los cuernos?	☐	☐	☐	☐
7. rompe contigo?	☐	☐	☐	☐
8. se olvida de llamarte el día de tu cumpleaños?	☐	☐	☐	☐

Paso 2 Entrevista a un compañero (una compañera) de clase para saber cómo respondió a las preguntas del **Paso 1.**

Paso 3 Prepara un breve resumen explicando si tú y tu compañero/a de clase perdonan fácilmente o guardan rencor. Básate en lo que dijo en la entrevista.

Actividad C Consejos

En parejas, lean las situaciones a continuación y escriban dos o tres oraciones como respuesta a lo que debe hacer cada persona para resolver su problema.

MODELO: A mi novio le gusta discutir sobre pequeñeces (*little things*). Me castiga verbalmente, me guarda rencor y no me habla por varios días. ¿Qué debo hacer? →
¡No mereces sufrir tanto! Debes decirle que no te gusta pelear. Si no se arrepienta de sus acciones y no quiere hacer las paces, debes romper con él.

1. Mi novio es demasiado posesivo. Siempre quiere saber dónde y con quién estoy. Si salgo con mis amigas, me busca y se pelea conmigo en público. ¿Qué debo hacer?

2. Mi novia es muy desconfiada. Cree que le oculto secretos y que le miento. La verdad es que la quiero mucho y no tengo ninguna intención de lastimarla. ¿Qué debo hacer?

3. Mi novio de hace cinco años me dice que quiere casarse conmigo y tener hijos. No puedo imaginar mi vida sin él, pero tampoco quiero casarme ahora. ¿Qué debo hacer?

Actividad D ¿Cómo termina la relación?

Paso 1 En parejas, hagan una lista de por lo menos seis de las razones por las cuales dos personas terminan una relación amorosa.

MODELO: Una de las personas se enamora de otra persona.

Paso 2 Indiquen cuál de las siguientes formas de terminar es más apropiada para cada situación del **Paso 1.**

1. romper con él/ella inmediatamente

2. no contestar las llamadas de la otra persona hasta que deje de (*until he/she stops*) llamar

3. mandarle un correo electrónico explicándole por qué ya no quieres salir con él/ella

4. hablarle francamente de tus razones para terminar, aunque la otra persona se lastime

5. pedirle a un amigo (una amiga) que termine la relación por ti

6. ¿ ?

MODELO: Si una de las personas se enamora de otra persona, es mejor romper con él/ella inmediatamente.

Gramática

A menos que no quieras...   Obligatory Subjunctive

In addition to being used with expressions of wishing and hoping, the sub-junctive is also used with conjunctions of contingency* such as *in order that, so that, provided that,* and *without,* among others. See the chart for a list of expressions of contingency in Spanish and examples of their use with the sub-junctive.

If there is no change in subject in the dependent clause, **antes de que** and **para que** shorten to **antes de** and **para** and are followed by an infinitive instead of the subjunctive. Compare the sentences below.

Voy a preparar café **antes de que vengan** los invitados.	*I'm going to make coffee before the guests come.*
Voy a preparar café **antes de estudiar.**	*I'm going to make coffee before studying.*
Lo escribo **para que entiendas** mejor.	*I'll write it down so (that) you understand better.*
Lo escribo **para recordarlo** más tarde.	*I'll write it down to remember it later.*

THE SUBJUNCTIVE WITH CONJUNCTIONS OF CONTINGENCY		
a menos que	*unless*	Vamos a la fiesta **a menos que** Marta no **quiera.** *We're going to the party unless Marta doesn't want to.*
antes (de) que	*before*	Tengo que llamar al banco **antes de que cierre.** *I have to call the bank before it closes.*
con tal (de) que	*provided* (*that*)	Voy a salir esta noche **con tal de que** me **paguen.** *I'm going out tonight provided that they pay me.*
en caso de que	*in case*	Llévate una chaqueta **en caso de que haga** frío. *Take a jacket in case it's cold.*
para que	*so* (*that*)	Te llevo en auto **para que** no **tengas** que caminar. *I'll drive you so you don't have to walk.*
sin que	*without*	No compro la casa **sin que** me **ofrezcan** el trabajo. *I won't buy the house without their offering me the job.*

*A *contingency* is an action or event that is dependent on something else.

DE SOL Y VIENTO

In **Episodio 7,** you will see a scene in which Jaime offers to help the Sánchez family. Part of this conversation follows.

JAIME
He cometido un grave error.
Ojalá no sea tarde para ayudarles a Uds. y para que su hija
me _____.[1]

ISABEL
¿María Teresa perdonar? ¡Huy!
¡Es durísima[a]! Va a ser muy
difícil... A menos que Ud.,
don Jaime, _____[2] su
perdón.

Selecting from the following options, which verb do you think best fits in each space above?

1. a. mienta
   b. lastime
   c. perdone
2. a. compre
   b. merezca
   c. necesite

[a]*very tough*

Actividad E ¿Cierto o falso?

Indica si las siguientes oraciones sobre los personajes de *Sol y viento* son ciertas o falsas.

	CIERTO	FALSO
1. Carlos puede vender la viña con tal de que doña Isabel y María firmen el contrato.	☐	☐
2. María conoce a Jaime antes de que Jaime conozca a Carlos.	☐	☐
3. Jaime no puede renunciar a (*quit*) su trabajo sin que Rassner se enoje.	☐	☐
4. Jaime no tiene que hacer mucho para que María lo perdone.	☐	☐
5. Doña Isabel no puede resolver su problema con Carlos a menos que don Paco la ayude.	☐	☐

Actividad F ¿Es lógico?

Escoge la opción más lógica para cada situación a continuación. En algunos casos hay más de una respuesta lógica.

1. Los padres trabajan para que sus hijos...
   a. tengan comida y ropa.
   b. reciban educación en colegios (*schools*) privados.
   c. puedan tener su propio auto en la preparatoria (*high school*).
2. Los estudiantes sacan una A en sus clases con tal de que...
   a. entreguen la tarea incompleta.
   b. saquen buenas notas en los exámenes.
   c. falten a (*skip*) clase con frecuencia.
3. Muchos no pueden pasar mucho tiempo al aire libre sin que...
   a. se aburran de tantas cosas que hacer.
   b. les piquen (*bite*) los insectos.
   c. les dé una insolación.
4. Uno no debe salir con sus amigos a menos que...
   a. no tenga un examen muy importante.
   b. tenga dinero.
   c. esté enfermo.
5. Es bueno llevar herramientas (*tools*) cuando uno viaja en auto en caso de que...
   a. se pinche una rueda.
   b. se descomponga (*breaks down*) el auto.
   c. otro conductor necesite ayuda.

Actividad G ¿Qué haces cuando sales?

Indica si haces las siguientes cosas cuando sales con tus amigos.

Cuando salgo con mis amigos...	SÍ	NO
1. llevo mi propio auto en caso de que no me divierta y quiera ir a otra fiesta.	☐	☐
2. me visto muy bien para que los demás me miren.	☐	☐
3. saco dinero del cajero automático antes de que vayamos a un club o restaurante.	☐	☐
4. ofrezco pagar algunas bebidas a menos que me falte dinero.	☐	☐
5. salgo a cualquier sitio con tal de que volvamos a casa para (*by*) las 2:00 de la mañana.	☐	☐
6. llevo dinero extra para regresar a casa en taxi.	☐	☐

Actividad H En la universidad

Paso 1 Lee las oraciones a continuación y llena los espacios en blanco con información verdadera para ti.

MODELO: Le presto (*I loan*) _____ a un amigo para que _____. →
Le presto mi libro de química a un amigo para que pueda hacer la tarea.

1. Le presto _____ a un amigo para que pueda _____.
2. Trato de tomar _____ créditos cada semestre (trimestre) con tal de que _____.
3. Hago ejercicio _____ veces a la semana a menos que _____.
4. Limpio mi apartamento cada _____ días (semanas) para que _____.
5. Todas las noches, antes de acostarme yo _____.
6. Llevo dinero extra cuando voy a _____ en caso de que _____.

Paso 2 Entrevista a un compañero (una compañera) de clase con las oraciones que escribiste en el **Paso 1** para saber si hace lo mismo que tú.

MODELO: ¿Tratas de tomar doce créditos cada semestre con tal de que la universidad ofrezca los cursos que necesitas?

Paso 3 Prepara un resumen sobre los resultados de tu entrevista.

MODELO: Yo trato de tomar doce créditos cada semestre con tal de que la universidad ofrezca los cursos que necesito. En cambio, Jonah trata de tomar quince créditos con tal de que no tenga que trabajar.

SOL Y VIENTO

Antes de ver el episodio

Actividad A ¿Qué recuerdas?

Indica si las siguientes oraciones son ciertas o falsas, según lo que sabes de la trama (*plot*) de *Sol y viento*.

		CIERTO	FALSO
1.	Don Paco es dueño de un restaurante en Chile.	☐	☐
2.	El esposo de doña Isabel ya ha muerto.	☐	☐
3.	Doña Isabel se preocupa por la viña.	☐	☐
4.	Jaime sabe que Carlos y María son hermanos.	☐	☐
5.	María sigue respetando a Jaime.	☐	☐

Actividad B Repaso

Antes de ver el **Episodio 7,** repasa las escenas que estudiaste en las actividades **De *Sol y viento*** en cada sección gramatical. Esas actividades te pueden ayudar con la comprensión.

Actividad C ¿Qué falta?

En el **Episodio 7** Jaime y Mario van a hablar del tiempo que falta para llegar a «Sol y viento». Llena los espacios en blanco con las opciones a continuación. Puedes verificar tus respuestas después de ver el episodio.

JAIME: ¿Estamos lejos?
MARIO: En automóvil, a siete minutos. A pie, cuarenta y cinco minutos, más o menos. Menos si se toma _____¹ por ahí...
JAIME: Me voy a pie. Nos vemos en la viña.
MARIO: ¡Don Jaime! ¡El sol está picando fuerteª! ¡Que no le dé _____²!

1. a. la autopista (*highway*)
  b. un atajo (*shortcut*)
2. a. un infarto (*heart attack*)
  b. una insolación (*heatstroke*)

ªpicando... *really beating down*

Actividad D El episodio

Ahora mira el episodio. Si hay algo que no entiendes bien, vuelve a ver la escena.

Después de ver el episodio

Actividad A ¿Qué recuerdas?

Contesta las preguntas a continuación según lo que recuerdas del **Episodio 7.**

1. Mario no pudo arreglar (*fix*) la rueda pinchada (*flat tire*) porque no tenía...
   a. herramientas (*tools*)   **b.** gato (*tire jack*)   **c.** repuesto (*spare*)

2. Jaime sufrió una insolación antes de llegar a la casa de los Sánchez. ¿Cierto o falso?
   a. cierto   **b.** falso

3. Según don Paco, Bartel Aquapower hizo mucho daño a la ecología de este país.
   a. el Brasil   **b.** Bulgaria   **c.** Bolivia

4. Jaime renuncia a (*quits*) su trabajo con Bartel Aquapower. ¿Cierto o falso?
   a. cierto   **b.** falso

5. Doña Isabel le dijo a Jaime que María no _____ fácilmente.
   a. se enamora   **b.** perdona   **c.** se divierte

Actividad B ¿Lo captaste?

Vuelve a la **Actividad C** de **Antes de ver el episodio** para verificar tus respuestas. Si es necesario, vuelve a ver la escena en cuestión.

Actividad C En resumen

Completa la siguiente narración con las palabras y expresiones apropiadas de la lista a la derecha.

En este episodio, a Mario y Jaime _____[1] una rueda camino a la viña. Como Mario no tenía _____,[2] Jaime decidió seguir a pie. En ruta a la viña, Jaime sufrió una _____[3] y se desmayó.[a] Mientras Jaime se recuperaba en casa de doña Isabel, don Paco _____[4] que Bartel Aquapower quería construir una represa en el valle, lo cual le haría[b] mucho daño tanto al medio ambiente como a _____[5] mapuche. Jaime comprendió el error de _____[6] y en una conversación con Andy, renunció a su trabajo con Bartel Aquapower.

la comunidad
insolación
le informó
repuesto
se les pinchó
sus acciones

[a]se... *passed out*   [b]*would cause*

Detrás de la cámara

Have you noticed that while María and Jaime switched to the use of **tú** in a previous episode, Mario has continued to use **usted** with Jaime? Even though Mario feels the need to comment on María and Jaime's relationship, he and Jaime are not friends and are not of the same age group. Mario is, in effect, an employee of Jaime's. However, Jaime does use **tú** when addressing Mario. You may also have noticed that Traimaqueo uses **tú** with Carlos, although he is technically employed by the family. What is different here is that Traimaqueo has known Carlos since the latter was a little boy. The use of **tú** was natural in that adult—child relationship. That Traimaqueo now works for Carlos has not changed that fundamental and earlier pattern of interaction. María, of course, when finding out what Jaime has been up to, immediately drops the **tú** and reverts to **usted**. Did you catch this in the previous episode?

RESUMEN DE VOCABULARIO

Para expresar los sentimientos

abrazar (c)	to hug
acariciar	to caress
amar	to love
besar	to kiss
darle (*irreg.*) **escalofríos a alguien**	to give someone chills
despreciar	to despise
estimar	to think highly of
extrañar	to miss (*someone*)
no aguantar	not to be able to stand, put up with
ponérsele (*irreg.*) **la piel de gallina a alguien**	to get goosebumps
querer (*irreg.*)	to love
sonrojarse	to blush
tenerle (*irreg.*) **cariño a alguien**	to be fond of someone
trabársele la lengua a alguien	to get tongue-tied

Cognados: adorar, detestar, respetar
Repaso: caerle (*irreg.*) **bien/mal a alguien, gustar, odiar, tenerle** (*irreg.*) **envidia a alguien**

Para describir la personalidad

atento/a	considerate
cariñoso/a	affectionate
comprensivo/a	understanding
coqueto/a	flirtatious
detallista	detail-oriented
encantador(a)	charming
engañador(a)	deceitful
entrometido/a	nosy; meddlesome
fiel	faithful
mandón (mandona)	bossy
porfiado/a	persistent
resuelto/a	determined
seductor(a)	seductive
sensible	sensitive
tacaño/a	stingy
vengativo/a	vengeful

Cognados: cruel, emocional, espontáneo/a, generoso/a, íntimo/a, nostálgico/a, posesivo/a, romántico/a, sentimental
Repaso: apasionado/a, cabezón (cabezona), celoso/a, divertido/a, orgulloso/a

proud   headstrong   jealous

Las relaciones personales

arrepentirse (ie, i) (de)	to be sorry (about); to regret
castigar (gu)	to punish
comprometerse (con)	to get engaged (to)
confiar (confío) (en)	to trust (in)
conquistar	to succeed in seducing someone
discutir	to argue
engañar	to deceive; to cheat on
guardar(le) rencor (a alguien)	to hold a grudge (against someone)
hacer (*irreg.*) **las paces con**	to make up with
ocultar(le) secretos (a alguien)	to hide secrets (from someone)
perdonar	to forgive
romper con	to break up with
salir (*irreg.*) **con**	to go out with
seducir (zc)	to seduce
terminar	to end (*a relationship*)
traicionar	to betray
la amistad	friendship
el noviazgo	engagement

to yell

Repaso: casarse (con), divorciarse de, enamorarse de, estar enamorado/a de, gritar, lastimar, llevarse *to hurt* bien/mal con, mentir (ie, i), merecer (zc), pelearse; la boda, el divorcio *to deserve*

Otras palabras y expresiones

darse (*irreg.*) **la mano**	to shake hands
esperar	to hope
saludar	to greet
ojalá que	I hope, wish that
los celos	jealousy
la pareja	couple
el respeto	respect
a menos que	unless
antes (de) que	before
con tal (de) que	provided (that)
en caso de que	in case
para que	so (that)
sin que	without

Sin alternativa[a]

¿De qué hablan María y Carlos? ¿Por qué crees que María parece enojada? ¿Ha descubierto[b] algo relacionado con la venta de la viña?

MARÍA: ...después que murió papá, te dejé sola con Carlos y no he cumplido con lo mío[c] para mantener la viña.

ISABEL: Hija, cada uno tiene su destino en la vida. Carlos ha tenido el suyo y tú tienes otro.

MARÍA: Hablando de Carlos, tengo que mostrarte[d] algo...

ISABEL: Tenemos que hablar, Carlos. También estaba hablando con tu papá... y creo que él estaría de acuerdo[e] con lo que quiero decirte.

CARLOS: ¿Y qué es lo que me quieres decir?

[a]Sin... *No choice* [b]*discovered* [c]*no... I haven't done my share* [d]*show you* [e]*estaría... would agree*

8A

El dinero y las finanzas

IN THIS LESSON, YOU WILL LEARN:

- to talk about money and your personal finances
- the present progressive to talk about what you are doing at the moment
- to talk about debts you have and how to pay them off
- the conditional to talk about what you would do in certain situations
- to talk about the economy
- the imperfect subjunctive to talk about hypothetical events and how you would respond to them

In addition, you will prepare for **Episodio 8** of the film *Sol y viento.*

◄

Los cajeros automáticos son una parte importante de la vida moderna.

The following media resources are available for *Sol y viento: En breve*

Episodio 8 of *Sol y viento*

Online *Manual de actividades*

Interactive CD-ROM

Online Learning Center Website

PRIMERA PARTE

Vocabulario

Talking About Money | **¿Cómo manejas el dinero?** | **Your Personal Finances**

En el banco

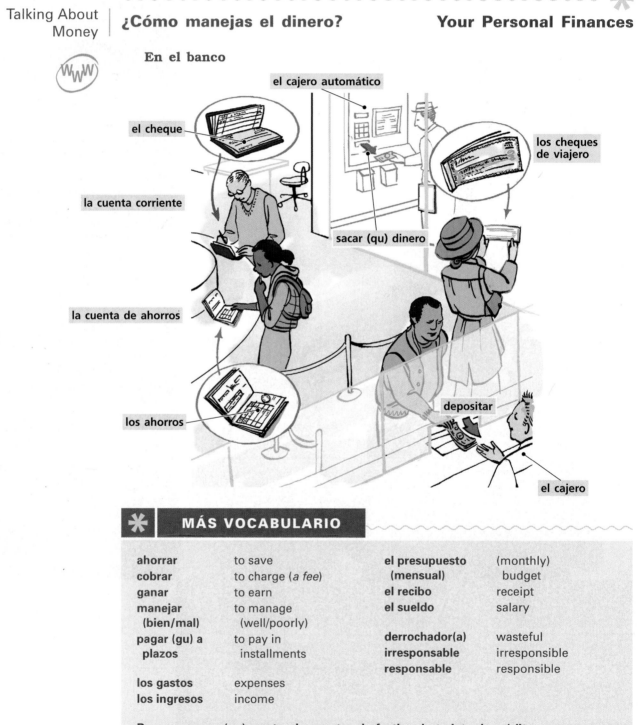

el cajero automático

el cheque

los cheques de viajero

la cuenta corriente

sacar (qu) dinero

la cuenta de ahorros

los ahorros

depositar

el cajero

✳ MÁS VOCABULARIO

ahorrar	to save	**el presupuesto**	(monthly)
cobrar	to charge (*a fee*)	**(mensual)**	budget
ganar	to earn	**el recibo**	receipt
manejar	to manage	**el sueldo**	salary
(bien/mal)	(well/poorly)		
pagar (gu) a	to pay in	**derrochador(a)**	wasteful
plazos	installments	**irresponsable**	irresponsible
		responsable	responsible
los gastos	expenses		
los ingresos	income		

Repaso: cargar (gu), gastar; la cuenta, el efectivo, la tarjeta de crédito

COMUNICACIÓN ÚTIL

Notice that Spanish has a number of ways to say *to save* and *to spend*. Be sure not to confuse these verbs and their meanings.

ahorrar	to save (*money*)	Necesitamos **ahorrar** más.
guardar	to save, keep (*things*)	¿Me **guardas** este recibo, por favor?
gastar	to spend (*money*)	**Gasté** demasiado en el centro comercial hoy.
pasar	to spend (*time*)	Elisa y Marcos **pasan** mucho tiempo juntos.

Vistazo cultural

Los cajeros automáticos

Hace pocos años, era necesario llevar una gran cantidad de cheques de viajero o de dinero en efectivo para viajar al extranjero. Para cambiar dólares norteamericanos en la moneda[a] del país de destino, el turista tenía que pagar las altas comisiones que cobraban algunos bancos y casas de cambio.[b] Afortunadamente todo eso ha cambiado gracias a los cajeros automáticos, esas máquinas maravillosas que te dan el dinero que necesitas, dónde y cuándo lo necesitas. Con sólo introducir en el cajero una tarjeta de crédito o bancaria y un código personal, se obtiene en efectivo la moneda del país donde uno se encuentre.[c] Tanto en España como en Latinoamérica los cajeros automáticos aceptan la mayoría de las tarjetas de crédito e incluso algunas tarjetas bancarias. Además, las transacciones son, por lo general, mucho más baratas que en los bancos o casas de cambio. Sin embargo, puede ocurrir que un cajero automático en el extranjero se trague[d] la tarjeta si no la reconoce. Por eso, siempre es conveniente apuntar los datos de la tarjeta en un lugar seguro,[e] para poder anularla[f] sin dificultad. Y claro, ¡siempre es buena idea llevar otra tarjeta de repuesto[g]!

▲ Los cajeros automáticos, como este en México, han facilitado las oportunidades de sacar dinero en el extranjero.

[a]*currency* [b]*casas... currency exchange offices* [c]*donde... wherever one may be* [d]*se... swallows* [e]*safe* [f]*to cancel it* [g]*de... spare*

Actividad A   Definiciones

Empareja cada palabra o frase con la definición apropiada.

1. ____ el cajero automático
2. ____ las cuentas
3. ____ el efectivo
4. ____ el presupuesto
5. ____ el recibo
6. ____ el cheque
7. ____ el sueldo
8. ____ los gastos
9. ____ la cuenta corriente
10. ____ la tarjeta de crédito

a. lo que uno prepara para manejar bien el dinero cada mes y no gastar demasiado
b. el conjunto (*entirety*) de lo que una persona gasta
c. cosa que uno escribe y firma para pagar las cuentas o el alquiler
d. máquina que se usa para sacar dinero
e. lo que uno gana cada semana, mes o año
f. lo que nos mandan cada mes las compañías por servicios de crédito, electricidad, gas, etcétera
g. prueba (*proof*) de una compra
h. lo que uno saca del cajero automático
i. lo que uno utiliza en vez de pagar en efectivo
j. uno deposita el dinero aquí para luego poder escribir cheques

Actividad B   Preguntas y respuestas

Paso 1   Escoge la respuesta apropiada para cada pregunta a continuación.

1. ____ ¿Me da el recibo, por favor?
2. ____ ¿Cómo prefiere pagar?
3. ____ ¿Dónde prefiere depositar este cheque?
4. ____ ¿Lo va a cargar en su tarjeta de crédito?
5. ____ ¿Cuánto desea sacar?
6. ____ ¿Se puede pagar con cheque?

a. En mi cuenta de ahorros, por favor.
b. Mil pesos, por favor.
c. No, sólo en efectivo o con tarjeta de crédito.
d. Si es posible, con un cheque de viajero.
e. Claro que sí. Aquí lo tiene.
f. No, lo voy a pagar en efectivo.

Paso 2   ¿Cuáles son algunos lugares posibles donde se puede escuchar cada pregunta y respuesta del **Paso 1**?

Actividad C   ¿Cómo manejan el dinero?

Paso 1   Indica la actitud hacia el dinero que tiene cada persona a continuación. Utiliza los adjetivos de la lista.

derrochador   irresponsable   responsable   tacaño

1. _____ Tengo un presupuesto mensual e intento seguirlo estrictamente. No soy rico, pero ahorro un poco cada mes y prefiero pagar en efectivo para no gastar más de lo que tengo.

2. _____ Tengo mucho dinero, pero no me gusta gastarlo. Cuando voy a un restaurante con amigos siempre pagamos a media (*we always split the check*); yo nunca invito (*offer to pay*). No quiero que mis amigos se aprovechen (*take advantage*) de mí porque soy rico.

3. _____ Soy estudiante y no trabajo. Pero los estudiantes tenemos muchos gastos —ropa nueva para cada estación del año y dinero para salir con los amigos tres veces a la semana. De vez en cuando, los invito a tomar algo. Tengo varias tarjetas de crédito, pero a veces no tengo el dinero suficiente para pagarlas.

4. _____ Trabajo mucho y también gano mucho. Me gusta vivir por el momento: compro mucha ropa cara y de moda, ceno todas las noches en los mejores restaurantes y viajo por todas partes del mundo. También compro los últimos aparatos electrónicos, aunque nunca los uso.

Paso 2 ¿Te pareces a alguien del **Paso 1**? ¿De qué manera? Prepara una oración para luego compartirla con la clase.

MODELO: Soy (un poco/bastante/muy) _____ porque...

Actividad D Entrevista

Paso 1 Hazle a un compañero (a una compañera) las preguntas a continuación y apunta sus respuestas.

1. ¿Tienes muchos gastos cada mes?
2. ¿Puedes ahorrar un poco de dinero cada mes?
3. Por lo general, ¿cómo prefieres pagar tus compras?
4. ¿Tienes un presupuesto mensual?
5. ¿Sabes cuánto dinero tienes en tu cuenta corriente?
6. Si quieres comprar algo pero no tienes suficiente dinero, ¿lo compras? ¿Cómo pagas?
7. Antes de salir con tus amigos, ¿te pones un límite en lo que puedes gastar?
8. ¿Guardas los recibos después de ir de compras?
9. ¿Sueles gastar más de lo que ganas o ganas más de lo que gastas?

Paso 2 Contesta las siguientes preguntas utilizando la información que te dio tu compañero/a en el **Paso 1.**

1. ¿Qué adjetivo describe mejor la habilidad de manejar el dinero que tiene tu compañero/a?

   ☐ responsable   ☐ irresponsable

2. ¿Tienes alguna sugerencia que hacerle a él/ella?

   Creo que (no) debe...

3. En tu opinión, ¿quién maneja mejor el dinero, tú o tu compañero/a? ¿Por qué?

Paso 3 Comparte tus respuestas del **Paso 2** con la clase. ¿Está de acuerdo el compañero (la compañera) a quien entrevistaste?

Gramática

¿Qué estás haciendo? The Present Progressive

In addition to using the present indicative to express what someone is doing right now, Spanish also uses the *present progressive*, which is formed with the verb **estar** + a present participle. The present participle is formed by adding **-ando** to the stem of **-ar** verbs and **-iendo** to the stem of **-er** and **-ir** verbs.

Los niños **están jugando** en el jardín.	*The kids are playing (right now) in the yard.*
¿Qué **estás comiendo**?	*What are you eating?*

Also note the following.

- Stem-changing **-ir** verbs also exhibit a stem change in the present participle, as indicated in the chart on the next page. Note also the spelling change for **-er** and **-ir** verbs whose stem ends in a vowel (e.g., **leer** → **le-**): a **y** is used instead of an **i.**

Estoy **leyendo.** ¿Qué quieres?	*I'm reading. What do you want?*

- As with infinitive constructions, object and reflexive pronouns can either precede the conjugated verb (**estar**) or be attached to the present participle. In the latter case, a written accent is added to maintain the original stress of the verb.

Pedro **se** está duchando.	*Pedro is taking a shower.*
Pedro está duchándo**se.**	

- In Spanish, the regular present tense, not the present progressive, is used to express actions that are repeated or that extend over a long period of time. It is also used for impending or planned actions.

REPEATED OR EXTENDED ACTIONS AND EVENTS:

Siempre lo **llama.**	*She's always calling him.*
Trabaja para la compañía Bartel Aquapower.	*He's working for Bartel Aquapower.*

IMPENDING OR PLANNED ACTIONS:

Llegamos pronto.	*We're arriving soon.*
¿A qué hora **vienes**?	*What time are you coming?*

✳ MÁS GRAMÁTICA

To express that an event or action has been going on or continuing over a period of time, Spanish uses the verb **seguir** + present participle.

¿Sigues trabajando para la misma compañía?
Are you still working for the same company?

Sigo esperando tu respuesta.
I keep on (I'm still) waiting for your reply.

FORMING THE PRESENT PROGRESSIVE		
estar	+	PRESENT PARTICIPLE
estoy estamos estás estáis está están está están	+	habl~~ar~~ → habl**ando** com~~er~~ → com**iendo** viv~~ir~~ → viv**iendo**
STEM-CHANGING -*ir* VERBS		
e → i: servir, pedir, decir		s**i**rviendo, p**i**diendo, d**i**ciendo
o → u: dormir		d**u**rmiendo
i → y		
leer → le- + -iendo → le**y**endo		
oír → o- + -iendo → o**y**endo		
construir → constru- + -iendo → constru**y**endo		

DE SOL Y VIENTO

In **Episodio 8** of *Sol y viento,* you will watch a scene in which María confronts her brother Carlos. Part of their exchange follows.

CARLOS
¿Qué **estás intruseando**[a]?

MARÍA
¡Si no lo hago, vas a seguir _____ a todos!

CARLOS
Me puedes preguntar y te respondo... lo que no me gusta es que te metas a[b] mi oficina sin mi permiso.

Selecting from the following options, what is it that María thinks Carlos will continue doing?

a. engañándonos   **b.** ayudándonos   **c.** molestándonos

[a]*intruding upon*   [b]*que... you're going into*

Actividad E ¿Quién lo está haciendo?

Escoge al personaje de la lista que corresponda a las oraciones a continuación.

1. _____ Está trabajando en la excavación con su profesora.
2. _____ Está esperando recibir el contrato firmado.
3. _____ Se está enterando (*finding out*) de lo que ha hecho Carlos.
4. _____ Está enamorándose de María.
5. _____ Está tratando de vender los terrenos de la familia.
6. _____ Está visitando a unos amigos en Chile.
7. _____ Está pensando mucho en su esposo.
8. _____ Está intentando comprar los terrenos de «Sol y viento».

Actividad F ¿Dónde están?

Empareja cada una de las acciones a continuación con el lugar más apropiado.

1. _i_ Está buscando un libro.
2. _e_ Está comiendo.
3. _h_ Está tomando una cerveza.
4. _a_ Está durmiendo la siesta.
5. _j_ Está preparando la cena.
6. _b_ Está sacando dinero.
7. _c_ Está haciendo ejercicio.
8. _g_ Está duchándose.
9. _d_ Está viendo una película.
10. _f_ Está esperando.

a. la habitación
b. el banco
c. el gimnasio
d. el cine
e. el comedor
f. el consultorio del médico
g. el baño
h. el bar
i. la biblioteca
j. la cocina

Actividad G ¿Qué estoy haciendo?

Piensa en una actividad. Luego, dale a un compañero (una compañera) algunas pistas sobre esa actividad, *sin revelar* lo que es. ¿Puede él/ella deducir cuál es la actividad?

MODELO: E1: Tengo un libro.
E2: ¿Estás leyendo?
E1: No. Estoy en un lugar particular.
E2: ¿Estás estudiando?
E1: No. Estoy en Barnes & Noble.
E2: ¡Ah! Estás comprando un libro.
E1: ¡Sí!

Actividad H ¿Qué hacías? ¿Qué sigues haciendo?

Paso 1 En una hoja de papel aparte haz una lista de cinco de las actividades que hacías cuando asistías a la escuela secundaria. Incluye por lo menos dos actividades relacionadas con el dinero.

MODELO: Trabajaba en un restaurante para ganar dinero.

Paso 2 Intercambia tu lista con la de otra persona. Hazle preguntas a tu compañero/a para averiguar si sigue haciendo cada actividad de la lista o no.

MODELO: ¿Sigues trabajando en un restaurante para ganar dinero?

Paso 3 ¿Cuáles son las actividades que tu compañero/a sigue haciendo hoy en día? ¿Son las mismas actividades, más o menos, que sigues haciendo tú?

Enfoque lingüístico

Los verbos y los sustantivos

As you have learned, just because two languages have an "equivalent" structure does not mean that their uses are equivalent. In the case of **-ndo** and *-ing,* you have seen that Spanish **-ndo** cannot be used to mean impending or planned events or to mean repeated and extended events as *-ing* can in English. In addition, **-ndo** can never be used as a noun as *-ing* can be in English. Spanish must use a "real" noun or, in many cases, an infinitive.

> **Gastar** dinero es fácil. **Ganar**lo, no.　　*Spending money is easy. Earning it isn't.*

Languages vary as to how they derive nouns from verbs and how they derive verbs from nouns. English is a language with great flexibility. For example, from the noun *supersize* comes a verb: *Would you like to supersize that?* English speakers also often play with language to make up verbs, as in *I'll FedEx it to you* or *I Googled it and found lots of sites.* Such inventing of verbs rarely occurs in Spanish. So make sure you keep nouns and verbs in their respective places and don't use **-ndo** forms as nouns.

SOL Y VIENTO: Enfoque cultural

En el **Episodio 8,** mientras todos se preparan para la recepción, María va a ayudar a Traimaqueo con algo bastante pesado.[a] Él le dice «¡Cuidado![b] ¡Cuidado! Ay, gracias, m'hija.[c]» Claro, ya sabes que María no es hija de Traimaqueo. Es muy común entre los hispanohablantes emplear de forma afectuosa los términos **hijo** o **hija** al dirigirse[d] a una persona más joven. **Tío** y **tía** son utilizados para demostrar cariño a una persona mayor, como lo hace María con don Paco. Paco es amigo de la familia —no es pariente— pero María lo quiere mucho, y por eso le dice **tío Paco.**

En el **Episodio 4** ya viste a Yolanda llamar a Traimaqueo **viejo.** Entre parejas, es frecuente que se llamen **viejo** o **vieja** como muestra de la intimidad y cariño entre ellos. Compara esto con el inglés, en que *my old lady* y *the old man* no son términos tan cariñosos. **Viejo** y **vieja** también se usan entre amigos íntimos y, a veces, entre otros miembros de la familia.

▲ ¿Crees que usa términos de cariño esta pareja tejana (de Texas)?

[a]*heavy*　[b]*Careful!*　[c]*mi hija*　[d]*addressing*

Vocabulario

Talking About
Payments, Loans,
and Debts

Las deudas

More on Personal Finances

Alicia González tiene muchas **deudas** (*debts*).

Sacó **un préstamo** (*loan*) para poder pagar los estudios...

...y también para comprar un auto nuevo.

Ahora, va a comprar una casa y necesita pagar **una hipoteca** (*mortgage*).

Además de sus deudas, tiene otros gastos, como...

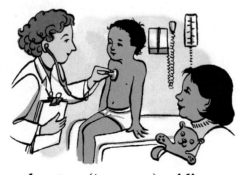

...**el seguro** (*insurance*) **médico** para ella y su familia

y **el seguro de automóvil** en caso de un accidente.

✱ MÁS VOCABULARIO

amortizar (c) una deuda (una hipoteca)	to pay off a debt (a mortgage)
deber	to owe
pagar (gu) de una vez	to pay off all at once
pedir (i, i) prestado/a	to borrow
prestar	to lend
la comisión	commission
los intereses	interest
el seguro	insurance
antirrobo	antitheft
contra incendios	fire
de vida	life
de vivienda	homeowner's

▒ Vistazo cultural

El seguro médico

El seguro médico es uno de los gastos que les preocupa a muchos norteamericanos. El seguro médico en los Estados Unidos está en manos de compañías privadas y en la mayoría de los casos es bastante caro. Por eso sólo las personas con un empleo fijo o con suficiente dinero tienen acceso a una protección médica asegurada. Desafortunadamente, el resto de la población queda sin protección. Este no es el caso en algunos países hispanos, como Cuba y España, entre otros. En Cuba los gastos médicos de todos los ciudadanos[a] corren a cargo del estado.[b] Es decir que todos tienen acceso al seguro médico y no tienen que pagar nada cuando consultan con un médico o van a un hospital. En España, un porcentaje del sueldo de los españoles va directamente a la Seguridad Social (un organismo oficial del estado) que se dedica a cubrir[c] los gastos médicos de los ciudadanos. En muchos otros países hispanos, existen los dos tipos de seguros: seguro público y privado. Por ejemplo, en la Argentina, los ciudadanos que tienen empleo fijo o suficiente dinero pueden acceder a una buena protección médica en clínicas y hospitales privados. Los que no pueden tener acceso a ese tipo de seguro automáticamente tienen un seguro público que les ofrece protección, aunque no es necesariamente muy buena. En todo el mundo el seguro médico es un tema fundamental de la sociedad. La diferencia se encuentra en la forma de solucionar el problema. Mientras que en algunos países hispanos el estado parece tener un papel[d] más activo en la solución del problema, en los Estados Unidos es la responsabilidad del ciudadano solucionar sus propios problemas médicos.

[a]*citizens*   [b]corren... *are covered by the state*   [c]*covering*   [d]*role*

Actividad A Definiciones

Empareja cada palabra o frase con la definición apropiada.

1. ___ los intereses
2. ___ una deuda
3. ___ el seguro
4. ___ un préstamo
5. ___ una hipoteca
6. ___ la comisión

a. lo que uno saca para poder comprar un coche
b. los pagos que hay que hacer si uno no puede pagar la cuenta de una vez
c. lo que se necesita para comprar una casa
d. obligación que uno tiene de pagarle algo a alguien
e. contrato para proteger una casa, un coche, etcétera
f. lo que recibe el agente de bienes raíces (*real estate agent*) por vender una casa

Actividad B ¿Tienes seguro?

Paso 1 Escoge la opción más apropiada, según tu caso, para cada tipo de seguro.

	LO TENGO.	NO LO TENGO, PERO DEBO TENERLO.	NO LO TENGO Y NO LO NECESITO AHORA.
1. seguro de automóvil	☐	☐	☐
2. seguro de vida	☐	☐	☐
3. seguro de vivienda	☐	☐	☐
4. seguro antirrobo	☐	☐	☐
5. seguro contra incendios	☐	☐	☐
6. seguro médico	☐	☐	☐

Paso 2 Si no tienes algunos de los seguros mencionados en el **Paso 1,** explica por qué.

MODELO: No tengo seguro de vida porque no tengo esposo/a ni hijos.

Paso 3 En tu opinión, ¿cuál de los seguros es más importante para ti tener ahora? ¿Por qué?

Paso 4 Compara tus respuestas de los **Pasos 1** a **3** con las de tres compañeros. ¿Coinciden algunas de sus respuestas con las tuyas? ¿Están todos de acuerdo en cuanto a cuál es el seguro más importante?

Actividad C   Las deudas que tenemos

Paso 1   Llena la tabla a continuación con información sobre las deudas que tienes ahora. Si no tienes ninguna deuda ahora, pon la información sobre las deudas que esperas (*you expect*) tener dentro de cinco años.

	DEUDA	AÑO EN QUE EMPEZÓ	LA ESTOY AMORTIZANDO AHORA.	LA PIENSO AMORTIZAR EN...
MODELO:	los estudios	dos mil tres (2003)	no	dos mil ocho (2008)
1.				
2.				
3.				

Paso 2   Haz una encuesta entre otros estudiantes para averiguar cuáles son las deudas que tienen. ¿Cuál es la deuda más común entre todos? ¿Cuáles son las deudas que esperan tener en el futuro?

Actividad D   Cómo salir de las deudas

Paso 1   Mucha gente tiene tantas deudas que no saben cómo van a amortizarlas todas. En grupos de tres o cuatro estudiantes, hagan una lista de siete sugerencias para ayudar a un amigo (una amiga) a limitar sus gastos y mejorar su crédito.

MODELO: No comas tanto en restaurantes.

Paso 2   Ahora pongan las sugerencias en orden de importancia. (1 = más importante)

Paso 3   Cada grupo va a presentar su lista a la clase. ¿Estás de acuerdo con las sugerencias de los otros grupos? ¿Qué grupo tiene el mejor plan para salir de deudas?

Gramática

¿Qué harías?

Introduction to the Conditional

You have already seen the expression **me gustaría** used to talk about what you *would* like (lit: what *would please* you). Unlike English, which forms the conditional using *would* plus a main verb, Spanish marks the conditional by adding a set of endings to the infinitive. As the chart indicates, **-ar, -er,** and **-ir** verbs all have the same conditional endings, a form of **-ía-.** Some verbs have irregular stems but all use the regular endings.

Conditional verb forms allow you to express what you *would* do, given a particular situation or circumstance.

No sé qué **haría** en tu situación.	*I don't know what I would do in your situation.*
Sería buena idea mantener un presupuesto.	*It would be a good idea to maintain a budget.*
Te dije que te **ayudaría.**	*I told you that I would help you.*

CONDITIONAL FORMS (REGULAR VERBS)					
hablar		**comer**		**vivir**	
hablaría	hablaríamos	comería	comeríamos	viviría	viviríamos
hablarías	hablaríais	comerías	comeríais	vivirías	viviríais
hablaría	hablarían	comería	comerían	viviría	vivirían
hablaría	hablarían	comería	comerían	viviría	vivirían

IRREGULAR CONDITIONAL FORMS		

decir: **dir-**
haber:* **habr-**
hacer: **har-**
poder: **podr-**
poner: **pondr-**   +   -ía   -íamos
querer: **querr-**   -ías   -íais
saber: **sabr-**   -ía   -ían
salir: **saldr-**   -ía   -ían
tener: **tendr-**
venir: **vendr-**

---

*Note that since the verb **hay** is a form of **haber,** the conditional of **hay** is **habría.**

Remember that when *would* implies something that you *used to do* in the past as a habitual action, the imperfect is used, not the conditional.

Siempre **comíamos** en restaurantes mexicanos.

We always would (used to) eat in Mexican restaurants.

DE SOL Y VIENTO

In **Episodio 8** of *Sol y viento,* you will watch a scene in which doña Isabel confronts her son Carlos about how he's been managing the winery. Part of their conversation follows.

ISABEL
Quizá eso te lo hubiera podido perdonar.[a]
Pero, ¿engañarnos a nosotras? ¿Engañar a los
vecinos, a la comunidad del valle? Nos has
puesto en una posición muy difícil, Carlos.

CARLOS
¡Tuve que hacerlo, mamá! ¡Las inversiones[b]
estaban a mi nombre! ¡No tenía nada! ¡Sólo
la venta de la viña _____ las deudas!

Which verb in the conditional do you think best fits in the blank?

a. cobraría

b. debería

c. pagaría

[a]Quizá... *I might have been able to forgive you for that.* [b]*investments*

Actividad E ¿Quién lo dijo?

Indica el personaje de la lista que se relaciona con cada afirmación a continuación.

1. _____ dijo que conseguiría las firmas de doña Isabel, María y los vecinos.

2. _____ dijo que jamás aprobaría la venta de «Sol y viento».

3. _____ dijo que iría a Chile para ayudar a doña Isabel.

4. _____ dijo que averiguaría (*he/she would find out*) lo que Carlos había hecho.

5. _____ dijo que haría todo lo posible para conseguir el perdón de María.

Actividad F ¿Qué cosas prestarías?

Paso 1 Indica si prestarías las siguientes cosas y a quiénes se las prestarías.

¿Le prestarías a alguien...	SÍ, A CASI TODO EL MUNDO.	SÓLO A MI FAMILIA O A ALGUNOS AMIGOS DE CONFIANZA (*trustworthy*).	NO. NO SE LO/LA/LOS PRESTARÍA A NADIE.
1. tu coche?	☐	☐	☐
2. cinco dólares?	☐	☐	☐
3. cien dólares?	☐	☐	☐
4. el libro de español?	☐	☐	☐
5. tu camiseta favorita?	☐	☐	☐
6. tus apuntes de una clase?	☐	☐	☐
7. tu computadora?	☐	☐	☐

Paso 2 Ahora indica si pedirías prestadas las siguientes cosas y a quiénes.

¿Le pedirías prestado a alguien...	SÍ, A CASI TODO EL MUNDO.	SÓLO A MI FAMILIA O A ALGUNOS AMIGOS DE CONFIANZA.	NO. NO SE LO/LA/LOS PEDIRÍA PRESTADO/A/OS A NADIE.
1. su coche?	☐	☐	☐
2. cinco dólares?	☐	☐	☐
3. cien dólares?	☐	☐	☐
4. el libro de español?	☐	☐	☐
5. su camiseta favorita?	☐	☐	☐
6. sus apuntes de una clase?	☐	☐	☐
7. su computadora?	☐	☐	☐

Paso 3 Compara tus respuestas del **Paso 1** y del **Paso 2**. ¿Eres una persona que se siente más cómoda (*comfortable*) prestando o pidiendo prestado? ¿Por qué?

Actividad G   ¿Eres arriesgado/a (*daring*)?

Paso 1   A continuación hay una lista de preguntas para determinar si alguien es arriesgado/a o aventurero/a. Primero, lee las primeras seis preguntas. Luego, escribe dos preguntas más, utilizando el condicional.

	NO, NO LO HARÍA.	SÍ, LO HARÍA.	DEPENDE DE LA SITUACIÓN.
1. ¿Viajarías solo/a a otro país?	☐	☐	☐
2. ¿Comerías carne de serpiente (*snake*)?	☐	☐	☐
3. ¿Invertirías (*Would you invest*) tu dinero en una empresa desconocida?	☐	☐	☐
4. ¿Vivirías en un lugar muy lejos de tu familia?	☐	☐	☐
5. ¿Te casarías con alguien de otra religión, cultura o idioma?	☐	☐	☐
6. ¿Irías a una playa nudista?	☐	☐	☐
7. ¿ ?	☐	☐	☐
8. ¿ ?	☐	☐	☐

Paso 2   Ahora entrevista a un compañero (una compañera) utilizando las preguntas del **Paso 1.** Incluye las dos preguntas que escribiste. Apunta sus respuestas.

Paso 3   Indica si tu compañero/a es arriesgado/a o no. Prepara dos oraciones que justifiquen tu opinión, pero no las compartas (*share*) con tu compañero/a.

MODELO: <u>   (Nombre)   </u> es bastante arriesgado/a porque comería carne de serpiente.

Paso 4   Comparte tus oraciones con la clase. ¿Está tu compañero/a de acuerdo con tu evaluación?

Actividad H   ¿Qué harías?

Paso 1   Escribe cinco oraciones que describan, en orden de importancia para ti, lo que harías con un millón de dólares. Puedes usar los verbos de la lista, si quieres.

ahorrar	dar	regalar
comprar	invertir	viajar

Paso 2   Compara lo que tú harías con lo que harían tres compañeros. Apunta lo que te dicen.

Paso 3   Tomando en cuenta lo que tus compañeros indicaron en el **Paso 2,** ¿hay algún adjetivo (algunos adjetivos) que describa(n) mejor a tu grupo?

altruista	generoso	pragmático
derrochador	materialista	responsable

TERCERA PARTE

Vocabulario

Talking About the Economy | **La economía**

✳ **Local and World Markets**

 ¿Cómo va la economía? Como muchas otras cosas, la economía también pasa por ciclos...

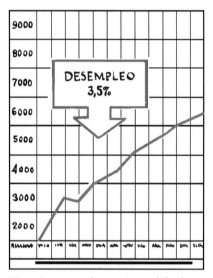

Hay épocas de **prosperidad** en las que hay **una alza** (*rise*) en **la Bolsa de valores** (*stock market*) durante varios meses, y hay una baja **tasa de desempleo** (*unemployment rate*).

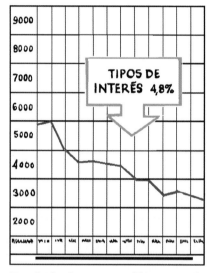

También hay **recesión** cuando **los tipos de interés** (*interest rates*) son muy bajos y la Bolsa de valores va **bajando.**

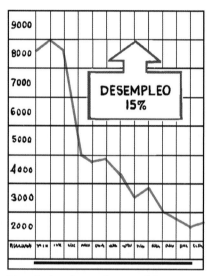

También hay **depresión, una baja** drástica en la Bolsa de valores y, a la vez, **una subida** drástica de la tasa de desempleo.

✳ **MÁS VOCABULARIO**

invertir (ie, i)	to invest	**los países en vías de**	developing countries
subir	to go up	**desarrollo**	
		la pobreza	poverty
las acciones	stocks	**la recuperación**	recovery
los bienes fabricados	manufactured goods	**la riqueza**	wealth
los bienes raíces	real estate		
la informática	information technology	**Cognados:** exportar, importar; los automóviles, la
las inversiones	investments	electrónica, la inflación, los metales preciosos, los
el mundo de los espectáculos	entertainment industry	productos farmacéuticos, los textiles
los países desarrollados	developed countries		

La economía de todos los países depende mucho de la venta a buen precio de los productos de exportación.

Los productos agrícolas y comestibles

el azúcar — el cacao — el café — el tabaco

Los recursos naturales

el acero — la energía — la madera — el petróleo

≋ Vistazo cultural

El producto nacional bruto[a]

Uno de los indicadores de la riqueza de un país es el producto nacional bruto (PNB),[b] es decir, la riqueza o los ingresos que genera cada habitante de un país. A continuación se puede ver el PNB por habitante (en dólares estadounidenses) de algunos países hispanohablantes.

País	PNB	País	PNB
la Argentina	$12.900	España	$18.000
Bolivia	$2.600	Guatemala	$3.700
Chile	$10.100	Honduras	$2.700
Colombia	$6.200	México	$9.100
Costa Rica	$6.700	el Paraguay	$4.750
Cuba	$1.700	el Perú	$4.550
el Ecuador	$2.900	el Uruguay	$9.300
El Salvador	$4.000	Venezuela	$6.200

▲ El PNB de algunos países hispanohablantes (2000)

[a]producto… *Gross National Product* [b]*GNP*

Actividad A Las acciones

Empareja la categoría de acciones con una compañía correspondiente.

1. ___ los textiles
2. ___ el mundo de los espectáculos
3. ___ los automóviles
4. ___ la informática
5. ___ los productos farmacéuticos
6. ___ la electrónica
7. ___ los metales preciosos

a. Sony
b. Microsoft
c. Tiffany
d. Gap
e. Volkswagen
f. Time-Warner
g. GlaxoSmithKline

Actividad B ¿Qué exportan?

Paso 1 Según el mapa, ¿qué países exportan los siguientes productos?

1. café
2. pescado
3. petróleo
4. tabaco
5. azúcar
6. automóviles
7. bananas
8. cacao

Paso 2 Mira otra vez el **Vistazo cultural** de la página 429. ¿Ves alguna relación entre los países que tienen un alto o bajo PNB y los productos que exportan?

Los países que exportan _____ por lo general tienen un PNB más alto que los países que exportan _____.

Actividad C ¿Desarrollado o en vías de desarrollo?

A continuación hay una lista de condiciones económicas, políticas y sociales. Indica si cada una de las condiciones se refiere, en términos generales, a un país desarrollado o un país en vías de desarrollo.

	PAÍS DESARROLLADO	PAÍS EN VÍAS DE DESARROLLO
1. alto PNB	☐	☐
2. economía inestable	☐	☐
3. inflación incontrolable	☐	☐
4. acceso de la mayoría de los habitantes a servicios de salud, educación y recreación	☐	☐
5. inseguridad política	☐	☐
6. la riqueza en manos de pocos	☐	☐
7. altas tasas de desempleo	☐	☐

Actividad D ¿Cómo va la economía?

Paso 1 Indica si, en tu opinión, estas condiciones económicas caracterizan la economía en una época de prosperidad, de recesión o de depresión.

	PROSPERIDAD	RECESIÓN	DEPRESIÓN
1. bajos tipos de interés	☐	☐	☐
2. una baja drástica de precios	☐	☐	☐
3. baja tasa de desempleo	☐	☐	☐
4. sigue el alza de la Bolsa de valores	☐	☐	☐
5. una baja moderada del PNB	☐	☐	☐
6. una subida drástica de la tasa de desempleo	☐	☐	☐
7. la Bolsa de valores sigue bajando	☐	☐	☐
8. una subida de confianza (*confidence*) de los consumidores	☐	☐	☐
9. una expansión rápida de la economía	☐	☐	☐

Paso 2 En grupos de tres estudiantes, contesten las siguientes preguntas.

1. ¿Cómo caracterizarían Uds. la economía de este país hoy en día? ¿Estamos en una época de prosperidad, de recesión o de depresión?

2. ¿Cuánto tiempo hace que estamos en esta situación?

NAVEGANDO LA RED

Busca información sobre la economía actual (*current*) de algún país hispanohablante. ¿Va subiendo o bajando la Bolsa de valores? ¿Cuál es la tasa de desempleo? Según la información que obtengas (*that you obtain*), ¿está el país en una época de prosperidad, de recesión o de depresión?

Gramática

| **Si tuviera más dinero...**

Hypothetical Statements; Introduction to the Imperfect Subjunctive

In both English and Spanish, clauses with the words *if*/**si** are used to speculate about possible situations. These situations or conditions can be real or they can be hypothetical. For example, the English sentence *If I have money, I spend it right away* represents a real condition. The speaker does *x* under the condition *y*. But in the sentence *If I had the money, I would spend it right away*, the speaker implies that he or she has no money, and the statement therefore represents an *unreal* or *hypothetical* situation. Notice that English uses different verb forms to convey an unreal situation: present tense (real) versus past tense (unreal). Spanish also uses different verb forms in hypothetical *if* or **si** clauses, but they're different than those used in English.

In Spanish, if the **si** clause represents a real situation, the verb in the **si** clause is in the present tense and the verb in the main clause can either be in the present or the future. For an unreal or hypothetical condition, the verb in the **si** clause is in the *imperfect subjunctive,* and the verb in the main clause is in the conditional. The imperfect subjunctive is formed by taking the third-person plural of the preterite, minus the **-on** ending, and adding the endings **-a, -as, -a, -amos, -ais, -an,** as indicated in the chart on the next page.

Si **tuviéramos** tiempo,... ...lo **podríamos** hacer.

If we had time (but we don't), ... *we could do it.*

Si me **sintiera** mejor,... ...**haría** ejercicio.

If I felt better (but I don't), ... *I would exercise.*

- Note that stem-changing **-ir** verbs in the preterite also have the same vowel change in all forms of the imperfect subjunctive:

  dormir: d**u**rmiera, d**u**rmieras, d**u**rmiera, d**u**rmiéramos, d**u**rmierais, d**u**rmieran

  pedir: p**i**diera, p**i**dieras, p**i**diera, p**i**diéramos, p**i**dierais, p**i**dieran

- Verbs that undergo a change from **i → y** in the third-person preterite also keep the **y** in all forms of the imperfect subjunctive:

  creer: cre**y**era, cre**y**eras, cre**y**era, cre**y**éramos, cre**y**erais, cre**y**eran

  oír: o**y**era, o**y**eras, o**y**era, o**y**éramos, o**y**erais, o**y**eran

FORMING THE IMPERFECT SUBJUNCTIVE

hablar → hablar~~on~~		comer → comier~~on~~		vivir → vivier~~on~~	
hablar**a**	hablár**amos**	comier**a**	comiér**amos**	vivier**a**	viviér**amos**
hablar**as**	hablar**ais**	comier**as**	comier**ais**	vivier**as**	vivier**ais**
hablar**a**	hablar**an**	comier**a**	comier**an**	vivier**a**	vivier**an**
hablar**a**	hablar**an**	comier**a**	comier**an**	vivier**a**	vivier**an**

IRREGULAR VERBS IN BOTH THE PRETERITE AND IMPERFECT SUBJUNCTIVE

VERB	THIRD-PERSON PLURAL PRETERITE	IMPERFECT SUBJUNCTIVE	VERB	THIRD-PERSON PLURAL PRETERITE	IMPERFECT SUBJUNCTIVE
decir:	dijer~~on~~	**dijera**	poner:	pusier~~on~~	**pusiera**
estar:	estuvier~~on~~	**estuviera**	querer:	quisier~~on~~	**quisiera**
haber:	hubier~~on~~	**hubiera**	saber:	supier~~on~~	**supiera**
hacer:	hicier~~on~~	**hiciera**	ser:	fuer~~on~~	**fuera**
ir:	fuer~~on~~	**fuera**	tener:	tuvier~~on~~	**tuviera**
poder:	pudier~~on~~	**pudiera**	venir:	vinier~~on~~	**viniera**

EXAMPLES OF HYPOTHETICAL STATEMENTS

Si **pudiera,** Manolo **se mudaría** a Chicago.   *If he could, Manolo would move to Chicago.*
Si **hiciéramos** eso, **ahorraríamos** mucho dinero.   *If we did that, we'd save a lot of money.*

DE SOL Y VIENTO

In **Episodio 4** of *Sol y viento,* you watched a conversation between María and Diego about Diego's future. Part of their conversation follows.

MARÍA
Diego, sólo tú puedes escoger tu futuro. Pero te digo que _____¹ una pena[a] si _____² tus estudios. Tienes mucho talento.

DIEGO
Gracias, profesora. Es que... bueno... mi familia. Mi papá sobre todo. Quiere que trabaje con él, en los negocios de la familia.

Which verb forms do you think belong in the blanks?

1. a. es   **b.** fuera   **c.** sería

2. a. dejaras   **b.** dejas   **c.** dejarías

[a]*shame*

Actividad E ¿Lo perdonarías?

Paso 1 Si tú fueras María, ¿perdonarías a Jaime? ¿Bajo qué circunstancias lo perdonarías? Escoge las razones que te parezcan aceptables.

Lo perdonaría...

1. ___ si me pidiera perdón.

2. ___ si renunciara a (*he quit*) su trabajo con Bartel Aquapower.

3. ___ si nos hiciera una oferta (*offer*) mejor.

4. ___ si me dijera que me quería.

5. ___ si decidiera mudarse a Chile.

Paso 2 Compara las razones que has elegido con las de otra persona. En la opinión de Uds., ¿es perdonable la conducta de Jaime?

Actividad F ¿Cómo reaccionarías?

Paso 1 Indica cómo reaccionarías en cada situación.

1. Si un mendigo (*beggar*) me pidiera dinero en la calle, yo...

   a. seguiría caminando.

   b. le daría un poco de dinero.

   c. le diría que no tengo nada.

2. Si supiera que la novia de un amigo había ligado con (*had gotten together with*) otro hombre, yo...

   a. no haría nada.

   b. hablaría con ella.

   c. hablaría con mi amigo.

3. Si me quedara atrapado/a en un ascensor (*elevator*), yo...

   a. estaría tranquilo/a porque lo arreglarían pronto.

   b. me pondría a pensar en (*about*) cómo salir de allí.

   c. me pondría muy nervioso/a.

4. Si recibiera un regalo de alguien que no me gustara, yo...

   a. se lo devolvería.

   b. le daría las gracias y me quedaría con el regalo.

   c. no le daría las gracias, pero me quedaría con el regalo.

5. Si supiera que mi novio/a salió con otra persona, yo...

   a. rompería inmediatamente con él/ella.

   b. saldría con otra persona también.

   c. lo/la perdonaría si se arrepintiera de sus acciones.

Paso 2 Comparte tus respuestas con otras tres personas. ¿En qué situaciones reaccionarían Uds. de la misma manera?

Actividad G Una encuesta

Paso 1 Contesta las siguientes preguntas. Inventa una situación hipotética para el número siete y luego contéstala.

1. Si tuvieras la oportunidad de viajar a un país hispanohablante, ¿adónde irías?
2. Si no asistieras a esta universidad, ¿qué harías?
3. Si pudieras conocer a cualquier persona, viva o muerta, ¿a quién te gustaría conocer?
4. Si compraras un auto nuevo, ¿qué modelo comprarías?
5. Si pudieras estar en otro lugar ahora mismo (*right now*), ¿dónde estarías?
6. Si cambiaras de especialización, ¿qué especialización escogerías?
7. Si _____, ¿_____?

Paso 2 Ahora, hazles las mismas preguntas a tres compañeros y apunta sus respuestas.

Paso 3 ¿Tienen Uds. algunas respuestas en común? Compártanlas con la clase.

Actividad H ¿Bajo qué circunstancias?

Indica bajo qué circunstancias harías las siguientes cosas, utilizando el imperfecto de subjuntivo.

1. Estudiaría en otra universidad si...
2. Viviría en otro país si...
3. Me divorciaría si...
4. Compraría un coche nuevo si...
5. Me sentiría muy feliz si...
6. Estaría muy avergonzado/a si...
7. Le ocultaría un secreto a un amigo si...
8. Dejaría de hablarle a alguien si...
9. Me casaría si...
10. Tendría celos de mi mejor amigo/a si...

Actividad I ¿Y su profesor(a)?

Paso 1 Con un compañero (una compañera), escriban respuestas que crees que daría su profesor(a) a cinco de las situaciones de la **Actividad G.**

MODELO: Si nuestra profesora tuviera la oportunidad de viajar a un país hispanohablante, iría a Cuba.

Paso 2 Lean sus oraciones a la clase. ¿Qué piensa su profesor(a)? ¿Está de acuerdo con lo que Uds. dicen?

RESUMEN DE VOCABULARIO

En el banco

ahorrar	to save
cobrar	to charge (*a fee*)
ganar	to earn
manejar (bien/mal)	to manage (well/poorly)
pagar (gu) a plazos	to pay in installments
sacar (qu) dinero	to withdraw money
los ahorros	savings
el/la cajero/a	teller
el cheque de viajero	traveler's check
la cuenta corriente	checking account
la cuenta de ahorros	savings account

Cognados: depositar; el cheque
Repaso: cargar (gu), gastar; el cajero automático,
la cuenta, el efectivo, la tarjeta de crédito

Las finanzas personales

amortizar (c) una deuda	to pay off a debt
(una hipoteca)	(a mortgage)
deber	to owe
pagar (gu) de una vez	to pay off all at once
pedir (i, i) prestado/a	to borrow
prestar	to lend
la deuda	debt
los gastos	expenses
la hipoteca	mortgage
los ingresos	income
el préstamo	loan
el presupuesto (mensual)	(monthly) budget
el recibo	receipt
el sueldo	salary
el seguro	insurance
antirrobo	antitheft
contra incendios	fire
de automóvil	car
de vida	life
de vivienda	homeowner's
médico	medical
derrochador(a)	wasteful
irresponsable	irresponsible
responsable	responsible

Cognados: la comisión, los intereses

La economía

bajar	to go down
invertir (ie, i)	to invest
subir	to go up
las acciones	stocks
la alza	rise (*stock market*)
la baja	fall
los bienes fabricados	manufactured goods
los bienes raíces	real estate
la Bolsa de valores	stock market
la informática	information technology
las inversiones	investments
el mundo de los	entertainment
espectáculos	industry
los países desarrollados	developed countries
los países en vías de	developing
desarrollo	countries
la pobreza	poverty
la recuperación	recovery
la riqueza	wealth
la subida	rise
la tasa de desempleo	unemployment rate
los tipos de interés	interest rates

Cognados: exportar, importar; la inflación,
la prosperidad, la recesión
Repaso: la depresión

Los productos de exportación

el acero	steel
el azúcar	sugar
el cacao	cocoa
el comestible	food item
la madera	wood
el producto agrícola	agricultural product

Cognados: el automóvil, la electrónica, la energía,
los metales preciosos, los productos farmacéuticos,
el tabaco, los textiles
Repaso: la banana, el café, el pescado, el petróleo,
los recursos naturales

LECCIÓN

8B

Los medios de comunicación[a]

El derecho (*right*) al voto es una necesidad en toda sociedad libre. ¿Con cuánta frecuencia votas tú? (Mendoza, la Argentina)

OBJETIVOS

IN THIS LESSON, YOU WILL LEARN:

■ to talk about the media, keeping up with current events, and types of TV programs

■ to talk about future events using the future tense

■ to talk about how the media presents information and how we react to it

■ to use the subjunctive to express doubt and disbelief

■ to talk about societal concerns

■ to use the subjunctive to talk about what you want to happen

In addition, you will watch **Episodio 8** of the film *Sol y viento*.

◄

The following media resources are available for *Sol y viento: En breve*

Episodio 8 of *Sol y viento*

Online *Manual de actividades*

Interactive CD-ROM

Online Learning Center Website

[a]Los... *Media*

Vocabulario

| Talking About Current Events | ¿Cómo te informas? | Getting Information ✳ |

La prensa y las noticias

el periódico   el titular   el noticiero   el accidente

la presentadora

EL DIARIO

El presidente propone su plan de paz

La bolsa sufre otra caída

Manifestaciones contra la guerra

El pronóstico del tiempo 29°

noticias 24

la noticia   la cadena

el pronóstico del tiempo   el artículo

el reportero   la testigo

✳ MÁS VOCABULARIO

estar (*irreg.*) al corriente	to be caught up (*with current events*)
informarse	to be informed; to inform oneself
el acontecimiento	happening, event
la noticia	piece of news
las noticias (internacionales, locales, nacionales)	(international, local, national) news
la prensa	press
el reportaje	report
la revista	magazine

A ver

Documental
23.00 (A&E Mundo). Moulin Rouge. Una cámara se interna tras bambalinas en el célebre club parisino, para mostrar que no todo es glamour y felicidad en vísperas de una premiere.

Biografía
21.00 (Film & Arts). Perfiles: Michael Douglas. Un resumen de la vida y carrera de este famoso actor de Hollywood. Con entrevistas a su padre Kirk Douglas y Oliver Stone.

Reportaje
22.00 (National Geographic). Tabú: curanderos. Conozca las técnicas de un chamán boliviano, un sanador indígena norteamericano y una hechicera etíope para curar enfermedades.

Misceláneo
13.00 (HBO). We stand alone together: The men of Easy Company. Conozca a los sobrevivientes de la Easy Company en que se inspiró la miniserie "The band of brothers".

Estreno
23.00 (MTV). Soda Stereo: La leyenda. Un novedoso documental que hace un recorrido por los 15 años de carrera de la banda pop más reconocida de latinoamérica. Con entrevistas exclusivas, fotos e imágenes de backstage. Artistas como Shakira, Marcelo Moura y Daniel Melero dan su testimonio sobre la importancia de Soda Stereo en el rock latino.

¿Qué hay de ver en la televisión?

el **anuncio publicitario**	commercial
la **comedia**	sitcom
el **concurso**	game show; contest
el **documental**	documentary
el **drama**	drama
el **programa de entrevistas**	talk show
el **programa deportivo**	sports program
el **reality**	reality show
la **telenovela**	soap opera

≈ Vistazo cultural

La programación en español en los Estados Unidos

En 1961 se creó el primer canal en español en los Estados Unidos en San Antonio, Texas. Hoy, más de cuarenta años después, este canal local de San Antonio forma parte de la cadena *Univisión,* que ocupa el quinto[a] lugar entre las cadenas más vistas del país y la más vista por los hispanos en los Estados Unidos. Además de *Univisión* en los Estados Unidos hay otras cadenas en español, entre ellas *Telemundo, Galavisión* y *TeleFutura.* Desde el principio de los años noventa la audiencia de las cadenas en español en los Estados Unidos ha seguido creciendo un 14% cada año, más que cualquier otra cadena de televisión. Además, *Univisión* es la cadena más vista entre los habitantes de algunas ciudades norteamericanas como Los Ángeles, Miami y San Antonio. Entre todas las acciones relacionadas con los medios de comunicación de Wall Street, es el más valorado debido a su rápido crecimiento.[b] Aunque la programación de estas cadenas incluye programas de entrevistas, documentales, programas de música y telenovelas de México y Sudamérica, el noticiero de *Univisión* se ha destacado[c] por presentar noticias internacionales, sobre todo de Latinoamérica, que no se pueden recibir en otros noticieros norteamericanos. Según algunos críticos de la prensa norteamericana, las cadenas en español son las únicas cadenas de la televisión norteamericana en que realmente se puede recibir noticias internacionales. Es decir, los noticieros de las cadenas principales normalmente sólo presentan noticias relacionadas con los asuntos[d] norteamericanos. Si presentan algún acontecimiento que ocurre fuera del país, casi siempre está relacionado con algún interés político o económico de los Estados Unidos.

▲ Jorge Ramos y María Elena Salinas, presentadores del noticiero de Univisión

[a]*fifth* [b]*growth* [c]*stood out* [d]*issues*

Actividad A   Definiciones

Tu profesor(a) va a leer descripciones de las palabras a continuación. Pon el número de la descripción al lado de la palabra que corresponde.

a. ___ el pronóstico del tiempo

b. ___ el presentador (la presentadora)

c. ___ el artículo

d. ___ el titular

e. ___ el/la testigo

Actividad B   Asociaciones

Empareja cada palabra con un ejemplo de la televisión.

1. ___ el noticiero   **a.** *Biography on A&E*

2. ___ la telenovela   **b.** *ABC, CBS, NBC, FOX*

3. ___ el concurso   **c.** *All My Children, Days of Our Lives*

4. ___ la cadena   **d.** *Oprah*

5. ___ el documental   **e.** *Survivor*

6. ___ el drama   **f.** *Law and Order, Six Feet Under*

7. ___ el programa de   **g.** *ABC World News Tonight*
          entrevistas
                          h. *Who Wants to Be a Millionaire?*
8. ___ el reality

Actividad C   ¿Estás al corriente?

Paso 1   Indica cuántas veces por semana te informas de lo que pasa en el mundo por los medios de comunicación mencionados a continuación.

	CADA DÍA	DE 3 A 5 VECES POR SEMANA	CASI NUNCA
1. Leo el periódico de la universidad.	☐	☐	☐
2. Leo un periódico nacional o local.	☐	☐	☐
3. Leo las noticias en el Internet.	☐	☐	☐
4. Leo una revista semanal (*weekly*).	☐	☐	☐
5. Miro el noticiero de una cadena principal (ABC, CBS, NBC, Univisión).	☐	☐	☐
6. Miro las noticias de una cadena de noticias (CNN, FOX News, MSNBC).	☐	☐	☐
7. Escucho la radio.	☐	☐	☐

Paso 2   Compara tus respuestas con las de tres compañeros de clase. Luego, prepara algunas oraciones para indicar a la clase las preferencias de tu grupo.

MODELO: En nuestro grupo nos informamos por el periódico de la universidad. Lo leemos casi todos los días. Casi nunca miramos el noticiero de una cadena principal.

Paso 3 Escucha las preferencias de los otros grupos. ¿Cuál es el medio de comunicación preferido por la clase para estar al corriente? ¿Refleja el estilo de vida de un estudiante universitario típico?

Actividad D ¿Qué miramos en la tele (*TV*)?

Paso 1 A continuación hay una tabla con varios tipos de programas televisivos. Llena la primera columna (**yo**) con el promedio (*average*) de horas que pasas por semana mirando ese tipo de programa.

TIPO DE PROGRAMA	YO	E1	E2	E3
1. las noticias				
2. las telenovelas				
3. los documentales				
4. los concursos				
5. los dramas				
6. los programas deportivos				
7. los programas de entrevistas				
8. los realities				
Total de horas				

Paso 2 De los tipos de programas que ves con mucha frecuencia, ¿cuál es el que nunca te pierdes (*miss*)?

MODELO: Veo muchos concursos. Nunca me pierdo *Jeopardy*.

Paso 3 Comparte tus respuestas con las de tres compañeros. Apunta sus respuestas en la tabla.

Paso 4 Ahora calcula el promedio de las horas de cada tipo de programa que ve tu grupo. Luego Uds. van a compartir esa información con toda la clase.

NAVEGANDO LA RED

Busca en la red un periódico de un país hispanohablante e imprime la página principal. ¿Cuál es el titular principal del periódico? En dos oraciones, indica de qué se trata el artículo. ¿Es una noticia sobre un evento político, económico, nacional o internacional? ¿Ya sabías algo de la noticia?

Gramática

¿Qué pasará?   Introduction to the Future Tense

You have learned to express future events in several ways in Spanish.

simple present:	Mañana me **voy** para España.
	Tomorrow I'm going to Spain.
ir + **a** + *infinitive:*	**Voy a trabajar** esta noche.
	I'm going to work tonight.
pensar + *infinitive:*	**Pienso estudiar** un año más.
	I think I'll study another year.
subjunctive:	**No creo que llegue** Juan esta tarde.
	I don't think Juan will arrive this afternoon.

In addition to the aforementioned constructions, Spanish also uses the simple *future tense.* Unlike the English future, which requires the auxiliary verb *will*, no auxiliary is needed in Spanish. The simple future is formed by using the infinitive as the stem and adding future-tense endings. The endings are the same for **-ar** and **-er/-ir** verbs.

estudiar + **é** = estudiar**é**	*I will study*
comer + **é** = comer**é**	*I will eat*
dirigir + **é** = dirigir**é**	*I will direct*

Verbs that have irregular stems in the conditional have the same irregular stems in the future tense. As happens with the conditional, these verbs are irregular in their stems only; all endings are the same as those for regular verbs.

COMUNICACIÓN ÚTIL

The simple future tense can also be used to express conjecture about what is going on at the present time.

¿Dónde **estará** César?	*Where can César be? (I wonder where César is.)*
Estará para llegar.	*He must be about to arrive.*
¿En qué **trabajará**?	*I wonder what his job is.*

FUTURE FORMS (REGULAR VERBS)					
trabajar		**ser**		**ir**	
trabajar**é**	trabajar**emos**	ser**é**	ser**emos**	ir**é**	ir**emos**
trabajar**ás**	trabajar**éis**	ser**ás**	ser**éis**	ir**ás**	ir**éis**
trabajar**á**	trabajar**án**	ser**á**	ser**án**	ir**á**	ir**án**
trabajar**á**	trabajar**án**	ser**á**	ser**án**	ir**á**	ir**án**

IRREGULAR FUTURE FORMS

decir: **dir-**
haber: **habr-**
hacer: **har-**
poder: **podr-**
poner: **pondr-**   +   -é   -emos
querer: **querr-**   -ás   -éis
saber: **sabr-**   -á   -án
salir: **saldr-**   -á   -án
tener: **tendr-**
venir: **vendr-**

DE SOL Y VIENTO

In **Episodio 9** of *Sol y viento,* don Paco will propose something important to María and doña Isabel, but he also talks to María about her future involvement with the winery. Read the following exchange and insert the verbs **tendrás** and **podrás** into the correct blanks.

PACO
Y tú, María, _____[1] que estar más comprometida[a] con la viña e incluso hacerte cargo del[b] negocio. ¿Crees que _____[2] hacerlo?

MARÍA
Oh, eh... No sé... Yo, de negocios... sé muy poco.

[a]*involved* [b]hacerte... *taking charge of the*

Actividad E ¿Probable o no?

Indica si crees que cada oración es probable o no.

		ES PROBABLE.	NO ES PROBABLE.
1.	Jaime se quedará en Chile por el resto de su vida.	☐	☐
2.	Carlos vendrá a la viña algún día.	☐	☐
3.	Doña Isabel se enojará con Carlos.	☐	☐
4.	María y Jaime se casarán.	☐	☐
5.	Traimaqueo asumirá más responsabilidades en la viña.	☐	☐
6.	Don Paco invertirá dinero en la viña.	☐	☐
7.	María dejará de ser (*will quit being*) profesora.	☐	☐

¡Exprésate!

You can use the future tense in *if/then* statements to tell under what conditions something might happen or to offer advice. This will be useful in some of the activities in this section.

Si dejas de fumar, **gozarás** de mejor salud.

Si quieres ser médico, no **tendrás** vida social mientras estudias.

If you quit smoking, you'll enjoy better health.

If you want to be a doctor, you won't have a social life during your studies.

Actividad F En el futuro

Indica en qué tipo de profesión una persona tendrá las siguientes experiencias en el futuro. Puede haber más de una posibilidad para cada oración. Escoge entre las profesiones de la lista.

abogado/a (*lawyer*), bibliotecario/a (*librarian*), biólogo/a, diseñador(a) de sitios (*web designer*), médico/a (*doctor*), profesor(a), psicólogo/a, reportero/a

Si una persona desea ser _____,...

1. ayudará a muchas personas.
2. pasará mucho tiempo en un laboratorio.
3. tendrá que practicar la habilidad de escuchar.
4. nunca ganará mucho dinero.
5. le será difícil tener vida social al principio.
6. necesitará un compañero (una compañera) de vida comprensivo/a.
7. pasará mucho tiempo sentada (*seated*).

Actividad G Para el año 2020

Entre todos, indiquen cuáles de las siguientes ideas son probables o posibles pero poco probables para el año 2020.

	PROBABLE	POSIBLE, PERO POCO PROBABLE
1. Una mujer será presidenta del país.	☐	☐
2. Los hispanos llegarán a formar el 40% de la población del país.	☐	☐
3. Los autos funcionarán con energía solar.	☐	☐
4. La Unión Europea adoptará el inglés como idioma oficial.	☐	☐
5. Los homosexuales podrán casarse legalmente en cualquier estado del país.	☐	☐
6. Todos los cursos de idiomas en las universidades serán «virtuales».	☐	☐
7. Ciertos campos de estudio no se ofrecerán más en la universidad.	☐	☐
8. Los futuros estudiantes universitarios pagarán el doble por la matrícula de lo que pagan hoy.	☐	☐

Actividad H Si dejas de...

Paso 1 Escribe tres oraciones sobre algo que haces con frecuencia.

MODELO: Compro mucha ropa. Me gusta mucho estar de moda (*in style*).

Paso 2 Pásale tus oraciones a otra persona, quien escribirá algo que te podrá pasar si dejas de hacer esa actividad. Luego, esa persona le pasará tus oraciones a una tercera persona, quien añadirá algo más sobre lo que has escrito.

MODELO: Si dejas de preocuparte tanto por la moda, tendrás dinero para otras cosas...

Paso 3 Al final, alguien debe devolverte las oraciones con las ideas escritas por las otras personas. ¿Estás de acuerdo con lo que te dicen tus compañeros? ¿Vas a seguir sus consejos?

◀

¿Qué pasará entre Jaime y María?
¿Se quedará Jaime en Chile?

SEGUNDA PARTE

Vocabulario

No me convence.

Functions of the Media

Pepita y Gonzalo están casados, pero tienen opiniones muy distintas en cuanto a la parcialidad de los presentadores de los noticieros.

GONZALO: ¿Puedes creer lo que está diciendo? ¡Este presentador es totalmente **parcial**!

PEPITA: No **exageres.** Yo creo que es muy **objetivo.**

También, los dos prefieren diferentes tipos de programas.

GONZALO: ¡Tienes que ver esto, amor! **Se trata de** un hombre que tiene que elegir a una esposa entre quince mujeres guapísimas.[a]

PEPITA: Me parece **una pérdida de tiempo.** Además de ser **cursi,** presenta **una imagen distorsionada** de la mujer.

GONZALO: ¡Qué va![b] Me **entretiene** y es muy **gracioso.**

[a]*gorgeous*   [b]¡Qué... *No way!*

✳ MÁS VOCABULARIO

Me parece...	It seems . . .
aburrido/a	boring
atrevido/a	daring
chocante	shocking
controvertido/a	controversial
cursi	tacky
entretenido/a	entertaining
gracioso/a	funny
una pérdida de tiempo	a waste of time

Cognados: apropiado/a, distorsionado/a, escandaloso/a, exagerado/a, inapropiado/a, informativo/a, interesante, objetivo/a, ridículo/a, sensacionalista, violento/a

dañar	to harm
distraer (*like* **traer**)	to distract
entretener (*like* **tener**)	to entertain
ser (*irreg.*) **parcial (a favor de / en contra de)**	to be biased (in favor of / against)
tratarse de	to be about

Cognados: controlar, criticar (qu), educar (qu), escapar, exagerar, manipular

las imágenes	images

〰 Vistazo cultural

Los realities

A principios de los años setenta, salió una serie en la televisión pública (PBS) en los Estados Unidos en la que las cámaras de televisión seguían a una familia norteamericana de clase media. El objetivo del programa era mostrarle[a] al público norteamericano «la realidad» de una familia de esa época. Casi cuarenta años más tarde, el fenómeno de los realities se extiende por todo el mundo, incluyendo los países hispanos. De hecho, versiones de algunos programas como *Big Brother* y *American Idol* se estrenaron[b] en España antes que en los Estados Unidos con los nombres de *Gran hermano* y *Operación triunfo*, respectivamente. Aunque existen muchas semejanzas en los realities entre países diferentes, muchas veces los productores crean o adaptan programas según las normas

▲ Una escena de *Gran hermano* (*Big Brother*), un programa reality de España

culturales de cada país. Por ejemplo, un programa que ha tenido mucho éxito en Sudamérica es el programa *Camino a la gloria*. Debido a la importancia del fútbol en la cultura hispanoamericana, en este programa se trata de futbolistas jóvenes que sueñan con jugar profesionalmente algún día. Los futbolistas pasan por unos entrenamientos[c] duros y a lo largo del programa un jurado[d] va eliminando, uno por uno, a los futbolistas. El ganador del concurso no sólo gana mucha fama, sino también recibe un contrato para jugar con un club profesional de fútbol.

[a]*to show* [b]*se... made their debuts* [c]*tryouts* [d]*panel of judges*

Actividad A   Definiciones

Empareja cada palabra o frase con la definición apropiada.

1. ___ manipular
2. ___ criticar
3. ___ entretener
4. ___ ser parcial
5. ___ dañar

a. divertir, distraer
b. favorecer una perspectiva y no otra
c. distorsionar
d. causar mal
e. censurar (*to judge*) las acciones de otro

Actividad B   Los programas televisivos

Indica si estás de acuerdo o no con las siguientes afirmaciones.

	ESTOY DE ACUERDO.	NO ESTOY DE ACUERDO.
1. La telenovela es ahora el tipo de programa más popular en los Estados Unidos.	☐	☐
2. La violencia en los medios de comunicación sólo refleja lo que pasa en la sociedad, no la influye.	☐	☐
3. Los medios de comunicación contribuyen a la violencia en la sociedad.	☐	☐
4. Los presentadores de los noticieros nos informan de las noticias sin ofrecer sus opiniones personales.	☐	☐
5. La objetividad en la prensa no existe.	☐	☐
6. Por lo general, la televisión tiene más influencia que los padres en la formación de los valores sociales de los niños norteamericanos.	☐	☐
7. «El sexo vende» en los anuncios publicitarios.	☐	☐
8. Los medios de comunicación perpetúan muchos estereotipos negativos sobre ciertos grupos minoritarios.	☐	☐

Actividad C   ¿Es apropiado para los niños o no?

Paso 1 Piensa en tres de los programas de televisión que, en tu opinión, no son apropiados para los niños.

En mi opinión, _____, _____ y _____ no son programas apropiados para los niños.

Paso 2 Ahora piensa en las razones por las que esos tres programas no son apropiados para los niños. Puedes utilizar algunas palabras de la lista a continuación. Luego vas a leer tus oraciones a la clase.

Vocabulario útil

el contenido denso (*heavy*)
el contenido sexual

el lenguaje fuerte (*strong language*)
la violencia

A causa de... , creo que _____ no es un programa apropiado para los niños.

Paso 3 Escucha las oraciones de tus compañeros. ¿Mencionan algunos de los mismos programas y razones?

Actividad D ¿Qué te parece ese programa?

Paso 1 En tu opinión, ¿a qué programa de televisión se puede aplicar cada adjetivo?

1. gracioso
2. cursi
3. controvertido
4. sensacionalista
5. chocante

Paso 2 Compara tus respuestas con las de un compañero (una compañera). Sigue el modelo.

MODELO: E1: Me parece que *The Simpsons* es un programa muy gracioso.
E2: A mí también me parece gracioso.

o

A mí no. Me parece más gracioso *Scrubs*.

Actividad E ¿Qué imágenes se presentan en los programas televisivos?

Paso 1 Vas a trabajar con un compañero (una compañera) de clase. A cada pareja su profesor(a) le va a asignar uno de los grupos sociales a continuación. Pensando en algunos programas televisivos específicos, tú y tu compañero/a deben escoger varios adjetivos que describan la imagen que se presentan de esas personas.

1. las mujeres
2. los afroamericanos
3. los hispanos
4. los homosexuales
5. las agrupaciones religiosas (cristianos, judíos, musulmanes [*Muslims*])

Adjetivos posibles:

atractivos/as	inteligentes	ricos/as
delgados/as	locos/as	sofisticados/as
fanáticos/as	perezosos/as	tontos/as
fuertes	pobres	trabajadores/as
graciosos/as	promiscuos/as (*promiscuous*)	violentos/as

Paso 2 Comparen los adjetivos que escogieron con los de otras parejas que describieron el mismo grupo social. ¿Escogieron los grupos los mismos adjetivos? ¿Creen que los programas televisivos presentan una imagen positiva o negativa de ese grupo? ¿Es una imagen realista o es exagerada?

Paso 3 Ahora compartan sus respuestas con toda la clase. ¿Qué grupo social tiene la imagen más positiva? ¿la más negativa?

Gramática

Expressing
Disbelief

Dudo que lo sepa.

Subjunctive of Doubt, Denial, and Uncertainty

In addition to using the subjunctive after expressions such as **ojalá, esperar que,** and certain adverbial expressions, the subjunctive is also used after expressions of doubt, denial, and uncertainty. Compare the two sentences below:

Creo que nos **dicen** la verdad.	*I think they're telling us the truth.*
No creo que nos **digan** la verdad.	*I don't think they're telling us the truth.*

In the first sentence, the statement *they're telling us the truth* is true in the mind of the speaker. However, in the second sentence, the speaker doubts the truth of the proposition. Because of this lack of affirmation, the subjunctive is used in the dependent clause. As the chart on the next page indicates, the subjunctive is "triggered" anytime an expression is used to express doubt, denial, or render uncertain the truth of a statement.

Note that when **no** precedes expressions of doubt or denial, the indicative is used. This is because the negation of doubt or denial is, in actuality, an affirmation.

No dudo que vienen.	*I don't doubt they're coming. = I believe they are.*
No niego que es verdad.	*I don't deny it's true. = I believe it is.*

Some expressions, upon first glance, may not seem to express doubt or denial. However, they do express uncertainty (the speaker isn't sure whether something is true or not) and require the subjunctive.

Es posible que **diga** la verdad.	*It's possible he's telling the truth. (The speaker doesn't know if he really is or not.)*
Es probable que **vayan** pronto.	*It's likely they'll leave soon. (The speaker doesn't know whether they will or not.)*

COMUNICACIÓN ÚTIL

Although in this section you will be using the present subjunctive only after expressions of doubt and denial, the imperfect subjunctive can also be used when the verb expressing doubt is in a past-tense form.

No pensaba que **fuera** verdad.	*I didn't think it was true.*
No podíamos creer que **ocurriera**.	*We couldn't believe it happened.*

Furthermore, a form called the present perfect subjunctive is used to express that someone presently disbelieves or denies that something *has happened*.

Dudo que lo **hayas hecho**.	*I doubt (that) you've done it.*
No es posible que **hayan roto**.	*It's not possible that they've split up.*

The present perfect subjunctive is formed by using the present subjunctive form of the verb **haber** (**haya, hayas, haya,** and so forth) and the past participle.

THE SUBJUNCTIVE WITH EXPRESSIONS OF DOUBT, DENIAL, AND UNCERTAINTY	
no (poder) creer/pensar	**No puedo creer** que te **guste** ese programa. *I can't believe you like that show.* **No pienso** que **sea** verdad. *I don't think it's true.*
dudar	**Dudamos** que **vengan.** *We doubt they're coming.*
no estar (*irreg.*) seguro/a de	**No está segura de** que **se casen.** *She's not sure they're getting married.*
negar (ie) (gu)	¿**Niegas** que lo **sepa?** *Do you deny that she knows?*
no es cierto/seguro/verdad	**No es cierto** que **haya** un examen hoy. *It's not true that there's a test today.*
(no) es posible / es imposible	**No es posible** que **sea** tan tarde ya. *It's not possible that it's so late already.* **Es posible** que **vayan** a otro lugar. *It's possible they'll go somewhere else.*
(no) es probable	**No es probable** que ese programa **continúe.** *It's not likely that program will continue.* **Es probable** que mis hijas **estudien** en la misma universidad. *It's likely that my daughters will study in the same university.*

DE SOL Y VIENTO

In **Episodio 8** of *Sol y viento,* you will watch a scene in which doña Isabel confronts Carlos about his business dealings. Part of their exchange follows.

ISABEL
No puedo creer que _____ mi hijo. También tengo aquí unos documentos falsificados. ¡Falsificados! ¡Con mi nombre y el de tu hermana!

Which verb form do you think belongs in the blank?

a. eres   **c.** seas

b. es   **d.** sea

Besides **no puedo creer,** what other expressions could doña Isabel have used? Would these expressions change the verb in the blank?

Actividad F Predicciones

Paso 1 Completa las predicciones sobre lo que crees que va a pasar con los personajes de *Sol y viento*, utilizando las siguientes expresiones.

Es probable que   Es posible que   Dudo que

1. _____ María perdone a Jaime.

2. _____ Jaime vuelva a trabajar con Bartel Aquapower.

3. _____ Jaime trabaje para «Sol y viento».

4. _____ Carlos se quede como administrador de «Sol y viento».

5. _____ Diego deje sus estudios para trabajar con su familia.

6. _____ Jaime y María se casen algún día.

Paso 2 Comparte tus predicciones con la clase. ¿Están todos de acuerdo?

Actividad G ¿Estás de acuerdo?

Indica si estás de acuerdo o no con las siguientes afirmaciones sobre los concursos en la televisión.

	ESTOY DE ACUERDO.	NO ESTOY DE ACUERDO.
1. Es probable que los concursos sean aún (*even*) más atrevidos en los próximos años.	☐	☐
2. Es posible que duren mucho tiempo los matrimonios entre personas que se casan en un concurso.	☐	☐
3. Es dudoso que los ganadores de los programas sean famosos por más de un mes.	☐	☐
4. No es cierto que los resultados de los programas sean predeterminados.	☐	☐
5. Es posible que los concursantes (*contestants*) se olviden de (*forget about*) las cámaras durante la filmación del programa.	☐	☐

Actividad H La prensa norteamericana

Paso 1 Indica si se usa el indicativo (I) o el subjuntivo (S) con las expresiones a continuación.

creo que + ___   no creo que + ___

es dudoso que + ___   no es dudoso que + ___

es verdad que + ___   no es verdad que + ___

es probable que + ___   es improbable que + ___

Paso 2 Usando las expresiones del **Paso 1,** expresa tus opiniones sobre las siguientes afirmaciones.

MODELO: Los norteamericanos están bien informados de las noticias internacionales. →
No es verdad que los norteamericanos estén bien informados de las noticias internacionales.

La prensa norteamericana...

1. ...es independiente de las ideas de los partidos políticos (*political parties*) principales.
2. ...es parcial a favor de una agenda conservadora.
3. ...se preocupa demasiado por la vida privada de los políticos.
4. ...normalmente favorece al gobierno.
5. ...presenta muchas noticias internacionales.
6. ...es sensacionalista.

Actividad I ¿Qué imagen tendrían?

Paso 1 Para muchas personas en el mundo, la única imagen que tienen de los Estados Unidos es lo que les presentan los medios de comunicación. Tu profesor(a) va a mencionar algunos programas de televisión y películas norteamericanos. Apúntalos en los espacios en blanco.

PELÍCULAS	PROGRAMAS DE TELEVISIÓN
1. _____	1. _____
2. _____	2. _____
3. _____	3. _____

Paso 2 Con un compañero (una compañera), escriban por lo menos tres oraciones que describan la imagen que alguien de otro país tendría de los Estados Unidos si sólo viera los programas y películas mencionados en el **Paso 1**. Usa los temas a continuación como guía.

la diversidad cultural
el nivel económico
el racismo
la religión
la tecnología
la violencia

MODELO: Es probable que piense que somos un país muy violento. /
Es posible que piense que somos muy violentos.

Paso 3 Compartan con la clase las oraciones que Uds. escribieron. Según las descripciones de sus compañeros, escojan una de las siguientes afirmaciones. ¿Tendría alguien de otro país una imagen positiva o negativa de los Estados Unidos? ¿Sería una imagen realista o exagerada?

☐ Dudo que esa persona tenga una imagen muy positiva.
☐ Es posible que su imagen sea realista.

TERCERA PARTE

Vocabulario

Talking About Being
a Valuable Member
of Society

La responsabilidad cívica   **Civic Duty and Citizenship**

Sonia es muy activa en su comunidad.

Vota en todas **las elecciones.**

Participa en **las reuniones cívicas.**

Trabaja de **voluntaria** en una
organización que ayuda a los niños.

De vez en cuando, participa en
manifestaciones.

El gobierno[a] y la responsabilidad cívica   [a]*government*

apoyar	to support
ayudar	to help
eliminar	to eliminate
protestar	to protest
el/la ciudadano/a	citizen
el deber	duty
el derecho	right
la ley	law
la libertad	liberty, freedom
la política	politics; policy
la preocupación	worry
la sociedad	society

✳ MÁS VOCABULARIO

el analfabetismo	illiteracy
los derechos humanos	human rights
el desempleo	unemployment
el hambre (*f.*)	hunger
la pérdida de los valores tradicionales	loss of traditional values
la protección del medio ambiente	environmental protection
el SIDA (síndrome de inmunodeficiencia adquirida)	AIDS

Cognados: la corrupción, el crimen violento, la discriminación, la drogadicción, la inmigración ilegal, el terrorismo, la violencia doméstica

Vistazo cultural

El voto obligatorio

Se ha notado en los últimos años la apatía[a] de los votantes norteamericanos en las elecciones. De hecho, apenas[b] el 50% de los votantes ejerce su derecho en las elecciones presidenciales. En algunos países, votar no es un derecho sino una obligación. Entre los países hispanohablantes, hay varios que tienen leyes que obligan a los ciudadanos a votar: la Argentina, Bolivia, Chile, Costa Rica, Guatemala, el Ecuador, México, el Perú y el Uruguay. Aunque en algunos países no tiene consecuencias por no cumplir con la ley, en otros las consecuencias de la abstención pueden ser mínimas, como una multa[c] de $20, o pueden ser más severas. En el Perú, durante los tres meses después de las elecciones, los ciudadanos tienen que llevar una tarjeta con un sello[d] que confirme que han votado. Si no tienen la tarjeta, no pueden recibir ciertos beneficios del gobierno. En Bolivia, también hay que llevar una tarjeta como prueba de haber votado para poder recibir el sueldo en el banco.

▲ En Guatemala, como en otros países hispanos, el voto es obligatorio.

La idea del voto obligatorio tiene sus defensores y sus críticos. Los que defienden esta política afirman que las elecciones democráticas son más legítimas si la mayor parte de la población participa. Además, si la democracia es el gobierno del pueblo, es la responsabilidad de todo el pueblo participar en las elecciones. Por otro lado, los que critican la política del voto obligatorio afirman que infringe sobre el derecho de elección,[e] fundamental en una sociedad democrática. ¿Qué crees tú? ¿Sería buena idea tener una ley del voto obligatorio en este país?

[a]*apathy* [b]*hardly* [c]*fine* [d]*seal, stamp* [e]*choice*

Actividad A Definiciones

Empareja las definiciones con la palabra o frase correspondiente.

1. ___ el terrorismo
2. ___ el desempleo
3. ___ la inmigración
4. ___ el analfabetismo
5. ___ la drogadicción
6. ___ el SIDA
7. ___ la discriminación
8. ___ la violencia doméstica

a. el movimiento de personas de un país a otro

b. una enfermedad (*disease*) que causa que el cuerpo humano no pueda protegerse de otras enfermedades

c. la condición de no saber leer ni escribir

d. actos de violencia para causar miedo entre la gente

e. tratar peor a un grupo de personas que a otro

f. la condición de no tener trabajo

g. actos de violencia que un miembro de una familia comete contra otros de la misma familia

h. la condición de depender físicamente de alguna sustancia química

Actividad B La responsabilidad cívica

Paso 1 Indica si las actividades a continuación son sólo buenas ideas o si son deberes de los ciudadanos.

	ES BUENA IDEA, PERO NO ES UN DEBER.	ES UN DEBER DE TODO CIUDADANO.
1. votar en las elecciones nacionales y locales	☐	☐
2. participar en una manifestación cuando uno no está de acuerdo con una ley o disposición (*regulation*)	☐	☐
3. pagar los impuestos (*taxes*) a tiempo	☐	☐
4. participar en las reuniones cívicas	☐	☐
5. informarse de la política del país	☐	☐
6. apoyar a las fuerzas armadas (*armed forces*)	☐	☐
7. avisar a la policía si uno presencia (*witnesses*) algún crimen	☐	☐
8. trabajar de voluntario/a para una causa u organización	☐	☐

Paso 2 ¿Cuántas de las actividades del **Paso 1** has hecho o haces ahora? Da un ejemplo.

MODELO: Trabajo de voluntario con la organización *Habitat for Humanity.*

Paso 3 Comparte tus respuestas de los **Pasos 1** y **2** con la clase. Según las respuestas de tus compañeros, ¿cuál de las siguientes afirmaciones describe mejor a tu clase?

☐ Somos una clase que participa muy activamente en la sociedad.

☐ Somos una clase que participa de forma más o menos activa en la sociedad.

☐ Somos una clase apática (*apathetic*).

Actividad C ¿Qué opinas?

Paso 1 Indica tu opinión sobre las ideas a continuación, utilizando una de las siguientes expresiones. **¡OJO!** Hay que usar el subjuntivo con **No creo que...**

Creo que...   No creo que...

1. es necesario perder algunas libertades para proteger el país contra el terrorismo.
2. los inmigrantes ilegales deben tener los mismos derechos que los ciudadanos.
3. el matrimonio es un derecho para todos, no sólo para los heterosexuales.
4. existe menos discriminación ahora que desde hace cinco años.
5. la edad para tomar bebidas alcohólicas debe ser la misma que la edad para votar.
6. votar en las elecciones debe ser obligatorio para todos los ciudadanos.
7. es buena idea aprobar (*to pass*) leyes más estrictas para la compra y posesión de armas.

Paso 2 Entrevista a un compañero (una compañera) para saber qué opina de las ideas del **Paso 1.**

Paso 3 ¿Estás de acuerdo con tu compañero/a? Prepara unas oraciones para compartir con la clase.

MODELOS: (No) Creemos que...

(Nombre) cree que... , pero yo no.

Actividad D Preocupaciones sociales

Paso 1 Tu profesor(a) va a asignarles a grupos de tres personas una preocupación social. En tu grupo, contesta las siguientes preguntas sobre esa preocupación.

1. ¿A quiénes afecta este problema?
2. ¿Cuáles son las causas del problema?
3. ¿Cuáles son las consecuencias?
4. ¿Sería fácil o difícil resolver el problema?
5. ¿Se puede aprobar leyes para combatir (*combat*) el problema?
6. ¿Qué pueden hacer los estudiantes universitarios para ayudar a resolver el problema?
7. ¿Cuál es el mayor obstáculo para resolver el problema?

Paso 2 Cada grupo va a presentar sus ideas a la clase. ¿Cuál de las preocupaciones tiene una solución más realista que las otras?

Gramática

Talking About
What You Want
to Happen

¿Qué quieres que haga?

**Subjunctive of Volition
and Desire**

In addition to the uses of the subjunctive that you have already learned, Spanish also uses the subjunctive after certain verbs of volition or desire. Note that, unlike with the subjunctive with expressions of doubt, making a statement negative does not change the need to use the subjunctive. That is, whether the expression is **quiere** or **no quiere,** for example, the subjunctive will appear in the dependent clause.

THE SUBJUNCTIVE WITH EXPRESSIONS OF VOLITION AND DESIRE		
decir (*irreg.*)	*to tell* (*someone to do something*)	Juan me **dice** que **vaya** a verlo. *Juan tells me to go see him.*
desear	*to want, desire*	**Deseamos** que el gobierno **haga** algo más efectivo para combatir el terrorismo. *We want the government to do something more effective to combat terrorism.*
es necesario / es preciso	*it's necessary*	**Es necesario** que todos **hagamos** algo de nuestra parte para eliminar la discriminación. *It's necessary that we all do our fair share to eliminate discrimination.* **Es preciso** que los políticos nos **escuchen.** *It's necessary that the politicians listen to us.*
insistir en	*to insist*	Mi padre **insiste en** que yo **piense** bien en el asunto. *My father insists that I think hard about the matter.*
(no) permitir	*to permit, allow*	**No puedo permitir** que **manejes.** *I can't allow you to drive.*
prohibir (**prohíbo**)	*to prohibit, forbid*	Te **prohíbo** que se lo **digas.** *I'm forbidding you to tell her.*
querer (*irreg.*)	*to want*	**Quiero** que me **escuches** un momento. *I want you to listen to me for a moment.*
recomendar (**ie**)	*to recommend*	El médico me **recomienda** que **haga** más ejercicio. *The doctor recommends that I exercise more.*
sugerir (**ie**)	*to suggest*	El profesor nos **sugiere** que **estudiemos** mucho para el examen. *The professor suggests that we study a lot for the test.*

DE SOL Y VIENTO

In **Episodio 8** of *Sol y viento,* you will watch a scene in which doña Isabel asks Yolanda where Carlos is. Part of their exchange follows.

ISABEL
¿Has visto a Carlos?

YOLANDA
No, señora. ¿Quiere que _____¹?

ISABEL
Sí, por favor. Dile que _____² hablarle y que me _____³ en el jardín.

Which verb forms do you think belong in the parts of the dialogue that are missing?

1. a. lo busco   **b.** lo busque   **c.** lo busqué

2. a. necesito   **b.** necesite   **c.** necesité

3. a. busca   **b.** busque   **c.** busqué

◐ Enfoque lingüístico

La ambigüedad de ciertos verbos

It may seem that a word means what a word means, regardless of the circumstance. But consider that a verb out of context may not capture its usual meaning in another context. For example, if you heard *to run* you might think of the action of moving very quickly with your legs. However, this is not the meaning in *she's running for office* or *my nose is running.*

The two verbs *tell* and *insist* are also ambiguous. On the one hand, they can be used in such contexts as *I'm telling you, John lies* and *I insist that John doesn't lie (isn't lying).* On the other hand, the words *tell* and *insist* can be used in contexts such as *I tell John not to lie* and *I insist that John not lie.* In the latter two cases, you could substitute verbs such as *command, demand,* or *order,* and the sense is retained: *I insist/demand that John not lie.* Note that you cannot do this in the first two examples, that is, *I'm telling you, John lies* cannot be *I'm demanding of you that John lies*!

Why is this important? In learning a language, you have to think about the meaning of a verb in context. The first two example sentences above require the indicative when they are expressed in Spanish.

I'm telling you, John lies.	**Te digo que John miente.**
I insist that John doesn't lie (isn't lying).	**Insisto en que John no miente.**

For the other two example sentences, the subjunctive is required in Spanish.

I tell John not to lie.	**Le digo a John que no mienta.**
I insist that John not lie.	**Insisto en que John no mienta.**

All languages have such ambiguities or multiple meanings, and this should not be a novel concept for you at this point. However, it is good to keep such things in mind because you wouldn't want to commit the *faux pas* of saying to someone **Insisto en que John mienta,** thereby implying that you are the source of John's lying habits!

Actividad E ¿Cierto o falso?

Indica si las siguientes oraciones son ciertas o falsas, según lo que ya sabes de *Sol y viento.*

	CIERTO	FALSO
1. Doña Isabel le dice a Yolanda que busque a Carlos.	☐	☐
2. Don Paco le recomienda a Jaime que vuelva a California.	☐	☐
3. María y doña Isabel no permiten que «Sol y viento» se venda.	☐	☐
4. María le sugiere a Diego que continúe con sus estudios.	☐	☐
5. Carlos no desea que Jaime hable con su madre, doña Isabel.	☐	☐
6. Doña Isabel quiere que María trabaje más en la viña.	☐	☐

Actividad F ¿Qué quieren?

Indica si, por lo general, quieren las siguientes cosas los conservadores o los liberales.

Quieren que el gobierno...	LOS CONSERVADORES	LOS LIBERALES
1. ...apruebe más leyes para controlar la compra y la posesión de armas de fuego.	☐	☐
2. ...apruebe más leyes contra el aborto (*abortion*).	☐	☐
3. ...baje los impuestos.	☐	☐
4. ...reduzca el presupuesto del ejército.	☐	☐
5. ...elimine la pena de muerte (*death penalty*).	☐	☐
6. ...permita el matrimonio entre los homosexuales.	☐	☐
7. ...proteja los valores tradicionales.	☐	☐
8. ...haga algo más efectivo para proteger el medio ambiente.	☐	☐
9. ...sea más pequeño.	☐	☐

Actividad G Nuestros hijos

Paso 1 Indica si harías las siguientes cosas cuando tengas hijos. Si ya los tienes, indica si haces las cosas o no.

	SÍ	NO
1. Voy a prohibirles que fumen.	☐	☐
2. Voy a permitirles que practiquen cualquier deporte.	☐	☐
3. Voy a prohibirles que asistan a fiestas con bebidas alcohólicas.	☐	☐
4. Voy a permitirles que vean la televisión durante la cena.	☐	☐

	SÍ	NO
5. Voy a prohibirles que tengan novio/a hasta los dieciséis años.	☐	☐
6. Voy a decirles que asistan a la iglesia (al templo, a la mezquita [*mosque*]) conmigo.	☐	☐
7. Voy a prohibirles que se levanten de la mesa hasta que terminen toda la comida de su plato.	☐	☐
8. Voy a recomendarles que consigan un trabajo de media jornada (*part-time*) a los dieciséis años.	☐	☐
9. Voy a permitirles que se queden en casa solos cuando voy de viaje.	☐	☐

Paso 2 Comparte tus respuestas con las de tres compañeros. Luego, contesta las siguientes preguntas.

1. ¿Quién va a ser (es) el padre / la madre más estricto/a?
2. ¿Quién va a ser (es) el padre / la madre menos estricto/a?
3. ¿Quién sería (es) el padre / la madre que estuviera más de acuerdo con tus ideas?

Actividad H ¿Qué le recomiendas?

Paso 1 Con un compañero (una compañera), termina las siguientes recomendaciones para un(a) estudiante nuevo/a en tu universidad.

1. Le recomiendo que viva en...
2. (No) Le recomiendo que tome clases de...
3. Le recomiendo que se aproveche de (*take advantage of*)...
4. Le recomiendo que no vaya a...
5. Le recomiendo que (no) coma en...
6. Le recomiendo que compre...

Paso 2 Ahora escriban dos recomendaciones más para el mismo (la misma) estudiante.

Paso 3 Compartan sus recomendaciones con la clase. ¿Están todos de acuerdo con las recomendaciones?

Actividad I Soluciones a los problemas

Paso 1 Escoge una de las preocupaciones sociales de la página 455. Trabajando con un compañero (una compañera), escribe cuatro oraciones que ofrezcan soluciones posibles al problema. Pueden utilizar las siguientes expresiones. **¡OJO!** No se olviden de usar el subjuntivo.

Es necesario que...   Queremos que...

Es recomendable que...   Se debe prohibir que...

Paso 2 Ahora compartan sus oraciones con otro grupo. ¿Qué piensan Uds. de las recomendaciones del otro grupo? ¿Están de acuerdo con ellas? ¿Son prácticas las recomendaciones? Respondan a cada recomendación, utilizando las siguientes expresiones.

¡Es una buena idea!   No creo que sea práctica.

(No) Estoy de acuerdo.   Me parece bien/mal porque...

SOL Y VIENTO

Antes de ver el episodio

Actividad A ¿Qué recuerdas?

A continuación hay unas paráfrasis (*paraphrases*) de lo que han dicho ciertos personajes en el episodio previo. De los personajes a continuación, ¿puedes indicar quién lo dijo y a quién se lo dijo?

1. «¡El sol está picando fuerte!» _____ se lo dijo a _____.
2. «Ya le dije que esta tierra no se vende.» _____ se lo dijo a _____.
3. «¿Comprende el daño de una represa en la zona?» _____ se lo dijo a _____.
4. «Quizás no me merezca que me perdone.» _____ se lo dijo a _____.
5. «Si pasan cinco días más, no va el negocio.» _____ se lo dijo a _____.

Actividad B ¿Qué falta?

En este episodio, doña Isabel se enfrenta con (*confronts*) Carlos. Lee el diálogo.

ISABEL: ¡Aquí hay más deudas que en todo el tiempo de la administración de tu papá! ¿Qué has hecho con el dinero de «Sol y viento»?

CARLOS: Mamá, estos son tiempos diferentes. El negocio es mucho más difícil.

ISABEL: ¿Me crees tonta? ¿Qué hiciste con el dinero de «Sol y viento»?

CARLOS: _____

¿Qué crees que dice Carlos en el espacio en blanco?

a. Invertí las ganancias (*earnings*) de la viña en varias compañías de tecnología.
b. Me enteré (*I found out*) de que papá había muerto sin pagar muchas de sus deudas y las tuve que pagar yo.

Actividad C El episodio

Ahora mira el episodio. Si hay algo que no entiendes bien, puedes volver a ver la escena en cuestión.

Después de ver el episodio

Actividad A ¿Qué recuerdas?

Contesta las siguientes preguntas sobre el **Episodio 8.**

1. Por fin Carlos le convence a María de que firme los papeles para vender «Sol y viento».

   a. cierto   **b.** falso

2. ¿Cuál fue la especialización de Jaime?

   a. economía   **b.** ecología   **c.** administración de empresas

3. ¿Quién invita a Jaime a la recepción de «Sol y viento»?

   a. Paco   **b.** Isabel

4. ¿Qué hizo Carlos con el dinero de «Sol y viento»?

   a. Lo depositó en una cuenta de ahorros en el extranjero.

   b. Lo usó para pagar las deudas de su padre.

   c. Lo invirtió en compañías de tecnología.

Actividad B ¿Lo captaste?

Verifica tus respuestas de la **Actividad B** en **Antes de ver el episodio.** Si es necesario, puedes ver el episodio de nuevo.

Actividad C Utilizando el contexto

¿Pudiste deducir el significado de las palabras y expresiones que aparecen en letra cursiva a continuación?

> YOLANDA: ¿Así vas a estar vestida para la recepción?
> MARÍA: No. Me voy a poner un vestido más tarde porque...
> YOLANDA: *¡Deja!* Yo me encargo de las flores. *Mejor anda a cambiarte* ahora mismo. ¡Ya van a llegar los invitados!

Actividad D En resumen

Completa la siguiente narración con las palabras y expresiones apropiadas de la lista a la derecha.

En este episodio, María _____[1] que Carlos _____[2] al resto de la familia y a los vecinos. María _____[3] explicaciones a su hermano, pero Carlos _____[4] que sólo él _____[5] el derecho de manejar los negocios de la viña. Luego, María _____[6] a su madre. Entonces doña Isabel _____[7] a su hijo qué _____[8] con el dinero de la viña. Parece que Carlos _____[9] en malas inversiones. A causa de este engaño, Isabel _____[10] a su hijo dos opciones.

descubrió
engañaba
había hecho
le dio
le pidió
le preguntó
lo había perdido
respondió
se lo contó todo
tenía

Detrás de la cámara

You may recall that Carlos said his sister is not interested in helping to run the winery and that she has other interests. You may have also noticed Carlos' resentment when he says this. Although his pride would keep him from admitting it, Carlos has always been jealous of his younger sister. María is smart and independent, and she has enjoyed much success in her career apart from the family business. Carlos, on the other hand, continuously tries to prove himself and is filled with envy and self-doubt because of his sister's success. As a result, his insecurity has led him to make some unwise decisions in the family business as well as in his personal life.

RESUMEN DE VOCABULARIO

Verbos

dudar	to doubt
estar (*irreg.*) **seguro/a de**	to be sure
insistir en	to insist
negar (ie) (gu)	to deny
permitir	to permit, allow
prohibir (prohíbo)	to prohibit, forbid
recomendar (ie)	to recommend

es imposible	it's impossible
es preciso	it's necessary
(no) es cierto	it's (not) certain
(no) es posible	it's (not) possible
(no) es probable	it's (not) likely
(no) es seguro/a	it's (not) certain
(no) es verdad	it's (not) true

Repaso: es necesario, decir (*irreg.*)**, desear, querer** (*irreg.*)**, sugerir (ie, i)**

La prensa y las noticias

estar (*irreg.*) **al corriente**	to be caught up (*with current events*)
informarse	to be informed; to inform oneself

el acontecimiento	happening, event
la cadena	network
los medios de comunicación	media
la noticia	piece of news
las noticias	news
internacionales	international
locales	local
nacionales	national
el noticiero	newscast
el/la presentador(a)	anchorman, anchorwoman

el pronóstico del tiempo	weather report
el reportaje	report
el/la testigo	witness
el titular	headline

Cognados: el accidente, el artículo, el/la reportero/a
Repaso: el periódico, la revista

Los programas televisivos

dañar	to harm
distraer (*like* **traer**)	to distract
entretener (*like* **tener**)	to entertain
ser (*irreg.*) **parcial**	to be biased
a favor de	in favor of
en contra de	against
tratarse de	to be about

el anuncio publicitario	commercial
el concurso	game show; contest
el programa de entrevistas	talk show
el programa deportivo	sports program
la telenovela	soap opera

atrevido/a	daring
chocante	shocking
controvertido/a	controversial
cursi	tacky
entretenido/a	entertaining
gracioso/a	funny
parcial	biased

Cognados: controlar, criticar (qu), educar (qu), escapar, exagerar, manipular; la comedia, el documental, el drama, la imagen, el reality; apropiado/a, distorsionado/a, escandaloso/a, exagerado/a, inapropiado/a, informativo/a, objetivo/a, ridículo/a, sensacionalista, violento/a
Repaso: aburrido/a, interesante

El gobierno y la responsabilidad cívica

apoyar	to support
aprobar (ue)	to pass (*a law*)
ayudar	to help

el/la ciudadano/a	citizen
el deber	duty
el derecho	right
la ley	law
la libertad	liberty, freedom
la manifestación	demonstration
la política	politics; policy
la reunión cívica	town meeting
el/la voluntario/a	volunteer

Cognados: eliminar, participar, protestar, votar; la elección

Preocupaciones de la sociedad

el analfabetismo	illiteracy
los derechos humanos	human rights

el hambre (*f.*)	hunger
la pérdida de los valores tradicionales	loss of traditional values
el SIDA (síndrome de inmunodeficiencia adquirida)	AIDS

Cognados: la corrupción, el crimen violento, la discriminación, la drogadicción, la inmigración ilegal, el terrorismo, la violencia doméstica
Repaso: el desempleo, la protección del medio ambiente

Otras palabras y expresiones

el impuesto	tax
la pérdida de tiempo	waste of time

Un brindis por el futuro

Antes de ver el episodio

Actividad A ¿Qué recuerdas?

Contesta cada pregunta con información verdadera, según lo que sabes de *Sol y viento* hasta el momento.

1. ¿Qué palabra describe mejor la actitud de Carlos ante su hermana, María? ¿Está resentido, celoso o enojado Carlos?
2. ¿Cómo supo doña Isabel de los documentos falsificados por Carlos?
3. Jaime dijo que no lo invitaron a la recepción para degustar el vino. ¿Por qué fue, entonces?
4. Cuando doña Isabel confrontó a Carlos en el jardín, le dijo que le quedaban dos opciones. ¿Cuáles eran?
5. Al final del **Episodio 8,** don Paco dijo que María debía escuchar algo. ¿Qué debe escuchar?

Actividad B ¿Qué falta?

Lee la siguiente presentación (*introduction*) y brindis que da doña Isabel al principio del **Episodio 9.** ¿Puedes deducir las palabras y expresiones que faltan?

ISABEL: Señoras y señores: primero que nada, en nombre de mi _____,[1] quiero agradecer vuestra presencia en esta importante ocasión. Para la viña «Sol y viento», es un orgullo que Uds. la visiten. ¡Y espero que el vino que vamos a degustar esta noche _____[2] uno de los mejores que hayan probado en su vida! También les _____[3] presentar a don Francisco Aguilar, gran amigo de nuestra familia y apreciado socio[a] de la viña «Sol y viento». Él ha venido desde México a probar nuestro vino. Bueno, sin más, les quiero _____[4] nuestra nueva cosecha. ¡Salud!

[a]*partner*

Actividad C El episodio

Ahora mira el episodio. Si hay algo que no entiendes bien, puedes volver a ver la escena en cuestión.

Después de ver el episodio

Actividad A ¿Qué recuerdas?

Contesta cada pregunta según lo que recuerdas del episodio.

1. ¿Qué preguntas hacen los vecinos e invitados? ¿Qué rumores han oído?
2. Don Paco hace un anuncio en público que para la familia implica la salvación de la viña. ¿Qué anuncia él?

Actividad B ¿Lo captaste?

Verifica tus respuestas para la **Actividad B** en **Antes de ver el episodio.** Puedes volver a ver la escena si es necesario.

Actividad C Usando el contexto

Utiliza el contexto y la situación para deducir el significado de las expresiones en letra cursiva. Puedes volver a ver esa parte del episodio si quieres.

> INVITADA: Isabel, ¿qué hay de los rumores de que van a vender «Sol y viento»?
> INVITADO: Yo también escuché algo así. *¿Qué hay de cierto?*[1]
> ISABEL: *Mientras me quede un soplo de vida, ¡no le pasará nada a esta viña ni a estas tierras!*[2] *¡Aquí no se venderá nada!*[3]

1. …   2. …   3. …

Actividad D En resumen

Completa la siguiente narración con las palabras y expresiones apropiadas de la lista a la derecha.

Ya sabes que, antes de comenzar la recepción para degustar el vino de la nueva cosecha de «Sol y viento», don Paco le habla a María. Le _____[1] que escuche a su corazón y que no se guíe solamente _____[2] su cerebro.

La degustación del vino empieza con una presentación de doña Isabel. _____[3] da a los invitados la bienvenida[a] y luego hace un brindis por la nueva cosecha. Después de probar el vino, algunos vecinos le preguntan sobre algunos rumores que circulan de que _____[4] la viña. Doña Isabel, con aire de mujer decidida, dice: «_____[5] me quede un soplo de vida, no se venderá nada.»

dice
les
mientras
por
se vende

[a]da… *she welcomes the guests*

Actividad E Las pruebas de Jaime

Paso 1 Al final de la escena con Jaime, María le dice: «No, en serio. No eres tan malo. Pero tienes mucho que probar todavía... » En grupos de tres, indiquen qué cosas debería hacer Jaime para pasar la prueba. Luego presenten sus ideas a los demás.

Paso 2 La clase entera debe determinar si las relaciones entre María y Jaime tienen futuro o no. ¿De qué dependen estas relaciones entre ellos? Hagan una lista en la pizarra con todas las ideas posibles.

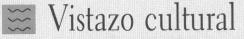

Vistazo cultural

El futuro del español

El español es la segunda lengua más estudiada en los Estados Unidos. Según las cifras del ACTFL (*American Council on the Teaching of Foreign Languages*), el 69% de los estudiantes secundarios[a] que estudian una segunda lengua optan por el español. En segundo rango[b] está el francés con el 16%. Las cifras son similares para el nivel universitario. El español también es una de las lenguas más estudiadas en otros países, como, por ejemplo, en el Japón y la China. ¿Por qué es tan popular estudiar español?

Como estudiante que ha elegido al español como materia, tú podrías contestar la pregunta mejor que nadie. Sin embargo, aquí se ofrecen unas cifras que quizás no conozcas: más de 35 millones de personas en los Estados Unidos son de ascendencia[c] hispana. De esos 35 millones, 28 millones dicen que el español es su primera lengua o, en el caso de las personas bilingües, una de sus primeras lenguas.

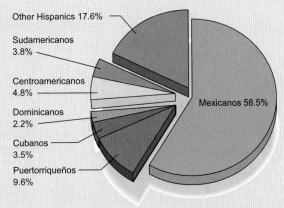

La ascendencia de los varios grupos hispanos en los Estados Unidos
Total population based on U.S. census, 2000 estimate* 35.3 million

Other Hispanics 17.6%
Sudamericanos 3.8%
Centroamericanos 4.8%
Dominicanos 2.2%
Cubanos 3.5%
Puertorriqueños 9.6%
Mexicanos 58.5%

* Source: Census Bureau. The Hispanic Population: Information from the 2000 Census.

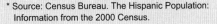

▲ La ascendencia de los varios grupos hispanos en los Estados Unidos

Se da la impresión entonces de que el español se está convirtiendo en una verdadera segunda lengua en este país. Pero la verdad es que no. Esas 28 millones de personas que dicen que el español es su primera lengua o una de sus primeras lenguas sólo forman el 10% de la población total de este país. Sin embargo, como va creciendo la población hispana en este país, seguramente crecerá el número de personas que hablan español. Y claro, la importancia del español seguirá creciendo a medida que[d] se reconozcan el poder económico y político de los 21 países donde el español es la lengua oficial.

[a]*high school* [b]*place* [c]*ancestry* [d]*a... as*

SPANISH-ENGLISH VOCABULARY

This Spanish-English Vocabulary contains all the words that appear in the text, with the following exceptions: (1) most identical cognates that do not appear in the chapter vocabulary lists; (2) verb forms; (3) diminutives in -ito/a; (4) absolute superlatives in -ísimo/a; and (5) most adverbs in -mente. Active vocabulary is indicated by the number of the lesson in which a word or given meaning is first listed (P = **Lección preliminar**). Vocabulary that is glossed in the text is not considered to be active vocabulary, and no lesson number is indicated for it. Only meanings that are used in this text are given.

Gender is indicated except for masculine nouns ending in -o, feminine nouns ending in -a, and invariable adjectives. Stem changes and spelling changes are indicated for verbs: **dormir (ue, u); llegar (gu)**.

Because **ch** and **ll** are no longer considered separate letters, words with **ch** and **ll** are alphabetized as they would be in English. The letter **ñ** follows the letter **n: añadir** follows **anuncio,** for example.

The following abbreviations are used:

adj.	adjective	*m.*	masculine
adv.	adverb	*Mex.*	Mexico
Arg.	Argentina	*n.*	noun
aux.	auxiliary	*neut.*	neuter
conj.	conjunction	*obj.*	object
def. art.	definite article	*p.p.*	past participle
d.o.	direct object	*pl.*	plural
f.	feminine	*poss.*	possessive
fam.	familiar	*prep.*	preposition
form.	formal	*pron.*	pronoun
gram.	grammatical term	*refl.*	reflexive
indef. art.	indefinite article	*s.*	singular
inf.	infinitive	*Sp.*	Spain
inv.	invariable	*sub. pron.*	subject pronoun
i.o.	indirect object	*v.*	verb
irreg.	irregular		

A

a to, at (1B); **a continuación** following; **a la derecha de** to the right of (2A); **a la izquierda de** to the left of (2A); **a la misma hora** at the same time (1A); **a la(s)…** at … o'clock (1A); **a menos que** unless (7B); **a menudo** often; **a pesar de** *prep.* in spite of, despite; **¿a qué hora?** at what time? (1A); **a solas** alone (1B); **llegar (gu) a tiempo** to arrive on time (1A)

abajo below, underneath

abierto/a (*p.p. of* **abrir**) open

abogado/a lawyer

abogar (gu) por to advocate

abordar to board

aborto abortion

abrazar (c) to embrace (7B)

abrigo overcoat (2B)

abril *m.* April (1B)

abrir (*p.p.* **abierto/a**) to open (1B)

abrochar(se) (el cinturón) to fasten (one's seatbelt)

absoluto/a absolute; complete

abstención *f.* abstention

abstracto/a abstract

abuelo/a grandfather, grandmother (3A); *pl.* grandparents

aburrido/a bored (1B); boring (2B)

aburrir(se) to bore (oneself) (7A)

abusar de to abuse (*someone*)

acá here

acabar to finish; **acabar de** + *inf.* to have just (*done something*)

academia academy

académico/a academic

acampar to camp (6B)

acaparado/a monopolized

acariciar to caress (7B)

acaso: por si acaso just in case

acceder a to consent to

acceso access

accesorio accessory

accidente *m.* accident (8B)

acción *f.* action; **Día** (*m.*) **de Acción de Gracias** Thanksgiving (4A); *pl.* stocks (8A)

aceite *m.* oil; **aceite de oliva** olive oil
aceptable acceptable
aceptación *f.* acceptance
aceptar to accept
acerca de about
acero steel (8A)
acertar (ie) to guess right
ácido acid
aclaración *f.* clarification
acomodar to settle; to make comfortable
acompañar to accompany; to go with
acondicionado: aire (*m.*) **acondicionado** air conditioning
aconsejar to advise
acontecimiento event, happening (8B)
acostarse (ue) to go to bed (2A)
acostumbrarse a to get used to, to become accustomed to
actitud *f.* attitude
actividad *f.* activity
activista *m., f.* activist
activo/a active
acto act
actor *m.* actor
actriz *f.* (*pl.* **actrices**) actress
actual current; contemporary
actualidad *f.:* **en la actualidad** currently
actuar (actúo) to act
acuario Aquarius
acuático/a aquatic
acuerdo agreement; **estar** (*irreg.*) **de acuerdo** to agree; **ponerse** (*irreg.*) **de acuerdo** to come to an agreement
adaptable adaptable (5A)
adaptarse to adapt
adecuado/a appropriate
adelante *adv.* ahead
además moreover; **además de** besides
adentro *adv.* inside
adicional additional
adiós good-bye
adivinar to guess
adjetivo adjective
administración *f.* administration; **administración de empresas** business administration (P)
administrador(a) administrator
admirador(a) fan, admirer
admirar to admire
adolescencia adolescence
adolescente *m., f.* adolescent, teenager (5A)
¿adónde? where (to)? (1B)
adoptar to adopt
adoptivo/a adopted (3A)
adorar to adore, worship (7B)
adquirido/a acquired; **síndrome** (*m.*) **de inmunodeficiencia adquirida (SIDA)** Acquired Immune Deficiency Syndrome (AIDS) (8B)
adquisición *f.* acquisition

aduana *s.* customs; **pasar por la aduana** to go through customs (6A)
adulto/a adult; **edad** (*f.*) **adulta** adulthood
adverbio adverb
advertir (ie, i) (de) to warn (about)
aéreo/a: línea aérea airline
aeróbico aerobic; **hacer** (*irreg.*) **ejercico aeróbico** to do aerobics (4A)
aeropuerto airport (6A)
afán *m.* desire
afectar to affect (7A)
afectuoso/a affectionate
afeitarse to shave (5A)
aficionado/a fan; **ser** (*irreg.*) **aficionado/a (a)** to be a fan (of) (4A)
afirmación *f.* statement
afirmar to affirm
afirmativo/a *adj.* affirmative
afluencia throng, horde
afortunadamente fortunately, luckily
África Africa (6B)
africano/a *n., adj.* African
afroamericano/a *n., adj.* African-American
afuera *adv.* outside; *n. pl.* suburbs, outskirts (2A)
agencia agency; **agencia de viajes** travel agency (6A)
agenda electrónica electronic organizer, PDA (personal digital assistant) (5A)
agente *m., f.* agent; **agente de inmobilaria** real estate agent; **agente de viajes** travel agent (6A)
agitado/a agitated, shaken
agosto August (1B)
agradable pleasant (1B)
agradar to please (5A)
agradecer (zc) to thank (3A)
agradecido/a thankful
agregar (gu) to add
agrícola *adj. m., f.* agricultural (8A)
agrio/a sour (3B)
agrupación *f.* group
agrupar to group
agua *f.* (*but* **el agua**) water (3B); **agua corriente** running water; **agua del grifo** tap water; **agua potable** drinking water; **contaminación** (*f.*) **del agua** water pollution (6B); **esquiar (esquío) en el agua** to water ski (4A)
aguacate *m.* avocado (3B)
aguado/a watered down
aguafiestas *m., f. s.* party-pooper (4A)
aguantar to endure; **no aguantar** not to be able to stand, put up with (7B)
ahí there
ahora now (1A)
ahorrar to save (8A)
ahorros *pl.* savings (8A); **cuenta de ahorros** savings account (8A)
aimará *m.* Aimara (language)

aire *m.* air; **aire acondicionado** air conditioning; **al aire libre** outdoors (6B); **contaminación** (*f.*) **del aire** air pollution (6B)
aislado/a isolated
ajedrez *m.* chess (4A)
ajeno/a foreign
ajo garlic
al (*contraction of* **a** + **el**) to the; **al aire libre** outdoors (6B); **al este de** to the east of (2A); **al horno** baked (3B); **al igual que** just like; **al lado de** beside (2A); **al norte de** to the north of (2A); **al oeste de** to the west of (2A); **al sur de** to the south of (2A); **al vapor** steamed (3B)
alarma *m.* alarm
alarmante alarming
alberca (*Mex.*) swimming pool
alcachofa artichoke
alcanzar (c) (una meta) to reach, achieve (a goal)
alcoba bedroom
alcohol *m.* alcohol
alcohólico/a *adj.* alcoholic; **bebida alcohólica** alcoholic drink
alegrarse to get, become happy (7A)
alegre happy (1B)
alegría happiness
alemán *m.* German (*language*) (P)
alergia allergy (7A)
alérgico/a allergic
alfombra rug; carpet (4B)
algo something, some (3B)
algodón *m.* cotton (2B)
alguien someone, anyone (1B)
algún, alguno/a/os/as some, any (3B)
alianza alliance
aliento breath; **mal aliento** bad breath
alimenticio/a nutritional
alimento food item (3B)
aliviar to alleviate
allá (way) over there
allí there (2B); over there (2B)
almacén *m.* department store (2A)
almendrado/a almond-shaped
almohada pillow
almorzar (ue) (c) to eat lunch (2A)
almuerzo lunch (3B)
alojamiento lodging (6A)
alojarse to stay (*in a place*) (6A)
alpinismo rock climbing; **practicar (qu) el alpinismo de rocas** to rock climb (6B)
alquilar to rent (4B); **se alquila** for rent (4B)
alquiler *m.* rent (1A)
alrededor de *prep.* around (2A)
alternativa *n.* alternative, choice
alterno/a alternating
alto/a tall (3A); high; **en voz alta** aloud; **zapatos de tacón alto** high-heeled shoes (2B)

altruista *adj. m., f.* altruistic

altura height

alubia bean

aluminio aluminum; **lata de aluminio** aluminum can (6B)

alza rise (8A)

amable friendly

amante *m., f.* lover

amar to love (7B)

amargo/a bitter (3B)

amarillo/a yellow (2B)

Amazonas: río Amazonas Amazon River

amazónico/a *adj.* Amazon

ambicioso/a ambitious (1B)

ambiente *m.* atmosphere; **medio ambiente** environment (6B)

ambigüedad *f.* ambiguity

ambos/as *pl.* both

amenaza threat

americano/a American; **fútbol** (*m.*) **americano** football (4A)

amerindio/a *adj.* indigenous to the Americas

amigo/a friend

amistad *f.* friendship (7B)

amor *m.* love

amoroso/a affectionate, loving

amortizar (c) una deuda to pay off a debt (8A); **amortizar una hipoteca** to pay off a mortgage (8A)

amplio/a ample, broad

amueblado/a furnished (4B)

amuleto amulet

analfabetismo illiteracy (8B)

análisis *m. inv.* analysis

analista *m., f.* analyst; **analista de sistemas** systems analyst

analítico/a analytical

anaranjado/a orange (*color*) (2B)

andar *irreg.* to walk; **andar en bicicleta** to ride a bicycle (4A); **rueda de andar** treadmill (4A)

andino/a Andean

anfitrión, anfitriona host, hostess

ángel *m.* angel

anglohablante *m., f.* English speaker; *adj.* English-speaking

angloparlante *m., f.* English speaker

animal *m.* animal

animar to encourage; to animate; to energize

aniversario anniversary

anoche *adv.* last night

anotar to note, take note of

ansioso/a worried, anxious (5B)

Antártida Antarctica (6B)

ante *prep.* before; faced with; in the presence of

antemano: de antemano ahead of time

anteojos *pl.* glasses (*vision*)

antepasado/a ancestor

antes *adv.* before; **antes de** (*prep.*) + *inf.* before (*doing something*); **antes (de) que** *conj.* before (7B)

anticipación *f.*: **con dos horas de anticipación** two hours ahead of time

anticipar to anticipate, foresee

antiguo/a old

antioxidante antioxidizing

antirrobo/a antitheft; **seguro antirrobo** antitheft insurance (8A)

antropología anthropology (P)

antropólogo/a anthropologist

anuncio advertisement; announcement; **anuncio publicitario** commercial (8B)

añadir to add

año year (1B); **cada año** each year; **¿cuántos años cumples?** how many years old are you (*turning*) (*fam. s.*)? (4A); **cumplir... años** to be ... old (*on a birthday*) (4A); **hace... años** ... years ago; **tener** (*irreg.*)**... años** to be ... years old (2A)

apagar (gu) to turn off (*light*) (5A)

aparato appliance; **aparato doméstico** household appliance (4B); **aparato electrónico** electronic device (5A)

aparecer (zc) to appear

aparente apparent

apariencia appearance

apartamento apartment (4B)

aparte *adv.* apart; besides; **hoja de papel aparte** separate piece of paper

apasionado/a passionate (1B)

apatía apathy

apático/a apathetic

apellido last name; **¿cuál es su apellido?** what's his/her last name? (P); **¿cuál es tu apellido?** what's your (*fam. s.*) last name? (P); **mi apellido es...** my last is ... (P)

apenas *adv.* hardly; barely

aperitivo appetizer

apetecer (zc) to appeal, be pleasing (5A)

aplicarse (qu) to apply oneself

apodarse to be nicknamed

apoyar to support (8B)

apoyo support

apreciar to appreciate

aprender to learn (1B)

apresurar to rush

aprobar (ue) to approve, pass (8B)

apropiado/a appropriate (8B)

aprovecharse (de) to take advantage (of)

aproximadamente approximately

apuntar to note, jot down

apunte *m.* note; **tomar apuntes** to take notes (1A)

apurado/a hurried, rushed

aquel, aquella *adj.* that (over there) (2B); *pron.* that one (over there) (2B)

aquello *neut. pron.* that (2B)

aquellos/as *adj.* those (over there) (2B); *pron.* those ones (over there)

aquí here (2B)

árabe *n., adj. m., f.* Arab

árbol *m.* tree; **árbol genealógico** family tree; **subirse a los árboles** to climb trees (5A)

archipiélago archipelago, group of islands

archivo archive, file (5A)

área *f.* (*but* **el área**) area

arena sand

argentino/a *n., adj.* Argentine

arma *f.* (*but* **el arma**) **de fuego** firearm

armado/a armed; **fuerzas armadas** armed forces

armario closet (4B)

armonía harmony, agreement

arquitecto/a architect

arquitectura architecture; **arquitectura paisajista** landscape architecture

arreglar to fix

arrepentirse (ie, i) (de) to be sorry (about); to regret (7B)

arriba *prep.* up

arriesgado/a daring, risk-taking

arrogante arrogant (1B)

arroz *m.* rice (3B)

arruinar to ruin

arte *m.* (*but* **las artes**) art (P)

arterial: presión (*f.*) **arterial** blood pressure (7A)

artículo article (8B)

artista *m., f.* artist

artístico/a artistic

ascendencia heritage

ascensor *m.* elevator

asegurado/a insured

asesinar to murder

así thus, so; **así así** so-so, fair; **así que** so (that), therefore

Asia Asia (6B)

asiático/a *n., adj.* Asian

asiáticoamericano *n., adj.* Asian-American

asiento chair (6A)

asignar to assign

asistente (*m., f.*) **de vuelo** flight attendant (6A)

asistir (a) to attend (1B)

asociación *f.* association

asociado/a associated; **Estado Libre Asociado** Free Associated State, Commonwealth

asociar to associate; to combine

aspecto aspect; appearance

aspiración *f.* aspiration, hope

aspiradora vacuum (4B); **pasar la aspiradora** to vacuum (4B)
aspirina aspirin (7A)
astronomía astronomy (P)
astrónomo/a astronomer
astuto/a astute, clever (1B)
asumir to assume
asunto subject, topic, issue
atacar (qu) to attack
atajo shortcut
atención f. attention
atender (ie) to wait on (6A)
atentado n. attack
atento/a considerate (7B)
atlántico/a: océano Atlántico Atlantic Ocean
atleta m., f. athlete (4A)
atlético/a athletic
atracción f. attraction; pl. amusements
atractivo/a attractive
atrapado/a trapped
atrasado/a backward
atravesar (ie) to cross; to run through (river)
atrevido/a daring (8B)
atún m. tuna (3B)
audiencia audience
auditorio/a auditorium (P)
aumentar to augment, increase
aumento n. increase
aun adv. even
aún adv. still, yet
aunque although
ausencia absence
Australia Australia (6B)
auto car
autobús m. bus (6A); **parada de autobuses** bus stop (2A)
autoconsciente m., f. self-conscious
automático/a automatic; **cajero automático** ATM (2A); **contestador** (m.) **automático** answering machine (5A)
automóvil m. automobile (8A); **seguro de automóvil** car insurance (8A)
autonomía individual political entity or region (Sp.)
autónomo/a autonomous
autoridad f. authority
autorizar (c) to authorize
autostop m.: **hacer** (irreg.) **autostop** to hitchhike
avance m. advance
avanzar (c) to advance
ave f. (but **el ave**) bird; pl. poultry (3B)
aventurarse to risk
aventurero/a adventurous
avergonzado/a embarrassed (7A)
averiguar (averigüo) to find out
avión m. airplane (6A)

ayer yesterday (4A)
ayuda n. help; **pedir (i, i) ayuda** to ask for help
ayudante m., f. helper; assistant
ayudar to help (8B)
ayuntamiento city (town) hall
azteca n. m., f.; adj. Aztec
azúcar m. sugar (8A); **cañaveral** (m.) **de azúcar** sugar cane field
azul blue (2B)

B

bailar to dance (1A); **salir** (irreg.) **a bailar** to go dancing
baile m. dance
baja n. fall (stocks) (8A)
bajar to go down (8A); **bajar de** to get off (6A); **bajar de peso** to lose weight
bajo prep. under
bajo/a adj. short (height); low (3A); **los Países Bajos** The Netherlands
balcón m. balcony (4B)
bambalina: tras bambalinas behind the scenes
banana banana (3B)
bancario/a adj. banking, financial
banco bank (2A)
banda band
bandeja tray
bandera flag
bañar to bathe; **bañarse** to take a bath (5A)
bañera bathtub (4B)
baño bathroom (4B); **con baño (privado)** with a (private) bathroom (6A); **traje** (m.) **de baño** bathing suit (2B)
bar m. bar (2A)
barato/a inexpensive, cheap (2B)
barbacoa n. barbecue
barco ship, boat; **navegar (gu) en barco** to sail (4A)
barra bar; **barra de frutas** fruit bar (3B); **barra de granola** granola bar (3B)
barrer (el piso) to sweep (the floor) (4B)
barrio neighborhood (2A)
basar to base, support
base f. base, foundation; **a base de** based on
básico/a basic
basquetbol m. basketball (4A); **jugar (ue) (gu) al basquetbol** to play basketball
bastante adv. somewhat, rather (1B)
basura garbage; **sacar (qu) la basura** to take out the trash (4B)
basurero landfill (6B)
bata robe (2B)
bebé m., f. baby
beber to drink (1B)

bebida n. drink; **bebida alcohólica** alcoholic drink
béisbol m. baseball (4A)
beisbolista m., f. baseball player
belleza beauty
bello/a beautiful
beneficios pl. benefits
berenjena eggplant
besar to kiss (7B)
beso n. kiss
biblioteca library (P)
bibliotecario/a librarian
bicicleta bicycle; **andar** (irreg.) **en bicicleta** to ride a bicycle (4A)
bien adv. well; **caerle** (irreg.) **bien a alguien** to like someone (5A); **combinar bien** to go well with (clothing) (2B); **llevarse bien con** to get along well with (5A); **manejar bien** to manage well (8A); **¿me queda bien?** does it fit me? (2B); **pasarlo bien** to have a good time (4A); **portarse bien** to behave well (5A); **quedarle bien** to fit well
bienes m. pl.: **bienes fabricados** manufactured goods (8A); **bienes raíces** real estate (8A)
bienestar m. well-being
bilingüe bilingual
bilingüismo bilingualism
billar m. s. pool, billiards
billete m. ticket (Sp.)
biodegradable: producto biodegradable biodegradable product (6B)
biografía biography
biología biology (P)
biólogo/a biologist
bistec m. steak (3B)
blanco/a white (2B); **vino blanco** white wine (3B)
blando/a soft (3B)
blindar to shield
blusa blouse (2B)
boca mouth (7A)
bocacalle f. intersection
boda wedding (5B); **padrino de boda** groomsman
bodega wine cellar
bolero love song
boleto ticket (6A)
bolígrafo pen
boliviano/a n., adj. Bolivian
bolsa purse (2B); **Bolsa de valores** stock market (8A)
bolso pocketbook; handbag
bonito/a pretty
bono voucher
borrador m. eraser (P)
bosque m. **(lluvioso)** (rain)forest (6B)
botana (Mex.) appetizer
botas pl. boots (2B)

botella bottle; **botella de plástico** plastic
bottle (6B); **botella de vidrio** glass
bottle (6B)
botón m. button
botones m. inv. bellhop (6A)
Brasil m. Brazil
brasileño/a Brazilian
bravo/a wild
brazo arm (7A)
brécol m. broccoli
bretaña: Gran Bretaña Great Britain
breve adj. brief
brillar to shine
brindar to toast
brindis m. toast (4A)
británico/a adj. British
bróculi m. broccoli (3B)
bruto/a: producto nacional bruto gross
national product
bucear to snorkel (6B)
buen, bueno/a good (1B); **buen provecho**
enjoy your meal; **buenas noches** good
night (P); **buenas tardes** good
afternoon/evening (P); **buenos días**
good morning (P); **es buena idea** it's a
good idea (2B); **estar** (irreg.) **a buen
precio** it's a good price; **estar** (irreg.)
en buena forma to be in good shape
(4A); **hace buen tiempo** it's good
weather (1B)
bufanda scarf (2B)
burlador(a) adj. seducer
burlarse de otros to make fun of others
buscar (qu) to look for (1A); **estoy
buscando...** I'm looking for . . . (2B)
búsqueda n. search; **hacer** (irreg.)
una búsqueda to do a search (5A)

C

caballero gentleman
caballo horse; **montar a caballo** to go
horseback riding (6B)
cabello hair
cabeza head (7A); **dolor** (m.) **de cabeza**
headache
cabezón(a) headstrong (5A)
cacahuete m. peanut; **mantequilla de
cacahuete** peanut butter (3B)
cacao cocoa (8A)
cacique m. chief (of a tribe)
cada inv. each (1A); **cada año** each year;
cada día every day; **cada mes** each
month; **cada uno** each one; **cada vez**
each time; **cada vez más** more and
more
cadena (TV) network (8B)
caer(se) irreg. to fall; **caerle bien/mal a
alguien** to (dis)like someone (5A);
dejar caer to drop; **¿en qué día (mes)
cae... ?** what day (month) is . . . ?

café m. (**descafeinado**) (decaffeinated)
coffee (3B); **café con leche** coffee
with milk; **charlar en un café** to chat
in a cafe (6B); **tomar café** to drink
coffee (1A)
cafetera coffeepot (4B)
cafetería cafeteria (P)
caída n. drop
caja box; cashier's station, checkout
counter (2B); **caja de cartón**
cardboard box (6B)
cajero/a teller (8A); **cajero automático**
ATM (2A)
cajón m. large box
calcetines m. pl. socks (2B)
calculadora calculator (5A)
calcular to calculate
cálculo calculus
calendario calendar
calidad f. quality
caliente hot; **chocolate** (m.) **caliente** hot
chocolate (3B); **té** (m.) **caliente** hot
tea (3B)
callar to silence someone; **callarse** to
shut up
calle f. street (6A)
calmado/a calm
calmante m. tranquilizer
calor m. heat; **hace (mucho) calor** it's
(very) hot (1B)
caloría calorie; **quemar calorías** to burn
calories (4A)
calvo/a bald (3A)
calzar (c): ¿qué número calza? what size
shoe do you (form. s.) wear? (2B)
cama bed (4B); **cama matrimonial** queen
bed (4B); **cama sencilla** twin bed (4B);
hacer (irreg.) **la cama** to make the
bed (4B)
cámara digital digital camera (5A)
camarero/a waiter, waitress
camarones m. pl. shrimp (3B)
cambiar (por) to change, exchange (for);
cambiar de canal to change
channels (5A)
cambio change; **en cambio** on the other
hand
caminar to walk (4A)
camino road; **camino a** on the way to
camión m. truck; bus (Mex.)
camisa shirt (2B)
camiseta T-shirt (2B)
campanario bell tower
campaña campaign
campeonato championship (4A)
campesino/a peasant
camping: hacer (irreg.) **camping** to go
camping (6B)
campo country(side); field (of work); **¿cuál
es tu campo?** what's your major? (P)
canadiense n., adj. Canadian

canal m. canal; **cambiar de canal** to
change channels (5A); **canal de
televisión** television channel
canario canary
cancelar to cancel
cancha (de tenis) (tennis) court (4A)
canción f. song
candidato/a candidate
canoa canoe; **remar en canoa** to go
canoeing (6B)
canoso/a: pelo canoso gray hair (3A)
cansado/a tired (7A)
cansarse to tire (7A)
cantante m., f. singer
cantar to sing (1A)
cantidad f. quantity
cañaveral (m.) **de azúcar** sugar
cane field
caótico/a chaotic (1B)
capa de ozono ozone layer (6B)
capilla chapel (2A)
cápita: renta per cápita per capita
income
capital f. capital (city)
capitán m. captain
captar to grasp
cara n. face (7A)
característica characteristic
caracterizar (c) to characterize
carbohidrato carbohydrate (3B)
cardíaco/a: infarto cardíaco heart attack
cardiopatía cardiopathy
cargar (gu) to charge
cargo: hacerse (irreg.) **cargo de** to take
charge of (something)
Caribe m. Caribbean (Sea)
caribeño/a n., adj. of or from the
Caribbean
caries f. inv. cavity
cariño affection; **tenerle** (irreg.) **cariño a
alguien** to be fond of someone (7B)
cariñoso/a affectionate (7B)
carnaval m. carnival; **Martes** (m.) **de
Carnaval** Mardi Gras (4A)
carne f. meat (3B); **carne de res** beef (3B)
carnero n. ram
carnicería butcher's shop
caro/a expensive (2B)
carrera major; career; **¿qué carrera
haces?** what's your (fam. s.) major? (P)
carretera highway
carro m. car
carta letter
cartel m. poster (4B)
cartelera billboard
cartera wallet (2B)
cartón m. cardboard; **caja de cartón**
cardboard box (6B)
casa house (4B); **casa particular** private
residence (4B); **casa privada** private
residence (4B); **compañero/a de casa**

housemate (4B); **limpiar la casa (entera)** to clean the (whole) house (4B); **regresar a casa** to go home (1A)

casado/a married (3A)

casamentero/a matchmaker

casarse (con) to marry, get married (5B)

casi almost; **casi nunca** almost never; **casi siempre** almost always

caso case; **en caso de que** conj. in case (7B)

castaño/a brown (3A)

castellano n. Spanish (language)

castellano/a adj. Castilian

castigar (gu) to punish (7B)

castillo castle

casualidad f. chance; coincidence

catalán/catalana n., adj. Catalonian

catálogo n. catalog

cataratas pl. waterfall (6B)

catástrofe f. catastrophe

catedral f. cathedral (2A)

categoría category; class

catolicismo Catholicism

católico/a n., adj. Catholic

catorce fourteen (1A)

causa cause; **a causa de** because of

causar to cause

cautela caution

cazuela casserole

CD: reproductor (m.) **de CD** CD player (5A)

cebolla onion (3B)

celebración f. celebration

celebrar to celebrate (4A)

célebre famous

celos pl. jealousy (7B); **tener** (irreg.) **celos** to be jealous

celoso/a jealous; **estar** (irreg.) **celoso/a** to be jealous (7A)

celular: (teléfono) celular cell phone (5A)

cena dinner (3B)

cenar to eat/have (for) dinner (3B); **cenar en un restaurante elegante** to eat in a fancy restaurant (6B)

cenizas pl. ashes

censurar to judge

centígrado/a centigrade

centro downtown (2A); **centro comercial** shopping center, mall (2A); **centro estudiantil** student center/union (2A)

Centroamérica Central America

centroamericano/a n., adj. of or from Central America

cepas pl. vine stocks

cepillo brush

cerca de prep. close to (2A)

cerdo pork; **chuleta de cerdo** pork chop (3B)

cereal (cocido) (cooked) cereal (3B)

cerebral cerebral (1B)

cerebro brain (8A)

ceremonia ceremony

cero zero (1A)

cerrar (ie) to close (2A)

cerveza beer; **tomar cerveza** to drink beer (1A)

chamán m. shaman

champiñones m. pl. mushrooms (3B)

champú m. shampoo

chapulín m. grasshopper

chaqueta jacket (2B)

charadas: juego de charadas charades

charlar to chat (1A); **charlar en un café** to chat in a cafe (6B)

chatarro/a: comida chatarra junk food

chau ciao

cheque m. check (8A); **cheque de viajero** traveler's check (8A)

chequear to check

chícharo pea (3B)

chico/a n. m., f. boy, girl (P); adj. small

chileno/a n., adj. Chilean

chimpancé m. chimpanzee

chisme m. gossip; **contar (ue) chismes** to gossip

chismear to gossip

chismoso/a gossipy (1B)

chiste m. joke

chocante shocking (8B)

chocar (qu) to run into; **chocarse con** to bump into

chocolate m. chocolate; **chocolate caliente** hot chocolate (3B)

chubasco rainstorm

chuleta de cerdo pork chop (3B)

cibercafé m. cybercafe

ciclismo cycling; **hacer** (irreg.) **ciclismo estacionario** to ride a stationary bike (4A)

cielo sky; heaven

cien, ciento one hundred (2A); **ciento uno/a** (2B); **por ciento** percent

cien mil one hundred thousand (5B)

ciencia science; **ciencias naturales** natural sciences (P); **ciencias políticas** political science (P); **ciencias sociales** social sciences (P)

científico/a scientist; adj. scientific

cierto/a certain; true

cifra number, figure

cigarrillo cigarette

cima top

cinco five (1A)

cincuenta fifty (2A)

cine m. movie theater (2A); the movies; **ir** (irreg.) **al cine** to go to the movies

cinta cassette

cintura waist

cinturón m. belt (2B); **abrocharse el cinturón** to fasten one's seatbelt

circulación f. circulation; traffic

círculo circle

circunstancia circumstance

cirugía surgery

cirujano/a surgeon

cita appointment; date (5A)

ciudad f. city (2A)

ciudadano/a citizen (8B)

cívico/a civic; **responsabilidad** (f.) **cívica** civic duty (8B); **reunión** (f.) **cívica** town meeting (8B)

civil: ingeniería civil civil engineering (P); **ingeniero/a civil** civil engineer

civilización f. civilization

clarificación f. clarification

claro/a clear; light

clase f. class (P); **clase media** middle class; **clase turística** coach (6A); **compañero/a de clase** classmate; **primera clase** first class (6A); **¿qué clases tienes este semestre/trimestre?** what classes do you (fam. s.) have this semester/quarter? (P); **sala de clase** classroom (P); **tengo una clase de...** I have a(n) . . . class (P); **tomar una clase** to take a class (1A)

clasificación f. classification

clasificar (qu) to classify

clave f. key

clic: hacer (irreg.) **clic** to click (5A)

cliente m., f. customer (2B)

clima m. climate

clínica clinic

coágulo clot

cobrar to charge (a fee) (8A)

cocido/a cooked (3B); **cereal** (m.) **cocido** cooked cereal (3B)

coche m. car

cocina kitchen; cooking (4B)

cocinar to cook (4A)

cocinero/a cook (6A)

codiciado/a coveted

código code

codo elbow (7A)

coexistir to coexist

cognado cognate

coincidencia coincidence

coincidir to coincide

cola tail (of an animal); line (of people); **hacer** (irreg.) **cola** to wait (stand) in line (6A)

colaborar to collaborate

colección f. collection

coleccionar to collect; **coleccionar estampillas** to collect stamps (4A); **coleccionar monedas** to collect coins (4A)

colega m., f. colleague

colegio high school

colesterol m. cholesterol

colgar (ue) (gu) to hang

coliflor f. cauliflower (3B)

colina hill (6B)

colocar (qu) to place

colombiano/a *n., adj.* Colombian
colonia colony
colonizar (c) to colonize (5B)
color *m.* color
colorear to color (5A)
columna column
comandante commander
combatir to fight
combinación *f.* combination
combinar to combine; **combinar bien** to go well with (*clothing*) (2B)
combustibles (*m.*) **fósiles** fossil fuels (6B)
comedia comedy (8B)
comedor *m.* dining room (4B)
comentar to comment, make comments on; to discuss
comentario comment; remark; *pl.* commentaries
comenzar (ie) (c) to begin
comer to eat (1B); **dar** (*irreg.*) **de comer** to feed
comercial: centro comercial shopping center, mall (2A)
comercio business (P); **Tratado de Libre Comercio (TLC)** North American Free Trade Agreement (NAFTA)
comestible *m.* food item (8A)
cometer to commit
cómico/a funny, comical (1B); **tiras cómicas** comics (5A)
comida food; meal; **comida chatarra** junk food; **comida rápida** fast food (3B)
comienzo *n.* beginning
comisión *f.* commission (8A)
como as, like; **tan pronto como** as soon as
¿cómo? how (1B); **¿cómo es?** what is he/she/it like? (3A); what are you (*form. s.*) like? (3A); **¿cómo se llama (él/ella)?** what's his/her name? (P); **¿cómo se llega a... ?** how do you get to . . . ? (6A); **¿cómo te llamas?** what's your (*fam. s.*) name? (P)
cómoda dresser (4B)
comodidades *f. pl.* amenities, conveniences
cómodo/a comfortable
compañero/a companion; **compañero/a de casa** housemate (4B); **compañero/a de clase** classmate; **compañero/a de cuarto** roommate (4B)
compañía company
comparación *f.* comparison
comparar to compare
compartir to share
compasión *f.* compassion
competición *f.* competition
competidor(a) competitive
competir (i, i) to compete (4A)
complemento *gram.* pronoun

completar to complete
completo/a complete; **pensión** (*f.*) **completa** room and all meals (6A)
comportamiento behavior
comportarse to behave, act
composición *f.* composition
comprar to buy (2B); **comprar recuerdos** to buy souvenirs (6B)
compras purchases; **de compras** shopping (2B)
comprender to understand (1B); to encompass
comprensivo/a understanding (7B)
comprometer to compromise; to involve; **comprometerse (con)** to get engaged (to) (7B)
compuesto/a *adj.* compound
compulsivo/a compulsive
computación *f.* computer programming
computadora computer (P); **computadora portátil** laptop computer (5A)
común *adj.* common
comunicación *f.* communication; **medios** (*pl.*) **de communication** media (8B); *pl.* communications (P)
comunidad *f.* community
con with (P); **con baño privado** with a private bathroom (6A); **con frecuencia** frequently; **con tal (de) que** provided (that) (7B)
concentración *f.* concentration
concentrar to concentrate; to focus; **concentrarse en** to concentrate in, be concentrated in
concepto concept, idea
concierto concert; **ir** (*irreg.*) **a un concierto** to go to a concert (6B)
conclusión *f.* conclusion
concordancia *gram.* agreement
concurso contest; game show (8B)
condición *f.* condition
condicional *m. gram.* conditional
condimentos condiments
condominio condominium (4B)
conducir *irreg.* to drive; **sacar (qu) la licencia de conducir** to get a driver's license (5A)
conducta conduct, behavior
conductor(a) driver
conectar to connect (5A)
conejo rabbit
conexión *f.* connection
confesar (ie) to confess
confiable trustworthy
confiado/a confident (1B)
confianza trust
confiar (confío) (en) to trust (in) (7B)
confidente confident
confirmar to confirm
conflicto conflict; **resolver (ue) conflictos** to resolve conflicts

confrontación *f.* confrontation
confrontar to confront
confundido/a confused (7A)
confundir to confuse; **confundirse** to get confused (7A)
confusión *f.* confusion
confuso/a confusing
congelación *n. f.* freezing
congelado/a frozen
congelador *m.* freezer
congelar to freeze; **congelarse** to freeze up (*the screen*) (5A)
conjunto outfit; entirety
conmigo with me
conocer (zc) to know, be familiar with (*someone, something*) (3A)
conocido/a acquaintance
conocimiento awareness; *pl.* knowledge
conquista conquest (5B)
conquistar to conquer (5B); to succeed in seducing someone (7B)
consecuencia consequence
conseguir (i, i) (g) to get, obtain (4B); **conseguir + *inf.*** to succeed in (*doing something*) (4B)
consejo piece of advice; *pl.* advice
consenso consent
consentido *n.* whim, fancy
consentido/a indulged, spoiled
conservación *f.* conservation
conservador(a) conservative (1B)
conservar to preserve, conserve (6B)
consideración *f.* consideration
considerar to consider
consistir en to consist of
consolar (ue) to console
constante *adj.* constant
constitución *f.* constitution
constituir (y) to constitute
construir (y) to build (6B)
consultar to consult
consultorio doctor's office (7A)
consumidor(a) *n.* consumer
consumir to eat; to use up
consumo consumption
contabilidad *f.* accounting (P)
contacto contact
contador(a) accountant
contaminación *f.* pollution; **contaminación del agua** water pollution (6B); **contaminación del aire** air pollution (6B)
contaminar to contaminate (6B)
contar (ue) to count (2A); to tell (2A); **contar chismes** to gossip
contener (*like* **tener**) to contain
contenido *s.* contents
contento/a happy (7A)
contestador (*m.*) **automático** answering machine (5A)
contestar to answer

contexto context
contigo *fam. s.* with you
continente *m.* continent (6B)
continuación *f.* continuation; **a continuación** following
continuar (continúo) to continue
continuo/a continuous
contra: en contra opposed
contraer (*like* **traer**) to contract
contrario *n.* opposite, contrary
contraseña password (5A)
contraste *m.* contrast
contratar to hire
contrato lease (4B)
contribución *f.* contribution
contribuir (y) to contribute
controlar to control (8B); to inspect
controvertido/a controversial (8B)
convencer (z) to convince
conversación *f.* conversation
convertir (ie, i) to change; **convertirse en** to turn into
coordinación *f.* coordination
copa (wine) glass (6A)
copiar to copy (5A)
coqueto/a flirtatious (7B)
corazón *m.* heart (7A)
corbata necktie (2B)
cordillera mountain range (6B)
correcto/a correct
corregir (i, i) (j) to correct
correo mail (2A); post office; **correo electrónico** e-mail (5A)
correr to run (1B)
correspondencia correspondence
corresponder to correspond
correspondiente *adj.* corresponding
corriente *n. f.* current; *adj.* current, present; **agua** (*f.* [*but* **el agua**]) **corriente** running water; **cuenta corriente** checking account (8A); **estar** (*irreg.*) **al corriente** to be caught up (*with current events*) (8B)
corrupción *f.* corruption (8B)
cortar(se) to cut (oneself) (7A)
cortés courteous
corto/a short (*except height*) (3A); **de corto plazo** short term (2B); **pantalones** (*m. pl.*) **cortos** shorts (2B)
cosa thing; **poner** (*irreg.*) **las cosas en orden** to put things in order (4B)
cosecha harvest
coser to sew
cosmético/a: cirugía cosmética cosmetic (plastic) surgery
cosmopolita *adj. m., f.* cosmopolitan
costa coast (6B)
costar (ue) to cost (2A)
costilla rib
costo cost, price

costumbre *f.* custom
cotidiano/a daily
creador(a) creative (1B)
crear to create
creativo/a creative
crecer (zc) to grow
creciente *adj.* growing
crédito credit (1A); **tarjeta de crédito** credit card (2B)
creencia belief
creer (y) (que) to think, believe (that) (1B); **creo que le queda un poco grande** I think it's a bit big on you (2B)
crema cream; **queso de crema** cream cheese (3B)
crianza upbringing
crimen *m.* crime; **crimen violento** violent crime (8B)
crisis *f.* crisis
cristiano/a *n., adj.* Christian
criticar (qu) to criticize (8B)
crítico/a critic
cronológico/a chronological
crucero cruise ship
crudo/a raw (3B)
cruel cruel (7B)
cruzar (c) to cross (6A)
cuaderno notebook
cuadra (city) block (6A)
cuadrado/a squared; **metros cuadrados** square meters (4B); **pies** (*m.*) **cuadrados** square feet (4B)
cuadro painting (4B); statistical chart; **de cuadros** plaid (2B)
cual: tal cual just as
¿cuál(es)? what? which? (1B); **¿cuál es su apellido?** what's his/her last name? (P); **¿cuál es su talla?** what size do you** (*form. s.*) wear? (2B); **¿cuál es tu apellido?** what's your (*fam. s.*) last name? (P); **¿cuál es tu campo?** what's your major? (P)
cualquier(a) any
cuando when(ever); **de vez en cuando** once in a while (3B)
¿cuándo? when? (1B)
cuanto: en cuanto as soon as; **en cuanto a** with regard to; **en unos cuantos días** in a few days (1B)
cuánto *pron.* **¿a cuánto sale?** how much is it?; **¿cuánto hay de aquí a... ?** how far is it from here to . . . ? (6A)
¿cuántos/as? how many? (1B); **¿cuántos años cumples?** how many years old are you (*turning*) (*fam. s.*)? (4A); **¿cuántos años tiene... ?** how old is . . . ?; **¿cuántos años tienes?** how old are you (*fam. s.*)?
cuarenta forty (2A)
cuarto *n.* quarter (*of an hour*); fourth; room (4B); **compañero/a de cuarto** roommate

(4B); **menos cuarto** a quarter to (*hour*) (1A); **servicio de cuarto** room service (6A); **y cuarto** a quarter past (*hour*) (1A)
cuarto/a fourth (4A)
cuatro four (1A)
cuatrocientos/as four hundred (2B)
cuatrocientos/as mil four hundred thousand (5B)
cubano/a *n., adj.* Cuban
cubierto/a (*p.p. of* **cubrir**) covered
cubiertos *pl.* silverware (6A)
cubrir (*p.p.* **cubierto/a**) to cover
cuchara spoon (6A)
cuchillo knife (6A)
cuello neck (7A)
cuenta bill (6A); check; **cuenta corriente** checking account (8A); **cuenta de ahorros** savings account (8A); **darse** (*irreg.*) **cuenta de** to realize
cuento story
cuerda cord; **saltar la cuerda** to jump rope
cuerno horn; **ponerle** (*irreg.*) **los cuernos (a alguien)** to be unfaithful to (someone)
cuero leather (2B)
cuerpo body; **partes** (*f. pl.*) **del cuerpo** parts of the body (3A)
cuestión *f.* question
cuidado care
cuidar (de) to take care (of)
culpa fault
culto devotion (*to a god or belief*)
cultura culture
cumpleaños *m. inv.* birthday (4A)
cumplido compliment
cumplir (con) to fulfill, carry out; **¿cuántos años cumples?** how many years old are you (*turning*) (*fam. s.*)? (4A); **cumplir... años** to be . . . old (*on a birthday*) (4A); **cumplir las promesas** to keep one's word
cuñado/a brother-in-law, sister-in-law; *pl.* siblings-in-law
curandero/a healer
curar to cure
cursi tacky (8B); cheesy
cursivo/a: letra (*s.*) **cursiva** italics
curso course
cuyo/a/os/as whose

D

dama lady; **dama de honor** bridesmaid
dañar to hurt, harm (8B)
dañino/a harmful
daño damage, hurt
dar *irreg.* to give (3B); **dar de comer** to feed; **dar la vuelta a** to go around

(*something*); **dar las gracias** to thank; **dar un paseo** to take a walk (4A); **dar una fiesta** to throw a party (4A); **darle escalofríos a alguien** to give someone chills (7B); **darle rabia (a alguien)** to make (someone) angry; **darse cuenta de** to realize; **darse la mano** to shake hands (7B)

dato piece of information; *pl.* data, facts

de *prep.* of (P); from (P); **de compras** shopping (2B); **de corto/largo plazo** short/long term; **de cuadros** plaid (2B); **¿de dónde eres?** where are you (*fam. s.*) from? (P); **de estatura mediana** of medium height (3A); **de ida** one-way (6A); **de ida y vuelta** round-trip (6A); **de la mañana** in the morning (A.M.) (1A); **de la noche** in the evening (night) (P.M.) (1A); **de la tarde** in the afternoon (1A); **de las… hasta las…** from . . . (*hour*) to (*hour*) (1A); **de lunares** polka-dotted (2B); **de nada** you're welcome; **¿de qué tamaño es… ?** what size is . . . ? (4B); **de rayas** striped (2B); **de repente** suddenly; **de venta** for sale (4B); **de vez en cuando** once in a while (3B); **es de…** it's made of . . . (2B); **soy de…** I'm from . . . (P)

debajo de under, below (2A)

deber *n. m.* duty (8B)

deber + *inf.* ought to, should (*do something*); to owe (8A)

debido a due to

débil weak

década decade (5B)

decidido/a decisive

decidir to decide

decir *irreg.* (*p.p.* **dicho/a**) to say (2A)

decisión *f.* decision

declaración *f.* statement

declarar to declare

dedicación *f.* dedication

dedicarse (qu) a to dedicate oneself to

dedo finger (7A); **dedo del pie** toe (7A)

deducción *f.* deduction

deducir (*like* **conducir**) to deduct; to infer

defecto defect

defender (ie) to defend

defensor(a) *n.* defender; *adj.* defensive

definición *f.* definition

definir to define

definitivo/a definitive

deforestación *f.* deforestation (6B)

degustar vinos to go wine tasting (6B)

dejar to leave; **dejar caer** to drop; **dejar de** + *inf.* to stop (*doing something*); **dejar en paz** to leave alone; **dejar perplejo/a (a alguien)** to leave (someone) perplexed; **dejar (una) propina** to leave a tip (6A)

del (*contraction of* **de** + **el**) of/from the

delante de in front of (2A)

delgado/a thin (3A)

delicado/a delicate

delicioso/a delicious

demandar to demand

demás: los/las demás others (4A)

demasiado *adv.* too, too much

demasiado/a *adj.* too much; *pl.* too many

democracia democracy

democrático/a democratic

demostrar (ue) to demonstrate; to show

demostrativo/a demonstrative

denotar to denote; to indicate

densidad *f.* density

denso/a heavy

dentista *m., f.* dentist

dentro (de) in, within, inside; **dentro de poco** soon (1B); **por dentro** within, (on the) inside

depender de to depend on

dependiente/a salesperson (2B)

deporte *m.* sport; **practicar (qu) un deporte** to practice a sport (1A)

deportivo/a *adj.* sport; **programa** (*m.*) **deportivo** sports show (8B)

depositar to deposit (8A)

depresión *f.* **(económica)** (economic) depression (5B)

deprimido/a depressed (5B)

deprimir(se) to depress, become depressed (7A)

derecha *n.* right-hand side; **a la derecha (de)** to the right (of) (2A); **doblar a la derecha** to turn right

derecho *n.* right (*legal*) (8B); law; **derechos humanos** human rights (8B); **seguir (i, i) (g) derecho** to continue straight ahead (6A)

derramar to spill

derrocar (qu) to defeat

derrochador(a) wasteful (8A)

derrotar to defeat

desafío *n.* challenge

desafortunadamente unfortunately

desagradable unpleasant

desahogarse (gu) con to take it out on

desarrollado/a developed; **país** (*m.*) **desarrollado** developed country (8A)

desarrollar to develop

desarrollo (sustenible) (sustainable) development; **país** (*m.*) **en vías de desarrollo** developing country (8A)

desastre *m.* **(natural)** (natural) disaster (5B)

desastroso/a disastrous

desaventajado/a disadvantaged

desayunar to eat/have (for) breakfast (3B)

desayuno breakfast (3B)

descafeinado/a decaffeinated (3B); **café** (*m.*) **descafeinado** decaffeinated coffee

descansar to rest (1A)

descapotable convertible

descargar (gu) to download (5A)

descendiente *m., f.* descendant

descomponer (*like* **poner**) decompose (6B)

desconectar to unplug, disconnect

desconfiado/a untrusting (1B)

desconocido/a unknown

describir (*p.p.* **descrito/a**) to describe (1B)

descripción *f.* description

descubrir (*p.p.* **descubierto**) to discover (5B)

descubrimiento discovery (5B)

descuento discount

descuidar to neglect

desde *prep.* from; **desde la(s)… hasta la(s)…** from . . . until . . . (*time*)

desear to want, desire (1A)

desechable disposable; **producto desechable** disposable product (6B)

desechos *pl.* wastes

desempleo unemployment; **tasa de desempleo** unemployment rate (8A)

deseo *n.* wish, desire

desierto desert (6B)

desilusionado/a disillusioned

desleal disloyal (1B)

desobedecer (zc) to disobey (3A)

despacio/a slow

despedirse (i, i) to say good-bye

despegar (gu) to take off (*plane*)

despejado/a clear; **está despejado** it's clear (*weather*) (1B)

desperdiciar to waste (6B)

desperdicios *pl.* waste (6B)

despertador *m.* alarm clock

despertarse (ie) to wake up (2A)

despreciar to despise (7B)

después *adv.* after; **después de** *prep.* after; **después (de) que** *conj.* after

destacado/a outstanding

destacar (qu) to stand out

destino destination; destiny, fate

destrucción *f.* destruction

detalle *m.* detail

detallista *adj. m., f.* detail-oriented (7B)

detergente *m.* detergent (4B)

determinar to determine

detestar to detest (7B)

detrás de *adv.* behind (2A)

deuda debt (8A); **amortizar (c) una deuda** to pay off a debt (8A)

devoción *f.* devotion

devolver (ue) (*p.p.* **devuelto/a**) to return (*something*)

devoto/a devout

devuelto/a (*p.p. of* **devolver**) returned

día *m.* day (1A); **buenos días** good morning (P); **cada día** every day; **Día de Acción de Gracias** Thanksgiving (4A); **Día de la Madre (del Padre)** Mother's (Father's) Day; **Día de los Enamorados** St. Valentine's Day (4A); **Día de los Reyes Magos** Epiphany (January 6), Day of the Magi; **Día de San Patricio** St. Patrick's Day (4A); **Día de San Valentín** St. Valentine's Day (4A); **día del santo** saint's day; **Día del Trabajo** Labor Day; **día festivo** holiday (4A); **¿en qué día cae... ?** what day is . . . ?; **hoy en día** nowadays; **¿qué día es hoy?** what day is it today? (1A); **todos los días** every day (1A)

diabetes *f.* diabetes

dialecto dialect

diálogo dialogue

diario *m.* newspaper

diario/a *adj.* daily

dibujar to draw (4A)

dibujo drawing

diccionario dictionary

dicho/a (*p.p. of* **decir**) said

diciembre *m.* December (1B)

dictador(a) dictator

dictadura dictatorship

diecinueve nineteen (1A)

dieciocho eighteen (1A)

dieciséis sixteen (1A)

diecisiete seventeen (1A)

diente *m.* tooth; **lavarse los dientes** to brush one's teeth (5A)

dieta *n.* diet

dietético/a: refresco dietético diet soft drink (3B)

diez ten (1A)

diez mil ten thousand (5B)

diferencia difference; **a diferencia de** unlike

diferenciar (de) to be different (from)

diferente (de) different (from/than)

difícil difficult (5B)

dificultad *f.* difficulty

difundirse to diffuse, spread

digestivo/a digestive

digital: cámara digital digital camera (5A)

Dinamarca Denmark

dinamismo dynamism, quality of being dynamic

dinero money (2B); **sacar (qu) dinero** to withdraw money (8A)

dinosaurio dinosaur

dios(a) god, goddess

diplomático/a diplomat

dirección *f.* direction; address (4B)

directo/a direct; straight; **vuelo directo** direct flight (6A)

director(a) director

dirigir (j) to direct; **dirigirse a** to direct oneself toward

disco: disco compacto compact disc; **disco duro** hard drive (5A)

discoteca discotheque (2A)

discreto/a discreet (1B)

discriminación *f.* discrimination (8B)

disculpar to excuse

disculpas: pedir (*irreg.*) **disculpas** to apologize

discusión *f.* discussion

discutir to discuss; to argue (7B)

diseñador(a) designer; **diseñador(a) de sitios** Web site designer

diseñar to draw; to design

disfrutar to enjoy

disponible available

disposición *f.* disposition

dispositivo device

dispuesto/a ready, willing

disquete *m.* diskette (5A)

distancia distance; **mando a distancia** remote control (5A)

distante distant; far away

distinción *f.* distinction

distinguir (g) to distinguish

distinto/a different, distinct

distorsionado/a distorted (8B)

distorsionar to distort

distraer (*like* **traer**) to distract (8B)

distribución *f.* distribution

distrito (federal) (federal) district

diversidad *f.* diversity

diversión *f.*: **ir** (*irreg.*) **a un parque de diversiones** to go to an amusement park (6B)

diverso/a diverse

divertido/a fun (1B)

divertir (ie, i) to entertain (4A); **divertirse** to enjoy oneself (5B)

dividirse to divide

divinidad *f.* divinity, god-like being

divorciado/a divorced (3A)

divorciarse to divorce, get divorced (5B)

divorcio divorce (5B)

doblar to turn (6A); **doblar a la derecha/izquierda** to turn right/left

doble double

doce twelve (1A)

doctor(a) doctor

doctorado doctoral degree

documental *m.* documentary (8B)

documento document; **guardar documentos** to save documents (5A)

dólar *m.* dollar

doler (ue) to hurt, ache (7A)

dolor *m.* pain; **dolor de cabeza** headache

doméstico/a domestic; **aparato doméstico** household appliance (4B); **quehaceres** (*m.*) **domésticos**

household chores (4B); **violencia doméstica** domestic violence (8B)

dominación *f.* domination

dominante dominant

dominar to dominate

domingo Sunday (1A)

dominicano/a *n., adj.* of or from the Dominican Republic

dominio *n.* control

don *m.* gift, skill; *title of respect used with a man's first name*

¿dónde? where? (1B); **¿de dónde eres?** where are you (*fam. s.*) from? (P)

doña *title of respect used with a woman's first name*

dormir (ue, u) to sleep (2A); **dormirse** to fall asleep (5A)

dormitorio bedroom

dos two (1A)

dos mil two thousand (5B)

dos millones two million (5B)

doscientos/as two hundred (2B)

doscientos mil two hundred thousand (5B)

drama *m.* drama (8B)

drástico/a drastic

droga drug

drogadicción *f.* drug addiction (8B)

ducha shower (4B)

ducharse to shower, take a shower (5A)

duda doubt; **sin duda** without a doubt

dudar to doubt (8B)

dudoso/a doubtful

dueño/a owner (4B)

dulce *adj.* sweet (3B); *n. pl.* candy (3B); **pan** (*m.*) **dulce** sweet bread (*Mex.*) (3B)

duración *f.* duration

durante during

durar to last

durmiente: la Bella Durmiente Sleeping Beauty

duro/a hard; firm; **disco duro** hard drive (5A)

DVD: reproductor (*m.*) **de DVD** DVD player (5A); **sacar (qu) un DVD** to rent a DVD (4A)

E

e and (*used instead of* **y** *before words beginning with* **i** *or* **hi**)

echar to throw out (6B); **echar un vistazo** to look over; **echar una siesta** to take a nap

ecología ecology

ecológico/a ecological

economía economy (8A); *s.* economics (P)

económico/a economic; **depresión** (*f.*) **económica** economic depression (5B); **nivel económico** economic level

ecoturismo ecotourism
ecoturista *m., f.* ecotourist
ecoturístico/a *adj.* ecotourist
ecuatoriano/a *n., adj.* Ecuadorean
edad *f.* age (2A); **edad adulta** adulthood
edición *f.* edition
edificio building (P)
educación *f.* education
educar (qu) to educate (8B)
educativo/a educational
efectivo: en efectivo cash (money) (2B)
efecto effect; **efecto invernadero** greenhouse effect (6B)
eficaz (*pl.* **eficaces**) effective
egoísta *adj. m., f.* selfish, egotistical (1B)
ejecutivo/a executive
ejemplificar (qu) to exemplify
ejemplo example; **por ejemplo** for example
ejercer (z) to engage in
ejercicio exercise; **hacer** (*irreg.*) **ejercicio** to exercise (4A); **hacer** (*irreg.*) **ejercicio aeróbico** to do aerobics (4A)
ejército army
el *def. art. m.* the (P); **el/la mayor** the oldest (3A); **el/la menor** the youngest (3A)
él *sub. pron.* he (P); *obj. of prep.* him
elección *f.* election (3B)
electricidad *f.* electricity
eléctrico/a electric; **ingeniería eléctrica** electrical engineering (P); **ingeniero/a eléctrico/a** electrical engineer
electrónica *n. s.* electronics (8A)
electrónico/a *adj.* electronic; **agenda electrónica** electronic organizer, PDA (personal digital assistant) (5A); **aparato electrónico** electronic device (5A); **correo electrónico** e-mail (5A)
elegante elegant; **cenar en un restaurante elegante** to eat in a fancy restaurant (6B)
elegir (i, i) (j) to choose; to elect
elemento element
elevar to elevate, raise
eliminar to eliminate (8B)
ella *sub. pron.* she (P); *obj of prep.* her
ellos/as *sub. pron.* they (P); *obj. of prep.* them
embargo: sin embargo *conj.* however
emborracharse to get drunk
emergencia emergency
emocionado/a moved
emocional emotional (7B)
emocionante exciting (5B)
empanada turnover pie or pastry
emparejar to match
emperador(a) emperor, empress
empezar (ie) (c) to begin (2A); **empezar a** + *inf.* to begin to (*do something*)

empleado/a employee
emplear to use
empleo job; **anuncio de empleo** job ad
empresa company; **administración** (*f.*) **de empresas** business administration (P)
empresarial of or related to business
en in (2A); **en cambio** on the other hand; **en caso de que** in case (7B); **en cuanto** as soon as; **en cuanto a** with regard to; **en punto** on the dot (*time*) (1A); **¿en qué día/mes cae... ?** what day/month is . . . ?; **¿en qué puedo servirle?** how may I help you? (2B); **en unos cuantos días** in a few days (1B)
enamorado/a (de) in love (with) (7A); **Día** (*m.*) **de los Enamorados** St. Valentine's Day (4A)
enamorarse (de) to fall in love (with) (5A)
encantado/a nice to meet you
encantador(a) delightful, charming (7B)
encantar to love (5A); **encantarle** to charm, delight (*someone*); to love (*thing*)
encargarse (de) to take charge (of)
encender (ie) to turn on (5A)
enchufe *m.* connection
encima de on top of (2A)
enclave *m.* enclave
encontrar (ue) to find (2B); **encontrarse con** to get together (meet) with
encuentro *n.* get-together; (chance) meeting (5B)
encuesta survey
energía energy (8A)
enérgico/a energetic (1B)
enero January (1B)
enfermarse to get sick (7A)
enfermedad *f.* sickness; disease
enfermero/a *n.* nurse (7A)
enfermo/a *n.* sick person; *adj.* sick; **estar** (*irreg.*) **enfermo/a** to be sick (7A)
enfoque *m.* focus
enfrentarse a to face, confront
enfrente de across from (2A); in front of (2A)
engañador(a) deceitful (7B)
engañar to deceive (7B); to cheat on (7B)
engañoso/a deceitful
enlace *m.* link (5A)
enlatado/a canned
enojado/a angry (5B)
enojarse to get mad (7A)
enorme enormous
ensalada salad; **ensalada mixta** tossed salad (3B)
enseñanza education
enseñar to teach (1A); to show
entender (ie) to understand (2A)
enterarse de to find out about

entero/a entire, whole; **limpiar la casa entera** to clean the whole house (4B)
enterrar (ie) to bury
entonces then
entrada entrance; ticket
entrante: la semana entrante next week (1B)
entrar (**en** + *place*) to enter (*a place*)
entre between (1B)
entregar (gu) to hand in
entrelazar (c) to intertwine
entrenamiento training
entrenar to train
entretanto meanwhile
entretener (*like* **tener**) to entertain (8B)
entretenido/a amused, entertained, fun (8B)
entretenimiento entertainment, amusement
entrevista interview; **programa** (*m.*) **de entrevistas** talk show (8B)
entrevistar to interview
entrometerse to meddle
entrometido/a nosy (7B); meddlesome (7B)
entusiasmado/a enthusiastic; excited
enviar (envío) to send (5A)
envidia envy; **tenerle** (*irreg.*) **envidia (a alguien)** to be envious (of someone) (7A)
envidioso/a envious
episodio episode
época era, age
equilibrado/a well-balanced
equipado/a equipped
equipaje *m.* luggage (6A); **facturar el equipaje** to check luggage (6A)
equipo team (4A)
equivalente equivalent
equivaler (*like* **valer**) to be equivalent; to be equal
equivocarse (qu) to be mistaken
error *m.* error, mistake
erupción *f.* eruption
escala scale; ladder; layover; **hacer** (*irreg.*) **escala** to make a stopover (6A)
escalada: practicar (qu) la escalada to rappel
escalar montañas to go mountain climbing
escalofríos *pl.* chills; **darle** (*irreg.*) **escalofríos a alguien** to give someone chills (7B)
escandaloso/a scandalous (8B)
escapar (de) to escape (from) (8B)
escasez (*pl.* **escaseces**) *f.* scarcity
escena scene
esclavo/a slave
escoba broom (4B)
escoger (j) to choose
escoliosis *f.* scoliosis

esconder to hide

escondite (*m.*): **jugar (ue) (gu) al escondite** to play hide and seek (5A)

escorpión *m.* scorpion

escribir (*p.p.* **escrito/a**) to write (1B)

escrito/a (*p.p. of* **escribir**) written

escritor(a) writer

escritorio desk (P)

escuchar to listen (to) (1A)

escuela school (2A); **escuela secundaria** high school

escultor(a) sculptor

escultura sculpture

escurrir to drain

ese/a *adj.* that (2B); *pron.* that (one) (2B)

eso *neut. pron.* that (2B)

esos/esas *adj.* those (2B); *pron.* those (ones) (2B)

espacio space

espaguetis *m. pl.* spaghetti (3B)

espalda back (*of a person*) (7A)

espantoso/a scary

español *n. m.* Spanish (*language*) (P)

español(a) *n.* Spaniard; *adj.* Spanish; **tortilla española** *omelette made of eggs, potatoes, and onions* (3B)

espárragos *pl.* asparagus (3B)

especial special

especialidad *f.* specialty

especialista specialist

especialización *f.* specialization, major

especie *f. s.* species; **especies en peligro de extinción** endangered species (6B)

específico/a specific

espectáculo spectacle, sight; show; **mundo de los espectáculos** entertainment industry (8A); **ver** (*irreg.*) **un espectáculo** to see a show (6B)

espejo mirror (4B)

espera: sala de espera waiting room (6A)

esperanza hope (7B)

esperar to hope; to wait for

espinacas *pl.* spinach

espíritu *m.* spirit

esponja sponge (4B)

espontáneo/a spontaneous (7B)

esposo/a husband, wife (3A); *pl.* married couple

espuma foam

esquiar (esquío) (en el agua) to (water) ski (4A)

esquina corner (*street*)

estable *adj.* stable (5B)

establecer (zc) to establish (5B)

establecimiento establishment

estación *f.* season (1B); station; **estación del tren** train station (2A)

estacionar to park

estacionario stationary; **hacer** (*irreg.*) **ciclismo estacionario** to ride a stationary bike (4A)

estadio stadium (2A)

estado *n.* state; condition; **estado físico** physical condition (7A); **Estado Libre Asociado** Free Associated State, Commonwealth; **Estados Unidos** United States

estadounidense *n., adj.* of or from the United States

estallar to explode

estampilla stamp; **coleccionar estampillas** to collect stamps (4A)

estanco tobacco shop (2A)

estante *m.* bookshelf (4B)

estantería *s.* shelves, bookcase

estar *irreg.* to be (P); **está despejado** it's clear (*weather*) (1B); **está lloviendo** it's raining (1B); **está nevando** it's snowing (1B); **está nublado** it's cloudy (1B); **estar a buen precio** to be a good price; **estar a nombre de...** to be in...'s name; **estar al corriente** to be caught up (*with current events*) (8B); **estar celoso/a** to be jealous (7A); **estar de acuerdo** to agree; **estar en (buena) forma** to be in (good) shape (4A); **estar enfermo/a** to be sick (7A); **estar harto/a (de)** to be sick (of), fed up (with); **estar listo/a** to be ready; **estar por** + *inf.* to be about to (*do something*); **estar seguro/a de** to be sure of (8B); **estoy buscando...** I'm looking for... (2B); **sólo estoy mirando** I'm just looking (2B)

estatua statue

estatura: de estatura mediana of medium height (3A)

estatus *m.* status

este *m.* east; **al este de** to the east of (2A)

este/a *adj.* this (2B); *pron.* this (one) (2B); **esta noche** tonight (1B)

este... uh ... (*pause sound*)

estelar: hora estelar prime time

estéreo (portátil) (portable) stereo (5A)

estereotipado/a stereotyped

estereotipo *n.* stereotype

estilo style

estimar to think highly of (7B)

estimulante stimulating (1B)

estimular to stimulate

estímulo stimulus

esto *neut. pron.* this (2B)

estómago stomach (7A)

estos/as *adj.* these (2B); *pron.* these (ones) (2B)

estrategia strategy

estratégico/a strategic

estrecho/a close

estrella star

estrenar to debut

estreno debut

estrés *m.* stress; **sufrir de estrés** to suffer from stress

estresado/a stressed

estricto/a strict

estrofa verse

estructura structure

estructural structural

estudiante *m., f.* student (P)

estudiantil *adj.* student; **centro estudiantil** student center/union (2A); **residencia estudiantil** dormitory (P)

estudiar to study (1A); **estudio...** I study ..., I'm studying ... (P); **¿qué estudias?** what are you (*fam. s.*) studying?

estudio study; *pl.* studies, schooling; **estudios de posgrado** graduate studies; **estudios interdepartamentales** interdisciplinary studies (P); **estudios latinos** Latino studies (P); **estudios sobre el género** gender studies (P)

estudioso/a studious

estufa stove (4B)

estupendo/a stupendous

estupidez *f.* (*pl.* **estupideces**) stupid thing

etapa step, stage

ética *s.* ethics

etiope *adj. m., f.* Ethiopian

etiqueta etiquette

etnicidad *f.* ethnicity

étnico/a ethnic

etnografía ethnography, study of the races of people

Europa Europe (6B)

europeo/a *adj.* European

evaluación *f.* evaluation

evaluar (evalúo) to evaluate

evento event (5B)

evidencia evidence

evidente evident

evitar to avoid

evolucionar to evolve

exacto/a exact

exageración *f.* exaggeration

exagerado/a exaggerated (8B)

exagerar to exaggerate (8B)

examen *m.* test; **examen médico** medical exam (7A)

examinar to examine (7A)

excavación *f.* excavation

excelencia excellence

excelente excellent

excéntrico/a eccentric (1B)

excepción *f.* exception

excepcional exceptional

excepto *adv.* except
excesivo/a excessive
excluir (y) to exclude
exclusivo/a exclusive
excursión *f.* excursión; **ir** (*irreg.*) **de excursión** to go on a hike, go hiking (6B)
excusa excuse
exhibir to exhibit
exigencias *pl.* demands
exigente demanding
exigir (j) to demand
exilado/a exiled
exilio exile
existir to exist
éxito success (5B); **tener** (*irreg.*) **éxito** to be successful (5B)
exitoso/a successful
exótico/a exotic; strange
expandir to expand
expansión *f.* expansion
expectativa expectation; **tener** (*irreg.*) **expectativas** to have expectations
expedir (i, i) to expedite; to issue
experiencia *n.* experience
experimentar to test, try out; to experience
experimento experiment
experto/a *n., adj.* expert
explicación *f.* explanation
explicar (qu) to explain
exploración *f.* exploration (5B)
explorador(a) explorer
explorar to explore (5B)
explosión *f.* explosion
explosivo/a explosive (1B)
explotar to exploit
exponer (*like* **poner**) to expose, report
exportación *f.* exportation; **productos de exportación** export products (8A)
exportador(a) exporter
exportar to export (8A)
expresar to express (7B)
expresión *f.* expression
expulsado/a expelled; thrown out
expulsar to eject
exquisito/a exquisite
extender (ie) to extend
extendido/a extended; **familia extendida** extended family (3A)
extensión *f.* extension
exterior *m.* exterior
extinción *f.* extinction; **especies** (*f. pl.*) **en peligro de extinción** endangered species (6B)
extranjero *n.* abroad; **ir** (*irreg.*) **al extranjero** to go abroad (6A)
extranjero/a *n.* foreigner; *adj.* foreign
extrañar to miss (*someone*) (7B); to be strange

extraño/a strange
extraordinario/a extraordinary
extraviar (extravío) to lose (*something*)
extremista *n., adj. m., f.* extremist
extremo *n.* extreme
extrovertido/a extroverted (1B)

F

fábrica factory (6B)
fabricado/a manufactured; **bienes** (*m. pl.*) **fabricados** manufactured goods (8A)
fabricar (qu) to make
fácil easy
facilidad *f.* ease; facility
facilitar to facilitate, make easy
factor *m.* factor, cause
facturar el equipaje to check luggage (6A)
facultad *f.* department (P)
falda skirt (2B)
falla error
falsificado/a falsified
falso/a false
falta *n.* lack (6B)
faltar to be missing, lacking
familia family (3A); **familia extendida** extended family (3A); **visitar a la familia** to visit one's family (1A)
familiar *adj.* pertaining to a family
famoso/a famous
fanático/a fan, enthusiast
fantástico/a fantastic
farmacéutico/a *n.* pharmacist (7A); *adj.* pharmaceutical; **producto farmacéutico** pharmaceutical product (8A)
farmacia pharmacy (2A)
fascinante fascinating
fascinar to fascinate (5A)
fatal awful
fatiga fatigue
favor *m.* favor; **hacerle** (*irreg.*) **un favor a alguien** to do someone a favor; **por favor** please
favorecer (zc) to favor
favorito/a favorite
fax *m.:* **máquina fax** fax machine (5A)
febrero February (1B)
fecha date (*calendar*) (5B)
federal: distrito federal federal district
felicidad *f.* happiness
felicitación *f.* congratulations; **tarjeta de felicitación** greeting card
felicitar to congratulate
feliz (*pl.* **felices**) happy (5B)
femenino/a feminine
fenómeno phenomenon
feo/a ugly (3A)
fertilizante *m.* fertilizer

festivo: día (*m.*) **festivo** holiday (4A)
fiar (fío) to trust; **(no) ser** (*irreg.*) **de fiar** to be (un)reliable
ficción *f.* fiction; **ciencia ficción** science fiction
fiebre *f.* fever; **tener** (*irreg.*) **fiebre** to have a fever (7A)
fiel faithful (7B)
fiesta party (4A); **dar** (*irreg.*) **una fiesta** to throw a party (4A); **Fiesta de las Luces** Hanukkah (4A); **fiesta de sorpresa** surprise party (4A)
fiestero/a fond of parties
figura figure
fijar to arrange, set up; **fijarse en** to take note of, notice
fijo/a fixed; **precio fijo** fixed price (2B)
filete *m.* fillet
filmación *f.* filming
filmar to film
filosofía philosophy (P)
filosófico/a philosophical
fin *m.* end; **con fines de lucro** for profit; **fin de semana** weekend (1A); **poner** (*irreg.*) **fin a** to end; **por fin** finally
final *m.* end; *adj.* final
finalizar (c) to finalize
finanzas (*pl.*) **personales** personal finances (8A)
firmar to sign (4B)
física *s.* physics (P)
físico/a physicist; **estado físico** physical condition (7A)
flagrante flagrant
flan *m.* flan (*baked custard*) (3B)
flor *f.* flower
florecer (zc) to flourish
florido/a flowery; **Pascua Florida** Easter (4A)
fluvial *adj. related to rivers*
fólico: ácido fólico folic acid
folleto brochure
fondo fund
forestal *adj.* forest
forjar to create
forma form, shape; **estar** (*irreg.*) **en (buena) forma** to be in (good) shape (4A)
formación *f.* formation
formar to form
formato format
foro forum
fortalecer (zc) to strengthen (4A)
fortuna luck
forzado/a forced
fósil *m.* fossil; **combustibles** (*m.*) **fósiles** fossil fuels (6B)
foto picture; **sacar (qu) fotos** to take pictures
foto(grafía) photo(graph); photography
fotografiado/a photographed

fotógrafo/a photographer
fracasar to fail (5B)
fracaso failure (5B)
frágil fragile
francamente frankly
francés *m.* French (*language*) (P)
francés, francesa *n., adj.* French
franja strip (*of land*)
frase *f.* phrase
frecuencia frecuency; **con frecuencia** frequently
frecuente frequent
fregar (ie) (gu) to scrub (4B)
frente a *prep.* in the face of; versus; facing
fresco/a fresh; cool; **hace fresco** it's cool (*weather*) (1B)
frijol *m.* bean
frío *n.*: **hace (mucho) frío** it's (very) cold (*weather*) (1B)
frío/a *adj.* cold
frito/a (*p.p. of* **freír**) fried; **huevo frito** fried egg (3B); **papas fritas** French fries (3B)
frontera border
frustración *f.* frustration
frustrado/a frustrated (7A)
frustrar(se) to frustrate (7A)
fruta fruit (3B); **barra de frutas** fruit bar (3B)
frutería fruit store
fuego fire; **arma** (*f.* [*but* **el arma**]) **de fuego** firearm
fuente *f.* source; fountain
fuera de outside (of); **por fuera** (on the) outside
fuerte strong (4A)
fuerza strength
fumar to smoke
función *f.* function
funcionar to function, work (*machines*) (5A)
fundación *f.* foundation; founding (5B)
fundamental basic
funicular *m.* funicular, railway
furioso/a furious (7A)
fusilamiento shooting
fútbol *m.* soccer (4A); **fútbol americano** football (4A)
futbolista *m., f.* soccer player
futuro *n.* future
futuro/a *adj.* future

G

gallego Galician (*language spoken in the region of Galicia in northwest Spain*)
galleta cookie (3B); **galleta salada** cracker (3B)

gallina hen (9A); **ponérsele** (*irreg.*) **la piel de gallina a alguien** to get goosebumps (7B)
gamba shrimp (*Sp.*)
ganador(a) winner
ganancias *pl.* earnings
ganar to win (4A); to earn (8A)
ganas *pl.*: **tener** (*irreg.*) **ganas de** + *inf.* to feel like (*doing something*)
ganga bargain (2B)
garaje *m.* garage (4B)
garantizar (c) to guarantee
garganta throat (7A)
gárgaras *pl.*: **hacer** (*irreg.*) **gárgaras** to gargle
gasolina gasoline
gastar to spend (2B)
gastos *pl.* expenses (8A)
gastronomía gastronomy, cuisine
gato/a cat (3A)
gemelo/a twin (3A)
gemir (i, i) to groan, moan; to howl
genealógico/a genealogical; **árbol** (*m.*) **genealógico** family tree
generación *f.* generation
general: en general in general
generalización *f.* generalization
generar to generate
genérico/a generic
género gender; genre; **estudios sobre el género** gender studies (P)
generoso/a generous (7B)
gente *f. s.* people; **rozarse (c) con la gente** to mingle with people (4A)
geografía geography
geográfico/a geographical
geometría geometry
gerente *m., f.* manager
gesto gesture
gimnasia: hacer (*irreg.*) **gimnasia** to work out (4A)
gimnasio gymnasium (2A)
globalizado/a globalized
gobernador(a) governor
gobierno government (8B)
golf *m.* golf (4A)
golfo gulf (6B)
gordito/a chubby (3A)
gordo/a fat
gorra baseball cap (2B)
gozar (c) de to enjoy
grabar to record (5A)
gracias thank you; **dar** (*irreg.*) **las gracias** to thank; **Día** (*m.*) **de Acción de Gracias** Thanksgiving (4A)
gracioso/a funny (8B)
graduación *f.* graduation (5B)
graduarse (me gradúo) to graduate (5B)
gramática grammar
gran, grande large, big (1B); great (1B); **creo que le queda un poco grande**

I think it's a bit little on you (2B); **Gran Bretaña** Great Britain
granola: barra de granola granola bar (3B)
grasa *n.* fat
grasoso/a greasy
gratis *adv. inv.* free (*of charge*)
grave serious
gregario/a gregarious (1B)
grifo tap, faucet; **agua** (*m.*) **del grifo** tap water
gris gray (2B)
gritar to yell, shout (9A)
grosero/a rude
grueso/a thick
grupo group
guapo/a handsome (3A); good-looking (3A)
guaraní *m.* Guarani (*indigenous language of Paraguay*)
guardar (documentos) to keep, save (documents) (5A); **guardar(le) rencor (a alguien)** to hold a grudge (against someone) (7B)
guatemalteco/a *n., adj.* Guatemalan
guerra war (5B); **guerra civil** civil war; **Guerra Fría** Cold War
guía *m., f.* guide (*person*); *f.* guidebook
guiar (guío) to guide
guisante *m.* pea
guitarra guitar; **tocar (qu) la guitarra** to play the guitar (1A)
gustar(le) to be pleasing (*to someone*) (3B); **me gusta…** I like …; **te gusta…** you (*fam. s.*) like …
gusto taste; pleasure; **mucho gusto** pleased to meet you (P)

H

haber *irreg.* to have (*aux.*)
habichuela bean
hábil skillful; proficient
habilidad *f.* ability; skill
habitación *f.* (dorm) room (2A)
habitante *m., f.* inhabitant
habitar to live
hablante *m., f.* speaker
hablar to speak (1A)
hacer *irreg.* (*p.p.* **hecho/a**) to make (2A); to do (2A); **hace** + *time* *time* ago (7A); **hace** + *time* + **que** + *present* it's been (*time*) since …; **hace (mucho tiempo)** (a long time) ago; **hace… años** … years ago; **hace buen/mal tiempo** it's good/bad weather (1B); **hace (mucho) calor/frío** it's (very) hot/cold (1B); **hace fresco** it's cool (*weather*) (1B); **hace sol** it's sunny (1B); **hace (mucho) viento** it's (very) windy (1B);

hacer autostop to hitchhike; **hacer camping** to go camping (6B); **hacer ciclismo estacionario** to ride a stationary bike (4A); **hacer clic** to click (5A); **hacer cola** to stand in line (6A); **hacer ejercicio** to exercise (4A); **hacer ejercicio aeróbico** to do aerobics (4A); **hacer el salto bungee** to bungee jump (6B); **hacer escala** to make a stopover (*on a flight*) (6A); **hacer gárgaras** to gargle; **hacer gimnasia** to work out (4A); **hacer kayak** to kayak (6B); **hacer la cama** to make the bed (4B); **hacer la maleta** to pack a suitcase (6A); **hacer las paces con** to make up with (7B); **hacer novillos** to skip/cut school (5A); **hacer rafting** to go rafting (6B); **hacer trucos** to do tricks; **hacer un viaje** to take a trip (6A); **hacer una búsqueda** to do a search (5A); **hacer** *zapping* to channel surf (5A); **hacerle un favor a alguien** to do someone a favor; **hacerse cargo de** to take charge (*of something*); **¿qué carrera haces?** what's your (*fam. s.*) major? (P)

hacia toward

hambre *f.* (*but* **el hambre**) hunger (8B); **tener** (*irreg.*) **hambre** to be hungry

hamburguesa hamburger (3B)

harto/a: estar (*irreg.*) **harto/a** (**de**) to be sick (of), fed up (with)

hasta *prep.* until; **de las… hasta las…** from (*hour*) to (*hour*) (1A); **hasta luego** until (see you) later; **hasta que** *conj.* until

hay (*from* **haber**): **(no) hay** there is/are (not) (P); **hay que** + *inf.* it's necessary + *inf.* (2B)

hechicero/a *adj.* magic; bewitching

hecho *n.* fact; **de hecho** in fact

hecho/a (*p.p. of* **hacer**) made; done

helado *n.* ice cream (3B); **té** (*m.*) **helado** iced tea (3B)

hemisferio hemisphere

hepatitis *f.* hepatitis

heredar to inherit

herencia heritage; inheritance

herida *n.* wound

hermanastro/a stepbrother, stepsister (3A)

hermandad (*f.*) **de mujeres** sorority

hermano/a brother, sister (3A); **medio/a hermano/a** half brother, half sister (3A); *m. pl.* siblings

herramienta tool

hídrico/a of or related to water

hierba herb; grass

hígado liver (7A)

hijastro/a stepson, stepdaughter (3A)

hijo/a son, daughter (3A); **hijo/a único/a** only child (3A); *m. pl.* children

hipertensión *f.* hypertension

hipoteca mortgage (8A); **amortizar (c) una hipoteca** to pay off a mortgage (8A)

hipotético/a hypothetical

hispano/a *n., adj.* Hispanic

Hispanoamérica Latin America

hispanohablante *m., f.* Spanish speaker

historia story; history (P)

histórico/a historical

historieta anecdote; short story; tale

hogar *m.* home (4B)

hoja leaf; sheet of paper; **hoja de papel aparte** separate piece of paper

¡hola! hello! hi! (P)

hombre *m.* man (P); **hombre de negocios** businessman

hombro shoulder (7A)

homenaje *m.* homage

homicidio homicide

homogéneo/a homogeneous

honesto/a honest, sincere (1B)

honor *m.* honor

hora hour; time; **a la misma hora** at the same time (1A); **¿a qué hora… ?** at what time … ? (1A); when … ? (1A); **con dos horas de anticipación** two hours ahead of time; **¿qué hora es?** what time is it? (1A); **¿tiene Ud. la hora?** do you (*form. s.*) have the time? (1A); **¿tienes la hora?** do you (*fam. s.*) have the time? (1A)

horario schedule (1A)

hormiga ant

horno stove (4B); **al horno** baked (3B)

horrible terrible, horrible

hospital *m.* hospital (2A)

hostilidad *f.* hostility

hotel *m.* hotel (2A)

hoy en día nowadays; **¿qué día es hoy?** what day is today? (1A)

hueso bone (7A)

huésped(a) guest

huevo egg (3B); **huevo frito** fried egg (3B); **huevos revueltos** scrambled eggs (3B)

humanidades *f., pl.* humanities (P)

humano human

humano/a *adj.* human; **derechos humanos** human rights (8B)

humilde humble (1B)

humillación *f.* humiliation

humo smoke

humor *m.* humor; mood; **estar** (*irreg.*) **de buen/mal humor** to be in a good/bad mood

huracán *m.* hurricane (5B)

I

Ibérico/a: Península Ibérica Iberian Peninsula

ida: de ida one-way (6A); **de ida y vuelta** round-trip (6A)

idea idea; **es buena idea** it's a good idea (2B)

identificar (qu) to identify; **identificarse con** to identify with

idioma *m.* language (P)

iglesia church (2A)

igual equal; **al igual que** just like

igualmente likewise, same here (P)

ilegal illegal

imagen *f.* (*pl.* **imágenes**) image (8B)

imaginar to imagine

imaginario/a imaginary

imaginativo/a imaginative (1B)

impaciente impatient (5A)

impactar to have an impact

impacto *n.* impact

imperfecto *gram.* imperfect (tense)

imperio empire

impermeable *m.* raincoat (2B)

importado/a *n.* imported

importancia importance

importante important

importar to matter; to be important (5A); to import (8A); **importarle un pito** not to care about

imposible impossible; **es imposible** it's impossible (8B)

impresión *f.* impression

imprimir to print

impuesto *n.* tax (8B)

impulsivo/a impulsive

impulso impulse

inadecuado/a inadequate

inanimado/a inanimate

inapropiado/a inappropriate (8B)

inca *n. m., f.* Inca

incaico/a Incan

incendio fire; **seguro contra incendios** fire insurance (8A)

incertidumbre *f.* uncertainty

incluir (y) to include

incluso/a including

incompleto/a incomplete

incontrolable uncontrollable

inconveniente inconvenient

incorporar to incorporate

increíble incredible, unbelievable

indefinido/a indefinite

independencia independence (5B)

independiente independent

independizarse (c) to become independent

indicador *m.* indicator

indicar (qu) to indicate

indiferencia indifference

indiferente indifferent (1B)
indígena *n. m., f.* indigenous (person);
  adj. m., f. indigenous, native
indigenismo indigenism
indio/a *n.* Indian
indirecto/a indirect
indiscreto indiscreet (1B)
indispensable essential
indómito/a untamed
indudablemente undoubtedly
industria industry
inesperado/a unexpected
inestabilidad *f.* instability
inestable unstable
infarto (cardíaco) heart attack
infiel *adj. m., f.* unfaithful
infierno hell
infinitivo/a *gram.* infinitive
inflación *f.* inflation (8A)
inflexión *f.* inflection
influencia influence
influir (y) en to influence
información *f.* information
informado/a informed
informarse to inform oneself (8B)
informática computer science (P);
  information technology (8A)
informativo/a informative (8B)
informe *m.* report
infraestructura infrastructure
infringir (j) to infringe
infundado/a unfounded
ingeniería (civil/eléctrica/mecánica)
  (civil/electrical/mechanical)
  engineering (P)
**ingeniero/a (civil, eléctrico/a,
  mecánico/a)** (civil, electrical,
  mechanical) engineer
ingenuo/a naive (1B)
Inglaterra England
inglés *n. m.* English (*language*) (P)
inglés, inglesa *adj.* English
ingresos *pl.* income (8A)
inicial *adj.* initial
iniciar to initiate, begin
inmediatamente immediately
inmigración *f.* **(ilegal)** (illegal)
  immigration (8B)
inmigrante *m., f.* immigrant (5B)
inmobiliaria: agente (*m., f.*) **de
  inmobiliaria** real estate agent
inmóvil unmoving
inmunodeficiencia: SIDA (síndrome
  [*m.*] **de inmunodeficiencia adquirida)**
  AIDS (Acquired Immune Deficiency
  Syndrome) (8B)
inodoro toilet (4B)
inolvidable unforgettable
inquieto/a restless
inquilino/a tenant (4B)
inseguridad *f.* insecurity

inseguro/a insecure
insistir en to insist on (8B)
insolación *f.* heat stroke
inspirar to inspire
instalaciones *f. pl.* facilities
instalar to install; **instalarse en** to settle
  into (*a house*)
instantáneo/a: mensajero instantáneo
  instant messenger
instituto institute
instrucción *f.* instruction
insuficiente insufficient
integración *f.* integration
integridad *f.* integrity
inteligencia intelligence
inteligente intelligent (1B)
intención *f.* intention
intenso/a intense
interacción *f.* interaction
intercambiar to exchange
intercambio *n.* exchange
**interdepartamental: estudios
  interdepartamentales** interdisciplinary
  studies (P)
interés *m.* interest; *pl.* interest (*finance*)
  (8A); **tipos de interés** interest
  rates (8A)
interesante interesting (1B)
interesar to interest, be
  interesting (5A)
interior *adj.* indoor (6B)
internacional international; **noticias**
  (*pl.*) **internacionales** international
  news (8B)
internar to confine
Internet *m.* Internet (5A)
interno/a internal; **órgano interno**
  internal organ (7A)
interpretación *f.* interpretation
interpretar to interpret, explain
interrogativo/a interrogative
intimidad *f.* intimacy
íntimo/a intimate, private; close
  (*relationship*) (7B)
intoxicante poisonous; intoxicating
introducir (zc) to introduce
introvertido/a introverted (1B)
inundación *f.* flood (5B)
invadir to invade (5B)
invasión *f.* invasion (5B)
inventar to invent
invernadero greenhouse; **efecto
  invernadero** greenhouse
  effect (6B)
inversión *f.* investment (8A)
invertir (ie, i) to invest (8A)
investigación *f.* research
investigador(a) researcher
investigar (gu) to research
invierno winter (1B)
invitado/a guest

invitar to invite
inyección *f.* injection; **ponerle** (*irreg.*)
  una inyección (a alguien) to give
  (someone) a shot (7A)
ir *irreg.* to go (1B); **ir a** + *inf.* to be going
  to (*do something*) (1B); **ir a un
  concierto** to go to a concert (6B); **ir a
  un parque de diversiones** to go to an
  amusement park (6B); **ir al cine** to go
  to the movies; **ir al extranjero** to go
  abroad (6A); **ir de excursión** to go on a
  hike, go hiking (6B)
irresponsable irresponsible (8A)
irritado/a irritated (7A)
irritante irritating, annoying
irritar(se) to irritate (get irritated) (7A)
isla island (6B)
italiano/a *n., adj.* Italian
izquierda *n.* left-hand side; **a la izquierda
  de** to the left of (2A); **doblar a la
  izquierda** to turn left

J

jabón *m.* soap (4B)
jamás never, not ever (3B)
jamón *m.* ham (3B)
japonés, japonesa *n., adj.* Japanese
jarabe *m.* **(para la tos)** (cough) syrup
jardín *m.* garden (4B)
jefe/a boss, chief
jerga slang, jargon
jitomate *m.* tomato (*Mex.*)
jornada work day; **de media jornada**
  part-time
joven *n. m., f.* (*pl.* **jóvenes**) young person
  (5A); *adj.* young
joya jewel
joyería jewelry store
jubilado/a retired
jubilarse to retire
judías verdes green beans (3B)
judío/a: pascua de los judíos
  Passover (4A)
juego game (4A); **juego de charadas**
  charades
jueves *m. inv.* Thursday (1A)
juez(a) (*m. pl.* **jueces**) judge
jugador(a) player
jugar (ue) (gu) to play (2A); **jugar a los
  videojuegos** to play video games (5A);
  jugar al escondite to play hide and
  seek (5A)
jugo juice (3B)
julio July (1B)
junio June (1B)
junto/a together
jurado panel of judges
jurar to swear (*an oath*)
justificar (qu) to justify
justo/a *adj.* fair

juvenil *adj.* youth
juventud *f.* youth (5A)
juzgar (gu) to judge

K

kayak: hacer (*irreg.*) **kayak** to kayak (6B)
kilo(grama) *m.* kilogram
kilómetro kilometer (4A)

L

la *f. def. art.* the (P); *d.o.* her, it, you (*f. form. s.*); **a la una** at one o'clock (1A); **es la una** it's one o'clock (1A)
labio lip
laboratorio laboratory
lacio/a: pelo lacio straight hair (3A)
lácteo/a dairy; **producto lácteo** dairy product (3B)
lado *n.* side; **al lado de** beside (2A)
ladrillo brick
lago lake (6B)
lámpara lamp (4A)
lana wool (2B)
langosta lobster (3B)
lanza: punta de lanza spearhead
lanzar (c) to throw, fling; **lanzarse** to break into (*career*)
lápiz *m.* (*pl.* **lápices**) pencil (P)
largo/a long (3A); **a lo largo de** throughout; **de largo plazo** long-term
las *f. pl.* the (P); *d.o.* you (*f. form. pl.*); them; **a las…** at … o'clock (1A)
lástima compassion; shame; **lástima que…** too bad that …
lastimar(se) to hurt (oneself) (7A)
lata de aluminio aluminum can (6B)
latino/a *adj.* Latino, Latina; **estudios latinos** Latino studies (P)
Latinoamérica Latin America
latinoamericano/a *n., adj.* Latin American
lavabo sink (bathroom) (4B)
lavadora washing machine (4B)
lavaplatos *m. inv.* dishwasher (4B)
lavar to wash (4B); **lavarse los dientes** to brush one's teeth (5A)
le *i.o. s.* to/for him, her, it, you (*form. s.*)
leal loyal (1B)
lealtad *f.* loyalty
lección *f.* lesson
leche *f.* milk (3B); **café** (*m.*) **con leche** coffee with milk
lechuga lettuce (3B)
lector(a) reader
lectura *n.* reading
leer (y) to read (1B)
legalmente legally

legítimo/a legitimate
lejano/a distant, far
lejía *n.* bleach (4B)
lejos de *adv.* far away from (2A)
lengua tongue; language (P); **lengua extranjera** foreign language; **sacar (qu) la lengua** to stick out one's tongue (7A); **trabársele la lengua a alguien** to get tongue-tied (7B)
lenguaje *m.* language
lentes *m. pl.* glasses (*vision*)
lento/a slow
les *i.o. pl.* to/for you (*form. pl.*), them
letra letter (*of the alphabet*); lyrics; **letra cursiva** italics; *pl.* humanities
levantar to lift, raise up; **levantar pesas** to lift weights (4A); **levantarse** to get up (5A)
léxico vocabulary
ley *f.* law (8B)
leyenda legend
liberal liberal (1B)
libertad *f.* liberty, freedom (8B)
libertino/a libertine
libra pound (*weight*)
libre free (unfettered); **al aire libre** outdoors (6B); **Estado Libre Asociado** Free Associated State, Commonwealth; **ratos libres** free time (4A)
librería bookstore (P)
libro book (P)
licencia license; **sacar (qu) la licencia de conducir** to get a driver's license (5A)
licor *m.* liquor
ligarse con to get together with
ligero/a *adj.* light
limitar to limit
límite *m.* limit
limón *m.* lemon (3B)
limonada lemonade
limpiar to clean; **limpiar la casa (entera)** to clean the (whole) house (4B)
limpieza *n.* cleaning; cleanliness; **producto de limpieza** cleaning product (4B)
lindo/a pretty
línea line; **línea aérea** airline; **patinar en línea** to inline skate (4A)
lingüístico/a linguistic
lío problem; **meterse en líos** to get into trouble (5A)
lista list
listo/a ready (1B); clever, smart (2B); **estar** (*irreg.*) **listo/a** to be ready; **ser** (*irreg.*) **listo/a** to be clever
literatura literature (P)
llamada *n.* (telephone) call
llamar to call (1A); **¿cómo se llama (él/ella)?** what's his/her name? (P);

¿cómo te llamas? what's your (*fam. s.*) name? (P); **llamar por teléfono** to call on the phone (1A); **llamarse** to be called; **me llamo…** my name is … (P)
llanura flatland, prairie (6B)
llave *n. f.* key
llegada arrival
llegar (gu) to arrive; **¿cómo se llega a… ?** how do you get to … ? (6A); **llegar a tiempo** to arrive on time (1A)
llenar to fill
lleno/a full
llevar to take, carry (1A); to wear (*clothing*) (2B); **llevar… créditos** to have … credits (1A); **llevarse bien/mal con** to get along well/poorly with (5A)
llorar to cry (7A)
llover (ue) to rain; **está lloviendo** it's raining (1B); **llueve** it's raining (1B)
lluvia rain
lluvioso/a rainy; **bosque** (*m.*) **lluvioso** rain forest (6B)
lo *d.o.* him, it, you (*m. form. s.*); **lo que** what, that which (1B)
local local; **noticias locales** local news (8B)
localizador *m.* pager
localizarse (c) to be located
loco/a mad, crazy
lógico/a logical
lograr + *inf.* to succeed (*in doing something*)
lomo loin
longitud *f.* duration
los *def. art. m. pl.* the (P); *d.o.* them, you (*form. pl.*); **los años veinte (treinta)** the twenties (thirties) (5B); **los/lás demás** others (4A)
lucha *n.* fight; struggle
lucro: con fines de lucro for profit
luego then; **hasta luego** until (see you) later
lugar *m.* place (2A)
lujo luxury; **hotel** (*m.*) **de lujo** luxury hotel (6A)
lunar *m.:* **de lunares** polka-dotted (2B)
lunes *m. inv.* Monday (1A); **el (los) lunes** on Monday(s) (1A)
luz *f.* (*pl.* **luces**) light (P); electricity; **Fiesta de las Luces** Hanukkah (4A)

M

madera wood (8A)
madrastra stepmother (3A)
madre *f.* mother (3A); **madre soltera** single mother (3A)
madrina godmother
madrugada early morning hours

maestría *n.* mastery, skill; master's degree

maestro/a (de primaria, secundaria) (elementary, high school) teacher

magia *n.* magic

magos *pl.*: **los Reyes** (*m.*) **Magos** the Magi (Three Wise Men); **Día** (*m.*) **de los Reyes Magos** Epiphany (January 6), Day of the Magi

maíz *m.* corn (3B); **palomitas de maíz** popcorn (3B); **tortilla de maíz** corn tortilla (3B)

mal, malo/a *adj.* bad (1B); sick (2B); **caerle** (*irreg.*) **mal a alguien** to dislike someone (5A); **hace mal tiempo** it's bad weather (1B); **llevarse mal con** to get along poorly with (5A); **manejar mal** to manage poorly (8A); **pasarlo mal** to have a bad time (4A); **portarse mal** to misbehave (5A); **quedarle mal** to fit poorly

maldad *n. f.* evil

maleta suitcase; **hacer** (*irreg.*) **la maleta** to pack a suitcase (6A)

maletero skycap, porter (6A)

maletín *m.* briefcase

malicioso/a malicious (1B)

mamá mom; mother

mandar to send; to order (5A)

mandato *n.* command

mando a distancia remote control (5A)

mandón, mandona bossy (7B)

manejar (bien/mal) to manage (well/poorly) (8A)

manera manner, way

manifestación *f.* demonstration (8B)

manifestar(se) (ie) to manifest, show

manipular to manipulate (8B)

mano *f.* hand (7A); **darse** (*irreg.*) **la mano** to shake hands (7B)

mansión *f.* mansion

mantel *m.* tablecloth

mantener (*like* **tener**) to maintain; to support; **mantenerse a raya** to keep (*something*) away

mantequilla butter (3B); **mantequilla de cacahuete** peanut butter (3B)

manual *m.* workbook

manufacturado/a manufactured

manzana apple (3B); city block (6A)

mañana *n.* morning; *adv.* tomorrow (1A); **de la mañana** in the morning (A.M.) (1A); **hasta mañana** until (see you) tomorrow; **pasado mañana** the day after tomorrow (1B); **por la mañana** in the morning (1A)

mapa *m.* map (6A)

máquina machine; **máquina fax** fax machine (5A)

mar *m., f.* sea, ocean (6B)

maravilloso/a marvelous

marca brand name (2B)

marcar (qu) to mark

mareado/a nauseated, dizzy

marearse to get nauseated, sick (*boat, car, plane*) (6A)

marido husband (3A)

marino/a *adj.* marine

mariscos *pl.* shellfish (3B); seafood (3B)

marrón *adj. m., f.* brown (2B)

martes *m. inv.* Tuesday (1A); **Martes de Carnaval** Mardi Gras (4A)

marzo March (1B)

más *adv.* more; **cada vez más** more and more; **es más** what's more; **más... que** more . . . than (3A)

mascota *n.* pet (3A)

masculino/a masculine

matar to kill

matemáticas mathematics (P)

materia subject (*school*) (P)

material *m.* material

materialista *m., f.* materialist

materno/a maternal (3A)

matrícula tuition

matrimonial: cama matrimonial queen bed (4B)

matrimonio matrimony, marriage (5B)

mayo May (1B)

mayor older (3A); **el/la mayor** the oldest

mayoría majority

me *d.o.* me; *i.o.* to/for me; *refl. pron.* myself; **me gusta...** I like . . . (1A); **me llamo** my name is (P); **me parece(n)...** it/that seems . . . to me; **¿me podría traer... ?** could you (*form. s.*) bring me . . . ? (6A)

mecánico/a mechanic; **ingeniería mecánica** mechanical engineering (P); **ingeniero/a mecánico/a** a mechanical engineer

media *n.* average

mediano/a *adj.* medium; average (2B); **de estatura mediana** of medium height (3A)

medianoche *f.* midnight (1A); **a medianoche** at midnight

medias *pl.* stockings (2B); pantyhose (2B)

medicación *f.* medication

medicina medicine (7A)

médico/a *n.* doctor (7A); *adj.* medical; **examen** (*m.*) **médico** medical exam (7A); **seguro médico** medical insurance (8A); **servicios médicos** medical services

medidas *pl.* measures

medio *n. s.* means, middle; **medio ambiente** environment (6B); **medios de comunicación** media (8B)

medio/a *adj.* half; middle; **clase** (*f.*) **media** middle class; **medio/a hermano/a** half

brother/sister (3A); **media pensión** room and one other meal (usually breakfast) (6A); **y media** half past (*hour*) (1A)

medioambiental environmental

mediodía *m.* noon, midday (1A); **a mediodía** at noon

meditar to meditate (4A)

mediterráneo/a *adj.* Mediterranean

mejillas cheeks (3A)

mejor better (3A)

mejorar to improve

melodrama *m.* melodrama

membresía membership

memoria memory

memorizar (c) to memorize (1A)

mencionar to mention

mendigo/a beggar

menor younger (3A); **el/la menor** the youngest

menos less; least; **a menos que** *conj.* unless (7B); **menos cuarto** a quarter to (*hour*) (1A); **menos... que** less . . . than (3A); **por lo menos** at least

mensaje *m.* message (5A)

mensajero/a messenger; **mensajero instantáneo** instant messenger

mensual monthly; **presupuesto mensual** monthly budget (8A)

mentalidad *f.* mentality

mente *f.* mind

mentir (ie, i) to lie (4B)

mentira lie

mentiroso/a liar (5A)

mentón *m.* chin (3A)

menú *m.* menu (6A)

menudo: a menudo often

mercadeo marketing

mercado market (2A)

mercancías *pl.* goods

merecer (zc) to deserve (3A)

merendar (ie) to snack (3B)

meridional southern

merienda *n.* snack (3B)

mérito merit

mermelada jam (3B)

mes *m.* month (1B); **cada mes** each month; **¿en qué mes cae... ?** ¿ what month is . . . ?; **una vez al mes** once a month (1B)

mesa table (P)

mesero/a waiter, waitress (6A)

meseta plateau (6B)

mesita end table (4B)

mestizaje *m.* mixing of races

mestizo/a *n.* mixed-race person

meta goal; **alcanzar (c) una meta** to reach a goal

metales (*m.*) **preciosos** precious metals (8A)

meteorológico/a meteorological

meterse to pick a fight; **meterse en líos** to get into trouble (5A)
metódico/a methodical (1B)
metro meter (4A); **metros cuadrados** square meters (4B)
mexicano/a *n., adj.* Mexican
mexicanoamericano/a *n., adj.* Mexican-American
mezcla mixture
mezquita mosque
mí *obj. of prep.* (4B)
mi(s) *poss.* my (4B); **mi apellido es…** my last name is . . . (P); **mi nombre es…** my name is . . . (P)
microondas *m. s.* microwave (4B)
microscopio microscope
miedo fear; **tener(le)** (*irreg.*) **miedo (a alguien)** to be afraid (of someone) (7A)
miembro/a member
mientras *adv.* meanwhile (5B); **mientras que** *conj.* while
miércoles *m. inv.* Wednesday (1A)
migración *f.* migration (5B)
migratorio/a migratory
mil thousand, one thousand (2B)
militar *adj.* military
milla mile (4A)
millón *m.* (**de**) million (5B)
millonario millionaire
mina *n.* mine
miniserie *f.* miniseries
minoría minority
minoritario/a *adj.* minority
minuto minute
mío/a/os/as *poss.* my, (of) mine (2B)
mirar to look (at), watch (1A); **sólo estoy mirando** I'm just looking (2B)
misceláneo/a miscellaneous
misión *f.* mission
mismo/a same; self; **a la misma hora** at the same time (1A)
misterio mystery
mitad *f.* half
mito myth
mitología mythology
mixto/a mixed; **ensalada mixta** tossed salad (3B)
mochila backpack (P)
moda fashion (2B); **de moda** in style
modelo model; *m., f.* model (*fashion*)
módem *m.* modem (5A)
modernización *f.* modernization
moderno/a modern
modesto/a modest
mojado/a wet
molestar to bother (3A)
momento moment, instant
moneda currency; coin; **coleccionar monedas** to collect coins (4A)
monitor *m.* monitor (5A)

monótono/a monotonous
montaña mountain (6B); **escalar montañas** to go mountain climbing (6B)
montar a caballo to go horseback riding (6B)
morado/a purple (2B)
mórbido/a morbid
moreno/a dark-skinned (3A)
morir(se) (**ue, u**) (*p.p.* **muerto/a**) to die (4B); **ya murió** he/she already died (3A)
moro/a *n.* Moor; *adj.* Moorish
morrón *m.* blow, bang, hit
mortalidad *f.* mortality
mosquetero: los Tres Mosqueteros The Three Musketeers
mostrador *m.* counter (*kitchen, etc.*)
mostrar (**ue**) to show (*something to someone*)
motivo motive, reason
motor *m.* engine, motor
mover (**ue**) to move (around); **moverse** to move (*houses*)
móvil: teléfono móvil cell phone
movimiento movement
mozo bellhop
muchacho/a boy, girl
mucho *adv.* a lot, much (1A)
mucho/a *adj.* much, a lot (of) (P); **hace mucho calor** it's very hot (1B); **hace mucho frío** it's very cold (1B); **hace mucho viento** it's very windy (1B); **mucho gusto** pleased to meet you (P); **pasar mucho tiempo** to spend a lot of time (1A)
mudanza move (5B)
mudarse to move (*to another house*) (5B)
mueble *m.* piece of furniture (4B)
muerte *f.* death (5B); **pena de muerte** death penalty
muerto/a (*p.p. of* **morir**) dead
muestra example
mujer *f.* woman (P); wife (3A); **hermandad** (*f.*) **de mujeres,** sorority; **mujer de negocios** businesswoman; **mujer policía** policewoman; **mujer político** (female) politician; **mujer soldado** (female) soldier
mujeriego *n.* womanizer
muleta crutch
multa fee, fine
multinacional multinational
mundial *adj.* world
mundo world; **mundo de los espectáculos** entertainment industry (8A)
muñeca wrist; doll (5A)
muro wall
músculo muscle
museo museum; **visitar un museo** to visit a museum (4A)

música music (P)
músico/a musician
musulmán, musulmana *n., adj.* Muslim
muy very (1A)

N

nacer (**zc**) to be born (5B)
nacido/a born; **recién nacido/a** newborn baby (5B)
nacimiento birth (5B)
nación *f.* nation
nacional national; **noticias** (*pl.*) **nacionales** national news (8B); **producto nacional bruto** gross national product
nada nothing; none (3B); **de nada** you're welcome
nadador(a) swimmer
nadar to swim (4A)
nadie nobody, not anybody (3B)
nahuatl *m.* Nahuatl (*language of the Aztecs*)
naranja orange (*fruit*) (3B)
nariz *f.* nose (3A); **tener** (*irreg.*) **la nariz tapada** to have a stuffed-up nose (7A)
narración *f.* narration
narrar to narrate
natación *f.* swimming (4A)
nativo/a *adj.* native, indigenous
natural *adj.* natural; **ciencias naturales** natural sciences (P); **desastre** (*m.*) **natural** natural disaster (5B); **recursos naturales** natural resources (6B)
naturaleza nature (6B)
navegar (**gu**) (**la red**) to navigate; to surf (the Web) (1A); **navegar en barco** to sail (4A)
Navidad *f.* Christmas (4A)
navideño/a *adj.* Christmas
necesario/a necessary; **es necesario** it's necessary (2B)
necesidad *f.* necessity
necesitar to need (1A); **necesitar** + *inf.* to need to (*do something*)
neerlandés, neerlandesa *adj.* Dutch
negación *f.* negation
negar (**ie**) (**gu**) to deny (8B)
negativo/a *adj.* negative
negocio business; **hombre** (*m.*) **de negocios** businessman; **mujer** (*f.*) **de negocios** businesswoman
negrita: en negrita in boldface type
negro/a *adj.* black (2B)
nervioso/a nervous (5B)
nevar (**ie**) to snow; **está nevando** it's snowing (1B); **nieva** it's snowing (1B)
nevera freezer (4B)
ni… ni neither . . . nor
nieto/a grandson, granddaughter (3A); *pl.* grandchildren

ningún, ninguno/a *adj.* no, not any (3B)

ninguno/a *pron.* none, not any (3B)

niñero/a baby-sitter; nanny (5A)

niñez *f.* (*pl.* **niñeces**) childhood (5A)

niño/a child; boy, girl (5A)

nivel *m.* level; **nivel económico** economic level

no no; not; **no aguantar** not to be able to stand, put up with (7B); **no es cierto** it's not true (8B); **no es posible** it's not possible (8B); **no es seguro/a** it's not sure (8B); **no es verdad** it's not true (8B); **no obstante** nevertheless; **no ser de fiar** to be unreliable; **todavía no sé** I still don't know (P); **ya no** no longer

noche *f.* night; **buenas noches** good night (P); **de la noche** in the evening (night); **esta noche** tonight (1B); **Noche Vieja** New Year's Eve (4A); **por la noche** in the evening (night); **todas las noches** every night (1A)

Nochebuena Christmas Eve (4A)

nocivo/a unhealthy, noxious

nocturno/a *adj.* nighttime

nombrar to name

nombre *m.* name; **estar** (*irreg.*) **a nombre de...** to be in . . . 's name; **mi nombre es...** my name is . . . (P)

nominar to nominate

norma norm

norte *m.* north; **al norte de** to the north of (2A)

Norteamérica North America (6B)

norteamericano/a *n., adj.* North American (*from the United States* or Canada)

nos *d.o.* us; *i.o.* to/for us; *refl. pron.* ourselves; **nos vemos** see you around

nosotros/as *sub. pron.* we (P); *obj. of prep.* us

nostálgico/a nostalgic (7B)

nota note

notable good

notar to note, notice

noticia piece of news; *pl.* news (8B); **noticias (internacionales, locales, nacionales)** (international, local, national) news (8B)

noticiero newscast, news show (8B)

novecientos/as nine hundred (2B)

novecientos mil nine hundred thousand (5B)

novedoso/a *adj.* novel

novela *n.* novel (1B)

novelista *m., f.* novelist

noventa ninety (2A)

noviazgo engagement (7B)

noviembre November (1B)

novillos: hacer (*irreg.*) **novillos** to skip/cut school (5A)

novio/a boyfriend, girlfriend; bride, groom (5B)

nube *f.* cloud

nublado/a cloudy; **está nublado** it's cloudy (1B)

nublar to darken

nudista *adj. m., f.* nudist

nuestro/a/os/as *poss.* our (1A)

nueve nine (1A)

nuevo/a new

nuez (*pl.* **nueces**) nut

número number (1A); **¿qué número calza?** what size shoe do you (*form. s.*) wear? (2B)

numeroso/a numerous

nunca never, not ever; **casi nunca** almost never

O

o or; **o... o** either . . . or

ó or (*used between two numbers to avoid confusion with zero*)

obedecer (zc) to obey (3A)

obediencia obedience

obediente obedient (5A)

objetividad *f.* objectivity

objetivo/a objective (8B)

objeto *n.* object

obligación *f.* obligation

obligar (gu) to obligate, require

obligatorio/a required

obra *n.* work (of art)

observación *f.* observation

observador(a) observer

obsesión *f.* obsession

obstáculo obstacle

obstante: no obstante nevertheless

obtener (*like* **tener**) to obtain, get

obvio/a obvious

ocasión *f.* occasion

ocasionar to cause

occidental *adj.* western

océano ocean (6B); **océano Atlántico** Atlantic Ocean; **Pacífico** Pacific Ocean

ochenta eighty (2A)

ocho eight (1A)

ochocientos/as eight hundred (2B)

ochocientos mil eight hundred thousand (5B)

ocio leisure time

octubre October (1B)

ocultar(le) secretos (a alguien) to hide secrets (from someone) (7B)

ocupación *f.* occupation

ocupado/a busy

ocupar to occupy

ocurrir to occur

odiar to hate (4B)

odio hatred

oeste *m.* west; **al oeste de** to the west of (2A)

ofender(se) to offend (get offended) (7A)

ofensivo/a offensive

oferta *n.* offer

oficina office (P)

oficio job, occupation; trade

ofrecer (zc) to offer (3A)

oír *irreg.* to hear (2A)

ojalá que I hope, wish that (7B)

ojo eye

oleada *n.* wave

oliva: aceite (*m.*) **de oliva** olive oil

olvidar to forget

once eleven (1A)

opción *f.* option

operación *f.* operation

opinar to think, believe

opinión *f.* opinion

oportunidad *f.* opportunity

optativo/a optional

optimista *n. m., f.* optimist; *adj.* optimistic (1B)

opuesto/a opposite

oración *f.* sentence

orden *m.* order (*chronological*); **poner** (*irreg.*) **las cosas en orden** to put things in order (4B)

ordenador *m.* computer (*Sp.*)

ordenar to order, put in order (6A)

orejas (outer) ears (3A)

orgánico/a organic

organismo organism

organización *f.* organization

organizado/a organized (1B)

organizar (c) to organize

órgano organ; **órgano interno** internal organ (7A)

orgullo pride

orgulloso/a (de) proud (of) (5B)

orientación *f.* orientation, direction

origen *m.* (*pl.* **orígenes**) origin; **¿de qué origen es/son... ?** what is/are . . . 's (national) origin?

os *d.o.* you (*fam. pl. Sp.*); *i.o.* to/for you (*fam. pl. Sp.*); *refl. pron.* yourselves (*fam. pl. Sp.*)

oscurecer (zc) to get dark

oscuro/a dark (5B)

oso *n.* bear

otoño fall (*season*) (1B)

otorgar (gu) to award

otro/a other; another (1B)

oyente *m., f.* listener

ozono ozone; **capa de ozono** ozone layer (6B)

P

paciencia patience
paciente *m., f.* patient (7A); *adj.* patient (5A)
pacífico/a peaceful (5B); **océano Pacífico** Pacific Ocean
padecer (zc) de to suffer from (7A)
padrastro stepfather (3A)
padre *m.* father (3A); *pl.* parents; **padre soltero** single father (3A)
padrino godfather; **padrino de boda** groomsman
pagar (gu) to pay (for) (1A); **pagar a plazos** to pay in installments (8A); **pagar de una vez** to pay off all at once (8A)
página page; **página web** Web page (5A)
pago payment
país *m.* country (2A); **país desarrollado** developed country (8A); **país en vías de desarrollo** developing country; **País Vasco** Basque country; **los Países Bajos** The Netherlands
paisaje *m.* landscape (6B)
paisajista *adj. m., f.:* **arquitectura paisajista** landscape architecture
pájaro bird (9A)
palabra word
palabrota swear word
palomitas (*pl.*) **de maíz** popcorn (3B)
pampa pampa, prairie
pan *m.* bread; **pan dulce** sweet bread (*Mex.*) (3B); **pan tostado** toast (3B)
pana corduroy
panadería bakery
panceta *Arg.* bacon
panqueque *m.* pancake (3B)
pantalla screen (*movie, computer*) (P)
pantalones *m.* pants (2B); **pantalones cortos** shorts (2B)
papa potato; **papas fritas** French fries (3B); **puré** (*m.*) **de papas** mashed potatoes (3B)
papá *m.* dad, father; daddy
papel *m.* role, part; paper; **hoja de papel aparte** separate piece of paper; **toalla de papel** paper towel (4B)
papitas *pl.* potato chips (3B)
paquete *m.* package
par *m.* pair; **un par de** a couple of
para for; in order to (1B); **para** + *inf.* in order to (*do something*) (2B); **para que** so (that) (7B)
paracaidismo skydiving; **practicar (qu) el paracaidismo** to skydive (6B)
parada de autobuses bus stop (2A)
paráfrasis *f.* paraphrase
paraguayo/a *n., adj.* Paraguayan
parapente *m.:* **practicar (qu) el parapente** to hang glide

parar to stop
parcial biased (8B); **ser** (*irreg.*) **parcial** to be biased (8A)
parcialidad *f.* bias
parecer (zc) to look; to seem (like) (5A); **me parece(n)...** it/that seems . . . to me; **parece ser** it seems to be, he/she seems . . . (1B); **parecerse (a)** to resemble (3A)
parecido/a (a) similar (to)
pared *f.* wall; **pintar las paredes** to paint the walls (4B)
pareja couple (7B); mate; partner; *pl.* pairs
paréntesis *m. inv.* parenthesis
pariente *m., f.* relative (3A)
parque *m.* park (2A); **ir** (*irreg.*) **a un parque de diversiones** to go to an amusement park (6B)
párrafo paragraph
parte *f.* part; **partes del cuerpo** parts of the body (3A)
participar to participate (8B)
particular particular; private; **casa particular** private residence (4B)
partido game (4A); **partido político** political party
pasa raisin (3B)
pasado/a *adj.* past; spoiled (*food*) (3B); **pasado mañana** the day after tomorrow (1B)
pasajero/a *n.* passenger (6A)
pasaporte *m.* passport (6A)
pasar (mucho) tiempo to pass, spend (a lot of) time (1A); **pasar a ser** to become; **pasar la aspiradora** to vacuum (4B); **pasar por la aduana** to go through customs (6A); **pasar por seguridad** to go through security (6A); **pasarlo bien/mal** to have a good/bad time (4A)
pasatiempo pastime
Pascua: Pascua (de los judíos) Passover (4A); **Pascua (Florida)** Easter (4A)
pasear to walk, stroll; **sacar (qu) a pasear** to take for a walk
paseo *n.* walk, stroll; **dar** (*irreg.*) **un paseo** to take a walk (4A)
pasión *f.* passion
paso step
pastel *m.* pastry; cake (3B); *pl.* pastries (3B); **porción** (*f.*) **de pastel** slice of cake (3B)
pastilla pill (7A)
patata potato (*Sp.*)
paterno/a paternal (3A)
patinar (en línea) to (inline) skate (4A)
patio courtyard, patio (4B)
patria homeland

Patricio: Día (*m.*) **de San Patricio** St. Patrick's Day (4A)
patrio/a patriotic
pavo turkey (3B)
paz *f.* (*pl.* **paces**) peace; **dejar en paz** to leave alone; **hacer** (*irreg.*) **las paces** to make up with (7B)
peca *n.* freckle (3A)
pecado *n.* sin
pecho chest (7A); **tomarse algo muy a pecho** to take something to heart (7A); to feel something intensely (7A)
peculiaridad *f.* peculiarity
pedagogía pedagogy; education
pedazo piece
pedir (i, i) to ask for (2B); to order (2B); **pedir ayuda** to ask for help; **pedir disculpas** to apologize (*to someone*); **pedir prestado/a** to borrow (8A)
pegado/a stuck on; close together
peinado hairdo
peinar to comb
pelar to peel
pelearse to fight (5A)
película movie (1A); **ver** (*irreg.*) **una película** to watch a movie
peligro danger; **especies** (*f. pl.*) **en peligro de extinción** endangered species (6B)
peligroso/a dangerous
pelirrojo/a red-headed (3A)
pelo (canoso/lacio/rizado/rubio) (gray/straight/curly/blond) hair (3A)
pena shame; penalty; sorrow; **pena de muerte** death penalty
península Ibérica Iberian Peninsula
pensar (ie) to think (2A); **pensar de** to think of; **pensar en** to think about
pensión *f.* boardinghouse (6A); **media pensión** room and one other meal (usually breakfast) (6A); **pensión completa** room and all meals (6A)
peor worse (3A)
pepino (de mar) (sea) cucumber
pequeñeces *f. pl.* little things
pequeño/a little, small (2B)
per cápita: renta per cápita per capita income
perder (ie) to lose (2A); **perder peso** to lose weight
pérdida loss; **pérdida de tiempo** waste of time (8B); **pérdida de los valores tradicionales** loss of traditional values (8B)
perdón *m.* forgiveness
perdonable forgivable
perdonar to forgive (7B); to pardon, excuse
perezoso/a lazy
perfeccionista *m., f.* perfectionist

perfecto/a perfect
perfil *m.* profile
periférico peripheral device
periódico newspaper (1B)
periodista *m., f.* journalist
permiso permission
permitir to allow (8B)
pero but (1A)
perpetuar (perpetúo) to perpetuate
perplejo/a perplexed (7A); **dejar perplejo/a (a alguien)** to leave (someone) perplexed
perro dog (3A)
persistente persistent
persona person (1B)
personaje *m.* character (*fictional*)
personal personal; **finanzas personales** personal finances (8A)
personalidad *f.* personality (1B)
perspectiva perspective
pertenecer (zc) to belong
peruano/a Peruvian
pesa weight; **levantar pesas** to lift weights (4A)
pesado/a heavy
pesar(se) to weigh (oneself); **a pesar de** *prep.* in spite of, despite
pescado fish (*food*) (3B)
pescar (qu) to fish (6B)
pesimista *n. m., f.* pessimist; *adj.* pessimistic (1B)
peso weight; **bajar de peso** to lose weight; **perder (ie) peso** to lose weight
pesquero/a *adj.* fishing
pesticida *m.* pesticide (6B)
petróleo petroleum (oil) (6B)
pez *m.* (*pl.* **peces**) fish (*alive*)
piano piano; **tocar (qu) el piano** to play the piano (1A)
picante hot, spicy (3B)
picar (qu) to bite; to nibble (4A)
picoso/a spicy (3B)
pie *m.* foot (7A); **a pie** on foot; **dedo del pie** toe (7A); **pies cuadrados** square feet (4B)
piel *f.* skin (3A); **ponérsele** (*irreg.*) **la piel de gallina a alguien** to get goosebumps (7B)
pierna leg (7A)
pijama *m. s.* pajamas (2B)
pila (recargable) (rechargeable) battery
piloto/a pilot
pinchado/a: rueda pinchada flat tire
pintar to paint (4A); **pintar las paredes** to paint the walls (4B)
pintor(a) painter
pintoresco/a picturesque
pirámide *f.* pyramid
piscina swimming pool (4A)

piso floor (4B); flat, apartment (*Sp.*) (4B); **barrer el piso** to sweep the floor (4B)
pista track (4A)
pito: importarle un pito not to care about
pizarra chalkboard (P)
pizza pizza (3B); **porción** (*f.*) **de pizza** slice of pizza (3B)
placer *m.* pleasure
plancha iron (4B)
planchar (la ropa) to iron (the clothes) (4B)
planear to plan
planeta *m.* planet
planificación *f.* planning
plano city map (6A)
planta floor (*of a building*) (*Sp.*) (4B)
plástico plastic; **botella de plástico** plastic bottle (6B)
plátano banana
plato plate (6A); prepared dish; *pl.* dishes (4B); **primer (segundo, tercer) plato** first (second, third) course (6A)
playa beach (6B)
plaza square, plaza (2A)
plazo term; **de corto/largo plazo** short/long term; **pagar (gu) a plazos** to pay in installments (8A)
pluma pen (P)
plumero feather duster (4B)
población *f.* population
poblado/a populated
pobre *adj.* poor (1B)
pobreza poverty (8A); **umbral** (*m.*) **de la pobreza** poverty line
poco/a *adv.* little (1B); *adj.* little; *pl.* few; **dentro de poco** in a little while (1B); **un poco** a little (1B)
poder *m.* power
poder *irreg.* to be able to, can (2A); **¿en qué puedo servirle?** how may I help you (*form. s.*)? (2B); **¿me podría traer...?** could you (*form. s.*) bring me...? (6A); **¿puedo probarme...?** may I try on...? (2B)
poema *m.* poem
poemario collection of poetry
poesía poetry
poeta *m., f.* poet
polémico/a controversial
policía *f.* police force; *m.* policeman; **mujer** (*f.*) **policía** policewoman
poliéster *m.* polyester (2B)
poliomielitis *f.* polio
politeísta *adj. m., f.* polytheist, believing in more than one god
política *s.* politics (8B); policy (8B)
político, mujer (*f.*) **político** politician
político/a political; **ciencias políticas** political science (P); **partido político** political party

pollo chicken (3B)
polvo *n.* dust; **quitar el polvo** to dust (4B)
poner *irreg.* (*p.p.* **puesto/a**) to put (2A); **poner alto el volumen** to turn the volume up high; **poner fin a** to end; **poner las cosas en orden** to put things in order (4B); **ponerle los cuernos (a alguien)** to be unfaithful (to someone); **ponerle una inyección (a alguien)** to give (someone) a shot (7A); **ponerse** to get, become (*emotion*); **ponerse de acuerdo** to come to an agreement; **ponérsele la piel de gallina a alguien** to get goosebumps (7B)
por for (4B); because of (4B); by, through, around; **estar** (*irreg.*) **por** + *inf.* to be about to + *inf.*; **llamar por teléfono** to call on the telephone (1A); **pasar por la aduana** to go through customs (6A); **por ciento** percent; **por dentro** within, (on the) inside; **por ejemplo** for example; **por favor** please; **por fin** finally; **por fuera** (on the) outside; **por la mañana/tarde/noche** in the morning/afternoon/evening (night) (1A); **por lo menos** at least; **por primera vez** for the first time; **¿por qué?** why? (1B); **por supuesto** of course
porcentaje *m.* percentage
porción *f.* (**de pastel, pizza**) slice (of cake, pizza) (3B)
porfiado/a persistent (7B)
porque because (1B)
portada home page (*Web*); cover (*book*)
portarse bien/mal to behave well/ badly (5A)
portátil portable; **computadora portátil** laptop computer (5A); **estéreo portátil** portable stereo (5A)
portero/a doorperson (4B); building manager (4B)
portugués *m.* Portuguese (*language*)
poseer (y) to possess
posesión *f.* possession
posesivo/a possessive (7B)
posgrado/a graduate; **estudios de posgrado** graduate studies
posibilidad *f.* possibility
posible possible
posición *f.* position
positivo/a positive
postre *m.* dessert (3B)
potable: agua (*f.* [*but* **el agua**]) **potable** drinking water
práctica *n.* practice
practicar (qu) to practice (1A); **practicar el alpinismo de rocas** to rock climb (6B); **practicar la escalada** to rappel; **practicar el paracaidismo** to skydive (6B); **practicar el parapente** to hang

glide; **practicar el yoga** to do yoga
(4A); **practicar un deporte** to practice
a sport (1A)
pragmático/a pragmatic
precavido/a cautious (5A)
precio (fijo) (fixed) price (2B); **estar**
(*irreg.*) **a buen precio** to be a
good price
precioso/a precious; valuable; **metales**
(*m.*) **preciosos** precious metals (8A)
preciso/a precise (1B); **es preciso** it's
necessary (8B)
precolombino/a pre-Columbian (before
Columbus)
predeterminado/a predetermined
predicción *f.* prediction
predominar to dominate
preferencia preference
preferir (ie, i) to prefer (2A)
pregunta *n.* question
preguntar to ask (questions)
preliminar preliminary
premio award; prize
prenda article of clothing (2B)
prender (las luces) to turn on (the
lights)
prensa *n.* press (8B)
preocupación *f.* worry (8B);
concern (8B)
preocupado/a worried (7A)
preocuparse (por) to worry
(about) (7A)
preparar to prepare (1A)
preparativo preparation
preparatoria high school
preposición *f.* preposition
presencia presence
presenciar to witness
presentación *f.* presentation;
introduction (P)
presentador(a) anchorman,
anchorwoman (8B)
presentar to present; to introduce; to
show (*a film*)
presente *n. m., adj. m. f.* present (*time*)
preservar to preserve, maintain
presidencia presidency
presidencial presidential
presidente/a president
presión *f.* pressure; **presión arterial**
blood pressure (7A)
prestado/a borrowed; **pedir (i, i)**
prestado/a to borrow (8A)
préstamo *n.* loan (8A); **sacar (qu) un**
préstamo to take out a loan
prestar to loan, lend (8A)
presumido/a conceited (9A)
presupuesto (mensual) (monthly)
budget (8A)
pretérito *gram.* preterite (tense)
pretexto pretext, excuse

prevalente prevalent
preventivo/a: señales (*f. pl.*) **preventivas**
warning signs
previo/a previous
primaria: (escuela) primaria
elementary school; **maestro/a de**
primaria elementary school
teacher
primavera spring (*season*) (1B)
primer, primero/a first; **por primera vez**
for the first time; **primer (segundo,**
tercer) plato first (second, third)
course (6A); **primera clase** first
class (6A)
primo/a cousin (3A); *pl.* cousins
principal *adj.* main, principal
principio beginning
prisa: tener (*irreg.*) **prisa** to be in a hurry
privacidad *f.* privacy
privado/a private; **casa privada** private
residence (4B); **con baño privado** with
a private bath (6A)
privilegiado/a privileged
probabilidad *f.* probability
probable probable; **es probable** it's
probable (8B)
probador *m.* dressing room (2B)
probar (ue) to try on; **¿puedo**
probarme... ? may I try on . . . ? (2B);
probarse to try on (2B)
problema *m.* problem
problemático/a problematic
procesar to process
proceso process
producción *f.* production
producir *irreg.* to produce
producto product; **producto**
biodegradable biodegradable product
(6B); **producto de limpieza** cleaning
product (4B); **producto desechable**
disposable product (6B); **producto**
farmacéutico pharmaceutical product
(8A); **producto lácteo** dairy product
(3B); **producto nacional bruto** gross
national product; **productos de**
exportación export products (8A)
productor(a) producer
profesión *f.* profession
profesional *adj.* professional
profesor(a) professor (P)
profundo/a deep
programa *m.* program; **programa de**
entrevistas talk show (8B); **programa**
deportivo sports show (8B); **programa**
televisivo television program (8B)
programación *f.* programming
programador(a) (computer)
programmer
prohibir (prohíbo) to prohibit (8B)
prólogo prologue
promedio *n.* average

promesa promise; **cumplir las promesas**
to keep one's word
prometer to promise
promiscuo/a promiscuous
pronombre *m.* pronoun
pronóstico del tiempo weather
report (8B)
pronto soon; **tan pronto como** as
soon as
pronunciación *f.* pronunciation
pronunciar to pronounce
propiedad *f.* property
propina tip (6A); **dejar (una) propina** to
leave a tip (6A)
propio/a own
proporcionar to give
propósito purpose; aim; intention; **a**
propósito by the way
prosperidad *f.* prosperity (8A)
próspero/a prosperous
protección *f.* protection
proteger (j) to protect (6B)
proteína protein
protestar to protest (8B)
provecho: buen provecho enjoy your
meal
provincia province, region
provocar (qu) to provoke
proximidad *f.* proximity
próximo/a next (1B)
prueba *n.* quiz, test
psicología psychology (P)
psicólogo/a psychologist
psiquiatra *m., f.* psychiatrist
publicación *f.* publication
publicar (qu) to publish
publicitario/a: anuncio publicitario
commercial (8B)
público *n.* public; audience; **teléfono**
público public telephone (P)
publico/a *adj.* public
pueblo small town
puerro leek
puerta door (P)
puerto (sea)port
puertorriqueño/a *n., adj.* Puerto Rican
pues... well . . .
puesto *n.* stand; **puesto que** given that
pulir to polish (4B)
pulmón *m.* lung (7A)
pulsar to click
punta de lanza spearhead
punto point; period; **en punto** on the dot
(*time*) (1A); **punto de vista** point of
view
puntual punctual; **ser** (*irreg.*) **puntual** to
be punctual (1A)
puntualidad *f.* punctuality
puré (*m.*) **de papas** mashed
potatoes (3B)
púrpura purple

Q

que that, which; than; **creer que** to think that (1B); **hasta que** *conj.* until; **lo que** what, that which (1B); **más** + *adj.* + **que** more + *adj.* + than; **tener** (*irreg.*) **que** + *inf.* to have to (*do something*)

¿qué? what? (1B); **¿a qué hora... ?** at what time ... ?, when ... ? (1A); **¿por qué?** why? (1B); **¿qué carrera haces?** what's your (*fam. s.*) major? (P); **¿qué clases tienes este semestre/trimestre?** what classes do you (*fam. s.*) have this semester/quarter? (P); **¿qué día es hoy?** what day is today? (1A); **¿qué estudias?** what are you (*fam. s.*) studying? (P); **¿qué hora es?** what time is it? (1A); **¿qué número calza?** what size shoe do you (*form. s.*) wear? (2B); **¿qué trae... ?** what comes with ... ? (6A)

quechua *m.* Quechua (*language*)

quedar to be located (2A); **creo que le queda un poco grande** I think it's a bit big on you (2B); **¿me queda bien?** does it fit me? (2B); **quedarle bien/mal** to fit well/ poorly; **quedarse** to stay (*in a place*) (6A); **quedarse con** to keep (*an object*)

quehacer *m.* chore; **quehaceres domésticos** household chores (4B)

queja complaint

quejarse (de) to complain (about)

quemar to burn; **quemar calorías** to burn calories (4A)

querer *irreg.* to want (2A); to love (7B); **quiere decir** it means

queso cheese (3B); **queso de crema** cream cheese (3B)

quien(es) who, whom

¿quién(es)? who?, whom? (1B)

química chemistry (P)

quince fifteen (1A)

quinientos/as five hundred (2B)

quinientos mil five hundred thousand (5B)

quiosco kiosk

quitar to remove, take away; **quitar el polvo** to dust (4B); **quitarse** to take off (*clothing*)

quizá(s) perhaps

R

rabia rage; **darle** (*irreg.*) **rabia (a alguien)** to make (someone) angry

racismo racism

radio *f.* radio (*medium*)

rafting: hacer (*irreg.*) **rafting** to go rafting (6B)

raíz *f.* (*pl.* **raíces**) root; **bienes** (*m. pl.*) **raíces** real estate (8A)

ramo bouquet

rápido *adv.* fast

rápido/a *adj.* fast, quick; **comida rápida** fast food (3B)

raro/a strange; rare; **raras veces** infrequently, rarely

rascacielos *m. s.* skyscraper (2A)

rasgar (gu) to tear, rip

rasgo feature, trait (3A)

rato *n.* while, short time; **ratos libres** free time (4A)

ratón *m.* mouse (*animal*); mouse (*computer*) (5A)

raya stripe; **de rayas** striped (2B); **mantenerse** (*like* **tener**) **a raya** to keep (*something*) away

rayo ray; **rayos X** X-rays (7A)

raza race (*people*)

razón *f.* reason

razonable reasonable

reacción *f.* reaction

reaccionar to react (7A)

real real; royal

realidad *f.* reality

realista *adj. m., f.* realistic

reality *m.* reality show (*TV*) (8B)

realizar (c) to attain, achieve

realmente really

rebaja sale (2B)

rebelde rebellious

recargable rechargeable; **pila recargable** rechargeable battery

recargar (gu) to recharge

recepción *f.* reception

recesión *f.* recession (8A)

receta recipe; prescription (7A)

recibir to receive (1B)

recibo receipt (8A)

reciclaje *m.* recycling (6B)

reciclar to recycle (6B)

recién recently; **recién nacido/a** newborn baby (5B)

reciente recent

recipiente *m.* container

recíproco/a reciprocal

recitar to recite

recoger (j) to pick up

recomendable recommendable

recomendación *f.* recommendation

recomendar (ie) to recommend (8B)

reconocer (zc) to recognize (3A)

reconocido/a renowned

recordar (ue) to remember (2A)

recorrido trip, journey

recorte *m.* clipping (*of a magazine*)

recreación *f.* recreation

recreo recess (5A)

recuerdo memory; souvenir; **comprar recuerdos** to buy souvenirs (6B)

recuperación *f.* recuperation (8A)

recuperarse to recuperate

recurrir a to turn to

recurso resource; **recursos naturales** natural resources (6B)

red *f.* net; Internet; **navegar (gu) la red** to surf the Web (1A)

redacción *f.* composition

reducir *irreg.* to reduce

reembolso reimbursement

reemplazar (c) to replace

reenviar (reenvío) to forward

referencia reference

referir(se) (ie, i) (a) to refer (to)

refinado/a refined

reflejar to reflect

reflexivo/a reflexive

refresco soft drink (3B); **refresco dietético** diet soft drink (3B)

refrigerador *m.* refrigerator (4B)

regalar to give (*as a gift*) (3B)

regalo gift (4A)

regatear to bargain (2B)

regateo bargaining

regimen *m.* diet

región *f.* region

regresar to return (*to a place*); **regresar a casa** to go home (1A)

regulador(a) regulator

regular to regulate

reinado *n.* reign

reírse (i, i) to laugh (7A)

relación *f.* relationship

relacionado/a (con) related (to)

relacionarse to relate, be related to

relajado/a relaxed (7A)

relajante *adj.* relaxing

relajarse to relax

relatar to relate, tell

relato tale, story

religión *f.* religion

religioso/a religious

rellenar to fill

relleno/a (de) stuffed (with)

reloj *m.* clock (P); watch (P)

remar to row; **remar en canoa** to go canoeing (6B)

remedio remedy

remolino pinwheel

Renacimiento Renaissance

rencor *m.* anger; **guardar(le) rencor (a alguien)** to hold a grudge (against someone) (7B)

renovar (ue) to renew

renta per cápita per capita income

renunciar a to quit (*a job*); to give up

repartir to distribute

repasar to review (1A)

repaso review

repente: de repente suddenly

repetir (i, i) to repeat (2B)

repleto/a overflowing

reportaje *m.* report (8B)

reportar to report
reportero/a reporter (8B)
represa dam
representante *m., f.* representative
representar to represent
represivo/a repressive
reproductor (*m.*) **de CD/DVD/vídeo** CD/DVD/video player (5A)
república republic; **República Dominicana** Dominican Republic
requerir (**ie, i**) to require
requisito requirement
res *f.*: **carne** (*f.*) **de res** beef (3B)
resaltar to highlight
resentido/a resentful
reserva reserve; reservation (*hotel*)
reservación *f.* reservation (6A)
reservado/a reserved (1B)
resfriado *n.* cold (*sickness*); **tener** (*irreg.*) **un resfriado** to have a cold (7A)
resfriarse (me resfrío) to catch a cold
residencia estudiantil residence hall, dormitory (P)
resolución *f.* resolution
resolver (**ue**) (*p.p.* **resuelto/a**) (**conflictos**) to resolve (conflicts)
respectivo/a respective
respetar to respect (7B)
respeto respect (7B)
respetuoso/a respectful
respirar to breathe (7A)
responder to respond, answer
responsabilidad *f.* responsibility; **responsabilidad cívica** civic duty (8B)
responsable responsible (8A)
respuesta response, answer
restaurante *m.* restaurant (2A); **cenar en un restaurante elegante** to eat in a fancy restaurant (6B)
resto rest, remainder; *pl.* remains; remnants
restricción *f.* restriction
resuelto/a (*p.p. of* **resolver**) determined (7B)
resultado result
resultar to turn out, result
resumen *m.* summary
resumir to sum up
retirar to withdraw
retrasar to delay, retard
retroproyectora projector
reunión *f.* (**cívica**) (town) meeting (8B)
reunirse (me reúno) to get together
revelar to reveal
revisar to check, inspect
revista magazine (1B)
revolución *f.* revolution (5B)
revuelto/a (*p.p. of* **revolver**): **huevos revueltos** scrambled eggs (3B)
rey *m.* king; **Día** (*m.*) **de los Reyes Magos** Epiphany (January 6), Day of the Magi

rico/a rich, wealthy (2B); delicious (2B)
ridículo/a ridiculous (8B)
rincón *m.* corner
riñón *m.* kidney
río river (6B)
ríoplatense *adj.* pertaining to the **río de la plata** (*Platte River*)
riqueza *s.* riches, wealth (8A)
ritmo rhythm
rito rite; ceremony
rivalidad *f.* rivalry
rizado/a curly (3A); **pelo rizado** curly hair (3A)
robar to rob, steal
robo break-in
roca rock; **practicar** (**qu**) **el alpinismo de rocas** to rock climb (6B)
rodear to surround
rodilla knee (7A)
rogar (**ue**) (**gu**) to beg
rojo/a red (2B)
románico/a *adj.* Romance (*language*)
romántico/a romantic (7B)
romper (*p.p.* **roto/a**) to break; **romper con** to break up with (7B); **romperse** to break (a bone) (7A)
roncar (**qu**) to snore
ronda *n.* round
ropa clothing (2B)
rosado/a pink (2B)
rosario rosary
rosbif *m.* roast beef (3B)
rosquilla bagel (3B)
rostro *n.* face
roto/a (*p.p. of* **romper**) broken
rozarse (**c**) **con la gente** to mingle with people (4A)
rubí *m.* ruby
rubio/a blond(e) (3A); **pelo rubio** blond hair (3A)
rueda wheel; **rueda de andar** treadmill (4A); **rueda pinchada** flat tire
ruido noise
rumor *m.* rumor
ruso/a *n., adj.* Russian
ruta route

S

sábado Saturday (1A)
saber *irreg.* to know (*facts, information*) (3A); to find out (*about something*); **saber** + *inf.* to know how to (*do something*) (3A); **todavía no sé** I still don't know (P)
sabio/a wise (1B)
sabor *m.* taste, flavor
sabroso/a savory, tasty
sacar (**qu**) to take out; **sacar a pasear** to take for a walk; **sacar dinero** to withdraw money (8A); **sacar fotos** to

take pictures; **sacar la basura** to take out the trash (4B); **sacar la lengua** to stick out one's tongue (7A); **sacar la licencia de conducir** to get a driver's license (5A); **sacar un préstamo** to take out a loan; **sacar un vídeo/DVD** to rent a video/DVD (4A); **sacarle sangre** to draw blood (7A)
sacerdote *m.* priest
sacrificarse (**qu**) to sacrifice oneself
safari *m.* safari
sal *f.* salt
sala living room (4B); **sala de clase** classroom (P); **sala de espera** waiting room
salado/a salty (3B); **galleta salada** cracker (3B)
salchicha sausage (3B)
salida exit; way out
salir *irreg.* to leave (2A); to go out (2A); **¿a cuánto sale?** how much is it?; **salir a bailar** to go dancing; **salir con** to go out with (7B)
salsa salsa (3B)
saltar to jump; **saltar la cuerda** to jump rope
salto: hacer (*irreg.*) **el salto bungee** to bungee jump (6B)
salud *f.* health (7A)
saludable healthy
saludar to greet (7B)
saludo greeting
salvar to save (6B)
san *apocopated form of* **santo**
sandalia sandal (2B)
sándwich *m.* sandwich (3B)
sangre *f.* blood; **sacarle** (**qu**) **sangre** to draw blood (7A)
sanguíneo/a *adj.* blood
santería *religion of African origin practiced in the Caribbean*
santo/a *n., adj.* saint
se *refl. pron.* herself, himself, itself, yourself (*form. s.*), themselves, yourselves (*form. pl.*)
se alquila for rent (4B)
secadora dryer (4B)
sección *f.* section
seco/a dry
secreto *n.* secret; **ocultar(le) secretos (a alguien)** to hide secrets (from someone) (7B)
secundario/a secondary; **escuela secundaria** high school; **maestro/a de secundaria** high school teacher
seda silk (2B)
sedentario/a sedentary
sediento/a thirsty
seducir (**zc**) to seduce (7B)
seductor(a) seductive (7B)
seguida: en seguida right away

seguir (i, i) (g) to follow (2B); **seguir derecho** to continue straight ahead (6A)
según according to
segundo/a adj. second; **segundo plato** second course (6A)
seguramente surely
seguridad f. safety; **pasar por seguridad** to go through security (6A)
seguro insurance; **seguro antirrobo** antitheft insurance (8A); **seguro contra incendios** fire insurance (8A); **seguro de automóvil** automobile insurance (8A); **seguro de vida** life insurance (8A); **seguro de vivienda** homeowner's insurance (8A); **seguro médico** medical insurance (8A)
seguro/a adj. sure; safe; **estar** (irreg.) **seguro/a de** to be sure of (8B); **(no) es seguro** it's (not) certain (8B)
seis six (1A)
seiscientos/as six hundred (2B)
seiscientos mil six hundred thousand (5B)
selección f. selection; national team (soccer)
seleccionar to select, choose
sello seal, stamp
selva (tropical) (tropical) jungle (6B)
semáforo signal; traffic light
semana week (1A); **fin** (m.) **de semana** weekend (1A); **semana entrante** next week (1B); **semana pasada** last week
semanal weekly
semejante similar
semejanza similarity
semestre m. semester
semilla seed
senador(a) senator
sencillo/a simple (1B); **cama sencilla** twin (single) bed (4B)
sendero path
seno breast (of a person)
sensación f. sensation
sensacionalista m., f. sensationalist (8B)
sensible sensitive (7B)
sentarse (ie) to sit down
sentido n. sense; **sentido de dirección** sense of direction; **sentido del humor** sense of humor
sentimental sentimental (7B)
sentimiento feeling, emotion (7B)
sentir (ie, i) to feel (4B); **sentirse** to feel (emotion, health) (5A); **sentirse** + adj., adv. to feel + adj., adv.
señal f. sign; signal; **señales preventivas** warning signs
señalar to point out
señor (Sr.) man; Mr.
señora (Sra.) woman; Mrs.
señorita (Srta.) young woman; Miss, Ms.

separación f. separation
separado/a separated (3A)
septentrional northern
septiembre September (1B)
ser irreg. to be (P); **¿cómo es?** what is he/she/it/like? (3A); what are you (form. s.) like? (3A); **¿cuál es su apellido?** what's his/her last name? (P); **¿cuál es tu apellido?** what's your (fam. s.) last name? (P); **¿de dónde eres?** where are you (fam. s.) from? (P); **era** he/she/it was, you (form. s.) were (1B); **es buena idea** (2B); **es de...** it's made of . . . (2B); **es imposible** it's impossible (8B); **es la una** it's one o'clock (1A); **es necesario** it's necessary (2B); **es preciso** it's necessary (8B); **es probable** it's probable (8B); **mi apellido es...** my last name is . . . (P); **mi nombre es...** my name is . . . (P); **parece ser** it seems to be; he/she seems . . . (1B); **pasar a ser** to become; **¿qué hora es?** what time is it? (1A); **ser aficionado/a** to be a fan (4A); **(no) ser de fiar** to be (un)reliable; **ser parcial** to be biased (8A); **ser puntual** to be punctual (1A); **son de...** they're made of . . . (2B); **soy de...** I'm from . . . (P)
serie f. series
serio/a serious (1B)
serpiente f. snake
servicio service; **servicio de cuarto** room service (6A); **servicios médicos** medical services; **servicios sociales** social services
servilleta napkin (6A)
servir (i, i) to serve (2B); **¿en qué puedo servirle?** how may I help you? (2B)
sesenta sixty (2A)
sesión f. session
setecientos/as seven hundred (2B)
setecientos mil seven hundred thousand (5B)
setenta seventy (2A)
sexo sex
si if (1B)
sí yes; **sí, por supuesto** yes, of course
SIDA (síndrome [m.] **de inmunodeficiencia adquirida)** AIDS (Acquired Immune Deficiency Syndrome) (8B)
siempre always (3B)
siesta nap; **echar una siesta** to take a nap
siete seven (1A)
siglo century (5B); **siglo XXI** twenty-first century (5B)
significado meaning
significar (qu) to mean
significativamente significantly

signo n. sign (horoscope)
siguiente following; next
silencioso/a silent, quiet
silla chair (P)
sillón m. armchair (4B)
simbolizar (c) to symbolize
símbolo symbol
simbología symbology
similitud f. similarity
simpático/a friendly, nice (1B)
sin without (4B); **sin duda** without a doubt; **sin embargo** conj. however; **sin que** without (7B)
sincero/a sincere
sincretismo syncretism, consolidation of different religious doctrines
síndrome m. syndrome; **síndrome de inmunodeficiencia adquirida (SIDA)** Acquired Immune Deficiency Syndrome (AIDS) (8B)
sino but (rather)
sinónimo synonym
sinopsis f. synopsis
síntoma m. symptom
sinuoso/a winding
siquiera: ni siquiera not even
sistema m. system; **analista** (m., f.) **de sistemas** systems analyst
sitio place, location; site; **diseñador(a) de sitios** Web site designer
situación f. situation
situado/a situated, located
sobras pl. leftovers (3B)
sobre about; on, on top of (4B)
sobresaliente excellent
sobrino/a nephew, niece (3A)
social social; **ciencias sociales** social sciences (P); **servicios sociales** social services; **trabajador(a) social** social worker
sociedad f. society (8B)
socio/a associate; partner
socioeconómico/a socioeconomic
sociolingüístico/a sociolinguistic
sociología sociology (P)
sofá m. sofa (4B)
sofisticado/a sophisticated
soja soy(bean) (3B)
sol m. sun; **hace sol** it's sunny (1B); **tomar el sol** to sunbathe (1B)
solamente only (1A)
solas: a solas alone (1B)
soldado, mujer (f.) **soldado** soldier
soler (ue) + inf. to be in the habit of / be accustomed to (doing something) (2A)
sólido/a solid
solitario/a solitary
sólo (solamente) adv. only; **sólo estoy mirando** I'm just looking (2B)
solo/a alone

soltero/a single, unmarried (3A); **madre** (*f.*) **soltera** single mother (3A); **padre** (*m.*) **soltero** single father (3A)
solución *f.* solution
solucionar to solve
sombrero hat
sonar (ue) to ring
soneto sonnet
sonreír (i, i) to smile
sonrisa smile
sonrojarse to blush (7B)
soñador(a) dreamer (1B)
soñar (ue) (con) to dream (about) (5A)
sopa soup (3B)
soplo breeze; breath
soporte *m.* support
sorprendente surprising
sorprender to surprise
sorpresa surprise; **fiesta de sorpresa** surprise party (4A)
sospechar to suspect
sospechoso/a untrusting (1B)
sostener (*like* **tener**) to hold up, support
sótano basement
su(s) *poss.* his, her, its, their, your (*form. s., pl.*) (1A); **¿cuál es su apellido?** what's his/her last name? (P)
subdivisión *f.* subdivision; subsection
subida rise (8A)
subir to rise, go up (8A); **subir a** to board (6A); **subirse a los árboles** to climb trees (5A)
subjuntivo *gram.* subjunctive (mood)
sublevarse to revolt
subrayar to underline
suburbio suburb
suceder to happen
sucesión *f.* succession
suceso event, happening
sucio/a dirty
sudadera sweatshirt (2B)
Sudamérica South America (6B)
sudamericano/a *n., adj.* South American
sudar to sweat (4A)
suegro/a father-in-law, mother-in-law (3A)
sueldo (mínimo) (minimum) wage, salary (8A)
suelo floor
sueño *n.* dream; **tener** (*irreg.*) **sueño** to be sleepy (7A)
suerte *f.* luck; **tener** (*irreg.*) **suerte** to be lucky
suéter *m.* sweater (2B)
suficiente sufficient, enough
sufrir to suffer
sugerencia suggestion
sugerir (ie, i) to suggest (4B)
suicidio suicide
sujeto *n.* subject

sumar to add
superar to exceed
supermercado supermarket (2A)
supuesto/a (*p.p. of* **suponer**) supposed; **por supuesto** of course
sur *m.* south; **al sur de** to the south of (2A)
surfear to surf (6B)
suroeste *m.* southwest
suspender to suspend
sustancia substance
sustancial substantial
sustantivo noun
sustentable: desarrollo sustentable sustainable development
sustitución *f.* substitution
sustituir (y) to substitute
suyo/a/os/as *poss.* your, of yours (*form. s., pl.*); his, of his; her, of hers; their, of theirs (2B)

T

tabaco tobacco (8A)
tacaño/a greedy, stingy (7B)
tacón *m.* heel (*shoe*); **zapatos de tacón alto** high-heeled shoes (2B)
tal such, such a; **con tal de que** *conj.* provided that (7B); **¿qué tal?** how's it going?; **tal vez** perhaps
talento talent
talentoso/a talented
talla size (*clothes*) (2B); **¿cuál es su talla?** what size do you (*form. s.*) wear? (2B)
tamaño size (4B); **¿de qué tamaño es... ?** what size is . . . ? (4B)
también also, too
tampoco neither, not either (3B)
tan so; **tan... como** as . . . as (3A); **tan pronto como** as soon as
tanto *adv.* so much
tanto/a *adj.* so much; such; *pl.* so many; **tanto/a/os/as... como** as much/many . . . as (3A)
tapada: tener (*irreg.*) **la nariz tapada** to have a stuffed-up nose (7A)
tardar to take time (*to do something*)
tarde *n. f.* afternoon, evening; **buenas tardes** good afternoon/evening (P); **de la tarde** in the afternoon, evening (P.M.) (1A); **por la tarde** in the afternoon/evening (1A)
tarde *adv.* late (1A)
tarea homework (2A); task
tarifa rate, price, fare
tarjeta card (4A); **tarjeta de crédito** credit card (2B); **tarjeta de felicitación** greeting card
tasa rate, level; **tasa de desempleo** unemployment rate (8A)

taxista *m., f.* taxi driver
taza cup (*coffee*) (6A)
tazón *m.* bowl
te *d.o.* you (*fam. s.*); *i.o.* to/for you (*fam. s.*); *refl. pron.* yourself (*fam. s.*); **¿cómo te llamas?** what is your (*fam. s.*) name? (P); **te gusta...** you (*fam. s.*) like . . . (1A)
té (*m.*) **(caliente/helado)** (hot/iced) tea (3B)
teatro theater
teclado keyboard (5A)
técnica technique
técnico/a *n.* technician; *adj.* technical
tecnología technology
tecnológico/a technological
tejido/a woven
telefónica telephone company
teléfono telephone; **llamar por teléfono** to call on the telephone (1A); **teléfono celular** cell phone (5A); **teléfono público** public telephone (P)
telenovela soap opera (8B)
telepático/a telepathic
televidente *m., f.* television viewer
televisión *f.* television (*medium*); **canal** (*m.*) **de televisión** television channel; **ver** (*irreg.*) **la televisión** to watch TV
televisivo/a *adj.* television; **programa** (*m.*) **televisivo** television program (8B)
televisor *m.* television (*set*) (P)
tema *m.* theme, topic
temer to fear
temperatura temperature; **tomar(le) la temperatura** to take (*someone's*) temperature (7A)
temporada season (*sports*)
temprano early (1A)
tendencia tendency
tender (ie) to tend to
tenedor *m.* fork (6A)
tener *irreg.* to have (2A); **tener... años** to be . . . years old (2A); **tener celos** to be jealous; **tener éxito** to be successful (5B); **tener expectativas** to have expectations; **tener fiebre** to have a fever (7A); **tener ganas de** + *inf.* to feel like (*doing something*); **tener hambre** to be hungry; **tener la nariz tapada** to have a stuffed-up nose (7A); **tener prisa** to be in a hurry; **tener que** + *inf.* to have to (*do something*); **tener sueño** to be sleepy (7A); **tener suerte** to be lucky; **tener un resfriado** to have a cold (7A); **tenerle cariño a alguien** to be fond of someone (7B); **tenerle envidia (a alguien)** to be envious (of someone) (7A); **tenerle miedo (a alguien)** to be afraid (of someone) (7A); **tengo una clase de...** I have a(n) . . . class (P); **¿tiene Ud. la hora?** do you (*form. s.*) have the time? (1A)

tenis *m.* tennis (4A); **cancha de tenis** tennis court (4A); **zapatos de tenis** tennis shoes (2B)

tensión *f.* tension; **tensión arterial** blood pressure

tenso/a tense (7A); stressed

tentación *f.* temptation

terapeuta *m., f.* therapist

tercer, tercero/a third; **tercer plato** third course (6A)

terco/a stubborn

terminación *f.* ending

terminar to finish (7B)

término term

termostato thermostat

terraza terrace

terremoto earthquake (5B)

terrenos *pl.* lands

terrestre terrestrial

territorio territory

terrorismo terrorism (8B)

terrorista *n. m., f.* terrorist

testigo *n. m., f.* witness (8B)

testimonio testimony

textiles *m., pl.* textiles (8A)

texto text; **libro de texto** textbook

ti *obj. of prep.* you (*fam. s.*) (4B)

tibio/a warm

tiburón *m.* shark

tiempo weather (1B); time; **a tiempo** on time; **¿cuánto tiempo hace que... ?** how long has it been since . . . ?; **hace buen/mal tiempo** it's good/bad weather (1B); **hace (mucho) tiempo** (a long time) ago; **llegar (gu) a tiempo** to arrive on time (1A); **pasar (mucho) tiempo** to spend (a lot of) time (1A); **pérdida de tiempo** waste of time (8B); **pronóstico del tiempo** weather report (8B)

tienda store, shop (2A)

tierra earth, land

tijeras *pl.* scissors

timbre *m.* bell; ring (*tone*)

tímido/a timid (1B)

tinto/a: **vino tinto** red wine (3B)

tío/a uncle, aunt (3A); *pl.* aunts and uncles

típico/a typical

tipo type; **tipos de interés** interest rates (8A)

tiras cómicas comics (5A); cartoons

tirar to throw out (6B)

titular *m.* headline (8B)

titularse to be titled

título title

tiza chalk (P)

toalla (de papel) (paper) towel (4B)

tocar (qu) (el piano / la guitarra) to play (the piano / the guitar) (1A); to touch

tocino bacon (3B)

todavía still, yet; **todavía no sé** I still don't know (P)

todo/a all; every; **todas las noches** every night (1A); **todos los días** every day (1A)

tolerante tolerant

tomar to take (1A); to drink (1A); **tomar apuntes** to take notes (1A); **tomar café** to drink coffee (1A); **tomar cerveza** to drink beer (1A); **tomar el sol** to sunbathe (1B); **tomar una clase** to take a class (1A); **tomar(le) la temperatura** to take (*someone's*) temperature (7A); **tomarse algo muy a pecho** to take something to heart (7A); to feel something intensely (7A)

tomate *m.* tomato (3B)

tono tone

tontería foolish thing

tonto/a silly, foolish (1B)

topacio topaz

torbellino whirlwind

tormentoso/a stormy

toronja grapefruit (3B)

torpe clumsy (5A)

torre *f.* tower (2A)

torta cake

tortilla (de maíz) *thin cake made of cornmeal or flour* (3B); **tortilla española** *omelette made of eggs, potatoes, and onions* (*Sp.*) (3B)

tortuga turtle (9A)

tos *f.* cough; **jarabe** (*m.*) **para la tos** cough syrup

tostada de pan a la francesa French toast (3B)

tostado/a toasted; **pan** (*m.*) **tostado** toast (3B)

trabajador(a) *adj.* hardworking (1B); *n.* worker; **trabajador(a) social** social worker

trabajar to work (1A)

trabajo work, job; **Día** (*m.*) **del Trabajo** Labor Day

trabársele la lengua a alguien to get tongue-tied (7B)

tradicional traditional; **pérdida de valores tradicionales** loss of traditional values (8B)

traducir (*like* **conducir**) to translate

traer *irreg.* to bring (2A); **¿me podría traer... ?** could you (*form. s.*) bring me . . . ?; **¿qué trae... ?** what comes with . . . ? (6A)

tráfico traffic

tragedia tragedy

traicionar to betray (7B)

traje *m.* suit (2B); **traje de baño** bathing suit (2B)

trama plot (*of a story*)

tranquilo/a calm, peaceful

transacción *f.* transaction

transición *f.* transition

tránsito traffic

transmitir to transmit

transparente transparent

transporte *m.* transportation (6A)

trapo rag (4B)

tras *adv.* behind

tratado treaty; **Tratado de Libre Comercio (TLC)** North America Free Trade Agreement (NAFTA)

tratamiento treatment

tratar to treat; to deal with; **tratarse de** to be about (8B)

través: a través de through, by means of

travieso/a mischievous (5A)

trece thirteen (1A)

treinta thirty (1A); **los años treinta** the thirties (2A)

treinta y dos thirty-two (2A)

treinta y uno thirty-one (2A)

tren *m.* train; **estación** (*f.*) **del tren** train station (2B)

tres three (1A)

tres mil three thousand (5B)

trescientos/as three hundred (2B)

trescientos mil three hundred thousand (5B)

trimestre *m.* quarter (*school*)

triste sad (1B)

triunfo triumph

tropical: selva tropical tropical jungle (6B)

trotar to jog (4A)

trozo piece, chunk

truco trick

tú *sub. pron.* you (*fam. s.*) (P)

tu(s) *poss.* your (*fam. s.*) (1A); **¿cuál es tu apellido?** what's your (*fam. s.*) last name? (P)

tumultuoso/a tumultuous (5B)

turista *n. m., f.* tourist

turístico/a *adj.* tourist; **clase** (*f.*) **turística** tourist class (6A)

tutearse to address each other as **tú**

tuyo/a/os/as *poss.* your, of yours (*fam. s.*) (2B)

U

u or (*used instead of* **o** *before words beginning with* **o** *or* **ho**)

ubicación *f.* location

ubicado/a located

último/a last

umbral (*m.*) **de la pobreza** poverty line

un, uno/a *indef. art.* a, an; one (P); *pl.* some, any; **a la una** at one o'clock (1A); **es la una** it's one o'clock (1A); **un poco de** a little (of) (P); **una vez al mes** once a month (1B)

único/a only; **hijo/a único/a** only child (3A)

unión *f.* union

universidad *f.* university (P)

universitario/a of or pertaining to the university

uno one (1A); **cada uno** each one

urbano/a urban

uruguayo/a *n., adj.* Uruguayan

usar to use; to wear (*clothing*)

uso *n.* use

usted (Ud.) *sub. pron.* you (*form. s.*) (P); *obj. of prep.* you (*form. s.*)

ustedes (Uds.) *sub. pron.* you (*form. pl.*) (P); *obj. of prep.* you (*form. pl.*)

usuario/a user

útil useful

utilizar (c) to utilize, use

uva grape

V

vaca cow

vacación *f.* vacation; **de vacaciones** on vacation

vacío/a empty

vainilla vanilla

Valentín: Día (*m.*) **de San Valentín** St. Valentine's Day (4A)

válido/a valid

valiente brave

valle *m.* valley (6B)

valor *m.* value; **Bolsa de valores** stock market (8A); **pérdida de valores tradicionales** loss of traditional values (8B)

valorar to value

vano/a vain

vapor steam; **al vapor** steamed (3B)

vaqueros jeans (2B)

variación *f.* variation

variar (varío) to vary

variedad *f.* variety

varios/as *pl.* various

vasco: País (*m.*) **Vasco** Basque country

vaso glass (*water*) (6A)

vecindad *f.* neighborhood (4B)

vecindario neighborhood

vecino/a neighbor (4B)

vegetal *m.* vegetable

vegetariano/a vegetarian (3B)

vehículo vehicle

veinte twenty (1A); **los años veinte** the twenties (5B)

veinticinco twenty-five (1A)

veinticuatro twenty-four (1A)

veintidós twenty-two (1A)

veintinueve twenty-nine (1A)

veintiocho twenty-eight (1A)

veintiséis twenty-six (1A)

veintisiete twenty-seven (1A)

veintitrés twenty-three (1A)

veintiún, veintiuno/a twenty-one (1A)

velo veil

velocidad *f.* speed

vendaje *m.* bandage

vendedor(a) salesperson; vendor

vender to sell (2B)

vengativo/a vengeful (7A)

venir *irreg.* to come (2A)

venta sale; **de venta** for sale (4B)

ventaja advantage

ventana window (P)

ver *irreg.* (*p.p.* **visto/a**) to see (1B); **nos vemos** see you around; **ver la televisión** to watch TV; **ver un espectáculo** to see a show (6B); **ver una película** to watch a movie

verano summer (1B)

veras: de veras really

verbo verb

verdad *f.* truth

verdadero/a true

verde green (2B); unripe; **judías verdes** green beans (3B)

verdura vegetable (3B)

vergüenza shame

verificar (qu) to check, verify

verso line (of poetry)

vestido *n.* dress (2B)

vestir (i, i) to dress (2B); **vestirse** to get dressed (2B)

veterano/a veteran

veterinario/a veterinarian

vez *f.* (*pl.* **veces**) times; **a veces** sometimes; **cada vez** each time; **cada vez más** more and more; **de vez en cuando** once in a while (3B); **la próxima vez** the next time; **la última vez** the last time; **muchas veces** often; **pagar (gu) de una vez** to pay off all at once (8A); **raras veces** infrequently, rarely; **tal vez** perhaps; **una vez (al mes)** once (a month) (1B)

vía way; path; **país** (*m.*) **en vías de desarrollo** developing country (8A)

viajar to travel, take a trip (1A)

viaje *m.* trip; **agencia de viajes** travel agency (6A); **agente** (*m., f.*) **de viajes** travel agent (6A); **hacer** (*irreg.*) **un viaje** to take a trip (6A)

viajero/a traveler (6A); **cheque** (*m.*) **de viajero** traveler's check (8A)

vida life; **seguro de vida** life insurance (8A)

vídeo video; **reproductor** (*m.*) **de vídeo** video player (5A); **sacar (qu) un vídeo** to rent a video (4A)

videocámara camcorder (5A)

videojuego video game; **jugar (ue) (gu) a los videojuegos** to play video games (5A)

vidrio glass; **botella de vidrio** glass bottle (6B)

viejo/a *n.* elderly person; **Noche** (*f.*) **Vieja** New Year's Eve (4A)

viento wind; **hace (mucho) viento** it's (very) windy (1B)

viernes *m. inv.* Friday (1A)

vigilar to watch (over); to supervise

villano/a villain; antagonist

vino wine (3); **degustar vinos** to go wine tasting (6B); **vino blanco** white wine (3B); **vino tinto** red wine (3B)

viña vineyard

violencia violence; **violencia doméstica** domestic violence (8B)

violento/a violent (8B); **crimen** (*m.*) **violento** violent crime (8B)

virtud *f.* virtue

visitar to visit (1A); **visitar a la familia** to visit one's family (1A); **visitar un museo** to visit a museum (4A)

víspera eve; day before

vista view (4A); **punto de vista** point of view

vistazo glance; **echar un vistazo** to look over

vitalicio/a for life

viudo/a widowed (3A); widower, widow

vivienda housing (4B); **seguro de vivienda** homeowner's insurance (8A)

vivir to live (1B)

vivo/a alive (3A)

vocabulario vocabulary

vocal *f.* vowel

volante *m.* steering wheel

volar (ue) to fly

volcán *m.* volcano (6B)

volcánico/a volcanic

vólibol *m.* volleyball (4A)

volumen *m.* volume; **bajar el volumen** to lower the volume; **poner** (*irreg.*) **alto el volumen** to turn the volume up high

voluntario/a volunteer (8B); **trabajar de voluntario/a** to volunteer

volver (ue) (*p.p.* **vuelto/a**) to return (*to a place*) (2A); **volver a** + *inf.* to (*do something*) again

vos *fam. s.* you (*used instead of* **tú** *in certain countries of Central and South America*)

vosotros/as *sub. pron.* you (*fam. pl. Sp.*) (P); *obj. of prep.* you (*fam. pl. Sp.*)

votante *m., f.* voter

votar to vote (8B)

voto: derecho al voto right to vote

voz *f.* (*pl.* **voces**) voice; **en voz alta** aloud

vuelo (directo) (direct) flight (6A);
  asistente (*m., f.*) **de vuelo** flight
  attendant (6A)
vuelta *n.* turn; **dar** (*irreg.*) **la vuelta a** to
  go around (*something*); **de ida y vuelta**
  adj. round-trip (6A)
vuelto/a (*p.p. of* **volver**) returned
vuestro/a/os/as *poss.* your (*fam. pl. Sp.*),
  of yours (*fam. pl. Sp.*) (1A)

W

web Web (World Wide Web); **página
  web** Web page (5A)

X

X: rayos X X-rays (7A)

Y

y and (P); **y cuarto** quarter past (*hour*)
  (1A); **y media** half past (*hour*) (1A)
ya already; **ya murió** he/she already died
  (3A); **ya no** no longer
yeso cast (*for a broken bone*)
yo *sub. pron.* I (P)
yoga *m.* yoga; **practicar (qu) el yoga** to
  do yoga (4A)
yogur *m.* yogurt (3B)

Z

zanahoria carrot (3A)
zapatería shoe store
zapatilla slipper (2B)
zapato shoe (2B); **zapatos de cuero**
  leather shoes; **zapatos de tacón alto**
  high-heeled shoes (2B); **zapatos de
  tenis** tennis shoes, sneakers (2B)
zapping: **hacer** (*irreg.*) *zapping* to
  channel surf (5A)
zona zone
zumo juice (*Sp.*)

INDEX

This index is divided into two parts: Part I (Grammar) covers topics in grammar, structure, and usage. Part II (Topics) lists cultural topics, maps, countries, and vocabulary topics treated in the text. Other general topics appear alphabetically.

Part I: Grammar

Part II: Topics

CREDITS

ABOUT THE AUTHORS

BILL VANPATTEN was, until recently, Professor of Spanish and Second Language Acquisition at the University of Illinois at Chicago where he was also the Director of Spanish Basic Language. His areas of research are input and input processing in second language acquisition and the effects of formal instruction on acquisitional processes. He has published widely in the fields of second language acquisition and language teaching and is a frequent conference speaker and presenter. He is also the lead author of *Sol y viento* (2005, McGraw-Hill), *¿Sabías que... ?*, Fifth Edition (2008, McGraw-Hill), and *Vistazos*, Second Edition (2006, McGraw-Hill). He is also the lead author and designer of *Destinos* and co-author with James F. Lee of *Making Communicative Language Teaching Happen*, Second Edition (2003, McGraw-Hill). He is also the author of *Input Processing and Grammar Instruction: Theory and Research* (1996, Ablex/Greenwood) and *From Input to Output: A Teacher's Guide to Second Language Acquisition* (2003, McGraw-Hill), and he is the editor of *Processing Instruction: Theory, Research, and Commentary* (2004, Erlbaum). When not engaged in academic activities, he writes fiction and performs stand-up comedy.

MICHAEL J. LEESER is Assistant Professor of Spanish in the Department of Modern Languages and Linguistics at Florida State University, where he is also Director of the Spanish Basic Language Program. Before joining the faculty at Florida State, he taught a wide range of courses at the secondary and postsecondary levels, including courses in Spanish language and Hispanic cultures, teacher preparation courses for secondary school teachers, and graduate courses in communicative language teaching and second language acquisition. He received his Ph.D. in Spanish (Second Language Acquisition and Teacher Education) from the University of Illinois at Urbana-Champaign in 2003. His research interests include input processing during second language reading as well as second language classroom interaction. His research has appeared in journals such as *Studies in Second Language Acquisition* and *Language Teaching Research*. He also co-authored the CD-ROM, along with Bill VanPatten and Mark Overstreet, for *¿Sabías que... ?*, Fifth Edition (2008, McGraw-Hill), as well as the first edition of *Sol y viento*.

GREGORY D. KEATING is Assistant Professor of Linguistics and Second Language Acquisition in the Department of Linguistics and Oriental Languages at San Diego State University. Before joining the faculty at San Diego State, he taught courses in communicative language teaching and Spanish teacher education at the University of Illinois at Chicago, where he received his Ph.D. in Hispanic Linguistics and Second Language Acquisition. His areas of research include Spanish sentence processing, the role instruction plays in language acquisition, psycholinguistics, and the acquisition of Spanish syntax and vocabulary. His doctoral research explores the relationship between language processing and grammatical competence in the acquisition of Spanish gender agreement. He is a frequent presenter at conferences in the United States and Mexico. He is also a recipient of several teaching awards, including one from the University of Notre Dame, where he received his M.A. in Spanish Literature. In addition to teaching and research, he has supervised many language courses and teaching assistants and has assisted in the coordination of technology-enhanced lower-division Spanish language programs. He is also a co-author of the first edition of *Sol y viento*.